A
ATLAS a

TO
LONDON
AND SUBURBS

Containing 23,000 Streets, over 9,000 more than any other
Atlas Index.

Featuring House Numbers along main roads, L.C.C. Street
Name Changes and L.P.T.B. Underground and Trolley Bus
Developments.

CONTENTS:

MAPS

	Pages
Picture Map of Central London	2-3
Theatreland	4
Cinemaland	5
Shopping Centres and Parking Places	6
Clubland	7
Underground Railways (L.P.T.B.) of London and Suburbs	8-9
Key to 84 Sectional Maps	10-11
84 Sectional Maps of London and Suburbs	12-95
Places of Interest :—	
Museums, Art Galleries, Public Buildings, etc.	96

INDEX AND GUIDE

Places of Interest, and General Information	97-111
L.C.C. Street Name Changes	112-118
Index to 23,000 Streets with Postal Districts	123-228

THE ONLY QUICK MAP REFERENCE SUPPLEMENT
TO ALL OLD AND NEW STREET NAMES

See inside Back Cover for coloured Pictorial Map

These Maps are based upon the Ordnance Survey Map with the
sanction of the Controller of H.M. Stationery Office

GEOGRAPHERS' MAP CO., LTD.
24-27, HIGH HOLBORN, W.C.I.

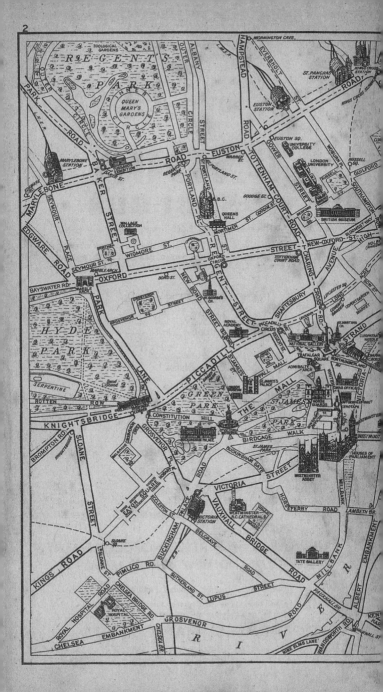

3

PICTURE MAP
OF
CENTRAL LONDON

Scale

Underground Stations (L.T.B)
Interchange

Copyright

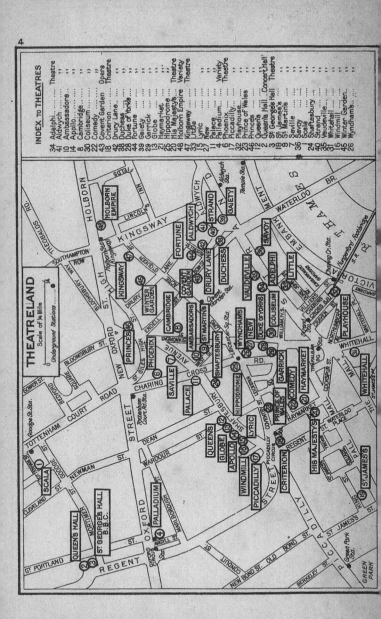

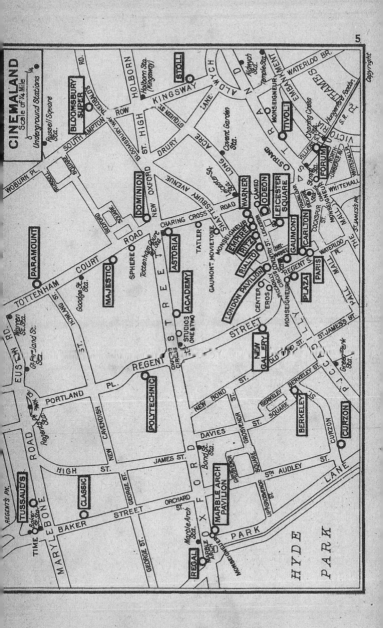

SHOPPING CENTRES AND PARKING PLACES

Parking Places shown thus ////
Garages ▲
Underground Stations (L.P.T.) ○

Scale.
0 — ¼ MILE

ALDERSGATE ST.
GOSWELL RD.
FARRINGDON RD.
CLERKENWELL RD.
ROSEBERY AV.
KINGS CROSS RD.
GRAY'S INN ROAD
St. Pancras
King's Cross
St. Pancras
Euston
HAMPSTEAD RD.
ALBANY ST.
Maryl ebone
MARYLEBONE RD.
Edgware Rd.
HARROW RD.
Royal Oak
Paddington
Bishops Bridge Rd.
Queens Rd.
WESTBOURNE GROVE
BAYSWATER RD.
Whiteley's
Bradley's
PEMBRIDGE
Notting Hill Gate
CHURCH ST.
KENSINGTON GARDENS
KENSINGTON HIGH ST.
Derry & Toms
Ponting's
Barker's
EARL'S COURT RD.
CROMWELL RD.
Gloucester Rd.
QUEEN'S GATE
EXHIBITION RD.
South Kensington
BROMPTON RD.
Harrods
Goochs
KNIGHTSBRIDGE
SLOANE STREET
Woollands
Harvey Nichols
Peter Jones
Sloane Square
Victoria
BUCKINGHAM PALACE RD.
GROSVENOR PL.
Coach Sta.
Gorringes
Army & Navy Stores
Parnell's
MILLBANK
Houses of Parliament
Westminster
WHITEHALL
THE MALL
ST. JAMES'S PARK
PICCADILLY
GREEN PARK
HYDE PARK
Serpentine
Hyde Park Corner
PARK LANE
OXFORD STREET
REGENT STREET
Selfridges
Marshall & Snelgrove
Debenham & Freebody
Bourne & Hollingsworth
Maples
Heals
Catesby's
Dickins & Jones
Liberty's
Gamages
Wallis
Nicholson's
Swan & Edgar
Civil Service Stores
Hampton's
Waring & Gillow
Shoolbred's
Druce
Cozens
Paddington
Lancaster Gate
BLACKFRIARS RD.
BLACKFRIARS BR.
NEW BR.
FLEET ST.
HOLBORN
HIGH HOLBORN
NEW OXFORD ST.
TOTTENHAM CT. RD.
CHARING CROSS RD.
ALDWYCH
STRAND
Charing Cross
Covent Garden
THAMES
VICTORIA EMBANKMENT
WATERLOO BR.
Waterloo
YORK RD.
WATERLOO RD.
S.R.

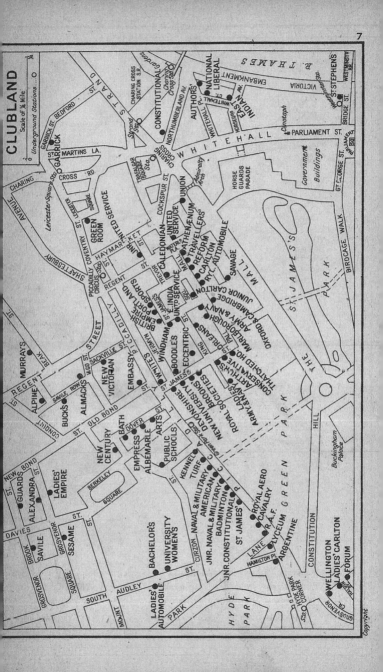

UNDERGROUND RAILWAYS
(LONDON PASSENGER TRANSPORT)
OF
LONDON AND SUBURBS

Scale of Miles

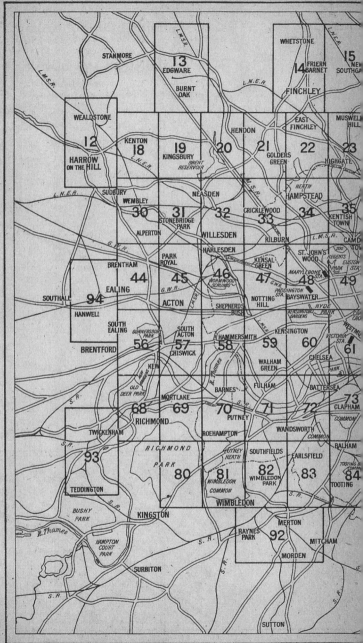

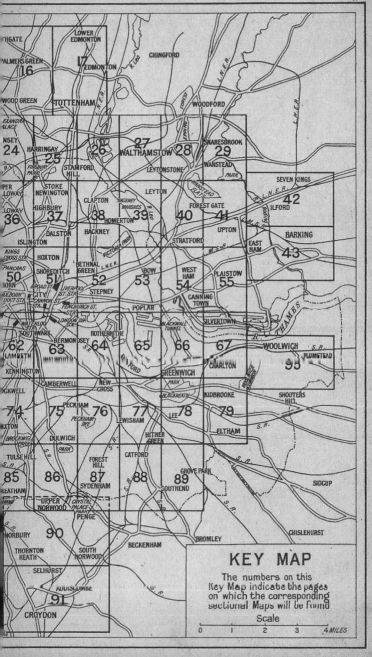

KEY MAP

The numbers on this Key Map indicate the pages on which the corresponding sectional Maps will be found

Scale

0   1   2   3   4 MILES

Railways & Stations
Underground Railways & Stations (L.P.T.)
Bus & Trolleybus Routes
House numbers....152

Interchange Stations...⊕

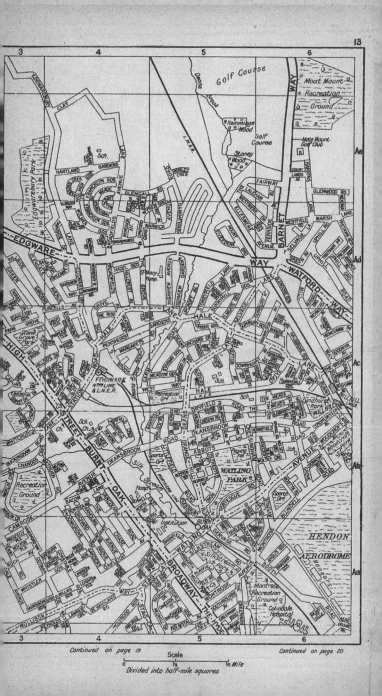

Continued on page 19

Scale

0   ¼   ½ Mile

Divided into half-mile squares

Continued on page 20

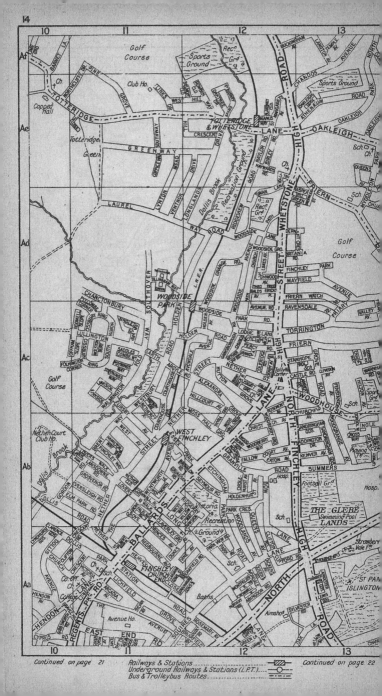

Continued on page 21

Railways & Stations .... ▱▱
Underground Railways & Stations (L.P.T.) .... ⊙—
Bus & Trolleybus Routes .... ═══

Continued on page 22

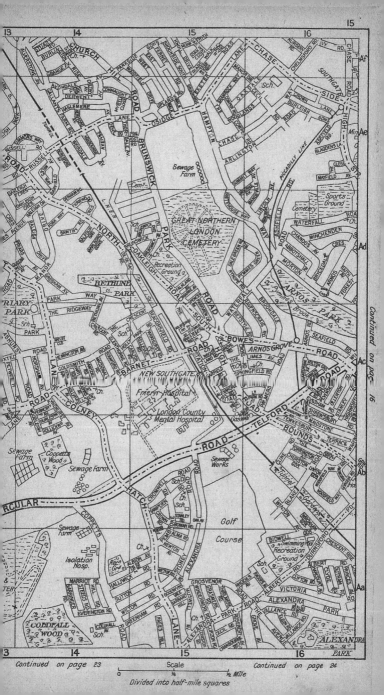

Scale

0   ¼   ½ Mile

Divided into half-mile squares

Continued on page 15

Continued on page 24

Continued on page 25

Railways & Stations
Underground Railways & Stations (L.P.T.)
Bus & Trolleybus Routes

House numbers...152

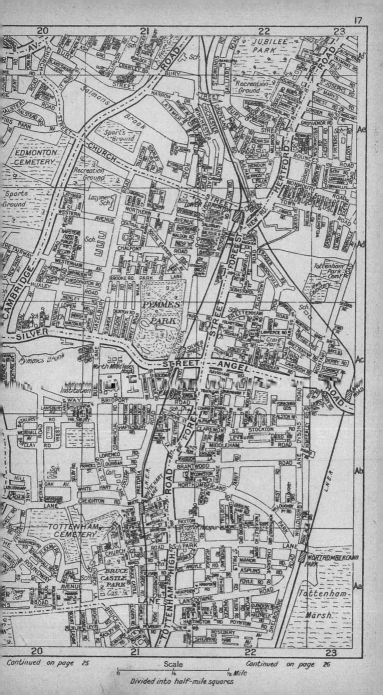

Continued on page 12

Continued on page 30

Interchange Stations ..... ⊙

Railways & Stations ....
Underground Railways & Stations (L.P.T.) ...
Bus & Trolleybus Routes ....

House numbers 253

Continued on page 20

Continued on page 31

EDGWARE RD.

THE HYDE

STAG LANE

KINGSBURY

KINGSBURY ROAD

Roe Green Park

ROE GREEN LANE

HAY LANE

Maternity Hosp.

WINCHESTER RD.

PRINCES

BERKELEY

BRAMPTON RD.

FRYENT

Sports Ground

KENTON LANE

SLOUGH LANE

HIGH STREET

CHURCH LANE

Barn Hill Recreation Ground

BARN HILL

HILL BARN

Recreation

BURGESS AV.

Recreation

ELTHORNE RD.

SUNNYMEAD

MEADOW

REEVES

WOODSMEAD RD.

Willesden Cemetery (proposed)

MALLARD WAY

Queensbury RD.

LAVENDER AV.

DUNSTER DR.

DEANSCROFT AV.

QUEENS WALK

GREENHILL

SALMON STREET

TUDOR GDS.

WOOD LANE

CHURCH DR.

BEVERLEY

SANDHURST

DRIVE

NORTH AVENUE

FAIRWAY

TEWKESBURY GDS.

TINTERN AV.

Eaton Gra. Recreation Gro.

BACON LANE

GOLDSMITH AV.

Sports Grd.

GROVE

EVELYN

ROSE CRESCENT

FAIRFIELDS

HIGHFIELD

Kingsbury

LEWGARS AV.

BRIAR WOOD GDS.

STEWART CLO.

Bush Fm.

Lit. Bush

Sch.

Hill Fm.

LANGDON DR.

ROSSDALE DR.

KINGSMERE PK.

PADDOCKS

WELLS RD.

WILLISDON

Ch.

Scale

0   ¼   ½ Mile

Divided into half-mile squares

A

B

C

D

3   4   5   6

Continued on page 19

Continued on page 32

Railways & Stations ....
Underground Railways & Stations (L.P.T.)...
Bus & Trolleybus Routes ....

House numbers..... 253

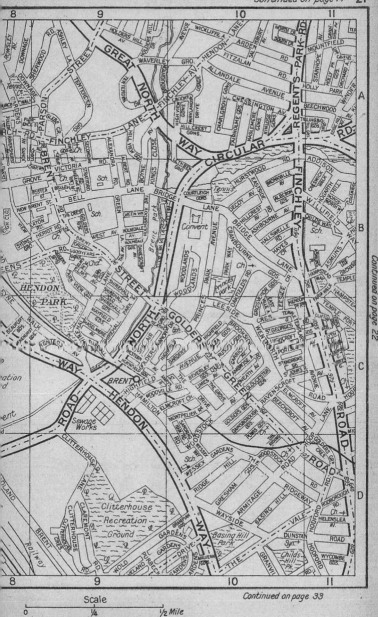

Continued on page 22

Scale

0   ¼   ½ Mile

Divided into half-mile squares

Continued on page 14

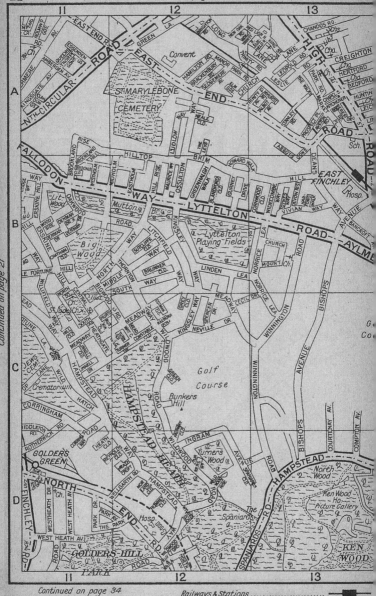

Continued on page 21

Continued on page 34

Railways & Stations
Underground Railways & Stations (L.P.T.)
Bus & Trolleybus Routes

House numbers..... 253

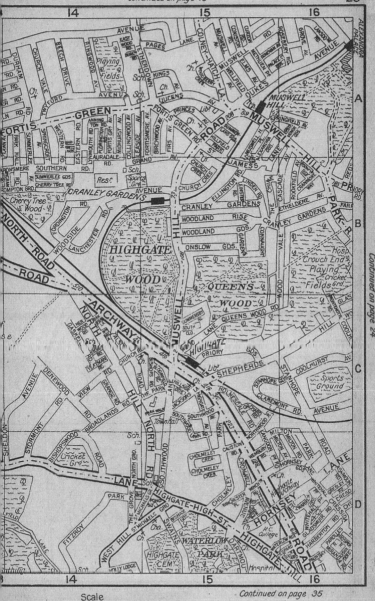

Continued on page 24

Continued on page 35

Scale

0 ¼ ½ Mile

Divided into half-mile squares

16 17 18 19

ALEXANDRA PALACE
ALEXANDRA
Television A.B.B.C.
ALEXANDRA PALACE
PARK

NOEL PK. & WOOD GRN.
Baths
CAXTON
GLADSTONE AV.
PELHAM
MAY
WESTERN
COBURG RD
HIGH
LYMINGTON RD
BLAKES
PELHAM
BEECH
RUSSELL
HEWITT

A

NEWLAND RD
SOUTH VIEW RD
HAWTHORN RD
BEECHWOOD RD
VIEW
LANE
Sch
EASTFIELD
BROOK RD
PEMBROKE
Gas Works
Reserv
Filter Beds
Pumping Sta.
MALVERN
RAVENSLEIGH
THE AVENUE
CLARSON
TURNPIKE LA. C. GREEN
WHITMARSH
WEST

PRIORY
ROAD
HIGH
CLOVELLY
PARK AVENUE
WARNER
REDSTON
NIGHTINGALE
RECTORY
Sch
TURNPIKE
LANE
SYDNEY
RALEIGH
HAMPDEN
LAUSANNE RD
FROBISHER
FALKLAND RD
HORNSEY
New River

B

PARK
BARRINGTON
CARYSFORT
PALACE
RD
PRIORY
PARK
HARINGEY
LIGHTFOOT RD
ROKESLY
ELMFIELD
ROSEBERY GDS.
WESTFIELD
GLEBE
RATHCOOLE
HAROLD
HARVEY
FAIRFAX RD
EFFINGHAM RD
BERESFORD
ALLISON
HEWITT
SEYMOUR
WARHAM

TOTTENHAM
ROAD
MIDDLE
BROADWAY
CROUCH
HALL
WESTON
Town Hall
FAIRLAND
FERME
NELSON
PARK
DENTON
UPLANDS
MAYFIELD
Sch
PEMBERTON
MATTISON
DUCKETT
CAVENDISH
BURGOYNE
HARINGAY
UMFREVILLE

C

CLIFTON
MOLSELEY
CRESCENT
COLERIDGE
HASLEMERE RD
CROUCH END HILL
CECILE
Christ Church
DICKENSON
ELLA
ELM G
Liverpool Reserv
RIDGE
GRANVILLE
OAK PARK
QUERNMORE
OAKFIELD
ALBANY
STAPLETON HALL
DAGMAR
HARINGAY

CROUCH END

D

HORNSEY LANE
HAZELVILLE
SUNNYSIDE
HORNSEY
WARTEMPSVILLE
HEATHVILLE
HOLLY
PARK
CROUCH HILL
BLYTHWOOD RD
PLEASANT
FLORENCE
VICTORIA
LANCASTER
CORNWALL
STROUD GREEN
CARLETON
REGINA
EVERSHOT
OXFORD RD
TOLLINGTON
PARK
FINS
PA

HORNSEY RD
HANLEY
STROUD GREEN
WADSTOCK
CHARTER

16 17 18 19

Continued on page 36
Continued on page 23

Railways & Stations ....
Underground Railways & Stations (L.P.T.) .. --·-○-·--
Bus & Trolleybus Routes ....

House numbers 253

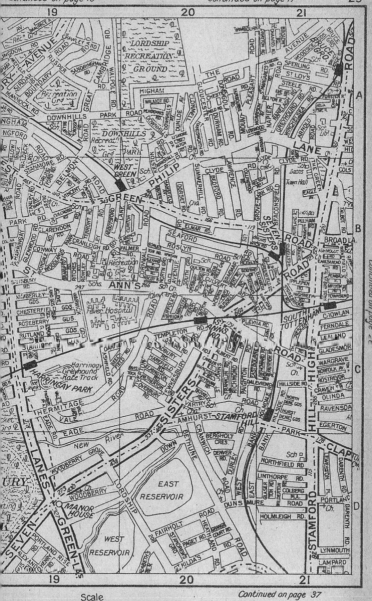

Scale

0   ¼   ½ Mile

Divided into half-mile squares

Continued on page 37

21 22 23 24

LOCKWOOD RESERVOIR

Sports Ground

HIGH RD.
REFORM RD.
DOWSETT
SEYMOUR
THACKERAY
SCOTLAND AV.
PARK VIEW RD.
CAREW RD.
MAFEKING RD.
BULLER RD.
ROAD
HOLCOMBE RD.
Recreation Ground

LANCASTER
GOLDSMI
SHAKES
BLACKHORSE

A

CHESTNUT
MITCHLEY RD.
SCALES RD.
SOMERSET RD.
ELBOURNE
GH CROSS
STATION RD.
Sch.

Sports Grd.
HOOKERS AV.
BLE
TAVI
CLIFT

TOTTENHAM (HALE)

FERRY LANE
FOREST

R. Lea Navigation
R. Lea
LOW MAYNARD RESERVOIR
HIGH MAYNARD RESERVOIR

BLACK HORSE ROAD

Hosp.
NEMOUTH
ANTILL RD.
SPRINGFIELD
EDITH RD.
BROAD

HAWARDEN RD.
EDWARD RD.
LLOYD
CORNWALLIS
COURTENAY

B

RES^R No 4
RES^R No 2
RES^R No 1
RES^R No 3

London Playing Fields

NEWTON
HERBERT
BERNARD RD.
FAIRVIEW
FAIRVIEW
PARK
ELM
GROVELANDS
ROAD
ROAD
ROAD
AVENUE
Recreation Ground
Sch.
ROAD

RESERVOIR No 5

COPPERMILL

WARWICK RES^R (EAST)

COPPERMILL LANE

C

PARK RD.
TIMBER
ALE
Imshot
Syr.
CASTLEWOOD
CRAVEN
WALK
LINGWOOD
Cricket Grd. High a.
SPRING HILL

WARWICK RES^R (WEST)

RACECOURSE RESERVOIR

Coppermill Br.

LAPTON

BRAYDON
KYVERDALE
OSBALDESTON RD.
FORBURG RD.
CHARDMORE RD.
COMMON
ASHTEAD
SPRING
SPRING HILL

SPRINGFIELD PARK

SPRINGFIELD

D

COMMON
AVENUE
MORESBY RD.
HOLM
HOMBER
LANE
HARRINGTON HILL
BAKERS HILL

W. LTHAMSTOW MARSHES

R. LEA

ARGALL AV.

21 22 23 24

Continued on page 38
Continued on page 25

Railways & Stations ....
Underground Railways & Stations (L.P.T.) ...
Bus & Trolleybus Routes ....

House numbers 253

Continued on page 28

Continued on page 39

Scale

0   ¼   ½ Mile

Divided into half-mile squares

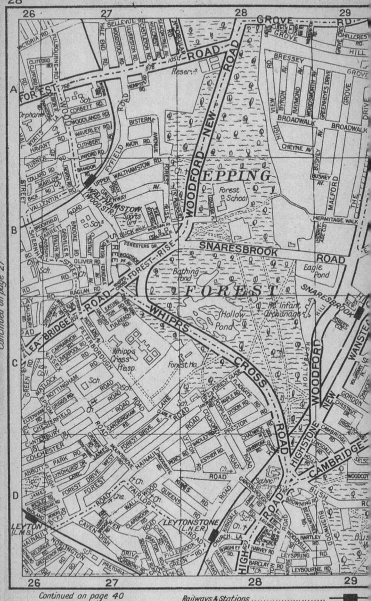

Continued on page 27

Continued on page 40

Railways & Stations ....
Underground Railways & Stations (L.P.T.)... ●–●–●
Bus & Trolleybus Routes ....

House numbers 253

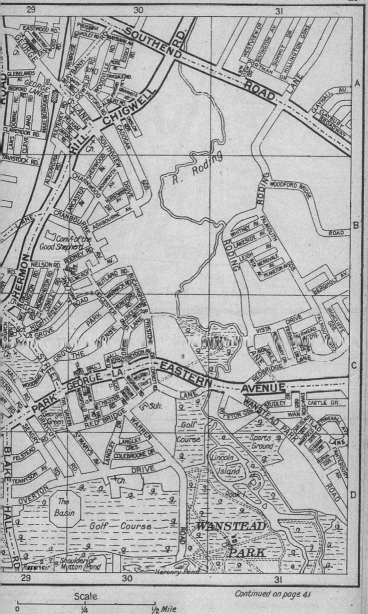

Continued on page 41

Scale

0   ¼   ½ Mile

Divided into half-mile squares

Continued on page 12

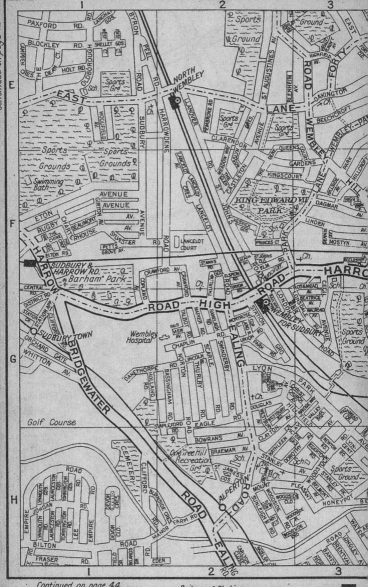

Continued on page 44

Interchange Stations---- ⊙

Railways & Stations ....
Underground Railways & Stations (L.P.T.)...
Bus & Trolleybus Routes ....

House numbers 253

Continued on page 32

CLARENDON AV.
BARN
KING
TOWN HALL
MOUNT
TUDOR
AVENUE FORTY LANE
KINGSBURY LANE
OLD CHURCH
BIRCHEN
AV.
AV.
Sports Grd.
Wembley Park
Chalkhill Ho.
THE DRIVE
ROAD
BRAEMAR
NEASDEN LA.
BROOK
CHALK HILL
BARN HILL ROAD
WYNDT
ST.
E
AVENUE
BRIDGE
BARN HILL
THE GREST
LOUGHTON
VERNEY
CROFT
NUTCAL
THE
AVENUE
FLASHUB
WAY
ROAD
AYLESBURY
WEST THE
DRIVE
ST.
DRIVE
LOUGHTON
VILLAGE
EASE DRIVE
Rest.
WAY
Sewage
Works

EMPIRE WAY
Empire Pool
Car Parking
Railway
Works

WEMBLEY
HILL
Wembley
Stadium
Greyhound
Race Track
Oakington Farm
PARK VIEW
THE GROVE
MONKS
R. Brent
ROAD
F

OAKINGTON
MANOR
AVENUE WAY
DRIVE
CHIPPENHAM AV.
RecreationGround
ROAD
RECREATION
GRESHAM RD.
VIVIAN
TUDOR
COURT NTH
BRENT
WAY
St. JS. WAY
ST.
Ch.
Willesden
BERKHAMSTED
REEDS
TUDOR
COURT STH.
R. Brent
GARDEN
WAY
Isolation
Hosp.
Soh!
TOKYNGTON AV.
NETTLEDEN
CHALK
Ch.
WEMBLEY
Old Filter
Beds
CIRCULAR
NORMANS MEAD
Recreation
Grd.
Soh!
G
Rest.
TOKYNGTON
VICTORIA
WYLD
CONDUIT
Tokyngton Com. Rd
BRENTFIELD
MITCHELL
Feeder
SIBBON AV.
Rest.
AVENUE
MONKS
NORTH
Canal
LEICESTER
Soh!
STONEBRIDGE
WAY
CROUCH
ALRIC
ROAD
HAZELDEAN
STONEBRIDGE
PARK
ROAD
HILL
CONDUIT
WYBORNE WAY
WYBRIDGE WAY
BARRY
MELVILLE
FAWOOD
ROAD
CASHLEY
CRAVEN
H
HEATHER PARK DRIVE
GONS.
AVENUE
SOUTH CIRCULAR
RecreationGround
Soh!
BRETT
SIDE
CRAVEN PK.
SHAKESPEARE
SHRUDSBURY
CARLYLE AV.
MILTON
CHELSEA RD.

Scale
0   1/4   1/2 Mile
Divided into half-mile squares

Continued on page 45

3   4   5   6

Continued on page 20

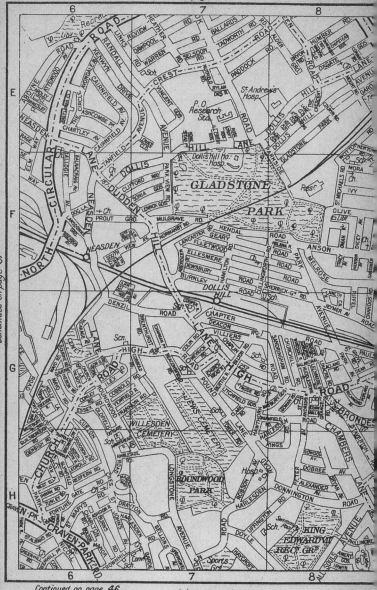

Continued on page 46

Railways & Stations ....
Underground Railways & Stations (L.P.T.)...
Bus & Trolleybus Routes ....

House numbers 253

Continued on page 34

Scale

0   1/4   1/2 Mile

Divided into half-mile squares

Continued on page 22

Continued on page 33

Continued on page 48

Interchange Stations ---- ⊙

Railways & Stations ....
Underground Railways & Stations (L.P.T.)...
Bus & Trolleybus Routes ....

House numbers 253

Continued on page 36

Continued on page 49

Scale

0   ¼   ½ Mile

Divided into half-mile squares

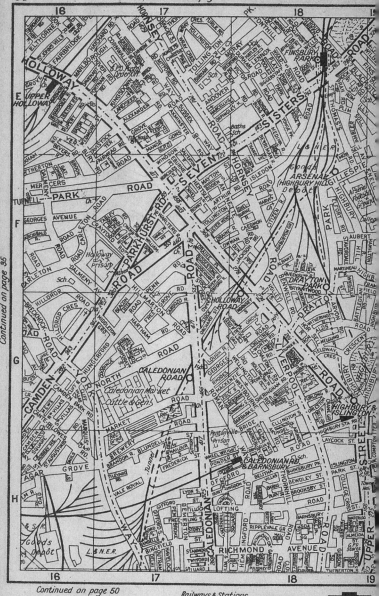

Continued on page 35

Continued on page 50

Interchange Stations....

Railways & Stations ....
Underground Railways & Stations (L.P.T.)...
Bus & Trolleybus Routes ....

House numbers..... 253

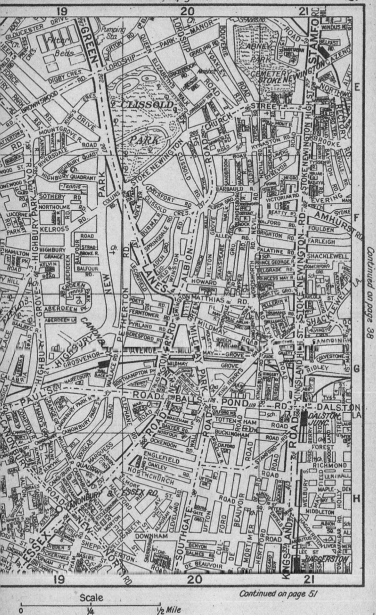

Continued on page 38
Continued on page 51

Scale

0   ¼   ½ Mile

Divided into half-mile squares

Continued on page 37

Continued on page 52

Railways & Stations ....
Underground Railways & Stations (L.P.T.) .....
Bus & Trolleybus Routes ....

House numbers 253

Continued on page 40

Continued on page 53

Scale

0   ¼   ½ Mile

Divided into half-mile squares

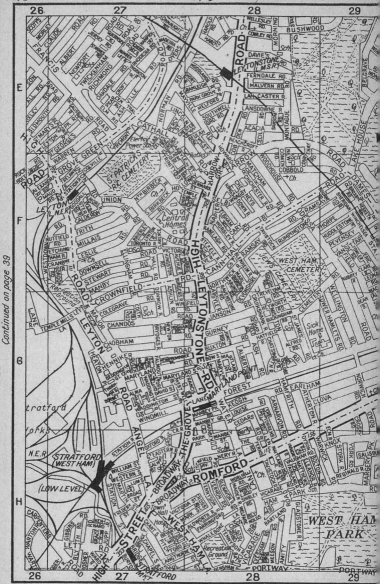

Continued on page 39

Continued on page 54

Railways & Stations ....
Underground Railways & Stations (L.P.T.)...
Bus & Trolleybus Routes ....

House numbers 253

Continued on page 42

Continued on page 43

Continued on page 55

Scale

0   ¼   ½ Mile

Divided into half-mile squares

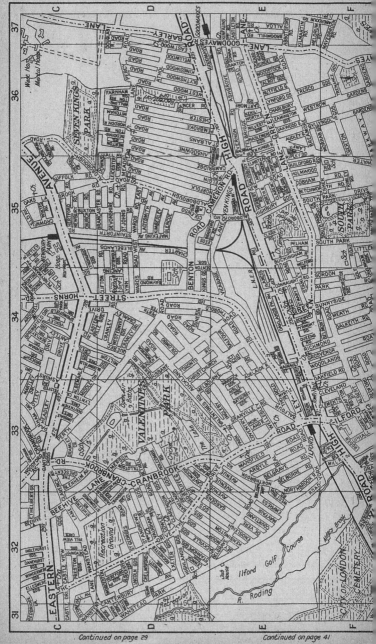

Continued on page 29   Continued on page 41

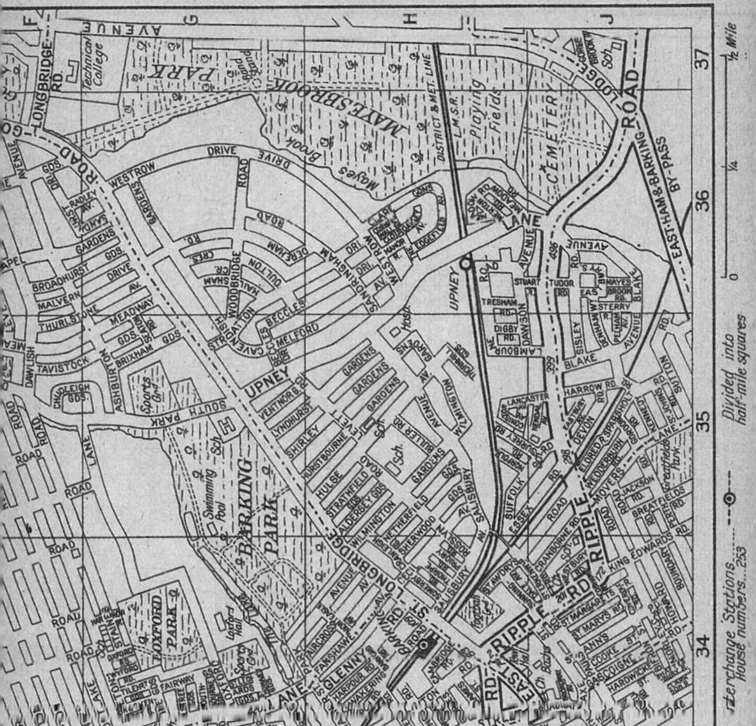

MAYESBROOK PARK

LONGBRIDGE RD.

Technical College

AVENUE

UPNEY LANE

CEMETERY

EAST-HAM & BARKING BY-PASS

RIPPLE ROAD

RIPPLE RD.

BARKING PARK

LONGBRIDGE ROAD

SOUTH PARK

UPNEY

RIVER RODING

Recreation Grd.

REYNOLDS ROAD

Gasometer

LONDON ROAD

BARKING

HIGH STREET

ROMFORD ROAD

ILFORD

Continued on page 41

Continued on page 55

Divided into half-mile squares

½ Mile

Railways & Stations ....
Underground Railways & Stations
Interchange Stations ....
Bus & Trolleybus Routes ....
House numbers. 253

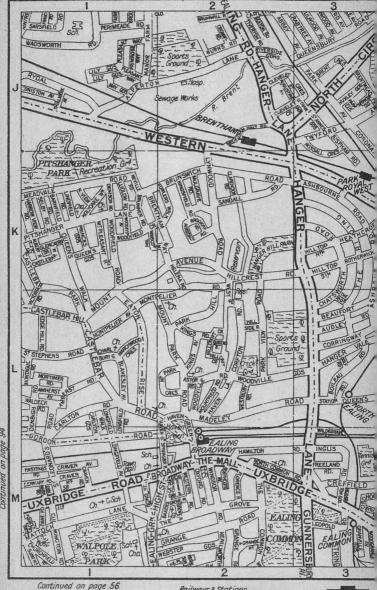

Continued on page 94

Interchange Stations..... ◉

Railways & Stations ....
Underground Railways & Stations (L.P.T.)...
Bus & Trolleybus Routes ....

House numbers..... 253

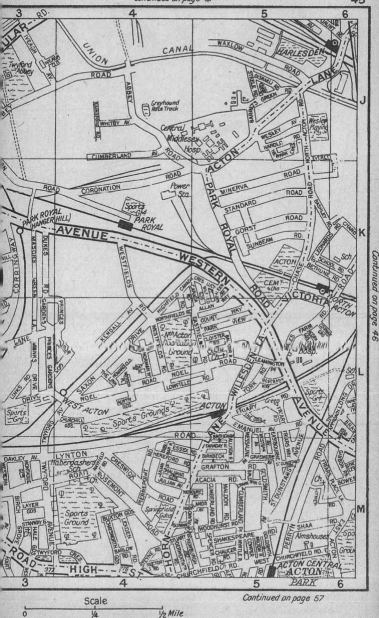

Scale

0   1/4   1/2 Mile

Divided into half-mile squares

Continued on page 46

Continued on page 45

Interchange Stations ..... ⊙

Railways & Stations ....
Underground Railways & Stations (L.P.T.)...
Bus & Trolleybus Routes ....

House numbers 253

Continued on page 48

Scale

0   ¼   ½ Mile

Divided into half-mile squares

Continued on page 60

Interchange Stations ---- ◎

Railways & Stations ....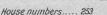
Underground Railways & Stations (L.P.T.) ...
Bus & Trolleybus Routes ....

House numbers..... 253

Continued on page 50

Continued on page 61

Scale

0   ¼   ½ Mile

Divided into half-mile squares

Continued on page 49

Continued on page 62

Interchange Stations ----- ⊙

Railways & Stations ....
Underground Railways & Stations (L.P.T.) ...
Bus & Trolleybus Routes ....
Tram Routes ....

House numbers 253

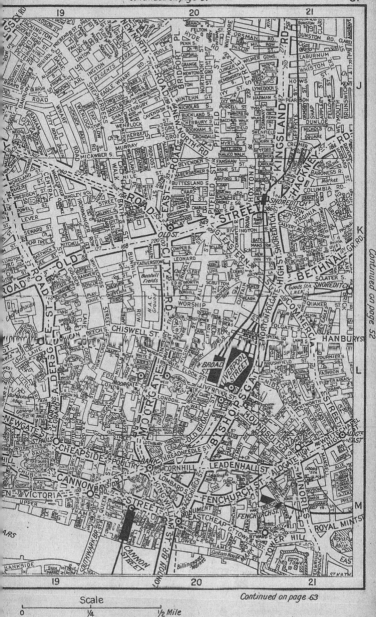

Continued on page 52

Continued on page 63

Scale

0   ¼   ½ Mile

Divided into half-mile squares

Continued on page 51

Continued on page 64

Interchange Stations ---- ⊙

Railways & Stations ....
Underground Railways & Stations (L.P.T.) ---
Bus & Trolleybus Routes ....

House numbers 253

Continued on page 54

Continued on page 65

Scale

0   ¼   ½ Mile

Divided into half-mile squares

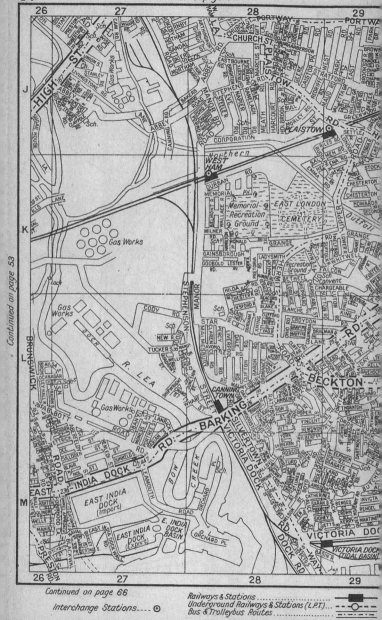

Continued on page 53

Railways & Stations ....
Underground Railways & Stations (L.P.T.) ..
Bus & Trolleybus Routes ....

House numbers 253

Continued on page 43

Scale

0   1/4   1/2 Mile

Divided into half-mile squares

Continued on page 94

GUNNERSBURY

Miniature
Golf Course

PARK

GUNNERSBURY

SOUTH EALING

EALING-LA

POPES

NORTHFIELDS

LITTLE EALING

WEST EALING

BOSTON

GREAT

BRENTFORD

HIGH

BRENTFORD (G.W.R.)

KEW BRIDGE (S.R.)

KEW BRIDGE ROAD

KEW

KEW GARDENS

GARDENS

Interchange Stations ···· ⊙

Railways & Stations ....
Underground Railways & Stations (L.P.T.) ... --○--
Bus & Trolleybus Routes ....

House numbers 253

Continued on page 58

Continued on page 69

Scale

0   ¼   ½ Mile

Divided into half-mile squares

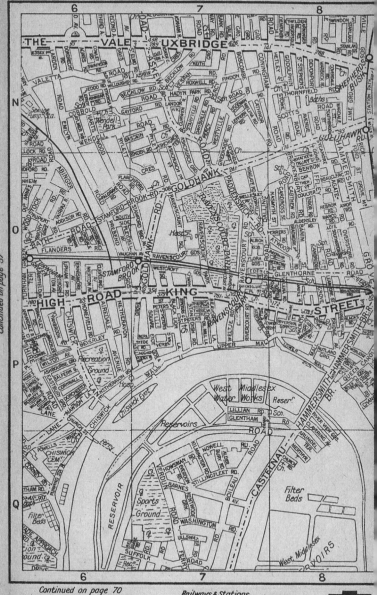

Interchange Stations..... ⦿

Railways & Stations ....
Underground Railways & Stations (L.P.T.)...
Bus & Trolleybus Routes ....

House numbers..... 253

Continued on page 60

Continued on page 71

Scale

0   ¼   ½ Mile

Divided into half-mile squares

Continued on page 48

Continued on page 59

Continued on page 72

Interchange Stations ----⊙

Railways & Stations ....
Underground Railways & Stations (L.P.T.) ....
Bus & Trolleybus Routes ....
Tram Routes ....
House numbers 253

D E   14   15   16

PARK

PARK LANE

PICCADILLY

ST JAMES'S ST

PALL MALL

THE MALL

N

Stanhope Gate

CURZON

GREEN PARK

Band Stand

ROTTEN ROW

GREEN PARK

London Mus.

ROAD

Albert Gate

HYDE PARK CORNER

CONSTITUTION HILL

THE PARK

KNIGHTSBRIDGE

St George's Hosp.

BIRDCAGE WALK

ST JAMES'S PALACE

SLOANE

GROSVENOR PLACE

Buckingham Palace

GARDENS

Wellington Barracks

ST JAMES'S PARK

PETTY FRANCE

STR

O

BELGRAVE

GROSVENOR

Royal Mews

GROSVENOR

ROAD

Bromley Vic Palace

VICTORIA

HORS

EATON

SQUARE

HOBART

BELGRAVE

VICTORIA

VAUXHALL

Westminster School Playground

VIN

SLOANE

EATON

Coach Station

BUCKINGHAM PALACE

BELGRAVE

BRIDGE

STREET

ROAD

SLOANE

EBURY

ROAD

SUTHERLAND

GEORGE'S

WAY

P

CHELSEA

ST

PIMLICO

Barracks

CHELSEA BRIDGE

CANAL

LUPUS

ROAD

RD

ROYAL HOSPITAL

ROAD

Chelsea Barracks

Royal Hospital

GROSVENOR

ROYAL

EMBANKMENT

CHELSEA

CHELSEA BR

QUEENS

CHELSEA

REACH

Electric Power Sta.

R I V

NINE ELMS

Q

NORTH DRIVE

Running Track

Goods Depôt S.R.

NINE ELMS

CRINGLE ST

Gas Works

B A T T E R S E A

CENTRAL AV

Gas Wks

ROAD

Goods Depôt

P A R K

BATTERSEA PK

15

16

Scale

0   1/4   1/2 Mile

Divided into half-mile squares

Continued on page 62

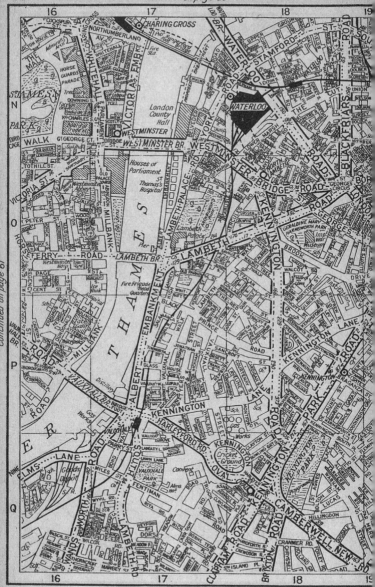

Continued on page 61

Interchange Stations ⊙

Railways & Stations ....
Underground Railways & Stations (L.P.T.) ....
Bus & Trolleybus Routes ....
Train Routes ....

House numbers 253

Continued on page 64

Continued on page 75

Scale

0   ¼   ½ Mile

Divided into half-mile squares

Continued on page 52

Continued on page 63

Continued on page 76

Railways & Stations	....
Underground Railways & Stations (L.P.T.)	---
Bus & Trolleybus Routes	....
Tram Routes	....
House numbers	 253

Continued on page 66

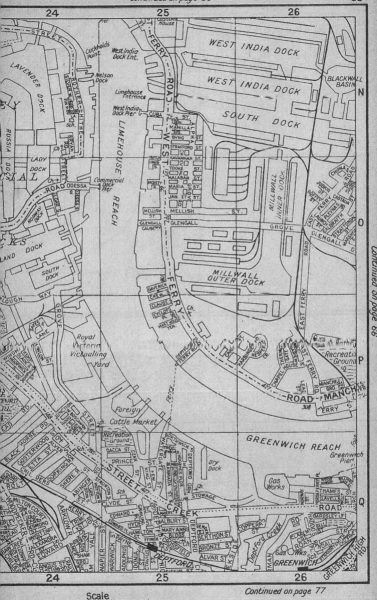

Scale
0   ¼   ½ Mile
Divided into half-mile squares

Continued on page 77

Continued on page 65

Railways & Stations ....
Underground Railways & Stations (L.P.T.) ..
Bus & Trolleybus Routes ....
Tram Routes ....

House numbers 253

Continued on page 95

29   **30**   **31**

ROYAL VICTORIA DOCK

CONNAUGHT

ROYAL ALBERT DOCK

RD.

PONTOON DOCK

Recreat'n Ground

ORIENTAL RD.

ROAD

N

WICH

THAMES RD.

FACTORY RD.

SILVERTOWN

KNIGHTS

BRADFIELD

T H A M E S

O

Wharf

Jetty

RIVERSIDE

HERRINGHAM

HARRINGTON WAY

BOWATER R.

SIEMENS

WARSPITE ST.

WESTFIELD

ROAD

WOOLWICH CHURCH ST.

ANCHOR & HOPE

MARYON PARK

Tramway Depot

Charlton Greyhound Race Track

LOMBARD WAY

LANE

CHARLTON

RD.

CHURCH

Sch.

P

MORDEN

VICTORIA

TROUGHTON

ROAD

Charlton Athletic Football Ground

MARYON WILSON PARK

WOODLAND

LITTLE HEATH

AVENUE

ELLISCOMBE

THE VILLAGE

CHARLTON PK. RD.

Q

BRAMSHOT

EVERSLEY R.

ROAD

HORNFAIR

Charlton House

CHARLTON PARK

Cricket Grd.

CHARLTON

CANBERRA

MONTCALM

ROAD

PARK

LANE

29   **30**   **31**

Continued on page 79

Scale

0   ¼   ½ Mile

Divided into half-mile squares

Interchange stations ..... ⊚

Railways & Stations ....
Underground Railways & Stations (L.P.T.) ...
Bus & Trolleybus Routes ....

House numbers 253

Continued on page 70

Scale

0   ¼   ½ Mile

Divided into half-mile squares

Continued on page 69

RESE... Water Works

Barn Elms (Ranelagh Club)

CUMBERLAND RD.
WESTMORELAND RD.
GERARDE
NASSAU
LONSDALE RD.
PROMENADE
BARNES
BARNES BRIDGE
CHURCH ROAD
CASTELNAU
Lyric Rd.
STATION RD.
HIGH ST.
WESTMINSTER
THORNE PASS
CHARLES ST.
ARCHWAY
RAILWAY
Recn Grd
Cricket Grd
BARNES
ROAD

BARN ELMS PARK
Polo Ground
Polo Ground
Beverley Brook

RANELAGH AV.
MILL HILL RD.
LANE
LOWER RICHMOND RD.
Barnes Cem
Putney Cem
Hosp.

BARNES COMMON
RIDE
LOWER

UPR RICHMOND RD. 500.
472 ROAD
UPPER RICHMOND ROAD
QUEENS RIDE
ROCKS
DRYBURGH
ERRINGHAM
LANDFORD
CLARENDON

Open Air Baths
Polo Ground
The Priory (Mental Hosp.)
Clarence Ho.
Roehampton
Club
Golf Course
Convent of the Sacred Heart
Grove Ho.
CLARENCE LANE
Pavilion

ROEHAMPTON LANE
DUNGARVAN AV.
LANGSIDE AV.
PUTNEY PARK AV.
DOVER
HUNTINGFIELD RD.
HUNTINGFIELD
ELMSHAW RD.
HAWKESBURY
PARKSTEAD RD.
CRESTWAY
HIGHDOWN RD.
PARKMEAD
COPPICE DR.
WESTMEAD
ROEHAMPTON HIGH ST.
Playing Fields
Roehampton Hosp.
Sch.

PUTNEY
HOWARD'S
HAZLEWELL
CHARTFIELD AV.
COLINETTE RD.
DEUTRY RD.
PARKFIELDS
GENOA
WESTL...
PUTNEY LANE
PORTSMOU...

PUTNEY
HEATH

Continued on page 81

Interchange Stations ----⊙

Railways & Stations ....
Underground Railways & Stations (L.P.T.) ... --○--
Bus & Trolleybus Routes ....

House numbers 253

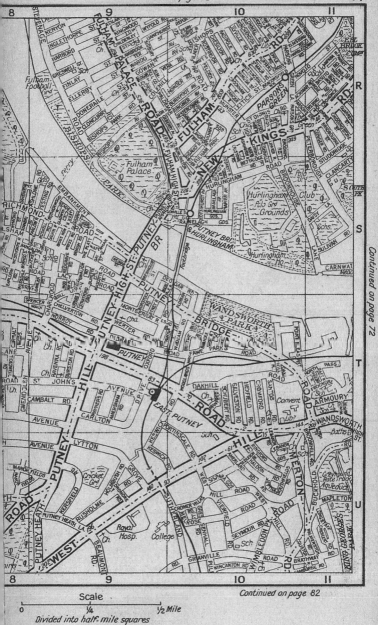

Continued on page 72

Scale

0   ¼   ½ Mile

Divided into half-mile squares

Continued on page 60

Continued on page 71

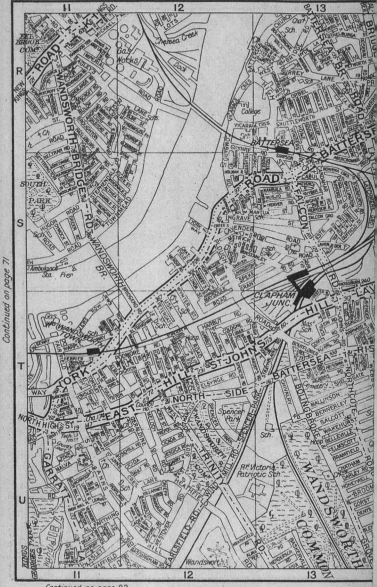

Continued on page 83

Railways & Stations ....
Underground Railways & Stations (L.P.T.)...
Bus & Trolleybus Routes ....
Tram Routes ....
House numbers 253

Continued on page 74

Continued on page 84

Scale

0   1/4   1/2 Mile

Divided into half-mile squares

Continued on page 73

Railways & Stations ....
Underground Railways & Stations (L.P.T.) ...
Bus & Trolleybus Routes ....
Tram Routes ....
House numbers 253

Continued on page 76

Continued on page 86.

Scale

0   1/4   1/2 Mile

Divided into half-mile squares

Continued on page 75

Interchange Stations ..... ⊙

Railways & Stations	
Underground Railways & Stations (L.P.T.)...	
Bus & Trolleybus Routes	
Tram Routes	
House numbers 253	

Continued on page 78

Continued on page 88

Scale

0   ¼   ½ Mile

Divided into half-mile squares

Continued on page 77

Continued on page 89

Railways & Stations ....
Underground Railways & Stations (L.P.T.)....
Bus & Trolleybus Routes ....
Tram Routes ....
House numbers 253

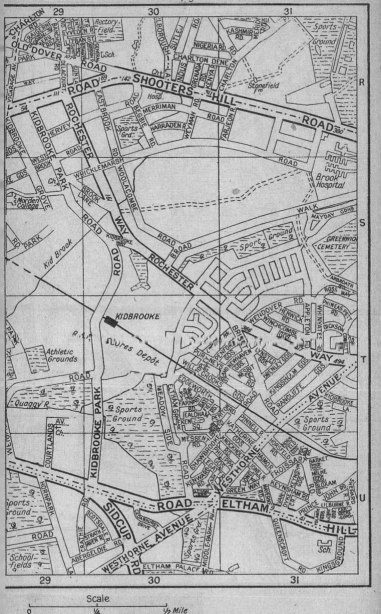

Scale

0   ¼   ½ Mile

Divided into half-mile squares

R I C H M O N D

White Lodge

Leg of Mutton Pond

Pen Ponds

Spankers Hill Wood

P A R K

Beverley Br.

Robin Hood Gate

Isabella Plantation

KINGSTON VALE

Sch.
Ch.
ROBIN HOOD LANE
DERWENT AV.
ULLSWATER CRES.
WATER CLOSE
GRASMERE AV.
ULLSWATER CRES.
KINGSTON
KINGSTON ROAD
RIDING
RYDAL GDNS.

Kenry Ho.

HILL
COOMBE WOOD RD.
COOMBE PARK
COOMBE PARK

Warren Ho.

HARBERTS RD.
KINGSTON WARREN
ROAD

Coombe Hill Golf Course

Railways & Stations	....
Underground Railways & Stations (L.P.T.)	...
Bus & Trolleybus Routes	....

Continued on page 82

Continued on page 92

Scale

0 ¼ ½ Mile

Divided into half-mile squares

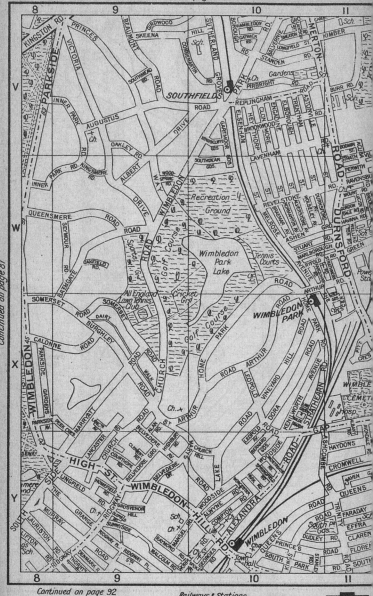

SOUTHFIELDS

Recreation Ground

Wimbledon Park Lake

Tennis Courts

WIMBLEDON PARK

All England Lawn Tennis Club

Golf Course

Park

HIGH ST.

WIMBLEDON HILL

Continued on page 81

Interchange Stations.....⊙

Railways & Stations ....
Underground Railways & Stations (L.P.T.)... – – –
Bus & Trolleybus Routes ....
Tram Routes ....
House numbers..... 253

Continued on page 84

Scale

0　　　　¼　　　　½ Mile

Divided into half-mile squares

Continued on page 83

TOOTING JUNC.

Railways & Stations ....
Underground Railways & Stations (L.P.T.)...
Bus & Trolleybus Routes ....
Tram Routes ....
House numbers 253

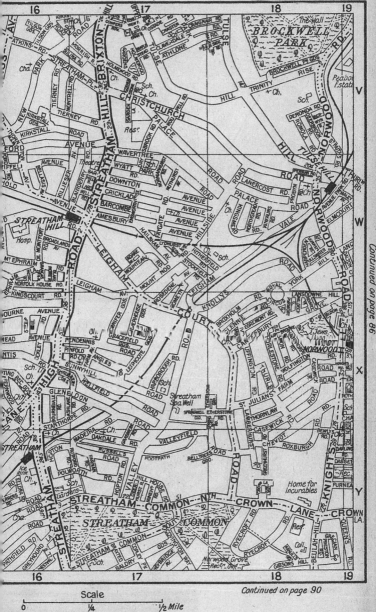

Continued on page 86

Continued on page 90

Scale

0   ¼   ½ Mile

Divided into half-mile squares

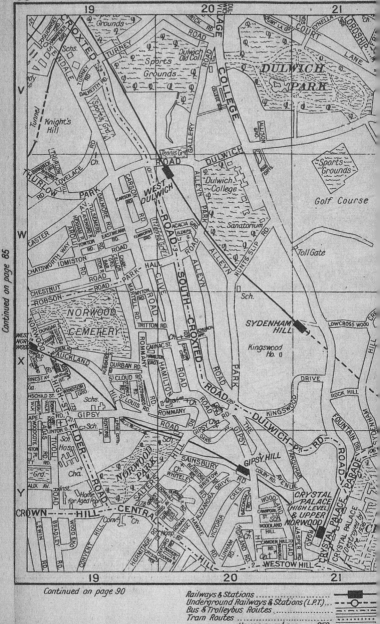

Continued on page 85

Railways & Stations ....
Underground Railways & Stations (L.P.T.)....
Bus & Trolleybus Routes ....
Tram Routes ....
House numbers 253

Continued on page 88

Scale

0   ¼   ½ Mile

Divided into half-mile squares

Continued on page 87

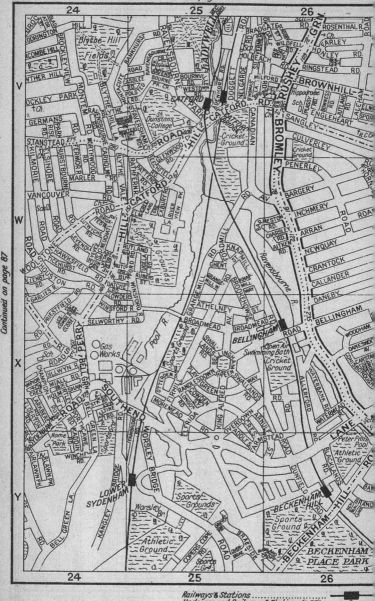

Railways & Stations ....
Underground Railways & Stations (L.P.T.)...
Bus & Trolleybus Routes ....
Tram Routes ....
House numbers 253

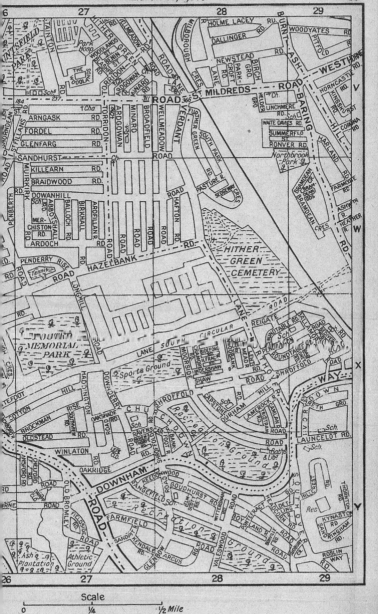

Continued on page 87

Continued on page 86

Continued on page 85

ELMERS END

AUCKLAND

ROAD

LONDON

HIGH ROAD

STREATHAM

MITCHAM ROAD

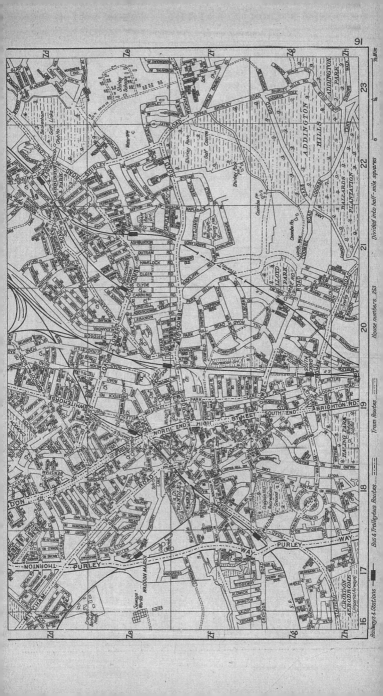

ADDINGTON PARK

ADDINGTON HILLS

SHIRLEY

UPPER SHIRLEY ROAD

Shirley Park Golf Course

ASHBURTON RD.
OUTRAM
HAVELOCK RD.
ELGIN
CLYDE
CANNING RD.
LEBANON

LLOYD PARK

NORTH END HIGH STREET
SOUTH END   BRIGHTON RD.

PURLEY   WAY   PURLEY   WAY

THORNTON   PURLEY

MITCHAM   WADDON MARSH

CROYDON AERODROME (Aerodrome)

23

22

21

20

19

18

17

16

½ Mile

¼

0

Divided into half-mile squares

House numbers, 253

Railways & Stations ——
Tram Routes ——
Bus & Trolleybus Routes ——

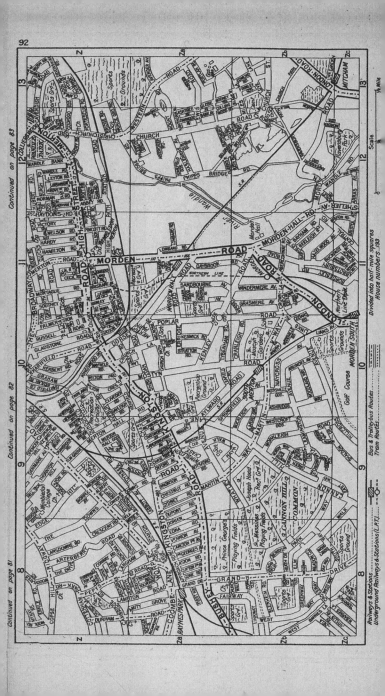

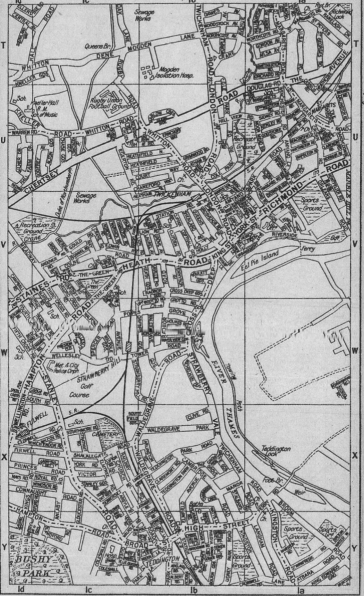

Continued on page 68

Railways & Stations
Underground Railways & Stations (L.P.T.)
Bus & Trolleybus Routes
House numbers 152

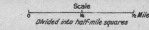

Scale

0   ¼   ½ Mile

Divided into half-mile squares

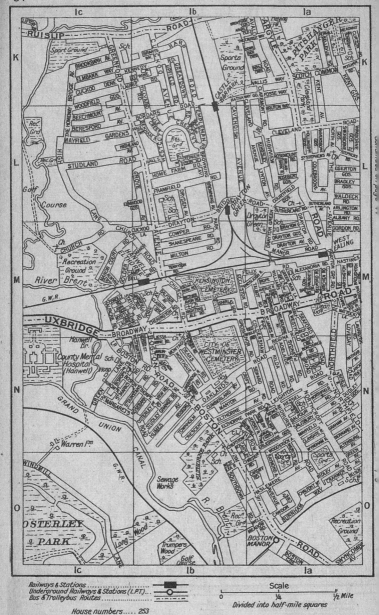

continued on page 95

Railways & Stations
Underground Railways & Stations (L.P.T.)
Bus & Trolleybus Routes

House numbers 253

Scale

0   ¼   ½ Mile

Divided into half-mile squares

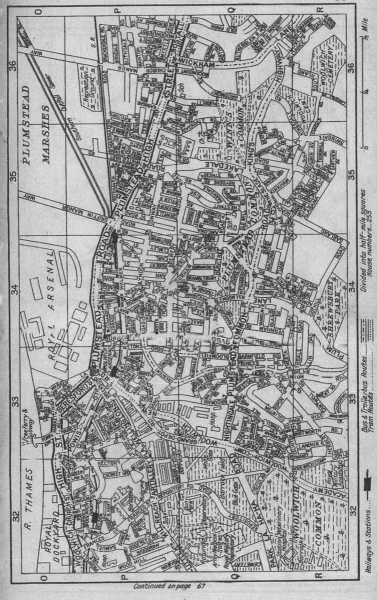

Continued on page 67

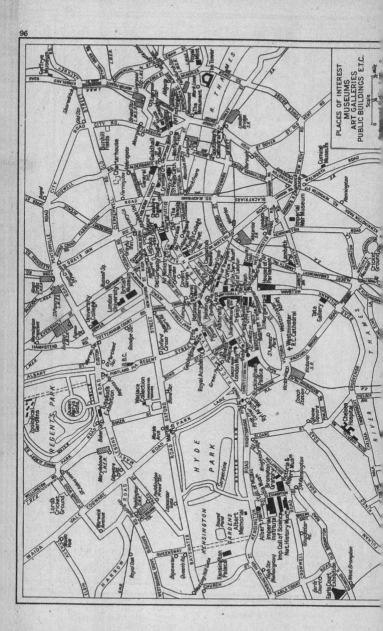

PLACES OF INTEREST
MUSEUMS
ART GALLERIES
PUBLIC BUILDINGS E.T.C.

PLACES OF INTEREST

Each place described is followed by a reference in brackets to its position on the Map. The first letter and number refer to the Map square and the last number to the Map page on which it will be found.

The nearest station to each place of interest is given in brackets after the address. Main Line Railway Stations are in italics and followed by the letter *R*. Underground Stations are followed by a letter denoting their respective line. Thus : B = Bakerloo ; C = Central ; D = District & Metropolitan ; N = Northern ; P = Piccadilly.

ACADEMY OF ARTS, ROYAL, BURLINGTON HOUSE, PICCADILLY, S.W.1 (Station : Piccadilly BP), was founded by George III in 1768, its first president being Sir Joshua Reynolds. An annual exhibition of pictures and sculpture, selected by Royal Academicians from the work of living artists is opened here on the first Monday in May and closes on the first Monday in August. Its opening is the first event of the London " season." OPEN DAILY 9 A.M. TO 7 P.M. ADMISSION 1/6. ON AUGUST BANK HOLIDAY OPEN TILL 10 P.M.: ADMISSION 1/-. THE GIBSON AND DIPLOMA GALLERIES with their permanent collection of old and modern pictures are OPEN DAILY THROUGHOUT THE YEAR FROM 11 a.m. TO 4 p.m. ADMISSION FREE. Important exhibitions of the works of Old Masters frequently take place at Burlington House during the winter. (15M 49)

ADMIRALTY, WHITEHALL, S.W.1 (Stations : Trafalgar Sq. B ; Strand, N). The nerve centre of the British Navy. The administration is enabled to keep in touch with the entire fleet in all parts of the world by means of the wireless installation which can be seen on the roof of the new building. The old building dates from 1722, the handsome screen being added in 1760 by Adam. Amongst many portraits inside, there is one of Samuel Pepys. Office hours : 10 a.m. to 5 p.m. (16N 62)

ADMIRALTY ARCH, TRAFALGAR SQUARE, S.W.1. (Stations : Trafalgar Sq. B ; Strand N). This large triple archway designed by Sir Aston Webb opens on to the Mall and the quiet of St. James's Park. State and Royal processions pass through it on their way between Buckingham Palace and Westminster Abbey. The rooms over the Arch contain the valuable Admiralty Library. (16N 62)

AGRICULTURAL HALL, UPPER STREET, ISLINGTON, N.1 (Station : Angel N). The scene of large cattle, horse and dog shows and trade exhibitions. At Christmas time this hall of 206 681 square feet is packed with people visiting the World Fair. (18J 50)

ALBERT EMBANKMENT, S.E.1 and S.E.11 (Stations : Westminster D ; Lambeth Nth. B ; *Vauxhall R*). The only embankment to have been built on the much neglected south side of the Thames. It runs between Vauxhall and Westminster Bridges and, amongst the buildings along it are Lambeth Palace, St. Thomas's Hospital and Doulton's Pottery Works. (17P 62)

ALBERT HALL, ROYAL, KENSINGTON GORE, S.W.7 (Station : Sth. Kensington DP). This enormous building which can hold over 10,000 people is famous for its concerts, political and other meetings, boxing contests and exhibitions of all kinds. Built at a cost of £200,000, it was opened in 1871 as a memorial to the Prince Consort, who had conceived the idea of a Hall of Arts and Sciences. The organ, with its 9,000 pipes is one of the largest in the world. (12N 60)

ALBERT MEMORIAL, KENSINGTON GARDENS, S.W.7 (Station : Sth. Kensington DP). Designed by Sir Gilbert Scott, it was erected as a memorial to the Prince Consort at a cost of £120,000. Intended to show Albert's very genuine interest in the culture of England, it lends itself, paradoxically enough, to much artistic criticism. (12N 60)

ALEXANDRA PALACE, MUSWELL HILL, N.22 (Stations : *Alexandra Palace R* ; Turnpike La. P ; *Wood Green R*). A large building open to the public and situated in grounds where there is entertainment of all kinds—racing, concerts, boating, swimming, dancing, ice skating, firework displays and trade shows. ADMISSION FREE, EXCEPT ON BANK HOLIDAYS AND DURING SPECIAL EVENTS WHEN ADMISSION IS 1/-. Part of the building has been taken over by the B.B.C. for its television transmission. (16A 23)

APSLEY HOUSE, HYDE PARK CORNER, S.W.1 (Station : Hyde Pk. Corner P). This Adams building was bought by the famous Duke of Wellington. It is still in the family and is the town residence of the present Duke. (14N 61)

ARTILLERY MEMORIAL, ROYAL, HYDE PARK CORNER, S.W.1 (Station : Hyde Pk. Corner P). A fine memorial by Jagger commemorating the Royal Artillery dead of the Great War. (14N 61)

BANK OF ENGLAND, THREADNEEDLE STREET, E.C.2 (Station : Bank CN). In spite of post-war financial problems, the Bank of England is still considered synonymous with security. Its first business in 1694 was to raise a loan of about £1,000,000 for the Government, then at war with France. It now has upwards of £525,000,000 in its vaults. The building, already several times enlarged since the early 18th century, has recently been rebuilt by Sir Herbert Baker. The armed guard, which is on duty here every night, is a reminder of the attack made on the Bank during the Gordon Riots. (20M 51)

BATTERSEA PARK (Stations: *Battersea Pk. R*; Sloane Sq. D and Bus 19). Lies betwee Chelsea and Albert Bridges on the south side of the river, and has a boating lake, tenni courts and a bandstand where Sunday concerts are given. (14R 73)

BETHNAL GREEN MUSEUM, CAMBRIDGE ROAD, E.3 (Stations: *Cambridge Heath R Bethnal Grn. R,* Bus 42). A branch of the Victoria and Albert Museum, it contains very fine collection of textiles, which date from 1685 when the Huguenots founded th Spitalfield silk weaving industry. The Children's Gallery with its dolls' houses and toy of several centuries is especially popular. Other exhibits include ceramics, furniture boots and shoes, showing the history of these local trades. The pictures include water colours and chiefly 19th-century British and foreign paintings. The Museum is OPEI ON WEEKDAYS FROM 10 A.M. TO 6 P.M.; MON. and THURS. 10 A.M. to 10 P.M.; SUNDAY 2.30 P.M. TO 6 P.M. ADMISSION FREE. (22K 52)

BILLINGSGATE FISH MARKET, LOWER THAMES STREET, E.C.3 (Stations: Marl Lane D; Monument D). Formerly a market for goods of various kinds, Billingsgat was, in the 17th century, restricted to dealing in fish. Opening every morning at 5 a.m it presents an almost mediæval scene with the fish porters loading high baskets of fish o to their heads and carrying them to carts or 20th-century lorries. And these fish porters amidst all the noise and screaming, still flavour their language with the proverbial " Bil lingsgate." (20M 51)

BLACKFRIARS BRIDGE, E.C.4 (Station: Blackfriars D). Built in 1770 as a memoria to William Pitt, Earl of Chatham, the bridge very soon changed its name of Pitt Bridg to that of the district of Blackfriars, so called after the black-habited Dominicans wh had their priory here from the 13th century until the Reformation. The bridge was rebuil in 1869, since when it has been considerably widened, and is now 108 ft., the wides bridge in London. (18M 50)

BLACKHEATH, S.E.3 (Station: *Blackheath R*; Buses 48, 54, 75, 21a, 108, 154). Adjoin Greenwich Park, and has been the scene of many historical events. It was here that Henry IV met Manuel Palæologus the Emperor of Constantinople in 1400, and that Henry VII welcomed Anne of Cleves. At Blackheath Wat Tyler, and later Jack Cade, gathered thei followers round them before advancing on London over Deptford Bridge. Here James introduced the game of golf to England and the Royal Blackheath Golf Club is th oldest golf club in this country. (27S 78)

BLACKWALL TUNNEL, E.14 (Station: *Poplar R*). This tunnel, 6,200 ft. long, unde the Thames to Greenwich was opened in 1897. The narrowness of the roadway only allow two streams of traffic but the building of a parallel tunnel at a cost of three million pound has been planned to relieve this congestion. (27N 66)

BOND STREET, W.1 (Stations: Bond St. C; Piccadilly BP). The world-famous fashionable shopping street of London. (15M 49)

BRITISH MUSEUM, GREAT RUSSELL STREET, W.C.1 (Stations: Russell Sq. P; Tot tenham Court Rd. BN). Originally founded in 1759 from the private collections of Si Hans Sloane and Sir Robert Cotton, it rapidly became the finest Museum in existence It contains an unrivalled collection of Assyrian, Babylonian, Egyptian, Greek and Roman sculpture, amongst which are the famous Elgin marbles. Coins and pottery, manuscripts historical documents, etc., all have their place in this gigantic museum. The Reading Room contains five million volumes which take up over 80 miles of shelving. Amongs notable people who have studied here are Thackeray and Karl Marx. The Museum is OPEN DAILY, 10 A.M. TO 6 P.M.; SUNDAYS 2 TO 6 P.M. ADMISSION FREE. The READING ROOM IS OPEN 9 A.M. TO 6 P.M., BUT ONLY TO TICKET-HOLDERS. Tickets may be obtained on written application to the Director. (16L 50)

BROADCASTING HOUSE, LANGHAM PLACE, W.1 (Station: Oxford Circus CB). The headquarters of the British Broadcasting Corporation, known as the B.B.C., this new building by Val Myer and M. T. Tudsbery was completed in 1932. (15L 49)

BROMPTON ORATORY, BROMPTON ROAD, S.W.7 (Station: Sth. Kensington DP) Built in the Italian Renaissance style during the 19th century, it is well-known for its fine musical services. At Christmas, this large Roman Catholic Church is thronged with people attending Midnight Mass. ADMISSION FREE DAILY 6 A.M. TO 10 P.M. BUT DURING SERVICES AND ON SATURDAY MORNINGS SIGHTSEEING IS NOT ALLOWED. Services: Sunday: Masses every half hour, from 6.30 to 9 a.m., and at 10, 10.45 and 12 noon. Services a 3.30 and 7 p.m. Weekdays: every half hour from 6.30 to 8.30 a.m. and at 10 a.m. Eve ning Service at 8 p.m. except Saturdays, when there is a service at 4.30 p.m. (13O 60)

BUCKINGHAM PALACE, S.W.1 (Station: St. James Pk. D). The London Palace of the King and Queen. When they are in residence the Royal Standard flies from the mas and the changing of the Guard takes place here (10 a.m.) instead of at St. James's Palace Rebuilt by the Duke of Buckingham in 1703, Buckingham Palace, as it was thereafte called, was bought by George III in 1761, enlarged by George IV, added to by Queen Victoria and refaced in 1913. Permission to visit the Royal Stables and Riding School can be obtained by writing to the Master of the Horse. (15N 61)

BUNHILL FIELDS, CITY ROAD, E.C.1 (Station: Old St. MN). For two centuries unti 1852 the chief Nonconformist burial ground. John Bunyan, Daniel Defoe, William Blak and John Wesley's mother are amongst the famous people buried here. Milton wrote

" Paradise Lost " in Bunhill Row and died there.   Charles Fox was buried in the adjoining Quaker Burial Ground, and John Wesley in the John Wesley Chapel opposite. (20K 51)

CALEDONIAN MARKET, CALEDONIAN ROAD, N.7 (Station : Caledonian Rd. P).   A cattle market on Mondays and Thursdays, it becomes a general market on Tuesdays and Fridays, on which two days rich and poor bargain-hunters mingle in the noisy, animated crowd. (17G 36)

CARLYLE'S HOUSE, 24, CHEYNE ROW, S.W.3 (Station : Sth. Kensington DP ; Bus 49)   The famous writer's life and period strongly pervade this house, which contains much of his property and has hardly been altered since he occupied it.   He lived there from 1834 until his death in 1881. (13Q 60)

CAVELL MEMORIAL, ST. MARTIN'S PLACE, W.C.2 (Station : Trafalgar Sq. B).   This statue, by Sir G. Frampton, was unveiled in 1920 in memory of Nurse Edith Cavell, whose heroism in the Great War led to her being shot for harbouring and assisting the escape of prisoners. (16M 50)

CENOTAPH, THE, WHITEHALL, S.W.1 (Station : Trafalgar Sq. B ; Strand N ; Westminster D).   Designed by Sir Edward Lutyens for the Peace Celebrations of August 3rd, 1919, it was erected in its present form as a perpetual memorial to " The Glorious Dead " of the Great War.   On November 11th of each year (anniversary of Armistice Day) crowds gather at the Cenotaph for the two minutes' silence, and the base is covered with wreaths laid by the King, members of the Government, etc., and mourners. (17N 62)

CENTRAL CRIMINAL COURT, OLD BAILEY, E.C.4 (Station : St. Pauls C).   Known as the Old Bailey, the present building was completed in 1907 on the site of Newgate Prison.   The lofty tower is surmounted by a bronze gilt figure of Justice.   The Court House can be visited on Tuesdays and Fridays from 10 a.m. to 4 p.m. or by special application to the Keeper.   When the Court sits, the Public Gallery, holding about 200 people, is open from 10.15 a.m. to 1.30 p.m.   During spectacular cases, a large crowd gathers outside the Old Bailey in the hope of gaining admission. (19L 51)

CENTRAL HALL, TOTHILL STREET, WESTMINSTER, S.W.1 (Station : Westminster D).   This large domed building almost opposite Westminster Abbey is the Methodists' London Headquarters.   The hall is, however, much used for courts, conferences and exhibitions. (16N 62)

CHARTERHOUSE, CHARTERHOUSE SQUARE, SMITHFIELD, E.C.1 (Station : Aldersgate D).   Founded in 1371, this Carthusian Monastery was dissolved by Henry VIII.   In 1611 it was endowed as a hospital for 80 old men and a school for 40 boys, but the school, now one of the famous public schools, was transferred to Godalming in 1872.   Charterhouse contains some of the finest early sixteenth century architecture in the country.   For admission APPLY TO THE PORTER'S LODGE ON MON., WED., FRI., 3 TO 5 p.m.   ADMISSION 1/-. (19L 51)

CHELSEA ROYAL HOSPITAL, ROYAL HOSPITAL ROAD, S.W.3 (Station : Sloane Sq. D ; Bus 39), was designed by Sir Christopher Wren and founded in 1682 by Charles II at the instigation, it is suggested, of Nell Gwynne, as a home for old or disabled soldiers.   The " Chelsea Pensioner " is a well-known figure in his summer scarlet or dark blue winter coat.   The building contains a fine statue of Charles II by Grinling Gibbons.   ADMISSION FREE.   The GARDENS are spacious and the Horticultural Society hold their Flower Show here in the Spring. (14P 61)

CHESHIRE CHEESE, THE OLD, WINE OFFICE COURT, 145, FLEET STREET, E.C.4 (Station : Blackfriars D).   An old and little-altered Inn, famous for its Pudding on Wednesdays and for its literary associations.   Tradition has it that Dr. Johnson, Boswell and Oliver Goldsmith were habitués of the " Cheshire Cheese," and nowadays one may often see some prominent journalist lunching here. (18M 50)

CITY CHURCHES
    Churches marked * survived the Great Fire of 1666.
    Churches marked † were restored after the Fire but not by Wren.
    All the remaining Churches were rebuilt or restored by Christopher Wren.

Name of Church and Situation	Nearest Station
Allhallows, Lombard Street, E.1.	Bank CN (20M 51)
Allhallows, Barking-by-the-Tower, Tower Hill, E.C.3	Mark La. D (20M 51)
Allhallows-on-the-Wall, London Wall, E.C.2	Liverpool St. CD (20L 51)
Austin Friars, Old Broad Street, E.C.2	Bank CN (20L 51)
Christ Church, Newgate Street, E.C.1	St. Pauls C (19L 51)
St. Alban, Wood Street, E.C.2	St. Pauls C (19L 51)
St. Alphage, London Wall, E.C.2	Moorgate DN (19L 51)
St. Andrew, Holborn Viaduct, E.C.1	Chancery La. C (18L 50)
St. Andrew-by-the-Wardrobe, Queen Victoria Street, E.C.4	Blackfriars D (18L 50)
St. Andrew Undershaft, Leadenhall Street, E.C.3	Liverpool St. CD (20M 51)
St. Anne & St. Agnes, Gresham Street, E.C.2	St. Pauls C (19L 51)
St. Augustine with St. Faith under St. Paul's, Old Change, E.C.4	St. Pauls C (19M 51)
St. Bartholomew-the-Great, Smithfield, E.C.1	Aldersgate D (19L 51)
St. Bartholomew-the-Less, Giltspur Street, E.C.1	St. Pauls C (19L 51)
St. Benet, Paul's Wharf, E.C.4	Blackfriars D (19M 51)
St. Botolph, Aldersgate Street, E.C.1	St. Pauls C (19L 51)

†St. Botolph, Aldgate, E.C.3 .. .. Aldgate D (21M 51)
†St. Botolph, Bishopsgate, E.C.2 .. .. Liverpool St. CD (20L 51)
St. Bride, Fleet Street, E.C.4 .. .. Blackfriars D (18M 50)
St. Clement, Eastcheap, E.C.3 .. .. Monument D (20M 51)
St. Dunstan-in-the-East, Lower Thames Street, E.C.3 .. .. Mark La. D (20M 51)
†St. Dunstan-in-the-West, Fleet Street, E.C.4 .. .. .. Temple D (18M 50)
St. Edmund, King and Martyr, Lombard Street, E.C.3 .. .. Bank CN (20M 51)
*St. Ethelburga-the-Virgin, Bishopsgate, E.C.2 .. .. .. Liverpool St. CD (20L 51)
*St. Etheldreda, Ely Place, E.C.1 .. .. Farringdon D (18L 50)
*St. Giles, Redcross Street, E.C.1 .. .. Moorgate DN (19L 51)
*St. Helen, Bishopsgate, E.C.2 .. .. Liverpool St.CD (20M 51)
St. James, Garlick Hill, E.C.4 .. .. Mansion Ho. D (19M 51)
*St. Katherine Cree, Leadenhall St. E.C.3 .. .. .. Aldgate D (20M 51)
St. Lawrence Jewry, Gresham Street, E.C.2 .. .. .. Bank CN (19L 51)
St. Magnus the Martyr, Lower Thames Street, E.C.3 .. Monument D (20 M 51)
St. Margaret, Lothbury, E.C.2 .. .. Bank CN (20M 51)
St. Margaret Pattens, Eastcheap, E.C.3 .. .. .. Monument D (20M 51)
St. Martin, Ludgate Hill, E.C.4 .. .. St. Pauls C (19M 50)
St. Mary Abchurch, Abchurch Lane, E.C.4 .. .. .. Monument D (20M 51)
St. Mary Aldermary, Queen Victoria Street, E.C.4 .. .. Mansion Ho. D (19M 51)
St. Mary-at-Hill, Monument Street, E.C.3 .. .. .. Monument D (20M 51)
St. Mary-le-Bow, Cheapside, E.C.2 .. .. Mansion Ho. D (19M 51)
St. Mary-the-Virgin, Aldermanbury, E.C.2 .. .. .. Moorgate DN (19L 51)
†St. Mary Woolnoth, Lombard Street, E.C.3 .. .. .. Bank CN (20M 51)
St. Michael Paternoster Royal, College Hill, E.C.4 .. .. Cannon St. D (19M 51)
St. Michael-upon-Cornhill, E.C.3 .. .. Bank CN (20M 51)
St. Mildred, Bread Street, E.C.4 .. .. Mansion Ho. D (19M 51)
St. Nicholas Cole Abbey, Queen Victoria Street, E.C.4 .. Mansion Ho. D (19M 51)
*St. Olave, Hart Street, E.C.3 .. .. Mark La. D (20M 51)
St. Peter-upon-Cornhill, E.C.3 .. .. Bank CN (20M 51)
St. Sepulchre, Newgate Street, E.C.2 .. .. .. St. Pauls C (19L 50)
St. Stephen, Coleman Street, EC.2. .. .. .. Bank CN (20L 51)
St. Stephen, Walbrook, E.C.4 .. .. Bank CN (20M 51)
St. Swithin, Cannon Street, E.C.4 .. .. Cannon St. D (20M 51)
St. Vedast, Foster Lane, E.C.2 .. .. St. Pauls C (19M 51)

CLEOPATRA'S NEEDLE, VICTORIA EMBANKMENT, W.C.2 (Station : Charing Cross BDN). An Egyptian obelisk, which about 3,500 years ago stood in front of the Temple of the Sun at Heliopolis. When it was being towed to England in 1877, this " Needle," 68½ ft. high and weighing 180 tons, had to be abandoned in the Bay of Biscay during a storm. It was recovered by another tug and ultimately reached its destination. (17M 50)

COLLEGE OF ARMS, or COLLEGE OF HERALDS, QUEEN VICTORIA STREET, E.C.4 (Station : Blackfriars D). The College deals with all matters relating to Heraldry and State Functions and consists of three Kings of Arms (Garter, Clarenceux, Norroy), six Heralds and four Pursuivants, all of whom are appointed by the Earl Marshal, the Duke of Norfolk. The building, Derby House, reconstructed by Wren after the Great Fire, was presented to the College by Queen Mary in 1555. OPEN FOR HERALDIC ENQUIRIES ON WEEKDAYS 10 A.M. TO 4 P.M. ADMISSION TO VIEW OBTAINABLE ON APPLICATION. (19M 51)

COUNTY HALL, BELVEDERE ROAD, S.E.1 (Station : Westminster D), is the administrative headquarters of the London County Council. Situated on the south side of the Thames, this fine building is by Ralph Knott and was opened by his late Majesty King George V in 1922. The building has already cost over three and a half million pounds and extensions are now being erected. ADMISSION TO PORTIONS OF THE COUNTY HALL ON SATURDAYS, EASTER AND WHIT MONDAYS AND AUGUST BANK HOLIDAY, 10.30 A.M. TO 12 NOON AND 1.30 TO 3.30 P.M. (17N 62)

COVENT GARDEN MARKET, SOUTHAMPTON STREET, STRAND, W.C.2 (Station : Covent Garden P). The famous and most important London market for vegetables, fruit and flowers. Originally the Convent Garden of Westminster, then an arcaded square by Inigo Jones, this open piazza lent itself to the selling of country produce, and quickly developed into the largest market of its kind in this country. The lovely flowers and animation of the whole scene make an early morning visit between 6 a.m and 9 a.m. (Tues., Thur., Sat.) well worth while. (17M 50)

CROSBY HALL, CHEYNE WALK, CHELSEA, S.W.3 (Station : Sth. Kensington DP, and Bus 49). A fifteenth-century building deriving its name from Sir John Crosby, whose home it originally was. It was removed from Bishopsgate to its present position in 1910. Richard, Duke of Gloucester, occupied it before he became King, and Crosby Hall therefore appears in Shakespeare's " Richard III." (13Q 60)

CRYSTAL PALACE, SYDENHAM, S.E.19 (Station : *Crystal Palace R*). Erected in Hyde Park as the Exhibition Building of 1851. Removed to Sydenham, it became a centre of amusement and was known for its early balloon trials, firework displays and brass band contests, until burnt down in 1936. For occasional exhibitions see newspapers. (21Y 87)

CUMING MUSEUM, WALWORTH ROAD, S.E.17 (Station : Elephant & Castle BN). Its relics of the Stone Age and the civilisations of Babylon, Egypt, Greece, Rome and Mexico, illustrate the development of man's work from prehistoric to recent times. OPEN MONDAY TO FRIDAY, 12 NOON TO 8.30 P.M.; SATURDAY, 10 A.M. TO 8.30 P.M.; SUNDAY, 6 TO 9 P.M. ADMISSION FREE. (19P 63)

CUSTOM HOUSE, LOWER THAMES STREET, E.C.3 (Stations : Monument D ; Mark Lane D), is where the Customs are levied by the Customs and Excise Commission. The first Custom House was erected in 1385 and after burning down was replaced by three others which suffered a similar fate. The present building (1815), by David Laing, lies a little to the west of its predecessors and has a river frontage of 488 ft. OPEN DAILY 10 A.M. TO 5 P.M. (20M 51)

DICKENS'S HOUSE, 48, DOUGHTY STREET, W.C.1 (Station : Russell Square P). Although the author lived here only from 1837 to 1839, " Oliver Twist," " Nicholas Nickleby " were written and the " Pickwick Papers " were completed during those two years. The house is now a Museum of Dickens Memorabilia, and the headquarters of the Dickens Fellowship. OPEN 10 A.M. TO 5 P.M. ADMISSION 6D. (17K 50)

DOCKS, THE, were built during the 19th century to deal with the ever-increasing trade of the Port of London, to day the largest port in the world. They stretch along the north side of the Thames from below the Tower to Tilbury and can be seen from the river in motor launches which run from Westminster Pier. They lie in the following order (the nearest station being given in italics) : St. Katherine's (21N 63), *Mark La. D* ; London (22N 64), *Shadwell D, Wapping D*, West India (25N 65), Millwall (26O 65), East India (27M 66), *Poplar R* ; Royal Victoria (29N 67), *Trains from Fenchurch St. R* ; Royal Albert and King George (31N 67), *East Ham D* ; Tilbury, *Trains from Fenchurch St. R.* The only Dock on the south side of the river is the Surrey Commercial Dock (24N 64), *Surrey Docks D.*

DONALDSON MUSICAL INSTRUMENTS, ROYAL COLLEGE OF MUSIC, PRINCE CONSORT ROAD, SOUTH KENSINGTON, S.W.7 (Station : Sth. Kensington DP). Contains a small collection of rare instruments. OPEN ON APPLICATION. (12O 60)

DOWNING STREET, WHITEHALL, S.W.1 (Stations : Trafalgar Sq. B, Westminster D). Bought as a messuage and built on towards the end of the 17th century by Sir George Downing, under whom Pepys unwillingly worked as a clerk at one time. No. 10, Downing Street is now world-famous as the home of the British Prime Minister and the scene of Cabinet Meetings. No. 11 houses the Chancellor of the Exchequer, and No. 12 is the Government Whip's Office. (16N 62)

DUKE OF YORK'S COLUMN, WATERLOO PLACE, S.W.1 (Stations : Piccadilly BP, Trafalgar Sq. B). This column, which stands above the steps leading down to St. James's Park, is 124 ft. high, and was erected in 1833 as a memorial to Frederick, Duke of York, the second son of George III. Famous for his debts and incapacity as Commander-in-Chief, he is the Duke of York who, in popular song, " led his ten thousand men up a hill and down again." View from top. ADMISSION 6D. (16N 62)

DULWICH PICTURE GALLERY, GALLERY ROAD, DULWICH, S.E.21 (Station : *Nth. Dulwich R*). Contains an outstanding collection of Flemish and Dutch art which had originally been bought as a nucleus for a Polish National Gallery before the partition of that country. Amongst the exhibits are Rembrandt's famous " Girl at a Window," and paintings by Ruisdael, Van de Velde, Cuyp, Van Dyck, Rubens, etc. Tiepolo, Velasquez, Murillo and Poussin, and fine examples of British 17th and 18th century portraiture are also exhibited. OPEN WEEKDAYS FROM 10 A.M TO 4, 5 OR 6 P.M. SUNDAYS : 2 P.M. TO 5 or 6 P.M. CLOSED ON SUNDAYS OCT. TO MARCH. ADMISSION FREE. (20V 86)

EARL HAIG, STATUE OF, WHITEHALL, S.W.1 (Station : Strand N). The third attempt to please a critical public has resulted in the present statue of Earl Haig by Eric Hardiman which was unveiled in 1937. (17N 62)

EARLS COURT, WARWICK ROAD, S.W.5 (Station : Earls Court DP, West Brompton D). Was known in pre-war days for its " Big Wheel " and other open-air attractions. But the present gigantic building by Howard Crane (completed in 1937) contains swimming pools, skating rinks, etc., besides large exhibition halls for motor and other shows. (11P 59)

FLEET STREET, E.C.4 (Station : Temple D). This well-known centre of the British news-paper industry is an unpretentious but exceedingly busy thoroughfare between the Strand and Ludgate Hill. Isaac Walton lived here near the corner of Chancery Lane. (18M 50)

FOREIGN OFFICE, WHITEHALL, S.W.1 (Stations : Westminster D, Trafalgar Sq. B). (16N 62)

GEFFRYE MUSEUM, KINGSLAND ROAD, E.2 (Station : *Shoreditch R*). The buildings are old Almshouses erected in 1715 by the Ironmongers' Company, and contain interesting exhibits of panelled rooms and shop fronts, furniture and ironwork preserved from demolished 16th, 17th and 18th century houses. OPEN 11 A.M. TO 6 P.M. SUNDAYS : 2 P.M. TO 6 P.M. CLOSED ON MONDAYS (EXCEPT BANK HOLIDAYS). ADMISSION FREE. (21K 51)

GENERAL POST OFFICE, KING EDWARD STREET, E.C.1 (Station : St. Pauls C). These eight enormous buildings were erected in 1913 to replace the old Post Office which was no longer able to cope with an ever-increasing postal business. The present G.P.O.

houses the whole administrative, postal, telephone and telegraph staff. The Post Restante Bureau is on the left of the Public Hall. OPEN 8 A.M. TO 9.30 P.M. The Telegraph Office in St. Martin's-le-Grand is always open. (19L 51)

GEOLOGY, MUSEUM OF PRACTICAL, EXHIBITION ROAD, SOUTH KENSINGTON, S.W.7 (Station: Sth. Kensington DP). Contains precious stones, fossils and models of famous diamonds; maps and specimens of the structure of Great Britain, and a section dealing with industrial geology and mineralogy. OPEN 10 A.M. TO 6 P.M. SUNDAYS: 2.30 P.M. TO 6 P.M. ADMISSION FREE. (12O 60)

GOLDSMITHS' HALL, GRESHAM STREET, E.C.2 (Station: St. Pauls C). The home of the Goldsmiths' Company, one of the twelve " Great " Livery Companies of the City of London. Since Henry III it has been responsible for the " Trial of the Pyx," the testing of newly-minted coins, which takes place annually. Gold and silver are hallmarked here with the " leopard's head." The Company possesses one of the most representative collections of antique plate in the country, a notable exhibit being Queen Elizabeth's coronation goblet. ADMISSION USUALLY OBTAINABLE ON WRITTEN APPLICATION. (19L 51)

GRAY'S INN, HOLBORN, W.C.1 (Station: Chancery Lane C). One of the four great Inns of Court, it possesses a fine Elizabethan Hall and Chapel. The catalpa tree in the Gardens was planted by Bacon when a student at this Inn. (18L 50)

GREEN PARK, PICCADILLY (Stations: Green Pk. P, Hyde Pk. Corner P). One of the Royal Parks of London, it possesses particularly lovely trees and is 53 acres in size. It was at one time larger, but the gardens of Buckingham Palace were extended by George III to take in part of it. On the Piccadilly side, the fine iron gateway of old Devonshire House is still standing. (15N 61)

GREENWICH HOSPITAL, ROMNEY ROAD, S.E.10 (Station: *Greenwich R.* Or in summer by boat from Westminster Pier), is on, or near, the site of the old Palace of Placentia, where Henry VIII, Queen Mary, and Queen Elizabeth were born. The present building by Wren was for centuries a hospital for seamen and is now a naval school. The Painted Hall with its paintings by Thornhill is visited by the public. (27Q 66)

GREENWICH OBSERVATORY. *See* OBSERVATORY, ROYAL.

GREENWICH PARK (Station: *Greenwich R.* Or in summer by boat from Westminster Pier). This Royal Park of almost 200 acres was laid out under Charles II by Le Nôtre, the designer of St. James's Park (q.v.). Fine trees, tame deer and the lovely view over Wren's elegant buildings beside the Thames well repay a visit. (27R 78)

GUILDHALL, THE, GRESHAM STREET, E.C.2 (Station: Bank CN), is the Town Hall of the City of London and dates from 1411-39. The original building, except the porch, the crypt with its lovely vaulting, and the structure of the Hall, was destroyed in the Great Fire of 1666. The Great Hall, which contains the famous " Gog and Magog " giant figures, is the scene of civic receptions, etc. Here the Livery Companies, whose banners hang from the walls, annually elect the new Lord Mayor and Sheriffs and give their famous banquet on Lord Mayor's Day (Nov. 9th.). Here, too, the Freedom of the City is bestowed. The Museum contains many relics of Roman, Anglo-Saxon and mediæval London, and the Art Gallery has representative examples of 19th-century English paintings. The library has an excellent general collection and is rich in valuable manuscripts and works relating to historical London. The Hall is OPEN 10 A.M. TO 5 P.M. ART GALLERY & MUSEUM 10 A.M. TO 4 OR 5 P.M. LIBRARY AND NEWS ROOM 10 A.M. TO 6 P.M. ADMISSION FREE. (19L 51)

HAMPSTEAD HEATH, N.W.3 (Station: Hampstead N) is a fine airy upland which, with the adjoining Parliament Hill, is almost 600 acres in size. Always a popular resort, the Heath is crowded with people, and children on Bank Holidays come to enjoy the Fair in the Vale of Health. Three famous inns, " Jack Straw's Castle," the " Bull and Bush " and " The Spaniards " stand near the Heath. (12E 34)

HAMPTON COURT PALACE, HAMPTON COURT (Station: *Hampton Court R*, or by bus or coach. In summer by boat from Westminster Pier). This magnificent palace is the largest in England. It was built by Cardinal Wolsey in 1515, but in 1526 when he was losing favour he presented it to Henry VIII. From then until the death of George II it was a favourite residence of English sovereigns. The palace contains many pictures amongst which are a Giorgione, a Tintoretto and two Rembrandts and also, in the Great Hall, very fine tapestries. The lovely grounds and gardens with the Maze were laid out by William III, and Wren's Orangery is famous for its magnificent Mantegna paintings. The gardens are OPEN FREE DAILY (SUNDAYS FROM 2 P.M.). STATE APARTMENTS ARE OPEN WEEKDAYS 10 A.M. TO 4, 5, OR 6 P.M. (EXCEPT FRI.). ADMISSION : FREE ON SUNDAYS ; 6D. ON SATURDAYS ; 1/- ON OTHER DAYS (CHILDREN 6D.)

HOME OFFICE, WHITEHALL, S.W.1 (Stations: Trafalgar Sq. B, Westminster D). (16N 62)

HOME OFFICE INDUSTRIAL MUSEUM, HORSEFERRY ROAD, S.W.1 (Station: St. James Pk. D), contains exhibits of methods and appliances for the promotion of safety and health amongst industrial workers. OPEN WEEKDAYS 10 A.M. TO 4 P.M. ADMISSION FREE. (16O 61)

HORNIMAN MUSEUM, LONDON ROAD, FOREST HILL, S.E.23 (Station: *Lordship La. R*). Contains weapons and exhibits of arts and crafts of primitive peoples, and objects

illustrating the evolution of animals and man. There is a fine Zoological Library. OPEN : WEEKDAYS 11 A.M TO 5.30, 6 OR 7 P.M. SUNDAYS : 2 P.M. TO 8 P.M. ADMISSION FREE. (22W 87)

HORSE GUARDS, WHITEHALL, S.W.1 (Stations : Charing Cross BDN, Trafalgar Sq. B). Rebuilt in 1742, these barracks are part of the old Whitehall Palace. Two mounted Life-guardsmen are always on sentry duty here and the Changing of the Guard daily at 11 a.m. is a picturesque sight. "The Trooping of the Colours," a magnificent ceremony, takes place on the King's birthday on the parade ground at the rear of the building. (16N 62)

HOUSES OF PARLIAMENT, PARLIAMENT SQUARE, S.W.1 (Station : Westminster D), stand throughout the world as a symbol of democratic government. Begun in 1840, on the site of the old Palace of Westminster, this is the largest building erected in England since the Reformation, and cost £3,000,000. When Parliament is sitting, a flag flies from Victoria Tower by day and by night a light burns in the Clock Tower above the famous Big Ben. ADMISSION TO BOTH HOUSES IS FREE ON SATURDAYS EASTER MON. AND TUES., WHIT. MON. AND TUES. AND AUGUST BANK HOLIDAY FROM 10 A.M. TO 3.30 P.M. Entrance at Victoria Tower. For ADMISSION to the HOUSE OF COMMONS during debates apply to an M.P. or to the Admission Order Office in St. Stephen's Hall. For ADMISSION to the HOUSE OF LORDS during debates a Peer's order must be obtained. (17O 62)

HYDE PARK (Stations : Hyde Park Corner P, Knightsbridge P, Lancaster Gate C, Marble Arch C). This Royal Park was presented to Henry VIII by the Abbey of Westminster. It is 360 acres large and is frequented by both rich and poor. On the south side from Hyde Park Corner westwards, many people take an early morning ride in Rotten Row before going to business ; while on Sundays the fashionable world congregates here. It is on Sundays, too, that the famous "tub-thumping" public orators near Marble Arch air their views to crowds of listeners. The Serpentine, a large lake in the centre of the Park, is now one of London's Lidos and in summer MIXED BATHING is allowed from May to September at a cost of 3d. WEEKDAYS : 6.30 A.M. TO DUSK ; SUNDAYS 6.30 A.M. TO 10 A.M. AND 2 P.M. TO 6 P.M. Boating is also available. (13M 48)

IMPERIAL INSTITUTE, IMPERIAL INSTITUTE ROAD, S.W.7 (Station : Sth. Kensington DP). Founded in order to promote an interest in the Empire, this building was opened by Queen Victoria in 1893. The exhibits show the geography, resources and commercial products of each country of the Empire. OPEN : 10 A.M. TO 5 P.M. ; SUNDAYS 2.30 TO 6 P.M. ADMISSION FREE. (12O 60)

IMPERIAL WAR MUSEUM, ST. GEORGE'S ROAD, LAMBETH (Station : Lambeth Nth. B), serves as a record of the Great War with its collection of military, naval and aerial trophies, its library of books and photographs and its picture gallery. The building was, originally Bethlem Royal Hospital or "Old Bedlam" which was moved here from Moorfields in 1815. The hospital is now at Beckenham. OPEN DAILY 10 A.M. TO 6 P.M. ; SUNDAYS 2.30 P.M. TO 6 P.M. ADMISSION FREE. (18O 62)

INDIA MUSEUM IMPERIAL INSTITUTE ROAD, S.W.7 (Station : Sth. Kensington DP). A branch of the Victoria and Albert Museum devoted to the portrayal of the life, art and religion of India and its surrounding countries. OPEN : DAILY 10 A.M. TO 6 P.M.; SUN-DAYS : 2.30 P.M. TO 6 P.M. ADMISSION FREE. (12O 60).

KENSINGTON GARDENS (Stations : High St. Kensington D, Lancaster Gate C, Queens Rd. C). Formerly the grounds of Kensington Palace, this is now a charming woodland park, where children gather at the Round Pond to sail their boats or cluster round the statue of Peter Pan. The Long Water should be seen from the bridge that divides it from the Serpentine. (12N 60)

KENSINGTON PALACE, KENSINGTON GARDENS, S.W.7 (Station : High St. Kensington D). Was purchased from a private owner by William III, for whom Wren built the south wing. Queen Victoria was born here and also Her Majesty Queen Mary. (11N 60).

KEN WOOD, HIGHGATE (Station : Golders Grn. N and Bus 102). This elegant mansion in the Adams' style with its fine collection of paintings, notably the series of Romney's portraits of Lady Hamilton, its Georgian furniture and the beautiful grounds which surround it, is part of the Iveagh Bequest to the nation. OPEN : DAILY 10 A.M. TO 5 P.M.; SUN-DAYS : 2.30 P.M. TO 5 P.M. ADMISSION FREE ; WED. AND FRI. 1/-. (13D 22)

KEW GARDENS (ROYAL BOTANIC GARDENS), KEW (Station : Kew Gardens D). These lovely gardens, ideally situated beside the Thames, were founded in 1759 by the widow of Frederick, Prince of Wales, and were extended by George III in 1772. A Museum of trees, plants and shrubs from all over the world, these gardens are, in addition, beautifully laid out. There are four Museums, a Palm House, a Lily Pond, etc. OPEN : DAILY 10 A.M. TO DUSK. ADMISSION : 1D., TUES. AND FRI. 6D., BANK HOLIDAYS FREE. (2Q 56)

LAMBETH BRIDGE, S.W.1 (Station : Westminster D). Was opened in 1932 in the place of a late 19th century suspension bridge. It harmonises with the modern blocks of offices along Millbank. (17O 62)

LAMBETH PALACE, LAMBETH ROAD, S.E.1 (Station : Lambeth Nth. B). For over 700 years the residence of the Archbishops of Canterbury. Its early English Chapel dates from the 12th century. ADMISSION to the Palace Tues. Thurs. and Sat. afternoons on written application to the Secretary. The LIBRARY with its 14,000 manuscripts is OPEN

MON., WED. AND FRI. 10 A.M. TO 4 OR 4.30 P.M., THURSDAYS 10 A.M. TO 1 P.M., BUT IS CLOSED FOR 6 WEEKS FROM SEPTEMBER 1ST. ADMISSION FREE. (17O 62)

LAW COURTS (ROYAL COURTS OF JUSTICE), STRAND, W.C.2 (Stations : Aldwych P. Temple D). These buildings, which were opened in 1882, cost about £1,000,000, but had to be enlarged in 1911. The Central Hall and the body of the 23 Courts are not open to the general public, but steps in the towers at the gateway lead up to the public galleries. (18M 50)

LEIGHTON HOUSE, 12, HOLLAND PARK ROAD, W.14 (Station : Kensington Olympia D). Built by the late Lord Leighton, P.R.A., this house contains many of that artist's pictures. The Arab Hall is noted for its collection of 14th and 17th century tiles. OPEN MON., TUES., THURS., 11 A.M. TO 3 P.M. WED. AND FRI., 11 A.M. TO 1 P.M. SAT., 11 A.M. TO 5 P.M. CLOSED ON SUNDAY. ADMISSION FREE. (10O 59)

LINCOLN'S INN, CHANCERY LANE, W.C.2 (Station : Chancery Lane C). One of the four Inns of Court which have the power of " calling to the Bar." The Library, built in 1842, is the finest Law Library in London and contains over 70,000 volumes and many fine MSS. Of architectural interest are the early 16th-century gateway to Chancery Lane, and the Inigo Jones chapel erected in 1623. (18L 50)

LLOYD'S, LEADENHALL STREET, E.C.3 (Station : Aldgate D). This world-renowned centre of marine insurance is named after Edward Lloyd's Coffee House, the 17th-century *rendezvous* of people interested in shipping. In 1928 Lloyd's moved to its present building from the Royal Exchange where it had been since 1774. With it moved the famous Lutine Bell, which is rung once for the loss or wreck of a ship and twice for good news. (20M 51)

LONDON BRIDGE, E.C.4 (Station : London Bri. N). The only bridge in London until the 18th century. The present bridge, however, dates from 1832, replacing Old London Bridge which, with its houses and shops on either side, formed such an intrinsic part of the City's history. (20M 51)

LONDON MUSEUM, LANCASTER HOUSE, S.W.1 (Stations : Green Pk. P, St. James Pk. D). Illustrates the domestic and social history of London from pre-Roman times to the present day. The collection of costumes, associated with the Royal Family, contains the coronation robes of his late Majesty King George V and Queen Mary. OPEN FROM 10 A.M. TO 6 P.M., SUNDAYS 2 P.M. TO 6 P.M. FROM NOVEMBER TO MARCH CLOSES AT 4 P.M. ADMISSION : TUES. 1/-; WED. AND THURS. 6D.; OTHER DAYS FREE. (15N 61)

LONDON STONE, ST. SWITHIN'S CHURCH, CANNON STREET, E.C.4 (Station : Cannon St. D). Possibly the oldest relic in the streets of London, this stone is believed to have been the millarium from which the Romans measured all distances out of the City. It was moved in 1798 to its present position in the Wall of the Church, the iron grille being added later. (20M 51)

MADAME TUSSAUD'S, MARYLEBONE ROAD, N.W.1 (Station : Baker St. BD). The world-famous waxwork exhibition where the visitor wanders amongst life-like historical and contemporary figures. OPEN DAILY 10 A.M. TO 10 P.M. ADMISSION 1/3; CHILDREN 6D. " CHAMBER OF HORRORS," 6D. EXTRA. (13L 48)

MANSION HOUSE, BANK, E.C.4 (Station : Bank CN). This, the first official residence of the Lord Mayors of London, was built in 1739. Until this time the Mayors had to receive in their own homes. The famous lavish banquets given by the Lord Mayor take place in the Egyptian Hall. The City Police Court is in the same building. For ADMIS-SION, WRITTEN APPLICATION TO BE MADE TO THE LORD MAYOR'S SECRETARY. (20M 51)

MARBLE ARCH, OXFORD STREET, W.1 (Station : Marble Arch C). Originally intended as an entrance to Buckingham Palace, this " triumphal arch " was made too narrow for the State Coach and became a gate into Hyde Park. Later, the park boundary was moved back and Marble Arch, now isolated, is an entrance to nowhere. Nearby, where Edgware Road intersects with Bayswater Road stood Tyburn Gallows, the scene of many executions. (14M 49)

MARLBOROUGH HOUSE, PALL MALL, S.W.1 (Station : Green Pk. P), was built by Wren in 1709 for the great Duke of Marlborough. It became State property and was the home of Edward VII when he was Prince of Wales, and George V until his accession. From 1911 until her death, it was the residence of Queen Alexandra. Queen Mary lives here when she is in London. (16N 61)

MINT, THE ROYAL, ROYAL MINT STREET, E.1 (Station : Mark La. D). Originally housed in the Tower of London, it was transferred to its present building in 1811. It is here that our silver and bronze coins are struck, as also medals, seals and a number of Colonial coinages. For ADMISSION, WRITTEN APPLICATION TO BE MADE IN ADVANCE TO THE DEPUTY MASTER. (Parties not to exceed six.) (21M 51)

MONUMENT, THE, E.C.3 (Station : Monument D). A fluted Doric column erected by Wren to commemorate the Great Fire of London. It is 202 ft. high, which is the distance to the house in Pudding Lane where the fire broke out. The view from the top well repays the climb of 345 steps. OPEN : MAR. 31ST TO SEPT. 30TH, 9 A.M. TO 6 P.M.; OCT. 1ST TO MAR. 30TH, 9 A.M. TO 4 P.M. ADMISSION 8D. (20M 51)

NATIONAL GALLERY, TRAFALGAR SQUARE, W.C.2 (Stations : Strand N, Trafalgar Sq. B). One of the most important picture galleries of the world, containing a representative collection of every European school of painting, and works by nearly all the great masters. The paintings are arranged according to school and period. The gallery was founded in 1824 with the Angerstein Collection of 38 pictures. OPEN : MON., TUES., WED., 10 A.M. TO 8 P.M.; THURS. FRI., SAT., 10 A.M. TO 5 P.M.; SUN., 2 P.M. TO 5 P.M. ADMISSION FREE, EXCEPT THURS. AND FRI., 6D. Free Lectures weekdays 11 a.m. and noon ; Sats. 2 and 3 p.m., and extra lectures Tues. 1 p.m., Wed. 6.30 p.m. (16M 50)

NATIONAL MARITIME MUSEUM, QUEEN'S HOUSE, ROMNEY ROAD, GREENWICH (Station : *Greenwich R*, or in summer by boat from Westminster Pier). Opened in 1937 by King George VI and Queen Elizabeth, it can be said to illustrate the naval history of the world. Harrison's 18th-century chronometers in the Navigation Room are of particular interest. One of the two rooms is devoted to Nelson, and contains the uniform in which he was killed at Trafalgar. The lovely building, housing the collection, is partly by Wren, but was originally designed for Henrietta Maria by Inigo Jones. OPEN WEEKDAYS 10 A.M. TO 6 P.M., SUN., 2.30 TO 6 P.M. ADMISSION FREE EXCEPT FRI., 6D.(27Q 66)

NATIONAL PORTRAIT GALLERY, ST. MARTIN'S PLACE, W.C.2 (Stations : Strand N, Trafalgar Sq. B). Makes British history vivid by its authentic portraits of the men, women and children who have contributed to its making. The portraits are arranged chronologically, starting with the Tudor dynasty until the present day. OPEN : Nov. TO FEB., 10 A.M. TO 4 P.M.; SUN., 2.30 P.M. TO 4.30 P.M.; MAR.—OCT., 10 A.M. TO 5 P.M. (THURS. & FRI. TO 4 P.M.) ; SUN., 2.30 TO 5.30 P.M. APRIL TO SEPT. 10 A.M. TO 6 P.M. (THURS. AND FRI. TO 5 P.M.) SUN. 2.30 TO 5.30 P.M. ADMISSION FREE, EXCEPT THURS. & FRI., 6D. (16M 50)

NATURAL HISTORY MUSEUM, CROMWELL ROAD, S.W.7 (Station : Sth. Kensington DP). A branch of the British Museum, it contains the finest Natural History collection in the world. Departments are devoted to botany, entomology, geology, mineralogy and zoology. OPEN : 10 A.M. TO 6 P.M., SUN., 2.30 P.M. TO 6 P.M. CLOSED GOOD FRIDAY AND CHRISTMAS DAY. ADMISSION FREE. Free Guide Lectures weekdays at 11.30 a.m. and 3 p.m.; Sun., 3 p.m. to 4.30 p.m. (12O 60)

NEW SCOTLAND YARD, VICTORIA EMBANKMENT, S.W.1 (Station : Westminster D). The headquarters of the Metropolitan Police and the Criminal Investigation Department. The present taste for detective novels has made Scotland Yard famous the world over. (17N 62)

OBSERVATORY, ROYAL, GREENWICH PARK, S.E.10 (Station : *Greenwich R*, or by boat in summer from Westminster Pier). Founded by Charles II to give exact data to navigators; since when all longitudes are calculated from its meridian. The meridian line can be seen a few yards from the building. Greenwich time is proverbial ; it is telegraphed to all important towns at 1 p.m., when the magnetic clock at the Observatory releases a previously hoisted time-ball. (27Q 66)

OLD BAILEY, *see* CENTRAL CRIMINAL COURT.

OLYMPIA, HAMMERSMITH ROAD, W.14 (Station : Kensington Olympia D). The scene of the Royal Tournament and of many important shows and exhibitions, it is particularly known to children for its Christmas Circus. (9O 59)

PARKES MUSEUM, 90, BUCKINGHAM PALACE ROAD, S.W.1 (Station : Victoria D). Contains exhibits relating to modern hygiene in architectural and food values ; disinfection, etc., for prevention of disease. OPEN : WEEKDAYS, 9.30 A.M. TO 5.30 P.M. (MON. 9.30 A.M. TO 7 P.M.). ADMISSION FREE. (15O 61)

PETTICOAT LANE," MIDDLESEX STREET, E.1 (Stations : Aldgate East D, Liverpool St. CD). The appropriately-named Street Market for secondhand clothes, etc., where, on Sunday mornings, bargain hunters or merely passers-by run the gauntlet of shouting and persuasive salesmen. (21L 51)

PICCADILLY CIRCUS, W.1 (Station : Piccadilly BP). The gay centre of London, is brilliantly illuminated at night by a variety of many coloured advertisements. The charming statue of Eros is by Sir Alfred Gilbert and the flower sellers sitting on the steps round its pedestal are an integral part of London life. (16M 49)

PUBLIC RECORD OFFICE, CHANCERY LANE, W.C.2 (Station : Chancery La. C). The fireproof storehouse of the State Documents. Here, amongst other interesting documents, are to be seen the Domesday Book, papers concerning the Gunpowder Plot, a letter from President Washington to George III and the log of Nelson's " Victory." OPEN : 2 P.M. TO 4 P.M. CLOSED SAT. AND SUN. ADMISSION FREE. (18L 50)

QUEEN VICTORIA MEMORIAL, THE MALL, S.W.1 (Stations : Green Pk. P, Victoria D). Stands in front of Buckingham Palace. Designed by Sir Thos. Brock, it is of white marble, the centre figure of the Queen being 13 ft. high. Groups on the remaining sides represent Justice, Truth and Motherhood, while the whole is surmounted by a winged Victory. (15N 61)

QUEEN'S HALL, LANGHAM PLACE, W.1 (Station : Oxford Circus BC). The centre of London orchestral music, this hall seats 2,414 people. (15L 49)

REGENT'S PARK (Stations: Baker St. BD, Regents Pk. B, St. Johns Wood D). Is named after George IV while Regent for his father. One of the largest London parks, it covers an area of 470 acres, and contains the Zoo (q.v.) and a large boating lake. In the summer open air plays are performed in Queen Mary's Gardens. The elegant terraces surrounding the Park are by John Nash. (14 J 49)

ROYAL ACADEMY OF ARTS, see ACADEMY OF ARTS, ROYAL.

ROYAL COLLEGE OF SURGEONS, LINCOLN'S INN FIELDS, W.C.2 (Stations: Chancery La. C., Holborn CP). Contains the Anatomical Museum founded by John Hunter, which has been greatly enlarged since his death. ADMISSION BY A MEMBER'S INTRODUCTION OR ON APPLICATION TO THE SECRETARY. OPEN WEEKDAYS 10 A.M. TO 5 P.M., SAT., 10 A.M. TO 1 P.M. LIBRARY OPEN 10 A.M. TO 6 P.M. ADMISSION FREE (17L 50)

ROYAL EXCHANGE, CORNHILL, E.C.3 (Station: Bank CN). Was opened by Queen Victoria in 1844, replacing two previous buildings on this site which in turn in 1666 and 1838 were both burnt down. Though the original Exchange of 1568 was modelled on the Antwerp Bourse, no business of this nature is now transacted here. In the Ambulatory there are many 19th-century frescoes of historical events. ADMISSION FREE. (20M 51)

ROYAL INSTITUTE OF PAINTERS. 195, PICCADILLY, W.1 (Station: Green Pk. P) From time to time gives an exhibition of contemporary painting. (16M 49)

ROYAL UNITED SERVICE MUSEUM, WHITEHALL, S.W.1 (Stations: Charing Cross BDN, Trafalgar Sq. B, Westminster D). Occupies Inigo Jones's Banqueting Hall; the only part ever to be completed of his design for the new Palace of Whitehall. The magnificent ceiling is by Rubens. Charles I passed through the Hall to be executed outside the northern window. The Museum deals with the naval and military history of Great Britain and contains a collection of Arms, Armour, Models and relics of famous soldiers and sailors, etc. OPEN: WEEKDAYS 10 A.M. TO 5 P.M. ADMISSION 1/-, EXCEPT WED. AND SAT. AFTERNOONS, 6D. SOLDIERS AND SAILORS AND PARTIES OF SCHOOLCHILDREN FREE. (17N 62)

ST. BARTHOLOMEW'S HOSPITAL, SMITHFIELD, E.C.1 (Station: St. Pauls C). Known as " Bart's," this is the oldest hospital in England, having been incorporated in an Augustinian Priory founded under Henry I by Rahere in 1123. It escaped the Great Fire. Frequently enlarged, the hospital now has over 10,000 in-patients and over 400,000 out-patients. The building contains paintings by Hogarth and portraits of famous doctors and surgeons by Reynolds, Lawrence, etc. OPEN: 9 A.M. TO 5 P.M. ADMISSION FREE. (19L 51)

ST. JAMES'S PALACE, S.W.1 (Stations: Green Pk. P, St. James Pk. D). Built in 1532 by Henry VIII on the site of a Leper Hospital, this Palace was from time to time used as a Royal Residence after the Palace of Whitehall was burnt down in 1698. Charles II, James II, Mary II and George IV were born here, and it was here that Charles I, took leave of his children before his execution. More recently it was known as the residence of Edward VIII while Prince of Wales. The main gateway, the Tapestry Room and the Chapel Royal (open to the public on Sundays) are all that remain of the original building. (16N 61)

ST. JAMES'S PARK (Stations: St. James Pk. D, Trafalgar Sq. B). These 93 acres were acquired by Henry VIII in 1531 to give him hunting near his Palace of Whitehall. It was under Charles II that the land was laid out by Le Nôtre, the French landscape gardener, to form one of the most charming of London's Royal Parks. (17N 61)

ST. PAUL'S CATHEDRAL, LUDGATE HILL, E.C.4 (Stations: Blackfriars D, Mansion House D, St. Pauls C). This is Sir Christopher Wren's masterpiece built to replace the much larger Old Cathedral after its destruction on the same site in the Great Fire of 1666. The most prominent of London's buildings, it is an immense Renaissance structure, its exterior length being 515 ft.; its width across transepts 250 ft. and the height from pavement to the top of the cross 365 ft. Amongst the many famous people buried here are Christopher Wren, Nelson, Wellington and Jellicoe; Florence Nightingale, Reynolds and Turner. OPEN WEEKDAYS, 9 A.M. TO 5 OR 6 P.M. ADMISSION FREE TO NAVE AND TRANSEPT, but visitors must not walk about during services. 627 steps lead to the Galleries and to the Great Ball. ADMISSION TO CRYPT, 6D.; LIBRARY, WHISPERING GALLERY AND STONE GALLERY, 6D.; GOLDEN GALLERY 1/-, BALL, 1/-. Services: Weekdays, 8 a.m., 10 a.m., 1.15 p.m., 4 p.m. (choral); Sundays, 7.45 a.m., 8 a.m., 10.30 a.m. (choral); 3.15 p.m. (choral); 7 p.m. (19M 51)

SASSOON, SIR PHILIP, HOUSE OF, 45, PARK LANE, W.1 (Station: Hyde Pk. Corner P). Is frequently opened to the public for very fine loan exhibitions of paintings, furniture or objets d'art. (14M 49)

SAVOY CHAPEL, SAVOY HILL, STRAND, W.C.2 (Stations: Aldwych P, Strand N). Is on the site of the old Palace of Savoy given to the Earl of Savoy by Henry III. It finally came into the hands of John of Gaunt, and it is believed that during this time Chaucer was married in the Chapel. Wat Tyler's rebels, however, destroyed the buildings in 1381 and John of Gaunt had to flee. The present chapel was erected as part of a hospital founded under the will of Henry VII. (17M 50)

SCIENCE MUSEUM, EXHIBITION ROAD, S.W.7 (Station: Sth. Kensington. DP). Contains a fine collection of scientific apparatus and models illustrating the development of

machinery, engineering, transport, optics, etc. Many of the exhibits can be operated by visitors. Of popular interest are Headley's locomotive, the oldest in existence ; Stephenson's " Rocket," Wilbur Wright's original aeroplane, and the aeroplane in which Alcock and Brown were the first to fly the Atlantic. OPEN : 10 A.M. TO 6 P.M.; SUNDAYS, 2.30 P.M. TO 6 P.M. ADMISSION FREE. (12O 60)

SMITHFIELD MARKET, SMITHFIELD, E.C.1 (Station : Aldwych P), is London's Central Market, known particularly as a meat market. A convenient size for jousting and for the Bartholomew Fair, this 3-acre site, able to contain many spectators, was a favourite place of execution during the 16th and beginning of the 17th century. Martyrs of all denominations were burnt here for their beliefs. In 1381 Wat Tyler was killed at Smithfield by the Lord Mayor. (19L 50)

SOANE'S MUSEUM (SIR JOHN SOANE'S), LINCOLN'S INN FIELDS, W.C.2 (Station : Holborn CP). Once the residence of the architect of the Bank of England, this 18th-century house contains architectural fragments and drawings collected by him. Egyptian, Greek and Roman antiquities, including the sarcophagus of Seti I ; and, above all, the best collection of Hogarth's work, eight scenes of his " The Rake's Progress," and four of his Election series. Paintings by Canaletto, Watteau, Reynolds and Turner are also to be seen. OPEN MAR. TO AUG.: TUES., WED., THURS. AND FRI., 10.30 A.M. TO 5 P.M. OCT. TO NOV., THURS. AND FRI., 10.30 A.M. TO 5 P.M. (4 P.M. NOV.). Other times on application to the Curator. ADMISSION FREE. (17L 50)

SOMERSET HOUSE, STRAND, W.C.2 (Stations: Aldwych P, Temple D). Was originally the Palace of Edward VI's first Protector, the Duke of Somerset, after whom it is named. At his execution the Palace was forfeited to the Crown. The present building dates from 1775 and houses the Registrar-General of Births, Deaths and Marriages, the Inland Revenue Office and the Probate Registry. On payment of 1/- the wills of John Milton, Nelson and Wellington may be seen. William Shakespeare's will is enclosed in a glass case. Office hours : 10 a.m. to 4 p.m. Sats.: 10 a.m. to 1 p.m. (17M 50)

SOUTHWARK CATHEDRAL, LONDON BRIDGE, S.E.1 (Station : London Bri. N). A superlative example of Gothic, hardly less fine than Westminster Abbey. Originally the church of an Augustinian Priory founded under Henry I, St. Saviour's was inaugurated as a Cathedral under its present name in 1905. John Harvard, founder of Harvard University, U.S.A., was baptised here in 1607. Exactly 300 years later a chapel and window were erected in his memory by Harvard students. Edmund Shakespeare, brother of William Shakespeare, Fletcher and Massinger are buried in the Cathedral. Services : 7.30 a.m., 8 a.m. and 5 p.m. Sundays : 8 a.m., 11 a.m., 6.30 p.m. ADMISSION FREE. (20N 63)

STAPLE INN, HOLBORN, W.C.1 (Station : Chancery La. C). Formerly one of the lesser Inns of Court and now the home of the Society of Actuaries, it is fronted by the best known Tudor houses in London. The peace and quiet of its enchanted quadrangle, reached through passing under an arch, is unbelievable after the noise and bustle of Holborn. Johnson lived in Staple Inn, as did in fiction a character of Dickens. (18L 50)

STOCK EXCHANGE, THE, THROGMORTON STREET, E.C.2 (Station : Bank CN). Although the public are not admitted to the buildings, they can see dealings between the stockbrokers after 4 p.m. when the Stock Exchange shuts and business continues in the " Street." (20M 51)

TEMPLE BAR, STRAND, W.C.2 (Stations : Temple D, Aldwych P), was the western entrance gate to the city of London, and is mentioned in records as far back as the 13th century. The last Temple Bar was erected by Wren in 1672, but was removed to Theobald's Park, Cheshunt, Herts., in 1878, where it stands to-day. The Griffin Monument opposite the Law Courts marks its original site. (18M 50)

TATE GALLERY, MILLBANK, S.W.1 (Station : Victoria D). Owes both name and existence to Sir Henry Tate who founded it in 1897. It contains examples of the British School from the 18th century to the present day and a section devoted to the Modern Foreign School. This latter, with its magnificent paintings of the French School, is the finest representative collection in Europe. OPEN : APRIL TO SEPT.: 10 A.M. TO 6 P.M., SUN. 2 P.M. TO 6 P.M. SEPT. TO APRIL, TO 4, 4.30 OR 5 P.M. ADMISSION FREE, EXCEPT TUES., WED., 6D. Free Lectures daily at 11 a.m., Sat. 11 a.m., 2 p.m., 3 p.m. (16P 62)

TEMPLE, FLEET STREET, E.C.4 (Stations : Aldwych P, Temple D). Comprises two Inns of Court, the Inner and Middle Temple and, since the suppression of the Knights Templars in the 14th century, has been the centre of legal law in England. The Temple Church of 1185, built in the round form adopted by this Order, is a fine example of early English architecture. It contains several effigies of Crusaders. The Church is OPEN WEEKDAYS 10.30 A.M. TO 4 OR 5 P.M., EXCEPT SATS. Sunday services 11 a.m., 3 p.m. ADMISSION FREE. Oliver Goldsmith was buried in the churchyard. Middle Temple Hall (the dining-hall of the Benchers and students) with its splendid hammer beam roof, carved screen and stained glass windows was opened by Queen Elizabeth in 1576. She is supposed to have seen Shakespeare acting in " Twelfth Night " on the dais at the end of the Hall. At No. 2, Crown Office Row, near the Hall, Charles Lamb was born. (18M 50)

TOWER BRIDGE, E.1 (Stations : London Bri. N, Mark La. D). Was designed by Barry and Jones and opened in 1894. The opening of the two drawbridges to allow the passage of large ships is one of the sights of London. A bell rings before the bridge opens, and all

traffic has to wait on either side; even pedestrians, for, since 1909, the footway 142 ft. above high water mark, has been closed. (21N 63)

TOWER OF LONDON, E.C.3 (Station : Mark La. D). Built in part by William the Conqueror as a fortress to guard the river approach to London, this is the most perfect example of a mediæval castle in England. The White Tower contains, besides its collection of armoury and execution relics, the finest early-Norman chapel in England. The Crown Jewels are housed in the Wakefield Tower. Anne Boleyn, Lady Jane Grey, Sir Walter Raleigh and other political prisoners were executed on Tower Green. OPEN : WEEKDAYS 10 A.M. TO 5 OR 6 P.M. CLOSED ON SUNDAYS. ADMISSION : To WHITE TOWER, 6D. (FREE SATS.) ; JEWEL HOUSE, 6D.; BLOODY TOWER, 6D. (21M 51)

TRAFALGAR SQUARE, S.W.1 and W.C.2 (Stations : Strand N, Trafalgar Sq. B). Laid out as a war memorial and named after the victory of Trafalgar, the Square was completed in 1841. In the centre rises Nelson's Column, 145 ft. high, so as to allow Nelson a view of the sea. The lions at the base are by Landseer. Facing Whitehall is a fine 17th-century equestrian statue of Charles I, the Martyr King. On the north side are the standard measures of length: inch, foot, etc. Trafalgar Square is often used for political demonstrations. (16M 50)

UNIVERSITY OF LONDON, WOBURN SQUARE, W.C.1 (Station : Russell Sq. P). This magnificent new building by James Holden was started in 1933 and will give to the London University the importance it deserves. Overshadowed by Oxford and Cambridge, it is at last coming into its own. (16L 50)

VICTORIA & ALBERT MUSEUM, CROMWELL ROAD, S.W.7 (Station : Sth. Kensington DP). Is the finest existing museum of industrial art, and illustrates artistic achievements throughout the centuries. The reference library is the most complete of its kind. The museum was founded by Queen Victoria and the Prince Consort, but the present buildings were opened by Edward VII in 1909. OPEN : 10 A.M. TO 6 P.M.; SUNDAYS : 2.30 P.M. TO 6 P.M. ADMISSION FREE. Free lectures daily at noon and 3 p.m. (13O 60)

VICTORIA EMBANKMENT (Stations from West to East: Westminster D, Charing Cross BDN, Temple D, Blackfriars D). This magnificent tree-lined thoroughfare skirts the Thames for over a mile and a quarter between Westminster and Blackfriars Bridge. Designed by Sir Joseph Bazelgatte, the engineer, it was completed in 1870 at a total cost of almost £2,000,000. Until then this part of London had been like Venice, the river lapping against the buildings. York House Water Gate, now high and dry, shows how much land was reclaimed from the Thames. (17M 50)

WALLACE COLLECTION, HERTFORD HOUSE, MANCHESTER SQUARE, W.1 (Station Bond St. C). Possesses the most representative collection in England of French 18th-century painting, sculpture, furniture and Sèvres porcelain. It includes, as well, master-pieces by Rembrandt, Van Dyck, Velasquez and Titian. Formed by the fourth Marquess of Hertford and his son Sir Richard Wallace, the collection was bequeathed to the nation by Lady Wallace in 1897 and opened in 1909. OPEN : 10 A.M. TO 5 P.M. SUNDAYS 2 P.M. TO 5 P.M. CLOSED GOOD FRIDAYS, CHRISTMAS EVE AND CHRISTMAS DAY. AD-MISSION FREE, EXCEPT TUES. AND FRI., 6D. Free Lectures daily at 3 p.m., Sat. noon No lectures Wed. (14L 49)

WAR OFFICE, WHITEHALL, S.W.1 (Stations : Strand N, Trafalgar Sq. B, Westminster D). (17N 62)

WATERLOO BRIDGE, W.C.2 (Stations : Temple D, Waterloo BN). Originally opened in 1817, Rennie's bridge became unsafe in 1924. It is hoped that the building of the new bridge, designed by Gilbert Scott, will be completed in 1940. (17M 50)

WATERLOO PLACE, PALL MALL, S.W.1 (Station : Trafalgar Sq. B). There is a fine view from here over St. James's Park. This quiet " backwater " is usually full of parked cars surrounding the several monuments and memorials of King Edward VII, the Crimean Monument, Scott, Florence Nightingale, etc. (16N 72)

WESTMINSTER ABBEY, PARLIAMENT SQUARE, S.W.1 (Station : Westminster D). The most interesting and historic religious building in England, and architecturally one of the masterpieces of the Middle Ages. Founded circa 800 it was planned and erected as a Royal Mausoleum by Henry III in memory of Edward the Confessor; and, in fact, until George II, all the Kings of England were buried within its precincts. All, too, have been crowned here with only two exceptions : Edward V, who was murdered before being crowned, and Edward VIII, who renounced the throne before his coronation. The famous Coronation Chair is in Edward the Confessor's Chapel. Many famous men are buried in the Abbey. Poet's Corner is well-known and here also is the tomb of the Unknown Warrior. OPEN : DAILY 8 A.M. TO 6.30 P.M., AND FROM APRIL 1ST TO SEPT. 30TH TO 7.30 P.M., BUT VISITORS MUST NOT WALK ABOUT DURING SERVICES. ADMISSION : FREE ; AMBULATORY AND CHAPELS, 6D., BUT FREE MON. CLOSED SUN. Services : Weekdays, 8 a.m., 10 a.m., 4 p.m.; Sundays, 8 a.m., 10.30 a.m., 3 p.m., 6.30 p.m. (16O 62)

WESTMINSTER BRIDGE, S.W.1 (Station : Westminster D). The second bridge to be built over the Thames in London, it was not even begun until 1739. Up to that time London Bridge had stood alone and the " Watermen " with their ferry boats had prospered. The present structure, however, dates from 1862. (17N 62)

WESTMINSTER CATHEDRAL, ASHLEY GARDENS, S.W.1 (Station : Victoria D). This Roman Catholic Cathedral, opened in 1903, is the first Cathedral built in England since the Reformation. The architect, John Francis Bentley, who was influenced by the Christian Byzantine style of St. Sophia at Constantinople, died a year before the building was completed. A lift serves the Campanile, which is 275 ft. high. Cardinals Manning and Wiseman are buried in the Cathedral. OPEN DAILY, BUT VISITORS MUST NOT WALK ABOUT DURING SERVICES. ADMISSION FREE, LIFT 1/-, CRYPT 6D. Services, Week-days : Every half-hour from 7 a.m. to 9 a.m., 10.30 a.m., 3.15 p.m. and 8.15 p.m. Sundays : Every half-hour from 6 a.m. to 9 a.m., 10.30 a.m., 12 noon, 3.15 p.m. and 7 p.m. (15O 61)

WESTMINSTER HALL, PARLIAMENT SQUARE, S.W.1 (Station : Westminster D). The only part of the old Palace of Westminster to survive the fire of 1834. Erected in 1097 by William Rufus, it was restored by Richard II, who was responsible for the magnificent oak roof spanning the 68 ft. width of the Hall. Many famous State trials have taken place here, among them those of Charles I, Sir Thomas More, Guy Fawkes and Warren Hastings. The lying-in-state of Edward VII and of his late majesty King George V brought thousands of mourners to Westminster Hall. OPEN SATURDAYS 10 A.M. TO 4.30 P.M.; Other days when Parliament is not in session, 10 A.M. TO 4 P.M.; When Parliament is in session, MON. AND THURS., 10 A.M. TO 2.45 P.M. ADMISSION FREE. (17O 62)

WHITECHAPEL ART GALLERY, WHITECHAPEL HIGH STREET, E.1 (Station : Aldgate East D). Special loan exhibits of great interest are frequently shown here. (21L 51)

ZOOLOGICAL GARDENS, REGENT'S PARK, N.W.1 (Stations : Camden Town N, Regents Pk. B, St. Johns Wood D). Is the finest " Zoo " in existence, and is visited by over two million people every year. The animals live in ideal conditions, and the Reptile, Monkey and Insect Houses and the Aquarium are specially arranged for a study of the inmates. Rides on the elephants and camels are a special attraction for the children. Feeding times are : Pelicans, 2.30 p.m.; Polar Bears, 3 p.m.; Eagles, 3.30 p.m. ; Lions, Tigers, etc., 4 p.m. (winter 3 p.m.) ; Seals and Sea Lions, 4.30 p.m. (winter 3.30 p.m.) ; Diving Birds, Noon. and 3.15 p.m.; Reptiles, Fri., 3 p.m. to 6 p.m.; Aquarium, Tues. and Fri. Noon. OPEN 9 A.M. TO SUNSET OR 7 P.M., BUT ON WED. AND THURS. IN JUNE, JULY AND AUG. UNTIL 11.30 P.M. ADMISSION 1/-, MONDAYS 6D., CHILDREN 6D. AQUARIUM 1/-, CHILDREN 6D. ADMISSION ON SUNDAYS, ONLY WITH A FELLOW'S ORDER. (14J 49)

GENERAL INFORMATION

MAIN LINE RAILWAY TERMINI

GREAT WESTERN
Paddington

LONDON, MIDLAND & SCOTTISH
Euston
St. Pancras

LONDON & NORTH-EASTERN
Fenchurch St.
Liverpool St.
King's Cross
Marylebone

SOUTHERN RAILWAY

Charing Cross London Bridge
Holborn Viaduct Victoria
Waterloo

The entire Transport System of London, consisting of Underground, Trams, Bus and Trolley Bus, is controlled by the London Passenger Transport Board, whose Headquarters are at 55, Broadway, Westminster, S.W.1. VIC 6800.

The Underground System is composed of 5 Lines : Bakerloo, Central, District & Metropolitan, Piccadilly, Northern. *See* Underground Map, pages 8 and 9.

TAXIS.—The minimum fare for one or two people is 9d., which covers the first two-thirds of a mile, after which 3d. has to be paid for each additional third of a mile. For each additional person there is an extra charge of 6d. Two children under 10 count as one adult.
Luggage.—A charge of 3d. is made for every article outside, and the same charge for more than two packages inside or for any one package inside which exceeds 2 ft. in length.

MOTOR COACHES.—Coaches for the whole of England have their Headquarters at Victoria and King's Cross Coach Stations. The prices are somewhat less than by rail, but seats should be booked in advance.

STEAMBOATS.—In summer there are various pleasure trips by boat both up and down the Thames starting at Westminster and Tower Pier.

LOST PROPERTY OFFICES.—Buses, Trams, Trolley Buses, Underground, 200, Baker St., N.W.1. **Main Line Railways.**—Main Stations. **Taxis, Streets, etc.**—109, Lambeth Rd., S.E.1.

LONDON PARKING PLACES

CITY OF LONDON
Finsbury Circus ec2
West Smithfield ec1

FINSBURY
Charterhouse Sq. ec1
Finsbury Sq. ec2

HACKNEY
Banbury Rd. e9
Boleyn Rd. e7
Clapton Sq. e5
Croston St. e8
Crozier Ter. e9
De Beauvoir Sq. n1
Evering Rd. n16
Homerton Gro. e9
Kenninghall Rd. e5
Roseberry Pl. e8
Smalley Rd. n16
Wilton Rd. e8

HAMMERSMITH
Mall Rd. w6

HAMPSTEAD
Broadhurst Gdns. nw6

HOLBORN
Bedford Row wc1
Bedford Sq. wc1
Bloomsbury Sq. wc1
North Crescent wc1
Red Lion Sq. wc1
South Crescent wc1

HOLBORN & WESTMINSTER
Kingsway wc2
Lincoln's Inn Fields wc2

KENSINGTON
Basil St. sw3
Campden Hill Rd. w8
Exhibition Rd. sw7
Hans Crescent sw1
Hans Rd. sw3
Hornton St. w8
Kensington Pk. Rd. w11
Kensington Sq. w8
Queen's Gate sw7
Royal Crescent w11
Bellefields Rd. sw9

LAMBETH
Bernay's Gro. sw9
Bessemer Rd. se5
Binfield Rd. sw4

Canterbury Rd. sw9
Chestnut Rd. se27
Ferndale Rd. sw9
Pulross Rd. sw9
Studley Rd. sw4
Trinity Sq. sw9
Tunstall Rd. sw9

LEWISHAM
Belmont Rd. se13
David's Rd. se23
Doggett Rd. se6

PADDINGTON
Queensway w2

ST. MARYLEBONE
Allsop Pl. nw1
Boston Pl. nw1
Boston St. nw1
Cavendish Sq. w1
Devonshire Pl. w1
Dorset Sq. nw1
King St. w1
Manchester Sq. w1
Portland Pl. w1

ST. PANCRAS
Fitzroy Sq. w1
Osnaburgh St. nw1
Osnaburgh Ter. nw1
Tolmer's Sq. nw1

SHOREDITCH
Britannia St. n1
Hoxton Sq. n1
Provost St. n1
Westmoreland Pl. n1

STEPNEY
Frederick Pl. e3
Mile End Rd. e1
Philpot St. e1
Sutton St. East, e1

WANDSWORTH
Alderbrook Rd. sw12
Baldry Gdns. sw16
Balham Gro. sw12
Blakenham Rd. sw17
Broomhill Rd. sw18
Burstock Rd. sw15
Burston Rd. sw15
Cato Rd. sw4
Deodar Rd. sw15
Eglantine Rd. sw18
Elmfield Rd. sw17
Embankment, The, sw15
Felsham Rd. sw18
Fullerton Rd. sw18

Geraldine Rd. sw18
Grafton Sq. South sw4
Laitwood Rd. sw12
Lochinvar St. sw12
Louisville Rd. sw17
Magdalen Rd. sw18
Montserrat Rd. sw15
Ormeley Rd. sw12
Otterburn St. sw17
Pathfield Rd. sw16
Pendennis Rd. sw16
Pinfold Rd. sw16
Polygon, The, sw4
Ravenna Rd. sw15
St. Luke's Rd. sw4
Shrubbery Rd. sw16
Stanthorpe Rd. sw16
Tremadoc Rd. sw4
Undine St. sw17
Upper Tooting Pk. sw17
Verran Rd. sw12
Voltaire Rd. sw4
Wavertree Rd. sw2
Westwell Rd. App. sw16
Woodbourne Av. sw16

WESTMINSTER
Ambrosden Av. sw1
Approach Rd. wc2
Berkeley Sq. w1
Caxton St. sw1
Cock Yd. w1
Conduit St. w1
George St. w1
Golden Sq. w1
Gt. Marlborough St. w1
Gt. Scotland Yd. sw1
Grosvenor Sq. w1
Grosvenor St. w1
Hanover Sq. w1
Horse Guards Av. sw1
Howard St. wc2
Matthew Parker St. sw1
North Row w1
Northumberland Av. wc2
Orchard St. w1
Piccadilly w1
Red Mews, w1
St. Ann's St. sw1
St. James's Sq. sw1
Savile Row w1
Soho Sq. w1
Thirleby Rd. sw1
Victoria Embkt. sw1
Waterloo Pl. sw1
Whitehall Court sw1
Whitehall Pl. sw1

WOOLWICH
General Gordon Pl. se18

COMPLETE LIST OF STREET NAME CHANGES WITH MAP REFERENCE

OLD NAME.	NEW NAME.	
Abbey Rd. W.11	Stoneleigh Rd.	9M 47
Abbey St. E2	Buckfast St.	22K 52
Abbot's Rd. NW6	Abbots Pl.	11H 34
Abingdon St. E2	Herald St.	22K 52
Abbotswell St. SE4	Abbotswell Rd.	25U 77
Acacia Rd. SE26	Hazel Gro.	23Y 87
Acorn St. SE5	Benhill Rd.	20R 75
Acorn St. SE18	Corn St.	31P 67
Acton St. E8	Arbutus St.	21H 37
Adam St. SE1	County St.	19O 63
Adam St. W1	Robert Adam St.	14L 49
Adams M. W1	Adams Row	14M 49
Adelaide Pl. NW3	Adelaide Clo.	14H 35
Adelaide Rd. SE4	Adelaide Av.	25T 77
Adelaide Rd. W12	Adelaide Gro.	7M 46
Agnes St. SE1	Whichcote St.	18N 62
Albany St. E1	Chudleigh St.	24M 52
Albany St. SE5	Keesey St.	20Q 63
Albemarle St. EC1	Albemarle Way	19K 50
Albert Cotts. SE18	Kidd Cotts.	32P 95
Albert Cotts. SW3	Hoadley Cotts.	13P 60
Albert Cotts. SW11	Alberta Cotts.	13T 72
Albert M. NW1	Albert Terr. M.	14H 35
Albert M. NW6	Abbey M.	11H 34
Albert M. W11	Bulmer M.	11M 47
Albert Rd. E8	Middleton Rd.	21H 38
Albert Rd. NW1 & NW8	Prince Albert Rd.	13J 48
Albert Rd. SE4	Darling Rd.	25S 77
Albert Rd. SE15	Consort Rd.	22R 76
Albert Rd. SW19	Albert Dri.	9W 82
Albert Sq. E1	Albert Gdns.	23M 52
Albert St. E1	Deal St.	22L 52
Albert St. E14	Drew St.	26M 53
Albert St. N1	Culpeper St.	18J 50
Albert St. W2	Consort St.	13L 48
Albion M. E. W2	Albion M.	13M 48
Albion M. N. W2	Connaught Clo.	13M 48
Albion M. W. W2	Albion Clo.	13M 48
Albion M. E3	Haven M.	25L 53
Albion Pl. E2	Ducal Pl.	21K 51
Albion Pl. W11	Alba Pl.	10L 47
Albion Rd. NW6	Harben Rd.	12H 34
Albion Rd. SE13	Albion Way	26T 78
Albion Rd. SE18	Woolwich Ch. St.	31P 67
Albion Rd. SW8	Albion Av.	16S 73
Albion St. E3	English St.	24K 53
Albion St. N1	Balfe St.	17J 50
Aldred Rd. SE17	Aldred St.	18Q 62
Alexandra Rd. N4	Alexandra Gro.	19D 25
Alexandra Rd. SE19	Alexandra Dri.	20Y 86
Alexandra Rd. W14	Milson Rd.	9O 59
Alfred Cotts. SW7	Montpelier Pl.	13O 60
Alfred M. W11	Ladbroke M.	10N 59
Alfred Pl. E2	Russia Pl.	23J 52
Alfred Pl. SW7	Thurloe St.	13O 60
Alfred St. N1	Elia St.	19J 50
Alfred St. SE1	Keyse Rd.	21O 63
Alfred St. SW1	Udall St.	16P 61
Alfred St. SW11	Alfreda St.	15R 73
Alfred's Pl. EC1	Alfred's Clo.	19L 51
Allen St. EC1	Dallington St.	19K 51
Allen St. N1	Hawes St.	19H 37
Allington St. SW2	Allington Rd.	17U 74
Alma Rd. E2	Doric Rd.	23J 52
Alma Rd. E3	Portia Rd.	24L 53
Alma Rd. N1	Harecourt Rd.	19G 37
Alma Rd. SE1	Alma Gro.	21P 63
Alma St. N.1	Cherbury St.	20J 51
Alpha Pl. N1	Omega Pl.	17J 50
Alpha Pl. NW5	Raglan St.	15G 35

NEW NAME.	
Abbey M. NW6.	11H 34
Abbots La. SE1.	20N 63
Abbots Pl. NW6.	11H 34
Abbotswell Rd. SE4.	25U 77
Aberavon Rd. E3.	24K 53
Abourne St. W9.	11K 48
Adams Row W1.	14M 49
Adderley St. E14.	26M 53
Addison Pl. W11.	9N 59
Adelaide Av. SE4.	25T 77
Adelaide Clo. NW3.	14H 35
Adelaide Gro. W12.	7M 46
Adelina Gro. E1.	23L 52
Adeline Pl. WC1.	16L 50
Adenmore Rd. SE6.	25V 88
Agar Gro. NW1.	16H 35
Ainsworth Rd. E9.	23H 38
Alba Pl. W11.	10L 47
Albemarle Way EC1.	19K 50
Albert Dri. SW19.	9W 82
Albert Gdns. E1.	23M 52
Albert Ter. M. NW1.	14H 35
Alberta Cotts. SW11.	13T 72
Albion Av. SW8.	16S 73
Albion Clo. W2.	13M 48
Albion M. W2.	13M 48
Albion Way SE13.	26T 78
Albyn Rd. SE8.	25R 77
Alders Ct. EC1.	19L 51
Aldersgate St. EC1.	19L 51
Aldred St. SE17.	18Q 62
Alexander Gro. N4.	19D 25
Alexandra Dri. SE19.	20Y 86
Alfreda St. SW11.	15R 73
Alfred's Clo. EC1.	19L 51
Alie St. E1.	21M 51
Allcroft Pass. NW5.	14G 35
Allenbury St. E2.	22K 52
Allen Edwards Rd. SW8.	16R 74
Allgood St. E2.	21J 52
All Hallows Ct. EC3.	20M 51
All Hallows Pl. SE1.	19N 63
Allingham St. N1.	19J 51
Allington Rd. SW2.	17U 74
Allington St. SW1.	15O 61
Allitsen Rd. NW8.	13J 48
Alloway Rd. E3.	24K 53
Alma Gro. SE1.	21P 63
Alpha Clo. NW1.	13K 48
Alpha Gro. E14.	25N 65
Alsen Cotts. N7.	18E 36
Alsen Pl. N7.	17E 36
Amberley Gro. SE26.	22Y 87
Amos Ct. E1.	22N 64
Ampton Pl. WC1.	17K 50
Amwell St EC1.	18K 50
Andrews Crosse WC2.	17M 50
Angel Wk. W6.	8P 58
Ann's Clo. SW1.	14N 61
Ansdell Ter. W8.	11O 60
Antrobus St. SW1.	15P 61
Apollo Pl. SW10.	12Q 60
Apostle Rd. E3.	24L 53
Apothecary St. EC4.	18M 50
Apsley St. E1.	23L 52
Arbutus St. E8.	21H 37
Archery Clo. W2.	13M 48
Arctic St. NW5.	15G 35
Argyle St. WC1.	17K 50
Argyle Wk. WC1.	17K 50

L.C.C. STREET NAME CHANGES.

OLD NAME.	NEW NAME.	
Alpha Rd. E14	Alpha Gro.	25N 65
Alpha Rd. NW1	Alpha Clo.	13K 48
Amberley Rd. SE26	Amberley Gro.	22Y 87
Anchor Alley EC4	Vintners Pl.	19M 51
Anchor St. E14	Lanyard St.	24L 53
Ancona Rd. N5	Aubert Rd.	19F 37
Angel Ct. WC2	Penley Ct.	18M 50
Angel Pl. W6	Angel Wk.	8P 58
Ann St. E14	Oceana Clo.	27M 54
Ann's Pl. SW1	Ann's Clo.	14N 61
Ann's Pl. SW9	Robsart Pl.	18R 74
Ann's Pl. SW10	Moravian Pl.	12Q 60
Anstey Rd. SE5	Bicknell Rd.	19S 75
Approach Rd. SE27	Station Rise	18W 85
Approach Rd. WC2	Temple Pl.	18M 50
Arcade, The SE1	Bridge Arcade	29N 63
Arcade, The SW6	Walham Grn. Arcade	11Q 60
Arcade, The SW7	Kensington Stn. Arcade	13O 60
Archer St. NW1	Curnock St.	16J 49
Archer St. SW8	Parry St.	17Q 62
Archer St. W11	Westbourne Gro.	10M 47
Argyle Pl. WC1	Argyle Wk.	17K 50
Arlington St. EC1	Arlington Way	18K 50
Army St. SW4	Littlebury Rd.	16S 73
Arthur M. N7	Arthur Pl.	17H 36
Arthur M. W2	Winsland M.	12L 48
Arthur Rd. N16	Gunstor Rd.	21F 37
Arthur St. E2	Cyprus Pl.	23J 52
Arthur St. E9	Brooksbank St.	23G 38
Arthur St. E14	Lawless St.	26M 53
Arthur St. SE15	Camelot St.	22Q 64
Arthur St. SE18	Arthur Gro.	34P 95
Arthur St. SW11	Rawson St.	14R 73
Arthur St. WC2	Earnshaw St.	16L 50
Artillery La. SE1	St. Olave's Ter.	21N 63
Artillery St. E1	Peace St.	22K 52
Arundel Pl. SW1	Shaver's Pl.	16M 50
Arundel St. N16	Arundel Gro.	21G 37
Ashburnham Rd. SE10	Asburnham Pl.	26R 77
Ashby Rd. N1	Ashby Gro.	19H 37
Athelstane Rd. E3	Athelstane Gro.	24J 53
Auckland Rd. E3	Zealand Rd.	24J 53
Augustus Rd. W.6	Brackenbury Gdns	8O 58
Avenue Cotts. SE5	Bethwin Cotts.	19Q 63
Avenue Rd. E3	Kitkat Ter.	25K 53
Avenue Rd. E5	Midhurst Rd.	22F 38
Avenue Rd. SE5	Bethwin Rd.	19Q 63
Avenue Rd. SE13	Romer Av.	26T 77
Avenue Rd. W6	Sycamore Gdns.	8N 58
Avenue, The E5	Warwick Retreat	22D 26
Avenue, The NW3	North End Av.	12D 22
Avenue, The SE3	Vicarage Av.	29R 79
Avenue, The SE3	Blackheath Gro.	28S 78
Avenue, The SE12	Somertrees Av.	29V 89
Avenue, The SE18	Sandy Hill Av.	33Q 95
Avenue, The SW2	Jebb Av.	17U 74
Avenue, The SW3	Sydney Clo.	13P 60
Avondale Rd. SE15	Avondale Rise	21S 75
Babmaes M. SW1	Babmaes St.	16M 49
Back Alley E3	Botolph Pass.	26K 53
Back Alley SE15	Rye Pass.	21S 76
Back La. SE10	Morden La.	26S 78
Back La. E15	Drover La.	22Q 64
Back La. SE18	Dairy La.	32P 95
Baker St. E1	Damien St.	22L 52
Baker St. E2	Bacton St.	23K 52
Baker St. SW9	Blackwell St.	18R 74
Baker St. WC1	Lloyd Baker St.	18K 50
Balchier Rd. SE22	Ryedale	22U 76
Ball Ct. EC1	Alders Ct.	19L 51
Barnfield Rd. SE19	Bristow Rd.	20Y 86
Bartlett's Bldgs. EC2	Bartlett's Pl.	20L 51

NEW NAME.	
Arline Ter. E2.	21K 51
Arlington Way EC1.	18K 50
Armoury Way SW18.	11T 71
Arthur Gro. SE18.	34P 95
Arthur Pl. N7.	17H 36
Arundel Gro. N16.	21G 37
Ashbridge St. NW8.	13K 48
Ashburnham Pl. SE10.	26R 77
Ashby Gro.	19H 37
Ashby St. EC1.	19K 51
Ashfield St. E1.	22L 52
Ashlar Pl. SE18.	33P 95
Ashmole St. SW8.	17Q 62
Aske St. N1.	20K 51
Askew Bldgs. W12.	7N 58
Astell St. SW3.	13P 60
Astle St. SW11.	14R 73
Athelstane Gro. E3.	24J 53
Athlone St. NW5.	15G 35
Atwood Rd. W6.	8O 58
Aubert Rd. N5.	19F 37
Aveline St. SE11.	18P 62
Avening Rd. SW18.	11U 71
Aviland St. W6.	9P 59
Avon Rd. SE4.	25S 77
Avondale Rise SE15,	21S 75
Axminster Rd. N7.	17E 36
Ayliffe Pl. SE1.	19O 63
Aylward St. E1.	23L 52
Ayres St. SE1.	19N 63
Babmaes St. SW1.	16M 49
Bacon Gro. SE1.	21O 63
Bacton St. E2.	23K 52
Badric Rd. SW11.	13S 72
Bagford St. N1.	20H 37
Bales Ct. EC4.	18L 50
Balfe St. N1.	17J 50
Ba'four St. SE17.	19O 63
Balham Sta. Rd. SW12	14V 84
Baltic Pass. EC1.	19K 51
Bancroft Rd. E1.	23K 52
Banks St. SW8.	17Q 62
Bantry St. SE5.	20R 75
Baptist Gdns. NW5.	14G 35
Barbauld Rd. N16.	20F 37
Barbican EC1.	19L 51
Bard Rd. W10.	9M 47
Bardsley La. SE10.	26Q 65
Bardsey Pl. E1.	23L 52
Barge Ho. St. SE1.	18M 50
Barlow Cotts. SE17.	20P 63
Barnabas Rd. E9.	24G 38
Barrie St. W2.	12M 48
Barter St. WC1.	17L 50
Bartholomew Clo. EC1.	19L 51
Bartholomew Pas. EC1.	19L 51
Bartholomew St. SE1.	20O 63
Bartlett's Pl. EC2,	20L 51
Bartley Rd. SW2.	17U 74
Barton Rd. W14.	9P 59
Basing Ct. SE15.	21R 75
Basing St. W11.	10L 47
Basire St. N1.	19H 37
Batchelor St. N1.	18J 50
Bate St. E14.	25M 53
Bath Row NW1.	15K 49
Bathway SE18.	33P 95
Batten St. SW11.	13S 72
Battersea Bri. Rd. SW11.	13G 60
Battersea Ch. Rd. SW11.	13R 72
Battishill St. N1.	18H 36
Baylis Rd. SE1.	18O 62

L.C.C. STREET NAME CHANGES.

OLD NAME.	NEW NAME.	NEW NAME.	
Bartley St. SW2	Bartley Rd. 17U 74	Baynes Ct. EC1.	18K 50
Barton St. W14	Barton Rd. 9P 59	Baynes St. NW1.	16H 35
Basing Pl. SE15 (part)	Basing Ct. 21R 75	Bayswater Rd. W2.	11M 48
Basing Rd. SE15	Bellenden Rd. 21R 75	Bazely St. E14.	26M 53
Basing Rd. W11	Basing St. 10L 47	Beaconsfield Wk. SW6	10R 71
Bath Ct. EC1	Baynes Ct. 18K 50	Beatty Rd. N16.	21F 37
Bath Pl. NW1	Bath Row 15K 49	Beatty St. NW1.	15J 49
Bath St. E1	Darling Row 22L 52	Beaumont Av. W14.	10P 59
Bath St. E14	Poplar Bath St. 26M 53	Beaumont Gro. E1.	23L 52
Bath St. SE1	Conquest St. 19O 62	Beaumont St. W1.	15L 49
Batson St. E14	Bate St. 25M 53	Becher Pl. W11.	9M 47
Bayswater Hill W2	Bayswater Rd. 11M 48	Beckenham Hill Rd. SE6.	
Beaconsfield Rd. SW6	Beaconsfield Wk. 10R 71		26Y 88
Beaumont Rd. W14	Beaumont Av. 10P 59	Becklow Gdns. W12.	7N 58
Beaumont St. E1	Beaumont Gro. 23L 52	Bective Pl. SW15.	10T 71
Beckenham Hill SE6	Beckenham Hill Rd. 26Y 88	Bede Rd. E3.	25L 53
Beckenham La. SE6	Beckenham Hill Rd. 26Y 88	Bedford Way WC1.	16K 50
Becklow Pl. W12	Becklow Gdns. 7N 58	Bekesbourne St. E14.	24M 53
Bedford Ct. SW9	Fenwick Ct. 16S 74	Belfort Rd. SE15.	23R 76
Bedford St. E1	Cavell St. 22L 52	Belgrave Gdns. NW8.	12J 48
Bedford St. E14	Ditchburn St. 27M 54	Belgrove St. WC1.	17K 50
Bedford Terr. SW3	Hemus Pl. 13P 60	Bell St. NW1.	13L 48
Beech St. SW8	Banks St. 17Q 62	Bellenden Rd. SE15.	21R 75
Belgrave Rd. NW8	Belgrave Gdns. 12J 48	Bell Grn. La. SE26.	24Y 88
Belgrave St. WC1	Belgrove St. 17K 50	Bell Inn Yd. EC3.	20M 51
Bell Ct. EC1	Brooke's Ct. 18L 50	Belmont Pk. SE13.	27T 78
Bell Ct. EC3	Blue Anchor Ct. 20M 51	Belmore Pl. SW8.	16R 73
Bell Ct. SE1	Bermondsey St. 20O 63	Bempton St. E2.	22J 52
Bell Terr. NW6	Springfield La. 11J 48	Bendall M. NW1.	13L 48
Bell Yd. EC1	Edison Sq. 20K 51	Bendmore Av. SE2.	36P 95
Bell Yd. EC3	Bell Inn Yd. 20M 51	Benhill Rd. SE5.	20R 75
Belmont Rd. SE13	Lockmead Rd. 27S 78	Bennett Gro. SE13.	26R 77
Bendall St. NW1	Bell St. 13L 48	Bermondsey St. SE1.	20O 63
Bendmore Rd. SE2	Bendmore Av. 36P 95	Berriman Rd. N7.	18E 36
Bennett St. SE13	Bennett Gro. 26R 77	Berry Pl. EC1.	19K 51
Bennett St. E1	Rathbone St. 16L 49	Besson Cotts. SE14.	23R 76
Bentinck St. SW1	Hatherley St. 16O 61	Bethwin Cotts. SE5.	19Q 63
Beresford St. SE5	John Ruskin St. 19Q 63	Bethwin Rd. SE5.	19Q 63
Berkley St. EC1	Briset St. 19L 50	Bicknell Rd. SE5	19S 75
Berkley Ct. OW11	Wildlich Ct. 14R 70	Diggerstaff St. N4.	10E 30
Berwick St. SW1	Guildhouse St. 15O 61	Big'and Pl. E1.	22M 52
Birdcage Wk. N16	Windus Wk. 21E 38	Billing Pl. SW10.	11Q 60
Birkbeck Rd. SE21	Birkbeck Hill 19W 86	Billing Rd. SW10.	11Q 60
Bishop's M. SW6	Coomer M. 10Q 59	Bingham St. N1.	20G 37
Bishop's Rd. E2	Bishop's Way 22J 52	Birkbeck Hill SE21.	19W 86
Bishop's Rd. W2	Bishop's Bri. Rd. 12L 48	Birkenhead St. WC1.	17K 50
Blackheath Pk. SE3 (part)	Foxes Dale 28S 78	Birkin St. SW8.	16R 73
Black Horse Yd. W1	Evelyn Yd. 16L 49	Bishop St. N1.	19H 37
Black Lion Ct. W1	Blore Ct. 16M 49	Bishop's Ter. SE11.	18O 62
Blk. Swan All. EC4	Blk. Swan Ct. 19M 51	Bishop's Way E2.	23J 52
Blake Rd. SW6	Blake Gdns. 11R 72	Bishop's Bri. Rd. W2.	12L 48
Blendon Rd. SE18	Blendon Terr. 34Q 95	Blackall St. EC2.	20K 51
Blenheim St. SW3	Astell St. 13P 60	Blackheath Gro. SE3.	28S 78
Blind La. SE18	Camdale Rd. 35R 95	Blackpool Rd. SE15.	22S 76
Blomfield St. W2	Blomfield Vills. 12L 48	Blk. Prince Rd. SE11.	17P 62
Bloomfield Rd. E3	Bede Rd. 25L 53	Blk. Swan Ct. EC4.	19M 51
Bloomsbury St. E14	Hilditch St. 26M 54	Blackwall Way E14.	27M 54
Blue Anchor La. SE15	Mission Pl. 21R 76	Blackwell St. SW9.	18R 74
Bolingbroke Rd. SW11	Bolingbroke Wk. 13R 72	Blake Gdns. SW6.	11R 72
Bolton Rd. W11	Portobello St. 10M 47	Blanchard Pl. E8.	22H 38
Bond St. SW8	Bondway 17Q 62	Blandford Pl. W1.	14L 49
Bond St. WC1	Cruikshank St. 18J 50	Blandford St. W1.	14L 49
Bonneville Rd. SW4	Bonneville Gdns 15U 73	Blean St. SW8.	16Q 62
Boston St. NW1	Taunton St. 13K 48	Blendon Ter. SE18.	34Q 95
Boundary M. W11	Powis M. 10L 47	Blenheim Gdns. SW4.	16U 72
Boundary Rd. W11	Swanscombe Rd. 9N 59	Bletchley St. N1.	20J 51
Bourdon St. W1 North West	Bourdon P. 15M 49	Bliss Cres. SE13.	26R 77
Bouverie St. W2	Bouverie Pl. 13L 48	Blomfield Vills. W2.	12L 48
Bow La. E14	Bazely St. 26M 53	Bloomfield Rd. SE18.	33Q 95
Bramcote Rd. SE16	Bramcote Gro. 22P 64	Bloomsbury Way WC1.	17L 50
Brampton Rd. E9	Bramshaw Rd. 23H 38	Blore Ct. W1.	16M 49
Brand St. N7	Rollet St. 18F 36	Blue Anchor Ct. EC3.	20M 51
Brand St. NW1	Lascelles St. 13K 48	Boadicea St. N1.	17J 50
Brandon Rd. SW2	Bartley Rd. 17U 74	Bocking St. E8.	22H 38

OLD NAME.	NEW NAME.
Brewer St. EC1	Paget St. 18K 50
Brewer St. SW1	Allington St. 15O 61
Brewer St. N. EC1	Friend St. 18K 50
Brewer's La. WC2	Hungerford La. 17M 50
Brewer's Yd. N1	Collins Yd. 19J 50
Brewer's Yd. NW3	Carlisle Yd. 12F 34
Brewhouse La. SW15	Brewhouse St. 9S 71
Bridge Rd. E14	Westferry Rd. 25M 53
Bridge Rd. NW1	Bridge App. 14H 35
Bridge Rd. W. SW11	Westbridge Rd. 13R 72
Bridge St. E1 & E3	Solebay St. 24K 53
Bridge St. E9	Ponsford St. 23G 38
Bridge St. SE10	Creek Rd. 26Q 65
Bridgewater St. NW1	Bridgeway St. 16J 49
Brighton Terr. SW8	Patcham Terr. 15R 73
Brindley St. W2	Brindley Rd. 11L 48
Britannia St. N1	Britannia Wk 20K 51
Broad St. E1	Highway, The 23M 52
Broad St. SE11	Black Prince Rd. 17P 62
Broad St. W1	Broadwick St. 16M 49
Broad St. WC2	High Holborn 17L 50
Broad Yd. N1	Quick Pl. 19J 50
Broadwall SE1 South-East	Hatfields 18N 62
Broadway SE8	Deptford B'way 25R 77
Broadway W6	Hammersmith B'way 8P 59
Broadway, The E8	Broadway Mkt 22J 52
Broadway, The EC4	Ludgate B'way 19M 50
Broadway, The SW6	Fulham B'way 11Q 59
Broker's All. WC2	Shelton St. 17M 50
Bromley St. E14	Brushwood St. 26L 53
Brook St. E1	Cable St. 23M 52
Brook St. SE11	Brook Dri. 18O 62
Brooklands Rd. SE3	Brooklands Pk. 29S 78
Broomhouse Rd. SW6 South from Hurlingham Rd.	Broomhouse La. 10S 71
Broughton Rd. N16	Barbauld Rd. 20F 37
Brown St. W1	Brown Hart Gdns. 14M 49
Brunswick M. W11	Westbourne Gro. M. 11M 47
Brunswick Pl. E1	Bardsey Pl. 23L 52
Brunswick Rd. N19	Macdonald Rd. 16E 35
Brunswick Rd. SE5	Brunswick Villas 20R 75
Brunswick Sq. SE5 East	St. Giles St. 20R 75
South	Brunswick Pk 20R 75
West	Benhill Rd. 20R 75
Brunswick St. E1	Brunehild St. 22M 52
Brunswick St. E8	Haggerston Rd. 21H 37
Brunswick St. E9	Cresset St. 23H 38
Brunswick St. E14	Blackwall Way 27M 54
Brunswick St. N1	Reid St. 18J 50
Buckingham M. N1	Railway St. 17J 50
Buckingham M. W11	Portobello Rd. 11M 47
Buckingham St. N1	Boadicea St. 17J 50
Buckingham St. SW1	Buckingham Pl. 15O 61
Buckingham St. W1	Greenwell St. 15K 49
Bull Ct. EC1	Memel Ct. 19K 51
Bull's Head Pass. EC2	Oat La. 19L 51
Bulstrode M. W1	Bulstrode Pl. 15L 49
Burdett St. E3	Purdy St. 26K 53
Burgoyne Rd. E3	Lanfranc Rd. 24J 53
Burlington Rd. W2	St. Stephen's Gdns. 11L 47
Burton St. SE17	Burton Gro. 20P 63
Bury Ct. EC2	Love La. 19L 51
Bury Pl. NW1	Bell St. 13L 48
Bury St. WC1	Bury Pl. 17L 50
Butcher Row SE8	Borthwick St. 25Q 65
Butler St. E1	Brune St. 21L 51
Buxton St. EC1	Hermit St. 18K 50
Byron St. NW1	Elgood St. 13K 48
Cadogan Ter. SW3	Cadogan Gdns. 14O 61
Calverley St. E1	Calverley Wk. 23L 52
Cambridge Circus E2	Cambridge Cres. 22J 52
Cambridge Pl. SE18	Cambridge Row 33Q 95
Cambridge Pl. W2	Norfolk Pl. 13L 48

NEW NAME.	
Boldero St. NW8.	13K 48
Bolingbroke Wk. SW11.	13R 72
Bondway SW8.	17Q 62
Bonhill St. EC2.	20K 51
Bonneville Gdns. SW4.	15U 73
Borthwick St. SE8.	25Q 65
Boscobel Pl. SW1.	14O 61
Boscobel St. NW8.	13K 48
Boswell St. WC1.	17L 50
Botolph Pass. E3.	26K 53
Boundary Rd. NW8.	12H 34
Bourchier St. W1.	16M 49
Bourdon Pl. W1.	15M 49
Bourdon St. W1.	15M 49
Bourlet Clo. W1.	15L 49
Bourne St. SW1.	14P 61
Bourne Ter. W2.	11L 48
Bouverie Pl. W2.	13L 48
Boyton Pl. NW1.	13L 48
Brackenbury Gdns. W6.	8O 58
Bradlaugh St. N1.	20J 51
Braes St. N1.	19H 37
Braganza St. SE17.	18P 62
Braidwood St. SE1.	20N 63
Bramcote Gro. SE16.	22P 64
Bramshaw Rd. E9.	23H 38
Bramwell Pl. SW8.	15S 73
Bredgar Rd. N19.	15E 35
Brenthouse Rd. E9.	23H 38
Brewer St. W1.	16M 49
Brewhouse St. SW15.	9S 71
Bridge App. NW1.	14H 35
Bridge Arcade SE1.	29N 63
Bridgefoot SE11.	17P 62
Bridgeman St. NW8.	13J 48
Bridgeway St. NW1.	16J 49
Bridport Ter. SW8.	16R 73
Bridstow Pl. W2.	11L 47
Brindley Rd. W2.	11L 48
Brinsley St. E1.	22M 52
Briset St. EC1.	19L 50
Bristow Rd. SE19.	20Y 86
Britannia Wk. N1.	20K 51
Brittany St. SE11.	17P 62
Britton St. EC1.	18L 50
Brixton Station Rd. SW9.	18S 74
Broadbent St. W1.	15 M 49
Broadley St. NW8.	13L 48
Broadway Mkt. E8.	22J 52
Broadwick St. W1.	16M 49
Brodlove Ct. E1.	23M 52
Brodlove La. E1.	23M 52
Brokesley St. E3.	25K 53
Bromfield St. N1.	18J 50
Bromley High St. E1.	26K 53
Brompton Pl. SW3.	13O 60
Brook Dri. SE11.	18O 62
Brook La. SE3.	29S 79
Brooke's Ct. EC1.	18L 50
Brooklands Pk. SE3.	29S 78
Brooksbank St. E9.	23G 38
Broomhouse La. SW6.	10S 71
Bros St. E8.	23J 52
Brough St. SW8.	17Q 62
Brownfield St. E14.	26M 53
Brown Hart Gds. W1.	14M 49
Browning M. W1.	15L 49
Brune St. E1.	21L 51
Brunehild St. E1.	22M 52
Brunswick Pk. SE5.	20R 75
Brunswick Villas SE5.	20R 75

L.C.C. STREET NAME CHANGES.

OLD NAME.	NEW NAME.
Cambridge Rd. E1 & E2	Cambridge Heath Rd. 23K 52
Cambridge Rd. SE12	Cambridge Dri. 29U 78
Cambridge Rd. W6	Cambridge Gro. 8O 58
Cambridge St. E2	Jersey Ter. 22K 52
Cambridge St. NW1	Camley St. 16J 50
Cambridge St. SE5	Tamerton St. 19Q 63
Cambridge St. W2	Kendal St. 13M 48
Cambridge Ter. W2	Sussex Gdns. 13L 48
Camden Gdns. W12	Shepherd's Gdns. 9N 59
Camden Sq. SE15	Rosemary Gdns. 21R 75
Camden St. E2	Ellsworth St. 22K 52
Camden St. N1	Camden Wk. 19J 50
Camden St. SE15	Gatonby St. 21R 75
Campbell Rd. N.4	Whadcoat St. 18E 36
Canal Bank SE1	Rodsley Pl. 22Q 64
Canal Bank SE8	Canal App. 24P 65
Canal Rd. N1	Orsman Rd. 20J 51
Canal Ter. NW1	Canal View 16H 35
Canning Pl. SE5	Canning Cross 20S 75
Cannon Pl. E1	Maples Pl. 22L 52
Canterbury M. SE17	Penton M. 18P 62
Canterbury Rd. N1	Wright St. 21G 37
Canterbury Rd. SE15 & 16	Ilderton Rd. 23Q 64
Canterbury Ter. N.1	Kingsbury Ter. 21G 37
Canterbury Ter. W9	Lanark Rd. 12K 48
Capener's Yd. SW1	Capener's Clo. 14N 61
Cardigan St. N1	Bagford St. 20H 37
Carey St. SW1	Rutherford St. 16O 61
Carlisle St. E2	Stenhouse St. 22K 52
Carlisle St. NW1 & NW8	Penfold St. 13K 48
Carlisle St. SE1	Carlisle La. 18O 62
Carlton M. SW11	Battersea Bri. Rd. 13Q 60
Carlton M. W9	Western M. 10L 47
Carlton Rd. E1	Portelet St. 23K 52
Carlton Rd. NW5	Grafton Rd. 15G 35
Carlton Rd. SW15	Carlton Dri. 9T 71
Carlton Sq. SE14	Pomeroy Sq. 23R 76
Carlton St. NW8	Kennet St. 13K 48
Caroline Pl. EC1	Sally Pl. 18K 50
Caroline Pl. SE18	Carolina Pl. 32P 95
Caroline Pl. SW3	Donne Pl. 13O 60
Caroline Pl. W6	Caroline Wk. 9Q 59
Caroline Pl. WC1	Mecklenburgh Pl. 17K 50
Caroline St. E5	Charnwood St. 22E 38
Caroline St. NW1	Carol St. 15H 35
Caroline St. SW1	Caroline Ter. 14P 61
Caroline St. WC1	Adeline Pl. 16L 50
Castlands Rd. SE6	
North-West	Burford Rd. 24W 88
South	Winsford Rd. 24W 88
Castle Ct. E1	Chess Ct. 21L 51
Castle Ct. EC4	Florio Ct. 18M 50
Castle St. EC1	Saffron St. 18L 50
Castle St. EC2	Epworth St. 20K 51
Castle St. SE1	Thrale St. 19N 63
Castle St. SW11	Shuttleworth Rd. 13R 72
Castle St. WC2	Shelton St. 17M 50
Castle Yd. EC4	Castle Yd. La. 19M 51
Catherine St. E2	Winkley St. 22J 52
Catherine St. EC1	Cranwood St. 20K 51
Catherine St. SE11	Worgan St. 17P 62
Catherine St. SW1	Catherine Pl. 15O 61
Cavendish Rd. W. NW8	Cavendish Clo. 13J 48
Caxton St. E3	Caxton Gro. 25K 53
Cedar Rd. SW6	Cedarne Rd. 11Q 60
Champion Pk. SE26	Champion Rd. 24X 88
Chancellor Rd. SE21	Chancellor Gro. 19W 86
Chandos St. WC2	
North-East	Chandos Pl. 17M 50
South	William IV St. 17M 50
Chapel Ct. N16	Slindon Ct. 21E 37
Chapel Ct. W1	Tenison St. 15M 49

NEW NAME.	
Brushwood St. E14.	26L 53
Bryan Rd. SE16.	24N 65
Brydges Pl. WC2.	16M 50
Buckfast St. E2.	22K 52
Buckingham Pl. SW1.	15O 61
Buckley St. SE1.	18N 62
Buckmaster Rd. SW11.	13T 72
Buller Sq. SE15.	21R 76
Bullivant St. E14.	26M 54
Bulmer M. W11.	11M 47
Bulstrode Pl. W1.	15L 49
Bunton St. SE18.	33P 95
Burder Rd. N1.	21G 37
Burford Rd. SE6.	24W 88
Burge St. SE1.	20O 63
Burgh St. N1.	19J 51
Burlington Pl. SW6.	10S 71
Burnham St. E2.	23K 52
Burrage Pl. SE18.	33Q 95
Burton Gro. SE17.	20P 63
Burton Pl. WC1.	16K 50
Bury Pl. WC1.	17L 50
Bush Cotts. SE18.	11T 71
Bute Gdns. W6.	9O 59
Byand Pl. E8.	21G 37
Cable St. E1.	23M 52
Cadogan Gdns. SW3.	14O 61
Cadogan La. SW1.	14O 61
Caedmon Rd. N7.	18F 36
Calderwood St. SE18.	33P 95
Caldwell St. SW9.	17R 74
Callcott St. W8.	11N 59
Calshot St. N1.	17J 50
Calverley Wk. E1.	23L 52
Calvin St. E1.	21L 51
Camberwell Pass. SE5.	19R 75
Camberwell Ch. St. SE5.	20R 75
Cambridge Cres. E2.	22J 52
Cambridge Dri. SE12.	29U 70
Cambridge Gro. W6.	8O 58
Cambridge Pass. E9.	23H 38
Cambridge Row SE18.	33Q 95
Cambridge Heath Rd. E1 & E2.	23K 52
Camdale Rd. SE18.	35R 95
Camden Wk. N1.	19J 50
Camden High St. NW1.	15H 35
Camdenhurst St. E14.	24L 53
Camelot St. SE15.	22Q 64
Camera Pl. SW10.	12Q 60
Camley St. NW1.	16J 50
Canal App. SE8.	24P 65
Canal View NW1.	16H 35
Canning Cross SE5.	20S 75
Canon Beck Rd. SE16.	23N 64
Canon Murnane Rd. SE1.	21O 63
Capener's Clo. SW1.	14N 61
Cardinal Bourne St. SE1	20O 63
Carlisle La. SE1.	18O 62
Carlisle St. SE1.	18O 62
Carlisle Yd. NW3.	12F 34
Carlton Dri. SW15.	9T 71
Carltoun St. NW5.	15G 35
Carnegie St. N1.	18J 50
Carol St. NW1.	15H 35
Carolina Pl. SE18.	32P 95
Caroline Ct. N7.	18G 36
Caroline Ter. SW1.	14P 61
Caroline Wk. W6.	9Q 59
Carpenter's Yd. EC3.	21M 51
Caslon St. EC1.	19 K 51

L.C.C. STREET NAME CHANGES.

OLD NAME.	NEW NAME.	
Chapel Rd. W11	St. Mark's Pl.	10M 47
Chapel St. E1	Drant St.	21L 51
Chapel St. E2	Arline Ter.	21K 51
Chapel St. N1	Chapel Mkt.	18J 50
Chapel St. SE18	Chapel Hill	32P 95
Chapel St. SW9	Mowll St.	18R 74
Chapel St. SW10	Camera Pl.	12Q 60
Chapel St. W6	School St.	8P 58
Chapel St. WC1	Rugby St.	17L 50
Charing Cross SW1 (Nos. 57-66)		
	Trafalgar Sq.	16N 62
Charles Pl. E1	Glamis Pl.	23M 52
Charles St. E1	Aylward St.	23L 52
Charles St. E14	Scurr St.	26M 53
Charles St. EC1	Greville St.	18L 50
Charles St. EC1	Viscount St.	19L 51
Charles St. N1	Yeate St.	20H 37
Charles St. N7	Corrall Rd.	18G 36
Charles St. NW1	Phœnix Rd.	16K 49
Charles St. SE1	Nicholson St.	18N 62
Charles St. SW7	Trevor St.	13N 60
Charles St. W11	Queensdale Pl.	9N 59
Charlotte Cotts. SE27	Charlotte Villas	19X 85
Charlotte M. WC1	Stedham Pl	17L 50
Charlotte Pl. SE18	Evins Pl.	34P 95
Charlotte Pl. SE27	Charlotte Villas	19X 85
Charlotte Pl. SW4	Charlotte Row	15S 73
Charlotte St. E2	Helston St.	21K 52
Charlotte St. EC2	Charlotte Rd.	20K 51
Charlotte St. N1	Carnegie St.	18J 50
Charlotte St. SE1	Rowcross St.	21P 63
Charlotte St. SE18	Perrott St.	34P 95
Charlotte St. SW3	Rysbrack St.	14O 61
Charlton St. W1	Hanson St.	15L 49
Chartham Rd. SE27	Chartham Gro.	18X 85
Chatham Pl. SE17	Balfour St.	20P 63
Chatham St. SW11	Dagnall St.	14R 73
Chatsworth Rd. SE27	Chatsworth Way	19W 86
Chelsea Gro. SW10	Cavaye Pl.	12P 60
Cheney St. NW1	Cheney Rd.	17J 50
Cheniston Gdns. W8.	North Wright's La.	11O 60
Chesnut Rd. SE18	Chestnut Rise	35Q 95
Chester M. NW1	Chester Ter. M.	15K 49
Chester M. N. SW1	Chester M.	15O 61
Chester Pl. SE18	Chester Gro.	34P 95
Chester Pl. W2	Strathearn Pl.	13M 42
Chester Pl. M. SW1	Chester Sq. M.	15O 61
Chester St. E2	Burnham St.	23K 52
Chester St. SW1	Chester Way	15O 61
Chester Ter. W1	Rowan Ter.	9O 59
Chesterfield St. WC1	Crestfield St.	17K 50
Chichester St. W2	Kinnaird St.	12L 48
Chilton St. SE8	Chilton Gro.	24P 64
Chislett Rd. NW6	Compayne Gdns.	11G 34
Chiswell St. SE5	Hopewell St.	20R 75
Christchurch Rd. NW3.	Christchurch Hill	13F 34
Christchurch St. SE10.	Christchurch Way	28P 66
Church Ct. E1	Amos Ct.	22N 64
Church Ct. EC2	St. Olave's Ct.	19M 51
Church Ct. EC4	St. Clement's Ct.	20M 51
Church La. N1	St. Mary's Path	19H 37
Church La. NW3	Perrin's La.	12F 34
Church La. SW11	Sunbury La.	13R 72
Church Pass. E1	Nantes Pass.	21L 51
Church Pass. EC3	All Hallows Ct.	20M 51
Church Pass. EC3	Church Cloisters	20M 51
Church Pass. EC3	St. James's Pass.	21M 51
Church Pass. N1	Dagmar Pass.	19H 37
Church Pass. SE5	Camberwell Pass.	19R 75
Church Pass. SE5	Churchyard Pass.	20R 75
Church Pass. SE10	St. Alfege Pass.	26Q 66
Church Pass. SE16	Peter Hills Wk.	23N 64
Church Pass. SE18	Church Hill	32O 95

NEW NAME.	
Castile Rd. SE18.	33P 95
Castlehaven Rd. NW1.	15H 35
Castlereagh St. W1.	13L 48
Castle Yd. La. EC4.	19M 51
Catherine Pl. SW1.	15O 61
Cato St. W1.	13L 48
Cavaye Pl. SW10.	12P 60
Cave St. N1.	18J 50
Cavell St. E1.	22L 52
Cavendish Clo. NW8.	13J 48
Cavendish Ret. SW8.	16R 74
Caxton Gro. E3.	25K 53
Cecilia Rd. E8.	21G 38
Cedarne Rd. SW6.	11Q 60
Central Pl. EC1.	19K 51
Cephas Av. E1.	23K 52
Chalcot Rd. NW1.	14H 35
Chalcot Sq. NW1.	14H 35
Chalton St. NW1.	16J 49
Chamberlain Cotts. SE5.	
	20R 75
Chambers Rd. N7.	17P 36
Champion Rd. SE26.	24X 88
Chancellor Gro. SE21.	19W 86
Chandos Pl. WC2.	17M 50
Chantry Pl. N.1.	19J 51
Chapel Hill SE18.	32P 95
Chapel Mkt. N1.	18J 50
Chapone Pl. W1.	19M 49
Charles Clo. NW1.	15H 35
Charlotte Rd. EC2.	20K 51
Charlotte Row SW4.	15S 73
Charlotte Ter. N1.	18J 50
Charlotte Villas SE27.	18X 85
Charlton Pk. La. SE7.	31R 79
Charmouth St. N1.	20J 51
Charnwood St. E5.	22E 38
Chart St. N1.	20K 51
Chartham Gro. SE27.	18X 85
Chatfield Rd. SW11.	12S 72
Chatsworth Way SE27.	19W 86
Chelsea Sq. SW3.	13P 60
Chelsea Manor Gdns. SW3.	
	13P 60
Chelsea Manor St. SW3.	
	13P 60
Cheltenham Rd. SE15.	23T 76
Cheney Rd. NW1.	17J 50
Chenies M. WC1.	16L 49
Chepstow Rd. W2.	11L 47
Cherbury St. N1.	20J 51
Cherry Pl. E1.	23L 52
Cheseman St. SE26.	22X 87
Cheshire Bldgs. E2.	22K 52
Cheshire St. E2.	21K 52
Chess Ct. E1.	21L 51
Chester Gro. SE18.	34P 95
Chester M. SW1.	15O 61
Chester Sq. M. SW1.	15O 61
Chester Ter. M. NW1.	15K 49
Chester Way SW1.	15O 61
Chestnut Ct. SW6.	10Q 59
Chestnut Rise SE18.	35Q 95
Chicksand St. E1.	21L 52
Chillingworth Rd. N7.	18G 36
Chiltern St. W1.	14L 49
Chilton Gro. SE8.	24P 64
Chivers Cotts. E14.	24M 53
Christchurch Hill NW3.	13F 34
Christchurch Pl. SW8.	16R 73
Christchurch Way SE10.	
	28P 66
Christian Pl. E1.	22M 52
Christie St. N19.	17E 36

L.C.C. STREET NAME CHANGES.

OLD NAME.	NEW NAME.	
Church Pass. SE18..	St. Margaret's Path	34Q 95
Church Pass. WC2	St. Giles Pass.	16M 50
Church Path E14	Morant Path	25M 53
Church Path W6	Lillie Wk.	10Q 59
Church Pl. W2	Unwin Pl.	12L 48
Church Pl. W10	St. John's Ter.	9K 47
Church Pl. WC2	Inigo Pl.	17M 50
Church Rd. E9	Barnabas Rd.	24G 38
Church Rd. N1	Northchurch Rd.	20H 37
Church Rd. NW3	Tasker Rd.	14G 35
Church Rd. SE23	Church Rise	23W 87
Church Rd. SW2	St. Matthew's Rd.	17U 74
Church Rd. SW11	Battersea Ch. Rd.	13R 72
Church Rd. W6	Atwood Rd.	8O 58
Church Row E2	St. Matthew's Row	21K 52
Church Row E14	Newell St.	25M 53
Church Row EC1	St. Luke's Row	19K 51
Church Row EC3	St. Katherine's Row	21M 51
Church Row EC4	St. Stephen's Row	21M 51
Church Row SW6	Church Gate	9S 71
Church Row WC2	Savoy Row	17M 50
Church St. E2	Redchurch St.	21K 51
Church St. N1	Gaskin St.	19H 37
Church St. N16..	Stoke Newington Ch. St.	20F 37
Church St. NW8. East	Lilestone St.	13L 48
Church St. SE1	Roper La.	21N 63
Church St. SE5..	Camberwell Church St.	20R 75
Church St. SE8	Deptford Ch. St.	25Q 65
Church St. SE10	Greenwich Ch. St.	26Q 66
Church St. SE13	Lee Church St.	28T 78
Church St. SE18	Woolwich Ch. St.	32O 95
Church St. SW3	Old Church St.	13P 60
Church St. SW8	Ashmole St.	17Q 62
Church St. W1	Romilly St.	16M 50
Church St. W2 West	Churchman St.	13L 48
Church St. W8	Kensington Ch. St.	11N 60
Church Ter. E9	St. Barnabas Ter.	23G 38
Church Ter. SE18	St. James's Villas	34Q 95
Church Ter. SW6	Christchurch Pl.	16R 73
Church Wk. NW3	Perrin's Wk.	12F 34
Church Wk. SE18 ..	Low Cross Wood La.	21X 86
Church Wk. SW18	Jew's Row	11T 72
Churchill Rd. E9	Churchill Wk.	23G 38
Circular Rd. SE18	Circular Way	32Q 95
Circus St. W1	Enford St.	13L 49
Circus, The SE10	Gloucester Circus	27R 78
Claremont Pl. E1	Cherry Pl.	23L 52
Claremont St. E2	Claredale St.	22J 52
Claremont Ter. SE17	Clare Ter.	20P 63
Clarence Cotts. SW9	Fenwick Cotts.	16S 74
Clarence La. N1	Clare La.	19H 37
Clarence M. NW1	Clarence Ter. M.	14K 49
Clarence M. W8	Old Ct. Pl.	11N 60
Clarence Rd. NW1	Clarence Way	15H 35
Clarence Rd. SW4	Clarence Av.	16U 73
Clarence St. E1	Cranberry St.	22K 52
Clarence St. EC1	Exchange St.	19K 51
Clarence St. N1	Burgh St.	19J 51
Clarence St. SE10	College App.	26Q 66
Clarence St. SE16	Canon Beck Rd.	23N 64
Clarence St. SW4	Clarence Wk.	17R 74
Clarence Ter. E5	Clarence Clo.	21J 51
Clarence Yd. N7	Tollington Rd.	17F 36
Clarendon Pl.W11	Clarendon Cross	10M 47
Clarendon Rd. SE13	Clarendon Rise	27T 78
Clarendon Rd. SW15	Clarendon Dri.	8S 70
Clarendon Sq. NW1		
East	Chalton St.	16J 49
North	Polygon Rd.	16J 49
South	Phœnix Rd.	16J 49
West	Werrington St.	16J 49
Clarendon St. NW1	Werrington St.	16J 49
Clarendon St. W2	Clarendon Cres.	11L 48

OLD NAME.	NEW NAME.	
Christina St. EC2.		20K 51
Christmas St. SE1.		20O 63
Chudleigh St. E1.		24M 52
Church Cloisters EC3.		20M 51
Church Gate SW6.		9S 71
Church Hill SE18.		32O 95
Church Rise SE23.		23W 87
Churchfields SE10.		26Q 65
Churchill Wk. E9.		23G 38
Churchman St. W2.		13L 48
Churchyd. Pass. SE5.		20R 75
Circular Way SE18.		32Q 95
Clapham Cres. SW4.		16T 73
Clapham High St. SW1.		16T 73
Clapham Manor St. SW4.		
		16S 73
Clapton Way E5.		22F 38
Clare La. N1.		19H 37
Clare Ter. SE17.		20P 63
Claredale St. E2.		22J 52
Clarence Av. SW4.		16U 73
Clarence Clo. E5.		21J 51
Clarence Ter. M. NW1.		14K 49
Clarence Wk. SW4.		17R 74
Clarence Way NW1.		15H 35
Clarendon Cres. W2.		11L 48
Clarendon Cross W11.		10M 47
Clarendon Dri. SW15.		8S 70
Clarendon Rise SE13.		27T 78
Clarges M. W1.		15N 61
Clark's Pass. SW8.		17Q 62
Clavell St. SE10.		26Q 65
Cleaver Sq. SE11.		18P 62
Clere St. EC2.		20K 51
Cleveland Ter. W2.		12L 48
Cleveland Way E1.		23L 52
Cliff Rd. NW1.		16G 36
Cliff Vills. NW1.		16G 36
Clifford's Row SW1.		14P 61
Clifton Av. W12.		7N 58
Clifton Rise SE14.		24R 77
Clifton Way SE15.		22R 76
Clissold Cres. N16.		20F 37
Cloth Ct. EC1.		19L 51
Clyde Vale SE23.		23W 87
Coal Wharf Rd. W12.		9N 59
Coalcroft Rd. SW15.		8T 70
Cobden Pl. SE15.		20Q 63
Coborn St. E3.		25K 53
Cockspur Ct. SW1.		16N 62
Coleman Clo. E1.		23N 64
Coleman Fields N1.		19H 37
Coley St. WC1.		18K 50
College App. SE10.		26Q 66
College Cres. N1.		18H 36
College Row E9.		23G 38
College Terr. E3.		24K 53
College Yd. NW5.		15F 35
Collent St. E9.		23H 38
Collingwood Pl. SE18.		33O 95
Collins Rd. N5.		19F 37
Collins Yd. N1.		19J 50
Colombo St. SE1.		18N 62
Comet Ho. Pl. SE8.		25R 77
Commercial Rd. E1 & E14.		
		22M 52
Commercial Way SE15.		21R 75
Commondale SW15.		8S 70
Compayne Gdns. NW6.		11G 34
Compton Sq. N1.		19G 37
Condell Rd. SW8.		16R 73
Condray St. SW11.		13R 72
Connaught Clo. W2.		13M 48
Conquest St. SE1.		19O 62:

OLD NAME.	NEW NAME.
Clark St. EC1	Pardon St. 19K 51
Clark's M. WC2	Dyott M. 16L 50
Clark(e)'s Pl. E3	St. Stephen's Rd. 24J 53
Clark's Pl. SW8	Clark's Pass. 17Q 62
Clay La. SE18	Erindale 35Q 95
Clayton St. N1	Tilloch St. 17H 36
Clement's La. WC2	St. Clement's La. 17M 50
Cleveland St. E1	Cleveland Way 23L 52
Clifton Hill SE14	Clifton Rise 24R 77
Clifton Pl. SW10	Cavaye Pl. 12P 60
Clifton Rd. NW1	Cliff Rd. 16G 36
Clifton Rd. SE4	Avon Rd. 25S 77
Clifton Rd. SE15	Clifton Way 22R 76
Clifton Rd. W12	Clifton Av. 7N 58
Clifton St. E14	Lax St. 25L 53
Clifton St. SW8	Courland St. 16R 74
Clifton St. W11	Poynter St. 9M 47
Clifton Vills. NW1	Cliff Vills. 16G 36
Clyde St. SW10	Redcliffe Pl. 12Q 60
Coach & Horses Yd. EC1	
	Bartholomew Clo. 19L 51
Cobden St. SE15	Cobden Pl. 20Q 63
Cock Yd. SE18	Ferry Pl. 33O 95
Cock Yd. W1	St. Anselm's Pl. 15M 49
Colchester St. EC3	Pepys St. 21M 51
Coleherne Ct. (part) SW5	
	Old Brompton Rd. 11P 60
Coleman St. E1	
East	Monza Pl. 23N 64
West	Coleman Clo. 23N 64
Coleman St. N1	Coleman Fields 19H 37
Coleman's Bldgs. W12	Askew Bldgs. 7N 58
College La. E9	College Row 23G 38
College M. NW5	College Yd. 15F 35
College Pl. SW3	Elystan Pl. 13P 60
College Rd. NW3	Eton College Rd. 14H 35
College St. E3	College Ter. 24K 53
College St. E9	Priestley St. 23G 38
College St. N1	College Cross 18H 36
College St. SE1	Jenkins St. 17N 62
College St. SW15	Wadham Rd. 10T 71
Collingwood St. SE1	Colombo St. 18N 62
Collingwood St. SE18	Collingwood Pl. 33O 95
Commercial Rd. SE1	Upper Ground 18N 62
Commercial Rd. SE15	Commercial Way 21R 75
Commercial Rd. E. E1 & E14	
	Commercial Rd. 22M 52
Compton St. N1	Bingham St. 20G 37
Compton St. WC1	Tavistock Pl. 17K 50
Conduit St. E5	Rossendale St. 22E 38
Connaught Sq. M. W2	Archery Clo. 13M 48
Cook's Cotts. SE17	Kinglake Pl. 20P 63
Cooper's Row E1	Minting Row 21M 52
Cordelia St. E3	Lear St. 24K 53
Cork St. SE5	Bantry St. 20R 75
Cornwall Rd. E2	Cornwall Av. 23K 52
Cornwall Rd. E9	Redruth Rd. 23H 38
Cornwall Rd. SW2 & SW4	
East from Lyham Rd.	Blenheim Gdns. 16U 74
Cornwall Rd. W11	
East	Westbourne Pk. Rd. 10L 47
West	Cornwall Cres. 10L 47
Cornwall St. SW6	Rumbold Rd. 11Q 60
Cornwall Rd. SE15	Furley Rd. 22R 76
Cottage Gro. E3	Rhondda Gro. 24K 53
Cottage Gro. SE17	Penrose Gro. 19P 63
Cottage Pl. E1	Adelina Gro. 23L 52
Cottage Pl. E2	Darsham Pl. 21K 52
Cottage Pl. SW1	Cottage Wk. 14O 61
Cottages, The E14	Chivers Cotts. 24M 53
Cottenham Rd. N19	Sussex Way 17D 24
Cotton St. EC1	Milliner St. 19L 51
County Ter. St. SE1	County St. 19O 63

	NEW NAME.
Cons St. SE1.	18N 62
Consort Rd. SE15.	22R 76
Consort St. W2.	13L 48
Conway St. W1.	15K 49
Coomer M. SW6.	10Q 59
Copperfield St. SE1.	19N 63
Cordelia St. E14.	26M 53
Corn St. SE18.	31P 67
Cornwall Av. E2.	23K 52
Cornwall Cres. W11.	10L 47
Corrall Rd. N7.	18G 36
Corsham St. N1.	20K 51
Cosser Ct. SE1.	18O 62
Cosser St. SE1.	18O 62
Cottage Wk. SW1.	14O 61
Coulgate St. SE4.	24S 77
County St. SE1.	19O 63
Courland St. SW8.	16R 74
Courtauld Pl. W1.	15L 49
Coventry Rd. E1 & E2.	22K 52
Cowley Gdns. E1.	23M 52
Coxmount Rd. SE7.	31P 67
Cramer St. W1.	14L 49
Cranberry St. E1.	22K 52
Cranbrook Ter. E2.	23J 52
Cranleigh St. NW1.	16J 49
Cranwood St. EC1.	20K 51
Crawford Rd. SE5.	19R 75
Creasy St. SE1.	20O 63
Creek St. SE10.	26Q 65
Creekside SE8.	25Q 65
Crellin Bldgs. E1.	22M 52
Crescent La. SW4.	15T 73
Crescent Row EC1.	19K 51
Cresset Rd. E9.	23H 38
Cresset St. SW4.	16S 73
Cressy Ct. E1.	23L 52
Crestfield St. WC1.	17K 50
Crockford Pl. NW1.	13L 48
Crombie M. SW11.	13S 72
Cross Key Ct. EC2.	20L 51
Cross Keys Clo. W1.	14L 49
Crowder St. E1.	22M 52
Crown Ct. WC2.	17L 50
Crown Works E2.	22J 52
Crozier Ct. EC1.	18K 50
Cruikshank St. WC1.	18J 50
Culmore Cross SW12.	15V 84
Culpeper St. N1.	18J 50
Cumberland Ter. M. NW1.	
	15J 49
Cunard Pl. EC3.	20M 51
Cundy St. SW1.	14P 61
Curnock St. NW1.	16J 49
Curtis St. SE1.	21O 63
Cut, The. SE1.	18N 62
Cyclops Pl. E14.	25P 65
Cypress Pl. W1.	15L 49
Cyprus Pl. E2.	23J 52
Dacre Pk. SE13.	28T 78
Dacre Pl. SE13.	28T 78
Dagmar Pass. N1.	19H 37
Dagnall St. SW11.	14R 73
Dairy La. SE18.	32P 95
Dallington St. EC1.	19K 51
Dalwood Pl. SE5.	20R 75
Damien St. E1.	22L 52
Danesdale Rd. E9.	24H 39
Daniel Gdns. SE15.	21Q 63
Danube St. SW3.	13P 60
Daplyn St. E1.	21L 52
Darling Rd. SE4.	25S 77
Darling Row E1.	22L 52
Darsham Pl. E2.	21K 52

L.C.C. STREET NAME CHANGES.

OLD NAME.	NEW NAME.
Coventry St. E1 & E2	Coventry Rd. 22K 52
Cowley St. E1	Cowley Gdns. 23M 52
Cranbrook Rd. E2	Cranbrook Ter. 23J 52
Craven St. N1	Corsham St. 20K 51
Crawford St. SE5	Crawford Rd. 19R 75
Creasy's Cotts. SW2	Sulina Rd. 16V 85
Creek St. SE8	Creekside 25R 77
Crescent Pl. WC1	Burton Pl. 16K 50
Crescent St. W11	Becher Pl. 9M 47
Cromwell Rd. N19	Ireton Rd. 16E 36
Cross Ct. N1	Graham Ct. 19J 51
Cross Ct. WC2	Crown Ct. 17L 50
Cross St. EC4	Gophir La. 20M 51
Cross Rd. E5	Rogate Rd. 22F 38
Cross Rd. SE5	Guildford Pl. 19R 75
Cross Rd. SE22	E. Dulwich Rd. 21T 75
Cross St. E2	Bempton St. 22J 52
Cross St. EC1	St. Cross St. 18L 50
Cross St. EC2	Lackington St. 20L 51
Cross St. SE1	Creasy St. 20O 62
Cross St. SE7	Eastmoor Pl. 31P 67
Cross St. SW3	Stackhouse St. 14O 61
Cross St. SW4	Cresset St. 16S 73
Cross St. WC1	Swinton Pl. 17K 50
Cross Keys M. W1	Cross Keys Clo. 14L 49
Crown Ct. EC2	Milton Ct. 19L 51
Crown Ct. EC2	Old Broad St. 20L 51
Crown Ct. EC3	Three Crown Ct. 21M 51
Crown Ct. EC4	Hood Ct. 18M 50
Crown Ct. SW6	Chestnut Ct. 10Q 59
Crown Ct. WC2	Andrews Crosse 17M 50
Crown Pl. SW11	Leitrim Pass. 14R 73
Crown Yd. E2	Crown Works 22J 52
Culmore Rd. SW12	Culmore Cross 15V 84
Cumberland M. NW1	Cumberland Ter. M. 15J 49
Cumberland St. N7	Ponder St. 17H 36
Curzon St. N1	Charmouth St. 20J 51
Doore St. SE13	Fludyer St. 28T 78
Dagmar Rd. N10	Dagnedale Rd. 74H 6?
Dane Av. SE5	Finsen Rd. 19T 75
Daniel St. SE15	Daniel Gdns. 21Q 63
Darnley Rd. W11	St. Ann's Villas 23H 38
Dartmouth Pl. SE7	Harden's Manorway 31Q 67
Dartmouth Pl. SE10	Dartmouth Hill 27R 78
Davis Pl. SW10	Apollo Pl. 12Q 60
Dawson St. W6	Aviland St. 9P 59
Dean St. E1	Deancross St. 23M 52
Dean St. EC4	Dean La. 18L 50
Dean St. N1	Bishop St. 19H 37
Dean Yd. E1	Chapone Pl. 16M 49
Dean's Ct. EC4	Bales Ct. 18L 50
Deauville Rd. SW4	Elms Cres. 15U 73
Defoe Rd. SW17	Garratt La. 13X 83
Denbigh M. W11	Denbigh Clo. 10M 47
Denbigh Rd. E3	Palon Clo. 25K 53
Denmark Pl. SE27	Denmark Wk. 19X 86
Denmark Rd. N1	Dewey Rd. 18J 50
Denmark St. E1	Crowder St. 22M 52
Denmark St. N1	Dignum St. 18J 50
Derby St. SW1	Derby Gate 17N 62
Derby St. WC1	St. Chad's St. 17K 50
Devonport M. W2	Radnor M. 13M 48
Devonport St. W2	Sussex Pl. 13M 48
Devonshire Rd. E9	Brenthouse Rd. 23H 38
Devonshire Rd. N7	Axminster Rd. 17E 36
Devonshire Rd. SE10	Devonshire Dri. 26R 77
Devonshire Rd. SW8	Allen Edwards Rd. 16R 74
Devonshire St. E1	Bancroft Rd. 23K 52
Devonshire St. N1	Devonia Rd. 19J 51
Devonshire St. SE15	Devon St. 22Q 64
Devonshire St. WC1	Boswell St. 17L 50
Devonshire Ter. E14	Mast House Ter. 25P 65
Digby Rd. N4	Digby Cres. 19E 37

NEW NAME.	
Dartmouth Hill SE10.	27R 78
Dartmouth Rd. SE23.	22X 87
Darwin Pl. SE17.	20P 63
Davenant St. E1.	22L 52
David M. W1.	14L 49
Davidge St. SE1.	18N 62
Dawes St. SE17.	20P 63
Deal St. E1.	22L 52
Dean La. EC4.	18L 50
Deancross St. E1.	23M 52
Denbigh Clo. W11.	10M 47
Denmark Wk. SE27.	19X 86
Deptford B'way SE8.	25R 77
Deptford Ch. St. SE8.	25Q 65
Deptford High St. SE8.	25Q 65
Derby Gate SW1.	17N 62
Derry St. W8.	11N 60
Devon St. SE15.	22Q 64
Devonia Rd. N1.	19J 51
Devonport Pass. E1.	23M 52
Devonshire Dri. SE10.	26R 77
De Walden St. W1.	15L 49
Dewar St. SE15.	21S 76
Dewar Yd. SE15.	21S 76
Dewey Rd. N1.	18J 50
Dewport St. W6.	9P 59
Dicken's Sq. SE1.	19O 63
Digby Cres. N4.	19E 37
Dingwall St. N1.	18J 50
Disney Pl. SE1.	19N 63
Ditchburn St. E14.	27M 54
Dobins Ct. EC2.	19L 51
Doddington Rd. SW11.	14R 73
Dombey St. WC1.	17L 50
Donegal Row N1.	18J 50
Donne Pl. SW3.	13O 60
Dorian St. E1.	22L 52
Doric Rd. E2.	23J 52
Dorset Rise EC4.	18M 50
Dorset Wk. SW9	1?6J 6?
Dorset Works N1.	20J 51
Dorville Cres. W6.	7O 58
Dove Rd. N1.	20G 37
Downs La. E5.	22F 38
Dragon Yd. WC1.	17L 50
Drant St. E1.	21L 51
Drew St. E14.	26M 53
Driver St. SW8.	15R 73
Drover La. SE15.	22Q 64
Dryden St. WC2.	17M 50
Drysdale St. N1.	21K 51
Ducal Pl. E2.	21K 51
Duchy Pl. SE1.	18N 62
Duchy St. SE1.	18N 62
Dudley Ct. EC2.	19L 51
Dudmaston M. SW3.	13P 60
Duke of York St. SW1.	16N 61
Duke St. Hill SE1.	20N 63
Dunbar Pl. SE27.	19X 86
Dunbridge Pl. E2.	22K 52
Dunbridge St. E2.	22K 52
Dunelm St. E1.	23L 52
Dunloe Pl. E2.	21J 52
Dunn's Pl. E8.	21F 37
Dunraven St. W1.	14M 49
Dunstable M. W1.	15L 49
Dunstans Gro. SE22.	22U 76
Dunton Rd. SE1.	21P 63
Durham Rise SE18.	34Q 95
Durweston St. W1.	14L 49
Duthie St. E14.	27M 54
Dutton St. SE10.	26R 77
Dyott M. WC2.	16L 50
Eaglet Pl. E1.	23L 52

L.C.C. STREET NAME CHANGES.

OLD NAME.	NEW NAME.
Doby Ct. EC2	Dobins Ct. 19L 51
Dock Yd. Rails SE18	Woolwich Ch. St. 32O 95
Doddington Gro. SW11	Doddington Rd. 14R 73
Dorset M. N1	Dorset Works 20J 51
Dorset St. SW8	Dorset Wk. 17Q 62
Dorset St. E1	Pitsea St. 23M 52
Dorset St. EC4	Dorset Rise 18M 50
Dorset St. N1	Dove Rd. 20G 37
Dorville Rd. W6	Dorville Cres. 7O 58
Douglas Pl. EC1	Pickburn Pl. 18K 50
Douglas Pl. W2	Redan Pl. 11M 48
Douglas Rd. SE13	Marischal Rd. 27T 78
Down Pl. SE18	Foreland St. 34P 95
Down St. SE18	Foreland St. 34P 95
Downsbury Rd. SW18	Sispara Gdns. 10U 71
Drayton Ter. SW10	Old Brompton Rd. 12P 60
Drive, The SE26	Hall Dri. 22Y 87
Duke St. E1	Fort St. 21L 51
Duke St. SE1	Duchy St. 18N 62
Duke St. SE1	Duke St. Hill. 20N 63
Duke St. NW8	Boldero St. 13K 48
Durham Rd. SE18	Durham Rise 34Q 95
Durham Vills. W8	Phillimore Pl. 11N 59
Eagle Pl. E1	Eaglet Pl. 23L 52
Eagle Pl. SE17	Kinglake Pl. 20P 63
Earl St. NW8	Broadley St. 13L 48
Earl St. SE1	Thomas Doyle St. 19O 62
Earl St. SE18	Earl Rise 34P 95
East Pl. N1	Northeast Pl. 18J 50
East St. E3	Coborn St. 25K 53
East St. E8	Bros St. 23J 52
East St. N1	Gifford St. 17H 36
East St. SE7	Eastmoor St. 31O 67
East St. SE18	Troy St. 33P 95
East St. SE27	Waring St. 19X 86
East St. W1	Chiltern St. 14L 49
East St. WC1	Dombey St. 17L 50
Eastbrook Rd. SE3 South.	Woolacombe Rd. 30S 79
E. Chapel St. W1	Trebeck St. 15N 61
E. Smithfield E1	
E. of Dock St.	Highway, The 21M 52
Eaton Cotts. SW1	Eaton Clo. 14P 61
Eaton Pl. E1	Shiloh St. 23L 52
Eaton Pl. E9	Purcell Pl. 23H 38
Eaton St. SE1	Greet St. 18N 62
Eaton Ter. NW8	Kingsmill Ter. 13J 48
Ebenezer Pl. E14	Elsmere Pl. 24L 53
Eccleston St. E. SW1	Eccleston St. 15O 61
Edith Rd. SE15	Gautrey Rd. 23S 76
Edmund St. NW1	Cheney Rd. 17J 50
Edmond's Pl. SE1	Lockyer Pl. 20N 63
Edward St. E1	Edwin St. 23K 52
Edward St. N1	Micawber St. 19J 51
Edward St. NW1	Varndell St. 15K 49
Edward St. SE1	Treveris St. 18N 62
Edward St. SW1	Osbert St. 16P 61
Edward St. W1	Broadwick St. 16M 49
Edward Ter. N1	Drysdale St. 21K 51
Edward Ter. NW6	Kilburn Pl. 11G 34
Edwardes Ter. W8	Kensington High St. 10O 59
Eglinton Rd. E3	Saxon Rd. 24J 53
Eldon Rd. NW3	Eldon Gro. 13F 34
Eleanor Rd. SE18	Castile Rd. 33P 95
Elgin Ter. W9	Lanark Rd. 11J 48
Elizabeth Cotts. SE15	Livesey Pl. 22Q 64
Elizabeth Pl. SW1	Elizabeth St. 14P 61
Elizabeth Pl. SW1	Clifford's Row 14P 61
Elizabeth Pl. SW15	Oakhill Pl. 10T 71
Elizabeth Pl. W2	Poplar Pl. 11M 48
Elizabeth St. SE17	Lytham St. 19P 63
Ellerslie Rd. SW4	Ellerslie Sq. 16T 74
Elm Gdns. W6	Bute Gdns. 9O 59
Elm Gro. W6	Bute Gdns. 9O 59

NEW NAME.	
Earl Rise SE18.	34P 95
Earlham St. WC2.	16M 50
Earlstoke St. EC1.	18K 50
Earnshaw St. WC2.	16L 50
Earsby St. W14.	10O 59
E. Dulwich Rd. SE22.	21T 75
Eastminster E1.	21M 51
Eastmoor Pl. SE7.	31P 67
Eastmoor St. SE7.	31O 67
E. Surrey Gro. SE15.	21R 75
Eastway E9.	25G 39
Eaton Clo. SW1.	14P 61
Ebson St. SW8.	15R 73
Eburne Rd. N7.	17F 36
Eccleston Pl. SW1.	15O 61
Eckford St. N1.	18J 50
Eden Row W6.	7O 58
Edis St. NW1.	14H 35
Edison Sq. EC1.	20K 51
Edward's Cotts. N1.	19H 37
Edwin St. E1.	23K 52
Elba Pl. SE17.	19O 63
Eldon Gro. NW3.	13F 34
Elf Row E1.	23M 52
Elgood St. NW1.	13K 48
Elia St. N1.	19J 50
Elizabeth Av. N1.	20H 37
Elizabeth Ct. SW1.	14P 61
Ellerman St. E14.	25M 53
E'lerslie Sq. SW4.	16T 74
Ellsworth St. E2.	22K 52
Elmington Rd. SE5.	20R 75
Elmley St. SE18.	34P 95
Elm Park La. SW3.	12P 60
Elms Cres. SW4.	15T 73
Elrington Rd. E8.	22H 38
Elsden M. E2.	23K 52
Elsmere Pl. E14.	24L 53
Elsynge Rd. SW18.	12T 72
Ely Cotts. SW8.	17Q 62
Ely Ct. EC1.	18L 50
E'ystan Pl. SW3.	13P 60
Emden St. SW6.	11R 72
Emily Vills. SW18.	11T 72
Empress Pl. SW6.	11P 59
Enderby St. SE10.	27P 66
Endsleigh Pl. WC1.	16K 50
Enford St. W1.	13L 49
English St. E3.	24K 53
Ensign St. E1.	22M 52
Epworth St. EC2.	20K 51
Erindale SE18.	35Q 95
Ernest Av. SE27.	19X 85
Escreet Gro. SE18.	32P 95
Esterbrooke St. SW1.	16P 61
Eton College Rd. NW3.	14H 35
Eton Garages NW3.	13G 34
Etty St. SE1.	17O 62
Evelyn Wk. N1.	20J 51
Evelyn Yd. W1.	16L 49
Eversholt Row NW1.	16K 50
Eversholt St. NW1.	16J 49
Everton Bldgs. NW1.	15K 49
Evins Pl. SE18.	34P 95
Excel Ct. WC2.	16M 50
Exchange St. EC1.	19K 51
Exmouth Mkt. EC1.	18K 50
Eyre St. Hill EC1.	18K 50
Fairfield Gro. SE7.	31Q 67
Fairholt St. SW7.	13O 60
Falconberg M. W1.	16L 50
Fann St. EC1.	19L 51
Farnfield St. E14.	26M 53
Farren Rd. SE23.	24W 87

L.C.C. STREET NAME CHANGES.

OLD NAME.	NEW NAME.
Elm Pl. E. SW3	Lecky St. 12P 60
Elm Row E1	Elf Row 23M 52
Elm St. SE18	Elmley St. 34P 95
Elm Pk. Gdns. M. SW3	Elm Pk. La. 12P 60
Elms Rd. SE21.	
East	Gilkes Cres. 20U 75
West	Gilkes St. 20U 75
Elms Rd. SW4 South-East	Elms Cres. 16U 73
Ely Pl. SE11	Geraldine St. 18O 62
Ely Pl. SW8	Ely Cotts. 17Q 62
Emden Rd. SW6	Emden St. 11R 72
Emily Pl. SW18	Emily Vills. 11T 72
Emma St. SW11	Hope St. 12S 72
Ernest Pl. SE27	Charlotte Villas 18X 85
Ernest St. SE1	Canon Murnane Rd. 21O 63
Ernest St. SE27	Ernest Av. 19X 85
Esher St. SE11	Aveline St. 18P 62
Essex St. E2	Wessex St. 23K 52
Essex St. E8	Bocking St. 22H 38
Essex St. N1	Shenfield St. 21J 51
Eton Rd. SE18	Vincent Rd. 33P 95
Eton Stables NW3	Eton Garages 13G 34
Eton St. NW1	Edis St. 14H 35
Eton St. SE18	Rudd St. 34P 95
Evelyn St. N1	Evelyn Wk. 20J 51
Exeter St. NW8	Ashbridge St. 13K 48
Exmouth St. EC1	Exmouth Mkt. 18K 50
Exmouth St. NW1	Starcross St. 16K 49
Fair St. E1	Dunelm St. 23L 52
Fairfield Rd. SE7	Fairfield Gro. 31Q 67
Falcon Ct. SE1	Lit. Dorrit Ct. 19N 63
Farm St. W1	South St. 15M 49
Feathers Ct. EC1	Fox Ct. 18L 50
Felix St. SE1	Etty St. 17O 62
Field Pl. SW8	Pulham Pl. 17Q 62
Field Pl. SW11	Play Pl. 12S 72
Finch St. E1	Hopetown St 21L 52
Finchley Rd. SE17	Forsyth Rd. 19Q 62
Fleur De Lis Ct. EC3	Houndsditch 20L 51
Flint St. E14	Holday St. 30L 60
Florence St. SE14	Florence Ter. 25R 77
Florence St. E. SE14	Omega St. 25R 77
Forster Clo. SW2	Tilson Gdns. 16V 85
Fountain Ct. EC2	Fountaine Ct. 19L 51
Fountain Ct. EC2	St. Matthew's Ct. 19M 51
Fountain Rd. SE19	Fountain Dri. 21X 86
Foxes La. SE3	Foxes Dale 28S 78
Fox's Bldgs. E2	Fox's Yd. 21K 51
Frances St. E2	Weymouth Pl. 21J 51
Frances St. SE1	Buckley St. 18N 62
Frances St. SW11	Condray St. 13R 72
Francis St. E2	Weymouth Pl. 21J 51
Francis St. N1	Charlotte Ter. 18J 50
Francis St. SW3	Petyward 13P 60
Francis St. W6	Dewport St. 9P 59
Francis St. WC1	Torrington Pl. 16L 49
Franklin St. NW5	Arctic St. 15G 35
Frederick Pl. E3	Aberavon Rd. 24K 53
Frederick Pl. E8	Frederick Ter. 21H 37
Frederick Pl. NW8	Mackennal St. 13J 48
Frederick Pl. WC1	Ampton Pl. 17K 50
Frederick St. SW1	Esterbrooke St. 16P 61
Friar St. SE1	Webber St. 19N 62
Furley St. SE15	Furley Rd. 22R 76
Gainsborough Rd. E3	Alloway Rd. 24K 53
Gainsborough Rd. E9	Eastway 25G 39
Garden Row SE13	Gentian Row 26S 77
Garden Row SW6	Wansdown Pl. 11Q 60
Garden Row SW9	Garden Clo. 17S 74
Garden St. SW1	Garden Ter. 16P 61
Garratt La. SW17	
South-East	Garratt Ter. 13X 83
Gaspar M. SW5 East	Gaspar Clo. 11O 60

NEW NAME.
Fenchurch Bldgs. EC3. 20M 51
Fenelon Pl. W14. 10O 59
Fenwick Cotts. SW9. 16S 74
Fenwick Ct. SW9. 16S 74
Ferdinand Rd. NW1. 15H 35
Ferry App. SE18. 33O 95
Ferry Pl. SE18. 33O 95
Ferry St. E14. 26P 65
Fife Ter. N1. 18J 50
Finsen Rd. SE5. 19T 75
Fitzhardinge St. W1. 14L 49
Flaxman Ct. W1. 16M 49
Fletcher La. SE1. 19N 63
Fletcher St. E1. 22M 52
Flitcroft St. WC2. 16M 50
Flood Wk. SW3. 13P 60
Florence Ter. SE14. 25R 77
Florio Ct. EC4. 18M 50
Fludyer St. SE13. 28T 78
Folgate St. E1. 21L 51
Foreland St. SE18. 34P 95
Foreman Ct. W6. 8P 59
Forset Clo. W1. 13L 48
Forsyth Rd. SE17. 19Q 62
Fort St. E1. 21L 51
Fortess Wk. NW5. 15F 35
Fortune Dri. SE19. 21X 86
Fortune St. EC1. 19K 51
Fountain Dri. SE19. 21X 86
Fountain St. E2. 21K 51
Fountaine Ct. EC2. 19L 51
Fownes St. SW11. 13S 72
Fox Ct. EC1. 18L 50
Foxes Dale SE3. 28S 78
Fox's Yd. E2. 21K 51
Frampton St. NW8. 13K 48
Frances St. SE18. 32P 95
Friary Rd. SE15. 22Q 64
Friend St. EC1. 18K 50
Fulham B'way SW6. 11Q 59
Fulham High Rd. SW6. 10S 71
Fulham Pal. Rd. W6. 8P 58
Furley Pl. SE15. 22Q 64
Furley Rd. SE15. 22R 76
Furrow La. E9. 23G 38
Garbutt Pl. W1. 14L 49
Garden Ter. SW1. 16P 61
Garden Clo. SW9. 17S 74
Garnet St. E1. 23M 52
Garratt La. SW17. 13X 83
Garratt Ter. SW17. 13X 83
Gaskin St. N1. 19H 37
Gaspar Clo. SW5. 11O 60
Gate M. SW7. 13N 60
Gathorne St. E2. 23J 52
Gatonby St. SE15. 21R 75
Gautrey Rd. SE15. 23S 76
Gavel St. SE17. 20O 63
Geary St. N7. 18G 36
Geffrye St. E2. 21J 51
Gentian Row SE13. 26S 77
George St. W1. 14L 49
Geraldine St. SE11. 18O 62
Gerrard Rd. N1. 19J 51
Gifford St. N1. 17H 36
Gilden Rd. NW5. 14G 35
Gilkes Cres. SE21. 20U 75
Gilkes St. SE21. 20U 75
Glamis Pl. E1. 23M 52
Glasshill St. SE1. 19N 63
Glasshouse Wk. SE11. 17P 62
Glasshouse Yd. EC1. 19L 51
Glebe St. SE16. 22O 64
Glebe Ter. E3. 26K 53
Glegg Pl. SW15. 9S 71

L.C.C. STREET NAME CHANGES.

OLD NAME.	NEW NAME.	NEW NAME.
Gee St. NW1	Polygon Rd. 16J 49	Glenalvon Pl. SE18. 31P 67
George St. NW1	Gower St. 16K 49	Glencarnock Av. E14. 27P 66
George St. SE18	Woolwich Ch. St. 32P 95	Glengall Gro. E14. 25O 65
George St. W1	St. George St. 15M 49	Globe Rd. E1. 23K 52
George Yd. WC2	Goslett Yd. 16M 50	Globe Ter. E2. 23K 52
Gerrard St. N1	Gerrard Rd. 19J 51	Globular Ct. E1. 22M 52
Gibson Cotts. W6	Theresa St. 7P 58	Gloucester Cir. SE10. 26R 78
Gibson Sq. N1 South	Theberton St. 18H 36	Gloucester Dri. N4. 19E 37
Gifford St. N1	Stanway St. 21J 51	Gloucester Gro. SE15. 20Q 63
Gladstone St. N19	Christie St. 17E 36	Gloucester Pl. NW1. & W1. 14L 49
Gladstone Rd. SW8	St. Joseph's St. 15R 73	
Gladstone St. SW8	Trenchold St. 17Q 62	Gloucester Way EC1. 18K 50
Glasshouse St. E1	John Fisher St. 21M 52	Godalming Rd. E14. 26L 53
Glasshouse St. SE11	Glasshouse Wk. 17P 62	Godfrey Rd. SE18. 32P 95
Glasshouse Yd. EC4	Playhouse Yd. 19M 50	Golding St. E1. 22M 52
Glebe Rd. E3	Glebe Ter. 26K 53	Golford Pl. NW1. 13K 48
Glebe Rd. SE16	Glebe St. 22O 64	Goodge Pl. W1. 16L 49
Glebe Rd. SE5	St. Giles Rd. 20R 75	Goodman St. E1. 21M 52
Gledhow Ter. SW5	Old Brompton Rd. 12P 60	Gophir La. EC4. 20M 51
Glengall Rd. E14	Glengall Gro. 25O 65	Goslett Yd. WC2. 16M 50
Glenview Rd. SE13	Nightingale Gro. 27U 78	Goswell Rd. EC1. 19K 51
Globe Ct. E1	Globular Ct. 22M 52	Gough Gro. E14. 25M 53
Globe Ct. SE11	Wake Ct. 17O 62	Gower Ct. WC1. 16K 49
Globe St. E1	Sampson St. 22N 64	Gower St. NW1. 16K 49
Gloucester Pl. SE10	Gloucester Circus 26R 78	Grace St. NW1. 16K 50
Gloucester Rd. N4	Gloucester Dri. 19E 37	Grafton Rd. NW5. 15G 35
Gloucester Rd. SE15	Gloucester Gro. 20Q 63	Grafton Way W1 & WC1. 16K 49
Gloucester St. EC1	Gloucester Way 18K 50	
Gloucester Ter. SW7	Old Brompton Rd. 12P 60	Grafton Yd. NW5. 15G 35
Godfrey St. SE18	Godfrey Rd. 32P 95	Graham Ct. N1. 19J 51
Golden Sq. NW3	Mount Sq., The 12F 34	Graham Ter. SW1. 14P 61
Goldsmith Sq. N16	St. Matthias Sq. 20G 37	Granby Ter. NW1. 15J 49
Goldsmith St. EC4	Pemberton Row 18L 50	Grange Gro. N1. 19G 37
Goldsmith St. WC2	Stukeley St. 17L 50	Grange St. N1. 20J 51
Goldsmith's Pl. NW6	Springfield La. 11J 48	Grant St. N1. 18J 50
Gordon Pl. WC1	Endsleigh Pl. 16K 50	Grantley St. E1. 23K 52
Gordon Rd. N16	Beatty Rd. 21F 37	Granville Gro. SE13. 26S 78
Gordon Rd. NW1	Beatty St. 15H 35	Grass Ct. EC3. 20M 51
Gordon St. N1	Quick St. 19J 51	Gt. Guildford St. SE1. 19N 63
Gough St. E14	Gough Gro. 25M 53	Greatorex St. E1. 21L 52
Gough St. SE18	Hough St. 33P 95	Greek Ct. W1. 16M 50
Grace St. N1	Shirley St. 18H 36	Green Dale SE5 & SE22. 20T 75
Grafton M. NW5	Grafton Yd. 15G 35	Greenberry St. NW8. 13J 48
Grafton Rd. N7	Eburne Rd. 17F 36	Greenfield Rd. E1. 22L 52
Grafton St. E1	Grantley St. 23K 52	Greenland Rd. NW1. 15H 35
Grafton St. W1 & WC1	Grafton Way 16K 49	Greenwell St. W1. 15K 49
Graham St. SW1	Graham Ter. 14P 61	Greenwich Ch. St. SE10. 26Q 66
Granby St. NW1	Granby Ter. 15J 49	
Grand Junct. Rd. W2	Sussex Gdns. 13M 48	Greenwich High Rd. SE10. 26 Q 65
Grange Rd. N1	Grange Gro. 19G 37	Greenwich Pk. St. SE10. 27Q 66
Grange Rd. NW1	Castlehaven Rd. 15H 35	
Grange Rd. SW4	Hannington Rd. 15S 73	Greenwich South St. SE10. 26R 77
Grange, The NW3	Parkhill Pl. 14G 35	
Granville Pl. WC1	Gwynne Pl. 18K 50	Greet St. SE1. 18N 62
Granville Rd. SE13	Granville Gro. 26S 78	Greville M. NW6. 11J 48
Gray St. E1	Dorian St. 22L 52	Greville St. EC1. 18L 50
Gray St. E14	Adderley St. 26M 53	Grosvenor Av. N5. 19G 37
Gray St. W1	Picton Pl. 14L 49	Grosvenor M. W1. 15M 49
Gray's Inn Pl. SW1	Osier Pl. 15O 61	Grotto Ct. SE1. 19N 63
Gt. Alie St. E1	Alie St. 21M 51	Grove Way SW9. 17R 74
Gt. Barlow St. W1	Cramer St. 14L 49	Guildford Gro. SE10. 26R 77
Gt. Bath St. EC1	Topham St. 18K 50	Guildford Pl. SE5. 19R 75
Gt. Bland St. SE1	Burge St. 20O 63	Guildhouse St. SW1. 15O 61
Gt. Charlotte St. SE1	Cut, The 18N 62	Gunstor Rd. N16. 21F 37
Gt. Chart St. N1	Chart St. 20K 51	Gwynne Pl. WC1. 18K 50
Gt. Chesterfield St. W1	Wheatley St. 14L 49	Haddo Ter. SE10. 26Q 65
Gt. Earl St. WC2	Earlham St. 17M 50	Haggerston Rd. E8. 21H 37
Gt. Garden St. E1	Greatorex St. 21L 52	Halcrow St. E1. 22L 52
Gt. Hermitage St. E1	Hermitage Wall 22N 64	Half Moon Ct. EC1. 19L 51
Gt. James St. N1	Purcell St. 20J 51	Halkin M. SW1. 14O 61
Gt. Pearl St. E1	Calvin St. 21L 51	Hall Dri. SE26. 22Y 87
Gt. Prescot St. E1	Prescot St. 21M 51	Hamilton Clo. NW8. 12K 48
Gt. Quebec St. W1	Upr. Montagu St. 14L 49	

OLD NAME.	NEW NAME.
Gt. Queen St. WC2	Remnant St. 17L 50
Gt. Saffron Hill EC1	Saffron Hill 18L 50
Gt. St. Andrew St. WC2	Monmouth St. 17M 50
Gt. Stanhope St. W1	Stanhope Gate 14N 61
Gt. Tongue Yd. E1	Tongue Alley 21L 52
Gt. Tower Hill EC3	Tower Hill 21M 51
Gt. White Lion St. WC2	Mercer St. 17M 50
Gt. Woodstock St. W1	Nottingham Pl. 14L 49
Green Bank SE1	Braidwood St. 20N 63
Green Lane SE5 & SE22	Green Dale 20T 75
Green La. SW11	Vicarage Cres. 12R 72
Green St. SW3	Mossop St. 13O 60
Green St. W2	N. Wharf Rd. 13L 48
Grn. Dragon Yd. WC1	Dragon Yd. 17L 50
Greenfield St. £1	Greenfield Rd. 22L 52
Greenfield St. E14	Brownfield St. 26M 53
Greenwich Rd. SE10	Greenwich High Rd. 26R 77
Grosvenor M. W1. East	Bourdon St. 15M 49
Grosvenor Rd. N5	Grovenor Av. 19G 37
Grosvenor St. E1	Mountmorres Rd. 23L 52
Grosvenor St. SE5	Urlwin St. 19Q 63
Grove SE1	Southwark Gro.
Grove Cotts. SE5	Chamberlain Cotts. 20R 75
Grove La. N16	Lampard Gro. 21D 25
Grove M. NW1	Bendall M. 13L 48
Grove M. W11	Portobello Rd. 10L 47
Grove Rd. NW8	Lisson Gro. 13K 48
Grove Rd. SW9	Grove Way 17R 74
Grove Rd. SW12	Weir Rd. 15V 84
Grove St. E1	Golding St. 22M 52
Grove, The NW3	Hampstead Gro. 12F 34
Grove, The NW5	Highgate Rd. 15F 35
Grove, The SE10	West Gro. 27R 78
Grove, The SE18	Rail Pl. 32O 95
Grove, The SW8	Vauxhall Gro. 17Q 62
Grove, The SW18	St. Ann's Hill 11U 72
Grove, The W6	Hammersmith Gro. 8O 58
Grove Vale Depôt Cotts. SE22	Vale End 21T 75
Guildford Rd. E14	Godalming Rd. 26L 52
Guildford Rd. SE15	Guildford Gro. 20R 77
Guildford St. SE1	Gt. Guildford St. 19N 63
Hackney Gro. E8	
North	Sylvester Path 22G 38
South East	Wilton Way 22G 38
Hale St. N1	Rees St. 19J 51
Half Moon Pass. EC1	Half Moon Ct. 19L 51
Halkin M. N. SW1	Halkin M. 14O 61
Hall Pl. SE15	Cheltenham Rd. 23T 76
Hall St. E3	Hedworth St. 25L 53
Hamilton M. NW8	Hamilton Clo. 12K 48
Hamilton Pl. N16	Ormsby Pl. 21F 37
Hamilton Rd. E3	Haverfield Rd. 24K 52
Hamilton Rd. N5	Hamilton Pk. 19F 37
Hamilton Rd. SE24	Mumford St. 18U 74
Hamilton St. NW1	Greenland Rd. 15H 35
Hampden St. NW1	Polygon Rd. 16J 50
Hampden St. W2	Hampden Cres. 11L 48
Hampshire St. SE11	Hampshire Pl. 17P 62
Handel St. SW18	Tonsley St. 11T 72
Hanover Ct. EC3	Carpenter's Yd. 21M 51
Hanover St. N1	Noel Rd. 19J 51
Hanover St. NW5	Gilden Rd. 14G 35
Hanover St. SE15	Highshore Rd. 21R 75
Hanover Ter. W11	Lansdowne Wk. 10M 47
Hardinge St. N1	Battishill St. 18H 36
Hare Ct. EC1	Lauderdale St. 19L 51
Hare St. E1	Harry St. 23L 52
Hare St. E2	Cheshire St. 21K 52
Harley M. S. W1	Wigmore St. 15L 49
Harley St. E3	Harley Gro. 25K 53
Harley St. SW11	Harleton St. 13R 72
Harper St. SE1	Harper Rd. 19O 63
Harrington Rd. SE18	Harrington Way 31O 67

NEW NAME.
Hamilton Pl. N5 19F 37
Hamilton Ter. NW8. 12J 48
Hammersmith B'way W6. 8P 59
Hammersmith Gro. W6. 8O 58
Hampden Cres. W2. 11L 48
Hampshire Pl. SE11. 17P 62
Hampshire Hog La. W6. 7P 58
Hampstead Gro. NW3. 12F 34
Hampstead High St. NW3. 12F 34
Handley St. SW11. 13R 72
Hannington Rd. SW4. 15S 73
Hanson St. W1. 15L 49
Harben Rd. NW6. 12H 34
Harden St. SE18. 31P 67
Harden's Manorway SE7. 31O 67
Harecourt Rd. N1. 19G 37
Harleton St. SW11. 13R 72
Harley Gro. E3. 25K 53
Harold Pl. SE11. 18P 62
Harper Rd. SE1. 19O 63
Harrington Way SE18. 31O 67
Harry St. E1. 23L 52
Hart Yd. EC1. 18L 50
Hartfield Ter. E3. 25J 53
Hatfields SE1. 18N 62
Hatherley St. SW1. 16O 61
Hatton Row NW8. 13K 48
Havelock Wk. SE23. 23W 87
Haven M. E3. 25L 53
Haverfield Rd. E3. 24K 52
Hawes St. N1. 19H 37
Hay Currie St. E14. 26L 53
Haydon Wk. E1. 21M 51
Hazel Gro. SE26. 23Y 87
Head St. E1. 23L 52
Headlam St. E1. 22L 52
Heath La. SE3. 28R 78
Hedworth St. E3. 25L 53
Heiron Cotts. SE17. 19Q 63
Helston St. E2. 21K 52
Hemus Pl. SW3. 13P 60
Henrietta Pl. W1. 15L 49
Henslowe Pass. SE1. 19N 63
Henstridge Pl. NW8. 13J 48
Herald St. E2. 22K 52
Herbal Hill EC1. 18L 50
Herbert Gro. N1. 20J 51
Hercules St. N7. 17F 36
Hermit St. EC1. 18K 50
Hermitage Wall E1. 22N 64
Herringham Rd. SE7. 31P 67
Hertford St. W1. 15N 61
Hester Rd. SW11. 13Q 60
High Holborn WC2. 17L 50
Highgate Rd. NW5. 15F 35
Highgate High St. N6. 15D 23
Highshore Rd. SE15. 21R 75
Highway, The E1. 21M 52
Hilditch St. E14. 26M 54
Hill Reach SE18. 32P 95
Hillgate St. W8. 11M 47
Hillingdon St. SE5 & SE17. 19Q 62
Hillrise Rd. N19. 17D 24
Hillyard St. SW9. 18R 74
Hind Gro. E14. 25M 53
Hoadley Cotts. SW3. 13P 60
Hobday St. E14. 26L 53
Hocking Bldgs. SE11. 18P 62
Hollar Rd. N16. 21F 37
Holloway Pass. E1. 22L 52

OLD NAME.	NEW NAME.
Harrow St. SE1	
North	Disney Pl. 19N 63
South	Sanctuary St. 19N 63
Hart St. SW11	Scholey St. 13R 72
Hart St. W1	Brown Hart Gdns. 14M 49
Hart St. WC1	Bloomsbury Way 17L 50
Hasted Rd. SE7 West to Charlton La.	
	Coxmount Rd. 31P 67
Hatfield St. SE1	Hatfields 18N 62
Havelock Pl. E2	Gathorne St. 23J 52
Havelock Rd. W14	Irving Rd. 9O 59
Havelock St. SE23	Havelock Wk. 23W 87
Haverstock St. NW1	Ferdinand Clo. 15H 35
Heath St. E1	Head St. 23L 52
Heath Ter. SE10	
East	Maidenstone Hill 26R 77
West	Dutton St. 26R 77
Henrietta St. E2	Allgood St. 21J 52
Henrietta St. W1	Henrietta Pl. 15L 49
Henry Pl. E5	Stoneham Pl. 22E 38
Henry St. E14	Stainsby Pl. 25L 53
Henry St. EC1	Steadman St. 19K 51
Henry St. NW8	Allitsen Rd. 13J 48
Henry St. SE1	Holyrood St. 20N 63
Henry St. SE11	Oval Way 17P 62
Henry St. SE18	Frances St. 32P 95
Henry St. SW11	Winders Rd. 13R 72
Henry St. WC1	Roger St. 17K 50
Henstridge Vills. NW8	Henstridge Pl. 13J 48
Herbert St. N1	Herbert Gro. 20J 51
Herbert Rd. SW9	Manor Ho. Rd. 17S 74
Herbert Rd. SW15	Bective Pl. 10T 71
Hercules Rd. N7	Hercules St. 17F 36
Hereford Bldgs. E2	Cheshire Bldgs. 22K 52
Hereford St. NW1	Sheringham St. 13L 48
Herne Gro. SE22	Dunstans Gro. 22U 76
Hertford Pl. E1	Globe Rd. 23K 52
High Rd. Kilburn NW6	
	Kilburn High Rd. 11H 33
High Rd. Lee SE12 & SE13	Lee High Rd. 27T 78
High St. Bloomsbury WC2	
	St. Giles High St. 16L 50
High St. Bromley E3	Bromley High St. 26K 53
High St. Camden Town NW1	
	Camden High St. 15H 35
High St. Clapham SW4	
	Clapham High St. 16T 73
High St. Deptford SE8	
	Deptford High St. 25Q 65
High St. Fulham SW6	Fulham High St. 10S 71
High St. Hampstead NW3	
	Hampstead High St. 12F 34
High St. Highgate N6	Highgate High St. 15D 23
High St. Homerton E9	Homerton High St. 23G 38
High St. Islington N1	Islington High St. 18J 50
High St. Lambeth SE1	
	Lambeth High St. 17O 62
High St. Notting Hill W11	
	Notting Hill Gate 11M 47
High St. Peckham SE15	
	Peckham High St. 21R 76
High St. Putney SW15	Putney High St. 9T 71
High St. Portland Town NW8	
	St. John's Wood High St. 13J 48
High St. Roehampton SW15	
	Roehampton High St. 7U 70
High St. St. John's Wood NW8	
	St. John's Wood High St. 13J 48
High St. St. Marylebone W1	
	Marylebone High St. 14L 49
High St. Shadwell E1	Highway, The 22M 52

Holmead Rd. SW6.	11Q 60
Holton St. E1.	23K 52
Holwood Pl. SW4.	16T 73
Holyrood St. SE1.	20N 63
Homerton High St. E9.	23G 38
Hood Ct. EC4.	18M 50
Hope St. SW11.	12S 72
Hopetown St. E1.	21L 52
Hopewell St. SE5.	20R 75
Hopton St. SE1.	19N 63
Horse Yd. N1.	19H 37
Horse & Groom Ct. SE11.	
	19P 62
Horseferry Pl. SE10.	26Q 65
Hough St. SE18.	33P 95
Houndsditch EC3.	20L 51
Hurst Cotts. SE13.	26S 77
Howley Ter. SE1.	18N 62
Hoxton St. N1.	20J 51
Hungerford La. WC2.	17M 50
Hunts Slip Rd. SE21.	20W 86
Hyde Pk. Cres. W2.	13M 48
Hyde's Pl. N1.	19H 37
Ilchester Gdns. W2.	11M 48
Ilderton Rd. SE15 & 16.	
	23Q 64
Inglebert St. EC1.	18J 50
Inigo Pl. WC2.	17M 50
Inn Yd. W1.	16L 49
Invermore Pl. SE18.	34P 95
Inverness St. NW1.	15H 35
Ireton Rd. N19.	16E 36
Irving Rd. W14.	9O 59
Irwin Av. SE18.	35R 95
Islington High St. N1.	18J 50
Islington Pk. St. N1.	18H 36
Iverna Ct. W8.	11O 60
Ivor Pl. NW1.	14K 49
Ivor St. NW1.	15H 35
Ivy Rd. SE4.	24T 77
Ivy Wk. N1.	20J 51
Jamaica Rd. SE16.	21O 64
Jamestown Rd. NW1.	15H 35
Jasper Rd. SE19.	21Y 86
Jebb Av. SW2.	17U 74
Jeddo Rd. W12.	6N 58
Jenkins St. SE1.	17N 62
Jerome St. E1.	21L 51
Jersey Terr. E2.	22K 52
Jew's Row SW18.	11T 72
Joan St. SE1.	18N 62
John Fisher St. E1.	21M 52
John Ruskin St. SE5.	19Q 63
Jowett St. SE15.	21R 75
Junction App. SE13.	26S 77
June Bldgs. E1.	23K 52
Keesey St. SE5.	20Q 63
Kelso Pl. W8.	11O 60
Kempt St. SE18.	33Q 95
Kendal St. W2.	13M 48
Kennings Way SE11.	18P 62
Kennington La. SE11.	17P 62
Kensal Pl. W10.	10K 47
Kensington Mall W8.	11M 48
Kensington Ch. St. W8.	
	11N 60
Kensington High St. W8. & W14.	10O 59
Kensington Stn. Arcade SW7.	13O 60
Kentish Town Rd. NW5.	
	15G 35
Kenworthy Rd. E9.	24G 39

L.C.C. STREET NAME CHANGES.

OLD NAME.	NEW NAME.
High St. Sydenham SE23 & SE26	
East .... Dartmouth Rd.	22X 87
West .... Kirkdale	22W 87
High St. Wandsworth SW18	
Wandsworth High St.	11T 71
High St. Wapping E1 . Wapping High St.	22N 64
High St. W. Norwood SE27	
Norwood High St.	19X 86
Hill St. EC2 .... Bonhill St.	20K 51
Hill St. SE1 .... Glasshill St.	19N 63
Hill St. SE18 .... Hill Reach	32P 95
Hill St. SW7 .... Trevor Pl.	13N 60
Hill's Pl. WC1 .... Chenies M.	16L 49
Hind St. E14 .... Hind Gro.	25M 53
Holford St. E1 .... Holton St.	23K 52
Holland Rd. N19 .... Spears Rd.	17D 24
Holland Rd. SW9	
North .... Lilford Rd.	18S 74
South East .... Minet Rd.	18S 74
Holland St. SE1 .... Hopton St.	19N 63
Holland St. SW9 .... Caldwell St.	17R 74
Homer St. SE1 .... Virgil St.	18O 62
Hope Cotts. SE13 .... Hurst Cotts.	26S 77
Hope Pl. N7 .... Caroline Ct.	18G 36
Hope St. E1 .... Monthope St.	21L 52
Hope St. N7 .... Geary St.	18G 36
Horace St. SW8 .... Luscombe St.	17Q 62
Horace St. W1 .... Cato St.	13L 48
Horse & Groom Yd. SE11	
Horse & Groom Ct.	19P 62
Horseferry Rd. E14 .... Highway, The	24M 53
Horseferry Rd. SE10 .... Horseferry Pl.	26Q 65
Howard St. E14 .... March St.	26M 53
Howard St. SW8 .... Bridport Ter.	16R 73
Howley Pl. SE1 .... Howley Ter.	18N 62
Hyde's Pl. E. N1 .... Hyde's Pl.	19H 37
Hyde's Pl. W. N1 ...... Edward's Cotts.	19H 37
Inverness Pl. SE18 .... Invermore Pl.	34P 95
Irwin St. SE18 .... Irwin Av.	35R 95
Iverna Gdns. W8	
South-East .... Iverna Ct.	11O 60
Ivy La. N1 .... Ivy Wk.	20J 51
Ivy La SE4 .... Ivy Rd.	24T 77
James Pl. E1 ...... Devonport Pass.	23M 52
James Pl. E8 .... Byland Pl.	21G 37
James Pl. SE1 .... Murphy Pl.	18O 62
James St. NW1 .... Jamestown Rd.	15H 35
James St. W2 .... Cleveland Ter.	12L 48
Jane St. SE1 .... Joan St.	18N 62
John St. SW11 .... Petergate	12T 72
John's Ct. SE17 .... Heiron Cotts.	19Q 63
Johnson St. E14 .... Ferry St.	26P 65
Johnson St. NW1 .... Cranleigh St.	16J 49
Johnson St. W8 .... Hillgate St.	11M 47
Joseph St. SE18 .... Glenalvon Pl.	31P 67
Kennard St. SW11 .... Astle St.	14R 73
Kensington Rd. W14 Kensington High St.	10O 59
Kent House La. SE26 .... Bell Grn. La.	24Y 88
Keppel St. SE1 .... Keppel Row	19N 63
Kidbrooke La. SE3 .... Brook La.	29S 79
Kidd St. SE18 .... Woodhill	31P 67
Kimberley Rd. SE15 .... Kimberley Av.	22S 76
King St. E1 .... Eastminster	21M 51
King St. E14 .... Ming St.	25M 53
King St. EC1 .... Smithfield St.	18L 50
King St. NW1 .... Plender St.	16J 49
King St. SW3 .... St. Luke's St.	13P 60
King St. W1 .... Blandford St.	14L 49
King St. W8 .... Derry St.	11N 60
Kg. Edward St. E1 ...... Kingward St.	22L 52
Kg. Edward St. N1 ...... Bromfield St.	18J 50
Kg. Edward St. SE1 .... Kg. Edward Wk.	18O 62
Kg. William St. SE10 .. Kg. William Wk.	26Q 66

NEW NAME.	
Keppel Row SE1.	19N 63
Keyse St. SE1.	21O 63
Keyworth Pl. SE1.	18O 62
Kidd Cotts. SE18	32P 95
Kiffen St. EC2.	20K 51
Kilburn Pl. NW6.	11G 34
Kilburn High Rd. NW6.	
	11H 33
Killick Cotts. N1.	17J 50
Killick St. N1.	17J 50
Kilner St. E14.	25L 53
Kimberley Av. SE15.	22S 76
King Edward Wk. SE1.	18O 62
Kinglake Pl. SE17.	20P 63
Kingly Ct. W1.	16M 49
King's Cres. N4.	19E 37
King's Gro. SE15.	22R 76
King's Ter. NW1.	16J 49
King's Bench St. SE1.	19N 63
Kingsbury Ter. N1.	21G 37
King's Head Pass. SW4.	
	16T 73
Kingshold Rd. E9.	23H 38
Kingsmill Ter. NW8.	13J 48
Kingswood Dri. SE21.	20X 86
Kingward St. E1.	22L 52
Kg. William Wk. SE10.	26Q 66
Kinloch St. N7.	18F 36
Kinnaird St. W2.	12L 48
Kinver Rd. SE26.	23X 87
Kirby Gro. SE1.	20N 63
Kirk St. WC1	17L 50
Kirkdale SE26.	22X 87
Kirkwood Pl.NW1.	14H 35
Kitcat Ter. E3.	25K 53
Lackington St. EC2.	20L 51
Ladbroke Mews W11.	10N 59
Lambeth High St. SE1.	17O 62
Lampard Gro. N16.	21D 25
Lanark Rd. W9	11Y 42
Lancaster Av. SE27.	19W 85
Lancaster Dri. NW3.	13G 34
Lancaster Gro. NW3.	13G 34
Landor Wk. W12.	7N 58
Lanfranc Rd.E3.	24J 53
Langford Clo. NW8.	12J 48
Langstone St. E14.	25L 53
Langton Gate EC1.	19K 51
Langton Rise SE23.	22V 87
Lansdowne Dri. E8.	22H 38
Landsdowne La. SE7.	30Q 67
Lansdowne Rise W11.	10M 47
Lansdowne Ter. WC1.	17K 50
Lansdowne Wk. W11.	10M 47
Lansdowne Way SW8.	16R 74
Lanyard St. E1.	24L 53
Lapse Wood Wk. SE23	22W 87
Lascelles St. NW1.	13K 48
Latimer Pl. W10.	8L 47
Lauderdale Ct. EC1.	19L 51
Laurier Rd. NW5.	15F 35
Lawes St. E3.	25L 53
Lewless St. E14.	26M 53
Lawrence Rd. E3.	25K 53
Lax St. E14.	25L 53
Layton Rd. N1.	18J 50
Lear St. E3.	24K 53
Leathermarket St. SE1.	
	20N 63
Lecky St. SW3.	12P 60
Lee Ch. St. SE13.	28T 78
Lee Hg. Rd. SE12 & 13	27T 78
Lefevre Gro. E3.	25J 53
Legge St. SE13.	26U 77

L.C.C. STREET NAME CHANGES.

OLD NAME.	NEW NAME.	
Kg. William St. WC2 ..	William IV. St.	17M 50
King's Pl. NW1	Plender Pl.	16J 49
King's Pl. W1	Blandford Pl.	14L 49
King's Rd. N4	King's Cres.	19E 37
King's Rd. NW1	St. Pancras Way	16H 35
King's Rd. SE15	King's Gro.	22R 76
King's Bench Wk. SE1..	King's Bench St.	19N 63
King's Head Yd. SW4	King's Head Pass.	16T 73
King's Head Yd. WC2	Mathews Yd.	17M 50
Kingswood Rd. SE21....	Kingswood Dri.	20X 86
Kinver Rd. N. SE26	Kinver Rd.	23X 87
Kinver Rd. S. SE26	Kinver Rd.	23X 87
Kirby St. SE1	Kirby Gro.	20N 63
Kirkwood Rd. NW1	Kirkwood Pl.	14H 35
Knott St. SE8	Creekside	25Q 65
Lamb La. SE10	Bardsley La.	26Q 65
Lambeth M. W1	Clarges M.	15N 61
Lanark Vills. W9	Lanark St.	12K 48
Lancaster M. NW8 ..	St. Edmund's Clo.	14J 49
Lancaster M. W11	St. Luke's M.	10L 47
Lancaster Pl. NW3	Lancaster Dri.	13G 34
Lancaster Rd. NW3	Lancaster Gro.	13G 34
Lancaster Rd. SE27	Lancaster Av.	19W 85
Lancaster St. W2	Barrie St.	12M 48
Landor Rd. W12	Landor Wk.	7N 58
Landseer Rd. E3	Lawrence Rd.	25K 53
Langdon Rd. N19	Bredgar Rd.	15E 35
Langford M. NW5	Allcroft Pass.	14G 35
Langford M. NW8	Langford Clo.	12J 48
Langton Av. EC1	Langton Gate	19K 51
Langton Rd. SE23	Langton Rise	22V 87
Langton St. E14	Langstone St.	25L 53
Langton St. EC1	Langton Gate	19K 51
Lansdowne M. WC1	Ormond M.	17K 50
Lansdowne Rd. SE13	Belmont Pk.	27T 78
Lansdowne Pl. WC1	Lansdowne Ter.	17K 50
Lansdowne Rd. E8	Lansdowne Dri.	22H 38
Lansdowne Rd. SE7	Landsdowne La.	30Q 67
Lansdowne Rd. SW8	Lansdowne Way	17R 74
Laurel Cotts. SW18	Bush Cotts.	11T 71
Lawfranc Rd. E3	Lanfranc Rd.	24J 53
Layton Rd. N1	Liverpool St.	18J 50
Lee St. E14	Kilner St.	25L 53
Lee St. SE18	St. Margaret's Ter.	34Q 95
Leicester St. E14	Duthie St.	27M 54
Leopold St. SE11	Leopold Wk.	17P 62
Lewis Rd. SE5	Padfield Rd.	19S 75
Lewis Rd. E. SE5	Southwell Rd.	19S 75
Lewisham Rd. NW5	Laurier Rd.	15F 35
Lincoln St. E3	Brokesley St.	25K 53
Linton St. NW1	Penfold Pl.	13L 48
Lion St. E14	Farnfield St.	26M 53
Litcham St. NW5	Athlone St.	15G 35
Lit. Alie St. E1	Alie St.	21M 51
Lit. Ann St. E1	Pace Pl.	22M 52
Lit. Baltic St. EC1	Baltic Pass.	19K 51
Lit. Barlow St. W1	St. Vincent St.	14L 49
Lit. Bath St. EC1	Eyre St. Hill	18K 50
Lit. Blenheim St. SW3	Danube St.	13P 60
Lit. Bridge St. E1	Solebay Pl.	24K 53
Lit. Cadogan Pl. SW1	Cadogan La.	14O 61
Lit. Cambridge Pl. E2	Dunloe Pl.	21J 52
Lit. Camden St. NW1	Selous St.	16J 49
Lit. Carlisle St. NW8 ..	Whitehaven St.	13L 48
Lit. Chapel St. W1	Sheraton St.	16M 49
Lit. Charles Pl. NW1	Charles Clo.	15H 35
Lit. Chatham Pl. SE17	Balfour St.	20P 63
Lit. Clayton St. SE11	Pegasus Pl.	18P 62
Lit. Cross St. N1	Shillingford St.	19H 50
Lit. Crown Ct. W1	Tisbury Ct.	16M 49
Lit. Cumming St. N1	Fife Ter.	18J 50
Lit. Dean St. W1	Bourchier St.	16M 49
Lit. Denmark St. WC2	Flitcroft St.	16M 50

NEW NAME.	
Leicester Ct. WC2.	16M 50
Leigh Hunt St. SE1.	19H 63
Leith Rd. E3.	24L 53
Leitrim Pass. SW11.	14R 73
Lendal Terr. SW4.	16S 74
Leo Yard EC1.	18K 50
Leon St. SE18.	33P 95
Leopold Wk. SE11.	17P 62
Lilestone St. NW8.	13L 48
Lilford Rd. SW9.	18S 74
Lillie Wk. W6	10Q 59
Lindfield St. E14.	25M 53
Lion Pass. EC1.	18J 50
Lisson Gro. NW8.	13K 48
Little St. EC1.	19K 50
Littlebury Rd. SW4.	16S 73
Lit. Dorrit Ct. SE1.	19N 63
Liverpool Gro. SE17.	19P 63
Livesey Pl. SE15.	22Q 64
Llewellyn St. SE16.	21O 64
Lloyd Baker St. WC1.	18K 50
Loaf Ct. E1.	21M 51
Lockmead Rd. SE13.	27S 78
Lockyer Pl. SE1.	20N 63
Lodge Rd. NW8.	13K 48
Lollard Pl. SE11.	18P 62
Lombard Wall SE7.	29P 67
London La. E8.	22H 38
London M. W2.	13L 48
Longleigh La. SE2.	36P 95
Longman St. E2.	23J 52
Longmoore St. SW1.	15P 61
Lonsdale Pl. N1.	18H 36
Lonsdale Rd. W11.	10M 47
Lord Hills Rd. W2.	11L 48
Lord North St. SW1.	17O 62
Lorne Clo. NW8.	13K 48
Lothian Rd. SW9.	18K 74
Lough Rd. N7.	17G 36
Love La. EC2.	19L 51
Low Cross Wood La. SE21.	
	21X 86
Lucas Rd. SE5 & SE17.	18Q 62
Ludgate B'way EC4.	19M 50
Lukin St. E1.	23M 52
Luscombe St. SW8.	17Q 62
Luxborough St. W1.	14L 49
Lyndhurst Terr. NW3.	13F 34
Lyndhurst Way SE15.	21R 75
Lytham St. SE17.	19P 63
Macbean St. SE18.	33P 95
Macbeth St. W6.	8P 58
Macclesfield Rd. EC1.	19K 51
Macdonald Rd. N19.	16E 35
Mackennal St. NW8.	13J 48
Mackenzie Rd. N7.	18G 36
MacLeod St. SE17.	19P 63
McMillan St. SE8.	25Q 65
Mackworth St. NW1.	15J 49
Maddams St. E3.	26L 53
Maidenstone Hl. SE10.	26R 77
Malcolm Pl. E2.	23K 52
Mall Studios NW3	14G 35
Mandarin St. E14.	25M 53
Manley Ct. N16.	21E 37
Manning St. E14.	24L 53
Manor St. SW3.	13P 60
Manor Ho. Rd. SW9.	17S 74
Maples Pl. E1.	22L 52
March St. E14.	26M 53
Marcilly Rd. SW18.	12T 72
Marcon Pl. E8.	22G 38
Margaret Gdns. SE1.	20O 63
Margery St. WC1.	18K 50

L.C.C. STREET NAME CHANGES.

OLD NAME.	NEW NAME.
Lit. Drummond St. NW1	Crace St. 16K 50
Lit. Duke St. SE1	Duchy Pl. 18N 62
Lit. Durweston St. W1 ..	Durweston St. 14L 49
Lit. East Pl. SE11	Lollard Pl. 18P 62
Lit. Earl St. WC2	Earlham St. 16M 50
Lit. Earl St. NW8	Miles Pl. 13K 48
Lit. Ebury St. SW1	Cundy St. 14P 61
Lit. Elm Pl. SW3	Lecky St. 12P 60
Lit. Essex St. N1	Tiptree St. 21J 51
Lit. Europa Pl. SW11	Morgan's Wk. 13Q 60
Lit. Exeter St. NW8	Whitehaven St. 13L 48
Lit. Goodge St. W1	Goodge Pl. 16L 49
Lit. Gower Pl. WC1	Gower Ct. 16K 49
Lit. Gray's Inn La. WC1 ..	Mt. Pleasant 18K 50
Lit. Grosvenor M. W1	Grosvenor M. 15M 49
Lit. Grosvenor St. W1 ..	Broadbent St. 15M 49
Lit. Grove St. NW8	Plympton St. 13K 48
Lit. Halifax St. E1	Tailworth St. 21L 52
Lit. Harcourt St. W1	Shillibeer Pl. 14L 49
Lit. Hermitage St. E1	Orton St. 22N 64
Lit. Holloway St. E1	Holloway Pass. 22L 52
Lit. Howland St. W1	Cypress Pl. 15L 49
Lit. Hunter St. SE1	Potier St. 20O 63
Lit. James St. N1	Tarlton St. 20J 51
Lit. James St. WC1	Northington St. 17L 50
Lit. John St. E1	Tailworth St. 21L 52
Lit. King St. NW1	King's Ter. 16J 49
Lit. Lant St. SE1	
North	Trundle St. 19N 63
South	Weller St. 19N 63
Lit. Leonard St. EC2	Blackall St. 20K 51
Lit. Liverpool St. SE17	Lytham St. 19P 63
Lit. Manor St. SW4	Prescott Pl. 16S 73
Lit. Marlborough Pl. SE1	Penry Pl. 21P 64
Lit. Mason St. SE17	Gavel St. 20O 63
Lit. Northampton St. EC1	Little St. 19K 50
Lit. Orford St. SW3	Rosemoor St. 13P 60
Lit. Paris St. SE1	Paris St. 17O 62
Lit. Pearl St. E1	Jerome St. 21L 52
Lit. Pierrepont Row N1 ..	Pierrepont Row 18J 50
Lit. Pulteney St. W1	Brewer St. 16M 49
Lit. Randolph St. NW1	Rousden St. 16H 35
Lit. Saffron Hill EC1	Herbal Hill 18L 50
Lit. St. Andrew St. WC2 ..	Monmouth St. 17M 50
Lit. South St. SE5	Dalwood Pl. 20R 75
Lit. Stamford St. SW6 ...	Sandford St. 12Q 60
Lit. Stanhope St. W1	Stanhope Row 15N 61
Lit. Suffolk St. SE1	Sudrey St. 19N 63
Lit. Surrey St. SE1	Davidge St. 18N 62
Lit. Sussex Pl. W2	Sussex Pl. 13M 48
Lit. Sutton St. EC1	Northburgh St. 19K 51
Lit. Thames St. SE10	Clavell St. 26Q 65
Lit. Tongue Yd. E1	Tongue Ct. 22L 52
Lit. Trafalgar Pl. SE17	Elba Pl. 19O 63
Lit. Turner St. E1	Rampart St. 22M 52
Lit. Union Pl. E1	Cressy Ct. 23L 52
Lit. Union St. NW1	Golford St. 13K 48
Lit. Welbeck St. W1	Welbeck Way 15L 49
Lit. White Lion St. WC2	Mercer St. 17M 50
Lit. Winchester St. SE1	Winchester Sq. 20N 63
Lit. Windmill St. SE1	Cons St. 18N 62
Lit. Woodstock M. W1 ...	Woodstock M. 15L 49
Liverpool St. N1	Layton Rd. 18J 50
Liverpool St. SE17	Liverpool Gro. 19P 63
Liverpool St. WC1	Birkenhead St. 17K 50
Lloyd's Pl. SW3	Brompton Pl. 13O 60
Lodge Pl. NW8	Lodge Rd. 13K 48
Lombard Rd. SE7	Lombard Wall 29P 67
Lombard St. E1	Daplyn St. 21L 52
Lombard St. S. E1	Leigh Hunt St. 19N 63
London Rd. E5	Clapton Way 22F 38
London St. E2	Dunbridge St. 22K 52

NEW NAME.	
Marina Pl. SW8.	16R 74
Mariner Pl. E14.	26M 53
Mariner St. E1.	22M 52
Marischal Rd. SE13.	27T 78
Market St. SE18.	33P 95
Marlborough Av. E8.	21J 52
Marlborough Gro. SE1.	21P 64
Marlborough Pl. NW8.	12J 48
Marshall Gdns. SE1.	18O 62
Martello St. E8.	22H 38
Martin Cres. SE16.	22O 64
Martin's Yd. SE1.	17N 62
Marybank SE18.	32P 95
Marylebone High St. W1.	14L 49
Maryon Rd. SE7.	31P 67
Massingham St. E1.	23K 52
Mast House Terr. E14.	25P 65
Mathews Yd. WC2.	17M 50
Matilda St. N1.	7J 50
Mayflower St. SE16.	23N 64
Mayplace La. SE18.	33Q 95
McCullum Rd. E3.	24J 53
Mecklenburgh Pl. WC1.	17K 50
Mell St. SE10.	28Q 66
Mellish St. E14.	25O 65
Melville St. N1.	19H 37
Memel St. EC1.	19K 51
Menotti Bldgs. E2.	22K 52
Mercator Rd. SE13.	27T 78
Mercer St. WC2.	17M 50
Merton Rise NW3.	13H 34
Micawber St. N1.	19J 51
Michael Rd. SW6.	11R 72
Middleton Gro. N7.	17G 36
Middleton Rd. E8.	21H 38
Middleton Way SE13.	27T 78
Midhurst Rd. E5.	22F 38
Midlothian Rd. E3.	24L 52
Miles Pl. NW8.	13K 48
Milford Rd. SE6.	25V 88
Mill Gdns. SE26.	22X 87
Milligan St. E14.	25M 53
Milligan St. E14.	25M 53
Milliner St. EC1.	19L 51
Mills Gro. E14.	26L 53
Milson Rd. W14.	9O 59
Milton Ct. EC2.	19L 51
Milton Gro. N16.	20F 37
Minet Rd. SW9.	18S 74
Ming St. E14.	25M 53
Minshull St. SW8.	16R 73
Minting Row E1.	21M 52
Mission Pl. SE15.	21R 76
Mitre Pass. EC3.	21M 51
Mitre Rd. SE1.	18N 62
Modbury Gdns. NW5.	14G 35
Modern Ct. EC1.	18L 50
Monmouth St. WC2.	17M 50
Montagu M. W6.	9P 59
Monthope St. E1.	21L 52
Montpelier Gro. NW5.	16G 35
Montpelier Pl. SW7.	13O 60
Monza Pl. E1.	23N 64
Moorhouse Rd. W2.	11L 47
Mora St. EC1.	19K 51
Morant Path E14.	25M 53
Moravian Pl. SW10.	12Q 60
Mordecai Pl. E1.	21L 52
Morden La. SE10.	26S 78
Morgan's Wk. SW11.	13Q 60
Morley St. SE1.	18O 62
Mornington Gro. E3.	25K 53

L.C.C. STREET NAME CHANGES.

OLD NAME.	NEW NAME.
London St. E14	
North	Bekesbourne St. 24M 53
South	Spert St. 24M 53
London St. N1	Treaty St. 17J 50
London St. SE10	Greenwich High Rd. 26Q 65
Long La. SE2	Longleigh La. 36P 95
Lorne Gdns. NW8	Lorne Clo. 13K 48
Lorrimore St. SE17	Olney Rd. 19P 63
Love Ct. E1	Brodlove Ct. 23M 52
Love La. E1	Brodlove La. 23M 52
Love La. E5	Downs La. 22F 38
Love La. SE3	Heath La. 27S 78
Love La. SE1	Fletcher La. 19N 63
Love La. SE18	Mayplace La. 33Q 95
Love La. SW9	Stockwell La. 17S 74
Lwr. Common SW15	Commondale 8S 70
Lwr. Parkfields SW15	Parkfields 8T 70
Lwr. Ashby St. EC1	Wyclif St. 18K 50
Lwr. Berkeley St. W1	Fitzhardinge St. 14L 49
Lwr. Bland St. SE1	Cardinal Bourne St. 20O 63
Lwr. Cedars M. SW4	Turnchapel M. 15S 73
Lwr. Charles St. EC1	Walmsley St. 18K 50
Lwr. Conduit M. W2	Smallbrook M. 12M 48
Lwr. Fenton St. E1	Mariner St. 22M 52
Lwr. Harden St SE18	Harden St. 31P 67
Lwr. John St. N1	Bradlaugh St. 20J 51
Lwr. Kennington La. SE11	
	Kennington La. 17P 62
Lwr. Market St. SE18	Polytechnic St. 33P 95
Lwr. North St. E14	Saltwell St. 25M 53
Lwr. Park Rd. SE15	Friary Rd. 22Q 64
Lwr. Pellipar Rd. SE18	Godfrey Rd. 32P 95
Lwr. William St. NW8	Greenberry St. 13J 48
Lwr. Wood St. SE18	Woodrow 32P 95
Lucas St. E1	Lukin St. 23M 52
Lyndhurst Rd. SE15	Lyndhurst Way 21R 75
Macclesfield St. EC1	Macclesfield Rd. 19K 51
Mall, The NW3	Mall Studios 14G 35
Mall, The NW3 North	Kensington Mall 11M 48
Mall, The W8 South-West	
	Palace Gdns. Ter. 11M 48
Manchester Bldgs. E2	Menotti Bldgs. 22K 52
Manchester M. NW6	Greville M. 11J 48
Manchester Rd. W10	Oldham Rd. 9M 47
Manchester St. WC1	
North-West	Argyle St. 17K 50
South	Whidborne St. 17K 50
Manning Pl. E14	Manning St. 24L 53
Manning Pl. NW1	Crockford Pl. 13L 48
Manor Gdns. SW3	Chelsea Manor Gdns. 13P 60
Manor Pl. E8	Marcon Pl. 22G 38
Manor Pl. W2	St. Philip's Pl. 12L 48
Manor St. SE18	Kempt St. 33Q 95
Manor St. SW3	Chelsea Manor St. 13P 60
Manor St. SW4	Clapham Manor St. 16S 73
Mansell Pass. E1	Haydon Wk. 21M 51
Mansfield St. E2	Whiston Rd. 21J 51
Mansfield St. SE1	Rotary St. 19O 62
Margaret Pl. SE1	Margaret Gdns. 20O 63
Margaret St. E9	Collent St. 23H 38
Margaret St. WC1	Margery St. 18K 50
Maria St. E2	Geffrye St. 21J 51
Market Row SE1	St. George's Mkt. 19O 63
Market St. E1	Trader St. 24L 52
Market St. E14	Cordelia St. 26M 53
Market St. EC2	Snowden St. 20L 51
Market St. N7	Wheelwright St. 17H 36
Market St. SE1	Leathermarket St. 20N 63
Market St. SE18	Bathway 33P 95
Market St. SW1	St. Alban's St. 16M 49
Market St. W1	Shepherd Mkt. 15N 61
Market St. W1	St. Michael's St. 13L 48
Marlborough Gate W2	Bayswater Rd. 12M 48
Mornington Ter. NW1.	15J 49
Morocco St. SE1.	20O 63
Morris Wk. SE18.	31P 67
Morrish Rd. SW2.	17V 85
Mortimer Sq. W11.	9M 47
Mossop St. SW3.	13O 60
Mostyn Gro. E3.	25J 53
Mount Gdns. SE26.	22W 87
Mt. Pleasant WC1.	18K 50
Mount Terr. E1.	22L 52
Mount, The NW3.	12F 34
Mount Sq., The NW3.	12F 34
Mountmorres Rd. E1.	23L 52
Mowll St. SW9.	18R 74
Moxon St. W1.	14L 49
Mumford Rd. SE24.	18U 74
Murphy Pl. SE1.	18O 62
Murray Gro. N1.	20J 51
Mursell Rd. SW8.	17R 74
Myddleton Pl. SE16.	22O 64
Myrtleberry St. E8.	21H 37
Nag's Head Depot SE1.	19N 63
Nantes Pass. E1.	21L 51
Napier Gro. N1.	19J 51
Needham Rd. W11.	11M 47
Nelson Gdns. E2.	22J 52
Nelson Rd. SE10.	26Q 66
Neville Pl. SE11.	17P 62
Newburgh St. W1.	16M 49
Newcastle Clo. EC4.	18L 50
New Cavendish St. W1.	15L 49
Newell St. E14.	25M 53
Newton Gro. N1.	20J 51
Newtown St. SW11.	15R 73
Nicholas Rd. E1.	23K 52
Nicholson St. SE1.	18N 62
Nightingale Gro. SE13.	27U 78
Noel Rd. N1.	19J 51
Norfolk Pl. W2.	13L 48
Norland Pl. W11.	10N 59
Norland Rd. W11.	9N 59
Norman Ct. E1.	22M 52
Norman Gro. E3.	24J 53
North Pass. SW18.	11T 71
Northbourne Rd. SW4.	16T 74
Northburgh St. EC1.	19K 51
Northchurch Rd. N1.	20H 37
Northeast Pl. N1.	18J 50
North End Av. NW3.	12D 22
North End Cres. W14. (part)	
	10P 59
Northiam St. E8.	22J 52
Northington St. WC1.	17L 50
Northumbria St. E14.	25M 53
Northwest Pl. N1.	18J 50
Northwick Dri. Har.	1aE 12
N. Wharf Rd. W2.	13L 48
Norwood High St. SE27	19X 86
Nottingham Pl. W1.	14L 49
Notting Hill Gate W11.	
	11M 47
Oakhill Pl. SW15.	10T 71
Oakley Gdns. SW3.	13Q 60
Oat La. EC2.	19L 51
Oceana Clo. E14.	27M 54
Old St. EC1.	20K 51
Old Barrack Yd. SW1.	13N 60
Old Broad St. EC2.	20L 51
Old Brompton Rd. SW5.	
& SW7	11P 60
Old Church St. SW3.	13P 60
Old Ct. Pl. W8.	11N 60
Oldershaw Rd. N7.	18G 36
Oldfield Gro. SE16.	23P 64

L.C.C. STREET NAME CHANGES.

OLD NAME.	NEW NAME.	NEW NAME.
Marlborough Rd. E8 ..	Marlborough Av.	21J 52
Marlborough Rd. NW8..	Marlborough Pl.	12J 48
Marlborough Rd. SE13	Mercator Rd.	27T 78
Marshall St. SE1	Marshall Gdns.	18O 62
Martha's Bldgs. EC1	Old St.	20K 51
Martin St. SE16	Martin Cres.	22O 64
Martin's Bldgs. SE1	Martin's Yd.	17N 62
Mary Pl. SE18	Marybank	32P 95
Mary St. E1	Bigland Pl.	22M 52
Mason's Av. SE18	Ashlar Pl.	33P 95
Mason's Ct. N16	Manley Ct.	21E 37
Mason's Ct. SE14	Besson Cotts.	23R 76
Mason's Pl. N16	Manley Ct.	21E 37
Matilda Cotts. SE10	Bardsley La.	26Q 65
Matilda St. E1	Christian Pl.	22M 52
May's Bldgs. E1	June Bldgs.	32K 52
Medland St. E14	Highway, The	24M 53
Meeting Ho. La. SE18		
	Ship & Half Moon Pass.	33O 95
Mercer St. E1	Shadwell St.	23M 52
Merton Rd. NW3	Merton Rise	13H 34
Merton Rd. W8	Kelso Pl.	11O 60
Middle Row EC1	Crescent Row	19K 51
Middle St. E8	Dunn's Pl.	21F 37
Miles St. SE10	Mell St.	28Q 66
Middle St. SE15	Jowett St.	21R 75
Middle St. SW7	Fairholt St.	13O 60
Middlesex St. N7	Alsen Pl.	17E 36
Middleton Rd. N7	Middleton Gro.	17G 36
Middleton Rd. SE13	Middleton Way	27T 78
Middleton Rd. SW11	Buckmaster Rd.	13T 72
Miles St. W6	Theresa Rd.	7P 58
Mill La. SE26	Mill Gdns.	22X 87
Mill La. SW2	Morrish Rd.	17V 85
Milton Pl. SW8	Belmore Pl.	16R 73
Milton Rd. E3	McCullum Rd.	24J 53
Milton Rd. N16	Milton Gro.	20F 37
Milton St. SW8	Minshull St.	16R 73
Mitre Ct. EC1	Crozier Ct.	18K 50
Mitre Ct. EC1	Ely Ct.	18L 50
Mitre Ct. EC1	Mitre Pass.	21M 51
Mitre Ct. N1	Upper St.	18H 36
Mitre St. SE1	Mitre Rd.	18N 62
Montagu M. W6	Shortlands M.	9P 59
Montagu St. W6	Shortlands	9P 59
Montague Pl. E14	Osborn Clo.	25M 53
Montague St. SE1	Stones End St.	19O 63
Montpelier Rd. N19	Rickthorne Rd.	17E 36
Montpelier Rd. NW5	Montpelier Gro.	16G 35
Montpelier Rd. W6	Worlidge St.	8P 59
Montpelier Rd. W11	Lansdowne Rise	10M 47
Montpelier Row W6	Worlidge St.	8P 59
Montpelier St. SE17	Pelier St.	19Q 63
Moore St. W1	Castlereagh St.	13L 48
Mordecai Pl. E1	Montague Pl.	21L 52
Moreland St. N4	Woodfall Rd.	18E 36
Moreton Gdns. SW5..	Old Brompton Rd.	11P 60
Moreton Ter. SE16	Truman St.	22O 64
Moreton Ter. SW5 ..	Old Brompton Rd.	11P 60
Mornington Rd. E3....	Mornington Gro.	25K 53
Mornington Rd. NW1 ..	Mornington Ter.	15J 49
Morris St. SE18	Morris Wk.	31P 67
Mortimer Rd. W11	Mortimer Sq.	9M 47
Mostyn Rd. E3	Mostyn Gro.	25J 53
Mostyn Rd. SW9	Lothian Rd.	18R 74
Motley St. EC2	Christina St.	20K 51
Mount St. E1	Mount Ter.	22L 52
Mount St. E2	Swanfield St.	21K 51
Mount St. SE7	Maryon Rd.	31P 67
Mount, The SE26	Mount Gdns.	22W 87
Mulberry Pl. EC1	Berry Pl.	19K 51
Munden Cotts. NW6	Kilburn Pl.	11G 34
Munton Rd. SE17 North-East	Balfour St.	19O 63

NEW NAME.	
Oldham Rd. W10.	9M 47
Olney Rd. SE17.	19P 63
O'Meara St. SE1.	19N 63
Omega Pl. N1.	17J 50
Omega St. SE14.	25R 77
Oranmore M. SW1.	16P 62
Orchardson St. NW8.	13K 48
Ordnance Cres. SE10.	27O 66
Ordnance Hill NW8.	13J 48
Orleston M. N7.	18G 36
Ormiston Gro. W12.	7M 46
Ormond Clo. WC1.	17L 50
Ormond M. WC1.	17K 50
Ormsby Pl. N16.	21F 37
Orsman Rd. N1.	20J 51
Orton St. E1.	22N 64
Osbert St. SW1.	16P 61
Osborn Clo. E14.	25M 53
Osier Pl. SW1.	15O 61
Osier St. E1.	23L 52
Oval Way SE11.	17P 62
Pace Pl. E1.	22M 52
Padbury Ct. E2.	21K 51
Padfield Rd. SE5 & SE24	
	19S 75
Paget Rise SE18.	33R 95
Paget St. EC1.	18K 50
Palace Gdns. Terr. W8.	
	11M 48
Palmerston Cres. SE18.	34Q 95
Pardon St. EC1.	19K 51
Parfett St. E1.	22L 52
Paris St. SE1.	17O 62
Park Vista SE10.	27Q 66
Parkfield Rd. SE14.	24R 77
Parkfields SW15.	8T 70
Parkgate Rd. SW11.	13Q 60
Park Hall Rd. SE21.	19W 86
Parkhill Pl. NW3.	14G 35
Parkway NW1.	15J 49
Parry St. SW8.	17Q 62
Parvin St. SW8.	16R 73
Passmore St. SW1.	14P 61
Pastor St. SE11.	19O 63
Patcham Terr. SW8.	15R 73
Paton Clo. E3.	25K 53
Paul M. SE17.	20Q 63
Peace St. E1.	22K 52
Pearman Pl. SE1.	18O 62
Peckham Hg. St. SE15.	21R 76
Pegasus Pl. SE11.	18P 62
Peggotty Pl. SE1.	19N 63
Pelier St. SE17.	19Q 63
Pemberton Row EC4.	18L 50
Pembroke Clo. SW1.	14N 61
Penfold Pl. NW1.	13L 48
Penfold St. NW1 & NW8.	
	13K 48
Penley Ct. WC2.	18M 50
Penrose Gro. SE17.	19P 63
Penry Pl. SE1.	21P 64
Pensbury Pl. SW8.	16R 73
Penton M. SE17.	18P 62
Penton Rise WC1.	17J 50
Penzance St. W11.	10M 47
Pepys St. EC3.	21M 51
Perrin's La. NW3.	12F 34
Perrin's Wk. NW3.	12F 34
Perrott St. SE18.	34P 95
Petergate SW11.	12T 72
Peter Hills Wk. SE16.	23N 64
Petyward SW3.	13P 60
Philchurch Pl. E1.	22M 52
Philip Pl. EC1.	19J 50

L.C.C. STREET NAME CHANGES.

OLD NAME.	NEW NAME.	
Murray St. N1	Murray Gro.	20J 51
Myrtle Cotts. SW15	Glegg Pl.	9S 71
Myrtle St. SE18	Bunton St.	33P 95
Nag's Head Yd. SE1	Nag's Head Depot	19N 63
Napier Rd. SE14	Walpole Rd.	24R 77
Napier St. N1	Napier Gro.	19J 51
Naylor's Yd. W1	Kingly Ct.	16M 49
Nelson Pl. E1	Winthrop Pl.	22L 52
Nelson Pl. SE1	Peggoty Pl.	19N 63
Nelson Sq. SE15	Furley Rd.	22R 76
Nelson St. E2	Nelson Gdns.	22J 52
Nelson St. EC1	Mora St.	19K 51
Nelson St. NW1	Beatty St.	15J 49
Nelson St. SE10	Nelson Rd.	26Q 66
Neptune St. E1	Wellclose St.	22M 52
Netley St. W9	Abourne St.	11K 48
Neville St. SE11	Neville Pl.	17P 62
New Ct. EC1	Modern Ct.	18L 50
New Ct. EC1	Cloth Ct.	19L 51
New Rd. SE18	Woolwich New Rd.	33Q 95
New Rd. SW8	Thessaly Rd.	15Q 61
New St. E8	Blanchard Pl.	22H 38
New St. EC1	Caslon St.	19K 51
New St. SE17	Braganza St.	18P 62
New St. W6	Hampshire Hog La.	7P 58
New Castle Pl. E1	Tyne Pl.	21L 51
New Castle St. E1	Tyne St.	21L 51
Newcastle St. E14	Glencarnock Av.	27P 66
Newcastle St. EC4	Newcastle Clo.	18L 50
Newcastle St. SE10	Enderby St.	27P 66
New Chesterfield St. W1	De Walden St.	15L 49
New Church St. SE16	Llewellyn St.	21O 64
New Cut SE1	Cut, The	18N 62
New Gravel La. E1	Garnet St.	23M 52
New Inn Yd. W1	Inn Yd.	16L 49
Newman St. SW11	Fownes St.	13S 72
Newton St. N1	Newton Gro.	20J 51
Nicholas St. E1	Nicholas Rd.	23K 52
Nightingale La. E1	Thomas More St.	21M 52
Nightingale La. SE10	Westgrove La	27R 78
Nile St. SE18	Ferry App.	33O 95
Noah's Ark All. SE1	Henslowe Pass.	19N 63
Noel St. N1	Noel Rd.	19J 51
Noel St. SE1	Christmas St.	20O 63
Norfolk Bldgs. E1	Crellin Bldgs.	22M 52
Norfolk M. W. W2	London M.	13L 48
Norfolk Rd. E8	Cecilia Rd.	21G 38
Norfolk Rd. W11	Needham Rd.	11M 47
Norfolk Rd. Villas W11	Needham Rd.	11M 47
Norfolk St. E1	Massingham St.	23K 52
Norfolk St. E14	St. Lawrence St.	27N 66
Norfolk St. N1	Melville St.	19H 37
Norfolk St. W1	Dunraven St.	14M 49
Norland Rd. N. W11	Norland Rd.	9N 59
Norland Stables W11	Norland Pl.	10N 59
Norman Bldgs. E1	Norman Ct.	22M 52
Norman Rd. E3	Norman Gro.	24J 53
Norman St. SW3	Sprimont Pl.	13P 60
Norris St. N1	Upwey St.	20J 51
North Cotts. N1	Compton Sq.	19G 37
North Ct. SE1	Cosser Ct.	18O 62
North Pl. NW8	Hatton Row	13K 48
North Pl. SW8	North Pass.	11T 71
North Rd. SW4	Northbourne Rd.	16T 74
North St. E8	Northiam St.	22J 52
North St. NW8	Frampton St.	13K 48
North St. SE1	Cosser St.	18O 62
North St. SE7	Herringham Rd.	31P 67
North St. SW1	Lord North St.	17O 62
North St. SW10	Billing Pl.	11Q 60
Northampton Pl. SW6	Durlington Pl.	10S 71
Northampton St. E1	Headlam St.	22L 52

	NEW NAME.	
Phillimore Pl. W8.		11N 59
Phillimore Wk. W8.		11N 59
Phoenix Rd. NW1.		16K 49
Pickburn Pl. EC1.		18K 50
Pickwick St. SE1.		19N 63
Picton Pl. W1.		14L 49
Pierrepont Row N1.		18J 50
Pitfield St. N1.		20J 51
Pitsea St. E1.		23M 52
Play Pl. SW11.		12S 72
Playhouse Yd. EC4.		19M 50
Plender Pl. NW1.		16J 49
Plender St. NW1.		16J 49
Pleshey Rd. N7.		16F 35
Plough M. SW11.		12T 72
Plough Way SE16.		24P 65
Plympton Pl. NW8.		13K 48
Plympton St. NW8.		13K 48
Polthorne St. SE18.		34P 95
Polygon Rd. NW1.		16J 49
Polytechnic St. SE18.		33P 95
Pomeroy Sq. SE14.		23R 76
Ponder St. N7.		17H 36
Ponler St. E1.		22M 52
Ponsford St. E9.		23G 38
Pope St. SE1.		21O 63
Poplar Pl. W2.		11M 48
Poplar Bath St. E14.		26M 53
Portelet Rd. E1.		23K 52
Portia Rd. E3.		24L 53
Portland Gro. SW8.		17R 74
Portland Rise N4.		19D 25
Portman Clo. W1.		14L 49
Portobello Rd. W11.		10L 47
Portobello St. W11.		10M 47
Potier St. SE1.		20O 63
Poulton St. E2.		23J 52
Powis M. W11.		10L 47
Pownall Pl. SW6.		10Q 59
Poynter St. W11.		9M 47
Pratt Wk. SE11.		17O 62
Prescot St. E1.		21M 51
Prescott Pl. SW4.		16S 73
Prestwood St. N1.		19J 51
Prideaux Pl. WC1.		18K 50
Priestley St. E9.		23G 38
Prince Albert Rd. NW1 & NW8.		13J 48
Princedale Rd. W11.		10M 47
Pr. of Wales Dr. SW11.		14R 73
Princes Way SW19.		9V 82
Princess Cres. N4.		19E 37
Princess Pl. SE1.		19O 63
Priory Ct. SW8.		16R 74
Priory Pk. SE3.		28T 78
Priory Terr. NW6.		11H 34
Priory Wk. SW10.		12P 60
Priter Way SE16.		22O 64
Prospect Vale SE18.		31P 67
Prospect Pl. E2.		23K 52
Prowse Pl. NW1.		15H 35
Pulham Pl. SW8.		17Q 62
Purcell Pl. E9.		23H 38
Purcell St. N1.		20J 51
Purdy St. E3.		26K 53
Putney High St. SW15.		9T 71
Qn. Caroline St. W6.		8P 58
Queen's Dri. N4.		19E 37
Queen's Gro. NW8.		13J 48
Queensberry Way SW7.		12O 60
Queensbury Path N1.		19H 37
Queensdale Pl. W11.		9N 59
Queensdale Wk. W11.		9N 59
Queensland M. N7.		18F 36

L.C.C. STREET NAME CHANGES.

OLD NAME.	NEW NAME.	
North End Rd. W14 (from Edith Rd. to Grove Ter.)	North End Cres.	10P 59
Northumberland St. E14	Northumbria St.	25M 53
Northumberland St. W1	Luxborough St.	14L 49
Norway St. EC1	Timber St.	19K 51
Nottingham Pl. E1	Parfett St.	22L 52
Oakley Cres. SW3	Oakley Gdns.	13Q 60
Oakley St. SE1	Baylis Rd.	18O 62
Old Barge Ho. St. SE1 ..	Upper Ground	18M 50
Old Dorset St. SW8	Dorset Wk.	17Q 62
Oldfield Rd. SE16	Oldfield Gro.	23P 64
Olney St. SE17	Olney Rd.	19P 63
Onslow Pl. SW7......	Old Brompton Rd.	12O 60
Orange St. E2	Satchwell Rd.	21K 52
Orange St. SE1	Copperfield St.	19N 63
Ordnance Rd. NW8	Ordnance Hill	13J 48
Ordnance Rd. SE10	Ordnance Cres.	27O 66
Ormiston Rd. W12	Ormiston Gro.	7M 46
Ormond Yd. WC1.........	Ormond Clo.	17L 50
Osborn Pl. E1	Chicksand St.	21L 52
Osborne Ter. SW8	Richborne Ter.	17Q 62
Oxford Rd. N1	Elizabeth Av.	20H 37
Oxford St. E1	Stepney Way	22L 52
Oxford Ter. W2	Sussex Gdns.	13L 48
Paddington St. N4	Biggerstaff St.	18E 36
Padfield St. SE24	Padfield Rd.	19S 75
Paget Rd. SE18	Paget Rise	33R 95
Palace St. NW5	St. Silas Pl.	14G 35
Palmer St. SE1	Theed St.	18N 62
Palmerston Rd. SE18 ..	Palmerston Cres.	34Q 95
Palmerston Rd. SW18......	Avening Rd.	11U 71
Palmerston St. SW11......	Newtown St.	15R 73
Paradise Pass. E9	Cambridge Pass.	23H 38
Paradise Pl. SE16........	Myddleton Pl.	22O 64
Paradise Pl. W1	Garbutt Pl.	14L 49
Paradise Rd. N5	Collins Rd.	19F 37
Paradise Row W6	Eden Row	7O 58
Paradise St. EC2.........	Clere St.	20K 51
Parad se St. W1.........	Moxon St.	14L 49
Park Cres. SW4	Clapham Cres.	16T 70
Park La. N16	Clissold Cres.	20F 37
Park La. NW1	Siddons La	14K 49
Park La. SE7............	Charlton Pk. La.	31R 79
Park Pl. E2	Yerwood Pl.	22K 52
Park Pl. E9	Ram Pl.	23G 38
Park Pl. E14	Milligan Pl.	25M 53
Park Pl. SE1............	Carlisle St.	18O 62
Park Pl. SE18	Park Vista	27Q 66
Park Pl. SW4 North..	St. Alphonsus Rd.	16T 73
South-East ..	Holwood Pl.	16T 73
Park Rd. E3.............	Leith Rd.	24L 53
Park Rd. SE14	Parkfield Rd.	24R 77
Park Rd. SE18 North ...	Waverley Rd.	34P 95
South ...	Waverley Cres.	34P 95
Park Rd. SE21	Park Hall Rd.	19W 86
Park Rd. SE23	Waldram Pk. Rd.	23W 87
Park Rd. SW11	Parkgate Rd.	13Q 60
Park Rd. SW18	Elsygne Rd.	12T 72
Park St. E2.............	Welwyn St.	25K 52
Park St. E14	Milligan St.	25M 53
Park St. N1.............	Islington Park St.	18H 36
Park St. N16	Yoakley Rd.	20F 37
Park St. NW1	Parkway	15J 49
Park St. SE10	Greenwich Park St.	27Q 66
Park St. SE13	Legge St.	26U 77
Park St. W10............	Latimer Pl.	8L 47
Parliament St. E2	Witan St.	22K 52
Parliament St. SE1.......	Speech St.	19O 63
Paul's All. EC4	St. Paul's All.	19M 51
Payne St. N1............	Cave St.	18J 50
Pearson St. SE10.........	Haddo Ter.	26Q 65
Pearson St. SW11.........	Batten St.	13S 72
Pelham St. E1	Woodseer St.	21L 52
Queensland Pl. N7.		18F 36
Queensland Rd. N7.		18F 36
Queensway W2.		11M 48
Quick Pl. N1.		19J 50
Quick St. N1.		19J 51
Radnor M. W2.		13M 48
Radnor Rd. SE15.		21Q 64
Radnor Wk. SW3.		13P 60
Raft Rd. SW18.		11T 71
Raglan St. NW5.		15G 35
Rail Pl. SE18.		32O 95
Railway Arcade SW9.		18T 74
Railway Ct. SE18.		32P 95
Railway Rise SE22.		21T 75
Railway St. N1.		17J 50
Railway Terr. SE13.		26U 77
Ram Cotts. SW18.		11T 72
Ram Pl. E9.		23G 38
Rampart St. E1.		22M 52
Randolph Av. W9.		11J 48
Rathbone St. W1.		16L 49
Ravenet St. SW11.		15R 73
Ravenscourt Pl. W6.		7O 58
Ravenscourt Rd. W6.		7O 58
Rawson St. SW11.		14R 73
Raynor Pl. N1.		19H 37
Reardon Path E1.		22N 64
Reardon St. E1.		22N 64
Rector St. N1.		19J 51
Redan Pl. W2.		11M 48
Redchurch St. E2.		21K 51
Redcliffe Pl. SW10.		12Q 60
Redcross Way SE1.		19N 63
Redruth Rd. E9.		23H 38
Rees St. N1.		19J 51
Regal La. NW1.		15J 49
Regency Pl. SW1.		16O 62
Regina St. NW1.		16J 49
Reid St. N1.		18J 50
Romnant St. WC2.		18T 51
Rhoda St. E2.		21K 51
Rhondda Gro. E3.		24K 53
Richborne Terr. SW8.		17Q 62
Richmond Av. N1.		18H 36
Richmond Ter. M. SW1.		17N 62
Richmond Way W12 & W14.		9N 59
Rickthorne Rd. N19.		17E 36
Riding Ho. St. W1.		15L 49
Riley Rd. SE1.		21O 63
Ritchie St. N1.		18J 50
River Pl. N1.		19H 37
Riverside Gdns. W6.		8P 58
Roberta St. E2.		22K 52
Robert Adam St. W1.		14L 49
Robsart Pl. SW9.		18R 74
Rochester Wk. SE1.		20N 63
Rodsley Pl. SE1.		22Q 64
Roehampton High St. SW15.		7U 70
Rogate Rd. E5.		22F 38
Roger St. WC1.		17K 50
Roland Way SW7.		12P 60
Rollet St. N1.		18F 36
Roman Rise SE19.		20Y 86
Roman Way N7.		17G 36
Romer Av. SE13.		26T 77
Romilly St. W1.		16M 50
Roper La. SE1.		21N 63
Rose Pass. EC1.		19K 51
Rose Wk. SE1.		21O 63
Rosemary Gdns. SE15.		21R 75
Rosemoor St. SW3.		13P 60

OLD NAME.	NEW NAME.		NEW NAME.	
Pembroke M. N. SW1	Pembroke Clo.	14N 61	Rossendale St. E5.	22E 38
Penry Rd. SE1	Marlborough Gro.	21P 64	Rotary St. SE1.	19O 62
Penton St. WC1	Penton Rise	17J 50	Rousden St. NW1.	16H 35
Percy Cotts. SW1	Old Barrack Yd.	13N 60	Rowan Terr. W6.	9O 59
Peter St. E2	Rhoda St.	21K 51	Rowcross St. SE1.	21P 63
Philip St. E1	Philchurch St.	22M 52	Rowland St. E1.	22L 52
Phillimore M. W8	Phillimore Wk.	11N 59	Ruby Triangle SE15.	22Q 64
Phillip's Ter. SW1	Old Barrack Yd.	13N 60	Rudd St. SE18.	34P 95
Phipps M. SW1 (part)	Eccleston Pl.	15O 61	Rugby St. WC1.	17L 50
Phœnix Pl. SE1	Holyrood St.	20N 63	Rumbold Rd. SW6.	11Q 60
Phœnix Pl. W11	Addison Pl.	9N 59	Rural Pl. SE14.	23R 76
Phœnix St. NW1	Phœnix Rd.	16J 50	Russia Pl. E2.	23J 52
Pitt St. SE15	E. Surrey Gro.	21R 75	Rutherford St. SW1.	16O 61
Pitt St. W1	Scala St.	16L 49	Rutland Gro. W6.	8P 58
Platt's La. NW3 (Nos. 58-66 even)			Rutland Wk. SE6.	25W 88
	Telegraph Hill	11E 34	Rye Pass. SE15.	12S 76
Playhouse Yd. EC1	Fortune St.	19K 51	Ryedale SE22.	22U 76
Pleasant Pass. NW1	Underhill Pass.	15J 49	Rysbrack St. SW3.	14O 61
Pleasant Pl. SW4	Triangle Pl.	16T 73	St. Alban's Gro. W8.	11O 60
Plough Ct. EC1	Barbican	19L 51	St. Alban's St. SW1.	16M 49
Plough La. E9	Furrow La.	23G 38	St. Alfege Pass. SE10	26Q 66
Plough Rd. SE18	Plough Way	24P 65	St. Alphonsus Rd. SW4.	
Plough Yd. EC3	Seething La.	21M 51		16T 73
Porson St. SW8	Ebson St.	15R 73	St. Andrew's Gro. N16.	20D 25
Portland Pl SW8 North..	Portland Gro.	17R 74	St. Andrew's Wk. E2.	22K 52
South	Mursell Rd.	17R 74	St. Ann's Hill SW18.	11U 72
Portland Rd. N4	Portland Rise	19D 25	St. Ann's Vills. W11.	23H 38
Portland St. E1	Westport St.	24M 52	St. Anselm's Pl. W1.	15M 49
Portman M. N. W1	Portman Clo.	14L 49	St. Barnabas Terr. E9.	23G 38
Portsdown Rd. W9	Randolph Av.	11J 48	St. Chad's St. WC1.	17K 50
Powis Rd. E14	Cyclops Pl.	25P 65	St. Clement's Ct. EC4.	20M 51
Pownall Rd. SW6	Pownall Pl.	10Q 59	St. Clement's La. WC2.	17M 50
Pratt St. SE11	Pratt Walk	17O 62	St. Cross St. EC1.	18L 50
Prebend St. NW1	Baynes St.	16H 35	St. Dionis Rd. SW6.	10R 71
Primrose St. E2	Allenbury St.	22K 52	St. Edmund's Clo. NW8.	
Pr. of Wales Rd. SW11..	Pr. of Wales Dri.	14R 73		14J 48
Princes Ct. E2	Padbury St.	21K 51	St. George St. W1.	15M 49
Princes Ct. WC2	Excel Ct.	16M 50	St. George's Mkt. SE1.	19O 63
Princes Pl. E2	Fountain St.	21K 51	St. George's Way SE15.	
Princes Rd. SE11	Black Prince Rd.	17P 62		20Q 63
Princes Rd. SW19	Princes Way	9V 82	[*. Giles Pass. WC2.	16M 50
Princes Rd. W11	Princedale Rd.	10M 47	St. Giles Rd. SE5.	20R 75
Prince's Sq. E1	Swedenborg Sq.	22M 52	St. Giles High St. WC2.	16L 50
Princes Sq. SE11	Cleaver Sq.	18P 62	St. James's App. EC2	20K 51
Princes St. SE16	Mayflower St.	23N 64	St. James's Av. E2.	23J 52
Prince's Yd. SE15	Dewar Yd.	21S 76	St. James's Gdns. W11.	9M 47
Prince's Yd. W2	Ilchester Gdns.	11M 48	St. James's Pass. EC3.	21M 51
Princess M. SE1	Princess Pl.	19O 63	St. James's Vlls. SE18.	34Q 95
Princess Rd. N4	Princess Cres.	19E 37	St. John's Av. SW15.	9T 71
Princess St. NW8	Boscobel St.	13K 48	St. John's Cres. SW9.	18S 74
Priory Gro. SW10	Priory Wk.	12P 60	St. John's Gro. N19.	16E 35
Priory La. SE3	Priory Pk.	28T 78	St. John's Terr. SE18.	34Q 95
Priory Pl. NW1	Prowse Pl.	15H 35	St. John's Terr. W10.	9K 47
Priory Pl. SW8	Priory Ct.	16R 74	St. John's Wood High St.	
Priory Rd. SW8	Lansdowne Way	16R 74	NW8.	13J 48
Priory St. NW1	Ivor St.	15H 35	St. Joseph's St. SW8.	15R 73
Prospect Pl. E14	Mariner Pl.	26M 53	St. Jude's Rd. E2.	22J 52
Prospect Pl. N1	Lonsdale Pl.	18H 36	St. Katherine's Row EC3.	
Prospect Pl. SE13	Railway Ter.	26U 77		21M 51
Prospect Pl. SE14	Rural Pl.	23R 76	St. Lawrence St. E14.	27N 66
Prospect Pl. SE18	Prospect Vale	31P 67	St. Lawrence Ter. W10.	10L 47
Prospect Row N1	Donegal Row	18J 50	St. Luke's Av. SW4.	16T 74
Prospect Row SE18	Prospect Vale	31P 67	St. Luke's M. W11.	10L 47
Prospect Ter. E2	Prospect Wk.	23K 52	St. Luke's Row EC1.	19K 51
Providence Pl. E2	Poulton St.	23J 52	St. Luke's St. SW3.	13P 60
Providence Pl. NW6	Kilburn Pl.	11G 34	St. Margaret's Gro. SE18.	
Providence Pl. SE1	Keyworth Pl.	18O 62		34Q 95
Providence Pl. SE1	Pearman Pl.	18O 62	St. Margaret's Pass. SE13.	
Providence Pl. SE8	Comet Ho. Pl.	25R 77		28T 78
Providence Pl. SW18	Ram Cotts.	11T 72	St. Margaret's Path SE18.	
Providence Pl. W12..	Shepherd's Bush Pl.	9N 59		34Q 95
Queen Sq. N7	Queensland Pl.	18F 36	St. Margaret's Ter. SE18.	
Queen St. E1	Rowland St.	22L 52		34Q 95

OLD NAME.	NEW NAME.
Queen St. NW1	Regina St. 16J 49
Queen St. W6	Qn. Caroline St. 8P 58
Queen's Bldgs. W1 ..	Tottenham Ct. Rd. 16L 49
Queen's Ct. SE1	Grotto Ct. 19N 63
Queen's M. NW1	Regal La. 15J 49
Queen's Pl. E1	Stutfield Pl. 22M 52
Queen's Pl. N1 North	Raynor Pl. 19H 37
South..	Queensbury Path 19H 37
Queen's Pl. SW8	Bramwell Pl. 15S 73
Queen's Pl. W11	Queensdale Wk. 9N 59
Queen's Rd. N4	Queen's Dri. 19E 37
Queen's Rd. NW8	Queen's Gro. 13J 48
Queen's Rd. SE23	Taymount Rise 22W 87
Queen's Rd. W2	Queensway 11M 48
Queen's Sq. SW8	St. Philip Sq. 15R 78
Queen's Ter. W1	Forset Clo. 13L 48
Queen's Yd.	Tottenham Ct. Rd. 16L 49
Queensberry M. E. SW7 East	
	Queensberry Way 12O 60
Radnor St. SE15	Radnor Rd. 21Q 64
Radnor St. SW3	Radnor Wk. 13P 60
Raglan Pl. NW5	Raglan St. 15G 35
Raglan St. SE23	Clyde Vale 23W 87
Railway App. SE4	Coulgate St. 24S 77
Railway App. SE13	Junction App. 26S 77
Railway App. SE23....	Lapse Wood Wk. 22W 87
Railway App. SW6	Station Path 10R 71
Railway App. SW9	Railway Arcade 18T 74
Railway Cotts. SE18	Railway Ct. 32P 95
Railway Pl. E2	Malcolm Pl. 23K 52
Railway Pl. SE18	Walmer Ter. 34P 95
Railway St. E14	Hay Currie St 26L 53
Ralph St. N7	Kinloch St. 18F 36
Ranelagh Rd. W2	Lord Hills Rd. 11L 48
Ranger Rd. SE19	Jasper Rd. 21Y 86
Rectory Gro. SE18	Escreet Gro. 32P 95
Rectory Rd. SW6	St. Dionis Rd. 10R 71
Redcross St. SE1	Redcross Way 19N 63
Red Lion St. EC2	Dudley Ct. 19L 51
Red Lion Pass. EC1	Lion Pass 19L 50
Red Lion Pass. EC1..	Bartholomew Pass. 19L 51
Red Lion Pass. NW1	Stanley Pass. 16J 50
Red Lion St. E1 North	Reardon St. 22N 64
South ..	Reardon Path 22N 64
Red Lion St. EC1	Britton St. 18L 50
Red Lion St. SE18	Leon St. 33P 95
Red Lion Yd. EC1	Leo Yd. 18K 50
Red Lion Yd. EC1	Warner Yd. 18K 50
Red Lion Yd. SW1	Cockspur Ct. 16N 62
Regent Pl. SW1	Regency Pl. 16O 62
Regent St. N1	Thoresby St. 19K 51
Regent St. SE10	Sparta Pl. 26R 77
Retreat, The SW8 ..	Cavendish Retreat 16R 74
Richard St. N1	Ritchie St. 18J 50
Richmond M. SW1	Richmond Ter. M. 17N 62
Richmond M. W2	St. Stephen's M. 11L 47
Richmond M. W2	Shrewsbury M. 11L 47
Richmond Pl. SW6	Empress Pl. 11P 59
Richmond Pl. SW8	Birkin St. 16R 73
Richmond Rd. N1	Richmond Av. 18H 36
Richmond Rd. W2	Chepstow Rd. 11L 47
Richmond Rd. W12 & W14	Richmond Way 9N 59
Richmond St. EC1	Shene St. 19K 51
Richmond St. N1	Matilda St. 17J 50
Richmond St. NW8	Orchardson St. 13K 48
Richmond Ter. SW8	Richborne Ter. 17Q 62
Riley St. SE1	Riley Rd. 21O 63
River St. E3	Maddams St. 26L 53
River St. N1	River Pl. 19H 37
River St. SW15	Waterman St. 9S 71
Robert St. E2	Roberta St. 22K 52
Robert St. E14	Mandarin St. 25M 53
Robert St. N1	Prestwood St. 19J 51

NEW NAME.

St. Mark's Pl. W11.	10M 47
St. Mark's Rise E8.	21G 37
St. Martin's Clo. NW1.	15H 35
St. Mary's Gdns. SE11.	18O 62
St. Mary's Gro. N1.	19G 37
St. Mary's Path N1.	19G 37
St. Mary's Wk. SE11.	18O 62
St. Matthew's Ct. EC2.	19M 51
St. Matthew's Rd. SW2.	
	17U 74
St. Matthew's Row E2.	21K 52
St. Matthias Sq. N16.	20G 37
St. Michael's Gro. N6.	15D 23
St. Michael's St. W2.	13L 48
St. Olave's Ct. EC2.	19M 51
St. Olave's Ter. SE1.	21N 63
St. Pancras Way NW1.	16H 35
St. Paul's All. EC4.	19M 51
St. Paul's Ter. SE17.	19P 62
St. Paul's Way E3.	25L 53
St. Paul's Yd. N7.	17H 36
St. Peter's Av. E2.	22J 52
St. Peter's Clo. E2.	22J 52
St. Peter's Way N1.	21H 37
St. Philip Sq. SW8.	15R 73
St. Philip's Pl. W2.	12L 48
St. Philip's Way N1.	19J 51
St. Rule St. SW8.	15S 73
St. Silas Pl. NW5.	14G 35
St. Stephen's Clo. SE1.	20O 63
St. Stephen's Gdns. W2.	
	11L 47
St. Stephen's Gro. SE12.	
	26S 78
St. Stephen's M. W2.	11L 47
St. Stephen's Rd. E3.	24J 53
St. Stephen's Row EC4	21M 51
St. Thomas's Way SW6.	
	10Q 71
St. Vincent St. W1.	14L 49
Saffron Hill EC1.	18L 50
Saffron St. EC1.	18L 50
Sale Pl. W2.	13L 48
Sally Pl. EC1.	18K 50
Salmon Bldgs. E14.	24M 53
Saltash St. E2.	23K 52
Saltwell St. E14.	25M 53
Sampson St. E1.	22N 64
Sanctuary St. SE1.	19N 63
Sandbrook Rd. N16.	20G 37
Sandford St. SW6.	12Q 60
Sandy Hill Av. SE18.	33Q 95
Sarum Rd. E3.	24L 53
Satchwell Rd. E2.	21K 52
Saunders Gro. W11.	9N 59
Saunders Ness Rd. E14.	26P 65
Savoy Row WC2.	17M 50
Savoy Way WC2.	17M 50
Saxon Rd. E3.	24J 53
Scala St. W1.	16L 49
Scholey Cotts. SW11.	13R 72
Scholey St. SW11.	13R 72
School St. W6.	8P 58
Schooner St. E14.	27P 66
Scurr St. E14.	26M 53
Seaham St. SW8.	16Q 62
Searle St. SW11.	13R 72
Seaton Pl. NW1.	15K 49
Sebastian St. EC1.	19K 51
Seething La. EC3.	21M 51
Sekforde St. EC1.	18K 50
Selous St. NW1.	16J 49
Seymour Clo. EC1.	18K 50

OLD NAME.	NEW NAME.

Robert St. SE18 North .... Polthorne St. 34P 95
Robert St. W1.......... Weighhouse St. 15M 49
Robert St. WC1................ Kirk St. 17L 50
Rochester Pl. N16
         Stoke Newington High St. 21F 37
Rochester St. SE1 ...... Rochester Wk. 20N 63
Rock Ter. SE18 .... Blendon Ter. 34Q 95
Rodney Pl. N1............ Wynford Pl. 17J 50
Rodney St. SE1 .... Pickwick St. 19N 63
Roland Houses SW7 (Nos. 1-4)
         Old Brompton Rd. 12P 60
Roland Mans. SW7 (Nos. 9-11)
         Old Brompton Rd. 12P 60
Roman Rd. N7 ....: Roman Way 17G 36
Roman Rd. SE19 .... Roman Rise 20Y 86
Rose Cot's. W6 .... Shortlands 9P 59
Rose Ct. EC1 .... Rose Pass. 19K 51
Rose Ct. SE1 .... Rose Walk 21O 63
Rosewell Av. SW2 .... Jebb Av. 17U 74
Rosoman St. EC1 North-West Amwell St. 18K 50
Royal Oak Pl. SE13 St. Margaret's Pass. 28T 78
Royal Oak Pl. SW1 .... Boscobel Pl. 14O 61
Rupert St. E1 .... Goodman St. 21M 52
Russell Rd. N7 .... Berriman Rd. 18E 36
Russell Rd. SE15 .... Blackpool Rd. 22S 76
Russell St. E1 .... Halcrow St. 22L 52
Russell St. SE26.......... Cheseman St. 22X 87
Russell St. SW9 .... Hillyard St. 18R 74
Russell St. SW11 .... Ravenet St. 15R 73
Rutland Rd. SE6.......... Rutland Wk. 25W 88
Rutland Rd. W6 .... Rutland Gro. 8P 58
Rutland St. E1 .... Ashfield St. 22L 52
Rutland St. NW1 .... Mackworth St. 15J 49
Rutland St. SW1 .... Antrobus St. 15P 61
Rutland St. SW8 .... Brough St. 17Q 62
Rye Dale SE22 .... Ryedale 22U 76
Ryder's Ct. WC2 .... Leicester Ct. 16M 50
Sadler's Bldgs. EC1........... Fanni St. 19L 51
St. Alban's Pl. SW1...... St. Alban's St. 16M 49
St. Alban's Rd. W8 .... St. Alban's Gro. 11O 60
St. Alban's Rd. W8 .... Victoria Gro. 12O 60
St. Alban's Rd. N. W8 ...... Ansdell Ter. 11O 60
St. Andrew's Rd. N16...St. Andrew's Gro. 20D 25
St. Andrew's St. E2 .... St. Andrew's Wk. 22K 52
St. Andrew's St. SW8 ...... St. Rule St. 15S 73
St. Ann's Rd. E3 .... Midlothian Rd. 24L 53
St. Ann's Rd. SW9 .... Southey Rd. 18R 74
St. Ann's Rd. SW18....... Marcilly Rd. 12T 72
St. Dunstan's Rd. E3 ...... Timothy Rd. 24L 53
St. George St. E1 .... Highway, The 22M 52
St. George's Rd. NW1 ...... Chalcot Rd. 14H 35
St. George's Rd. NW6 ...... Priory Ter. 11H 34
St. George's Rd. SE15.. St. George's Way 20Q 63
St. George's Sq. NW1 ...... Chalcot Sq. 14H 35
St. James's Gdns NW5.. Modbury Gdns. 14G 35
St. James's Pl. EC2 ...... St. James's App. 20K 51
St. James' Pl. SE18 .... Burrage Pl. 33Q 95
St. James's Pl. W11 .... Penzance St. 10M 47
St. James's Rd. E2 ...... St. James's Av. 23J 52
St. James's Rd. N7 ...... Mackenzie Rd. 18G 36
St. James's Rd. SW9 .. St. James's Cres. 18S 74
St. James's Sq. W11 .. St. James's Gdns. 9M 47
St. James's St. N1 .... Cantry St. 19J 51
St. James's Wk. EC1 South-East
         Sekforde St. 18K 50
St. John's Gdns. NW5.... Baptist Gdns. 14G 35
St. John's M. SW11 .... Plough M. 12T 72
St. John's Pk. N19 ...... St. John's Gro. 16E 35
St. John's Rd. N1 .... Pitfield St. 20J 51
St. John's Rd. SE8 .... Albyn Rd. 25R 77
St. John's Rd. SE18 ...... St. John's Ter. 34Q 95
St. John's Rd. SW9 ...... St. John's Cres. 18S 74
St. John's Rd. SW15 ...... St. John's Av. 9T 71

NEW NAME.	

Seymour Wk. SW10. 12P 60
Shacklewell Rd. N16. 21F 37
Shadwell St. E1. 23M 52
Shakspeare Wk. N16. 20F 37
Shaver's Pl. SW1. 16M 50
Shelton St. WC2. 17M 50
Shene St. EC1. 19K 51
Shenfield St. N1. 21J 51
Shepherd Mkt. W1. 15N 61
Shepherd's Gdns. W12. 9N 59
Sheraton St. W1. 16M 49
Sheringham St. NW1. 13L 48
Sherlock M. W1. 14L 49
Shepherd's Bush Pl. W12.
         9N 59
Shillibeer Pl. W1. 14L 49
Shillingford St. N1. 19H 37
Shiloh Pl. E1. 23L 52
Ship Pass. E1. 22N 64
Ship & Half Moon Pass.
     SE18. 33O 95
Shirley St. N1. 18H 36
Short Pl. SE18. 34P 95
Shortlands W6. 9P 59
Shrewsbury M. W2. 11L 47
Shuttleworth Rd. SW11.
         13R 72
Siddons La. NW1. 14K 49
Silk Pl. EC2. 19L 51
Silver Wk. SE16. 24N 65
Sispara Gdns. SW18. 10U 71
Skinner Pl. SW1. 14P 61
Slindon Ct. N16. 21E 37
Smallbrook M. W2. 12M 48
Smart's Pl. WC2. 17L 50
Smithfield St. EC1. 18L 50
Smithy St. E1. 23L 52
Smollett St. SW3. 13O 60
Snowden St. EC2. 20L 51
Solebay Pl. E1. 24K 53
Solebay St. E1 & E3 24K 53
Somers Cres. W2. 13L 48
Somertree Av. SE12. 29V 89
South St. W1. 15M 49
South Terr. SW7. 13O 60
Southampton Pl. WC1. 17L 50
Southampton Way SE5 20Q 63
Southern Gro. E3. 24K 53
Southey Rd. SW9. 18R 74
Southwark Gro. SE1. 19N 63
Southwell Rd. SE5. 19S 75
Sovereign St. W2. 12L 48
Spafield St. EC1. 18K 50
Sparta Pl. SE10. 26R 77
Spears Rd. N19. 17D 24
Speech St. SE1. 19O 63
Spencer Rise NW5. 15F 35
Spencer Wk. SW15. 9T 71
Spenser Gro. N16. 20F 37
Spert St. E14. 25M 53
Sprimont Pl. SW3. 13P 60
Spring Gro. E3. 25J 53
Spring Pass. SW15. 9S 71
Springfield La. NW6 11J 48
Springfield Rise SE26. 22X 87
Spurgeon St. SE1. 20O 63
Stackhouse St. SW3. 14O 61
Staffordshire St. SE15. 22R 76
Stainsby Pl. E14. 25L 53
Stamford Clo. NW3. 12E 34
Stanhope Gate W1. 14N 61
Stanhope Row W1. 15N 61
Stanhope Terr. W2. 13L 48
Stanley Gro. SW8. 14S 73

OLD NAME.	NEW NAME.
St. John's Pk. Rd. SE3..	Stratheden Rd. 29R 78
St. Jude's St. E2	St. Jude's Rd. 22J 52
St. Lawrence Rd. W10..St.	Lawrence Ter. 10L 47
St. Leonard St. SW1	Longmore St. 15P 61
St. Luke's Rd. SW4	St. Luke's Av. 16T 74
St. Margaret's Rd. SE18	
	St. Margaret Gro. 34Q 95
St. Mark's Rd. E8	St. Mark's Rise 21G 37
St. Mark's Rd. SE5 & SE17	Hillingdon St. 19Q 62
St. Mark's Rd. SW10	Billing Rd. 11Q 60
St. Martin's Pl. NW1 ..	St. Martin's Clo. 15H 35
St. Mary St. E1	Davenant St. 22L 52
St. Mary Abbot's Ter. (Nos. 31-49)	
	Kensington High St. 11N 60
St. Mary's Rd. N1	St. Mary's Gro. 19G 37
St. Mary's Sq. SE11....	St. Mary's Gdns. 18O 62
St. Mary's St. SE11	St. Mary's Wk. 18O 62
St. Nicholas Rd. SW17....	Trinity Cres. 14W 84
St. Paul's M. N7	St. Paul's Yd. 17H 36
St. Paul's M. SE17	Paul M. 20Q 63
St. Paul's Rd. E3	St. Paul's Way 25L 53
St. Paul's Rd. NW1	Agar Gro. 16H 35
St. Paul's Rd. SE17	
North-West	Westcott Rd. 19P 62
South-East..........	St. Paul's Ter. 19P 62
St. Peter St. E2	St. Peter's Av. 22J 52
St. Peter's Rd. E1	Cephas Av. 23K 52
St. Peter's Rd. N1	St. Peter's Way 21H 37
St. Peter's Rd. N7	Chambers Rd. 17F 36
St. Peter's Sq. E2	St. Peter's Clo. 22J 52
St. Philip St. N1	St. Philip's Way 19J 51
St. Stephen's Rd. SE13	St. Stephen's Gro. 26S 78
St. Stephen's Rd. W2	St. Stephen's Gdns. 11L 47
St. Stephen's Sq. E1 ..St.	Stephen's Clo. 20O 63
St. Stephen's Sq. W2..St.	Stephen's Gdns. 11L 47
St. Thomas's Rd. E3	Apostle Rd. 24L 53
St. Thomas's Rd. E9	Ainsworth Rd. 23H 38
St. Thomas's Rd. SW6	St. Thomas's Way 10Q 59
Sale St. W2	Sale Pl. 13L 48
Salisbury Rd. E8	Elrington Rd. 22H 38
Salisbury St. E3	Sarum Rd. 24L 53
Salisbury St. N1	Grange St.. 20J 51
Salisbury St. SE16	Wilson Gro. 22O 64
Samuel St. E14............	Camdenhurst St. 24L 53
Sarah Pl. SE18	Marybank 32P 95
Satchwell Rents E3	Satchwell Rd. 21K 52
Saunders Rd. W11..........	Saunders Gro. 9N 59
Saville St. W1	Hanson St. 15L 49
Seaton St. NW1	Seaton Pl. 15K 49
Sewell Rd. SW11	Chatfield Rd. 12S 72
Seymour Pl. EC1	Seymour Clo. 18K 50
Seymour Pl. SW10	Seymour Walk 12P 60
Seymour Row NW1	Eversholt Row 16K 50
Seymour St. NW1..........	Eversholt St. 16J 49
Seymour St. SW8	Driver St. 15R 73
Shaftesbury Rd. W6....	Ravenscourt Rd. 7O 58
Shaftesbury Rd. E. W6 ..	Ravenscourt Pl. 7O 58
Shaftesbury Rd. W.14	Fenelon Pl. 10O 59
Shakspeare Rd. N16....	Shakspeare Wk. 20F 37
Shepherd St. E1	Toynbee St. 21L 51
Shepherd's Pl. SE11..........	Harold Pl. 18P 62
Sherwood St. E3............	Lawes St. 25L 53
Ship All. W1	Flaxman Ct. 16M 49
Ship La. SE11	Bishop's Ter. 18O 62
Ship St. E1..................	Ship Pass. 22N 64
Ship St. E14................	Schooner St. 27P 66
Ship Yd. W1	Flaxman Ct. 16M 49
Short St. EC2	Silk Pl. 19L 51
Short St. N1	Aske St. 20K 51
Short St. SE18	Sunbury St. 32P 95
Short St. SE18	Short Pl. 34P 95
Shorter St. E1	Fletcher St. 22M 52
Shrubbery Rd. SE13....	Sundermead Rd. 26S 77

NEW NAME.	
Stanley Pass. NW1.	16J 50
Stanway St. N1.	21J 51
Star & Garter Yd. E1.	22M 52
Starcross St. NW1.	16K 49
Starfield Rd. W12.	7N 58
Station Cres. SE3.	29Q 66
Station Path SW6.	10R 71
Station Rise SE27.	18W 85
Steadman St. EC1.	19K 51
Stedham Pl. WC1.	17L 50
Stenhouse St. E2.	22K 52
Stepney Way E1.	22L 52
Stockwell La. SW9.	17S 74
Stoke Newington Ch. St. N16.	
	20F 37
Stoke Newington High St.	
N16.	21F 37
Stoneham Pl. E5.	22E 38
Stoneleigh Rd. W11.	9M 47
Stones End St. SE1.	19O 63
Stratford Villas NW1.	16H 35
Strathearn Pl. W2.	13M 48
Stratheden Rd. SE3.	29R 78
Stukeley St. WC2.	17L 50
Stutfield Pl. E1.	22M 52
Sudrey St. SE1.	19N 63
Suffolk Gro. SE16.	23P 64
Sulina Rd. SW2.	16V 85
Summer Gro. E3.	25J 53
Sun Alley EC2.	19L 51
Sunbury La. SW11.	13R 72
Sunbury St. SE18.	32P 95
Sundermead Rd. SE13.	26S 77
Surrey Steps WC2.	17M 50
Sussex Gdns. W2.	13L 48
Sussex Pl. W2.	13M 48
Sussex Way N7.	17E 36
Sussex Way N19.	17D 24
Sutherland Wk. SE17.	19P 62
Sutton Row W1.	16L 50
Sutton Wk. SE1.	17N 62
Swan Rd. SE16.	23N 64
Swanfield St. E2.	21K 51
Swanscombe Rd. W11.	9N 59
Swedenborg Sq. E1.	22M 52
Swinton St. WC1.	17K 50
Sycamore Gdns. W6.	8N 58
Sydney Clo. SW3.	13P 60
Sylvester Path E8.	22G 38
Tailworth St. E1.	21L 52
Tamerton St. SE5.	19Q 63
Tarlton St. N1.	20J 51
Tasker Rd. NW3.	14G 35
Taunton Pl. NW1.	13K 48
Tavistock Pl. WC1.	17K 50
Tavistock St. WC2.	17M 50
Taymount Rise SE23.	22W 87
Telegraph Hill NW3.	11E 34
Temple Pl. WC2.	18M 50
Tenison Ct. W1.	15M 49
Tennis St. SE1.	20N 63
Tenter St. E1.	21M 51
Thackeray Rd. SW8.	15S 73
Theberton St. N1.	18H 36
Theed St. SE1.	18N 62
Theresa Rd. W6.	7P 58
Theresa St. W6.	7P 58
Thessaly Rd. SW8.	15Q 61
Thomas Rd. E14.	25L 53
Thomas Doyle St. SE1.	19O 62
Thomas More St. E1.	21M 52
Thoresby St. N1.	19K 51
Thorndike St. SW1.	16P 61

L.C.C. STREET NAME CHANGES.

OLD NAME.	NEW NAME.		NEW NAME.	
Sidney Pl. EC1	Philip Pl.	19J 50	Thrale St. SE1.	19N 63
Sidney Rd. E9	Kenworthy Rd.	24G 39	Three Crown Ct. EC3.	21M 51
Sidney St. E2	Longman St.	23J 52	Three Nuns Ct. SE1.	19N 63
Sidney St. EC1	Wakley St.	19J 50	Thurloe St. SW7.	13O 60
Silver St. E1	Apsley St.	23L 52	Tilloch St. N1.	17H 36
Silver St. NW3	Mount, The	12F 34	Tilson Gdns. SW2.	16V 85
Silver St. SE16	Silver Wk.	24N 65	Timber St. EC1.	19K 51
Silver St. WC1	Barter St.	17L 50	Timothy Rd. E3.	24L 53
Simpson St. SW8	Blean St.	16Q 62	Tiptree St. N1.	21J 51
Skinner St. SW1	Skinner Pl.	14P 61	Tisbury Ct. W1.	16M 49
Smart's Bldgs. WC2	Smart's Pl.	17L 50	Tollington Rd. N7.	17F 36
Smith St. E1	Smithy St.	23L 52	Tompion St. EC1.	19K 50
Smith St. EC1	Tompion St.	19K 50	Tongue Alley E1.	21L 52
Smith St. SE5 & SE17	Lucas Rd.	18Q 62	Tongue Ct. E1.	22L 52
Smith's Cotts. N7	Alsen Cotts	18E 36	Tonsley St. SW18.	11T 72
Somers Pl. W2	Somers Cres.	13L 48	Topham St. EC1.	18K 50
Somerset St. SW11	Handley St.	13R 72	Torrington Pl. WC1.	16L 49
Somerset St. WC2	Savoy Way	17M 50	Tottenham Ct. Rd. W1.	16L 49
South Cres. SE13	Bliss Cres.	26R 77	Tower Hill EC3.	21M 51
South Gro. E3	Southern Gro.	24K 53	Toynbee St. E1.	21L 51
South Gro. N6 South.	St. Michael's Gro.	15D 23	Trader St. E1.	24L 52
South St. E1	Basire St.	19H 37	Trafalgar Av. SE15.	21P 63
South St. SE10	Greenwich South St.	26R 77	Trafalgar Gdns. E1.	24L 52
South St. SE17	Dawes St.	20P 63	Trafalgar Sq. SW1.	16N 62
South St. SW7	South Ter.	13O 60	Treaty St. N1.	17J 50
South St. SW10	Billing St.	11Q 60	Trebeck St. W1.	15N 61
South St. W6	Riverside Gdns.	8P 58	Trenchold St. SW8.	17Q 62
Southampton St. N1	Calshot St.	17J 50	Treveris St. SE1.	18N 62
Southampton St. SE5	Southampton Way	20Q 63	Trevor Pl. SW7.	13N 60
Southampton St. W1	Conway St.	15K 49	Trevor St. SW7.	13N 60
Southampton St. WC1	Southampton Pl.	17L 50	Triangle Pl. SW4.	16T 73
Southwick Cres. W2	Hyde Pk. Cres.	13M 48	Trinity Cres. SW17.	14W 84
Spectacle All. E1	White Church Pass.	21L 51	Trinity Garage SE1.	19O 63
Spencer Pl. EC1.	Goswell Rd.	19K 51	Trinity Gdns. SW9.	17T 74
Spencer Rd. N7	Caedmon Rd.	18F 36	Trio Pl. SE1.	19O 63
Spencer Rd. NW5	Spencer Rise	17F 35	Troy St. SE18.	33P 95
Spencer Rd. SW15	Spencer Wk.	9T 71	Truman St. SE16.	22O 64
Spencer St. E1	Brinsley St.	22M 52	Trundle St. SE1.	19N 63
Spencer St. N1	Shillingford St.	19H 37	Turnchapel M. SW4.	15S 73
Spencer St. SW11	Searle St.	13R 72	Tyers Gate SE1.	20N 63
Spenser Rd. N16	Spenser Gro.	20F 37	Tyne Pl. E1.	21L 51
Spring Gdns. SW8	Seaham St.	16Q 62	Tyne St. E1.	21L 51
Spring Gdns. SW15	Spring Pass.	9S 71	Udall St. SW1.	16P 61
Spring Gdn. Pl. E1	Stepney Way	24L 50	Underhill Pass. NW1.	15J 49
Spring Row NW5	Raglan St.	15G 35	Underwood Rd. E1.	22L 52
Spring St. E3	Spring Gro.	25J 53	Union Wk. E2.	21K 51
Spring St. N1	Braes St.	19H 37	Unwin Pl. W2.	12L 48
Springfield Rd. SE26	Springfield Rise	22X 87	Upper Ground SE1.	18N 62
Stafford Rd. SW9	Wynne Ter.	18S 74	Upper St. N1.	18H 36
Stafford St. SE15	Staffordshire St.	22R 76	Upr. Montagu St. W1.	14L 49
Stamford Pl. NW3	Stamford Clo.	12E 34	Upwey St. N1.	20J 51
Stamford Rd. SW6	Holmead Rd.	11Q 60	Urlwin St. SE5.	19Q 63
Stanhope St. W2	Stanhope Pl.	13L 48	Usk Ter. SW11.	12T 72
Stanhope Ter. NW1	Parkway	15J 49	Vale End SE22.	21T 75
Stanhope Ter. W2 (Nos. 7-14)	Bayswater Rd.	13L 48	Varndell St. NW1.	15K 49
Stanley Rd. N1	Burder Rd.	21G 37	Vauxhall Gro. SW8.	17Q 62
Stanley Rd. SW6	Michael Rd.	11R 72	Vernon Rise WC1.	17K 50
Stanley St. SW8	Stanley Gro.	14S 73	Vicarage Av. SE3.	29R 79
Star Ct. W1	Greek Ct.	16M 50	Vicarage Cres. SW11.	12R 72
Star Pl. E1	White's Gdns.	22M 52	Vicarage Gro. SE5.	20R 75
Star & Garter Yd. E1	Garter Yd.	22M 52	Victoria Cres. SE19.	20Y 86
Station App. SE16	Priter Way	22O 64	Victoria Dri. SW19.	9V 82
Station Rd. SE3	Station Cres.	29Q 66	Victoria Gro. W8.	12O 60
Station Rd. SE6	Adenmore Rd.	25V 88	Victoria Rise SW4.	15S 73
Station Rd. SE22	Railway Rise	21T 75	Victoria Way SE7.	29P 67
Station Rd. SW9	Brixton Station Rd.	18S 74	Victorian Gro. N16.	21F 37
Station Rd. SW12	Balham Station Rd.	14V 84	Victorian Rd. N16.	21F 37
Station Rd. W12.	Starfield Rd.	7N 58	Vincent Rd. SE18.	33P 95
Station Yd. NW5	Kentish Town Rd.	15G 35	Vine Hill EC1.	18K 50
Sterndale Rd. SW8	Condell Rd.	16R 73	Vine La. SE1.	20N 63
Stibbington St. NW1	Chalton St.	16J 49	Vinters Pl. EC4.	19M 51
Stone's Bldgs. SE11	Hocking Bldgs.	18P 62	Virgil St. SE1.	18O 62
			Viscount St. EC1.	19L 51

L.C.C. STREET NAME CHANGES.

OLD NAME.	NEW NAME.	NEW NAME.
Stoney La. SE1	Abbots La 20N 63	Vivian Gro. SE15. 22S 76
Straightsmouth SE10 North	Churchfields 26Q 65	Wadham Rd. SW15. 10T 71
Stratford Pl. NW1	Stratford Villas 16H 35	Wager St. E3. 25L 53
Sudbury Ct. Dri. Har.	Northwick Dri. 1aE 12	Waite Pl. SE15. 21Q 63
Suffolk Pl. NW1	Boyton Pl. 13L 48	Wake Ct. SE11. 17O 62
Suffolk St. E14	Ellerman St. 25M 53	Wakley St. EC1. 19J 50
Suffolk St. SE16	Suffolk Gro. 23P 64	Waldram Cres. SE23. 23W 87
Sugar Loaf Ct. E1	Loaf Ct. 21M 51	Waldram Pk. Rd. SE23.
Sugar Loaf Ct. EC3	Fenchurch Bldgs. 20M 51	23W 87
Summer St. E3	Summer Gro. 25J 53	Walham Grn. Arcade SW6.
Sun Ct. EC2	Cross Key Ct. 20L 51	11Q 60
Sun St. SE1	Pope St. 21O 63	Walk Pl. E1. 24K 53
Sun St. SE18	Sunbury St. 32P 95	Walmer Ter. SE18. 34P 95
Surrey Pl. WC2	Surrey Steps 17M 50	Walmsley St. EC1. 18K 50
Sussex Pl. EC3	Cunard St. 20M 51	Walpole Rd. SE14. 24R 77
Sussex Pl. SW7	Old Brompton Rd. 12P 60	Walter Ter. E1. 24L 52
Sussex Rd. N7	Sussex Way 17E 36	Wandsworth High St. SW18.
Sussex St. E14	Lindfield St. 25M 53	11T 71
Sutherland Pl. SE17	MacLeod St. 19P 63	Wansdown Pl. SW6. 11Q 60
Sutherland St. SE17	Sutherland St. 19P 63	Wapping High St. E1. 22N 64
Sutton Pl. W1	Falconberg M. 16L 50	Waring St. SE27. 19X 86
Sutton St. SE1	Sutton Wk. 17N 62	Warner Yd. EC1. 18K 50
Sutton St. W1	Sutton Row 16L 50	Warren Ct. N1. 18J 50
Swan La. SE16	Swan Rd. 23N 64	Warspite Rd. SE18. 31O 67
Swan Yd. E8	London La. 22H 38	Warwick Cotts. W6. 7P 58
Sydenham Hill Rd. SE26	Kirkdale 22X 87	Warwick Gro. E5. 22E 38
Tamar St. E3	Lefevre Gro. 25J 53	Warwick Retreat E5. 22D 26
Tavistock St. E2	Saltash St. 22K 52	Warwick Way SW1. 15P 61
Taylor's Bldgs. WC2	Brydges Pl. 16M 50	Watergate EC4. 18M 50
Temple St. E8	Myrtleburry St. 21H 37	Watergate Wk. WC2. 17M 50
Temple St. SE11	Pastor St. 19O 63	Waterloo Gdns. E2. 23J 52
Tennis Ct. SE1	Tennis St. 20N 63	Waterloo Row E14. 24M 53
Tenter St. E1	Tenter Ground 21M 51	Waterman St. SW15. 9S 71
Thackeray St. SW8	Thackeray Rd. 15S 73	Watts Gro. E3. 26L 53
Theberton St. W. N1	Theberton St. 18H 36	Waverley Cres. SE18. 34P 95
Theresa Cotts. W6	Theresa St. 7P 58	Waverley Rd. SE18. 34P 95
Theresa M. W6	Theresa St. 7P 58	Waverley Wk. W2. 11L 47
Thomas St. E14	Thomas Rd. 25L 53	Weaver Wk. SE27 19X 86
Thornhill Cotts. N1	Wynford Colls. 18J 50	Webber St. SE1. 18N 62
Thornhill Sq. SE5	Westmacott Gdns. 20Q 63	Welbeck Way W1. 15L 49
Three Tuns Pass. SE1	Three Tuns Ct. 19N 63	Weighhouse St. W1. 15M 49
Thurlow Pl. E2	Globe Ter. 23K 52	Weir Rd. SW12. 15V 84
Thurlow St. SW8	Pensbury Pl. 16R 73	Wellclose St. E1. 22M 52
Tottenham St. W10	Kensal Pl. 10K 47	Weller St. SE1. 19N 63
Tower St. E8	Martello St. 22H 38	Wellesley Ter. N1. 19K 51
Tower St. SE1	Morley St. 18O 62	Wellington Gdns. SE7. 30Q 87
Trafalgar Rd. SE15	Trafalgar Av. 21P 63	Wellington Wk. W6. 8P 58
Trafalgar Sq. E1	Trafalgar Gdns. 24L 52	Wellington Way E3. 25K 53
Trafalgar Sq. SE15	Buller Sq. 21R 76	Wells Rise NW8. 14J 49
Trafalgar Sq. SW3	Chelsea Sq. 13P 60	Wells Rd. W12. 8N 58
Triangle, The SE15	Ruby Triangle 22Q 64	Wells Way SE5. 20Q 63
Trinity M. SE1	Trinity Garage 19O 63	Wells Pk. Rd. SE26. 21X 87
Trinity Pl. N1	Bletchley St. 20J 51	Welwyn St. E2. 23K 52
Trinity Pl. SE1	Trio Pl. 19O 63	Werrington St. NW1. 16J 49
Trinity Rd. SE16	Bryan Rd. 24N 65	Wessex St. E2. 23K 52
Trinity Sq. SW9	Trinity Gdns. 17T 74	West Gro. SE10. 27R 78
Trinity St. N1	Batchelor St. 18J 50	West M. SW1. 15P 61
Trinity St. SE18	Warspite Rd. 31O 67	Westbourne Gro. W11. 10M 47
Troy Town SE15 North-West.	Dewar St. 21S 76	Westbourne Gro. W. W11.
Turner Rd. E13	Dacre Pk. 28T 78	11M 47
Twining St. WC2	St. Clement's La. 17M 50	Westbourne Ter. W2. 12L 48
Tyer's Gateway SE1	Tyers Gate 20N 63	Westbourne Pk. Rd. W11.
Underwood St. E1	Underwood Rd. 22L 52	10L 47
Union Bldgs. E2	Union Wk. 21K 51	Westbridge Rd. SW11. 13R 72
Union Ct. W6	Foreman Ct. 8P 59	Westcott Rd. SE17. 19F 62
Union M. N7	Orleston M. 18G 36	Western M. W9. 10L 47
Union M. W1	Bourlet Clo. 15L 49	Westferry Rd. E14. 25M 53
Union Pl. E1	Whitehead Pl. 23L 52	Westgrove La. SE10. 27R 78
Union Pl. EC1	Glasshouse Yd. 19L 51	Westhorpe Rd. SW15. 8S 71
Union Pl. SE1	Ayliffe Pl. 19O 63	Westland Pl. N1. 20K 51
Union Pl. W1	Courtauld Pl. 15L 49	Westmacott Gdns. SE5. 20Q 63
Union Rd. E14	Mellish St. 25O 65	Westmoor St. SE7. 30O 67
Union Rd. N17	Pleshey Rd. 16F 35	

L.C.C. STREET NAME CHANGES.

OLD NAME.	NEW NAME.
Union Rd. N16	Hollar Rd. 21F 37
Union Rd. SE1	Harper Rd. 19O 63
Union Rd. SE16	Jamaica Rd. 21O 64
Union Rd. SE21	Hunts Slip Rd. 20W 86
Union Sq. SE1	Dicken's Sq. 19O 63
Union St. E14	Bullivant St. 26M 54
Union St. EC4	Apothecary St. 18M 50
Union St. N1	Rector St. 19J 51
Union St. SE18	Macbean St. 33P 95
Union St. SW1	Passmore St. 14P 61
Union St. W1	Riding Ho. St. 15L 49
Union Ter. SW11	Usk Ter. 12T 72
Upr. Ashby St. EC1	Ashby St. 19K 51
Upr. Av. Rd. M. NW3	Adelaide Clo. 13H 34
Upr. Baker St. WC1	Lloyd Baker St. 18K 50
Upr. Bedford Pl. WC1	Bedford Way 16K 50
Upr. Bland St. SE1	Spurgeon St. 20O 63
Upr. Chadwell St. EC1	Inglebert St. 18J 50
Upr. Charles St. EC1	Sebastian St. 19K 51
Upr. Charlton St. W1	Hanson St. 15L 49
Upr. Colfe Rd. SE23	Farren Rd. 24W 87
Upr. Garden St. SW1	Thorndike St. 16P 61
Upr. George St. W1	George St. 14L 49
Upr. Gloucester Pl. NW1 & W1	Gloucester Pl. 14L 49
Upr. Grange Rd. SE1	Dunton Rd. 21P 63
Upr. Ground St. SE1	
Part	Barge Ho. St. 18M 50
Remainder	Upr. Ground 18M 50
Upr. Hamilton Ter. NW8	Hamilton Ter. 12J 48
Upr. Hornsey Rise N19	Hillrise Rd. 17D 24
Upr. Kennington La. SE11	
West	Bridgefoot 17P 62
Remainder	Kennington La. 17P 62
Upr. Manor St. SW3	Chelsea Manor St. 13P 60
Upr. Market St. SE18	Market St. 33P 95
Upr. Marylebone St. W1	New Cavendish St. 15L 49
Upr. Park Fields SW15	Coalecroft Rd. 8T 70
Upr. Park Pl. NW1	Ivor Pl. 14K 49
Upr. Rathbone Pl. W1	Rathbone St. 16L 49
Upr. Rupert St. W1	Winnett St. 16M 49
Upr. Russell St. SE1	Morocco St. 20O 63
Upr. Rutland Gate M. SW7	Gate M. 13N 60
Upr. Smith St. EC1	Earlstoke St. 18K 50
Upr. Vernon St. WC1	Prideaux St. 18K 50
Upr. Westbourne Ter. W2	Westbourne Ter. 12L 48
Upr. William St. NW8	Bridgeman St. 13J 48
Upr. Wimpole M. W1	Dunstable M. 15L 49
Upr. Yardley St. EC1	Yardley St. 18K 50
Urswicke Rd. SW11	Badric Rd. 13S 72
Vernon St. WC1	Vernon Rise 17K 50
Vicarage Rd. SE5	Vicarage Gro. 20R 75
Vicarage Rd. SW11	Vicarage Cres. 12R 72
Victoria Cotts. SW11	Scholey Cotts. 13R 72
Victoria Gro. N16	Victorian Gro. 21F 37
Victoria Gro. W. N16	Yorkshire Gro. 21F 37
Victoria M. E2	Elsden M. 23K 52
Victoria M. N7	Queensland M. 18F 36
Victoria M. NW8	Boundary Rd. 12H 34
Victoria M. SE13	Dacre Pl. 28T 78
Victoria M. SW11	Crombie M. 13S 72
Victoria Pl. N7	Queensland Pl. 18F 36
Victoria Pl. SE1	All Hallows Pl. 19N 63
Victoria Pl. SE15	Furley Pl. 22Q 64
Victoria Pl. SE27	Weaver Wk. 19X86
Victoria Pl. SW8	Marina M. 16R 74
Victoria Pl. W2	Bridstow Pl. 11L 47
Victoria Rd. N7	Chillingworth Rd. 18G 36
Victoria Rd. N16	Victorian Rd. 21F 37
Victoria Rd. NW1	Castlehaven Rd. 15H 35
Victoria Rd. SE7	Victoria Way 29P 67

NEW NAME.	
Westmoreland Ter. SW1.	15P 61
Weston Rise WC1.	17J 50
Westport St. E1.	24M 52
Weymouth Pl. E2.	21J 51
Weymouth Ter. E2.	21J 51
Wheatley St. W1.	14L 49
Whadcoat St. N4.	18E 36
Wharf Pl. E2.	22J 52
Wharfside EC4.	20M 51
Wheelwright St. N7.	17H 36
Whichcote St. SE1.	18N 62
Whidborne St. WC1.	17K 50
Whiston Rd. E2.	21J 51
White Ch. Pass. E1.	21L 51
Whitehaven St. NW8.	13K 48
Whitehead Pl. E1.	23L 52
White Horse Rd. E1.	24M 52
White's Gdns. E1.	22M 52
Wigmore Pl. W1.	15L 49
Wilditch St. SW11.	14R 73
William Rd. NW1.	15K 49
William IV St. WC2.	17M 50
Willow Pl. SW1.	16O 61
Willow Way SE26.	22X 87
Willshaw St. SE14.	25R 77
Wilson Gro. SE16.	22O 64
Wilton Row SW1.	14N 61
Wilton Villas N1.	20J 51
Wilton Way E8.	22G 38
Winchester Sq. SE1.	20N 63
Winchester Wk. SE1.	20N 63
Winders Rd. SW11.	13R 72
Windmill Dri. SW4.	15T 73
Windmill Wk. SE1.	18N 62
Windsor Gro. SE27.	19X 86
Windsor Wk. SE5.	20S 75
Windus Wk. N16.	21E 38
Winkley St. E2.	22J 52
Winnett St. W1.	16M 49
Winsford Rd. SE6.	24W 88
Winsland M. W2.	12L 48
Winthrop Pl. E1.	22L 52
Witan St. E2.	22K 52
Wood Clo. E2.	21K 52
Woodfall Rd. N4.	18E 36
Woodhall SE18.	31P 67
Woodin St. E14.	26L 53
Woodland Cres. SE10.	27Q 66
Woodland Wk. SE10.	28Q 66
Woodlands Way SW15.	10T 71
Woodrow SE18.	32P 95
Woodseer St. E1.	21L 52
Woodstock Gro. W12.	9N 59
Woodstock M. W1.	15L 49
Woodstock Ter. E14.	26M 53
Woolacombe Rd. SE3.	30S 79
Woolwich Ch. St. SE18.	31P 67
Woolwich New Rd. SE18.	33Q 95
Worgan St. SE11.	17J 62
Worlidge St. W6.	8P 59
Wren St. WC1.	17K 50
Wright Rd. N1.	21G 37
Wright's La. W8.	11O 60
Wyclif St. EC1.	18K 50
Wynford Cotts. N1.	17J 50
Wynford Pl. N1.	17J 50
Wynne Ter. SW9.	18S 74
Wynter St. SW11.	12T 72
Wythburn Pl. W1.	14L 49
Yardley St. EC1.	18K 50
Yeate St. N1.	20H 37

L.C.C. STREET NAME CHANGES.

OLD NAME.	NEW NAME.
Victoria Rd. SE15	Bellenden Rd. 21S 75
Victoria Rd. SE19	Victoria Cres. 20Y 86
Victoria Rd. SW4	Victoria Rise 15S 73
Victoria Rd. SW19	Victoria Dri. 9V 82
Victoria St. W2	Sovereign St. 12L 48
Victoria Yd. NW8	Boundary Rd. 12H 34
Victory Pl. SE15	Waite Pl. 21Q 63
Vine Cotts. W6	Shortlands 9P 59
Vine Pl. N1	Hoxton St. 20J 51
Vine St. EC1	Vine Hill 18K 50
Vine St. SE1	Vine La. 20N 63
Vine Yd. EC1	Aldersgate St. 19L 51
Vivian Rd. SE15	Vivian Gro. 22S 76
Wade's Pl. E1	Walk Pl. 24K 53
Waldram Rd. SE23	Waldram Cres. 23W 87
Walmer Rd. SE18	Walmer Ter. 34P 95
Walter St. E1	Walter Ter. 24L 52
Warner St. N7	Oldershaw Rd. 18G 36
Warner St. SE1	Bartholomew St. 20O 63
Warren M. N1	Warren Ct. 18J 50
Warren St. N1	Grant St. 18J 50
Warwick Gdns. W14 North-West	
	Kensington High St 10O 59
Warwick Pl. W6	Warwick Cotts. 7P 58
Warwick Pl. W.M. SW1	West M. 15P 16
Warwick Rd. E5..........	Warwick Gro. 22E 38
Warwick St. SW1	Warwick Way 15P 61
Water St. EC4	Watergate 18M 50
Waterloo Rd. E2	Waterloo Gdns. 23J 52
Waterloo St. E14	Waterloo Row 24M 53
Waterloo St. SE5	Elmington Rd. 20R 75
Waterloo St. W6	Macbeth St. 8P 58
Waterside EC4	Wharfside 20M 51
Waverley Rd. W2	Waverley Wk. 11L 47
Well St. E1	Ensign St. 22M 52
Wellesley St. N1	Wellesley Ter. 19K 51
Wellington M. SW1	Oranmore M. 16P 62
Wellington Pl. SE7 ..	Wellington Gdns. 30Q 67
Wellington Rd. E3	Wellington Way 24K 53
Wellington Rd. N7	Lough Rd. 17G 36
Wellington Rd. N16	Shacklewell Rd. 21F 37
Wellington Rd. SE7 ..	Wellington Gdns. 30Q 67
Wellington Rd. SE15	Belfort Rd. 23R 76
Wellington Rd. SW11	Hester Rd. 13Q 60
Wellington Rd. W6	Wellington Wk. 8P 58
Wellington St. E14	Woodin St. 26L 53
Wellington St. NW1	Inverness St. 15H 35
Wellington St. SE8	McMillan St. 25Q 65
Wellington St. SW3	Flood Wk. 13P 60
Wells M. W12	Wells Rd. 8N 58
Wells Rd. NW8	Wells Rise 14J 49
Wells Rd. SE26	Wells Pk. Rd. 21X 87
Wells St. SE5	Wells Way 20Q 63
Wells St. SW1	Babmaes St. 16M 49
Wells St. WC1	Wren St. 17K 50
West Pl. N1	Northwest Pl. 18J 50
West Pl. SE11	Geraldine St. 18O 62
West Pl. SW15	Glegg Pl. 9S 71
West St. SE7	Westmoor St. 30O 67
West St. W1	Newburgh St. 16M 49
Westbourne St. SW1	Bourne St. 14P 61
Westbourne Ter. N. W2	Bourne Ter. 11L 48
W. Bolton Gdns. SW5 Old Brompton Rd. 12P 60	
W. Chapel St. W1	Hertford St. 15N 61
Western Ter. W11	Lonsdale Rd. 10M 47
W. Grove Ter. SE10	Westgrove La. 27R 78
Westhorpe St. SW15	Westhorpe Rd. 8S 71
Westmoreland M. W1	Browning M 15L 49
Westmoreland Pl. N1	Westland Pl. 20K 51
Westmoreland Rd. W2 ..	Moorhouse Rd. 11L 47
Westmoreland St. SW1	
	Westmoreland Ter. 15P 61
Westmoreland St. W1	Beaumont St. 15L 49

NEW NAME.	
Yerwood Pl. E2.	22K 52
Yoakley Rd. N16.	20E 37
York Hill SE27.	18W 85
York Way N1 & N7.	17H 36
Yorkshire Gro. N16.	21F 37
Yorkshire Rd. E14.	24M 53
Zealand Rd. E3.	24J 53

OLD NAME.	NEW NAME.
Weston St. E3	Watts Gro. 26L 53
Weston St. WC1	Weston Rise 17J 50
Wetherby Ter. SW5 (Nos. 7-10)	
	Old Brompton Rd. 12P 60
Weymouth M. E2	Weymouth Ter. 21J 51
Wharf Rd. E2	Wharf Pl. 22J 52
Wharf Rd. E14 East..	Saunders Ness Rd. 26P 65
West..........	Ferry St. 26P 65
Wharf Rd. SW18	Raft Rd. 11T 71
Wharf Rd. W10	Bard Rd. 9M 47
Wharf Rd. W12	Coal Wharf Rd. 9N 59
Whiston St. E2	Whiston Rd. 22J 52
Whitecross St. SE1	Ayres St. 19N 63
White Hart Ct. EC3	Grass Ct. 20M 51
White Hart Ct. N16	
	Stoke Newington High St. 21F 37
White Hart St. SE11	Kennings Way 18P 62
White Hart Yd. EC1	Hart Yd. 18L 50
White Hind All. SE1	Henslowe Pass. 19N 63
White Horse St. E1	
North	White Horse Rd. 24M 52
South-West	Cable St. 24M 52
White Horse Yd. N1	Horse Yd. 19H 37
White Lion St. E1	Folgate St. 21L 51
Whitfield St. EC2	Kiffen St. 20K 51
Why's Yd. SW1	Eaton Clo. 14P 61
William M. NW1	Everton Bldgs. 15K 49
William St. E1	Ponler St. 22M 52
William St. EC4	Watergate 18M 50
William St. N1	Eckford St. 18J 50
William St. N1	Allingham Street 19J 51
William St. NW1	William Rd. 15K 49
William St. SE18	Calderwood St. 33P 95
William St. SW8	Parvin St. 16R 73
William St. W8	Callcott St. 11N 59
William St. W14	Earsby St. 10O 59
William Ter. NW6	Kilburn Pl. 11G 34
Williams Pl. NW8	Plympton Pl. 13K 48
Willoughby Rd. W12	Jeddo Rd. 6N 58
Willow St. E1	Osier St. 23L 52
Willow St. SE1	Curtis St. 20O 63
Willow St. SW1	Willow Pl. 16O 61
Willow Wk. NW5	Fortess Wk. 15F 35
Willow Wk. SE6	Milford Rd. 25V 88
Willow Wk. SE26	Willow Way 22X 87
Wilson St. E3	Wager St. 25L 53
Wilson St. E14	Mills Gro. 26L 53
Wilson St. SE14	Willshaw St. 25R 77
Wilson St. SW11	Wynter St. 12T 72
Wilson St. WC1	Coley St. 18K 50
Wilson St. WC2	Dryden St. 17M 50
Wilton Cres. M. SW1	Wilton Row 14N 61
Wilton St. N1	Wilton Villas 20J 51
Winchester Cotts. N1	Killick Cotts. 17J 50
Winchester Pl. E2	Dunbridge St. 22K 52
Winchester St. E2	Dunbridge St. 22K 52
Winchester St. N1	Killick St. 17J 50
Winchester St. SE1	Winchester Wk. 20N 63
Winchester Yd. SE1	Winchester Sq. 20N 63
Windmill Pl. SW4	Windmill Dri. 15T 73
Windmill Rd. SW4	Windmill Dri 15U 73
Windmill St. SE1	Windmill Wk. 18N 62
Windsor Rd. SE5	Windsor Wk. 20S 75
Windsor Rd. SE27	Windsor Gro. 19X 86
Windsor Ter. NW3	Lyndhurst Ter. 13F 34
Wood St. E2	Wood Clo. 22K 52
Wood St. SE11	Brittany St. 17P 62
Wood St. SE18	Woodhill 32P 95
Wood St. SE27	Dunbar Pl. 19X 86
Wood St. SW3	Smollett St. 13O 60
Woodland Pl. SE10	Woodland Cres. 27Q 66
Woodland Rd. N16	Sandbrook Rd. 20F 37
Woodland St. SE10	Woodland Wk. 28Q 66

OLD NAME.	NEW NAME.	
Woodlands Pl. SE1	Bacon Gro.	21O 63
Woodlands Rd. SW15	Woodlands Way	10T 71
Wood's Clo. E2	Wood Clo.	21K 52
Wood's Cotts. SE17	Barlow Cotts.	20P 63
Wood's Cotts. SE18	Bloomfield Rd.	33Q 95
Woodstock Rd. E14	Woodstock Ter.	26M 53
Woodstock Rd. W12	Woodstock Gro.	9N 59
Worcester St. E1	Reardon St.	22N 64
Worcester St. SE1	O'Meara St.	19N 63
Wright's Bldgs. E14	Salmon Bldgs.	24M 53
Wythburn M. W1	Wythburn Pl.	14L 49
Yardley St. EC1 South-East	Spafield St.	18K 50
York M. SW3	Dudmaston M.	13P 60
York M. N. W1	David M.	14L 49
York M. S. W1	Sherlock M.	14L 49
York Pl. EC1	Central Pl.	19K 51
York Pl. SE17	Darwin Pl.	20P 63
York Pl. W6	Fulham Pal. Rd.	8P 58
York Rd. E14	Yorkshire Rd.	24M 53
York Rd. N1 & N7	York Way	17H 36
York Rd. SE27	York Hill	18W 85
York Rd. By-Pass SW18	Armoury Way	11T 71
York St. SW1	Duke of York St.	16N 61
York St. WC2	Tavistock St.	17M 50
York Ter. SW4	Lendal Ter.	16S 74
York Ter. WC2	Watergate Wk.	17M 50

ADDENDA
TO STREET INDEX

Abbeydale Rd.Wem. 3H 30
Abbots Gdns. N2. 13A 22
Alexandra Rd. N9. 22Af 17
Alington Cres. NW9. 5D 19
All Saints Rd. SE3. 28S 78
Arbroath Rd. SE9. 31S 79
Avondale Av. Barn.
    14Ae 15
Basing Hill Wem. 3D 19
Besant Rd. NW2. 10F 33
Bideford Gdns. N.9.
    21Af 17
Birchen Clo. NW9. 5D 19
Bishop Rd. Barn. 15Af 15
Brampton Clo.Wem. 3D 19
Briar Clo. N13. 20Ad 16
Bromley Gdns. N9.
    20Ad 17
Brook Cres. N9. 22Ac 17
Brooke Rd. N9. 21Ad 17
Brookside N14. 15Ae 15
Brookside South N14.
    15Af 15
Brumwill Rd. Wem. 2J 44
Burlington Rise Barn.
    14Af 15
Calder Gdns. Wem. 3A 19
Carlisle Rd. Wem. 5A 19
Cecil Dri. NW11. 12C 22
Cedarhurst Dri. SE9.
    30U 79
Chetwynd Av. Barn.
    14Ae 15
Church Mount N2. 13B 22
Churchill Av. Wem. 1C 18
Close, The Wem. 5E 31
Coniscliffe Rd. N13.
    20Ad 16
Connaught Av. Barn.
    14Ae 15
Cornwall Rd. N18. 22Ac 17
Countisbury Rd. N9.
    21Af 17
Cragmuir Pk. Wem. 3H 31
Craig Pk. Rd. N18. 22Ac 17
Croft Clo. NW7. 6Ad 13
Cross St. N18. 22Ac 17
Cumberland Rd. Wem.
    3A 18
Cuthbert Rd. N18. 22Ac 17
De Haviland Rd. Wem.
    4Aa 13
Dene Rd. N20. 14Ae 15
Dennis Av. Wem. 3F 30
Densworth Gro. N9.
    23Ad 17
Depot Rd. N18. 22Ac 17
Devonia Gdns. N18.
    19Ab 16
Derwent Av. Barn. 14Ae 15
Doncaster Rd. N9. 22Ae 17

Durham Rd. N9. 22Ae 17
Elizabeth Ride N9.
    23Af 17
Ellanby Cres. N18. 22Ac 17
Fairway, The N13 20Ad 17
Friars Wk. Barn. 15Af 15
Fryent Cres. NW9. 6C 20
Fryent Way Wem. 4B 19
Gallants Farm Rd. Barn.
    14Ae 15
Galsworthy Rd. NW2.
    10F 33
Gibb's Grn. Edg. 5Ad 13
Gillum Clo. Barn. 14Ae 15
Goffers Rd. SE3. 27R 78
Gordon Gdns. Wem.
    4Aa 13
Grange Av. Barn. 14Af 15
Green Wk. NW4. 9B 21
Greenway Clo. NW9.
    5Aa 13
Hampton Rise Wem. 2C 18
Hampton Way N14.
    15Ae 15
Hare & Billet Rd. SE3
    &.SE10. 27R 78
Hazel Clo. N13. 20Ad 17
Hill View NW9. 6D 20
Hillside Gdns.Wem. 3C 18
Honeypot La. Wem. 3H 30
Horton Av. NW2. 10F 33
Kingscourt Wem. 2F 30
Knoll Dri. Barn. 15Af.15
Lancelot Ct. Wem. 2F 30
Langton Way SE3. 28R 78
Lansbury Av. N18. 20Ac 17
Lawley Rd. Barn. 15Af 15
Leith Clo. NW9. 5D 19
Leyburn Gro. N18. 22Ab 17
Linnell Rd. N18. 22Ac 17
Litchfield Rd. N9. 22Ae 17
Long Pond Rd. SE3 28R 78
Lovatt Clo. Edg. 4Ac 13
Lowther Rd. Wem. 3A 18
Mallard Way NW9. 5C 19
Manor Clo. Wem. 4B 19
Marnham Av. NW2. 10F 33
Maxwelton Clo. NW7.
    6Ad 13
Mayday Gdns. SE3. 31S 79
Merley Ct. NW9. 5D 19
Middledene NW7. 6Ad 13
Middlesborough Rd. N18.
    21Ab 17
Monk Frith Barn. 15Af 15
Monks Pk. Gdns. Wem.
    4G 31
Mountview NW7. 6Ad 13
Myrtle Clo. Barn. 14Ae 15
Newcombe Pk.Wem. 3H 30
New Pk. Av. N13. 20Ad 16

Northchurch Rd. Wem.
    3G 31
Northdene NW7. 6Ad 13
Northwick Av. Wem.
    1C 18
Oak Clo. Barn. 15Af 15
Oak Way Barn. 15Af 15
Oxford Clo. N9. 22Ae 17
Pembroke Rd. N13.
    20Ad 16
Pentland Clo. NW2. 9E 33
Petts Gro. Av. Wem. 1F 30
Plevna Rd. N9. 22Ad 17
Prevost Rd. N11. 15Ae 15
Prince Of Wales Rd. SE3.
    28S 78
Rainsford Rd. NW10 4J 45
Retreat Clo. Wem. 1B 18
Richmond Cres. N9.
    22Ae 17
Riverside Gdns. Wem.
    2J 45
Rylston Rd. N13. 20Ad 17
St. Alphege Rd. N9.
    23Af 17
St. Mary's Gdns. N9.
    23Ae 17
St. Mary's Rd. Barn.
    14Af 15
St. Michaels Av. Wem.
    4G 31
St. Thomas Rd. N14.
    17Af 16
Sandgate Rd. N18. 22Ac 17
Seaton St. N18. 22Ac 17
Sennen Rd. N9. 21Af 17
Southdene NW7. 6Ad 13
Strathcona Av. Barn.
    2D 18
Stuart Rd. Barn. 14Af 15
Talbot Pl. SE3. 28S 78
Thorndale Av. Barn.
    14Ae 15
Tillingbourne Gro. N3.
    11A 21
Trelawn Pk. Rd. NW7.
    6Ad 13
Tuncombe Rd. N9. 20Ad 17
Victor Gro. Wem. 2H 30
Victoria Ct. Wem. 4G 31
Water Rd. Wem. 3H 30
Wells Dri. NW9. 5D 19
Westcroft Way NW2.
    10F 33
Westmorland Rd. Wem.
    3A 18
Wimborne Rd. N9. 22Ae 17
Woodgrange Clo. Wem.
    2B 18
Woolmead Av. NW9.
    7C 20
Wycombe Rd. Wem. 4H 31

INDEX TO STREETS

Abbreviations.—App. for Approach; Ct. for Court; Gdns. for Gardens; La. for Lane; Mt. for Mount; Pk. for Park; Pl. for Place; Rd. for Road; Sq. for Square; St. for Street; Upr. for Upper; Wk. for Walk. Bar. for Barking; Barn. for Barnet; Bec. for Beckenham; Cro. for Croydon; Edg. for Edgware; Har. for Harrow; Ilf. for Ilford; Kin. for Kingston; Mer. for Merton; Mor. for Morden; Rich. for Richmond; Ted. for Teddington; Tot. for Tottenham; Twi. for Twickenham.

Abbeville Rd. sw4.	15U 73
Abbey Av. Wem.	2J 44
Abbey Gdns. nw8.	12J 48
Abbey La. e15.	27J 54
Abbey La. nw6.	11H 34
Abbey Mews. nw6.	11H 34
Abbey Rd. e15.	28J 54
Abbey Rd.	
nw8. 2-98, 1-117.	
nw6. 100, 119 & up.	
	11H 34
Abbey Rd. nw10.	4J 45
Abbey Rd. sw19.	12Z 91
Abbey Rd. w11.	9M 47
Abbey Rd. Bar.	33H 43
Abbey Rd. Cro.	18Zf 91
Abbey Rd. Ilf.	34C 42
Abbey St. e2.	22K 52
Abbey St. e13.	29K 55
Abbey St. se1.	21O 63
Abbey St. se18.	35P 95
Abbeyfield Rd. se16.	23P 64
Abbot St. e8.	21G 37
Abbots Dri. Har.	1aD 12
Abbot's La. se1.	20N 63
Abbot's Rd. e6.	31J 55
Abbot's Rd. nw6.	11H 34
Abbots Rd. Edg.	5Ab 13
Abbotsbury Rd. w14.	10O 59
Abbotsbury Rd. Mor.	11Za 92
Abbotsford Av. n15.	19B 25
Abbotsford Rd. Ilf.	37E 42
Abbotshall Av. n14.	16Ad 15
Abbotshall Rd. se6.	27W 89
Abbotsleigh Rd. sw16.	15X 84
Abbotstone Rd. sw15.	8S 71
Abbotswell St. se4.	25U 77
Abbotswood Rd. sw16.	16W 84
Abbott Av. sw20.	9Za 92
Abbott Rd. e14.	27H 54
Abbot's Pk. Rd. e10.	26D 28
Abchurch La. ec4.	20M 51
Abchurch Rd. Cro.	21Zd 91
Abdale Rd. w12.	8M 46
Aberconway Rd. Mor.	11Zb 92
Abercorn Gdns. Har.	2C 18
Abercorn Mews. nw8.	12J 48
Abercorn Pl. nw8.	12J 48
Abercrombie St. sw11.	13S 72
Aberdare Gdns. nw6.	12H 34
Aberdeen La. n5.	19G 37
Aberdeen Pk. n5.	19F 37
Aberdeen Pl. nw8.	12K 48
Aberdeen Rd. n5.	19F 37
Aberdeen Rd. n18.	22Ac 17
Aberdeen Rd. nw10.	7F 32
Aberdeen Rd. Cro.	19Zg 91
Aberdeen Rd. Har.	1bAa 12
Aberdeen Rd. Mit.	12Za 92
Aberdour Rd. Ilf.	37F 42
Aberdour St. se1.	20O 63
Aberfeldy St. e14.	27M 54
Abergeldie Rd. se12.	29U 79
Abernethy Rd. se13.	27T 78
Abersham Rd. e8.	21G 38
Abingdon Rd. n2.	12Aa 14
Abingdon Rd. sw16.	16Za 90
Abingdon Rd. w8.	11O 59
Abingdon St. sw1.	17O 62
Abingdon Villas w8.	11O 59
Abinger Rd. se8.	24Q 65
Abinger Rd. w4.	6O 58
Ablett St. se16.	22P 64
Aboyne Rd. nw10.	6E 32
Aboyne Rd. sw17.	12X 83
Abyssinia Rd. sw11.	13T 72
Acacia Av. n17.	20Ab 17
Acacia Av. Wem.	2F 30
Acacia Gro. se21.	20W 86
Acacia Pl. nw8.	13J 48
Acacia Rd. e11.	28E 40
Acacia Rd. e17.	24C 27
Acacia Rd. n22.	18Aa 16
Acacia Rd. nw8.	13J 48
Acacia Rd. se26.	23Y 87
Acacia Rd. sw16.	17Z 90
Acacia Rd. w3.	5M 45
Academy Rd. se18.	32R 95
Acanthus Rd. sw11.	14S 73
Acfold Rd. sw6.	11R 72
Achilles Rd. nw6.	10F 33
Achilles St. se14.	24R 77
Acklam Rd. w10.	10L 47
Ackmar Rd. sw6.	10P 71
Ackroyd Rd. se23.	23V 87
Ackworth St. se1.	20O 63
Acland Rd. nw2.	8G 32
Acland St. e14.	25L 53
Acol Rd. nw6.	11H 34
Acorn Gdns. w3.	5L 45
Acorn Pl. se15.	22R 76
Acorn St. se18.	31O 67
Acre La. sw2.	17T 74
Acre Rd. sw19.	12Y 83
Acre St. sw8.	16R 73
Acris St. sw18.	12T 72
Acton La. nw10.	5J 45
Acton La.	
w4. 1-287 & 2-280.	
w3. 317, 322, & up.	5O 57
Acton St. e8.	21H 37
Acton St. wc1.	17K 50
Acuba Rd. sw18.	11V 82
Ada Pl. e2.	22J 52
Ada Rd. se5.	20R 75
Ada St. e8.	22J 52
Ada St. e15.	28J 54
Adair Rd. w10.	10K 47
Adam St. w1.	14L 49
Adam St. wc2.	17M 50
Adam & Eve Mews. w8.	
	11O 60
Adams Gdns. se16.	23N 64
Adams Mews w1.	14M 49
Adamson Rd. e16.	29M 55
Adamson Rd. nw3.	13H 34
Adamsrill Rd. se26.	24X 87
Adare Wk. sw16.	17W 85
Adderley Gro. sw11.	14T 73
Adderley Rd. Har.	1bAa 12
Adderley St. e14.	26M 53
Addey St. se8.	25R 77
Addington Dri. n12.	13Ab 14
Addington Gro. se26.	24Y 87
Addington Rd. e3.	25K 53
Addington Rd. e16.	28L 54
Addington Rd. n4.	18C 24
Addington Rd. Cro.	18Ze 91
Addington Sq. se5.	19Q 63
Addington St. se1.	17N 62
Addiscombe Av. Cro.	21Ze 91
Addiscombe Gro. Cro.	20Zf 91
Addiscombe Rd. Cro.	20Zf 91
Addiscombe Ct. Rd. Cro.	
	20Ze 91
Addison Av. w11.	9N 59
Addison Cres. w14.	10O 59
Addison Gdns. w14.	9N 59
Addison Pl. w11.	9N 59
Addison Rd. e16.	29M 54
Addison Rd. e17.	26B 27
Addison Rd. se25.	21Zb 90
Addison Rd. w4.	6O 58
Addison Rd. w14.	10N 59
Addison Way. nw11.	11B 21
Addison Brdg.Pl.w14.	10O 59
Addle Hill ec4.	19M 51
Addle St. ec2.	19L 51
Adela Av. Mor.	8Zb 92
Adela St. w10.	9K 47
Adelaide Cotts. w7.	1bD 04
Adelaide Pl. se15.	21R 75
Adelaide Rd. e10.	26F 39
Adelaide Rd. nw3.	13H 34
Adelaide Rd. se4.	25T 77
Adelaide Rd. w12.	7M 46
Adelaide Rd. w13.	1aN 04
Adelaide Rd. Ilf.	34E 42
Adelaide Rd. Rich.	3S 68
Adelaide Rd. Ted.	1bY 93
Adelaide St. wc2.	17M 50
Adelaide St. Cro.	18Ze 91
Adelina Gro. e1.	23L 52
Aden Gro. n16.	20F 37
Aden Rd. Ilf.	34D 42
Aden Ter. n16.	20F 37
Adeney Rd. w6.	9Q 59
Adie Rd. w6.	8O 58
Adine Rd. e13.	29L 55
Adler St. e1.	21L 52
Adley St. e5.	24F 39
Admaston Rd. se18.	34Q 95
Admiral Pl. w10.	9K 47
Adolf St. se6.	25Y 88
Adolphus Rd. n4.	19E 37
Adolphus St. se8.	25Q 65
Adpar St. w2.	13L 48
Ædy's Rd. se15.	21S 75
Ægis Gro. sw8.	15Q 61
Aerodrome Rd. nw9.	6Aa 13
Aeroville. nw9.	6Aa 13
Affleck St. n1.	17J 50
Afghan Rd. sw11.	13S 72
Agamemnon Rd. nw6.	10F 33

Agar St. wc2.	17M 50	
Agate Rd. w6.	8O 58	
Agate St. e16.	29M 54	
Agatha St. e1.	22N 65	
Agave Rd. nw2.	8F 33	
Agincourt Rd. nw3.	14F 35	
Agnes Av. Ilf.	33F 42	
Agnes Rd. w3.	6N 58	
Agnes St. e14.	25L 53	
Agnes St. e16.	31N 67	
Agnew Rd. se23.	23V 87	
Aiden Av. e15.	28K 54	
Ailsa Av. Twi.	1aT 93	
Ailsa Rd. Twi.	1aT 93	
Ailsa St. e14.	27L 54	
Ainger Rd. nw3.	14H 35	
Ainsdale Rd. w5.	2K 44	
Ainsty St. se16.	23N 64	
Ainsworth Rd. e9.	23H 38	
Aintree Av. e6.	31J 55	
Aintree Rd. Wem.	1J 44	
Aintree St. sw6.	9Q 59	
Air St. w1.	16M 49	
Airedale Av. w4.	6P 58	
Airedale Rd. sw12.	14V 84	
Airedale Rd. w5.	1O 56	
Airlie Gdns. w8.	10N 59	
Airlie Gdns. Ilf.	33E 42	
Airy St. se13.	26S 77	
Aislibie Rd. se12.	28T 78	
Aitken Rd. se6.	26W 88	
Ajax Av. nw9.	6A 20	
Ajax Rd. nw6.	11F 33	
Akehurst St. sw15.	7U 70	
Akenside Rd. nw3.	13G 34	
Akerman Rd. sw9.	18R 74	
Alabama St. se18.	35R 95	
Alacross Rd. w5.	1N 56	
Alan Rd. sw19.	9X 82	
Alba Gdns. nw11.	10C 21	
Albacore Cres. se13.	26U 77	
Albany. w1.	15M 49	
Albany Pl. n7.	18F 36	
Albany Rd. e10.	25D 27	
Albany Rd. e12.	31G 41	
Albany Rd. e16.	29M 54	
Albany Rd. e17.	24C 27	
Albany Rd. n4.	18C 24	
Albany Rd. n18.	23Ac 17	
Albany Rd. se5.	20Q 63	
Albany Rd. sw19.	11X 82	
Albany Rd. w13.	1aL 94	
Albany Rd. Bre.	2Q 56	
Albany St. e1.	24M 52	
Albany St. n15.	19B 25	
Albany St. nw1.	15J 49	
Albany St. se5.	20Q 63	
Albatross St. se18.	35R 95	
Albemarle Gdns. Ilf.	33C 42	
Albemarle St. w1.	15M 49	
Alberton Gdns. nw11.	10B 21	
Albert Bdg. sw3.	13Q 60	
Albert Bridge Rd. sw11.		
	13Q 60	
Albert Dri. sw19.	9W 82	
Albert Embankment		
se1. 1-8.		
se11 9 & up.	17P 62	
Albert Gdns. nw6.	10J 47	
Albert Gro. sw20.	9Z 91	
Albert Gro. w3.	4N 57	
Albert Hall Mans. sw7.		
	12N 60	
Albert Pl. n3.	11Aa 14	
Albert Pl. w8.	11O 60	
Albert Rd. e8.	21H 38	
Albert Rd. e10.	27E 40	
Albert Rd. e17.	25C 27	
Albert Rd. e18.	30A 29	
Albert Rd. n4.	18D 24	
Albert Rd. n15.	20C 25	
Albert Rd. n22.	16Aa 15	
Albert Rd.		
nw1. 1-23.		
nw8. 31 & up.	13J 48	
Albert Rd. nw4.	9B 21	
Albert Rd. nw6.	10J 47	
Albert Rd. se15.	22R 76	
Albert Rd. se20.	23Z 92	
Albert Rd. se25.	21Zb 90	
Albert Rd. w5.	1K 44	
Albert Rd. Har.	1dA 12	
Albert Rd. Ilf.	33F 42	
Albert Rd. Rich.	2T 68	
Albert Rd. Ted.	1bY 93	
Albert Rd. Twi.	1bV 93	
Albert Sq. e1.	23M 52	
Albert Sq. e15.	28G 40	
Albert Sq. sw8.	17R 74	
Albert St. e1.	22L 52	
Albert St. n1.	18J 50	
Albert St. n11.	15Ac 15	
Albert St. n12.	12Ac 14	
Albert St. nw1.	15J 49	
Albert St. w2.	13L 48	
Albert Ter. e3.	26K 53	
Albert Ter. nw1.	14H 35	
Alberta St. se17.	18P 62	
Albion Av. n10.	15Aa 15	
Albion Gdns. w6.	7O 58	
Albion Gro. n16.	20F 37	
Albion Hill se13.	26S 77	
Albion Mews. w2.	13M 48	
Albion Pl. ec1.	19L 50	
Albion Rd. e8.	21H 38	
Albion Rd. e17.	27A 28	
Albion Rd. n16.	20F 37	
Albion Rd. nw6.	12H 34	
Albion Rd. se13.	26T 78	
Albion Rd. se18.	31P 67	
Albion Rd. Twi.	1cV 93	
Albion Sq. e8.	21H 37	
Albion St. e3.	24K 53	
Albion St. e15.	27H 40	
Albion St. n1.	17J 50	
Albion St. se16.	23O 64	
Albion St. w2.	13M 48	
Albion St. Cro.	18Ze 91	
Albion Yard se16.	23N 64	
Albion Villas Rd.se26	23W 87	
Albrighton Rd. se5.	20S 75	
Albury St. se8.	25Q 65	
Albyn Rd. se8.	25S 77	
Alcester Cres. e5.	22E 38	
Alconbury Rd. e5.	22E 38	
Aldborough Rd. Ilf.	35D 42	
Aldbourn Rd. Wem.	1G 30	
Aldbourne Rd. w12.	7M 46	
Aldbridge St. se17	20P 63	
Aldbury Av. Wem.	4G 31	
Aldebert Ter. sw8.	17R 74	
Aldeburgh St. se10.	29P 66	
Aldenham St. nw1.	16J 49	
Aldensley Rd. w6.	8O 58	
Alder Rd. sw14.	5S 69	
Alder St. e15.	21Q 63	
Alderbrook Rd. sw12.	14U 73	
Alderbury Rd. sw13.	7Q 58	
Aldergrove nw2.	8E 32	
Aldermanbury ec2.	19L 51	
Alderman's Hill. n13	17Ad 16	
Aldermaston St. w10	9L 47	
Alderminster Rd. se1.	21P 64	
Alderney Rd. e1.	23K 52	
Alderney St. sw1.	15P 61	
Aldersbrook La. e12.	32F 43	
Aldersbrook Rd.		
e11. 1-13.		
e12. 14, 19 & up.	29E 41	
Aldersey Gdns. Bar.	35H 43	
Aldersgate St. ec1.	19L 51	
Aldershot Rd. nw6.	10H 33	
Alderton Cres. nw4.	8B 20	
Alderton Rd. se24.	19S 75	
Alderton Rd. Cro.	21Zd 91	
Alderville Rd. sw6.	10R 71	
Aldford St. w1.	14M 49	
Aldgate ec3.	21M 51	
Aldgate Av. e1.	21M 51	
Aldgate High St. ec3.		
	21M 51	
Aldine St. w12.	9N 59	
Aldis St. sw17.	13Y 83	
Aldred Rd. nw6.	11F 33	
Aldred St. se17.	18Q 62	
Aldren Rd. sw17	12X 83	
Aldridge Rd.Villas. w11.		
	10L 47	
Aldrington Rd. sw16.	15X 84	
Aldwick Rd. Cro.	17Zf 91	
Aldworth Gro. se13.	26U 77	
Aldworth Rd. e15.	28H 40	
Aldwych wc2.	17M 50	
Alexander Av. nw10.	8H 32	
Alexander Pl. sw7.	13O 60	
Alexander Rd. n19.	17E 36	
Alexander Sq. sw3.	13O 60	
Alexander St. w2.	11L 48	
Alexandra Av. sw11.	14R 73	
Alexandra Av. w4.	5Q 57	
Alexandra Gdns. n10.	15A 23	
Alexandra Dri. se19.	20Y 86	
Alexandra Gdns. w4.	5Q 57	
Alexandra Gro. n12.	12Ac 14	
Alexandra Mans. nw6.		
	12H 34	
Alexandra Pl. se25.	20Zc 90	
Alexandra Rd. e10.	26F 40	
Alexandra Rd. e17.	25C 27	
Alexandra Rd. e18.	29B 29	
Alexandra Rd. n4.	19D 25	
Alexandra Rd. n8.	18A 24	
Alexandra Rd. n10.	15Aa 15	
Alexandra Rd. n11.	15Ac 15	
Alexandra Rd. n15.	20B 25	
Alexandra Rd. nw4.	9A 21	
Alexandra Rd. nw8.	11H 34	
Alexandra Rd. se20.	23Z 92	
Alexandra Rd. se25.	20Zc 90	
Alexandra Rd. se26.	23Z 90	
Alexandra Rd. sw14.	5S 69	
Alexandra Rd. sw19.	10Y 82	
Alexandra Rd. w4.	5N 57	
Alexandra Rd. w14.	9O 59	
Alexandra Rd. Cro.	20Ze 91	
Alexandra Rd. Kew.	3R 68	
Alexandra Rd. e16.	29L 54	
Alexandra St. se14.	24Q 65	
Alexandra Pk. Rd.		
n10. 1-121 & 2-126c.		
n22. 123-355 & 128-372.		
	15Aa 15	
Alexandria Rd. w13.	1aM 94	
Alexis St. se16.	22O 64	
Alfearn Rd. e5.	23F 33	
Alford Rd. sw8.	16R 74	
Alfoxton Av. n15.	19B 25	
Alfred Pl. sw7.	13O 60	

Alfred Pl. wc1.	16L 49
Alfred Rd. e15.	28G 40
Alfred Rd. se25.	21Zc 90
Alfred Rd. w2.	11L 48
Alfred Rd. w3.	5M 45
Alfred Rd. w13.	1aM 94
Alfred St. e3.	25K 53
Alfred St. e16.	29N 66
Alfred St. n1.	19J 50
Alfred St. sw1.	16P 61
Alfreda St. sw11.	15R 73
Alfreton St. se17.	20P 63
Alfriston Av. Cro.	16Zd 91
Alfriston Rd. sw11.	14T 73
Algarve Rd. sw18.	11V 83
Algernon Rd. nw4.	7C 20
Algernon Rd. nw6.	11H 33
Algernon Rd. se13.	26T 77
Algiers Rd. se13.	25T 77
Alice St. e16.	28M 54
Alice St. se1.	20O 63
Alicia Av. Har.	1B 18
Alicia Clo. Har.	1B 18
Alicia Gdns. Har.	1A 18
Alie St. e1.	21M 51
Aliwal Rd. sw11.	13T 72
Alkerden Rd. w4.	6P 58
Alkham Rd. n16.	21E 37
Allan Edwards Rd. sw8.	
	16R 74
Allan Way, w3.	5L 45
Allandale Av. Cro.	10A 21
Allanmouth Rd. e9.	25H 39
Allardyce St. sw4.	17T 74
Allas Rd. e2.	23K 52
Allcroft Rd. nw5.	14G 35
Allen Rd. n16.	20F 37
Allen Rd. Bec.	23Zb 90
Allen Rd. Cro.	18Ze 91
Allen St. n1.	10H 37
Allen St. w8.	11O 61
Allenby Rd. se23.	24W 88
Allendale Rd. se5.	19R 75
Allerford Rd. se6.	26X 88
Allerton Rd. n16.	19E 37
Allerton St. n1.	20J 51
Allestree Rd. sw6.	9Q 59
Alleyn Pk. se21.	20W 86
Alleyn Rd. se21.	20W 86
Allfarthing La. sw18.	11U 72
Allhallows La. ec4.	20M 51
Alliance Rd. e13.	30L 55
Alliance Rd. w3.	36R 90
Allingham St. n1.	19J 51
Allington Rd. nw4.	8B 20
Allington Rd. w10.	9J 47
Allington St. sw1.	15O 61
Allington St. sw2.	17U 74
Allison Gro. se21.	20V 86
Allison Rd. n8.	18B 24
Allison Rd. w3.	5M 45
Alloa Rd. se8.	24P 64
Alloa Rd. Ilf.	37E 42
All Saints' Rd. w3.	4N 57
All Saints' Rd. w11.	10L 47
All Saints' St. n1.	17J 50
Allsop Pl. nw1.	14K 49
Allsop St. nw1.	14K 49
All Souls Av. nw10.	8J 46
Alma Cres. Har.	1cE 12
Alma Gro. n1.	18J 50
Alma Gro. se1.	21P 63
Alma Pl. nw10.	8K 46
Alma Pl. Cro.	18Zc 90
Alma Rd. e2.	23J 52
Alma Rd. e3.	24L 53

Alma Rd. n1.	19G 37
Alma Rd. n10.	15Aa 15
Alma Rd. sw18.	11T 72
Alma Rd. Har.	1cE 12
Alma Sq. nw8.	12J 48
Alma St. e15.	27G 40
Alma St. n5.	20J 51
Alma St. nw5.	15G 35
Alma Ter. sw18.	12U 72
Almack Rd. e5.	23F 38
Almeida St. n1.	18H 36
Almeric Rd. sw11.	13T 72
Almington St. n4.	17D 24
Almond Av. w5.	2N 56
Almond Rd. n17.	22Ab 17
Almorah Rd. n1.	20H 37
Alnuick Av. e16.	31M 55
Alnwick Rd. e16.	30M 55
Alperton La. Wem.	1J 44
Alperton St. w10.	10K 47
Alpha Pl. nw6.	11J 47
Alpha Pl. sw3.	13P 60
Alpha Pl. N. nw6.	11J 48
Alpha Pl. W. nw6.	11J 48
Alpha Rd. e14.	25N 65
Alpha Rd. n18.	22Ab 17
Alpha Rd. se14.	25R 77
Alpha Rd. Cro.	20Ze 91
Alpha St. se15.	21S 76
Alphage Wk. Edg.	5Aa 13
Alpine Rd. se16.	23P 64
Alric Av. nw10.	5H 31
Alroy Rd. n4.	18C 24
Alsace St. se17.	20P 63
Alscot Rd. se1.	21O 63
Alsen Rd. n7.	18E 36
Alston Rd. n18.	22Ab 17
Alston Rd. sw17.	12X 83
Alt Gro. sw19.	10Z 92
Altenberg Ave. w13.	1aN 94
Altenburg Gdns. sw11.	14T 73
Althea St. sw6.	11S 72
Althorp Rd. sw17.	13V 83
Althorpe Rd. Har.	1cB 12
Altmore Av. e6.	32H 43
Alton Gdns. Twi.	1cU 93
Alton Rd. n15.	20A 25
Alton Rd. Cro.	17Zf 91
Alton Rd. Rich.	2T 68
Altyre Rd. Cro.	20Zf 91
Alvanley Gdns. nw3.	11G 33
Alvar St. se8.	25Q 65
Alveston Mews sw7.	12P 60
Alverston Av. Wem.	3D 19
Alverstone Av. n20.	14Af 15
Alverstone Av. sw19.	10W 82
Alverstone Rd. e12.	33F 42
Alverstone Rd. nw2.	8H 33
Alverton St. se8.	24Q 65
Alveston Av. Har.	1A 18
Alvey Mews se17.	20P 63
Alvey St. se17.	20P 63
Alvington Cres. e8.	21G 37
Alwyn Av. w4.	5P 57
Alwyn Gdns. w3.	4L 45
Alwyne La. n1.	19H 37
Alwyne Pl. n1.	19H 37
Alwyne Rd. n1.	19H 37
Alwyne Rd. sw19.	10Y 82
Alwyne Rd. w7.	1cM 94
Alwyne Sq. n1.	19G 37
Alwyne Villas n1.	19H 37
Alyth Gdns. nw11.	11C 21
Amberden Av. n3.	11A 22

Ambergate St. se17.	18P 62
Amberley Gdns. n9.	21Ae 17
Amberley Gro. se26.	22Y 87
Amberley Gro. Cro.	21Ze 91
Amberley Mews w9.	11K 48
Amberley Rd. e10.	26C 27
Amberley Rd. n9.	21Af 17
Amberley Rd. n13.	17Ad 16
Amberley Rd. w9.	11K 48
Ambler Rd. n4.	18E 36
Ambleside Av. sw16.	16X 84
Ambleside Rd. nw10.	6H 32
Ambrosden Av. sw1.	16O 61
Ambrose Av. nw11.	10C 21
Ambrose St. se16.	22P 64
Amelia St. e16.	30N 67
Amelia St. se17.	19P 63
Amen Corner ec4.	19M 51
America Sq. ec3.	21M 51
American Gdns. n4.	18D 24
Amerland Rd. sw18.	10U 71
Amersham Gro. se14.	24Q 65
Amersham Rd. se14.	24K 77
Amersham Rd. sw15	9T 71
Amersham Rd. Har.	1bC 12
Amersham Vale se14.	24R 77
Amery Gdns. nw10.	8H 32
Amery Rd. Har.	1aE 12
Amery's Pl. se17.	20P 63
Ames St. e2.	23J 52
Amesbury Av. sw2.	17W 85
Amherst Av. w13.	1L 44
Amherst Rd. w13.	1L 44
Amhurst Pk. n16.	20C 25
Amhurst Pass. e8.	21F 38
Amhurst Rd.	
e8. 1-233 & 2-240.	
n16.235, 240 & up.	21F 37
Amhurst Ter. e8.	21F 38
Amies St. sw11.	13S 73
Amity Gro. sw20.	8Za 92
Amity Rd. e15.	28G 40
Amner Rd. sw11.	14U 73
Amor Rd. w6.	8O 58
Amott Rd. se15.	21T 76
Amoy Pl. e14.	25M 53
Ampthill Sq. nw1.	16J 49
Ampton St. wc1.	17K 50
Amstey Rd. e16.	29L 55
Amwell St. ec1.	18J 50
Amyand La. Twi.	1aU 93
Amyand Pk. Gdns. Twi.	
	1aU 93
Amyand Pk. Rd. Twi.	
	1aU 93
Amyruth Rd. se4.	25U 77
Anatola Rd. n19.	15E 35
Ancaster Rd. Cro.	23Zb 90
Ancaster St. se18.	35R 95
Anchor Alley ec4.	19M 51
Anchor St. e14.	24L 53
Anchor St. se16.	22P 64
Anchor & Hope La. se7.	
	30P 67
Ancill St. w6.	9Q 59
Ancona Rd. n5.	19F 37
Ancona Rd. nw10.	7J 46
Ancona St. se18	35Q 95
Andalus Rd. sw9.	17S 74
Anderson St. sw3.	14P 61
Anderson's Rd. e9.	23G 38
Anderson's Wk. se11.	
	17P 62
Andoe Rd. sw11.	13S 72
Andover Pl. nw6.	11J 48
Andover Rd. n7.	17E 36

Andover Rd. Twi. 1cV 93
Andre St. E8. 22G 38
Andrew St. E14. 26M 54
Andrew St. F16. 31N 67
Andrew's Rd. E8. 22J 52
Anerley Gro. SE19. 21Z 90
Anerley Pk. SE20. 22Z 90
Anerley Rd.
  SE19. 1-69 & 54-120.
  SE20. 71, 122 & up. 21Z 90
Anerley St. sw11. 14R 73
Anerley Vale SE19. 21Z 90
Anerley Station Rd. SE20.
  22Za 92
Aneside Edg. 5Ac 13
Angel La. E15. 27H 40
Angel Pass. EC4. 20M 51
Angel Rd. E3. 22Ac 17
Angel Rd. N18. 22Ac 17
Angel Rd. w6. 8P 58
Angel St. EC1. 19L 51
Angell Rd. sw9. 18S 74
Angell Pk. Gdns. sw9. 18S 74
Angle St. E11. 28F 40
Angler's La. NW5. 15G 35
Angles Rd. sw16. 17X 85
Anglesea Rd. SE18. 33P 95
Anglesea St. E1. 22K 52
Angrave St. E8. 21J 51
Angus Gdns. NW9. 6Aa 13
Angus Rd. E13. 30K 55
Angus St. SE14. 24Q 65
Anhalt Rd. sw11. 13Q 60
Ankerdine Cres. SE18. 33R 95
Anlaby Rd. Ted. 1cY 93
Anley Rd. w14. 9N 59
Ann St. SE18. 34P 95
Annandale Rd. SE10. 28Q 66
Annandale Rd. w4. 6P 58
Annandale Rd. Cro. 21Zf 91
Anne St. E13. 29K 54
Annesley Av. NW9. 6A 19
Annesley Clo. NW10. 6E 32
Annesley Rd. N19. 15E 35
Annette Rd. N7. 17F 36
Annington Rd. N2. 14A 23
Annis Rd. E9. 24H 39
Ann's Av. SE1. 21Q 64
Ann's Row SE17. 20P 63
Annsworthy Av. Cro.
  19Zb 90
Ansdell Rd. SE15. 23S 76
Ansdell St. w8. 11O 60
Ansell Rd. sw17. 13X 83
Anselm Rd. sw6. 10Q 59
Ansford Rd. Bec. 27Y 89
Anson Rd. N7. 16F 35
Anson Rd. NW2. 8F 32
Anstey Rd. SE5. 19S 75
Anstey Rd. SE15. 21S 76
Antcliff St. E1. 23M 52
Anthony Rd. SE25. 21Zd 91
Anthony St E1. 22M 52
Antill Rd. E3. 24K 53
Antill Rd. N15. 21B 26
Antill Ter. E1. 23L 52
Anton St. E8. 22G 38
Antrim Rd. NW3. 14G 35
Antrobus Rd. w4. 4O 57
Antrobus St. sw1. 15P 61
Antwerp St. E8. 22J 52
Appach Rd. sw2. 17U 74
Appian Rd. E3. 25J 53
Apple Garth Bre. 2O 56
Appleby Rd. E8. 22H 38

Appleby St. E2. 21J 51
Appleford Rd. w10. 10K 47
Applegarth Rd. w14. 9O 59
Appleton Rd. SE9. 31T 79
Appold St. EC2. 20L 51
Approach Rd. E2. 23J 52
Approach Rd. sw20. 8Za 92
Approach, The w3. 6L 45
Aprey Gdns. NW4. 9A 21
April St. E8. 21F 38
Apsley Rd. E17. 24B 27
Apsley Rd. SE25. 22Zc 90
Apsley St. E1. 23L 52
Aquila St. NW8. 13J 48
Aquinas St. SE1. 18N 62
Arabin Rd. SE4. 24T 77
Arbery Rd. E3. 24K 53
Arbour Sq. E1. 23M 52
Arbuthnot Rd. SE14. 23S 76
Arcadia Av. N3. 11Aa 14
Arcadia St. E14. 25L 53
Arcadian Gdns. N22. 18Ab 16
Arch St. SE1. 19O 63
Archbishop's Pl. sw2. 17U 74
Archdale Rd. SE22. 21T 75
Archel Rd. w14. 10P 59
Archer Rd. SE25. 22Zb 90
Archer St. NW1. 16J 49
Archer St. sw8. 17Q 62
Archer St. w1. 16M 49
Archer St. w11. 10M 47
Archibald Rd. N7. 16F 36
Archibald St. E3. 25K 53
Archway Pl. sw4. 15T 73
Archway Rd.
  N19. 1-43 & 2-88.
  N6. 121-513 & 122-510.
    14C 23
Archway St. sw13. 6S 70
Arcola St. E8. 21G 37
Ardberg Rd. SE24. 19U 75
Arden Rd. N3. 10A 21
Arden St. sw8. 16Q 61
Ardfern Av. sw16. 17Zb 90
Ardfillan Rd. SE6. 27W 89
Ardgowan Rd. SE6. 27V 89
Ardilaun Rd. N5. 19F 37
Ardleigh Rd. N1. 20H 37
Ardley Cl. NW10. 6E 32
Ardlui Rd. SE27. 19W 86
Ardmere Rd. SE13. 27U 78
Ardoch Rd. SE6. 27W 89
Ardowell Av. Ilf. 34C 42
Ardwell Rd. sw2. 17W 85
Ardwick Rd. NW2. 11F 33
Argall Av. E10. 24D 26
Argyle Gdns. Edg. 4Aa 13
Argyle Pass. N17. 21Aa 17
Argyle Pl. w6. 8P 58
Argyle Rd. wc1. 17K 50
Argyle Rd. E1. 23K 52
Argyle Rd. E15. 28G 40
Argyle Rd. E16. 29M 55
Argyle Rd. N12. 11Ac 14
Argyle Rd. N17. 21Aa 17
Argyle Rd. N18. 22Ac 17
Argyle Rd. NW9. 7C 20
Argyle Rd. w13. 1aK 94
Argyle Rd. Ilf. 33E 42
Argyle Rd. Twi. 1cX 95
Argyle Sq. wc1. 17K 50
Argyle St. E11. 27E 40
Argyle St. wc1. 17K 50
Argyll Pl. w1. 15M 49
Argyll Rd. w8. 11N 59
Argyll St. w1. 15M 49

Arica Rd. SE4. 24T 78
Ariel Rd. NW6. 11G 33
Aristotle Rd. sw4. 16S 74
Arkindale Gdns. SE6. 26X 88
Arkley Cres. E17. 24C 27
Arkley Rd. E17. 24C 27
Arklow Rd. SE14. 24Q 65
Arkwright Rd. NW3. 12G 34
Arkwright St. E16. 28M 54
Arlesford Rd. sw9. 17S 74
Arline St. E2. 21K 51
Arlingford Rd. sw2. 18U 74
Arlington Gdns. w4. 4P 57
Arlington Gdns. Ilf. 32D 42
Arlington Rd. N14. 15Ae 15
Arlington Rd. NW1. 15H 35
Arlington Rd. w13. 1aL 94
Arlington Rd. Ted. 1bX 93
Arlington Rd. Twi. 1aU 93
Arlington Sq. N1. 19J 51
Arlington St. N1. 19J 51
Arlington St. sw1. 15N 61
Arlington Way EC1. 18K 50
Arlow Rd. N21. 18Ae 16
Armada St. SE8. 25Q 65
Armadale Rd. sw6. 10Q 59
Armagh Rd. E3. 25J 53
Arminger Rd. w12. 8N 59
Armitage Rd. NW11. 10D 21
Armitage Rd. SE10. 28P 66
Arms Yard EC2. 20L 51
Armstrong Pl. SE18. 33P 95
Armstrong Rd. w3. 6M 46
Armstrong St. SE18. 33P 95
Army St. sw4. 16S 73
Arne St. wc2. 17M 50
Arngask Rd. SE6. 27V 89
Arnold Circus E2. 21K 51
Arnold Rd. E3. 25K 53
Arnold Rd. N15. 21A 25
Arnold's Pl. SE1. 21O 63
Arnos Gro. N14. 16Ad 15
Arnos Rd. N11. 16Ac 15
Arnott St. SE1. 19O 63
Arnside St. SE17. 19Q 63
Arnulf St. SE6. 25X 88
Arnulls Rd. SE19. 18Y 92
Arnulls Rd. sw16. 18Y 85
Arodene Rd. sw2. 17U 74
Arpley Rd. SE20. 23Z 90
Arragon Gdns. sw16. 16Z 90
Arragon Rd. E6. 31J 55
Arragon Rd. Twi. 1bV 93
Arran Rd. SE6. 26W 88
Arras Av. Mor. 12Zc 92
Arrol Rd. Cro. 23Zb 90
Arrow Rd. E3. 26K 53
Arterberry Rd. sw20. 8Z 92
Artesian Rd. w2. 11L 47
Arthingworth St. E15. 28J 54
Arthur Rd. N7. 17F 36
Arthur Rd. N9. 21Ae 17
Arthur Rd. N16. 21F 37
Arthur Rd. sw9. 18R 74
Arthur Rd. sw19. 10X 82
Arthur St. E16. 31N 67
Arthur St. EC4. 20M 51
Arthur St. SE15. 22Q 64
Arthur St. SE18. 34P 95
Arthur St. sw7. 13O 60
Arthur St. wc2. 16L 50
Arthurdon Rd. SE4. 25U 77
Artillery La. E1. 21L 51
Artillery Pl. SE18. 32P 95
Artillery Row sw1. 16O 61
Artillery St. E1. 22K 52

Artillery St. se1.	21N 63	
Artizan St. e1.	21L 51	
Arundel Av. Mor.	10Zb 92	
Arundel Gdns. n21.	18Ae 16	
Arundel Gdns. w11.	10M 47	
Arundel Gdns Ilf.	36E 42	
Arundel Gro. n16.	20G 37	
Arundel Pl. n1.	18G 36	
Arundel Rd. e15.	28F 40	
Arundel Rd. n16.	21G 37	
Arundel Rd. Cro.	19Zd 91	
Arundel Sq. n7.	18G 36	
Arundel St. w1.	16M 49	
Arundel St. wc2.	18M 50	
Arundel Ter. sw13.	8Q 58	
Arvon Rd. n5.	18G 36	
Ascalon St. sw8.	15R 73	
Ascham St. nw5.	16F 35	
Ascot Rd. n15.	20B 25	
Ascot Rd. n18.	22Ac 17	
Ascot Rd. sw17.	14Y 84	
Ascot St. e16.	28L 54	
Ascott Av. w5.	2N 56	
Ash Gro. e8.	22J 52	
Ash Gro. n9.	20Af 17	
Ash Gro. n13.	19Ad 16	
Ash Gro. nw2.	9F 33	
Ash Gro. w5.	2N 56	
Ash St. e15.	28G 40	
Ash St. se17.	19O 63	
Ashbourne Av. e18.	30B 29	
Ashbourne Av. nw11.	10B 21	
Ashbourne Av. Barn.	14Ae 15	
Ashbourne Av. Har.	1cD 12	
Ashbourne Gro. nw7.	6Ac 13	
Ashbourne Gro. se22.	21T 75	
Ashbourne Gro. w4.	6P 58	
Ashbridge Rd. e11.	28D 28	
Ashbrook Rd. n19.	16D 24	
Ashburn Gdns. sw7.	12O 60	
Ashburn Pl. sw7.	12U 60	
Ashburne Clo. w5.	3K 44	
Ashburne Rd. w5.	3K 44	
Ashburnham Av. Har.	1bC 12	
Ashburnham Gdns Har.	1bC 12	
Ashburnham Gro. se10.	26R 77	
Ashburnham Rd. nw10.	8J 47	
Ashburnham Rd. se10.	26R 77	
Ashburnham Rd. sw10.	12Q 60	
Ashburnham Rd. Rich.	1aW 93	
Ashburton Av. Cro.	22Ze 91	
Ashburton Av. Ilf.	35G 43	
Ashburton Gro. n7.	18F 36	
Ashburton Rd. e16.	29L 54	
Ashburton Rd. Cro.	21Ze 91	
Ashbury Rd. sw11.	14S 73	
Ashby Rd. n1.	19H 37	
Ashby Rd. se4.	25S 77	
Ashby St. ec1.	19K 51	
Ashchurch Gro. w12.	7O 58	
Ashchurch Ter. w12.	7N 58	
Ashchurch Pk. Villas w12.	7O 58	
Ashcombe Gdns. Edg.	4Ad 13	
Ashcombe Pk. nw2.	6E 32	
Ashcombe Rd. sw19.	11Y 82	
Ashcombe St. sw6.	11S 72	
Ashcroft Rd. e3.	24K 53	
Ashdon Rd. nw10.	6H 32	
Ashdown St. nw5.	14G 35	
Ashen Gro. sw19.	10W 82	
Ashenden Rd. e5.	24F 39	
Ashfield Rd. n4.	19C 25	
Ashfield Rd. n14.	16Af 15	
Ashfield Rd. w3.	6M 46	
Ashford Av. n8.	17B 24	
Ashford Rd. e6.	32H 43	
Ashford Rd. e17.	25B 27	
Ashford Rd. e18.	30A 29	
Ashford Rd. n17.	21Aa 17	
Ashford Rd. nw2.	9F 33	
Ashford St. n1.	20K 51	
Ashgrove Rd. Ilf.	36E 42	
Ashington Rd. sw6.	10R 71	
Ashlake Rd. sw16.	16X 85	
Ashleigh Rd. se20.	22Zb 90	
Ashleigh Rd. sw14.	5S 69	
Ashley Cotts. w14.	10P 59	
Ashley Gdns. n13.	19Ac 16	
Ashley Gdns. Wem.	2E 30	
Ashley La. nw4 & nw7.	9A 21	
Ashley Pl. sw1.	15O 61	
Ashley Rd. e7.	30H 41	
Ashley Rd. n17.	22A 26	
Ashley Rd. n19.	17D 24	
Ashley Rd. sw19.	11Y 83	
Ashley Rd. Cro.	17Zc 90	
Ashley Rd. Rich.	2S 68	
Ashlin Rd. e15.	27G 40	
Ashling Rd. Cro.	21Ze 91	
Ashmead Rd. se8.	25S 77	
Ashmere Gro. sw2.	16T 74	
Ashmill St. nw1.	13L 48	
Ashmole Pl. sw8.	18Q 62	
Ashmore Rd. w9.	10J 47	
Ashmount Rd. n15.	21B 25	
Ashmount Rd. n19.	16D 23	
Ashness Rd. sw11.	14T 73	
Ashridge Clo. Har.	1C 18	
Ashridge Gdns. n13.	17Ac 16	
Ashridge Way Mor.	10Zc 92	
Ashstead Rd. e5.	22D 26	
Ashton St. e.14.	26M 54	
Ashton St. e15.	27G 40	
Ashton Ter. w14.	10P 59	
Ashtree Av. Mit.	12Za 92	
Ash Tree Dell nw9.	5B 19	
Ashurst Dri. Ilf.	33C 42	
Ashurst Rd. n12.	13Ac 15	
Ashurst St. sw11.	13R 72	
Ashurst Wk. Cro.	22Ze 91	
Ashvale Rd. sw17.	13X 83	
Ashville Rd. e11.	27E 40	
Ashwater Rd. se12.	29W 89	
Ashwell Gro. n18.	20Ac 17	
Ashwell Rd. e3.	24J 52	
Ashwin St. e8.	21G 37	
Ashworth Rd. w9.	11K 48	
Aske St. n1.	20K 51	
Askew Cres. w12.	7N 58	
Askew Rd. w12.	7N 58	
Askew St. e9.	23H 38	
Askham Rd. w12.	7N 58	
Aslett St. sw18.	11U 72	
Asmara Rd. nw2.	10F 33	
Asmun's Hill nw11.	11B 21	
Asmun's Pl. nw11.	11B 21	
Aspenlea Rd. w6.	9Q 59	
Aspinall Rd. se4.	23S 76	
Aspinden Rd. se16.	22P 64	
Aspland Gro. e8.	22G 38	
Aspley Rd. sw18.	11U 72	
Asplins Rd. n17.	22Aa 17	
Assam St. e1.	21L 52	
Assembly Pass. e1.	23L 52	
Astbury Rd. se15.	22R 76	
Astell St. sw3.	13P 60	
Astey's Row n1.	19H 37	
Astle St. sw11.	14R 73	
Astley Av. nw2.	9F 33	
Astley St. se1.	21P 63	
Aston Av. Har.	1C 18	
Aston Rd. sw20.	8Za 92	
Aston Rd. w5.	2L 44	
Aston St. e14.	24L 53	
Astonville St. sw18.	10V 82	
Astrop Ter. w6.	8N 58	
Astwood Mews sw7.	12O 60	
Asylum Rd. se15.	22Q 64	
Atalanta St. sw6.	9R 71	
Atbara Rd. Twi.	1aY 93	
Atheldene Rd. sw18.	11V 83	
Athelney St. se6.	25X 88	
Athelstane Rd. e3.	24J 53	
Athelstane Rd. n4.	18E 36	
Athelstone Rd. Har.	1cAa 12	
Athenæum Rd. n20.	13Ae 14	
Athenlay Rd. se15.	29U 76	
Atherden Rd. e5.	23F 38	
Atherfold Rd. sw9.	16S 74	
Atherton Rd. e7.	28G 40	
Atherton St. sw11.	13R 72	
Athlone Rd. sw2.	17V 85	
Athlone St. nw5.	15G 35	
Athol Rd. Ilf.	36D 42	
Athol St. e14.	27M 54	
Atkins Rd. e10.	26C 27	
Atkins Rd. sw12.	15V 84	
Atkinson St. se14.	24Q 65	
Atlantic Rd. sw9.	18T 74	
Atlas Gdns. se7.	30P 67	
Atlas Rd. e13.	29J 54	
Atley Rd. e3.	25J 53	
Atney Rd. sw15.	9T 71	
Atterbury Rd. n4.	18C 24	
Atterbury St. sw1.	16P 62	
Attewood Av. nw10.	5A 31	
Attneave St. wc1.	18K 50	
Atwell Rd. se15.	22S 76	
Atwell St. se15.	22S 76	
Atwood Av. Kew.	3R 69	
Aubert Pk. n5.	18F 36	
Aubrey Rd. e17.	26A 27	
Aubrey Rd. n8.	17C 24	
Aubrey Rd. w8.	10N 59	
Aubrey St. e7.	29F 40	
Aubrey Wk. w8.	10N 59	
Auckland Hill se27.	19X 86	
Auckland Rd. e3.	24J 53	
Auckland Rd. e10.	26E 39	
Auckland Rd. se19.	21Z 90	
Auckland Rd. sw11.	13T 72	
Auckland Rd. Ilf.	33D 42	
Auckland St. se11.	17P 62	
Audley Gdns. Ilf.	36E 42	
Audley Rd. nw4.	8C 20	
Audley Rd. w5.	3L 44	
Audley Rd. Rich.	2T 68	
Audrey Rd. Ilf.	33F 42	
Audrey St. e2.	22J 52	
Augusta St. e14.	26M 53	
Augustine Rd. w14.	9O 59	
Augustus Rd. sw19.	9V 82	
Augustus Rd. w6.	8O 58	
Augustus St. nw1.	15J 49	
Aulay St. se1.	21Q 64	
Aulton Pl. se11.	18P 62	
Aurelia Gdns. Cro.	17Zc 90	
Aurelia Rd. Cro.	17Zd 91	
Auriol Rd. w14.	9O 50	
Austin Friars ec2.	20L 51	

Austin Rd. sw11. 14R 73
Austin St. e2. 21K 51
Austral St. se11. 18O 62
Australian Av. ec1. 19L 51
Autumn St. e3. 25J 53
Avalon Rd. sw6. 11R 72
Avarn Rd. sw17. 14Y 84
Avebury Rd. e11. 27D 28
Avebury Rd. sw19. 10Z 92
Aveley Rd. e5. 22E 38
Aveline St. se11. 18P 62
Ave Maria La. ec4. 19M 51
Avenell Rd. n5. 19F 36
Avenons Rd. e13. 29L 54
Avenue Cres. w3. 4N 57
Avenue Gdns. sw14. 5S 69
Avenue Gdns. w3. 4N 57
Avenue Rd. e3. 25K 53
Avenue Rd. e5. 22F 38
Avenue Rd. e7. 29G 41
Avenue Rd. e11. 27F 40
Avenue Rd. n6. 16C 23
Avenue Rd. n12. 12Ac 14
Avenue Rd. n15. 20B 25
Avenue Rd.
 nw8. 1-91 & 2-86.
 nw3. 93, 88 & up. 13H 34
Avenue Rd. nw10. 6J 46
Avenue Rd. se13. 26T 77
Avenue Rd.
 se20. 1-55 & 2-50.
 Bec. remainder. 23Za 90
Avenue Rd. se25. 21Za 90
Avenue Rd. w3. 4N 57
Avenue Rd. w6. 8N 58
Avenue Rd. w13. 1aM 94
Avenue Rd. Bre. 1P 56
Avenue, The, e5. 22D 26
Avenue, The, e11. 30C 29
Avenue, The, n3. 11Aa 14
Avenue, The, n3. 15H 35
Avenue, The, n8. 18A 24
Avenue, The, n10. 16Aa 15
Avenue, The, n11. 15Ac 15
Avenue, The, n17. 20A 25
Avenue, The, nw3. 12D 22
Avenue, The, nw6. 9H 33
Avenue, The, se3. 28S 78
Avenue, The, se3. 29R 79
Avenue, The, se10. 27R 78
Avenue, The, se19. 20Y 86
Avenue, The, sw4. 14T 73
Avenue, The, sw17. 15W 84
Avenue, The, w4. 6O 57
Avenue, The, w13. 6L 44
Avenue, The, Cro. 20Zf 91
Avenue, The, Kew. 3R 68
Avenue, The, Twi. 1aT 93
Avenue, The, Wem. 3D 19
Avenue, The, e11. 29E 40
Avenue Pk. Rd. se27.
 18W 85
Averill St. w6. 9Q 59
Avery Row w1. 15M 49
Aveton Rd. n2. 13A 22
Aviary St. e16. 28L 54
Avignon Rd. se4. 23S 76
Avington Gro. se20. 22Z 90
Avoca Rd. sw17. 14X 84
Avon Rd. e17. 27A 28
Avondale Av. n12. 12Ac 14
Avondale Av. nw2. 6E 32
Avondale Rise se15. 21S 75
Avondale Rd. e16. 28L 54
Avondale Rd. e17. 25D 27
Avondale Rd. n2. 12Aa 14

Avondale Rd. n13. 18Ad 16
Avondale Rd. n15. 19B 25
Avondale Rd. sw14. 5S 69
Avondale Rd. sw19. 11Y 82
Avondale Rd. Har. 1bA 12
Avondale Sq. se1. 21P 64
Avondale Pk. Gdns. w11.
 9M 47
Avondale Pk. Rd. w11. 9M 47
Avonley Rd. se14. 23Q 64
Avonmore Rd. w14. 10O 59
Avonmouth St. se1. 19O 63
Awfield Rd. n17. 20Aa 17
Axe St. Bar. 34J 43
Axholme Av. Edg. 4Ab 13
Aybrook St. w1. 14L 49
Aycliffe Rd. w12. 7M 46
Aylesbury Rd. se17. 20P 63
Aylesbury St. ec1. 18K 50
Aylesbury St. nw10. 5E 31
Aylesford St. sw1. 16P 61
Aylestone Av. nw6. 9H 33
Ayliffe St. se1. 19O 63
Aylmer Rd. e11. 28D 28
Aylmer Rd. n2. 13B 22
Aylmer Rd. w12. 6N 58
Aylton St. se16. 23O 64
Aylward St. se23. 23W 87
Aylward Rd. sw20. 10Za 92
Aynhoe Rd. w14. 9O 59
Aynscombe La. sw14. 4S 69
Ayres St. se1. 19N 63
Ayrsome Rd. n16. 20E 37
Aysgarth Rd. se21. 20U 75
Aytoun Rd. sw9. 17S 74
Azenby Rd. se15. 21S 75
Azof St. se10. 28P 66

Baalbec Rd. n5. 19G 37
Babington Rd. nw4. 8A 20
Babington Rd. sw16. 16Y 84
Babmaes St. sw1. 16M 49
Bacchus Wk. n1. 20J 51
Baches St. n1. 20K 51
Back Hill ec1. 18K 50
Back La. nw3. 12F 34
Back La. se10. 26S 78
Back La. se15. 22Q 64
Back La. Bar. 34J 43
Back Rd. e17. 26B 28
Back Church La. e1. 22M 52
Bacon Gro. se1. 21O 63
Bacon La. nw9. 4A 19
Bacon La. Edg. 4Ab 13
Bacon St.
 e1. 1-21 & 2-22.
 e2. 23, 24 & up. 21K 51
Baden Rd. n8. 17A 24
Baden Rd. Ilf. 33G 43
Badgers Hole, Cro. 23Zg 91
Badlis Rd. e17. 25A 27
Badminton Rd. sw12. 14U 73
Badric Rd. sw11. 12S 72
Badsworth Rd. se5. 19R 75
Baggallay St. e3. 24L 53
Bagley's La. sw6. 11R 72
Bagshot St. se17. 20P 63
Baildon St. se8. 25R 77
Bailey St. se5. 19Q 63
Baillie's Wk. w5. 2N 56
Baker Rd. nw10. 6H 31
Baker St. e1. 22L 52
Baker St. e2. 23K 52
Baker St. sw9. 18R 74
Baker St. w1. 14L 49

Baker's Av. e17. 26C 27
Bakers End sw20. 9Za 92
Baker's Hill e5. 23D 26
Baker's La. n6. 14C 23
Baker's La. w5. 2M 44
Baker's Mews w1. 14L 49
Baker's Row e15. 28J 54
Baker's Row ec1. 18K 50
Balaam St. e13. 29K 55
Balaclava Rd. se1. 21P 63
Balchier Rd. se22. 22U 76
Balcombe St. nw1. 14K 49
Balcorne St. e9. 23H 38
Balderton St. w1. 14M 49
Baldock St. e3. 26J 53
Baldry Gdns. sw16. 17Y 85
Baldwin Cres. se5. 19R 75
Baldwin St. ec1. 20K 51
Baldwin Ter. n1. 19J 51
Baldwin's Gdns. ec1. 18L 50
Baldwyn Gdns. w3. 5M 45
Bale St. e1. 24L 52
Balfern Gro. w4. 6P 58
Balfern St. sw11. 13R 72
Balfour Av. w7. 1bM 94
Balfour Gro. n20. 14Ad 15
Balfour Pl. w1. 14M 49
Balfour Rd. n5. 19F 37
Balfour Rd. n9. 22Ad 17
Balfour Rd. se25. 21Zc 90
Balfour Rd. sw19. 11Z 92
Balfour Rd. w3. 5L 45
Balfour Rd. w13. 1aN 94
Balfour Rd. Har. 1cB 12
Balfour Rd. Ilf. 33E 42
Balgowan St. se18. 35P 95
Balham Gro. sw12. 14V 84
Balham Hill sw12. 15U 73
Balham Rd. n9. 22Ae 17
Balham High Rd.
 sw12. 1-197 & 2-222.
 sw17. 199, 224 & up.
 14W 84
Balham New Rd. sw12.
 15V 84
Balham Pk. Rd. sw12. 14V 84
Balham Station Rd. sw12.
 14V 84
Ball St. w8. 11N 60
Ballamore Rd. se12. 29X 89
Ballance Rd. e9. 24G 38
Ballantine St. sw18. 11T 72
Ballards La. n3&n12. 11Aa 14
Ballards Rd. nw2. 7E 32
Ballater Rd. sw2. 17T 74
Ballater Rd. Cro. 21Zg 91
Ballina St. se23. 23V 87
Ballingdon Rd. sw11. 14U 73
Balliol Rd. n17. 20Aa 17
Balliol Rd. w10. 9L 47
Ballnacraig Av. nw10. 6F 32
Balloch Rd. se6. 27W 89
Ballogie Av. nw10. 6F 32
Balls Pond Rd. n1. 20G 37
Balmes Rd. n1. 20H 37
Balmoral Gdns. w13. 1aN 94
Balmoral Gdns. Ilf. 36E 42
Balmoral Rd. e7. 30G 41
Balmoral Rd. e10. 26E 39
Balmoral Rd. nw2. 8G 32
Balmoral St. n19. 15E 35
Balmuir Gdns. sw15. 8T 70
Balthazar Rd. n17. 21A 26
Baltic St. ec1. 19K 51
Balvernie Gro. sw18. 10V 82
Bamford Av. Wem. 3H 30

Bamford Rd. Bar. 34H 43
Bamford Rd. Bec. 26Y 88
Bampton Rd. se23 23W 87
Banbury Rd. e9. 24H 38
Banbury St. sw.11 13R 72
Banchory Rd. se3. 29R 79
Bancroft Av. n2. 13B 22
Bancroft Rd. e1. 23K 52
Bandon Rd. e2. 23J 52
Bangalore St. sw15. 9S 71
Banim St. w6. 8O 58
Banister Rd. w10. 9J 47
Banister St. e9. 23G 38
Bank Av. Mit. 12Za 92
Bank End se1. 19N 63
Bankfoot Rd. Brom. 28Y 89
Bankhurst Rd. se6. 25V 88
Bankside se1. 19M 51
Bankton Rd. sw2. 18T 74
Bankwell Rd. se13. 28T 78
Banner St. ec1. 19K 51
Banning St. se10. 27P 66
Bannockburn Rd. se18 35P 95
Banstead Gdns. n9. 20Ad 17
Banstead St. se15. 22S 76
Banstock Rd. Edg. 5Ab 13
Banyard Rd. se18. 22O 64
Barandon St. w11. 9M 47
Barbara St. n7. 18G 36
Barbel St. se1. 18O 62
Barbers Alley e13. 29K 55
Barbers Rd. e15. 26J 53
Barbican ec1. 19L 51
Barbot St. n9. 22Ad 17
Barchard St. sw18. 11T 72
Barchester Rd. Har. 1cAa 12
Barchester St. e14. 26L 53
Barclay Rd. e11. 28D 28
Barclay St. n?. 30L 55
Barclay Rd. e17. 20C 21
Barclay Rd. sw6. 11Q 59
Barclay Rd. Cro. 20S 92
Barclay Rd. W. n18. 20Ab 17
Barclay St. nw1. 16J 49
Barcombe Av. sw2. 17W 85
Barden St. se18. 35R 95
Bardolph Rd. n7. 17F 36
Bardsley Rd. Mor. 11Zb 92
Bardwell St. n7. 17G 36
Barfett St. w10. 10K 47
Barfield Av. n20. 14Ad 15
Barfield Rd. e11. 28D 28
Barford St. n1. 18J 50
Barforth Rd. se15. 22T 76
Barge House St. se1. 18M 50
Bargery Rd. se6. 26W 88
Barham Rd. Cro. 19Zg 91
Baring Rd. se12. 29V 89
Baring Rd. Cro. 21Ze 91
Baring St. n1. 20J 51
Bark Pl. w2. 11M 48
Barkham Rd. n17. 20Ab 17
Barking Rd. e6. 32J 43
Barking Rd.
e16. 1-233 & 2-242.
e13. 235, 244 & up. 28L 54
Barkston Gdns. sw5. 11P 60
Barkworth Rd. se16. 22P 04
Barlborough St. se14. 23Q 64
Barlby Gro. w10. 8L 46
Barlby Rd. w10. 8L 46
Barley La. Ilf. 37D 42
Barlow Rd. w3. 4M 45
Barlow St. se17. 20P 63
Barmeston Rd. se6. 25W 88

Barmore St. sw11. 12S 72
Barmouth Rd. sw18. 12U 72
Barmouth Rd. Cro. 23Zf 91
Barn Hill nw10. 4D 19
Barn Rise Wem. 4D 19
Barn St. n16. 20E 37
Barn Way Wem. 4D 19
Barnabas Rd. e9. 24G 38
Barnabas St. sw1. 14P 61
Barnard Hill n10. 15Aa 15
Barnard Rd. sw11. 13T 72
Barnardo St. e1. 23M 52
Barnby Pl. e15. 27J 54
Barnby St. e15. 27J 54
Barnby St. nw1. 16J 49
Barnes Av. sw13. 7Q 58
Barnes St. e14. 24M 53
Barnes Ter. sw13. 6R 70
Barnet Gro. e2. 22K 52
Barnet La. n20. 10Af 14
Barnet Way Edg. 6Ad 13
Barnfield Av. Cro. 23Zf 91
Barnfield Rd. se18. 33Q 95
Barnfield Rd. se19. 20Y 86
Barnfield Rd. w5. 1K 44
Barnfield Rd. Edg. 5Aa 13
Barnham St. se1. 20N 63
Barn Hill Rd. nw10. 4E 31
Barnsbury Gro. n1. 18H 36
Barnsbury Pk. n1. 18H 36
Barnsbury Rd. n1. 18J 50
Barnsbury Sq. n1. 18H 36
Barnsbury St. n1. 18H 36
Barnsbury Ter. n1. 18H 36
Barnsdale Rd. w9. 10K 47
Barnsley St. e1. 22K 52
Barnwell Rd. sw2. 18T 74
Barnwood Rd. se16. 29N 67
Baron Rd. e16. 28L 54
Baron St. n1. 18J 50
Baroness Rd. e2. 21K 51
Baronet Rd. n17. 22Aa 17
Baron's Pl. se1. 18N 62
Barons, The Twi. 1aU 95
Barons Ct. Rd. w14. 10P 59
Baronsfield Rd. Twi. 1aU 95
Baronsmead Rd. sw13. 7R 70
Baronsmede w5. 3N 56
Baronsmere Rd. n2. 14B 23
Barque St. e.14 26P 66
Barratt Av. n22. 17aa 16
Barret's Grn. Rd. nw10. 5J 45
Barrett Rd. e17. 27B 28
Barrett St. w1. 14M 49
Barretts Gro. n16. 21F 37
Barrhill Rd. sw2. 17W 85
Barriedale se14. 24S 77
Barringer Rd. n10. 14Aa 15
Barrington Rd. e12. 33G 43
Barrington Rd. n8. 16B 24
Barrington Rd. sw9. 18S 74
Barrow Clo. n21. 19Ad 16
Barrow Rd. sw16. 16Y 84
Barrow Rd. Cro. 18Zh 91
Barrowgate Rd. w4. 5P 57
Barrow Hill Rd. nw8. 13J 48
Barrowell Grn. n21. 19Ad 16
Barrs Rd. nw10. 5G 31
Barry Av. n15. 21C 25
Barry Rd. nw10. 5H 31
Barry Rd. se22. 21U 75
Barset Rd. se15. 22S 76
Barston Rd. se27. 19W 86

Barth Rd. se18. 35P 95
Bartholomew Clo. ec1. 19L 51
Bartholomew La. ec2. 20M 51
Bartholomew Rd. nw5. 16G 35
Bartholomew Sq. ec1. 19K 51
Bartholomew St. se1. 20O 63
Bartholomew Villas nw5. 15G 35
Bartholomews Rd. e6. 32J 43
Bartle Av. e6. 31J 43
Bartlett St. Cro. 19Zg 91
Bartlett's Bldgs. ec4 18L 50
Bartley St. sw2. 17U 74
Barton Rd. w14. 9P 59
Barton St. sw1. 17O 62
Bartram Rd. se4. 24U 77
Bartrip St. e9. 24G 39
Barwick Rd. e7. 29F 41
Bashley Rd. nw10. 5K 45
Basil St. sw3. 14O 61
Basing Ct. se15. 21R 75
Basing Hill nw11. 10D 21
Basing Pl. e2. 21K 51
Basing Rd. se15 21R 75
Basing Rd. w11. 10L 47
Basinghall St. ec2. 20L 51
Baskerville Rd. sw18. 13U 72
Basket Gdns. se9. 31U 79
Basnett Rd. sw11. 14S 73
Bassano St. se22. 21T 75
Bassant Rd. se18. 35Q 95
Bassein Pk. Rd. w12. 7N 58
Bassett Rd. w10. 9L 47
Bassett St. nw5. 14G 35
Bassingham Rd. sw18. 12U 72
Bassingham Rd. Wem. 2G 30
Basterfield St. ec1. 19K 51
Bastion Rd. se2. 36Q 95
Bastwick St. ec1. 19K 51
Basuto Rd. sw6. 11R 71
Batavia Rd. se14. 24R 77
Batchelor Pl. se5. 20R 75
Bateman St. w1. 16M 50
Bateman's Row. ec2. 20K 51
Bates Cres. Cro. 18Zh 91
Bateson St. se18. 35P 95
Bath Gro. e2. 21J 52
Bath Pl. ec2. 21K 51
Bath Rd. e7. 31H 41
Bath Rd. e15. 28H 40
Bath Rd. n9. 23Ae 17
Bath Rd. w4. 6O 58
Bath Rd. Mit. 12Zb 92
Bath St. e1. 21J 52
Bath St. e1. 22L 52
Bath St. e14. 26M 53
Bath St. ec1. 20K 51
Bath Ter. se1. 19O 63
Bath Way se18. 33P 95
Bathgate Rd. sw19. 9W 82
Bathurst Gdns. nw10. 8J 46
Bathurst Gdns. Ilf. 33E 42
Bathurst Mews w2. 13M 48
Bathurst Rd. Ilf. 20Ab 17
Bathurst St. w2. 12M 48
Batley Rd. n16. 21F 37
Batoum Gdns. w6 8O 59
Batson St. w12. 7N 58
Batsworth Rd. Mit. 12Za 92
Batten St. sw11. 13S 72
Batten's Yard se15. 22R 76
Battersea Bridge sw3. 13Q 60

Battersea Rise sw11. 13T 72
Battersea Bridge Rd. sw11. 13R 72
Battersea Church Rd. sw11. 13R 72
Battersea Pk. Rd. sw8. 1-179 & 2-18 sw11. 20,181 & up 13R 72
Battery Pl. Rich. 2S 68
Battle Bridge La. se1.20N 63
Battlebridge Rd. nw1. 17J 50
Battledean Rd. n5. 18G 36
Batty St. e1. 22M 52
Bavent Rd. se5. 19S 75
Bawdale Rd. se22. 21U 75
Bawtree Rd. se14. 24Q 65
Bawtry Rd. n20. 14Ad 15
Baxendale St. e2. 21J 52
Baxter Rd. e16. 30M 55
Baxter Rd. n1. 20G 37
Baxter Rd. n18. 22Ac 17
Baxter Rd. Ilf. 33G 43
Bay St. e8. 21H 37
Bayer St. ec1. 19K 51
Bayfield Rd. se9. 30T 79
Bayford Rd nw10. 9K 47
Bayford St. e8. 22H 38
Bayham Pl. nw1. 16J 49
Bayham Rd. w13 1aM 94
Bayham Rd. Mor. 11Zb 92
Bayham St. nw1. 15H 35
Bayham Rd. w4. 5N 57
Bayley St. wc1. 16L 50
Baylin Rd. sw18. 11U 72
Baynes St. nw1. 16H 35
Bayonne Rd. w6. 9Q 59
Bayston Rd n16 21F 37
Bayswater Rd. w2. 11M 48
Baythorne St. e3. 25L 53
Bay Tree Rd. sw2. 17T 74
Bazely St. e14. 26M 53
Bazon St. se1. 18N 62
Beachboro' Rd. se6. 26X 89
Beachcroft Rd. e11. 28E 40
Beachy Rd. e3. 25H 39
Beacon Hill n7. 17G 36
Beacon Rd. se13. 27U 78
Beaconsfield Rd. e10. 27E 40
Beaconsfield Rd. e16. 28L 54
Beaconsfield Rd. e17. 25C 27
Beaconsfield Rd. e18. 28A 28
Beaconsfield Rd.n9. 22Ad 17
Beaconsfield Rd.n11.15Ac 15
Beaconsfield Rd.n15 21B 25
Beaconsfield Rd.nw10. 7G 32
Beaconsfield Rd. se3. 28R 78
Beaconsfield Rd. w4. 5O 57
Beaconsfield Rd. w5. 1N 56
Beaconsfield Rd.Cro.19Zd 91
Beaconsfield Rd. Twi.1aU 93
Beaconsfield Ter. w4. 4P 57
Beaconsfield Wk. sw6.10R 71
Beacontree Av. e17. 27A 28
Beacontree Rd. e11. 28D 28
Beadnell Rd. se23. 23V 87
Beadon Rd. w6. 8O 58
Beaford Gro. sw20. 9Zb 92
Beagle St. e1. 21M 51
Beak St. w1. 16M 49
Beal Rd. Ilf. 33E 42
Beale Rd. e3. 24J 53
Beale St. e13. 29J 54
Beamish Rd. n9. 22Ae 17
Bear Alley ec4. 18L 50
Bear Gdns. se1. 19N 63
Bear Lane se1. 19N 63

Bear St. wc2. 16M 50
Beardell St. se19. 20Y 86
Bearstead Rise se4. 24U 77
Beatrice Av. sw16. 17Zb 90
Beatrice Av. Wem. 3G 30
Beatrice Rd. e17. 25C 27
Beatrice Rd. n4. 18D 24
Beatrice St. e1. 22P 64
Beatrice St. e13. 29L 54
Beatson St. se16. 24N 64
Beauchamp Pl. sw3. 13O 60
Beauchamp Rd. e7. 30H 41
Beauchamp Rd. se19.19Za 90
Beauchamp Rd.se25.19Za 90
Beauchamp St. sw11.13T 72
Beauchamp Rd. Twi. 1bU 93
Beauchamp St. ec1. 18L 50
Beauclerc Rd. w6. 8O 58
Beaufort Av. Har. 1aA 12
Beaufort Gdns. se13 25S 77
Beaufort Gdns. nw4. 8C 21
Beaufort Gdns. sw3. 13O 60
Beaufort Gdns. Ilf. 33D 42
Beaufort Rd. w5. 3L 44
Beaufort St. sw3. 12P 60
Beaufoy Rd. e13. 29K 55
Beaufoy Rd. n17. 21Ab 17
Beaufoy Rd. sw11. 14S 73
Beaulieu Clo. nw9. 6A 20
Beaulieu Gdns. n21. 19Ae 16
Beaumont Av. w14. 10P 59
Beaumont Av. Rich. 2S 68
Beaumont Av. Wem. 1F 30
Beaumont Cres. w14. 10P 59
Beaumont Pl. w1. 16K 49
Beaumont Rd. e10. 26D 27
Beaumont Rd. e13. 30K 55
Beaumont Rd. n19. 17D 24
Beaumont Rd.sw19. 9U 71
Beaumont Rd. w4. 5O 57
Beaumont Sq. e1. 23L 52
Beaumont St. e1. 23L 52
Beaumont St. w1. 15L 49
Beauval Rd. se22. 21U 75
Beavor La. w6. 7P 58
Bebbington Rd. se18. 35P 95
Beccles Dri. Bar. 35G. 43
Beccles St. e14. 25M 53
Becher St. w11. 9M 47
Beck La. Cro. 23Zb 90
Beck Rd. e8. 22J 52
Beck Rd. e15. 27J 54
Beckenham Rd. n9. 20Ad 17
Beckenham Hill Rd. se6.
                      26Y 88
Beckford Rd. Cro. 21Zd 91
Becklow Rd. w12. 7N 58
Beckton Rd. e6 & e16.29L 54
Beckway St. se17. 20P 63
Beckwith Rd. se24. 19U 75
Beclands Rd. sw17. 14Y 84
Becmead Av. sw16. 16X 84
Becmead Av. Har. 1aB 12
Becondale Rd. se19. 20Y 86
Bective Rd. e7. 29F 41
Bective Rd. sw15. 10T 71
Beddingfield St. e15. 27G 40
Beddington Rd. Ilf. 36D 42
Beddome St. se17. 19P 63
Bedford Av. wc1. 16L 50
Bedford Clo. n10. 15Aa 15
Bedford Gdns. w8. 11N 59
Bedford Hill sw12. 15V 84
Bedford Pk. Cro. 19Ze 91
Bedford Pl. wc1. 17L 50
Bedford Pl. Cro. 19Ze 91

Bedford Rd. e6. 32J 43
Bedford Rd. e17. 25A 27
Bedford Rd. e18. 29A 29
Bedford Rd. n2. 13A 22
Bedford Rd. n8. 16C 24
Bedford Rd. n15. 20B 25
Bedford Rd. n22. 17Aa 15
Bedford Rd. sw4. 16T 74
Bedford Rd. w4. 5O 57
Bedford Rd. w13. 1aM 94
Bedford Rd. Har. 1dB 12
Bedford Rd. Ilf. 33F 42
Bedford Rd. Twi. 1dW 93
Bedford Row wc1. 17L 50
Bedford Sq. wc1. 16L 50
Bedford St. e1. 22L 52
Bedford St. e14. 27M 54
Bedford St. se17. 19P 63
Bedford St. wc2. 17M 50
Bedford Ter. n7. 18E 36
Bedford Wk. w8. 11N 59
Bedfordbury wc2. 17M 50
Bedgebury Rd. se9. 30T 79
Bedivere Rd. se12. 29X 89
Bedwardine Rd.se19.20Z 90
Bedwell Rd. n17. 20Aa 17
Beebey Rd. e16. 29L 55
Beech Dri. n2. 14A 23
Beech Gdns. w5. 2N 56
Beech Rd. n11. 17Ab 16
Beech Rd. sw16. 17Zb 90
Beech St. ec1. 19L 51
Beech St. sw8. 17Q 62
Beech Wk. nw7. 6Ac 13
Beechcroft Av. nw11. 10C 21
Beechcroft Gdns Wem. 3E 30
Beechcroft Rd. sw14. 4S 69
Beechcroft Rd. sw17.13W 83
Beechdale n21. 18Ae 16
Beechdale Rd. sw2. 17U 74
Beeches sw17. 13W 83
Beechfield Rd. n4. 19C 25
Beechfield Rd. se6. 25W 88
Beecholme Rd. e5. 22F 38
Beech House Rd. Cro.
                      19Zf 91
Beechmore Rd. sw11.14R 73
Beechmount Av. w7. 1cL 94
Beechwood Av. n3. 11A 21
Beechwood Av. Cro. 18Zb 90
Beechwood Av. Kew. 3R 69
Beechwood Rd. n8. 17A 24
Beehive La. Ilf. 32C 42
Beeleigh Rd. Mor. 11Zb 92
Beer La. ec3. 20M 51
Beethoven St. w10. 10J 47
Begbie Rd. se3. 30R 79
Begonia Wk. w12. 7M 46
Beira St. sw12. 15U 73
Belfast Rd. n16. 21E 37
Belfast Rd.se25. 22Zc 90
Belford Gro. se18. 32P 95
Belfour St. sw8. 16Q 62
Belgrade Rd. n16. 21F 37
Belgrave Gdns. nw8. 12J 48
Belgrave Mkt. Ilf. 32E 42
Belgrave Mews E. sw1.
                      14O 61
Belgrave Mews N. sw1.
                      14O 61
Belgrave Mews S. sw1.14O 61
Belgrave MewsW.sw1.14O 61
Belgrave Pl. sw1. 14O 61
Belgrave Rd. e10. 26D 28
Belgrave Rd. e11. 29E 40

Belgrave Rd. E13.	30K 55
Belgrave Rd. E17.	25C 27
Belgrave Rd. SE25.	21Zb 90
Belgrave Rd. sw1.	15P 61
Belgrave Rd. sw13.	6Q 58
Belgrave Rd. Ilf.	32E 42
Belgrave Rd. Mit.	12Za 92
Belgrave Sq. sw1.	14O 61
Belgrave St. E1.	24M 52
Belgrave St. wc1.	17K 50
Belgrave Wk. Mor.	12Zb 92
Belham St. SE5.	20R 75
Belhaven St. E3.	24K 53
Belinda Rd. sw9.	18S 74
Belitha Villas N1.	18H 36
Bell Grn. SE26.	24X 88
Bell La. E1.	21L 51
Bell La. NW4.	9B 21
Bell La. sw18.	11T 71
Bell La. Twi.	1bV 93
Bell Rd. E3.	20L 53
Bell St. NW1.	13L 48
Bell St. SE10.	26Q 65
Bell Yard wc2.	18M 50
Bellamy Dri. Har.	1aAa 12
Bellamy St. sw12.	14U 73
Bellasis Av. sw2.	16W 85
Bellefields Rd. sw9.	17S 74
Bellenden Rd. SE15.	21S 75
Belleville Rd. sw11.	13U 72
Bellevue Pk. Cro.	19Zb 90
Bellevue Rd. E17.	27A 28
Bellevue Rd. N11.	15Ac 15
Bellevue Rd. NW4.	9B 21
Bellevue Rd. sw13.	7R 70
Bellevue Rd. sw17.	13V 83
Belle Vue Ter. NW4.	9B 21
Bellew St. sw17.	12X 83
Bellingham Grn. SE6.	25X 88
Bellingham Rd. SE6.	26X 88
Bellot St. SE10.	28P 66
Belle Gdn. Rd. SE15.	21R 76
Belltrees Gro. sw16.	17Y 85
Bellwood Rd. SE15.	23T 76
Belmont Av. N9.	22Ae 17
Belmont Av. N13.	17Ac 16
Belmont Av. N15.	19A 25
Belmont Av. Wem.	3H 30
Belmont Clo. N20.	12Ae 14
Belmont Gro. SE13.	27S 78
Belmont Gro. w4.	5O 57
Belmont Hill SE13.	27S 78
Belmont Pk. SE13.	27T 78
Belmont Rd. E15.	28K 54
Belmont Rd. N15.	19B 25
Belmont Rd. SE13.	27S 78
Belmont Rd. SE25.	22Zc 90
Belmont Rd. sw4.	16S 73
Belmont Rd. w4.	5P 57
Belmont Rd. Har.	1bA 12
Belmont Rd. Ilf.	34F 42
Belmont St. NW5.	14H 35
Belmont Pk. Rd. E10.	26C 27
Belmore St. sw8.	16R 74
Belper St. N1.	18H 36
Belsham St. E9.	23G 38
Belsize Av. N13.	18Ab 16
Belsize Av. NW3.	13G 34
Belsize Av. w13.	1aO 94
Belsize Cres. NW3.	13G 34
Belsize Gro. NW3.	13G 34
Belsize La. NW3.	13G 34
Belsize Pk. NW3.	13G 34
Belsize Pk.Gdns. NW3.	13G 34
Belsize Rd. NW6.	11H 34
Belsize Sq. NW3.	13G 34
Belsize Ter. NW3.	13G 34
Belson Rd. SE18.	32P 95
Belton Rd. E7.	30H 41
Belton Rd. E11.	28F 40
Belton Rd. N15.	21A 25
Belton Rd. NW2.	7G 32
Beltran Rd. sw6.	11S 72
Belvedere Av. sw19.	9Y 82
Belvedere Bldgs. SE1.	19N 63
Belvedere Cres. SE1.	17N 62
Belvedere Dri. sw19.	9Y 82
Belvedere Gro. sw19.	9Y 82
Belvedere Rd. E10.	24D 27
Belvedere Rd. SE1.	17N 62
Belvedere Rd. sw19.	21Z 90
Belvoir Rd. SE22.	22V 87
Bemerton St. N1.	17H 36
Bemish Rd. sw15.	9S 71
Bemsted Rd. E17.	25A 27
Benares Rd. SE18.	35P 95
Benbow Rd. w6.	8O 58
Benbow St. SE8.	25Q 65
Benbury Clo. Bec.	26Y 88
Bendemeer Rd. sw15.	9S 71
Bendish Rd. E6.	31H 43
Bendmore Rd. SE2.	36P 95
Bendon Valley sw18.	11V 83
Benedict Rd. sw9.	17S 74
Benedict Rd. Mit.	12Zb 92
Benfield St. sw11.	12S 72
Bengal Rd. Ilf.	33F 42
Bengarth Dri. Har.	1aAa 12
Bengeo St. E16.	29M 54
Bengeworth Rd. SE5.	19S 75
Benham St. sw11.	12S 72
Benhill Rd. SE5.	20R 75
Benin St. SE13.	27V 89
Benjamin St. EC1.	18L 50
Ben Jonson Rd. E1.	24L 52
Benledi St. E14.	27M 54
Benn St. E9.	24M 54
Bennerley Rd. sw11.	13T 72
Dennot Rd. E13.	30L 55
Bennet St. sw1.	15N 61
Bennett Pk. SE13.	28S 78
Bennett St. SE1.	18N 62
Bennett St. SE13.	26R 77
Bennett St. w4.	6P 58
Benningholm Rd. NW7.	6Ac 13
Bennington Rd. N17.	20Aa 17
Bennis Av. Wem.	3F 30
Bensham Clo. Cro.	19Zc 90
Bensham Gro. Cro.	19Za 90
Bensham La. Cro.	18Zd 91
Bensham Manor Rd. Cro.	19Zc 90
Benson Av. E6.	31K 55
Benson Rd. SE23.	23V 87
Benson Rd. Cro.	18Zf 91
Benthal Rd. N16.	21E 38
Bentham Rd. E9.	23G 38
Bentinck St. w1.	15L 49
Bentley Dri. Ilf.	34C 42
Bentley Rd. N1.	21G 37
Benton Gdns Ilf.	34D 42
Benton Rd. Ilf.	34D 42
Benton's La. SE27.	19X 86
Bentworth Rd.w12.	7M 46
Benwell Rd.N7.	18F 36
Benworth St. E3.	25K 53
Benyon Rd. N1.	20H 37
Berber Rd. sw11.	14T 73
Berens Rd. NW10.	9K 47
Beresford Av. w7.	1cL 94
Beresford Av. Barn.	14Ae 15
Beresford Av. Wem.	3H 30
Beresford Rd. N2.	13A 22
Beresford Rd. N5.	20G 37
Beresford Rd. N8.	18B 24
Beresford Rd. Har.	1cB 12
Beresford St. SE18.	33P 95
Berestede Rd. w6.	7P 58
Berger Rd. E9.	23G 38
Bergholt Cres. N16.	20D 25
Berkeley Mews w1.	14L 49
Berkeley Rd. E12.	31G 43
Berkeley Rd. N8.	16C 24
Berkeley Rd. N15.	20C 25
Berkeley Rd. NW9.	4B 19
Berkeley Rd. sw13.	7R 70
Berkeley Sq. w1.	15M 49
Berkeley St. w1.	15M 49
Berkhamsted Av. Wem.	3G 31
Berkley Rd. NW1.	14H 35
Berkshire Gdns. N13.	18Ab 16
Berkshire Rd. E9.	25G 39
Bermondsey Sq. SE1.	20O 03
Bermondsey St. SE1.	20N 63
Bermondsey Wall SE16.	21N 64
Bermuda St. E1.	23M 52
Bernard Av. w13.	1aN 94
Bernard Gdns. sw19.	10Y 82
Bernard Rd. N15.	21B 26
Bernard St. wc1.	17K 50
Bernays Gro. sw9.	17T 74
Berne Rd. Cro.	19Zc 90
Berner St. E1.	22M 52
Berners Mews w1.	16L 49
Berners Rd. N1.	18J 50
Berners Rd. N22.	18Aa 16
Berners St. w1.	16L 49
Berridge Grn. Edg.	4Ab 13
Berridge Rd. SE19.	20Y 86
Derry Clo. N21.	19Ae 16
Berry St. EC1.	19K 51
Berry St. NW10.	6G 32
Berry Way w5.	2O 56
Berryfield Rd. SE17.	19P 63
Berrylands sw20.	8Zb 92
Berryman's La. SE26.	23Y 87
Berrymead Gdns. w3.	5N 57
Berrymead Rd. w4.	5O 57
Bert Rd. Cro.	19Zc 90
Bertal Rd. sw17.	12X 83
Berthon St. SE8.	25Q 65
Bertie Rd. NW10.	7G 32
Bertram Rd. NW4.	8C 20
Bertrham St. N19.	15E 35
Bertrand St. SE13.	26S 77
Berwick Rd. E16.	30M 55
Berwick Rd. E17.	25B 27
Berwick Rd. N22.	19Aa 16
Berwick St. w1.	16M 49
Berwyn Rd. SE24.	18V 85
Berwyn Rd. Rich.	4T 69
Beryl Rd. w6.	9P 59
Besley St. sw16.	15Y 84
Bessborough Gdns. sw1.	16P 61
Bessborough Pl. sw1.	16P 62
Bessborough Rd. sw15.	7V 81
Bessborough Rd. Har.	1cD 12
Bessborough St. sw1.	16P 62
Bessemer Rd. SE5.	19S 75
Besson St. SE14.	23R 76
Bestwood St. SE8.	23P 75
Betchworth Rd. Ilf.	35E 42
Bethecar Rd. Har.	1bB 12
Bethell Av. E16.	28K 54

Bethell Av. Ilf.	33D 42	
Bethnal Grn. Rd.		
E1. 1-99 & 2-94		
E2. 96, 101 & up.	21K 51	
Bethune Av. N11.	14Ac 15	
Bethune Rd. N16.	20D 25	
Bethune Rd. NW10.	5K 45	
Bethwin Rd. SE5.	19Q 63	
Betstyle Rd. N11.	15Ad 15	
Betterton St. WC2.	17M 50	
Bettridge Rd. SW6.	10S 71	
Betts St. E1.	22M 52	
Beulah Clo. Edg.	4Ae 13	
Beulah Cres. Cro.	19Za 90	
Beulah Gro. Cro.	19Zd 91	
Beulah Hill SE19.	18Y 85	
Beulah Rd. E11.	28E 40	
Beulah Rd. E17.	26B 27	
Beulah Rd. SW19.	10Z 92	
Beulah Rd. Cro.	19Zb 90	
Bevan St. N1.	19J 51	
Bevenden St. N1.	20K 51	
Beverley Clo. SW13.	7R 70	
Beverley Gdns.NW11.	10C 21	
Beverley Gdns. SW13.	6S 70	
Beverley Gdns.Har.	1aAa 12	
Beverley Gdns. Wem.	3D 19	
Beverley La. SW19.	6X 81	
Beverley Path. SW13	6S 70	
Beverley Rd. E6.	31K 55	
Beverley Rd.SE20.	22Za 90	
Beverley Rd. SW13.	6S 70	
Beverley Rd. W4.	6P 58	
Beversbrook Rd. N19.	16E 36	
Beverstone Rd. SW2.	17T 74	
Beverstone Rd. Cro.	18Zb 90	
Bevington Rd. W10.	10L 47	
Bevington St. SE16.	22O 64	
Bevis Marks. EC3.	20L 51	
Bewdley St. N1.	18H 36	
Bewley St. E1.	22M 52	
Bewlys St.SE27.	18Y 85	
Bewick St. SW8.	15S 73	
Bexhill Rd. N11.	16Ac 15	
Bexhill Rd. SE4.	25U 77	
Bexhill Rd. SW14.	4S 69	
Bianca Rd. SE15.	21Q 63	
Bibbsworth Rd. N3.	10Aa 14	
Bicester Rd. SW14.	3S 69	
Bickenhall Mans. W1.	14L 49	
Bickersteth Rd. SW17.	13Y 84	
Bickerton Rd. N19.	15E 35	
Bickley Rd. E10.	26D 27	
Bickley St. SW17.	13Y 83	
Bickmore St. E14.	26M 53	
Bidborough St. WC1.	17K 50	
Bidder St. E16.	27L 54	
Biddestone Rd. N7.	17F 36	
Biddulph Rd. W9.	11K 48	
Bideford Rd. SE12.	28X 89	
Bidwell Gdns. N11.	16Aa 15	
Bidwell St. SE15.	22R 76	
Bifron St. SW10.	12Q 60	
Bifron St. Bar.	34J 43	
Big Hill E5.	22D 26	
Biggerstaff Rd. E15.	27J 54	
Biggin Hill SE19	18Z 90	
Biggin Way SE19.	19Z 90	
Bigginwood Rd. SE19.	18Z 90	
Biggs Row. SW15.	9S 71	
Bigland St. E1.	22M 52	
Bignell Rd.SE18.	33Q 95	
Bignold Rd. E7.	29F 41	
Bigwood Rd. NW11.	11B 22	
Billingsgate St. SE10.	26Q 65	
Billington Rd. SE14.	23R 76	
Billiter Av. EC3.	20M 51	
Billiter Sq. EC3.	20M 51	
Billiter St. EC3.	20M 51	
Billson St. E14.	27P 66	
Bilton Rd. Wem.	1H 30	
Bina Gdns. SW5.	12P 60	
Binden Rd. W12.	7N 58	
Binfield Rd. SW4.	17R 74	
Binfield Rd. Cro.	20Zg 91	
Bingfield St. N1.	17H 36	
Bingham Pl.W1.	14L 49	
Bingham Rd. Cro.	21Ze 91	
Bingley Rd. E16.	30M 55	
Binns Rd. W4.	5P 57	
Birch Av. N13.	19Ad 16	
Birch Av. N21.	19Ad 16	
Birch Gro. SE12.	28V 89	
Birch Gro. W3.	3M 45	
Birch Hill Cro.	23Zg 91	
Birchanger Rd. SE25.		
	21Zc 90	
Birchdale Rd. E7.	30G 41	
Birchen Gro. NW9.	5E 31	
Birchfield St. E14.	25M 53	
Birchin La. EC3.	20M 51	
Birchington Rd. N8.	16C 24	
Birchington Rd. NW6.	11H 34	
Birchlands Av. SW12.	14R 84	
Birch Tree Way Cro.	22Ze 93	
Birchwood Av. N10.	15A 23	
Birchwood Ct. NW9.	5Aa 13	
Birchwood Rd. SW17.	15Y 84	
Bird St. W1.	14M 49	
Birdcage Wk. N16.	21E 38	
Birdcage Wk. SW1.	16N 51	
Birdhurst Av. Cro.	19Zg 91	
Birdhurst Gdns. Cro.	20Zg 91	
Birdhurst Rise Cro.	20Zg 93	
Birdhurst Rd. SE18.	12T 72	
Birdhurst Rd. SW18.	13Y 83	
Birdhurst Rd. Cro.	20Zg 91	
Bird-in-Bush Rd. SE15.		
	21Q 64	
Birkbeck Av. W3.	5M 45	
Birkbeck Gro. W3.	5N 57	
Birkbeck Hill SE21.	19W 86	
Birkbeck Pl. SE21.	19W 86	
Birkbeck Rd. E8.	21G 37	
Birkbeck Rd. N8.	17B 24	
Birkbeck Rd. N12.	12Ac 14	
Birkbeck Rd. N17.	21Aa 17	
Birkbeck Rd. SW19.	11Y 83	
Birkbeck Rd. W3.	5N 57	
Birkbeck Rd. W5.	1O 56	
Birkbeck Rd. Cro.	23Za 90	
Birkbeck Rd. Ilf.	34C 42	
Birkbeck St. E2.	22K 52	
Birkdale Rd. SE2.	36P 95	
Birkhall Rd. SE6.	27W 89	
Birley Rd. N20.	12Ae 14	
Birley St. SW11.	14S 73	
Birnam Rd. N4.	17E 36	
Birstall Rd. N15.	21B 25	
Biscay Rd. W6.	9P 59	
Bisendon Rd. Cro.	20 Ze 91	
Bisham Gdns. N6.	15D 23	
Bishop Ken Rd. Har.	1bAa 12	
Bishop King'sRd. W14.		
	10O 59	
Bishops Av. E13.	29H 41	
Bishop's Av. SW6.	9R 71	
Bishop's Av. N2.	13C 22	
Bishop's Rd. E2.	23J 52	
Bishop's Rd. N6.	15C 23	
Bishop's Rd. SW6.	10R 71	
Bishop's Rd. W2.	12L 48	
Bishops Rd. W7.	1cN 94	
Bishops Rd. Cro.	18Ze 91	
Bishop's Ter. SE11.	18O 62	
Bishops Wk. Cro.	23Zh 91	
Bishopsgate EC2.	20L 51	
Bishop's Pk. Rd. SW6.	9R 71	
Bishop's Pk. Rd. SW16.		
	17Za 90	
Bishopsthorpe Rd. SE26.		
	23X 87	
Bishopswood Rd. N6.	14D 23	
Bispham Rd. W5.	3J 44	
Bisson Rd. E15.	27J 54	
Bisterne Av. E17.	27A 28	
Bittern St. SE1.	19N 63	
Black Boy La. N15.	19B 25	
Blackall St. EC2.	20K 51	
Blackburn Rd. NW6.	11G 34	
Blackburne's Mews W1.		
	14M 49	
Black Eagle St. E1.	21L 51	
Blackett St. SW15.	8S 71	
Blackfriars Br. EC4.	18M 50	
Blackfriars Rd. SE1.	18N 62	
Blackheath Hill SE10.	26R 77	
Blackheath Pk. SE3.	28S 78	
Blackheath Rise SE13.	26S 77	
Blackheath Rd. SE10.	26R 77	
Blackheath Vale SE3.	28S 78	
Blackhorse La. E17.	24A 26	
Black Horse La. Cro.	21Zd 91	
Blackhorse Rd. E17.	24B 26	
Blackhorse Rd. SE8.	24Q 65	
Blacklands Rd. SE6.	26Y 88	
Blacklands Ter. SW3.	14P 61	
Black Lion La. W6.	7P 58	
Black Lion Yd. E1.	21L 52	
Blackmore's Gro. Ted.	1bY 93	
Blacks Rd. W6.	8P 58	
Blackshaw Rd. SW17.	12X 83	
Blackstock Rd.		
N4. 1-175 & 2-156.		
N5. 158, 177 & up.	19E 36	
Blackstone Rd. E8.	22H 38	
Blackstone Rd. NW2.	9F 33	
Blackthorn St. E3.	25L 53	
Blackthorne Av. Cro.		
	22Ze 91	
Blackwall La. SE10.	28P 66	
Blackwall Tunnell E14.		
	27 N 66	
Blackwall Way E14.	27M 54	
Blackwater St. SE22.	21U 75	
Blackwall Gdns. Edg.	4Ad 13	
Blackwood St. SE17.	19P 63	
Blagden's La. N14.	16Ae 15	
Blagdon Rd. SE13.	26U 77	
Blagrove Rd. W10.	10L 47	
Blair Av. NW9.	6D 20	
Blair St. E14.	27M 54	
Blairderry Rd. SW2.	17W 85	
Blake Av. Bar.	36J 43	
Blake Rd. E16.	28L 54	
Blake Rd. N11.	16Ab 15	
Blake Rd. SW6.	11R 72	
Blake Rd. Cro.	20Ze 91	
Blake Rd. Mit.	13Zb 92	
Blake Hall Cres. E11.	29E 41	
Blake Hall Rd. E11.	29E 29	
Blakeley Bldgs. SE10.	27N 66	
Blakeley Cotts. SE10.	27N 66	
Blakemore Rd.SW16.	16W 85	
Blakemore Rd. Cro.	17Zc 90	
Blakenham Rd. SW17.		
	14X 84	
Blakeney Clo. N20.	12Ae 14	

Blake's Rd. se15. 20Q 63
Blakesley Av. w5. 1L 44
Blakesley St. e1. 23M 52
Blakesware Gdns. n9.20Af 17
Blanchard Rd. e8. 22H 38
Blanche St. e16. 28L 54
Blanchland Rd. Mor.
  11Zc 92
Bland St. se9. 31T 79
Blandfield Rd. sw12. 14U 73
Blandford Clo. nw11. 12B 22
Blandford Mews w1. 14L 49
Blandford Rd. w4. 6O 58
Blandford Rd. w5. 2N 56
Blandford Rd. Cro. 23Zb 90
Blandford Rd. Ted. 1cY 93
Blandford Sq. nw1. 13K 48
Blandford St. w1. 14L 49
Blantyre St. sw10. 12Q 60
Blashford St. se13. 27V 89
Blawith Rd. Har. 1bB 12
Blechynden Mews w11.
  9M 47
Blechynden St.
  w11. 1-21 & 2-30.
  w10. 23, 32 & up. 9M 47
Blegborough Rd. sw16.
  15Y 84
Blendon Rd. se18. 34Q 95
Blendon Row se17. 20Q 63
Blenheim Av. Ilf. 33C 42
Blenheim Av. Wem. 2E 30
Blenheim Cres.w11. 10M 47
Blenheim Gdns. nw2. 8G 33
Blenheim Gro. se15. 21S 76
Blenheim Rd. e6. 31K 55
Blenheim Rd. e15. 28F 40
Blenheim Rd. e17. 24A 26
Blenheim Rd. n19. 17E 36
Blenheim Rd. n22. 18A 24
Blenheim Rd. nw8. 12J 48
Bolingbroke Rd. w14. 9O 59
Blenheim Rd. se20. 23Z 90
Blenheim Rd. sw20. 8Zb 92
Blenheim Rd. w4. 6O 58
Blenheim Ter. nw8. 12J 48
Blenkarne Rd. sw11.
  13U 72
Blessbury Rd. Edg. 5Ab 13
Blessington Rd. se13.
  27T 78
Blewett St. se17. 20P 63
Blind La. e6. 31K 55
Blissett St. se10. 26R 77
Blithdale Rd. se2. 36P 95
Blockhouse St. se15. 23Q 64
Blockley Rd. Har. 1aE 12
Blockley Rd. Wem. 1E 30
Bloemfontein Av. w12.8N 58
Bloemfontein Rd. w12. 7M 46
Blomfield Mews w2. 12L 48
Blomfield Rd. w9. 12L 48
Blomfield St. ec2. 20L 51
Blomfield St. w2. 12L 48
Blondel St. sw11. 14R 73
Blondin Av. w5. 1O 56
Blondin St. e3. 25J 53
Bloom Gro. se27. 18X 85
Bloomburg St. sw1. 16P 61
Bloomfield Rd. e3. 25L 53
Bloomfield Rd. n6. 15C 23
Bloomfield Rd. se18. 33Q 95
Bloomfield St. n17. 21Ab 17
Bloomfield Ter. sw1. 14P 61
Bloomhall Rd. se19. 20Y 86
Bloom Pk. Rd. sw6. 10Q 59
Bloomsbury Pl. w.1. 17L 50

Bloomsbury Sq. wc1. 17L 50
Bloomsbury St. wc1. 16L 50
Blossom St. e1. 21L 51
Blount St. e14. 24L 53
Bloxam Gdns. se9. 31U 79
Bloxhall Rd. e10. 24D 27
Blucher Rd. se5. 19R 75
Blue Anchor La. se15.21R 76
Blumer Gdns. Har. 2C 18
Blundell Rd. Edg. 6Ab 13
Blundell St. n7. 17H 36
Blunt Rd. Cro. 19Zg 91
Blurton Rd. e5. 23F 38
Blyth Rd. e15. 27H 40
Blytb Rd. e17. 24D 27
Blythe Hill se6. 25V 88
Blythe Rd. w14. 9O 59
Blythe St. e2. 22K 52
Blythe Vale se6. 24W 88
Blythe Hill La. se6. 24V 88
Blythswood Rd. Ilf. 36D 42
Blythwood Rd. n4. 17D 24
Boathouse Wk. se15. 21R 75
Bodmin Rd. Mor. 11Zc 92
Bodmin St. sw18. 11V 82
Bodney Rd. e8. 22G 38
Bognor St. se8. 16R 73
Bohemia Pl. e8. 23G 38
Bohn St. e1. 24L 52
Boileau Rd. sw13. 7Q 58
Boileau Rd. w5. 3L 44
Bolan St. sw11. 13R 72
Bolden St. se8. 26S 77
Boldero St. nw8. 13K 48
Boleyn Rd. e6. 31J 55
Boleyn Rd. e7. 29H 41
Boleyn Rd. n16. 21G 37
Bolina Rd. se16. 23P 64
Bolingbroke Gro. sw11.
  13T 72
Bolingbroke Rd. w14. 9O 59
Bolingbroke Wk. sw11.
  13R 72
Bollo Bridge Rd. w3. 4N 57
Bollo La.
  w4. 1-95 & 2-100,
  w3. 97-289. 4N 57
Bolney St. sw8. 17Q 62
Bolsover St. w1. 15L 49
Bolton Gdns. nw10. 9J 47
Bolton Gdns. sw5. 12P 60
Bolton Gdns. Ted. 1bY 93
Bolton Rd. e15. 28H 40
Bolton Rd. n18. 21Ac 17
Bolton Rd. nw8. 11H 34
Bolton Rd. nw10. 6H 32
Bolton Rd. w4. 4Q 57
Bolton Rd. w11. 10M 47
Bolton Rd. Har. 1cA 12
Bolton St. se5. 18Q 62
Bolton St. w1. 15N 61
Boltons, The sw10. 12P 60
Bolwell St. se11. 17P 62
Bombay St. se16. 22O 64
Bomore Rd. w11. 9M 47
Bonamy St. se1. 22P 64
Bonar Rd. se15. 21R 76
Bonchurch Rd. w11. 9L 47
Bonchurch Rd. w13. 1aN 94
Bond St. e15. 28G 40
Bond St. sw8. 17Q 62
Bond St. w4. 5P 57
Bond St. w5. 1M 44
Bond St. wc1. 18J 50
Bonfield Rd. se13. 27T 78
Bonham Rd. sw2. 17U 74

Bonheur Rd. w4. 5N 57
Bonhill St. ec2. 20K 51
Boniface St. se1. 17O 62
Bonner Rd. e2. 23J 52
Bonner St. e2. 23J 52
Bonnersfield Clo. Har.
  1bB 12
Bonnersfield La. Har. 1aB 12
Bonneville Rd. sw4. 15U 73
Bonnington Sq. sw8. 17Q 62
Bonny St. nw1. 15H 35
Bonser Rd. Twi. 1bW 93
Bonsor St. se5. 20Q 63
Bonville Rd. Bro. 28Y 89
Bonwell St. e2. 23K 52
Bookham St. n1. 20J 51
Boone St. se13. 28T 78
Boone's Rd. se13. 28T 78
Boord St. e14. 28O 66
Boot St. n1. 20K 51
Booth Rd. nw9. 6Aa 13
Booth St. e1. 21L 52
Boothby Rd. n19. 16E 35
Border Cres. se26. 22Y 87
Border Rd. se26. 22Y 87
Bordesley Rd. Mor. 11Zc 92
Boreham Rd. n22. 19Aa 16
Borgard Rd. se18. 32P 95
Borland Rd. se15. 23T 76
Borneo St. sw15. 8S 71
Borough Hill Cro. 18Zf 91
Borough Rd. Mit. 13Za 92
Borough Rd. se1. 19O 62
Borough High St. se1.
  19N 63
Borrett Rd. se17. 19P 63
Borrodale Rd. sw18. 11U 72
Borrowdale Av. Har.1aAa 12
Borthwick Rd. e15. 28F 40
Borthwick Rd. nw9. 7C 20
Bosbury Gdns. se6. 20X 89
Boscastle Rd. nw5. 15F 35
Boscawen St. se8. 24P 65
Boscombe Av. e10. 27D 28
Boscombe Rd. sw17. 14Y 84
Boscombe Rd. sw19. 11Z 92
Boscombe Rd. w12. 7N 58
Boss St. se1. 21N 63
Bostall Hill se2. 36P 95
Bostock St. e1. 22N 64
Boston Gdns. Cro. 17Zb 90
Boston Mews nw1. 14K 49
Boston Pl. nw1. 13K 48
Boston Rd. e6. 31K 55
Boston Rd. e17. 25C 27
Boston Rd. w7. 1bN 94
Boston Rd. Cro. 17Zd 91
Boston Rd. Edg. 5Ab 13
Boston St. e2. 22J 52
Boston Pk. Rd. Bre. 1P 55
Boston Thorpe Rd. w7.
  1cN 94
Boswell Rd. Cro. 19Zc 90
Bosworth Rd. n11. 17Ac 16
Bosworth Rd. w10. 10K 47
Botha Rd. e13. 30L 55
Bothwell St. w6. 9Q 59
Botolph La. ec3. 20M 51
Botolph Rd. e3. 26K 53
Botsford Rd. sw20. 9Za 92
Boulcott St. e1. 24M 52
Boulogne Rd. Cro. 19Zd 91
Bounces Rd. n9. 22Ae 17
Boundaries Rd. sw12.
  14W 84
Boundary La. se17. 19Q 63

Boundary Rd. E13. 30K 55
Boundary Rd. E17. 25C 27
Boundary Rd. N22. 19A 25
Boundary Rd. NW8. 12H 34
Boundary Rd. sw19. 12Y 83
Boundary Rd. w11. 9N 59
Boundary Rd. Bar. 34J 43
Boundary Row SE1. 18N 62
Boundary St. E2. 21K 51
Bounds Green Rd.
  N11 & N22. 16Ab 15
Bourdon Rd. SE20. 22Za 90
Bourdon St. w1. 15M 49
Bourke Rd. NW10. 6G 31
Bourn Av. N15. 20B 25
Bourne Av. N14. 17Ae 16
Bourne Hill N13. 17Ae 16
Bourne Pl. w4. 5P 57
Bourne Rd. E7. 29F 40
Bourne Rd. N8. 17C 24
Bourne St. Cro. 18Zf 91
Bourne Ter. w2. 11L 48
Bourne, The, N14. 17Ae 16
Bournemouth Rd. SE15.
  22S 76
Bournemouth Rd. sw19.
  10Z 92
Bourne's Pl. sw11. 13R 72
Bournevale Rd. sw16.
  16X 85
Bournville Rd. SE6. 25V 88
Bournewood Rd. SE6.
  36R 95
Bousfield Rd. SE14. 23S 76
Boutflower Rd. sw11. 13T 72
Bouverie Gdns. Har. 2C 18
Bouverie Rd. N16. 20E 37
Bouverie Rd. Har. 1dC 12
Bouverie St. EC4. 18M 50
Bouverie St. w2. 13L 48
Bovay Pl. N7. 17F 36
Bovay St. N7. 17F 36
Boveney Rd. SE23. 23V 87
Bovill Rd. SE23. 23V 87
Bovingdon Av. Wem. 4G 31
Bovingdon Rd. sw6. 11R 72
Bow La. EC4. 19M 51
Bow La. N12. 12Ab 14
Bow Rd. E3. 25K 53
Bow St. E15. 28G 40
Bow St. wc2. 17M 50
Bowater pl. SE3. 29R 79
Bowater Rd. SE18. 31O 67
Bow Common La. E3. 24L 53
Bowden St. SE11. 18P 62
Bowdon Rd. E17. 25C 27
Bowen Rd. Har. 1cC 12
Bowen St. E14. 26L 53
Bower Av. SE10. 28R 78
Bower Rd. E9. 25H 39
Bower St. E1. 23M 52
Bowerdean St. sw6. 11R 72
Bowes Rd.
  N13. 1-159 & 2-148
  N11. 150, 161 & up 17Ac 16
Bowes Rd. w3. 6M 45
Bowfell Rd. w6. 8Q 59
Bowick Av. E17. 25A 27
Bowland Rd. sw4. 16T 74
Bowles Rd. SE1. 21Q 64
Bowley St. E14. 24K 53
Bowling Grn. Clo.sw15.8V 81
Bowling Grn. La. EC1.18K 50
Bowling Grn. St. SE11.18Q 62
Bowling Grn. Wk. N1.20K 51
Bowman's Pl. N7. 17F 36

Bowness Rd. SE6. 26V 88
Bowood Rd. sw11. 14T 73
Bowrons Av. Wem. 2H 30
Bowyer St. SE5. 19Q 63
Box St. E3. 25L 53
Boxall Rd. SE21. · 20V 75
Boxley Rd. Mor. 12Zc 92
Boxley St. E16. 29N 67
Boxmoor Rd. Har. 1aA 12
Boxmoor St. w11. 9N 59
Boxworth Gro. N1. 18H 36
Boyce St. SE1. 18N 62
Boycroft Av. NW9. 5C 19
Boyd Rd. E16. 28M 54
Boyd Rd. sw19. 12Y 83
Boyd St. E1. 22M 52
Boyer Rd. NW6. 11K 47
Boyfield St. SE1. 19N 63
Boyland Rd. Bro. 28Y 89
Boyle St. w1. 15M 49
Boyne Av. NW4. 9B 21
Boyne Rd. SE13. 27S 78
Boyson Rd. SE17. 19Q 63
Boyne Ter. Mews w11.10N 59
Boyton Pl. NW1. 13L 48
Boyton Rd. N8. 17A 24
Brabant Rd. N22. 18Aa 16
Brabazon St. E14. 26L 53
Brabourn Gro. SE15. 22S 76
Bracewell Rd. w10. 8L 46
Bracey St. N4. 17E 36
Bracken Av. sw12. 14U 73
Bracken Gdns. sw13. 7R 70
Brackenbury Rd. N2. 12A 22
Brackenbury Rd. w6. 8O 58
Brackendale N21. 18Ae 16
Brackendale Rd. SE2. 36P 95
Brackley Rd. w4. 6P 58
Brackley Ter. w4. 6P 58
Bracklyn St. N1. 20J 51
Bracknell Gdns. NW3. 11F 34
Bracknell Way NW3. 11F 34
Bracton Rd. SE16. 23P 64
Brad St. SE1. 18N 62
Bradbourne St. sw6. 11R 71
Bradbury St. N16. 21G 37
Braddon Rd. Kew. 3S 68
Braddon St. SE16. 22N 64
Braddyll St. SE10. 27P 66
Braden St. w9. 11K 48
Bradenham Rd. Har. 1aA 12
Bradfield Rd. E16. 29N 67
Bradford Rd. SE26. 22X 87
Bradford Rd. w3. 6N 57
Bradford Rd. Ilf. 35D 42
Bradgate Rd. SE6. 25V 88
Brading Rd. sw2. 17U 74
Brading Rd. Cro. 17Zd 91
Bradiston Rd. w9. 10J 47
Bradley Gdns. w13. 1aL 94
Bradley Rd. N22. 17Aa 16
Bradley St. E16. 29L 54
Bradley St. sw8. 16Q 62
Bradmore Gro. w6. 8O 58
Bradmore La. w6. 8P 58
Bradmore Pk. Rd. w6. 8O 58
Bradstock Rd. E9. 24H 38
Bradwell St. E1. 24K 52
Brady St. E1. 22K 52
Braemar Av. N22. 17Aa 16
Braemar Av. NW10. 5E 31
Braemar Av. sw19. 10W 82
Braemar Av. Cro. 18Zb 90
Braemar Av. Wem. 2H 30
Braemar Gdns. NW9. 6Aa 13
Braemar Rd. E13. 29L 54

Braemar Rd. N15. 20B 25
Braemar Rd. w3. 4O 57
Braemar Rd. Bre. 2P 56
Braemar St. E2. 23K 52
Braeside Bec. 25Y 88
Braham St. E1. 21M 52
Braidwood Rd. SE6. 27W 89
Brailsford Rd. sw2. 18U 74
Braintree St. E2. 23K 52
Bramah Rd. sw9. 18R 74
Bramber Rd. N12. 13Ac 14
Bramber Rd. w14. 10Q 59
Bramble Gdns. w12. 7M 46
Bramblebury Rd. SE18.
  34Q 95
Bramcote Rd. SE16. 22P 64
Bramcote Rd. sw15. 8T 70
Bramdean Cres.SE12.29W 89
Bramdean Gdns.SE12.29W 89
Bramerton St. sw3. 13P 60
Bramfield Rd. sw11. 13U 72
Bramford Rd. sw18. 12T 72
Bramham Gdns. sw5. 11P 60
Bramhope La. SE7. 30Q 67
Bramley Clo. Cro. 18Zg 91
Bramley Cres. Ilf. 33C 42
Bramley Hill Cro. 18Zg 91
Bramley Mews w10. 9M 47
Bramley Rd. w5. 1O 56
Bramley Rd. w10. 9M 47
Bramley St. w10. 9L 47
Brampton Gro. NW4. 8B 20
Brampton Gro. Har. 1aA 12
Brampton Pk. E6. 31K 55
Brampton Rd. E9. 23H 39
Brampton Rd. E9. 23H 38
Brampton Rd. N15. 19B 25
Brampton Rd. NW9. 4B 19
Brampton Rd. Cro. 20Zd 91
Bramshill Gdns. N19. 15E 35
Bramshill Rd. NW10. 6J 46
Bramshot Av. SE7. 29Q 67
Bramston Rd. NW10. 7J 46
Bramwell St. sw8. 15S 73
Brancaster Rd. E12. 32G 43
Brancaster Rd. sw16.16W 85
Brancaster Rd. Ilf. 35D 42
Branch Hill NW3. 12E 34
Branch Pl. N1. 20J 51
Branch Rd. E14. 24M 53
Brand St. N7. 18F 36
Brand St. SE10. 26R 77
Brandlehow Rd. sw15.10T 71
Brandon Gro. Ilf. 33F 42
Brandon Rd. E17. 27B 28
Brandon Rd. N7. 17H 36
Brandon Rd. sw2. 17U 74
Brandon St. SE17. 19P 63
Brandram Rd. SE13. 27T 78
Brandreth Rd. sw17.14W 84
Brangbourne Rd. Bec. 26Y 88
Branksea St. sw6. 9Q 59
Branksome Av. N18. 21Ab 17
Branksome Rd. sw2. 17T 74
Branksome Rd. sw19.
  10Z 92
Branscombe Gdns. N21.
  18Af 16
Branscombe St. SE13. 26S 77
Branstone Rd. Kew. 3R 68
Branstone St. w10. 9K 47
Brantwood Rd.N17.21Ab 17
Brantwood Rd.SE24. 19T 75
Brassey Sq. sw11. 14S 73
Brassie Av. w3. 6L 45

Brathway Rd. sw18. 11U 71
Bravington Rd. w9. 10J 47
Braxfield Rd. se4. 24T 77
Braxted Pk. se16. 17Y 85
Bray Pl. nw1. 15J 49
Bray Pl. sw8. 14P 61
Brayard's Rd. se15. 22S 76
Braybrook St. w12. 6L 46
Brayburne Av. sw4. 16S 73
Braydon Rd. n16. 21D 26
Bread St. ec4. 19M 51
Bread St. Hill ec4. 19M 51
Breakspears Rd. se4. 25T 77
Bream St. e3. 25H 39
Breamore Rd. Ilf. 36E 42
Bream's Bldgs. ec1. 18L 50
Brechin Pl. sw7. 12P 60
Brecon Rd. w6. 9Q 59
Brecknock Rd.
  n7. 1-113 & 2-142.
  n19. 114, 115 & up. 16F 35
Bredon Rd. se5. 19S 75
Bredon Rd. Cro. 21Zd 91
Breer St. sw6. 11S 72
Bremen St. e8. 22H 38
Bremner Rd. sw7. 12O 60
Brenchley Gdns. se15.23U 76
Brenda Rd. sw17. 13W 83
Brendon Av. nw10. 6F 32
Brendon St. w1. 13L 48
Brendon Way n9. 21Af 17
Brenley Gdns. se9. 31T 79
Brent Cres. w5. 3J 44
Brent Grn. nw4. 9B 21
Brent Rd. e16. 29L 54
Brent Rd. se18. 33R 95
Brent St. nw4. 9B 21
Brent Way n3. 11Ab 14
Brent Way Wem. 4G 31
D..nfield Clo. nw 10. 9G 31
Brentfield Rd. nw10. 5G 31
Brentham Way w5. 1K 44
Brentham Halt Rd. w5.
  2J 44
Brenthurst Rd. nw10,
  7G 32
Brentmead Pl. nw10. 3J 44
Brentmead Pl. nw11. 9C 21
Brenton St. e14. 24L 53
Brent Pk. Rd. nw4. 8C 20
Brentvale Av. Wem. 3H 30
Brentview Rd. nw9. 7C 20
Brentwick Gdns. Bre. 2O 56
Brereton Rd. n17. 21Aa 17
Bressey Gro. e18. 28A 28
Brett Rd. e8. 22G 38
Brett Rd. nw10. 5H 31
Brettell St. se17. 20P 63
Brettenham Rd. n18. 22Ac 17
Brettenham Rd. E. n18.
  22Ac 17
Brewer Pl. se18. 33P 95
Brewer St. se18. 33P 95
Brewer St. w1. 16M 49
Brewery Rd. n7. 17H 36
Brewery Rd. se18. 34P 95
Brewhouse La. e1. 22N 64
Brewhouse La. sw15. 9S 71
Brewster Gdns. w10. 8L 46
Brewster Rd. e10. 26D 27
Briant St. se14. 23R 76
Briar Av. sw16. 17Z 90
Briar Rd. nw2. 8F 33
Briar Rd. sw16. 17Zb 90
Briar Rd. Har. 1B 18
Briar Rd. Twi. 1cV 93

Briar Wk. sw15. 8T 70
Briar Wk. Edg. 5Ab 13
Briarbank Rd. w13. 1aL 94
Briardale Gdns. nw3. 11E 33
Briarfield Av. n2. 12Aa 14
Briarwood Clo. nw6. 5C 19
Briarwood Rd. sw4. 16T 73
Briary Grn. n9. 21Ad 17
Briary La. n9. 21Ad 17
Brick La.
  e1. 1-165 & 2-226.
  e2. 167, 228 & up. 21L 51
Brick St. w1. 15N 61
Brickfield Rd. e3. 26K 53
Brickfield Rd. Cro. 18Za 90
Brickfields Rd. Har. 1cD 12
Brickwood Rd. Cro. 20Ze 91
Bride La. ec4. 18M 50
Bride St. n7. 18G 36
Bridewell Pl. ec4. 18M 50
Bridge Av. w6. 8P 58
Bridge Av. w7. 1cK 94
Bridge Gate n21. 19Af 16
Bridge La. nw11. 10B 21
Bridge Pl. Cro. 18Zg 91
Bridge Pl. Cro. 20Ze 91
Bridge Rd. e6. 32H 43
Bridge Rd. e15. 27H 40
Bridge Rd. e17. 24D 27
Bridge Rd. n9. 22Ad 17
Bridge Rd. n22. 17Aa 15
Bridge Rd. nw10. 4E 31
Bridge Rd. nw10. 6G 31
Bridge Rd. sw19. 13Z 92
Bridge Rd. Twi. 1aU 93
Bridge Rd. W. sw11. 13R 72
Bridge St.
  e1. 1-57 & 2-48.
  e3. 50, 59 & up. 24K 53
Bridge St. e9 23G 38
Bridge St. n10. 11J 45
Bridge St. se10. 26Q 65
Bridge St. sw1. 17N 62
Bridge Ter. e15. 27D 40
Bridgefield Gro. sw18. 11T 72
Bridgefoot se11. 17P 62
Bridgeman St. nw8. 13J 48
Bridgend Rd. sw18. 12T 72
Bridges Rd. sw19. 11Y 83
Bridgewater Rd. Wem. 1G 30
Bridgewater Sq. ec1. 19L 51
Bridgewater St. ec1. 19L 51
Bridgewater St. nw1. 16J 49
Bridgeway Wem. 3G 30
Bridgford St. sw18. 12W 83
Bridgman Rd. w4. 4O 57
Bridgman Rd. Ted. 1bY 93
Bridle La. w1. 16M 49
Bridlington Rd. n9. 22Af 17
Bridport Pl. n1. 20J 51
Bridport Rd. n18. 21Ac 17
Bridport Rd. Cro. 18Zb 90
Bridport St. nw1. 13K 48
Bridson St. se15. 23Q 64
Brief St. se5. 18R 74
Brierley Rd. e11. 27F 40
Brierly St. e2. 23K 52
Brig St. e14. 27P 66
Bright St. e14. 26L 53
Brightfield Rd. se12. 28U 78
Brightling Rd. se4. 23U 76
Brightlingsea Pl. e14. 24M 53
Brightman Rd. sw18. 12V 83
Brighton Av. e17. 25C 27
Brighton Rd. e15. 28J 54
Brighton Rd. n2. 12A 22

Brighton Rd. n16. 21F 37
Brighton Rd. Cro. 19Zg 91
Brighton Ter. sw9. 17T 74
Brightside Rd. se13. 27U 78
Brightwell Cres. sw17. 13Y 83
Brigstock Rd. Cro. 18Zc 90
Brim Hill nw11. 12B 22
Brimmington Rd. se15.
  22R 76
Brindley St. se14. 24R 77
Brindley St. w2. 11L 48
Brinsley Rd. Har. 1cAa 12
Brisbane Av. sw19. 11Z 92
Brisbane Rd. e10. 26E 39
Brisbane Rd. w13. 1aN 94
Brisbane Rd. Ilf. 34D 42
Brisbane St. se5. 20R 75
Briscoe Rd. sw19. 12Y 83
Briset Rd. se9. 31T 79
Bristol Gdns. sw15. 8V 81
Bristol Gdns. w9. 12K 48
Bristol Mews w9. 12K 48
Bristol Rd. e7. 31H 41
Bristol Rd. e15. 28H 40
Bristol Rd. Mor. 11Zc 92
Briston Gro. n8. 17C 24
Bristow St. n1. 20J 51
Britannia Gdns. n1. 20J 51
Britannia Pl. sw11. 12S 72
Britannia Rd. n12. 12Ad 14
Britannia Rd. sw6. 11Q 60
Britannia Rd. Ilf. 33F 42
Britannia Row n1. 19H 37
Britannia St. n1. 17K 50
Britannia St. wc1. 17K 50
British Gro. w4. 6P 58
British St. e3. 25K 53
Britten St. sw3. 13P 60
Britton St. ec1. 18L 50
Brixham Gdns. Ilf. 35G 43
Brixham Rd. e16. 29M 54
Brixton Hill sw2. 17U 74
Brixton Rd. sw9. 18S 74
Brixton Station Rd. sw9.
  18S 74
Broad Ct. wc2. 17M 50
Broad La. n8. 17B 24
Broad La. n15. 21D 26
Broad Sanctuary sw1.
  16O 62
Broad St. e1. 23M 52
Broad St. e15. 27H 40
Broad St. se11. 17P 62
Broad St. w1. 16M 49
Broad St. Ted. 1cY 93
Broad Wk. e18. 29A 28
Broad Wk. n21. 18Ae 16
Broad Wk. nw1. 14J 49
Broad Wk. se3. 30S 79
Broad Wk. Kew. 2Q 56
Broad Wk., The, w8. 12N 60
Broadfield Rd. se6. 27V 89
Broadfields Av. Edg. 4Ad 13
Broad Grn. Av. Cro. 18Zd 91
Broadhinton Rd. sw4.
  15S 73
Broadhurst Av. Edg. 4Ad 13
Broadhurst Gdns. nw6.11G 34
Broadhurst Gdns. Ilf. 36F 43
Broadlands Av. sw16.16W 85
Broadlands Rd. n6. 14C 23
Broadley Ter. nw1. 13K 48
Broadmead se6. 25X 88
Broadview Rd. sw16. 16Y 84
Broadwall se1. 18N 62
Broadwater Rd. n17.21Aa 17

Broadwater Rd.sw17.13X 83
Broadway, Plaistow e13.
    29K 55
Broadway e15. 27H 40
Broadway ec4. 19M 50
Broadway, Crouch End n8.
    17C 24
Broadway, Cricklewood
nw2. 9F 33
Broadway, Westminster
sw1. 16O 61
Broadway, Ealing w5.
    2M 44
Broadway, Hammersmith
w6. 8P 59
Broadway, Ealing w7. 1cM 94
Broadway, Bar. 34J 43
Broadway, Edg. 5Aa 13
Broadway Av. se25. 19Zc 90
Broadway Av. Bar. 34J 43
Broadway Av. Twi. 1aU 93
Broadway, The, e8. 22J 52
Broadway, The, n9. 22Ad 17
Broadway, The, nw7. 6Ac 13
Broadway, The sw19.11Z 92
Broad Way, The, Har.
    1bAa 12
Broadwick St. wc2. 16M 49
Brock Rd. e13. 30L 55
Brockham St. se1. 19O 63
Brockenhurst Gdns. nw7.
    6Ac 13
Brockenhurst Gdns. Ilf.
    34G 43
Brockenhurst Rd. Cro.
    22Ze 91
Brockham Dri. Ilf. 34C 42
Brockill Cres. se4. 24T 76
Brocklebank Rd. sw18.
    12V 83
Brocklehurst St. se14.
    23Q 64
Brockley Cross se4. 24S 77
Brockley Footpath se4
& se6. 23T 76
Brockley Gro. se4. 24U 77
Brockley Pk. se23. 24V 88
Brockley Rise se23. 24V 87
Brockley Rd. se4. 24U 77
Brockley View se23. 24V 88
Brockley Hall Rd. se4.
    24U 77
Brockman Rise se6. 27X 89
Brockwell Pk. Gdns. se24.
    18V 85
Brodia Rd. n16. 21E 37
Brodie St. se1. 21P 63
Brodrick Rd. sw17. 13W 83
Brograve Rd. n17. 22A 26
Broke Rd. e8. 22H 38
Broken Wharf ec4. 19M 51
Bromar Rd. se5. 20S 75
Bromehead Rd. e1. 23L 51
Bromehead St. e1. 23L 52
Bromells Rd. sw4. 16T 73
Bromfelde Rd. sw4. 16S 74
Bromley Rd. e10. 26C 27
Bromley Rd. e17. 25A 27
Bromley Rd. n17. 21aA 17
Bromley Rd. n18. 20Ad 17
Bromley Rd. se6 & Bec.
    26V 88
Bromley St. e1. 24L 52
Bromley Hall Rd. e14. 26L 54
Bromley High St. e3. 26K 53
Brompton Gro. n2. 14B 23

Brompton Sq. sw3. 13O 60
Brompton Rd.
sw1. 2-36 & 87-135.
sw3. 1-85 & 38, 137
& up. 13O 60
Brompton Pk. Rd. n8. 18A 24
Bromwich Av. n6. 15E 35
Bromyard Av. w3. 6M 46
Brondesbury Pk.
nw6. 1-97 & 2-64.
nw2. 66, 99 & up. 8G 32
Brondesbury Rd. nw6. 10J 47
Brondesbury Villas nw6.
    10J 47
Bronsart Rd. sw6. 9Q 59
Bronson Rd. sw20 9Za 92
Bronti Pl. se17. 19P 63
Bronze St. se8. 25Q 65
Brook Av. Edg. 4Ac 13
Brook Av. Wem. 3E 31
Brook Dri. se11. 18O 62
Brook Dri. Har. 1cA 12
Brook Green w6. 9O 59
Brook La. N. Bre. 1P 56
Brook Rd. n8. 18A 24
Brook Rd. n22. 18A 24
Brook Rd. nw2. 7D 20
Brook Rd. S. Bre. 2P 56
Brook Rd. Cro. 19Zb 90
Brook Rd. Ilf. 35C 42
Brook Rd. Twi. 1aU 93
Brook St. e1. 23M 52
Brook St. n17. 21A 26
Brook St. w1. 15M 49
Brook Wk. Edg. 5Ab 13
Brookbank Av. w7. 1cK 94
Brookbank Rd. se13. 25T 77
Brookdale n11. 16Ad 15
Brookdale Rd. e17. 25A 27
Brookdale Rd. se6. 25V 88
Brookdene Rd. se18. 35P 95
Brooke Av. Har. 1cE 12
Brooke Rd. e17. 27B 28
Brooke Rd.
n16. 1-147 & 2-160.
e5. 149, 162 & up. 22E 38
Brooke St. ec1. 18L 50
Brookehowse Rd. se6.25X 88
Brookfield Av. e17. 27B 28
Brookfield Cres. Har. 2B 18
Brookfield Pk. nw5. 15E 35
Brookfield Rd. e9. 24G 39
Brookfield Rd. n9. 22Ad 17
Brookfield Rd. w4. 5N 57
Brookfield Rd. w5. 2K 44
Brook Grn. Rd. w6. 8O 59
Brookhill Rd. se18. 33Q 95
Brookland Clo nw11. 11B 22
Brookland Hill nw11. 11A 22
Brookland Rise nw11. 11B 22
Brooklands Av. sw18.11W 82
Brooklands Dri. Wem. 1H 30
Brooklands Rd. se3. 29S 78
Brooklands Rd. sw8. 16R 73
Brooklands St. sw8. 16R 73
Brooklyn Av. se25. 22Zb 90
Brooklyn Gro. se25. 22Zb 90
Brooklyn Rd. se25. 22Zb 90
Brooklyn Rd. w12. 8N 58
Brookmill Rd. se8. 25R 77
Brooks La. w4. 3P 57
Brooks Rd. e13. 29J 54
Brooksbank St. e9. 23G 38
Brooksby St. n1. 18H 36
Brooksby's Wk. e9. 24G 38

Brookside Rd. n18. 22Ac 17
Brookside Rd. nw11. 10C 21
Brookside Rd. n19. 16E 35
Brookside Rd. nw11. 10C 21
Brookside Way Cro. 23Zd 91
Brooksville Av. nw6. 10H 33
Brookview Rd. sw16. 15X 84
Brookville Rd. sw6. 10Q 59
Brookwood Av. sw13. 6S 70
Brookwood Rd. sw18. 10V 82
Broom Rd. Twi. 1aX 93
Broomfield Av. n13. 17Ac 16
Broomfield La. n13. 17Ac 16
Broomfield Pl. w13. 1aM 94
Broomfield Rd. n13. 17Ac 16
Broomfield Rd. w13. 1aM 94
Broomfield Rd. Kew. 3Q 56
Broomfield St. e14. 26L 53
Broomgrove Gdns. Edg.
    4Ab 13
Broomgrove Rd. sw9. 17S 74
Broomhill Rd. sw18. 11U 71
Broomhill Rd. Ilf. 37E 42
Broomhouse Rd. sw6. 10S 71
Broomsleigh St. nw6. 10G 33
Broomwater Way Twi.
    1aY93
Broomwood Rd. sw11.13U 72
Broseley Gro. se26. 24Y 87
Brougham Rd. e8. 22H 38
Brougham Rd. w3. 5L 45
Brougham St. sw11. 14S 73
Broughton Av. n3. 9A 21
Broughton Rd. n16. 20F 37
Broughton Rd. sw6. 11R 72
Broughton Rd. w13 1aM 94
Broughton Rd. Cro. 17Zc 90
Broughton St. sw8. 15R 73
Brouncker Rd. w3. 4N 57
Brown St. w1. 13L 49
Brown St. w1. 14L 49
Brown Hart Gdns. w1.14M 49
Brown St. w1. 14M 49
Brownhill Rd. se6. 26V 88
Browning Av. w7. 1bL 94
Browning Rd. e11. 28D 28
Browning Rd. e12. 32H 43
Browning St. se17. 19P 63
Brownlow Mews wc1. 17K 50
Brownlow Rd. e7. 29F 41
Brownlow Rd. e8 21H 38
Brownlow Rd. n3. 11Ab 14
Brownlow Rd. n11. 17Ab 16
Brownlow Rd. nw.10 6H 32
Brownlow Rd. w13. 1aM 94
Brownlow Rd. Cro. 20Zg 91
Brownlow St. e8. 21H 37
Brownlow St. wc1. 17L 50
Brown's Rd. e13. 29J 54
Brown's Rd. e17. 25A 27
Brownswood Rd. n4 19E 37
Broxash Rd. sw11. 14U 73
Broxbourne Rd. e7. 29F 40
Broxholm Rd. se27. 18X 85
Broxted Rd. se6. 24W 88
Bruce Gro. n17. 21A 25
Bruce Rd. e3. 26K 53
Bruce Rd. nw10. 5H 31
Bruce Rd. se25. 20Zb 90
Bruce Rd. Har. 1bAa 12
Bruce Castle Rd. n17.
    21Aa 17
Bruce Gro. Rd. n17. 21A 25
Brudenell Rd. sw17. 14X 84
Brunel Rd. se16. 23N 64
Brunel St. e16. 28M 54

Brunner Clo. NW11. 12B 22
Brunner Rd. E17. 24B 27
Brunner Rd. W5. — 1K 44
Brunswick Av. N11. 14Ad 15
Brunswick Clo. EC1. 18K 50
Brunswick Ct. SE1. 20N 63
Brunswick Cres. N11. 15Ad 15
Brunswick Gdns. W8. 11N 60
Brunswick Gro. N11. 15Ad 15
Brunswick Pk. SE5. 20R 75
Brunswick Pl. N1. 20K 51
Brunswick Pl. SE19. 21Z 90
Brunswick Rd. E10. 26D 27
Brunswick Rd. E14. 26L 53
Brunswick Rd. N15. 21B 25
Brunswick Rd. N19. 16E 35
Brunswick Rd. W5. 2K 44
Brunswick Sq. WC1. 17K 50
Brunswick St. E1. 22M 52
Brunswick St. E2. 21J 51
Brunswick St. E9. 23H 38
Brunswick St. E7. 26B 27
Brunswick St. N1. 18J 50
Brunswick Villas SE5. 20R 75
Brunswick Pk. Rd. 15Ae 15
Brunton's Pl. E14. 24M 53
Brushfield St. E1. 21L 51
Brushwood St. E14. 26L 53
Brussells Rd. SW11. 12T 72
Bruton Mews. W1. 15M 49
Bruton Pl. W1. 15M 49
Bruton Rd. Mor. 11Zc 92
Bruton St. W1. 15M 49
Bruton Way W13. 1aL 94
Bryan Av. NW10. 8H 32
Bryan Pl. N1. 17J 50
Bryan Rd. SE16. 24N 65
Bryan St. N1. 18J 50
Bryanston Pl. W1. 14L 49
Bryanston Sq. W1. 14L 49
Bryanston St. W1. 14L 49
Bryanstone Rd. N8. 17C 23
Bryant Rd. SW16. 17Za 90
Bryant St. E15. 27H 40
Bryantwood Rd. N7. 18F 36
Brycedale Cres. N14. 16Ad 15
Bryden Gro. SE26. 24Y 87
Brydges Rd. E15. 27G 40
Bryett Rd. N7. 17E 36
Brymer Rd. SE5. 21Q 63
Brynmaer Rd. SW11. 14R 73
Bryony Rd. W12. 7M 46
Buccleuch Cotts. E5. 22D 26
Buchan Rd. SE15. 23S 76
Buchanan Gdns. NW10. 8J 46
Bucharest Rd. SW18. 12V 83
Buck Lane, NW.9. 5B 19
Buck St. NW1. 15H 35
Buck Walk E17. 27B 28
Buckenham St. SE1. 20O 63
Buckfast Rd. Mor. 11Zb 92
Buck Hill Walk W2. 13M 48
Buckhold Rd. SW18. 11U 71
Buckhurst St. E1. 22K 52
Buckingham Av. N20 12Af 14
Buckingham Av. Cro. 18Za 90
Buckingham Gates W1.16O 61
Buckingham Rd. E10. 26E 39
Buckingham Rd. E11. 30B 28
Buckingham Rd. E15.28G 40
Buckingham Rd. N1. 20G 37
Buckingham Rd. N22.
  17Aa 13
Buckingham Rd. NW10. 7J 46
Buckingham Rd. Edg. 3Ab 13
Buckingham Rd. Har. 1Cb 12

Buckingham Rd. Ilf. 35E 42
Buckingham St. N1. 17J 50
Buckingham St. SW1. 15O 61
Buckingham St. WC2. 17M 50
Buckingham Pal. Rd. SW1.
  15O 61
Buckland Cres. NW3. 13G 34
Buckland Rd. E10. 26E 39
Buckland St. N1. 20J 51
Buckle St. E1. 21M 52
Buckleigh Av. SW20. 9Zb 92
Buckler's Alley SW6. 10Q 59
Bucklersbury. EC4. 20M 51
Buckley Rd. NW6. 10H 33
Buckmaster Rd. SW11.13T 72
Bucknall St. WC2. 16L 50
Buckner Rd. SW2. 17T 74
Buckstone Rd. N18. 22Ab 17
Buckthorne Rd. SE4. 24U 76
Budge Row EC4. 20M 51
Budge's Wk. W2. 12M 48
Buer Rd. SW6. 10S 71
Buff Pl. SE5. 19R 75
Bulganak Rd. Cro. 19Zb 90
Bulinga St. SW1. 16P 62
Bulkeley Rd. SW16. 17Za 90
Bull La. N18. 21Ac 17
Bull Rd. E15. 28J 54
Bullen St. SW11. 13R 72
Buller Rd. N17. 22A 26
Buller Rd. N22. 18Aa 16
Buller Rd. NW10. 9K 47
Buller Rd. Bar. 35H 43
Buller Rd. Cro. 19Zb 90
Buller Sq. SE15. 21R 76
Bullscroft Edg. 4Ad 13
Bulow Rd. SW6. 11R 72
Bulstrode St. W1. 15L 49
Bulwer Rd. E11. 27D 28
Bulwer Rd. N18. 21Ac 17
Bungalow Rd. SE25. 20Zc 90
Bungay St. E14. 25M 53
Bunhill Row EC1. 20K 51
Bunker's Hill NW11. 12C 22
Bunns La. NW7. 6Ac 13
Bunting Bri. Rd. Ilf. 34C 42
Bunyan Rd. E17. 24A 27
Burbage Rd.
  SE24. 1-105 & 2-118.
  SE21. 107-139 & 134-174.
    19U 75
Burcham St. E14. 26M 53
Burchell Rd. E10. 26D 27
Burchell Rd. SE15. 22R 76
Burcote Rd. SW18. 12V 83
Burdenshott Av. SW14. 4S 69
Burdett Rd.
  E3. 1-219 & 2-230.
  E14. 221,232 & up.24K 53
Burdett Rd. Cro. 19Zd 91
Burdett Rd. Kew. 3S 68
Burdett St.SE1. 18O 62
Burford Gdns. N13. 18Ad 16
Burford Rd. E6. 31K 55
Burford Rd. E15. 27H 40
Burford Rd. SE6. 25W 88
Burford Rd. Bren. 2P 56
Burge St. SE1. 20O 63
Burges Rd. E6. 33H 43
Burgess Av. NW9. 5C 19
Burgess Hill NW2. 10F 33
Burgess Rd. E15. 27F 40
Burgess St. E14. 25L 53
Burghill Rd. SE26. 23X 87
Burghley Rd. E11. 28D 28

Burghley Rd. N8. 18A 24
Burghley Rd. NW5. 15F 35
Burghley Rd. SW19. 9X 82
Burgos Gro. SE10. 26R 77
Burgoyne Rd. E3. 24J 53
Burgoyne Rd. N4. 18C 24
Burgoyne Rd. SE25. 20Zb 92
Burgoyne Rd. SW9. 17S 74
Burgundy St. SE1. 21P 63
Burke St. E16. 28L 54
Burland Rd. SW11. 14T 73
Burleigh Gdns. N14. 16Af 15
Burleigh St. WC2. 17M 50
Burley Rd. E16. 30M 55
Burlington Arc. W1. 15M 49
Burlington Av. Kew 3R 69
Burlington Gdns. W1. 15M 49
Burlington Gdns.W3. 5N 57
Burlington Gdns. W4. 5P 57
Burlington La. W4. 5Q 57
Burlington Mews W. W2.
  10L 47
Burlington Rd. N10. 14A 23
Burlington Rd. N17. 22Aa 17
Burlington Rd. SW6. 10S 71
Burlington Rd. W2. 10L 47
Burlington Rd. W4. 4P 57
Burlington Rd. Cro. 19Za 90
Burma Rd. N16. 20F 37
Burman St. SE1. 18O 62
Burmester Rd. SW17. 12X 83
Burnaby Cres. W4. 4P 57
Burnaby Gdns. W4. 4P 57
Burnaby St. SW10. 12Q 60
Burnard Pl. N7. 18G 36
Burnbury Rd. SW12. 16V 84
Burne St. NW1. 13L 48
Burnett St. SE11. 17P 62
Burney St. SE10. 26Q 66
Burnfoot Av. SW6. 10R 71
Burnham Rd. Mor. 11Zc 92
Burnham St. E10. 26D 27
Burnham Way W13. 1aO 94
Burnley Rd. NW10. 7F 32
Burnley Rd. SW9. 17S 74
Burns Rd. NW10. 6H 32
Burns Rd. SW11. 14R 73
Burns Rd. Har. 1bA 12
Burns Rd. Wem. 2J 44
Burnsall St. SW3. 13P 60
Burnside Cres. Wem. 2H 30
Burnside St. E3. 24K 53
Burnt Ash Hill SE12. 29V 89
Burnt Ash Rd. SE12. 28U 78
Burnthwaite Rd. SW6. 10Q 59
Burnt Oak Edg. 4Ab 13
Burntwood La. SW17. 12W 83
Buross St. E1. 22M 52
Burr Rd. SW18. 11V 82
Burr St. E1. 21N 64
Burrage Gro. SE18. 34P 95
Burrage Rd. SE18. 34P 95
Burrard Rd. E16. 29M 55
Burrard Rd. NW6. 11F 33
Burrell St. SE1. 18N 62
Burroughs The, NW4. 8B 20
Burrows Mews W1. 18N 62
Burrows Rd. NW10. 8J 47
Burslem St. E1. 22M 52
Burstock Rd. SW15. 9T 71
Burston Rd. SW15. 9T 71
Burstowe Rd. SW20. 9Za 92
Burton Ct. SW3. 14P 61
Burton Gro. SE17. 20P 63
Burton Rd. NW6. 10H 33
Burton Rd. SW9. 18R 74

Burton St. wc1. 16K 50
Burtop Rd. sw17. 11W 83
Burwash Rd. se18. 34Q 95
Burwell Rd. e10. 24D 27
Bury Ct. ec3. 20M 51
Bury Rd. n22. 18A 24
Bury Rd. ec3. 20M 51
Bury St. n9. 21Af 17
Bury St. sw1. 16N 61
Bury St. wc1. 17L 50
Bury Wa. sw3. 18P 60
Busaco St. n1. 17J 50
Busby Pl. nw5. 16G 34
Busby St. e2. 21K 52
Bush La. ec4. 20M 51
Bush Rd. e11. 29D 28
Bush Rd. se8. 23P 64
Bush Rd. Kew 3Q 56
Bushberry Rd. e9. 24G 39
Bushell St. e1. 22N 64
Bushey Av. e18. 29B 28
Bushey Rd. e13. 30J 55
Bushey Rd. sw20. 8Za 92
Bushey Hill Rd. se5. 21R 75
Bushnell Rd. sw17. 15W 84
Bushwood e11. 29D 28
Bushwood Rd. Kew. 3Q 57
Bushy Pk. Gdns. Ted. 1dY 93
Busk St. e2. 21J 52
Butcher Row e14. 24M 52
Butcher's Row se8. 25Q 65
Butcher's Rd. e16. 29M 54
Bute Rd. Cro. 18Ze 91
Bute St. sw7. 12O 60
Butler Av. Har. 1cC 12
Butler Rd. Har. 1dC 12
Butler St. e1. 21L 51
Butler St. e2. 23K 52
Butler St. ec2. 20L 51
Butt St. se8. 25Q 65
Buttesland St. n1. 20K 51
Butts, The, Bren. 1Q 56
Buxted Rd. n12. 13Ac 15
Buxton Gdns.w3. 4M 45
Buxton Rd. e6. 31K 55
Buxton Rd. e15. 28G 40
Buxton Rd. e17. 24B 27
Buxton Rd. nw2. 8G 32
Buxton Rd. sw14. 6S 70
Buxton Rd. Cro. 18Zc 90
Buxton Rd. Ilf. 35C 42
Buxton St. e1. 21L 52
Byam St. sw6. 12S 72
Bye, The, w3. 6L 46
Byeway The, sw14. 4S 69
Bye Way, The, Har. 1bAa 12
Byfield Gdns. sw13. 7R 70
Byfield Rd. e17. 25C 27
Bygrove Rd. sw19. 12Y 83
Bygrove St. e14. 25L 53
Byne Rd. se26. 23Y 87
Byng Pl. wc1. 16K 50
Byng St. e14. 25N 65
Byrne Rd. sw12. 15W 84
Byron Av. e12. 31H 41
Byron Av. e18. 28A 28
Byron Av. nw9. 4A 19
Byron Hill, Har. 1cD 12
Byron Rd. e10. 26D 27
Byron Rd. nw9. 8E 32
Byron Rd. w5. 3M 44
Byron Rd. Har. 1bAa 12
Byron Rd. Har. 1bC 12
Byron Rd. Wem. 1E 30
Byron St. e14. 26L 53

Bythorn St. sw9. 17S 74
Byton Rd. sw17. 14Y 84
Byward St. ec3. 21M 51
Bywater St. sw3. 13P 61
Bywood Av. Cro. 23Zd 91
Cable St. e1. 22M 52
Cabul Rd. sw11. 13S 72
Cactus Wk. sw12. 6M 46
Cadbury Rd. se16. 21O 64
Caddington Rd. nw2. 10E 33
Cadell St. e2. 21J 52
Cader Rd. sw18. 12U 72
Cadet Pl. se10. 27P 66
Cadiz St. e1. 24L 52
Cadogan Av. sw3 13O 60
Cadogan Gdns. e18. 30A 29
Cadogan Gdns. n3. 11Aa 14
Cadogan Gdns. sw3. 14P 61
Cadogan Pl. sw1. 14O 61
Cadogan Sq. sw1. 14O 61
Cadogan St. sw3. 14P 61
Cadogan Ter. e9. 25H 39
Cadoxton Av. n15. 21C 26
Cæsar St. e2. 21J 51
Cæsar's Camp sw19. 7Y 81
Cahir St. e14. 25P 65
Caird St. w10. 10K 47
Cairn Av. w5. 1N 56
Cairnfield Av. nw2. 6E 32
Cairns Rd. sw11. 13T 72
Cairo Rd. e17. 26B 27
Caistor Rd. sw12. 14V 84
Caistor Pk. Rd. e15. 28J 54
Caithness Rd. w14. 9O 59
Calabria Rd. n5. 19G 37
Calais St. se5. 19R 74
Calbourne Rd. sw12. 14V 84
Calcutta St. e14. 25M 53
Caldecot Rd. se5. 19S 75
Calderon Pl. w10. 8L 47
Calderon Rd. e11. 27F 40
Calder's Row sw2. 17U 74
Caldervale Rd. sw4. 16U 73
Caldew St. se5. 20Q 63
Cale St. sw3. 13P 60
Caledon Rd. e6. 32J 43
Caledonia St. n1. 17J 50
Caledonian Rd.
   n1. 1-351 & 2-400.
   n7. 353, 402 & up. 17J 50
Caletock St. se10. 28P 66
Callandar Rd. se6. 26W 88
Callard Av. n13. 19Ac 16
Callcott Rd. nw6. 10H 33
Callow St. sw3. 12P 60
Calmington Rd. se5. 20Q 63
Calonne Rd. sw19. 8X 82
Calthorpe St. wc1. 18K 50
Calton Av. se21. 20U 75
Calverley Gdns. Har. 2C 18
Calverley Gro. n19. 16D 24
Calverley St. e1. 23L 52
Calverley St. w10. 9L 47
Calvert Av. e2. 21K 51
Calvert Rd. se10. 28Q 66
Calvert St. nw1. 14H 35
Calverton Rd. e6. 33J 43
Calvin St. e1. 21L 51
Calydon Rd. se7. 30Q 67
Cam Rd. e15. 27J 54
Camac Rd. Twi. 1cV 95
Cambalt Rd. sw15. 9T 71
Camberwell Gate se17.19Q 63
Camberwell Glebe se5.20R 75
Camberwell Grn. se5. 19R 75
Camberwell Gro. se5. 20R 75

Camberwell Rd. se5. 19Q 63
Camberwell New Rd. se5.
                    18Q 62
Camberwell Station Rd.
   se5.   19R 75
Camborne Av. w13. 1N 56
Camborne Rd. sw18. 11U 71
Camborne Rd. Cro. 21Zd 91
Cambray Rd. sw12. 16V 84
Cambria Rd. se5. 19S 75
Cambria St. sw6. 11Q 60
Cambrian Rd. e10. 25D 27
Cambrian Rd. Rich. 2U 68
Cambridge Av. nw6. 11J 48
Cambridge Cir. e2. 22J 52
Cambridge Cir. wc2. 16M 50
Cambridge Cotts. Kew. 3Q 56
Cambridge Cres. Twi. 1bX 93
Cambridge Dri. se12. 29U 73
Cambridge Gdns. n21.20Af 17
Cambridge Gdns. nw6. 11J 48
Cambridge Gdns. w10. 9L 47
Cambridge Gate nw1. 15K 49
Cambridge Gro. se20. 22Z 90
Cambridge Pk. e11. 29D 28
Cambridge Pl. nw6. 11J 48
Cambridge Pl. w2. 13L 48
Cambridge Pl. se18. 33Q 95
Cambridge Pl. w8. 11N 60
Cambridge Rd.
   e1. 1-83 & 2-148.
   e2. 150, 185 & up. 23K 52
Cambridge Rd. e11. 29C 28
Cambridge Rd. e17. 25C 27
Cambridge Rd. nw6. 11J 47
Cambridge Rd. se20.22Zb 90
Cambridge Rd. sw11. 13R 72
Cambridge Rd. sw13. 6S 70
Cambridge Rd. sw20. 8Z 92
Cambridge Rd. w4. 4P 57
Cambridge Rd. w6. 8O 58
Cambridge Rd. w7. 1bN 94
Cambridge Rd. Cro. 18Zd 91
Cambridge Rd. Bar. 34H 43
Cambridge Rd. Ilf. 35E 42
Cambridge Rd. Kew. 3Q 56
Cambridge Rd. Twi. 1bX 93
Cambridge Rd., The, n9
   & n18.   20Ab 17
Cambridge Sq. w2. 13L 48
Cambridge St. nw1. 16J 50
Cambridge St. se5. 19Q 63
Cambridge St. sw1. 15P 61
Cambridge St. w2. 13M 48
Cambridge Ter. nw1. 15K 49
Cambridge Ter. w2. 13L 48
Cambrook St. se15. 23Q 64
Camdale Rd. se18. 35R 95
Camden Av. se15. 21R 75
Camden Cres. n7. 16G 36
Camden Cres. nw1. 16G 35
Camden Gdns. w12. 9N 59
Camden Gdns. Cro. 18Zb 90
Camden Gro. se15. 21R 75
Camden La. n7. 16G 36
Camden Mews nw1. 16G 36
Camden Pass n1. 18J 50
Camden Rd. e11. 30C 29
Camden Rd. e17. 25C 27
Camden Rd.
   nw1. 1-227 & 2-282.
   n7. 229,284 & up. 15H 35
Camden Rd. se3. 28S 78
Camden Sq. nw1. 16H 36
Camden Sq. se15. 21R 75

Camden St. E2. 22K 52
Camden St. N1. 19J 51
Camden St. Nw1. 15H 35
Camden St. SE15. 21R 75
Camden Hill Rd. SE19.
20Y 86
Camden Pk. Rd. Nw1.16G 36
Camden Town High St.
Nw1. 15H 35
Camel Rd. E16. 31N 67
Camelford Rd. W11. 9L 47
Camellia St. Sw8. 16R 74
Camera Pl. Sw10. 12Q 60
Cameron Rd. Cro. 18Zd 91
Cameron Rd. Ilf. 35E 42
Camilla Rd. SE16. 22P 64
Camlan Rd. SE12. 28X 89
Camlet St. E2. 21K 51
Camomile St. EC3. 20L 51
Camp Rd. Sw19. 7Y 81
Campana Rd. Sw6. 11R 71
Campbell Rd. E3. 25K 53
Campbell Rd. E6. 31J 43
Campbell Rd. E17. 25B 27
Campbell Rd. N4. 18E 36
Campbell Rd. W7. 1cM 94
Campbell Rd. Cro. 18Zd 91
Campbell Rd. Twi. 1dV 93
Campbell St. W2. 12L 48
Campbell St. W6. 9P 59
Campdale Rd. N7. 16F 35
Campden Cres. Har. 1aE 12
Campden Cres. Wem. 1E 30
Campden Gro. W8. 11N 59
Campden Hill W8. 10N 59
Campden Rd. Cro. 20Zg 91
Campden St. W8. 11N 59
Campden Hill Gdns. W8.
10N 59
Campden Hill Rd. W8.
11N 59
Campden Hill Sq. W8.10N 59
Campion Rd. Sw15. 8T 70
Camplin Rd. Har. 2B 18
Camplin St. SE14. 23Q 64
Campsbourne Rd. N8. 17A 24
Campshill Rd. SE13. 26U 77
Camrose Av. Edg. 3Aa 13
Camrose St. SE2. 36P 95
Canada Av. N18. 19Ab 16
Canada Cres. W3. 4K 45
Canada Rd. W3. 5K 45
Canadian Av. SE6. 25V 88
Canal Gro. SE15. 22Q 64
Canal Pl. EC5. 21Q 63
Canal Rd. E3. 24K 53
Canal Rd. N1. 20J 51
Canal St. SE5. 20Q 63
Canal View Nw1. 16H 35
Canberra Rd. SE7. 30Q 67
Cancel St. SE17. 20P 63
Cancell Rd. Sw9. 18R 74
Candahar Rd. Sw11. 13S 72
Candler St. N15. 20C 25
Candy St. E3. 25H 39
Canfield Gdns. Nw6. 11H 34
Canfield Pl. Nw6. 12G 34
Canford Rd. Sw11. 14T 73
Canham Rd. SE25. 20Zb 90
Canham Rd. W3. 6N 57
Cann Hall Rd. E11. 28F 40
Canning Cres. N22. 18Aa 16
Canning Pl. SE5. 20S 75
Canning Pl. W8. 12O 60
Canning Rd. E15. 27J 54
Canning Rd. E17. 24B 27

Canning Rd. N5. 19E 37
Canning Rd. Cro. 20Ze 91
Canning Rd. Har. 1bA 12
Cannon Clo. Sw20. 8Zb 92
Cannon Hill N14. 17Ad 16
Cannon Hill Nw6. 11F 34
Cannon Pl. E1. 22L 52
Cannon Pl. Nw3. 12E 34
Cannon Rd. N8. 17B 24
Cannon Rd. N14. 17Ad 16
Cannon Row Sw1. 17N 62
Cannon St. EC4. 19M 51
Cannon Hill La. Sw20.
9Zb 92
Cannon St. Rd. E1. 22M 52
Canon St. N1. 19J 51
Canon Beck Rd. SE16.
23N 64
Canonbie Rd. SE23. 22V 87
Canonbury Av. N1. 19H 37
Canonbury Gro. N1. 19H 37
Canonbury La. N1. 19H 36
Canonbury Pl. N1. 19H 37
Canonbury Sq. N1. 19H 37
Canonbury St. N1. 19H 37
Canonbury Villas N1. 19H 37
Canonbury Pk. N. N1. 19G 37
Canonbury Pk. S. N1. 19G 37
Canon Murnane Rd. SE1.
21O 63
Canons Clo. Edg. 3Ac 13
Canons Dri. Edg. 3Ac 13
Canrobert St. E2. 22K 52
Cantelowes Rd. Nw1. 16G 36
Canterbury Av. Ilf. 31D 29
Canterbury Gro. SE27.
18X 85
Canterbury Pl. SE11. 18O 62
Canterbury Rd. E10. 26D 28
Canterbury Rd. N1. 21O 07
Canterbury Rd. Nw6. 10J 47
Canterbury Rd. Sw9. 18S 74
Canterbury Rd. Cro. 17Zd 91
Canterbury Rd. Har. 1dB 12
Canterbury Ter. N1. 21G 37
Canterbury Ter Nw6. 11J 47
Canterbury Ter w9. 12K 48
Cantire Pl. SE5. 19R 75
Cantley Dri. Ilf. 34C 42
Cantley Rd. W7. 1bN 94
Canton Bldgs. E14. 25M 53
Canton St. E14. 25M 53
Cantrell Rd. E3. 25L 53
Cantwell Rd. SE18. 33R 95
Canvoy St. SE1. 19N 63
Cape Gdns. Ilf. 36F 43
Capel Av. Cro. 17Zg 91
Capel Rd.
E7. 1-165.
E12. 166 & up. 29F 41
Capella Pl. SE10. 26R 77
Capern Rd. Sw18. 11V 83
Capland St. Nw8. 13K 48
Caple Rd. Nw10. 6J 46
Capri Rd. Cro. 21Ze 91
Capstone Rd. SE12. 28X 89
Capworth St. E10. 25D 27
Caradoc St. SE10. 27P 66
Carberry Rd. SE19. 20Z 90
Carberry Av. W3. 3N 56
Carburton St. W1. 15L 49
Cardiff Rd. W7. 1aO 94
Cardiff St. Sw18. 35R 90
Cardigan Gdns. Ilf. 36E 42
Cardigan Rd. E3. 25J 53

Cardigan Rd. Sw13. 7R 70
Cardigan Rd. w2. 11K 47
Cardigan Rd. Rich- 2U 68
Cardigan St. N1. 20H 37
Cardigan St. SE11. 18P 62
Cardinal Pl. Sw15. 9S 71
Cardinal Bourne St. SE1.
20O 63
Cardington St. Nw1. 16K 49
Cardozo Rd. N7. 17G 36
Cardre Way N12. 13Ac 14
Cargill Rd. Sw18. 11V 83
Cargreen Rd. SE25. 21Zc 90
Carholme Rd. SE23. 24W 88
Carisbrooke Rd. E17. 24B 27
Carker's La. Nw5. 15F 35
Carleton Rd. N7. 16F 36
Carlingford Rd. N15. 19A 25
Carlingford Rd. Nw3. 13F 34
Carlisle Av. w3. 6L 46
Carlisle Gdns. Har. 2C 18
Carlisle Gdns. Ilf. 31C 29
Carlisle Pl. Nw8. 12K 48
Carlisle Pl. Sw1. 15O 61
Carlisle Rd. E10. 25E 39
Carlisle Rd. N4. 18D 24
Carlisle Rd. N11. 15Ac 15
Carlisle Rd. Nw6. 10H 33
Carlisle Rd. Nw9. 5Aa 13
Carlisle St. SE1. 18O 62
Carlisle St. w1. 16M 49
Carlow St. Nw1. 15J 48
Carlsbad St. N1. 17J 50
Carlton Av. Har. 1aB 12
Carlton Av. Wem. 3D 18
Carlton Av. W. Har. 1aD 12
Carlton Clo. Edg. 3Ac 13
Carlton Gdns. sw1. 16N 61
Carlton Gdns. w5. 1L 44
Carlton Gro. SE15. 22R 76
Carlton Hill Nw8. 12J 48
Carlton Mews w9. 11J 48
Carlton Rd. E1. 23K 52
Carlton Rd. E11. 28D 28
Carlton Rd. E12. 31G 41
Carlton Rd. N4. 18D 24
Carlton Rd. N11. 15Ac 15
Carlton Rd. N15. 21A 25
Carlton Rd. Nw5. 15G 35
Carlton Rd. SE4. 25S 77
Carlton Rd. Sw14. 4S 69
Carlton Rd. Sw15. 9T 71
Carlton Rd. w4. 5N 57
Carlton Rd. w5. 1L 44
Carlton Sq. SE14. 23R 76
Carlton St. E16. 28L 54
Carlton St. Nw5. 15G 35
Carlton Vale Nw6. 11J 48
Carlton Ter. SE26. 22X 87
Carlton House Ter. Sw1.
16N 62
Carlwell St. Sw17. 13Y 83
Carlyle Av. Nw10. 5H 31
Carlyle Rd. E12. 31F 41
Carlyle Rd. w5. 1O 56

Carlyle Rd. Cro. 21Ze 91
Carlyle Sq. sw3. 13P 60
Carlyon Clo. Wem. 2H 30
Carlyon Rd. Wem. 2J 44
Carmalt Gdns. sw15. 8T 71
Carmarthen St. n1. 20H 37
Carmelite Rd. Har. 1cAa 12
Carmelite St. ec4. 18M 50
Carmen St. e14. 26L 53
Carmichael Rd. se25. 21Zc 90
Carminia Rd. sw17. 15W 84
Carnaby St. w1. 16M 49
Carnac St. se27. 19X 86
Carnarvon Rd. e10. 27C 28
Carnarvon Rd. e15. 28G 40
Carnecke Gdns. se9. 31U 79
Carnforth Rd. sw16. 16Y 84
Carnwath Rd. sw6. 11S 71
Carolina Rd. se19. 18Za 90
Carline Pl. e2. 21K 51
Caroline Pl. w2. 11M 48
Caroline Pl. wc1. 17K 50
Caroline St. e1. 24M 52
Caroline St. e5. 22E 38
Caroline St. nw1. 15H 35
Caroline St. wc1. 16L 50
Caroline Ter. sw1. 14P 61
Caroline Wk. w6. 9Q 59
Carpenter Gdns. n21 19Ae 16
Carpenter St. sw1. 16O 62
Carpenter's Rd. e15. 26H 39
Carr Rd. e17. 25A 27
Carr St. e14. 24L 53
Carrier St. wc2. 16L 50
Carrington Rd. Rich. 3T 68
Carrington St. w1. 15N 61
Carroun Rd. sw8. 17Q 62
Carson Rd. e16. 29L 55
Carson Rd. se21. 19W 86
Carstairs Av. se6. 26X 88
Carter La. ec4. 19M 51
Carter St. se17. 19P 63
Carteret St. sw1. 16O 62
Carthew Rd. w6. 8O 58
Carthew Villas w6. 8O 58
Carthusian St. ec1. 19L 51
Carting La. wc2. 17M 50
Carton St. w1. 14L 49
Cartwright Gdns. wc1.
 17K 50
Cartwright St. e1. 21M 52
Carver Rd. se24. 19U 75
Carville Cres. Bre. 2O 56
Carville St. n7. 18E 36
Cary Rd. e11. 28F 40
Carysfort Rd. n16. 20F 37
Carysfort Rd. n8. 16B 24
Cascade Av. n10. 16B 23
Casella Rd. se14. 23R 76
Casewick Rd. se27. 18X 85
Casimir Rd. e5. 23E 38
Casino Av. se24. 19T 75
Casket St. e2. 21K 51
Caslon St. ec1. 19K 51
Caspian St. se5. 19Q 63
Casselden Rd. nw10. 6H 31
Cassidy Rd. sw6. 11Q 59
Cassilda Rd. se2. 36P 95
Cassilis Rd. Twi. 1aT 93
Cassiobury Rd. e17. 24C 27
Cassland Rd. e9. 23H 38
Cassland Rd. Cro. 19Zb 90
Casslee Rd. se6. 24V 88
Casson St. e1. 21L 52
Castalia St. e14. 26O 65
Castellain Rd. w9. 11K 48

Castello Av. sw15. 8T 70
Casterton St. e8. 22G 38
Castlands Rd. se6. 25W 88
Castle Dri. Ilf. 31C 29
Castle La. sw1. 15O 61
Castle Rd. n12. 12Ac 14
Castle Rd. nw1. 15G 35
Castle St. e6. 31J 55
Castle St. ec1. 19L 51
Castle St. ec2. 20K 51
Castle St. wc2. 17M 50
Castle Way n12. 14Ac 15
Castlebar Hill w5. 1L 44
Castlebar Mews w5. 1K 44
Castlebar Pk. w5. 1K 44
Castlebar Rd. w5. 1L 44
Castledine Rd. se20. 22Z 90
Castlegate Rich. 2S 68
Castlemain Rd. se15. 20Q 63
Castlemaine Av. Cro. 20Zh 91
Castlenau sw13. 7Q 58
Castlereagh St. w1. 13L 49
Castleton Av. Wem. 2F 30
Castleton Rd. e17. 27A 28
Castleton Rd. Ilf. 37E 42
Castletown Rd. w14. 10P 59
Castle View Gdns. Ilf.
 32C 42
Castlewood Rd.
 n16. 1-121 & 2-102.
 n15. 110-132 & 123-151.
 22C 26
Castor St. e14. 25M 53
Caterham Rd. se13. 27T 78
Catesby St. se17. 20P 63
Catford Br. se6. 25V 88
Catford Hill se6. 25W 88
Catford Rd. se6. 25V 88
Cathall Rd. e11. 27E 40
Cathay St. se16. 22N 64
Cathcart Hill n19. 15F 35
Cathcart Rd. sw10. 12Q 60
Cathcart St. nw5. 15G 35
Cathedral St. se1. 20N 63
Catherina Ter. sw8. 17R 74
Catherine Gro. se10. 26R 77
Catherine Rd. n10. 20C 25
Catherine St. e2. 22J 52
Catherine St. e16. 28M 54
Catherine St. ec1. 20K 51
Catherine St. e11. 17P 62
Catherine St. sw1. 15O 61
Catherine St. wc2. 17M 50
Cathles Rd. sw12. 15U 73
Cathnor Rd. w12. 7N 58
Cathorne Rd. n22. 18Aa 16
Catlin St. se16. 22P 64
Cato Rd. sw4. 16S 74
Cato St. w1. 13L 48
Cator St. se26. 23Y 87
Cator St. se15. 21Q 63
Caulfield Rd. e6. 32H 43
Caulfield Rd. se15. 22S 76
Causeway Ted. 1bY 93
Causeway, The sw18. 8Y 81
Causeway, The sw18. 11T 72
Causeyware Rd. n9. 23Af 17
Causton Rd. n6. 15D 23
Causton St. sw1. 16P 62
Cautley Av. sw4. 15U 73
Cave Rd. e13. 30K 55
Cavell Rd. n17. 20Ab 17
Cavendish Av. n3. 11A 21
Cavendish Dri. e11. 27D 28
Cavendish Dri. Edg. 3Ac 13
Cavendish Gdns. Bar. 35G 43

Cavendish Gdns Ilf. 33D 42
Cavendish Gro. sw8. 16R 74
Cavendish Pl. w1. 15L 49
Cavendish Rd. n4. 18C 24
Cavendish Rd. n18. 22Ac 17
Cavendish Rd. nw6. 10H 33
Cavendish Rd. nw8. 13J 48
Cavendish Rd. sw12. 15U 73
Cavendish Rd. sw19. 12Z 92
Cavendish Rd. w4. 4R 69
Cavendish Rd. Cro. 18Ze 91
Cavendish Rd. West nw8.
 13J 48
Cavendish Sq. w1. 15L 49
Cavendish St. n1. 20J 51
Cavenham Gdns. Ilf. 34F 42
Caversham Av. n13. 18Ad 16
Caversham Rd. n15. 19B 25
Caversham Rd. nw5. 16G 35
Caversham St. sw3. 14P 61
Caverswall St. w12. 8L 46
Cavour St. se17. 19P 62
Cawdor Cres. w7. 1aO 94
Cawdor St. e14. 26M 54
Cawley Rd. e9. 24H 38
Cawnpore St. se19. 20Y 86
Caxton Gro. e3. 25K 53
Caxton Rd. n22. 18A 24
Caxton Rd. sw19. 11Y 83
Caxton Rd. w12. 9N 59
Caxton St. sw1. 16O 61
Cayley St. e14. 24L 53
Cazenove Rd. n16. 21E 37
Cecil Av. Bar. 34H 43
Cecil Av. Wem. 3F 30
Cecil Ct. wc2. 16M 50
Cecil Rd. e11. 28E 40
Cecil Rd. e13. 29J 55
Cecil Rd. n10. 15Aa 15
Cecil Rd. n14. 15Ae 15
Cecil Rd. nw9. 6A 20
Cecil Rd. nw10. 6H 31
Cecil Rd. sw19. 11Z 92
Cecil Rd. w3. 5L 45
Cecil Rd. Cro. 17Zd 91
Cecil Rd. Har. 1cAa 12
Cecil Rd. Ilf. 33F 43
Cecil St. e1. 23L 52
Cecile Pk. n8. 17C 24
Cedar Gro. w5 2N 56
Cedar Rd. n17. 21aA 17
Cedar Rd. nw2. 9F 33
Cedar Rd. sw6. 11Q 60
Cedar Rd. Cro. 20Ze 91
Cedar Rd. Ted. 1bY 93
Cedar Ter. Rich. 2S 68
Cedars Av. e17. 25B 27
Cedars Rd. e15. 28G 40
Cedars Rd. n9. 22Ad 17
Cedars Rd. n21. 19Ae 16
Cedars Rd. sw4. 15S 73
Cedars Rd. sw13. 7S 70
Cedars Rd. w4. 4P 57
Cedars Rd. Cro. 16Zf 91
Cedars Rd. Mor. 10Zb 92
Cedarville Gdns. sw16 17Z 90
Celia Rd. n19. 16F 35
Cemetery La. se7. 31Q 67
Cemetery Rd. e7. 28G 40
Cemetery Rd. n17. 21Aa 17
Centaur St. se1. 18O 62
Central Av. e11. 27E 40
Central Av. n9. 21Ad 17
Central Av. Twi. 1dT 93
Central Hill se19. 19Y 86

Central Rd. Mor. 11Zc 92
Central Rd. Wem. 1F 30
Central Sq. NW11. 11B 22
Central St. EC1. 19K 51
Central Pk. Rd.E6. 31K 55
Centre St. E2. 22J 52
Century Rd. E17. 24A 27
Cephas St. E1. 23K 52
Ceres Rd. SE18. 35P 95
Cerise Rd. SE15. 21R 76
Ceylon Rd. W14 9O 59
Ceylon St. SW8. 16Q 61
Chad St. E8. 24J 53
Chadbourn St. E14. 26L 53
Chadd St. E13. 29J 54
Chadwell St. EC1. 18J 50
Chadwick Rd. E11. 28C 28
Chadwick Rd. SE15. 21S 75
Chadwick St. SW1. 16O 62
Chadwin Rd. E13. 29L 55
Chaffinch Av. Cro. 23Zd 91
Chaffinch Clo. Cro. 23Zc 90
Chagford St. NW1. 13J 48
Chailey St. E5. 23F 38
Chalcot Cres. NW1. 14H 35
Chalcot Gdns. NW3. 14G 35
Chalcot Sq. NW1. 14H 35
Chalcroft Rd. SE13. 28N 78
Chaldon Rd. SW6. 9O 59
Chale Rd. SW2. 16U 74
Chalfont Av. Wem. 4G 31
Chalfont Grn. N9. 21Ad 17
Chalfont Rd. N7. 18G 36
Chalfont Rd. N9. 21Ad 17
Chalfont Rd. SE25. 21Zb 90
Chalfont Way W13. 1aO 94
Chalford Rd. SE21. 20X 86
Chalgrove Rd. E9. 23G 38
Chalgrove Rd. N17 22Aa 17
Chalk Rd. E13. 00J 55
Chalk Farm Rd. NW1. 15H 35
Chalkhill Rd. NW10. 4E 31
Challin St. SE20. 22Z 90
Challis Rd. Bren. 1P 56
Challoner St. W14. 10P 59
Chalmers St. SW8. 15R 73
Clalsey Rd. SE4. 25T 77
Chalton St. NW1. 16J 50
Chamber Gdns. N2. 13Aa 14
Chamber St. E1. 21M 52
Chamberlain Rd. N2. 12Aa 14
Chamberlain Rd. N9. 22Ad 17
Chamberlain St. NW1. 14H 35
Chamberlayne Rd. NW10.
8H 33
Chambers La. NW10. 8II 82
Chambord St. E2. 21K 51
Chameleon Rd. N17. 22Ab 17
Champion Av. E16. 29L 54
Champion Gro. SE5. 20S 75
Champion Hill SE5. 20S 75
Champion Pk. SE5. 20S 75
Champion Rd. SE26. 24X 88
Chancel St. SE1. 18L 50
Chancellor Rd. SE21. 19W 86
Chancellors Rd. W6. 8P 59
Chancellors St. W6. 8P 58
Chancery La. WC2. 18L 50
Chanctonbury Way N12.
11Ad 14
Chandler Av. E16. 29L 54
Chandler St. E1. 22N 64
Chandos Av. E17. 26A 27
Chandos Av. N14. 16Ad 15
Chandos Av. N20. 13Ae 14
Chandos Av. W5. 1O 56

Chandos Cres. Edg. 3Ab 13
Chandos Rd. E15. 27G 40
Chandos Rd. N2. 13A 22
Chandos Rd. N17. 21A 25
Chandos Rd. NW2. 8G 32
Chandos Rd. NW10. 6K 45
Chandos Rd. Har. 1cB 12
Chandos St. W1. 15L 49
Chandos St. WC2. 17M 50
Channelsea Rd. E15. 27J 54
Chant St. E15. 27H 40
Chantry Rd. SW9. 17S 74
Chapel Mkt. N1. 18J 50
Chapel Pl. SW1. 14O 61
Chapel Pl. W1. 15M 49
Chapel Rd. W11. 10M 47
Chapel Rd. SE27. 19X 85
Chapel Rd. Mit. 12Zb 92
Chapel Rd. Twi. 1aU 93
Chapel Row EC1. 18K 50
Chapel St. E2. 21J 51
Chapel St. E15. 27H 40
Chapel St. EC2. 19L 51
Chapel St. N2. 13A 22
Chapel St. NW1. 13L 48
Chapel St. NW1. 16K 50
Chapel St. SE18. 32P 95
Chapel St. SW1. 14O 61
Chapel St. W6. 8P 58
Chapel Wk. NW4. 9B 21
Chapel House St. E14. 26P 65
Chaplin Rd. E15. 28J 54
Chaplin Rd. NW2. 7G 32
Chaplin Rd. Wem. 2G 30
Chaplin St. SE23. 23W 87
Chapman Pk. NW10. 7G 32
Chapman Rd. E9. 25G 39
Chapman Rd. E13. 29J 54
Chapman Rd. Cro. 17Ze 91
Chapman St. E1. 22M 52
Chapman's Gdns. NW2. 7G 32
Chapter Rd. NW2. 7G 32
Chapter Rd. SE17. 19P 63
Chapter St. E7. 29G 41
Chapter St. SW1. 16P 61
Chard St. E16. 27L 54
Chardmore Rd. N16. 22D 26
Charford Rd. E16. 29L 55
Chargeable La. E13. 29K 54
Chargeable St. E16. 28K 54
Charing Cross SW1. 17N 62
Charing Cross Rd. WC2.
16M 50
Charlbert St. NW8. 13J 48
Charlbury Gdns. Ilf. 36E 42
Charlbury Gro. W5. 1L 44
Charlecote Gro. SE26. 22X 87
Charles Cres. Har. 1cC 12
Charles Pl. E1. 23M 52
Charles La. NW8. 13J 48
Charles Rd. E7. 30H 41
Charles Rd. E18. 28A 28
Charles Sq. N1. 20K 51
Charles St. E1. 23L 52
Charles St. E16. 30N 67
Charles St. EC1. 18K 50
Charles St. EC1. 18L 50
Charles St. EC1. 19L 51
Charles St. N1. 20H 37
Charles St. N7. 18G 36
Charles St. N17. 21Ab 17
Charles St. NW1. 16K 49
Charles St. SW1. 16M 49
Charles St. SW7. 13N 60
Charles St. SW13. 6S 70

Charles St. W1. 15N 61
Charles St. W5. 2M 44
Charles St. W11. 9N 59
Charles St. Cro. 19Zf 91
Charleston St. SE17. 19P 63
Charlesworth St. N7. 17H 36
Charleville Circus SE26.
22Y 87
Charleville Rd. W14. 10P 59
Charlgrove Gdns. N3. 10A 21
Charlmont Rd. SW17. 13Y 83
Charlotte Rd. SW13. 6R 70
Charlotte St. E2. 21K 52
Charlotte St. E16. 28M 54
Charlotte St. EC2. 20K 51
Charlotte St. N1. 18J 50
Charlotte St. SE18. 34P 95
Charlotte St. W1. 16L 49
Charlotte Ter. N1. 18J 50
Charlton Dene SE7. 30R 79
Charlton La. SE7. 31P 67
Charlton Pl. N1. 19J 50
Charlton Rd. E13. 29J 54
Charlton Rd. NW10. 6H 32
Charlton Rd.
SE3. 1-121 & 2-78.
SE7. 80, 123 & up. 29Q 67
Charlton Rd. Har. 2B 18
Charlton Way SE3. 27R 78
Charminster Av. SW19.
11Za 92
Charnock Rd. E5. 22F 38
Charnwood Av. SW19.
11Za 92
Charnwood Dri. E18. 30B 29
Charnwood Rd. SE25.
20Zc 90
Charrington St. NW1. 16J 49
Charsley Rd. SE6. 26W 88
Chart St. N1. 20K 51
Charter Av. Ilf. 35D 42
Charterhouse Av. Wem.
1F 30
Charterhouse Sq. EC1. 10L 51
Charterhouse St. EC1. 18L 50
Charteris Rd. N4. 18D 24
Charteris Rd. NW6. 10H 33
Chatfield Av. SW15. 8T 70
Chatham Rd. SE27. 18X 85
Chatham Rd. SE25. 22Zb 90
Chatley Av. NW2. 6E 32
Chase Gdns. Twi. 1cU 93
Chase Rd. N14. 16Af 15
Chase Rd. NW10. 5K 45
Chase Side N14. 16Af 15
Chase, The, SW4. 15S 73
Chase, The, SW16. 17Z 90
Chase, The, SW20. 9Za 92
Chase, The, Cro. 16Zg 91
Chase, The, Edg. 4Ab 13
Chase, Way N14. 15Ae 15
Chasefield Rd. SW17. 14X 84
Chaseley St. E14. 24M 53
Chase Side Av. SW20. 9Za 92
Chatfield Rd. SW11. 12S 72
Chatfield Rd. Cro. 18Ze 91
Chatham Av. N1. 20J 51
Chatham Close NW11. 11B 22
Chatham Pl. E9. 23G 38
Chatham Pl. SE17. 20P 63

Chatham Rd. E17. 24A 27
Chatham Rd. E18. 28A 28
Chatham Rd. sw11. 13U 72
Chatham St. SE17. 20P 63
Chatsworth Av. sw20. 9Za 92
Chatsworth Av. Wem. 3G 30
Chatsworth Gdns w3. 4M 45
Chatsworth Rd. E5. 23F 38
Chatsworth Rd. E15. 28G 40
Chatsworth Rd. Nw2. 9G 33
Chatsworth Rd. w4. 5Q 57
Chatsworth Rd. w5. 3K 44
Chatsworth Rd. Cro. 19Zg 91
Chatsworth Way SE27. 19W 86
Chatteris Rd. SE17. 19O 63
Chatterton Rd. N4. 19E 37
Chatto Rd. sw11. 14U 73
Chaucer Av. Kew. 3S 69
Chaucer Clo. N11. 16Ac 15
Chaucer Rd. E7. 29G 41
Chaucer Rd. E11. 29C 28
Chaucer Rd. SE24. 18U 74
Chaucer Rd. w3. 5M 45
Chauncey St. N9. 22Ad 17
Chauntler Rd. E16. 30M 55
Cheam Pl. SE5. 20Q 63
Cheapside EC2. 19M 51
Cheddington Rd. N18.
    20Ad 17
Chelford Rd. Bec. 27Y 89
Chelmer Rd. E9. 24G 38
Chelmsford Gdns. Ilf. 32D 42
Chelmsford Rd. E11. 27D 28
Chelmsford Rd. E17. 25C 27
Chelmsford Rd. N14. 16Af 15
Chelmsford Sq. Nw10. 8H 32
Chelmsford St. w6. 9P 59
Chelsea Bridge sw1. 15Q 61
Chelsea Embankment
    sw3. 14Q 61
Chelsea Bridge Rd. sw1
    14P 61
Chelsea Pk. Gdns. sw3.
    12Q 60
Chelsham Rd. sw4. 16S 74
Cheltenham Pl. w3. 4N 57
Cheltenham Pl. Har. 2A 18
Cheltenham Rd. E10. 26C 28
Cheltenham Ter. sw3. 14P 61
Chelverton Rd. sw15. 9T 71
Chelwood Gdns. Kew. 3R 69
Cheney St. Nw1. 17J 50
Cheneys Rd. E11. 28F 40
Chenies Mews wc1. 16L 49
Chenies Pl. Nw1. 16J 50
Chenies St. wc1. 16L 49
Cheniston Gdns. w8. 11O 60
Chepstow Cres. w11. 11M 47
Chepstow Cres. Ilf. 35C 42
Chepstow Pl. w2. 11M 48
Chepstow Rise. Cro. 20Zf 91
Chepstow Rd. w7. 1bN 94
Chepstow Rd. Cro. 20Zf 91
Chepstow Villas. w2 10M 47
Chequer St. EC1. 19K 51
Chequers Way N13. 19Ac 16
Cherington Rd. w7. 1bM 94
Cheriton Sq. sw17. 14W 84
Cherry Clo. sw20. 9Zb 92
Cherry Garth Bre. 2O 56
Cherry Gdn. St. SE16. 22O 64
Cherry Hill Gdns. Cro. 17Zg 91
Cherry Orchard Rd. Cro.
    20Ze 91
Cherry Tree Rd. N2. 14B 23
Cherrywood La. sw20. 9Zb 92

Chertsey Rd. E11. 27E 40
Chertsey Rd. w4. 3P 57
Chertsey Rd. Twi. 1cU 93
Chertsey St. sw17. 14Y 84
Chesham Cres. SE20. 23Za 90
Chesham Pl. sw1. 14O 61
Chesham Rd. SE20. 23Za 90
Chesham St. sw1. 14O 61
Chesham Ter. w13. 1aN 94
Cheshire St. E2. 22K 52
Chesholm Rd. N16. 21F 37
Cheshunt Rd. E7. 30H 41
Cheshunt Rd. N17. 19Aa 16
Chesilton Rd. sw6. 10R 71
Chesley Gdns. E6. 31K 55
Chesney St. sw11. 14R 73
Chesnut Rd. SE18. 35Q 95
Chessington Av. N3. 10A 21
Chesson Rd. w14. 10P. 59
Chester Gate Nw1. 15K 49
Chester Mews Nw1. 15K 49
Chester Mews sw1. 15O 61
Chester Pl. Nw1. 15J 49
Chester Pl. SE18. 34P 95
Chester Pl. w2. 13M 48
Chester Rd. E7. 31H 41
Chester Rd. E11. 30C 29
Chester Rd. E16. 28L 54
Chester Rd. E17. 24C 26
Chester Rd. N9. 23Ae 17
Chester Rd. N15. 20A 25
Chester Rd. N18. 22Ac 17
Chester Rd. N19. 15E 35
Chester Rd. Nw1. 15K 49
Chester Rd. Ilf. 36D 42
Chester Sq. sw1. 15O 61
Chester St. E2. 23K 52
Chester St. E11. 28E 40
Chester St. sw1. 15O 61
Chester Ter. Nw1. 15K 49
Chester Ter. sw1. 14P 61
Chester Way SE11. 18P 62
Chesterfield Gdns. N4. 19C 25
Chesterfield Gdns. w1.15N 61
Chesterfield Grove SE22
    21T 75
Chesterfield Rd. E10. 27C 28
Chesterfield Rd. w4. 5Q 57
Chesterfield st. w1 15N 61
Chesterfield St. wc1. 17K 50
Chesterfield Wk. SE10.
    27R 78
Chesterford Gdns. Nw3.
    12F 34
Chesterford Rd. E12 32G 43
Chesterton Rd. E13. 29K 54
Chesterton Rd. w10. 9L 47
Chesterton Ter. E13. 29K 54
Chestnut Av. E7 29F 41
Chestnut Av. N8. 17B 24
Chestnut Av. Bre. 2O 56
Chestnut Dri. E11. 29C 28
Chestnut Gro. sw12. 14V 84
Chestnut Gro. w5. 2N 56
Chestnut Rd. N17 21A 26
Chestnut Rd. SE27 19W 86
Chestnut Rd. sw20. 9Za 92
Chestnut Rd. Twi. 1cV 93
Chetwode Rd. sw17. 14W 84
Chetwynd Rd. Nw5 15F 35
Cheval Pl. sw7 13O 60
Cheval St. E14. 25O 65
Chevening Rd. Nw6. 9J 47
Chevening Rd. SE10. 28O 66
Chevening Rd. SE19. 19Z 90

Cheverton Rd. N19. 16D 24
Chevet St. E9. 24G 39
Cheviot Gdns. Nw2. 9E 33
Cheviot Gate Nw2. 10D 21
Cheviot Rd. SE27. 18Y 85
Chewton Rd. E17. 24B 27
Cheyne Ave. E18. 28A 28
Cheyne Gdns. sw3 13Q 60
Cheyne Row sw3. 13Q 60
Cheyne Wk. Nw4. 8B 21
Cheyne Wk.
    sw3. 1-90
    sw10. 91 & up 13Q 60
Cheyne Wk. Cro. 21Zf 91
Chichele Rd. Nw2 9F 33
Chicheley St. SE1. 17N 62
Chichester Gdns. Ilf. 32D 42
Chichester Mews w2. 12L 48
Chichester Pl. w2. 12L 48
Chichester Rd. E11. 28F 40
Chichester Rd. N9. 21Ae 17
Chichester Rd. Nw6. 11J 47
Chichester Rd. w2. 12L 48
Chichester Rd. Cro. 20Zf 91
Chichester St. sw1. 16P 61
Chicksand St. E1. 22L 52
Chiddingstone St. sw6.
    11R 71
Chigwell Hill E1. 22M 52
Chigwell Rd. E18. 30A 29
Chilcot St. E14. 26M 53
Childebert Rd. sw17. 15W 84
Childeric Rd. SE14. 24Q 65
Childerley St. sw6. 9R 71
Childers St. SE8. 24Q 65
Child's Pl. sw5. 11O 60
Child's St. sw5. 11O 60
Child's Way Nw11. 11B 21
Chillerton St sw17 14Y 84
Chiltern Gdns. Nw2. 9E 33
Chiltern Rd. E3. 25K 53
Chiltern St. w1. 14L 49
Chilton Av. w5 2O 56
Chilton Rd. Rich. 3S 68
Chilton St. E2. 21K 52
Chilton St. SE8. 24P 64
Chilver St. SE10. 28P 66
Chilworth Mews w2. 12L 48
Chilworth St. w2. 12M 48
Chimes Av. N13 18Ac 16
China Wlk. SE11 18O 62
Chine, The, N10. 15B 23
Chine, The, Wem. 1F 30
Chingford Rd. E17. 26A 27
Chip St. sw4. 16S 73
Chipka St. E14. 26O 65
Chipley St. SE14. 24Q 65
Chippendale St. E5. 23F 38
Chippenham Av. Wem.
    4G 31
Chippenham Gdns. Nw6.
    11K 47
Chippenham Mews w9.
    11K 47
Chippenham Rd. w9. 11K 47
Chipstead Av. Cro. 18Zc 90
Chipstead Gdns. Nw2. 8E 32
Chipstead St. sw6. 11R 72
Chisenhale Rd. E3. 24J 53
Chisholm Rd. Cro. 20Zc 91
Chisholm Rd. Rich. 2U 68
Chislehurst Av. N12 12Ab 14
Chiswell St. EC1 20L 51
Chiswell St. SE5. 20R 75
Chiswick Bridge w4. 4R 69
Chiswick La. w4. 6P 58

Chiswick Mall w4. 6P 58
Chiswick Rd. n9 22Ae 17
Chiswick Rd. w4. 5O 57
Chiswick Com. Rd.w4. 5O 57
Chiswick High Rd. w4. 5P 57
Chitty St. w1. 16L 49
Chitty St. Mews w1. 16L 49
Chivalry Rd. sw11. 13T 72
Chobham Rd. e15. 27G 40
Cholmeley Cres. n6. 15D 23
Cholmeley Pk. n6 15D 23
Cholmondly Av. nw10. 7J 46
Cholmondeley Wk. Rich. 1T 68
Choumert Gro. se15. 21S 76
Choumert Rd. se15. 21S 75
Choumert Sq. se15. 21S 76
Chrisp St. e14. 26L 53
Christ Church Av. n12. 12Ab 14
Christchurch Av. nw6. 9H 33
Christchurch Av. Har. 1aA 12
Christchurch Av. Ted. 1bY 93
Christchurch Av. Wem. 2G 30
Christchurch Gdns. Har. 1aA 12
Christchurch Grn. Wem. 2G 30
Christchurch Pass. nw3. 13F 34
Christchurch Pl. nw3 13F 34
Christchurch Rd. n8. 17C 24
Christchurch Rd. nw3. 13F 34
Christ Church Rd. sw2. 17V 85
Christ Church Rd.sw14. 4T 69
Christchurch Rd.sw19 12Z 92
Christchurch Rd. Ilf. 34D 42
Christchurch St. se10.28P 66
Christchurch St. sw3. 14P 61
Christian St. e1. 22M 52
Christie Rd. e9 24H 39
Christopher Rd. w7. 1aO 94
Christopher St. ec2. 20L 51
Chryssoll Rd. sw9. 18Q 62
Chubworthy St. se14. 24Q 64
Chudleigh Gdns. Ilf. 35F 43
Chudleigh Rd. nw6. 9H 33
Chudleigh Rd. se4. 25U 77
Chudleigh Rd. Twi. 1cU 93
Chumleigh St. se5. 20Q 63
Church App. se21. 20X 86
Church Av. sw14. 5S 69
Church Clo. Edg. 5Ac 13
Church Cres. e9. 23H 38
Church Cres. n3. 10Aa 14
Church Cresc. n10. 15B 23
Church Cresc. n20 13Ad 14
Church Dri. nw9. 5D 19
Church Dri. Wem. 4G 31
Church End.nw4. 8A 20
Church Fields Cro. 23Zb 90
Church Gdns. w5. 1N 56
Church Gro. se13. 26T 77
Church Hill e17. 26B 27
Church Hill n21. 18Af 16
Church Hill se18. 32O 90
Church Hill sw19. 10Y 82
Church Hill, Har. 1bD 12
Church La. e1. 21L 52
Church La. e11. 28D 28
Church La. e17. 26B 27
Church La. n1 19H 37
Church La. n2. 13A 22
Church La. n8. 17B 24
Church La. n17. 21Aa 17

Church La. n9. 22Ae 17
Church La. nw9. 5D 19
Church La. nw10. 6G 32
Church La. se7. 30P 67
Church La. sw17. 14Y 84
Church La. sw19 10Z 92
Church La. sw20 8Z 92
Church La. w5. 1N 56
Church La. w6. 8P 58
Church La. Har. 1bAa 12
Church La. Ted. 1bY 93
Church La. Twi. 1aV 93
Church Path e11. 29C 29
Church Path e14. 25M 53
Church Path n12 12Ac 14
Church Path sw14. 5S 69
Church Path sw19. 10Za 92
Church Path w4 5O 57
Church Path, Cro. 19Ze 91
Church Path, Mit. 13Zb 92
Church Pl. w10. 9K 47
Church Pl. w2. 12L 48
Church Rd. e10. 25D 27
Church Rd. e12. 31G 43
Church Rd. e17. 24A 27
Church Rd. n1. 20H 37
Church Rd. n6. 14C 23
Church Rd. n17. 21Aa 17
Church Rd. nw4. 8A 20
Church Rd. nw10. 6H 32
Church Rd. se19. 20Za 90
Church Rd. se23. 23W 87
Church Rd. sw2. 17U 74
Church Rd. sw13. 8Q 58
Church Rd. sw13. 7R 70
Church Rd. sw19. 9Y 82
Church Rd. w3. 4N 57
Church Rd. w6. 8O 58
Church Rd. w7. 1bM 94
Church Rd. Bat. 34H 45
Church Rd. Cro. 19Zf 91
Church Rd. Ilf. 35C 42
Church Rd. Mit. 12Za 92
Church Rd. Rich. 2T 68
Church Rd. Twi. 1cX 93
Church Row e2. 21K 52
Church Row ec3. 21M 51
Church Row e14. 25M 53
Church Row nw3. 12F 34
Church Row sw6. 9S 71
Church St. e1 21L 52
Church St. e2. 21K 51
Church St. e15. 28J 54
Church St. n1 19H 37
Church St. n9 21Ad 17
Church St. n16. 20F 37
Church St.
nw8 1-127 & 2-142
w2. 129, 144 & up 13L 48
Church St. se5. 20R 75
Church St. se10. 26Q 66
Church St. se18. 32O 95
Church St. sw8. 17Q 62
Church St. w1. 16M 50
Church St. w4. 6P 58
Church St. w8. 11N 60
Church St. Cro. 18Zf 91
Church St. Mit. 13Zb 92
Church St. Twi. 1bV 93
Church St. N. e15. 28J 54
Church Ter. e9. 23G 38
Church Ter. se13. 27T 78
Church Vale n2. 14A 23
Church Vale se23. 23W 87
Church Wk. n16. 20F 37

Church Wk. nw2. 11E 33
Church Wk. nw3. 12F 34
Church Wk. nw4. 8A.21
Church Wk. se26 21X 86
Church Wk. sw20. 8Zb 92
Church Wk. Bre. 1P 56
Church Wk. Rich. 2T 68
Church Way n20. 13Ad 14
Church Yd. ec2. 20L 51
Churchdown. se12. 27X 89
Churchfield Av. n12. 13Ac 14
Churchfield Rd. w7. 1cN 94
Churchfield Rd. w13. 1M 44
Churchfield Rd. Har. 1dA 12
Churchfield Rd. E.,w3. 5M 45
Churchfield Rd. W.w.3. 5M 45
Churchill Av. Har. 1aC 12
Churchill Gdns. w3. 4L 45
Churchill Rd. e9. 23G 38
Churchill Rd. e16. 30M 55
Church Hill Rd. e17. 26B 27
Churchill Rd. nw2. 8G 32
Churchill Rd. nw5. 15F 35
Church Hill Rd, Barn. 14Af 15
Churchill Rd. Edg. 3Ac 13
Churchley Rd. se26. 22X 87
Church Manor Way se2. 36P 95
Churchmead Rd. nw10. 7G 32
Church Ter. Rd. Rich. 2T 68
Churchway nw1. 16K 50
Churchwell Path e9. 23G 38
Church Yd. Row. se11. 19O 62
Churstone Av. e13. 30J 55
Churston Gdns. n11. 16Ab 15
Churton St. sw1. 16P 61
Chute St. sw17. 12Y 83
Cibber Rd. se23. 23W 87
Cicida Rd. sw18. 12U 72
Cicely Rd. se15. 22R 76
Cinnamon St. e1. 22N 61
Cintra Pk. se19. 21Z 90
Circle Gdns.sw19. 10Za 92
Circle, The, nw2. 6E 32
Circular Rd., n17. 21A 26
Circular Rd. se1. 19O 63
Circular Rd. se18. 32Q 95
Circus Pl. ec2. 20L 51
Circus Rd. nw8. 12J 48
Circus St. se10. 26R 77
Circus St. w1. 13L 49
Circus, The, se10. 27R 78
Circus, The, w3. 7M 46
Cirencester St. w2. 11L 48
Cissbury Ring N. n12. 11Ac 14
Cissbury Ring S. n12. 11Ac 14
Cissbury Rd. n15. 20B 25
Citizen Rd. n7. 18F 36
City Rd. ec1. 19J 51
City Gdn. Row n1. 19J 51
Clabon Mews sw7. 14O 61
Clack St. se16. 23N 64
Clacton Rd. e6 31K 55
Clacton Rd. e17. 24C 27
Claigmar Gdns. n3. 11Aa 14
Clairview Rd. sw16. 15X 84
Clairville Gdns. w7 1bM 94
Clancarty Rd. sw6. 11S 71
Clandon Gdns. n3. 11A 22
Clandon Rd. Ilf. 35E 42
Clandon St. se8. 25R 77
Clanricarde Gdns.w2. 11M 48
Clapham Cres. sw4. 16T 73
Clapham Rd. sw9 16S 74

Clapham Com. N. Side. sw4. 14T 73
Clapham Com. S. Side. sw4. 15T 73
Clapham Com. W. Side. sw4. 14T 73
Clapham High St. sw4. 16T 73
Clapham Pk. Rd. sw4. 16T 73
Clapton Com. E.5. 22D 26
Clapton Sq. E5. 23G 38
Clara Pl. SE18. 33P 95
Clare Gdns. Bar. 36H 43
Clare Mkt. wc2. 17M 50
Clare Rd. E7. 29F 40
Clare Rd. E11. 27C 28
Clare Rd. NW10. 7G 32
Clare St. E2. 22J 52
Claremont Av. Har. 2B 18
Claremont Gdns. Ilf. 35E 42
Claremont Pl. SE16. 23O 64
Claremont Rd. E7. 30G 41
Claremont Rd. E11. 27E 40
Claremont Rd. E17. 24A 27
Claremont Rd. N6. 15C 23
Claremont Rd. NW2. 9E 33
Claremont Rd. w9. 10J 47
Claremont Rd. w13. 1aK 94
Claremont Rd. Cro. 21Ze 91
Claremont Rd. Har. 1bAa 12
Claremont Rd. Ted. 1bX 93
Claremont Rd. Twi. 1aU 93
Claremont Sq. N1. 18J 50
Claremont St. E2. 22J 52
Claremont St. N18. 22Ab 17
Claremont St. SE10. 26Q 65
Clarence Av. SE5. 19R 75
Clarence Av. Ilf. 32C 42
Clarence Clo. E8. 21J 51
Clarence Gdns. N3. 10Aa 14
Clarence Gdns. NW1. 15K 49
Clarence Gate NW1. 14K 49
Clarence La. sw15. 6U 70
Clarence Mews. E5. 22G 38
Clarence Pl. E5. 22G 38
Clarence Rd. E5. 22F 38
Clarence Rd. E11. 27F 40
Clarence Rd. E12. 31G 41
Clarence Rd. E16. 28L 54
Clarence Rd. N15. 20B 25
Clarence Rd. N22. 17Ab 16
Clarence Gate sw1. 16N 61
Clarence Gro. NW1. 15H 35
Clarence Rd. NW1. 15H 35
Clarence Rd. NW6. 10H 33
Clarence Rd. sw4. 16U 73
Clarence Rd. sw19. 11Y 82
Clarence Rd. w4. 3P 57
Clarence Rd. Cro. 19Zd 91
Clarence Rd. Kew. 3R 68
Clarence St. E1. 22K 52
Clarence St. N1. 19J 51
Clarence St. SE10. 26Q 66
Clarence St. sw4. 17R 74
Clarence St. Rich. 2S 68
Clarence Ter. NW 1. 14K 49
Clarendon Gdns. NW4. 8A 20
Clarendon Gdns. w9. 12K 48
Clarendon Gdns. Ilf. 32D 42
Clarendon Gdns. Wem. 2E 30
Clarendon Pl. w2. 13L 48
Clarendon Pl. w11. 10M 47
Clarendon Rise SE13. 27T 78
Clarendon Rd. E11. 27D 28
Clarendon Rd. E17. 26C 27
Clarendon Rd. E18. 29A 29
Clarendon Rd. N8. 18A 24

Clarendon Rd. N15. 19B 25
Clarendon Rd. N18. 22Ab 17
Clarendon Rd. sw15. 8S 70
Clarendon Rd. sw19. 13Z 92
Clarendon Rd. w5. 2K 44
Clarendon Rd. w11. 9M 47
Clarendon Rd. Cro. 18Ze 91
Clarendon Rd. Har. 1bC 12
Clarendon Sq. NW1. 16J 49
Clarendon St. NW1. 16J 49
Clarendon St. sw1. 15P 61
Clarendon St. w2. 11L 48
Clarendon Ter. w9. 12K 48
Clarens St. SE0. 24W 88
Clareville Gro. sw7. 12P 60
Clareville St. sw7. 12P 60
Clarges St. w1. 15N 61
Claribel Rd. sw9. 18R 74
Clarina Rd. SE20. 23Z 90
Clarissa St. E8. 21J 51
Clark Rd. Ilf. 35E 42
Clark St. E1. 23L 52
Clark's Orchard SE16. 22N 64
Clark's Row. sw9. 18R 74
Clarkson Rd. Bar. 34J 43
Clarkson St. E2. 22K 52
Clarkson St. E16. 28L 54
Claude Rd. E10. 27E 40
Claude Rd. E13. 29J 55
Claude Rd. SE15. 22S 76
Claude St. E14. 25P 65
Claughton Rd. E13. 30J 55
Clave St. E1. 22N 64
Clavell St. SE10. 26Q 65
Claverdale Rd. sw2. 17V 85
Clavering Av. sw13. 8Q 58
Clavering Rd. E12. 31E 41
Claverley Gro. N3. 11Ab 14
Claverton St. sw1. 16P 61
Claxton Gro. w6. 9P 59
Clay La. Edg. 4Ae 13
Clay St. w1. 14L 49
Claybrook Rd. w6. 9P 59
Claygate Rd. w13. 1aN 94
Clay Hall Rd. E3. 25J 53
Claylands Rd. sw8. 17Q 62
Claypole Rd. E15. 27J 54
Clayponds La. N. Bre. 2O 56
Clayponds La. S. Bre. 2P 56
Clayton Av. Wem. 2G 30
Clayton Cres. Bre. 1P 56
Clayton Rd. SE15. 22R 76
Clayton St. N1. 17H 36
Clayton St. SE11. 18Q 62
Cleaver Sq. SE11. 18P 62
Cleaver St. SE11. 18P 62
Clegg St. E1. 22N 64
Clegg St. E13. 29J 55
Clematis St. w12. 7M 46
Clemence St. E14. 25L 53
Clement Rd. sw19. 9Y 82
Clement Rd. Cro. 23Zb 90
Clementina Rd. E10 24E 39
Clement's Inn wc2. 17M 50
Clement's La. wc4. 20M 51
Clement's La. wc2. 17M 50
Clements La. Ilf. 33F 42
Clements Pl. Bre. 1P 56
Clements Rd. E6. 32H 43
Clement's Rd. SE16. 22O 64
Clements Rd. Ilf. 33F 42
Clephane Rd. N1. 20G 37
Clerkenwell Clo. EC1. 18K 50
Clerkenwell Grn. EC1. 18K 50
Clerkenwell Rd. EC1. 18L 50
Cleve Rd. NW6. 11H 34

Clevedon Av. N12. 13Ac 14
Clevedon Rd. SE20. 23Za 90
Clevedon St. N16. 21E 37
Cleveland Av. sw20. 9Za 92
Cleveland Av. w4. 6O 58
Cleveland Gdns. N15. 19B 25
Cleveland Gdns. NW2. 9D 21
Cleveland Gdns. sw13. 6R 70
Cleveland Gdns. w2. 12L 48
Cleveland Mews. w1. 15L 49
Cleveland Rd. E18. 29A 29
Cleveland Rd. N1. 20H 37
Cleveland Rd. sw13. 6R 70
Cleveland Rd. w4. 5O 57
Cleveland Rd. w13. 1aL 94
Cleveland Rd. Ilf. 33F 42
Cleveland Row sw1. 16N 61
Cleveland Sq. w2. 12M 48
Cleveland St. E1. 23L 52
Cleveland St. w1. 15L 49
Cleveland Pk. Av. E17. 25B 27
Cleveley Cres. w5. 2J 44
Clevelys Rd. E5. 22E 38
Clever Rd. E16. 29M 55
Cleves Rd. E6. 31J 55
Clewer Cre. Har. 1cAa 12
Clifden Rd. E5. 23F 38
Clifden Rd. Bre. 1P 56
Clifden Rd. Twi. 1bV 93
Cliff St. E16. 28L 54
Cliff Ter. SE8. 25S 77
Cliff Villas NW1. 16G 36
Clifford Av. sw14. 4S 69
Clifford Gdns. NW10. 8J 47
Clifford Gro. SE20. 23Z 90
Clifford Rd. E16. 28L 54
Clifford Rd. E17. 26A 28
Clifford Rd. N2. 12Aa 14
Clifford Rd. SE25. 21Zb 90
Clifford Rd. Wem. 1H 30
Clifford St. w1. 15M 49
Clifford Way NW10. 7F 32
Clifford's Inn EC4. 18M 50
Cliffview Rd. SE13. 25T 77
Clift St. N1. 20J 51
Clifton Av. E17 24A 26
Clifton Av. N3. 10Aa 14
Clifton Av. Wem. 3G 30
Clifton Cres. SE15. 22R 76
Clifton Gdns. N15. 22C 26
Clifton Gdns. NW11. 11C 21
Clifton Gdns. w4. 5O 57
Clifton Gdns. w9. 12K 48
Clifton Hill NW8 12J 48
Clifton Hill. SE14. 24R 77
Clifton Pl. w2. 13M 48
Clifton Rd. E7. 31H 41
Clifton Rd. E16. 28L 54
Clifton Rd. N3. 12Aa 14
Clifton Rd. N8. 16C 24
Clifton Rd. N22 16Aa 15
Clifton Rd. NW1. 16G 36
Clifton Rd. NW10. 7J 46
Clifton Rd. SE4. 25S 77
Clifton Rd. SE15. 22R 76
Clifton Rd. SE25 20Zb 90
Clifton Rd. sw19. 8Y 82
Clifton Rd. w9. 12K 48
Clifton Rd. w12. 7N 58
Clifton Rd. Ilf. 34D 42
Clifton Rd. Twi. 1cX 93
Clifton St. E14. 25L 53
Clifton St. EC2. 20L 51
Clifton St. sw8. 16R 74
Clifton St. w11. 9M 47
Clifton Ter. N4. 18E 36

Clifton Villas w9. 12L 48
Clifton Wk. Wem. 2H 30
Clifton Pk. Av. sw20 8Za 92
Cline Rd. N11. 16Ab 15
Clinger St. N1. 20J 51
Clink St. SE1. 19N 63
Clinton Rd. E3. 24K 53
Clinton Rd. E7. 29F 41
Clinton Rd. N15. 20B 25
Clipstone St. w1. 15L 49
Clissold Rd. N16. 20F 37
Clitheroe Rd. sw9. 17S 74
Clitherow Av. w7. 1bN 94
Clitherow Rd. Bre. 1P 56
Clitterhouse Cres. NW2. 9D 21
Clitterhouse La. NW2. 9D 21
Clitterhouse Rd. NW2. 9D 21
Clive Rd. SE21. 20X 86
Clive Rd. sw19. 13Y 83
Clive Rd. Twi. 1bX 93
Clive St. E1. 23L 52
Cliveden Rd. N1. 14O 61
Cliveden Rd. sw19. 10Z 92
Cloak La. EC4. 19M 51
Clock Pl. SE17. 19P 63
Cloister Gdns. Edg. 5Ac 13
Cloister Gdns. Cro. 22Zd 91
Cloister Rd. NW2. 10E 33
Cloister Rd. w3. 5L 45
Clonbrock Rd. N16. 20F 37
Cloncurry St. sw6. 9R 71
Clonmel Rd. sw6. 10R 71
Clonmel Rd. Twi. 1dX 93
Clonmell Rd. N15. 20A 25
Clonmore St. sw18. 10V 82
Clorane Gdns. NW3. 11E 33
Close, The, N14. 16Ae 15
Close, The, N20. 11Ae 14
Close, The, Rich. 4S 69
Close, The, Wem. 2G 30
Cloth Fair EC1. 19L 51
Cloth St. EC1. 19L 51
Cloudesley Rd. sw17. 15W 84
Cloudesley Pl. N1. 18J 50
Cloudesley Rd. N1. 18J 50
Cloudesley Sq. N1. 18H 36
Cloudesley St. N1. 18J 50
Clova Rd. E7. 29G 40
Clovelly Av. NW9. 6A 20
Clovelly Gdns. w9. 21Af 17
Clovelly Rd. N8. 16B 24
Clovelly Rd. w4. 5N 57
Clovelly Rd. w5. 1N 56
Clowders Rd. SE6. 24X 88
Club Row E1. 21K 51
Clunbury St. N1. 20J 51
Cluny Pl. SE1. 20O 63
Clutton St. E14. 26L 53
Clyde Circ. N15 21B 25
Clyde Pl. E10. 26D 27
Clyde Rd. E16. 29N 67
Clyde Rd. N15. 20B 25
Clyde Rd. N22. 16Aa 15
Clyde Rd. Cro. 21Ze 91
Clyde St. SE8. 25O 65
Clyde St. sw10. 12O 60
Clyde Ter. SE23. 23W 87
Clydesdale Gdns. sw14. 3S 69
Clydesdale Rd. w11. 10L 47
Clyston St. sw8. 16R 73
Coalecroft Rd. sw15. 8T 70
Coate St. E2. 22J 52
Cobb St. E1. 21L 51
Cobbett Rd. SE9. 31T 79
Cobbett St. sw8. 17Q 62
Cobbold Rd. E11. 28F 40

Cobbold Rd. NW10. 6G 32
Cobbold Rd. w12. 6N 58
Cobden Rd. E11. 28E 40
Cobden Rd. SE25. 22Zc 90
Cobden St. E14. 26L 53
Cobden St. SE15. 20Q 63
Cobham Rd. N22. 19A 25
Cobham Rd. Ilf. 35E 42
Cobham St. NW8. 13J 48
Coborn Rd. E3. 24K 53
Coborn St. E3. 25K 53
Cobourg Rd. SE5. 21Q 63
Cobourg St. NW1. 16K 49
Coburg Rd. N22. 17A 24
Cochrane Rd. sw19. 9Z 92
Cochrane St. NW8. 13J 48
Cock La. EC1. 19L 50
Cock Yard w1. 15M 49
Cockspur St. sw1. 16N 62
Code St. E1. 21K 51
Codrington Hill SE23. 24V 88
Cody Rd. E15. 27L 54
Coin St. SE1. 18N 62
Coke St. E1. 22L 52
Colbeck Mews sw7. 11P 60
Colbeck Rd. Har. 1dC 12
Colberg Pl. N16. 21D 25
Colby Rd. SE19. 20Y 86
Colchester Av. E12. 32F 42
Colchester Rd. E10. 27D 28
Colchester Rd. E17. 25C 27
Colchester Rd. Edg. 5Ab 13
Colchester St. EC3. 22L 52
Colchester St. sw1. 16P 61
Coldbath Sq. EC1. 18K 50
Coldbath St. SE13. 26S 77
Cold Blow La. SE14. 23Q 64
Coldershaw Rd. w13. 1aM 94
Coldfall Av. N10. 14A 15
Cold Harbour E14. 27N 66
Coldharbour Ln.
 SE5. 1-199 & 2-200
 sw9. 201, 202 & up. 18T 74
Coldharbour Rd. Cro. 17Zg 91
Coldharbour Way Cro. 18Zg 91
Cole Rd. Twi. 1bU 93
Cole St. SE1. 19O 63
Colebrook Av. w13. 1aL 94
Colebrooke Dri. E11. 30D 29
Colebrook Rd. E17. 25B 27
Colebrook Rd. sw16. 16Za 90
Colebrooke Row N1. 19J 50
Coleford Rd. sw18. 11T 72
Colegrave Rd. E15. 27G 40
Colegrove Rd. SE15. 21Q 63
Coleherne Mews sw10. 11P 60
Coleherne Rd. sw10. 11P 60
Colehill La. sw6. 9R 71
Coleman Rd. SE5. 20Q 63
Coleman St. E1. 23N 64
Coleman St. EC2. 20L 51
Colenso Rd. E5. 23F 33
Colenso Rd. Ilf. 35D 42
Cole Pk. Rd. Twi. 1bU 93
Coleraine Rd. N8. 18A 24
Coleraine Rd. SE3. 28Q 66
Coleridge Av. E12. 31G 43
Coleridge Gdns. NW6. 12H 34
Coleridge Rd. E17. 25A 27
Coleridge Rd. N4. 18E 36
Coleridge Rd. N8. 16C 24
Coleridge Rd. N12. 12Ac 14
Coleridge Wk. NW11. 11B 21
Coles Green Rd. NW2. 7D 20
Coleshill Rd. Ted. 1cY 93

Colestown St. sw11. 13R 72
Colet Gdns. w6. 9P 59
Colfe Rd. SE23. 24W 87
Coligny St. sw18. 12T 72
Colin Close NW9. 6B 20
Colin Cres. NW9. 7B 20
Colin Gdns. NW9. 7B 20
Colin Rd. NW10. 7G 32
Colin St. E3. 26L 53
Colina Rd. N15. 19B 25
Colin Deep Gdns. NW4. 7B 20
Colin Deep La. NW9. 6A 20
Colin Pk. Rd. NW9. 6A 20
Colindale Av. NW9. 6A 19
Colinette Rd. sw15. 8T 70
Coliston Rd. sw18. 10U 71
Collamore Av. sw18. 13V 83
Collard Rd. E17. 26B 28
College Cres. NW3. 12G 34
College Gdns. N18. 21Ac 17
College Gdns. SE21. 20R 86
College Hill EC4. 19M 51
College La. E9. 23G 38
College La. NW5. 15F 35
College Place E17. 28B 28
College Place NW1. 16J 49
College Rd. E17. 26C 27
College Rd. N17. 21Ab 17
College Rd. N21. 18Ae 16
College Rd. NW10. 8J 46
College Rd.
 SE21. 1-111 & 2-120
 SE19. 122-160 20V 86
College Rd. sw19. 12Y 83
College Rd. Har. 1cC 12
College St. E3. 24K 53
College St. EC4. 19M 51
College St. N1. 18H 36
College St. SE1. 17N 62
College St. sw15. 10T 71
College Ter. N3. 11Aa 14
Collerston Rd. SE10. 28P 66
Collett Rd. SE16. 22O 64
Collier St. N1. 17J 50
Colliers Water La. Cro.18Zc 90
Collingbourne Rd. w12.7M 46
Collingham Gdns. sw5.11P 60
Collingham Pl. sw5. 11O 60
Collingham Rd. sw5. 11O 60
Collington St. SE10. 27P 66
Collingtree Rd. SE26. 22X 87
Collingwood Av. N10. 14A 23
Collingwood Rd. E17. 25C 27
Collingwood Rd. N15. 20B 25
Collingwood Rd. Mit. 13Za 92
Collingwood St. E1. 22K 52
Collingwood St. sw3. 13P 60
Collins St. SE3. 28S 78
Collinson St. SE1. 19N 63
Colls Rd. SE15. 23R 76
Colman Rd. E16. 30L 55
Colmar St. E1. 23K 52
Colmer Rd. sw16. 17Z 90
Colnbrook St. SE1. 18O 62
Colne Rd. E5. 24F 33
Colne Rd. N21. 20Af 17
Colne Rd. Twi. 1cV 93
Colne St. E13. 29K 54
Colney Hatch La.
 N10. 1-187 & 2-273
 N11. Remainder 14Ac 15
Cologne Rd. sw11. 12T 72
Colomb St. SE10. 28Q 66
Colombo Rd. Ilf. 34D 42
Colombo St. SE1. 18N 62
Colonnade wc1. 17K 50

Colson Rd. Cro. 20Ze 91
Colsterworth Rd. N15. 21B 26
Colston Rd. E7. 31H 41
Colston Rd. sw14. 5S 69
Coltman St. se10. 26Q 65
Columbia Rd. E2. 21K 52
Columbia Rd. E13. 28L 54
Colvestone Cres. E8. 21G 37
Colville Gdns. w11. 10L 47
Colville Rd. E11. 27F 40
Colville Rd. E17. 24A 27
Colville Rd. N9. 22Ae 17
Colville Rd. w3. 4O 57
Colville Rd. w11. 10M 47
Colville Sq. w11. 10M 47
Colville Ter. w11. 10M 47
Colvin Rd. E6. 31J 43
Colvin Rd. Cro. 17Zc 90
Colvin St. w6. 8O 58
Colwell Rd. se22. 21U 75
Colwick St. se8. 24P 65
Colwick Ter. se8. 24P 65
Colwith Rd. w6. 8Q 59
Colwood Gdns. sw19. 12Z 91
Colworth Gro. se17. 19P 63
Colworth Rd. E11. 28C 28
Colworth Rd. Cro. 21Ze 91
Colwyn Rd. nw2. 8E 32
Colwyn St. se1. 18O 62
Colyton Rd. se22. 22U 76
Combe Rd. w4. 6P 58
Combedale Rd. se10. 29P 67
Combemartin Rd. sw15.
                         10V 82
Comber Gro. se5. 19R 75
Combermere Rd. sw9. 17S 74
Comberton Rd. E5. 22E 38
Comboss Rd. E9. 25H 39
Comeragh Rd. w14. 10P 59
Comerford Rd. se4. 24T 77
Comet St. se8. 25R 77
Commerce Rd. n22. 17Aa 16
Commerce Way Cro. 17Zf 91
Commercial Rd. n18. 21Ab 17
Commercial Rd. se1. 18N 62
Commercial Rd. E.
  E1, 1–601 & 2–554
  E14, 556, 603 & up 22M 52
Commercial St. E1. 21L 51
Commercial Way se15.
                         21R 75
Commerell St. se10. 28P 66
Commodore St. E1. 24L 53
Common, The, w5. 2M 44
Commons St. E14. 25O 65
Commonwealth Rd. n17.
                         22Ab 17
Como Rd. se23. 24W 87
Compayne Gdns. nw6. 11G 34
Compton Av. E6. 31J 55
Compton Av. n1. 19H 37
Compton Av. n6. 13D 22
Compton Cres. n17. 19Ab 16
Compton Cres. w4. 4Q 57
Compton Rd. n1. 19G 37
Compton Rd. n21. 19Ae 16
Compton Rd. nw10. 9K 47
Compton Rd. sw19. 10Y 82
Compton Rd. Cro. 22Ze 91
Compton St. Ec1. 19K 51
Compton St. n1. 20G 37
Compton St. wc1. 17K 50
Compton Ter. n1. 19H 36
Comus Pl. se17. 20P 63
Comyn Rd. sw11. 13T 72
Conan St. w14. 10P 59

Concanon Rd. sw2. 17T 74
Condell Rd. sw8. 16R 73
Conder St. E14. 24L 53
Conderton Rd. se5. 19S 75
Condray St. sw11. 13R 72
Conduit La. Cro. 21Zh 91
Conduit Pl. w2. 12M 48
Conduit Rd. se18. 33P 95
Conduit St. E5. .22E 38
Conduit St. w1, 15M 49
Conduit Way nw10. 5G 31
Conewood St. n5. 19F 37
Congo Rd. se18. 35Q 95
Congreve St. se17. 20P 63
Conifer Gdns. sw16. 17X 85
Coniger Rd. sw6. 11R 71
Coningham Rd. w12. 7N 58
Coningsby Rd. n4. 18C 24
Coningsby Rd. w5. 1N 56
Conington Rd. se13. 26S 77
Conisborough Cres. se6.
                         26X 88
Coniston Av. Bar. 35H 43
Coniston Av. Wem. 1J 44
Coniston Gdns. nw9. 5B 19
Coniston Rd. n10. 15A 23
Coniston Rd. n17. 22Ab 17
Coniston Rd. Cro. 21Ze 91
Conlan St. w10. 9K 47
Conley Rd. nw10. 6G 32
Conley St. se10. 28P 66
Conn St. se8. 25Q 65
Connaught Av. sw14. 4S 69
Connaught Gdns. n10. 15B 23
Connaught Gdns. n13. 19Ac 16
Connaught Pl. w2. 14M 49
Connaught Rd. E11. 27E 40
Connaught Rd. E16. 30M 55
Connaught Rd. E17. 25C 27
Connaught Rd. nw10. 6H 32
Connaught Rd. w13. 1aM 94
Connaught Rd. Har. 1bAa 12
Connaught Rd. Ilf. 34E 42
Connaught Rd. Twi. 1dX 93
Connaught Sq. w2. 13L 48
Connaught St. w2. 13L 48
Connaught Way n13. 19Ac 16
Connor St. E9. 23J 52
Conolly Rd. w7. 1cM 93
Conquest St. se1. 19O 62
Conrad St. E9. 23H 38
Conroy St. sw8. 16Q 62
Cons St. se1. 18N 62
Constable Close nw11. 12C 22
Constable Gdns. Edg. 4Aa 13
Constance Rd. se22. 20T 75
Constance Rd. Cro. 18Zd 91
Constance St. E16. 31N 67
Constantine Rd. nw3. 14F 35
Constitution Hill sw1.
                         15N 61
Content St. se17. 19P 63
Convent Gdns. w5. 1O 56
Convent Gdns. w11. 10L 47
Conway Gdns. w3. 5L 45
Conway Rd. n14. 17Ad 16
Conway Rd. n15. 19B 25
Conway Rd. nw2. 8E 32
Conway Rd. se18. 35P 95
Conway Rd. sw20. 8Z 92
Conyer St. E3. 24J 53
Conyers Rd. sw16. 16Y 84
Cook St. E14. 26M 53
Cooke St. Bar. 34J 43
Cook's Rd. E15. 26J 53

Cook's Rd. se17. 19Q 62
Coolfin Rd. E16. 29M 55
Coolhurst Av. n8. 16C 23
Coolhurst Rd. n8. 16C 24
Coomassie Rd. w9. 10K 47
Coombe Av. Cro. 20Zg 91
Coombe La. sw20. 8Za 92
Coombe La. Cro. 22Zg 91
Coombe Pk. Kin. 5Y 80
Coombe Rd. n22 18Aa 16
Coombe Rd. se26. 22X 87
Coombe Rd. Cro. 19Zg 91
Coombe Wood Rd. Kin.
                         4Y 80
Coomb's St. n1. 19J 51
Coomer Rd. sw6. 10Q 59
Cooper Rd. nw10. 7G 32
Cooper Rd. Cro. 18Zg 91
Cooper St. E16. 28L 54
Cooper's La. E10. 26D 27
Cooper's Rd. se1. 21P 63
Cooper's Row Ec3. 21M 51
Coopersale Rd. E9. 24G 38
Cope Place w8 11O 59
Cope St. se16. 23P 64
Copeland Av. se15. 22S 76
Copeland Rd. E17 26C 27
Copeland Rd. se15. 22S 76
Copenhagen Pl. E14 25M 53
Copenhagen St. n1. 17J 50
Copers Cope Rd. Bec. 25Y 88
Copland Av. Wem. 1F 30
Copland Rd. Wem. 2G 30
Copleston Rd. se15. 21T 75
Copley Pk. sw16. 17Y 85
Copley St. E1. 23L 52
Copperas St. se8. 26Q 65
Copperfield Rd. E3. 24L 53
Copperfield St. sw1. 19N 63
Coppermill La. E17. 23C 26
Copper Mill La. sw17. 11X 83
Coppetts Rd. n10. 14Ab 15
Coppice Clo. sw20. 8Zb 92
Coppice Drive sw15 7U 70
Coppice Wk. sw20. 11Ae 14
Copse Hill sw20. 8Z 92
Copthall Av. Ec2. 20L 51
Copthall Bldgs. Ec2. 20L 51
Copthall Gdns. Twi. 1bV 93
Copthorne Av. sw12. 16R 84
Coptic St. wc1. 17L 50
Coral St. se1. 18N 62
Coram St. wc1. 17K 50
Corbet Pl. E1. 21L 51
Corbett Rd. E11. 30C 29
Corbett Rd. E17. 27A 28
Corbett St. se16. 23P 64
Corbridge Cres. E2. 22J 52
Corby Rd. nw10. 5J 45
Corbyn St. n4. 17D 24
Cordelia St. E14. 26M 53
Cording St. E14. 26L 53
Cordova Rd. E3. 24K 53
Corfield St. E2. 22K 52
Corfton Rd. w5. 2L 44
Corinne Rd. n19. 16F 35
Corinth Rd. n7. 17G 36
Cork St. se5. 20R 75
Cork St. w1. 15M 49
Cormont Rd. se5. 18R 74
Cornbury Rd. se16. 23P 64
Cornbury st. se17. 20P 63
Cornelia St. n7. 18H 36
Corney Rd. w4. 6Q 58
Cornflower Ter. se22. 22U 76

Cornford Gro. sw12. 15W 84
Cornhill ec3. 20M 51
Cornick St. se16. 22O 64
Cornthwaite Rd. e5. 23F 38
Cornwall Av. n3. 11Ab 14
Cornwall Av. n22. 17Aa 16
Cornwall Clo. Bar. 36H 43
Cornwall Gdns. sw7. 11O 60
Cornwall Gro. nw10. 8G 32
Cornwall Gro. w4. 6P 58
Cornwall Rd. e2. 23K 52
Cornwall Rd. e9. 23H 38
Cornwall Rd. n4. 18D 24
Cornwall Rd. n15. 20B 25
Cornwall Rd. se1. 18N 62
Cornwall Rd. w11. 10L 47
Cornwall Rd. Cro. 18Zf 91
Cornwall Rd. Har. 1dB 12
Cornwall Rd. Twi. 1aV 93
Cornwall St. e1. 22M 52
Cornwall St. sw1. 16P 61
Cornwall St. sw6. 11Q 60
Cornwall Ter. nw1. 14K 49
Cornwallis Av. n9. 23Ae 17
Cornwallis Gro. n9. 23Ae 17
Cornwallis Rd. e17. 24B 26
Cornwallis Rd. n9. 23Ae 17
Cornwallis Rd. n19. 17E 36
Cornwood Clo. n2. 13B 22
Corona Rd. se12. 29V 89
Coronation Rd. e13. 30K 55
Coronation Rd. nw10. 4K 45
Coronet St. n1. 20K 51
Corporation Rd. Cro.
22Zd 91
Corporation Row ec1. 18K 50
Corporation St. e15. 28J 54
Corporation St. n7. 17G 36
Corrance Rd. sw2. 17T 74
Corrie Av. n14. 16Ad 15
Corringham Rd. nw11. 11C 22
Corringham Rd. Wem. 4D 19
Corringway nw11. 11D 22
Corringway w5. 3L 44
Corsehill St. sw16. 15Y 84
Corsica St. n5. 19G 37
Corston St. se8. 24Q 65
Cortayne Rd. sw6. 10R 71
Corunna Rd. sw8. 15R 73
Corunna Ter. sw8. 15R 73
Cosbycote Av. se24. 19T 75
Cosmo Pl. wc1. 17L 50
Cossall St. se15. 22R 76
Costa St. se15. 21S 76
Cosway St. nw1. 13L 48
Cotall St. e14. 25L 53
Cote Av. sw16. 17Z 90
Coteford St. sw17. 14X 84
Cotesbach Rd. e5. 23F 38
Cotford Rd. Cro. 19Zb 90
Cotham St. se17. 19P 63
Cotherstone Rd. sw2. 17V 85
Cotleigh Rd. nw6. 11H 33
Cotman Clo. nw11. 12C 22
Cotman Gdns. Edg. 3Aa 13
Cotman St. sw18. 12T 72
Cotswold Gdns. e6. 31K 55
Cotswold Gdns. nw2. 9D 21
Cotswold Gdns. Ilf. 35D 42
Cotswold Gate nw2. 10D 21
Cotswold St. se27. 19X 85
Cottage Grn. se5. 20Q 63
Cottage Grove e3. 24K 53
Cottage Grove sw9. 17S 74
Cottage La. ec1. 19K 51
Cottage Pl. se11. 18Q 60

Cottage St. e14. 26M 53
Cottage Wk. sw3. 13O 60
Cottenham Rd. e17. 25B 27
Cottenham Rd. n19. 17D 24
Cottenham Pk. Rd. sw20.
8Z 92
Cottesbrook St. se14. 24Q 64
Cottesmore Gdns. w8. 11O 60
Cottingham Rd. se20. 23Z 90
Cottington St. se11. 18P 62
Cotton St. e14. 26M 53
Cotton's Gdns. e2. 21K 51
Cotton's La. e11. 28D 28
Cottrill Rd. e8. 22G 38
Coulgate St. se4. 24S 77
Coulson St. sw3. 14P 61
Councillor St. se5. 19R 75
Countess Rd. e17. 25A 27
Countess Rd. nw5. 16F 35
County Gro. se5. 19R 75
County Rd. Cro. 18Za 90
County St. se1. 19O 63
Coupland Ter. se18. 34Q 95
Courcy Rd. n8. 18A 24
Courland Grove sw8. 16R 74
Court Clo. Har. 2A 18
Court Dri. Cro. 17Zg 91
Court La. se21. 20U 75
Court Rd. se25. 21Zb 90
Court St. e1. 22L 52
Court Way nw9. 6A 20
Court Way w3. 5L 45
Court Way Twi. 1bU 93
Courtenay Av. n6. 13D 22
Courtenay Rd. e11. 28F 40
Courtenay Rd. e17. 24B 26
Courtenay Rd. sw19. 13Z 92
Courtenay Sq. se11. 18P 62
Courtenay St. se11. 18P 62
Courtfield Av. Har. 1bB 12
Courtfield Cres. Har. 1bB 12
Courtfield Gdns. sw5. 11O 60
Courtfield Gdns. sw13. 1aL 94
Courtfield Rd. sw7. 12O 60
Courthill Rd. se13. 26T 77
Courthope Rd. nw3. 14F 35
Courthope Rd. sw19. 9Y 82
Courthope Villas sw19. 9Z 92
Courthouse Rd. n3. 11Ab 14
Courthouse Rd. n12. 11Ac 14
Courtleigh Gdns. nw11.
10B 21
Courtman Rd. n17. 19Aa 16
Courtnell St. w2. 11L 47
Courtney Rd. n7. 18F 36
Courtney Rd. Cro. 18Zf 91
Courtrai Rd. se23. 24U 76
Cousin La. ec4. 19M 51
Couthurst Rd. se3. 30Q 67
Coutts Rd. e3. 24L 53
Coval Gdns. sw14. 4T 69
Coval Rd. sw14. 4T 69
Covent Gdn. wc2. 17M 50
Coventry Rd. se25. 21Zb 90
Coventry Rd. Ilf. 33E 42
Coventry St.
e1. 1-83 & 2-64
e2. 66, 85 & up. 22K 52
Coventry St. w1. 16M 50
Coverdale Rd. nw2. 9H 33

Coverdale Rd. w12. 8N 58
Coverdale Rd. Bar. 34J 43
Coverton Rd. sw17. 13X 83
Covington Gdns. se19. 18Z 90
Covington Way sw16. 17X 85
Cowan St. se5. 20Q 63
Cowbridge La. Bar. 33H 43
Cowcross St. ec1. 18L 50
Cowden St. se6. 25X 88
Cowdrey Rd. sw19. 11Y 83
Cowdry St. e9. 24G 39
Cowick Rd. sw17. 14X 84
Cowley La. e11. 28E 40
Cowley Rd. e11. 28E 40
Cowley Rd. e11. 29C 29
Cowley Rd. sw9. 18R 74
Cowley Rd. sw14. 5S 69
Cowley Rd. w3. 6N 58
Cowley Rd. Ilf. 32D 42
Cowley St. e1. 23M 52
Cowley St. sw1. 16O 62
Cowper Rd. n14. 15Ae 15
Cowper Rd. n16. 20F 37
Cowper Rd. n18. 22Ac 17
Cowper Rd. sw19. 12Y 83
Cowper Rd. w3. 5M 45
Cowper Rd. w7. 1bM 94
Cowper St. ec2. 20K 51
Cowper's Row sw2. 17V 85
Cowslip Rd. e18. 30A 29
Cox's Wk. se21. 21V 87
Coxson Pl. se1. 21N 63
Coxmount Rd. se7. 31P 67
Coxwell Rd. se18. 35P 95
Crabtree Av. Wem. 3J 44
Crab Tree La. sw6. 9Q 59
Craddock St. nw1. 14G 35
Cragnair Rd. sw2. 17V 85
Craigen Av. Cro. 22Ze 91
Craigerne Rd. se3. 29R 79
Craignish Av. sw16. 17Za 90
Crail Row se17. 20P 63
Cramer St. w1. 14L 49
Cramore Rd. se12. 28X 89
Crampton Rd. se20. 22Z 90
Crampton St. se17. 19P 63
Cranborne Rd. Bar. 34J 43
Cranbourn St. wc2. 16M 50
Cranbourne Av. e11. 29B 29
Cranbourne Gdns. nw11.
10B 21
Cranbourne Rd. e15. 27F 40
Cranbourne Rd. n10. 15Aa 15
Cranbrook Rise Ilf. 32D 42
Cranbrook Rd. e2. 23J 52
Cranbrook Rd. e16. 29N 67
Cranbrook Rd. e17. 25B 27
Cranbrook Rd. n17. 21Ab 17
Cranbrook Rd. se8. 25R 77
Cranbrook Rd. se19. 19Za 90
Cranbrook Rd. sw19. 9Z 92
Cranbrook Rd. w4. 6P 58
Cranbrook Rd. Ilf. 33C 42
Cranbrook St. e2. 23J 52
Cranbrook Pk. Rd. n22.
18Aa 16
Cranbury Rd. sw6. 11R 72
Crane Av. w3. 5M 45
Crane Av. Twi. 1bT 93
Crane Ct. ec4. 18M 50
Crane Gro. n7. 18G 36
Crane Rd. Twi. 1cV 93
Crane St. se10. 27Q 66
Craneford Way Twi. 1bU 93
Cranfield Rd. se4. 24S 77
Cranfield Villas se27. 19X 86

Cranford Gdns. N13. 17Ac 16
Cranford St. E1. 23M 52
Cranham Gdns. N9. 21Ad 17
Cranham Rd. SE16. 22P 64
Cranhurst Rd. NW2. 8G 33
Cranleigh Gdns. Bar. 34H 43
Cranleigh Gdns. Har. 2B 18
Cranleigh Rd. N15. 19B 25
Cranleigh Rd. SW19. 10Zb 92
Cranley Dri. Ilf. 34D 42
Cranley Gdns. N10. 15B 23
Cranley Gdns. N13. 18Ad 16
Cranley Gdns. SW7. 12P 60
Cranley Mews SW7. 12P 60
Cranley Pl. SW7. 12P 60
Cranley Rd. E13. 80L 55
Cranley Rd. Ilf. 34D 42
Cranmer Av. W13. 1aO 94
Cranmer Rd. E7. 30F 41
Cranmer Rd. SW9. 18Q 62
Cranmer Rd. Cro. 18Zf 91
Cranmer Rd. Edg. 4Ae 13
Cranmore Way N10. 16B 23
Cranston St. SW7. 24W 87
Cranswick Rd. SE16. 22P 64
Crantock Rd. SE6. 26W 88
Cranwich Rd. N16. 20D 25
Cranworth Gdns. SW9. 18R 74
Craster Rd. SW2. 17V 85
Crathie Rd. SE12. 29U 79
Crathorn St. SE13. 26S 77
Craven Av. W5. 1M 44
Craven Gdns. SW19. 11Y 82
Craven Hill W2. 12M 48
Craven Mews W5. 1M 44
Craven Pk. NW10. 6H 31
Craven Rd. NW10. 5H 31
Craven Rd. W2. 12M 48
Craven Rd. W5. 1M 44
Craven Rd. Cro. 22Ze 91
Craven St. N1. 20K 51
Craven St. WC2. 17M 50
Craven Ter. W2. 12M 48
Craven Wk. N16. 22D 26
Craven Hill Gdns. W2. 12M 48
Craven Pk. Rd. N15. 21C 25
Craven Pk. Rd. NW10. 6H 32
Crawford Av. Wem. 2F 30
Crawford Gdns. N13.
         19Ad 16
Crawford Pl. W1. 13L 48
Crawford Rd. SE5. 19R 75
Crawford Rd. Wem. 1F 30
Crawford St. E16. 28M 54
Crawford St. W1. 13L 48
Crawley Rd. E10. 26D 27
Crawley Rd. N9. 21Af 17
Crawley Rd. N22. 19A 25
Crawshay Rd. SW9. 18R 74
Crawthew Gro. SE22. 21T 75
Crayford Rd. N7. 17F 36
Crealock St. SW18. 11U 72
Creasy St. SE1. 20O 63
Crebor St. SE22. 22U 76
Credenhill St. SW16. 15Y 84
Crediton Hill NW6. 11G 34
Crediton Rd. E16. 29M 54
Crediton Rd. NW10. 9J 47
Credon Rd. E13. 30J 55
Credon Rd. SE16. 22P 64
Creechurch La. EC3. 21M 51
Creed La. EC4. 19M 51
Creek Rd. SE8. 25Q 65
Creek St. SE8. 25R 77
Creek St. SW11. 12S 72
Creek Pl. W6. 8P 58

Creeland Gro. SE6. 25S 88
Crefeld Rd. W6, 9Q 59
Creffield Rd.
   w5. 1-51 & 2-56.
   w3. 53, 58 & up. 3M 44
Creighton Av. E6. 31J 55
Creighton Av. N2. 13A 22
Creighton Rd. N17. 21Ab 17
Creighton Rd. NW6. 9J 47
Creighton Rd. W5. 1O 56
Crellin St. E1. 22M 52
Cremer St. E2. 21J 51
Cremorne Rd. SW10. 12Q 60
Crescent Gdns. SW19. 11X 82
Crescent Gro. SW4. 16T 73
Crescent La. SW4. 16T 73
Crescent Rise W2. 16Aa 15
Crescent Rd. E6. 30J 55
Crescent Rd. E10. 25E 39
Crescent Rd. E13. 29J 55
Crescent Rd. N3. 11Aa 14
Crescent Rd. N8. 16C 24
Crescent Rd. N9. 22Ae 17
Crescent Rd. N11. 14Ac 15
Crescent Rd. N22. 17Aa 15
Crescent Rd. SW20. 8Z 92
Crescent Rd. SE18. 33P 95
Crescent Rd. SE19. 21Z 90
Crescent Row EC1. 19K 51
Crescent St. N1. 17H 36
Crescent St. W11. 9M 47
Crescent, The. E17. 24C 27
Crescent, The. N11. 14Ac 15
Crescent, The. N15. 21C 25
Crescent, The. NW2. 8E 32
Crescent, The. NW8. 7R 70
Crescent, The. SW13. 11X 82
Crescent, The. Cro. 20Zd 91
Crescent, The. Har. 1aD 12
Crescent, The. Ilf. 33C 42
Crescent Way N12. 13Ab 14
Crescent Way SE4. 25T 77
Crescent Way SE16. 17Z 90
Crescent Wood Rd. SE26.
         21X 86
Cresford Rd. SW6. 11R 72
Creslow St. SE13. 27U 78
Crespigny Rd. NW4. 8C 20
Cressage Rd. Bre. 2P 56
Cressida Rd. N19. 16D 23
Cressingham Rd. SE13. 26S 78
Cressingham Rd. Edg. 5Ab 13
Cressington Rd. N16. 21F 37
Cresswell Pl. SW10. 12P 60
Cresswell Rd. SE25. 22Zb 90
Cressy Av. W4. 3P 57
Cressy Pl. E1. 23L 52
Cressy Rd. NW3. 14F 35
Crest Rd. NW2. 7E 32
Crest, The. N13. 18Ac 16
Crestway SW15. 7U 70
Crest Brook Av. N13. 19Ad 16
Creswick Rd. E3. 25K 53
Creswick Rd. W3. 4M 45
Creswick Wk. NW11. 11B 21
Creton St. SE18. 33P 95
Crew St. E14. 25O 65
Crewdson Rd. SW9. 18Q 62
Crewys Rd. NW11. 11E 33
Crewys Rd. SE15. 22S 76
Crichton St. SW8. 15S 73
Cricketfield Rd. E5. 22F 38
Cricklade Av. SW2. 17W 85
Cricklewood La. NW2. 9F 33

Crieff Rd. SW18. 12U 72
Criffel Av. SW2. 16W 85
Crimscott St. SE1. 21O 63
Crimsworth Rd. SW8. 16R 74
Crinan St. N1. 17J 50
Cringle St. SW8. 15Q 61
Crisp Rd. W6. 8P 58
Crispin Rd. Edg. 5Ab 13
Crispin St. E1. 21L 51
Cristowe Rd. SW6. 10R 71
Criterion Mews N19. 16E 36
Crockerton Rd. SW17. 13W 83
Crockford Pl. NW1. 13L 48
Crocus Wk. W12. 6M 46
Croft Gdns. W7. 1bN 94
Croft Rd. SW19. 12Z 92
Croft Rd. Har. 1aE 12
Croft St. SE8. 24P 64
Croft, The. NW10. 6J 46
Croft, The. Wem. 1F 30
Croftdown Rd. NW5. 15E 35
Crofton Rd. E13. 30K 55
Crofton Rd. SE5. 20R 75
Crofton Ter. Rich. 2S 68
Crofton Pk. Rd. SE4. 24U 77
Crofts Rd. Har. 1aB 12
Croftway NW3. 11F 34
Crogsland Rd. NW3. 14H 35
Croham Rd. Cro. 19Zg 91
Croham Manor Way Cro.
         20Zh 91
Croham Pk. Av. Cro. 20Zg 91
Croindene Rd. SW16. 17Za 90
Cromartie Rd. N19. 16D 24
Crome St. SE10. 29P 66
Cromer Rd. E10. 27D 28
Cromer Rd. SE25. 22Zb 90
Cromer Rd. SW17. 14Y 84
Cromer St. WC1. 17K 50
Cromer Villas Rd. SW18.
         10U 71
Cromford Rd. SW18. 10T 71
Crompton St. W2. 12K 48
Cromwell Av. N6. 15D 23
Cromwell Av. W6. 7P 58
Cromwell Cres. W8. 10O 59
Cromwell Gro. W6. 8O 59
Cromwell Pl. N6. 15D 23
Cromwell Pl. SW7. 12O 60
Cromwell Rd. E7. 30H 41
Cromwell Rd. E17. 26C 27
Cromwell Rd. N3. 12Aa 14
Cromwell Rd. N10. 15Ab 15
Cromwell Rd. N19. 16E 36
Cromwell Rd.
   sw7. 1-147 & 2-156.
   sw5. 147A, 158 & up.
         11O 60
Cromwell Rd. SW19. 11Y 82
Cromwell Rd. Cro. 19Zd 91
Cromwell Rd. Twi. 1bY 93
Cromwell Rd. Wem. 2J 44
Crondace Rd. SW6. 11R 71
Crondall St. N1. 20J 51
Cronin St. SE15. 21Q 63
Crooke Rd. SE8. 24P 64
Crooked Usage N3. 10A 21
Crooms Hill SW6. 10R 71
Croom's Hill SE10. 27Q 66
Cropley St. N1. 20J 51
Crosby Rd. E7. 29G 40
Crosby Row SE1. 20N 63
Crosby Sq. EC3. 20M 51
Cross Deep Twi. 1bW 93
Cross La. EC3. 20M 51
Cross La. N8. 17A 24

Cross Rd. E5. 22F 38
Cross Rd. N8. 17A 24
Cross Rd. E15. 15Ac 15
Cross Rd. N22. 18Ab 16
Cross Rd. sw19. 11Z 92
Cross Rd. Cro. 20Ze 91
Cross Rd. Har. 1aAa 12
Cross Rd. Har. 1cB 12
Cross St. E15. 28H 40
Cross St. E17. 24B 27
Cross St. EC1. 18L 50
Cross St. N1. 19H 37
Cross St. NW4. 7C 20
Cross St. sw4. 16S 73
Cross St. sw13. 6S 70
Cross. wc1. 17K 50
Crossfield Rd. N15. 19A 25
Crossfield Rd. NW3. 13G 34
Crossfield St. se8. 25Q 65
Crossford St. sw9. 17S 74
Crosslands Av. w5. 3N 56
Crossley St. N7. 18G 36
Cross Way N9. 21Af 17
Cross Way N12. 13Ab 14
Cross Way Edg. 4Ad 13
Cross Deep Gdns. Twi. 1bV 93
Crossland Rd. Cro. 18Zd 91
Crossway, N16. 21G 37
Crossway sw20. 8Zb 92
Crossway The Har. 1bAa 12
Crossways N22. 19Ab 16
Crossways, The, Wem. 4D 19
Croston St. E3. 22H 38
Crouch Hill
  N4. 1-79 & 2-60.
  N8. 62, 81 & up. 17C 24
Crouch Rd. NW10. 5G 31
Crouch End Hill N8. 16C 23
Crouch Hall Rd. N8. 16C 24
Crowborough Rd, sw17,
  17V 01
Crowhurst Rd. sw9. 18S 74
Crowland Rd. N15. 21C 25
Crowland Rd. Cro. 19Zc 90
Crowland Ter. N1. 20H 37
Crowlands Gdns. N14.
  17Af 16
Crowley Cres. Cro. 18Zg 91
Crown Ct. wc2. 17L 50
Crown Hill se19. 19Y 85
Crown Hill Cro. 19Zf 91
Crown La. N14. 16Ae 15
Crown La. sw16. 18Y 85
Crown La. w3. 6M 46
Crown La. Mor. 11Zb 92
Crown Pl. NW5. 15G 35
Crown Rd. N10. 15Ab 15
Crown Rd. N17. 22Ab 17
Crown Rd. Mor. 11Zb 92
Crown Rd. Twi. 1aU 93
Crown St. E16. 29M 54
Crown St. se5. 19Q 63
Crown St. w3. 4N 57
Crown St. Har. 1cD 12
Crown Ter. Rich. 3S 68
Crowndale Rd. NW1. 16J 49
Crownfield Av. Ilf. 35C 42
Crownfield Rd. E15. 27F 40
Crownhill Rd. NW10. 6H 32
Crown La. Gdns. sw16.
  18Y 85
Crownstone Rd. sw2. 17U 74
Crowther Av. Kew 2O 56
Crowther Rd. se25. 21Zc 90
Croxford Gdns. N22. 19Aa 16
Croxley Rd. w9. 10K 47

Croxted Rd.
  se21. 1-293 & 2-198.
  se24. 200, 295 & up.
  19V 86
Croydon Gro. Cro. 18Ze 91
Croydon Rd. E13. 28L 54
Croydon Rd. se20. 22Za 90
Croydon Rd. Cro. 23Zc 90
Croyland Rd. N9. 22Ae 17
Crozier Rd. se1. 17O 62
Crozier Ter. E9. 24G 38
Crucifix La. se1. 20N 63
Crudon St. N1. 19J 51
Cruikshank Rd. E15. 28G 40
Crummock Gdns. NW9. 6B 20
Crundale Av. NW9. 4B 19
Crutched Friars EC3. 21M 51
Crystal Ter. se19. 19Y 86
Crystal Pal. Parade se19.
  21Y 86
Crystal Pal. Rd. se22. 21U 75
Crystal Pal. Pk. Rd. se26.
  22Y 87
Cuba St. E14. 25N 65
Cubitt St. wc1. 17K 50
Cuckoo Dene w7. 1cK 94
Cuckoo La. w7. 1bM 94
Cudham St. se6. 26V 88
Cudworth St. E1. 22K 52
Culford Gdns. sw3. 14O 61
Culford Gro. N1. 20H 37
Culford Mews N1. 20G 37
Culford Rd. N1. 20H 37
Culling Rd. se16. 23O 64
Cullingworth Rd. NW10.
  7F 32
Culloden St. E14. 27M 54
Cullum St. E15. 27H 40
Culloss Rd. N15. 19B 25
Culross St. w1. 14M 49
Culverden Rd. sw12. 15W 84
Culverhouse Gdns. sw16.
  17X 85
Culverley Rd. se6. 26V 88
Culvert Pl. sw11. 14S 73
Culvert Rd. N15. 20B 25
Culvert Rd. sw11. 14R 73
Culworth St. NW8. 13J 48
Cumberland Av. NW10. 4J 45
Cumberland Cres. w14.
  10O 59
Cumberland Mkt. NW1.
  15K 49
Cumberland Pk. w3. 5M 45
Cumberland Rd. E12. 31G 41
Cumberland Rd. E13. 29L 55
Cumberland Rd. E17. 25C 27
Cumberland Rd. se25.
  22Zd 91
Cumberland Rd. sw13. 7R 70
Cumberland Rd. w3. 5M 45
Cumberland Rd. w7. 1bN 94
Cumberland Rd. Kew 3Q 56
Cumberland St. N7. 17H 36
Cumberland St. sw1. 15P 61
Cumberland Ter. N4. 18N 62
Cumberland Ter. NW1. 15J 49
Cumberland Ter. NW1. 15J 49
Cumberton Rd. N17. 20Aa 17
Cumbrian Gdns. NW2. 9E 33
Cumming St. N1. 18J 50

Cunard St. se5. 20Q 63
Cundy Rd. E16. 30M 55
Cunliffe St. sw16. 15Y 84
Cunningham Pk. Har. 1cB 12
Cunningham Pl. NW8. 12K 48
Cunningham Rd. N15. 21B 26
Cunnington St. w4. 5O 57
Cupar Rd. sw11. 14R 73
Curlew St. se1. 21N 63
Currie Rd. sw11. 12S 72
Currie St. sw8. 16Q 62
Cursitor St. EC4. 18L 50
Curtain Rd. EC2. 20K 51
Curtis St. se1. 21O 63
Curve, The, w12. 7M 46
Curwen Rd. w12. 7N 58
Curzon Av. Har. 1aAa 12
Curzon Cres. NW10. 6G 32
Curzon Rd. N10. 15Aa 15
Curzon Rd. Cro. 17Zd 91
Curzon St. N1. 20J 51
Curzon St. w1. 15N 61
Custance St. N1. 20J 51
Custom St. E16. 29M 55
Cut, The, se1. 18N 62
Cutcombe Rd. se5. 19S 75
Cuthbert Rd. E17. 27A 28
Cuthbert Rd. Cro. 18Zf 91
Cuthbert St. w2. 12L 48
Cuthill Rd. se5. 20R 75
Cutler St. E1. 21L 51
Cyclops Pl. E14. 25P 65
Cygnet St. E1. 21K 51
Cymon St. E2. 21K 52
Cynthia St. N1. 18J 50
Cypress Rd. se25. 20Za 90
Cypress Rd. Har. 1cAa 12
Cyprus St. N8. 10Aa 14
Cyprus Rd. N9. 21Ae 17
Cyprus St. E2. 23J 52
Cyprus Pl. se22. 21U 76
Cyrus St. EC1. 19K 51
Czar St. se8. 25Q 65

Dacca St. se8. 25Q 65
Dace Rd. E3. 25H 39
Dacre Pk. se13. 28T 78
Dacre Rd. E11. 28U 28
Dacre Rd. E13. 29J 55
Dacre Rd. Cro. 16Zd 91
Dacre St. se13. 28T 78
Dacre St. sw1. 16O 62
Dacres Rd. se23. 23X 87
Daffodil St. w12. 7M 46
Dafforne Rd. sw17. 14X 84
Dagenham Rd. E10. 25D 27
Dagmar Av. Wem. 3F 30
Dagmar Gdns. NW10 9J 47
Dagmar Rd. E9. 24H 39
Dagmar Rd. N4. 18C 24
Dagmar Rd. N22. 17Aa 15
Dagmar Rd. se5. 20R 75
Dagmar Rd. se25. 20Zc 90
Dagmar Ter. N1. 19H 37
Dagnal Rd. se25. 20Zc 90
Dagnall Pk. se25. 20Zc 90
Dagnall St. sw11. 14R 73
Dagnan Rd. sw12. 15U 73
Dagonet Rd. se12. 29X 89
Dahomey Rd. sw16. 15Y 84
Dainford Clo. Bec. 27Y 89
Daintry St. E9. 25G 39
Dairy Wk. sw19. 9X 82
Daisy La. sw6. 11S 71
Daisy Rd. E18. 30A 29
Dakin St. E14. 24L 53

Dalby St. nw5. 15G 35	Darien Rd. sw11. 12S 72	Dawson Pl. w2. 11M 47
Dalby Rd. sw18. 12T 72	Darlan Rd. sw6. 10R 71	Dawson Rd. nw2. 9F 33
Dalberg Rd. sw2. 18T 74	Darlaston Rd. sw19. 9Z 92	Dawson St. se18. 34P 95
Dale Av. Edg. 3Aa 13	Darley Rd. sw11. 13U 72	Dawson St. w6. 9P 59
Dale Gro. n12. 12Ac 14	Darling Rd. se4. 25S 77	Daybrook Rd. sw19. 11Za 92
Dale Rd. e16. 28L 54	Darling Row e1. 22L 52	Daylesford Av. sw15. 7S 70
Dale Rd. nw5. 14G 35	Darlington Rd. se27. 19Y 85	Daysbrook Rd. sw2. 17V 85
Dale St. w4. 6P 57	Darnley Rd. e9. 23H 38	Dayton Gro. se15. 23R 76
Dalebury Rd. sw17. 13W 83	Darrell Rd. se22. 21U 76	Deacon Rd. nw2. 7G 32
Dale Green Rd. n11. 15Ad 15	Dart St. w10. 10J 47	Deacon St. se17. 19O 63
Daleham Gdns. nw3. 13G 34	Dartmoor St. w8. 11N 59	Deadman's Hill, Wem. 4G 31
Daleham Mews nw3. 13G 34	Dartmouth Gro. se10. 27R 78	Deal Rd. sw17. 14Y 84
Dale Pk. Rd. se19. 19Za 90	Dartmouth Hill se10.	Deal St. e1. 22L 52
Daleside Rd. sw16. 15Y 84	27R 78	Dealtry Rd. sw15. 8T 70
Daleview Rd. n15. 21C 25	Dartmouth Rd. e16. 29M 54	Dean Court Wem. 1E 30
Dalgarno Gdns. w10. 8L 46	Dartmouth Rd. nw2. 9G 33	Dean Gdns. e17. 27B 28
Dalgleish St. e14. 24M 53	Dartmouth Rd. nw4. 7C 20	Dean Rd. nw2. 8G 32
Dalkeith Rd. se21. 19V 86	Dartmouth Rd. se23. 22X 87	Dean Rd. Cro. 19Zg 91
Dalkeith Rd. Ilf. 34F 42	Dartmouth Row se10. 27S 78	Dean St. e1. 23M 52
Dallas Rd. nw4. 8C 20	Dartmouth St. sw1. 16N 62	Dean St. e7. 29G 40
Dallas Rd. se26. 22X 87	Dartmouth Pk. Av. nw5.	Dean St. ec4. 18L 50
Dallin Rd. se18. 33R 95	15E 35	Dean St. n1. 19H 37
Dalling Rd. w6. 7O 58	Dartmouth Pk. Hill	Dean St. w1. 16L 49
Dallinger Rd. se12. 28V 89	nw5. 1-83 & 2-56	Dean Wk. Edg. 5Ab 13
Dallington St. ec1. 19K 51	n19. 72, 85 & up. 15D 23	Dean Bradley St. sw1. 17O 62
Dalmain Rd. se23. 23V 87	Dartmouth Pk. Rd. nw5.	Deanery Rd. e15. 28H 40
Dalmally Rd. Cro. 21Zd 91	15F 35	Deanery St. w1. 14N 61
Dalmeny Av. n7. 16F 36	Dartnell Rd. se5. 21Q 63	Dean Farrar St. sw1. 16O 62
Dalmeny Av. sw16. 18Za 90	Dartnell Rd. Cro. 20Zd 91	Deanhill Rd. sw14. 4T 69
Dalmeny Rd. n7. 16F 36	Dartrey Rd. sw10. 12Q 60	Dean's Bldgs. se17. 20P 63
Dalmore Rd. se21. 19W 86	Darvall Sq. sw18. 12T 72	Deans Clo. nw7. 5Ac 13
Dalrymple Rd. se4. 24T 77	Darvall St. sw18. 12T 72	Deans La. Edg. 5Ab 13
Dalston La. e8. 21G 38	Darville Rd. n16. 21F 37	Deans Rd. w7. 1bN 94
Dalton St. se27. 19W 85	Darwin Rd. n22. 19Aa 16	Deans Way n2. 13B 22
Dalwood Pl. se5. 20R 75	Darwin Rd. w5. 1P 56	Deans Way, Edg. 5Ac 13
Dalwood St. se5. 20R 75	Darwin St. se17. 20P 63	Deansbrook Rd. Edg. 20P 63
Dalyell Rd. sw9. 17S 74	Dashwood Rd. n8. 17C 24	Deanscroft Av. nw9. 5D 19
Dame St. n1. 19J 51	Dashwood Rd. sw8. 16R 73	Dean Stanley St. sw1. 17O 62
Dames Rd. e7. 29F 40	Dassett Rd. se27. 19Y 85	Dean Trench St. sw1. 16O 62
Danbrook Rd. sw16. 17Z 90	Datchelor Pl. se5. 20R 75	Deauville Rd. sw4. 15U 73
Danbury St. n1. 19J 51	Datchet Rd. se6. 24W 88	De Beauvoir Cres. n1. 20H 37
Danby St. se15. 21S 75	Date St. se17. 19P 63	De Beauvoir Rd. n1. 20H 37
Dancer Rd. sw6. 10R 71	Daubeney Rd. e5. 24F 39	De Beauvoir Sq. n1. 21H 37
Dancer Rd. Rich. 3S 68	Daubeny Rd. n17. 19Ab 16	Debnams Rd. se16. 23P 64
Dane Pl. e3. 24J 53	Dault Rd. sw18. 12U 72	De Burgh Rd. sw19. 12Z 92
Dane Rd. sw19. 12Z 92	Davenant Rd. n19. 16E 36	Decima St. se1. 20O 63
Dane Rd. w13. 1M 44	Davenport Rd. se6. 26U 77	Decoy Av. nw11. 10B 21
Dane Rd. Ilf. 34G 43	Daventry Av. e17. 25C 27	De Crespigny Pk. se5. 20S 75
Dane St. wc1. 17L 50	Daventry St. nw1. 13L 48	Dee Rd. e13. 28K 54
Daneby Rd. se6. 26X 88	Davey Rd. e9. 25H 39	Dee St. e14. 27M 54
Danecroft Rd. se24. 19T 75	Davey St. se15. 21Q 63	Deepdene Rd. se5. 19T 75
Danehurst Gdns. Ilf. 32C 42	David St. e15. 27G 40	Deepfield Cotts. nw9. 7B 20
Danehurst St. sw6. 9R 71	Davidge St. se1. 18N 62	Deerbrook Rd. se24. 18V 85
Danemere St. sw15. 8S 71	David's Rd. se23. 23W 87	Deerdale Rd. se24. 19T 75
Danes Rd. e5. 19R 75	Davidson Rd. Cro. 20Ze 91	Deerhurst Rd. nw2. 9G 33
Danescroft Av. nw4. 9B 21	Davies La. e11. 28E 40	Deerhurst Rd. sw16. 17Y 85
Daneswood Av. se6. 26X 88	Davies St. w1. 15M 49	Defoe Av. Kew 3Q 57
Danethorpe Rd. Wem. 1G 30	Davis Av. e1. 21L 52	Defoe Rd. n16. 20E 37
Daneville Rd. se5. 19R 75	Davis Rd. w3. 6N 58	Defoe Rd. sw17. 13X 83
Daniel Pl. nw4. 8C 20	Davis St. e13. 30K 55	De Frene Rd. se26. 24X 87
Daniel St. e2. 21K 52	Davis St. e14. 26O 66	Dekker Rd. se21. 20U 75
Daniel St. se15. 21Q 63	Davisville Rd. w12. 7N 58	Delacourt Rd. se3. 29R 79
Daniel's Rd. se15. 23R 76	Dawes Av. Twi. 1bT 93	Delafield Rd. se7. 30Q 67
Danson Rd. se17. 19P 63	Dawes Rd. sw6. 10Q 59	Delaford Rd. se16. 22P 64
Dante Rd. se11. 18O 62	Dawes St. se17. 20P 63	Delaford St. sw6. 10Q 59
Danvers Rd. n8. 16B 24	Dawlish Av. n13. 17Ac 16	Delamere Cres. w2. 11L 48
Danvers St. sw3. 13Q 60	Dawlish Av. sw18. 11W 83	Delamere Gdns. nw7. 5Ac 13
Daphne St. sw18. 11U 72	Dawlish Dri. Ilf. 35F 43	Delamere Rd. sw.20 9Z 92
D'Arblay St. w1. 16M 49	Dawlish Rd. e10. 26E 39	Delamere Rd. w2. 12L 48
Darby St. e1. 21M 52	Dawlish Rd. n17. 21A 26	Delamere Ter. w2. 12L 48
D'Arcy Dri. Har. 2B 18	Dawlish Rd. nw2. 9G 33	Delancey St. nw1. 15J 49
D'Arcy Gdns. Har. 2A 18	Dawlish St. sw8. 17Q 62	Delaporte Sq. sw18 12T 72
Darell Rd. Rich. 3S 69	Dawnay Gdns. sw18. 12W 83	De Laune St. se17. 18P 62
Darenth Rd. n16. 21D 25	Dawnay Rd. sw18. 12W 83	Delaware Rd. w9. 11K 48
Darfield Rd. se4. 24U 77	Dawpool Rd. nw2. 7E 32	Delhi Rd. n9. 21Af 17
Darfur St. sw15. 8S 71	Dawson Av. Bar. 35H 43	Delhi St. n1. 17H 36

Delia St. sw18. 11U 72
Dell, The, Wem. 1F 30
Dellow St. e1 22M 52
Deloraine St. se8. 25R 77
Delorme St. w6. 9Q 59
Delvan St. se18. 33Q 95
Delverton Rd. se17. 19P 62
Delvino Rd. sw6. 11R 71
De Montfort Rd. sw6. 16W 85
De Morgan Rd. sw6. 11S 72
Dempsey St. e1. 23L 52
Dempster Rd. sw18. 12T 72
Denbigh Gdns. Rich. 3T 68
Denbigh Pl. sw1. 15P 61
Denbigh Rd. e6. 31K 55
Denbigh Rd. e8. 25K 53
Denbigh Rd. nw10. 6H 32
Denbigh Rd. w11. 10M 47
Denbigh Rd. w13. 1L 44
Denbigh St. sw1. 15P 61
Denbigh Ter. w11. 10M 47
Dendy St. sw12. 14V 84
Dene, The, Wem. 2F 30
Denehurst Gdns. nw4. 8C 21
Denehurst Gdns. w3. 4N 57
Denehurst Gdns. Rich. 3S 69
Denewood Rd. n6. 14C 23
Denham Dri. Ilf. 34C 42
Denham Rd. n20. 14Ad 15
Denham St. se10. 29P 66
Denham Way Bar. 35J 43
Denholme Rd. w9. 10K 47
Denison Rd. sw19. 12Y 83
Denison Rd. w5. 1K 44
Denleigh Gdns. n21. 18Ae 16
Denman Dri. nw11. 11B 22
Denman Dri. N. nw11. 11B 22
Denman Dri. S. nw11. 11B 22
Denman Rd. se15. 21R 75
Denman St. se1. 7M 63
Denman St. w1. 16M 49
Denmark Av. sw19. 9Z 92
Denmark Gro. n1. 18J 50
Denmark Hill se5. 19R 75
Denmark Pl. sw27. 19X 86
Denmark Rd. n1. 18J 50
Denmark Rd. n8. 18B 24
Denmark Rd. nw6. 10J 47
Denmark Rd. se5. 19R 75
Denmark Rd. se25. 22Zc 90
Denmark Rd. sw19. 9Y 82
Denmark Rd. w13. 1M 44
Denmark Rd. Twi. 1cW 93
Denmark St. e1. 22M 52
Denmark St. e11. 28F 40
Denmark St. e13. 29L 55
Denmark St. n1. 18J 50
Denmark St. n17 22Aa 17
Denmark St. wc2. 16L 50
Denmark Ter. n19. 17E 36
Dennett Rd. Cro. 18Ze 91
Dennett's Gro. se14. 23R 76
Dennett's Rd. se14. 23R 76
Denning Av. Cro. 18Zg 91
Denning Rd. nw3. 13F 34
Dennington Av. Bar. 33H 43
Dennington Pk. Rd. nw6.
 11G 34
Dennis St. n1. 17J 50
Dennis Pk. Cres. sw20. 9Za 92
Denny Rd. n9. 22Ae 17
Denny St. se11. 18P 62
Densham Rd. e15. 28H 40
Denton Rd. n8. 18C 24
Denton Rd. n18. 21Ac 17
Denton Rd. nw10. 5H 31

Denton St. sw18. 11U 72
Dent's Rd. sw11. 13U 72
Denver Rd. n16. 20D 25
Denver St. sw3. 13O 60
Denzil Rd. nw10. 6G 32
Deodar Rd. sw15. 10S 71
Deptford Bridge se8. 25R 77
Deptford B'way se8. 25R 77
Deptford Green se8. 25Q 65
Deptford Church St. se8.
 25Q 65
Deptford Ferry Rd. e14.
 25P 65
Deptford High St. se8. 25Q 65
De Quincey Rd. n17. 20Aa 17
Derby Av. n12 12Ac 14
Derby Av. Har. 1cAa 12
Derby Rd. e9. 23H 38
Derby Rd. n15. 19B 25
Derby Rd. n18. 23Ac 17
Derby Rd. sw14. 4T 69
Derby Rd. sw19. 10Z 92
Derby Rd. Cro. 18Ze 91
Derby Hill se23. 23W 87
Derbyshire St. e2. 22K 52
Dereham Rd. Bar. 36G 43
Derek Av. Wem. 4G 31
Dericote St. e8. 22H 38
Dering Pl. Cro. 19Zg 91
Dering Rd. Cro. 19Zg 91
Dering St. w1. 15M 49
Derinton Rd. sw17. 14X 84
Dermody Gdns. se13. 27U 78
Dermody Rd. se13. 27U 78
Deronda Rd. se24. 18V 85
Derrick Gdns. se7. 30O 67
Dersingham Av. e12. 32G 43
Dersingham Rd. nw2. 10E 33
Derwent Av. n18. 20Ac 17
Derwent Av. nw7. 6Ac 10
Derwent Av. nw9. 6B 20
Derwent Cres. n12. 12Ad 14
Derwent Gdns. Har. 1C 18
Derwent Gro. se22. 21T 75
Derwent Rd. n13. 17Ad 16
Derwent Rd. se20. 22Za 90
Derwent Rd. w5. 1O 56
Derwent St. se10. 28P 66
Derwentwater Rd. w3. 4M 45
Desart St. e14. 26M 54
Desenfans Rd. se21. 20U 75
Desford Rd. e16. 28L 54
Desmond St. se14. 24Q 65
Despard Rd. n19. 16D 23
Detling Rd. Bro. 28Y 89
Detmold Rd. e5. 23E 38
Devas Rd. sw20. 8Z 92
Devas St. e3. 26K 53
De Vere Gdns. w8 12N 60
De Vere Gdns. Ilf. 32E 42
Deverell St. se1. 20O 63
Devereux Rd. sw11. 14U 73
Devon Clo. Wem. 1H 30
Devon Cres. Wem. 1H 30
Devon Gro. n4. 19C 25
Devon Rise n2. 13B 22
Devon Rd. n17. 21A 26
Devon Rd. Bar. 35J 43
Devoncourt Rd. n17. 20Aa 16
Devoncroft Gdns. Twi. 1bV 93
Devonport Gdns. Ilf. 32C 42
Devonport Rd. w12. 8N 58
Devonport St. e1. 23M 52
Devonport St. w2. 13M 48
Devon's Rd. e3. 26K 53

Devons Rd. e8. 25L 53
Devonshire Clo. w1. 15L 49
Devonshire Clo. E. w1. 15L 49
Devonshire Clo. S. w1. 15L 49
Devonshire Clo. W. w1. 15L 49
Devonshire Gdns. w4. 4Q 57
Devonshire Gro. se15. 22Q 64
Devonshire Pl. w1. 15L 49
Devonshire Pl. w4. 6P 57
Devonshire Rd. e9. 23H 38
Devonshire Rd. e15. 28F 40
Devonshire Rd. e16. 30M 55
Devonshire Rd. e17. 25C 27
Devonshire Rd. n7. 17E 36
Devonshire Rd. n13. 18Ac 16
Devonshire Rd. n17. 19Ab 16
Devonshire Rd. se10. 26R 77
Devonshire Rd. se23. 23W 87
Devonshire Rd. sw19. 13Z 92
Devonshire Rd. w4. 6P 58
Devonshire Rd. w5. 1O 56
Devonshire Rd. Cro. 19Zd 91
Devonshire Rd. Har. 1cB 12
Devonshire Rd. Ilf. 35D 42
Devonshire Sq. ec2. 21L 51
Devonshire St. e1. 23K 52
Devonshire St. ec3. 20L 51
Devonshire St. n1. 19J 51
Devonshire St. se15. 22Q 64
Devonshire St. w1. 15L 49
Devonshire St. w4. 6P 57
Devonshire St. wc1. 17L 50
Devonshire Ter. w2. 12M 48
Devonshire Hill La. n17.
 20Ab 91
Dewberry St. e14. 26L 53
Dewey St. sw17. 13Y 84
Dewhurst Rd. w14. 9O 59
Dewsbury Rd. nw10. 7F 32
Dewsbury Ter. nw1. 15H 35
D'Eynsford Rd. se5. 20R 75
Diamond St. se15. 20R 75
Diaamond Ter. se10. 27R 78
Diana Pl. nw1. 15K 49
Diana Rd. e17. 25A 27
Dibden St. n1. 19H 87
Dicey Av. nw2. 8F 32
Dickens Av. n2. 12Aa 14
Dicken's Rd. e6. 31J 55
Dicken's Sq. se1. 19O 63
Dickens St. sw8. 15R 73
Dickenson Rd. n8. 17C 24
Dickenson Rd. nw5. 15G 35
Dickenson's La. se25.
 21Zc 90
Dickson Rd. se9. 31T 79
Didcot St. sw11. 12T 72
Dieppe St. w14. 10P 59
Digby Rd. e9. 23G 38
Digby Rd. n4. 19E 37
Digby Rd. Bar. 35H 43
Digby St. e2. 23K 52
Diggon St. e1. 23L 52
Dighton Rd. sw18. 12T 72
Digswell St. n7. 18G 36
Dilke St. sw3. 14Q 61
Dillon Pl. n7. 18F 36
Dillwyn Rd. se26. 24X 88
Dilston Gro. se16. 22O 64
Dimsdale Dri. nw9. 5D 19
Dimsdale Rd. sw6. 10Q 59
Dingle La. e14. 25M 53
Dingley Pl. ec1. 19K 51
Dingley Rd. ec1. 19K 51
Dingwall Av. Cro. 19Zf 91

Dingwall Rd. sw18.	12V 83	
Dingwall Rd. Cro.	19Ze 91	
Dingwell Gdns. nw11.	11C 21	
Dinmont St. e2.	22J 52	
Dinsdale Rd. se3.	28Q 66	
Dinsmore Rd. se22.	15V 84	
Dirleton Rd. e15.	28J 54	
Disbrowe Rd. w6.	9Q 59	
Disney Pl. se1.	19N 63	
Disraeli Rd. e7.	29G 41	
Disraeli Rd. nw10.	5J 45	
Disraeli Rd. sw15.	9T 71	
Disraeli Rd. w5.	1N 56	
Diss St. e2.	21K 51	
Distaff La. ec4.	19M 51	
Distillery La. w6.	8P 59	
Distillery Rd. Bre.	2P 56	
Distin St. se11.	18P 62	
District Rd. Wem.	1G 30	
Dixie St. e1.	22K 52	
Dixon Rd. se14.	24R 77	
Dixon Rd. se25.	20Zb 90	
Dixon St. e14.	25M 53	
Dix's Pl. se1.	21O 63	
Dobree Av. nw10.	8H 32	
Dock Rd. e16.	28M 54	
Dock Rd. Bre.	1Q 56	
Dock St, e1.	21M 52	
Dockhead se1.	21N 63	
Dockley Rd. se16.	21O 64	
Doctor St. se17.	20Q 63	
Dod St. e14.	25M 53	
Dodbrooke Rd. se27.	18X 85	
Doddington Gro. se17.	18P 62	
Doddington Rd. sw11.	14R 73	
Dodson St. se1.	18O 62	
Doggett Rd. se6.	25V 88	
Dog La. nw10.	6F 32	
Dog Kennel Hill se22.	20S 75	
Dolben St. se1.	18N 62	
Dolby Rd. sw6.	10S 71	
Dolland St. se11.	17P 62	
Dollis Av. n3.	10Aa 14	
Dollis Pk. n3.	10Aa 14	
Dollis Rd. n3.	10Ab 14	
Dollis Hill Av. nw2.	8E 32	
Dollis Hill La. nw2.	8E 32	
Dolphin La. e14.	26M 53	
Dombey St. wc1.	17L 50	
Domingo St. ec1.	19K 51	
Dominion Rd. Cro.	20Zd 91	
Domville Gro. se5.	21P 63	
Donald Rd. e13.	30J 55	
Donald Rd. Cro.	17Zd 91	
Donald St. e3.	26K 53	
Donaldson Rd. nw6.	10J 47	
Donegal St. n1.	18J 50	
Doneraile St. sw6.	9R 71	
Dongola Rd. e13.	29K 55	
Dongola Rd. n15.	20A 25	
Dongola St. e1.	24L 53	
Donne Pl. sw3.	13O 60	
Donnington Rd. nw10.	8H 32	
Donnington Rd. Har.	1B 18	
Donovan Av. n10.	15A 23	
Doon St. se1.	18N 62	
Dora Rd. sw19.	10X 82	
Dora St. e14.	24L 53	
Dorchester Av. n13.	19Ad 16	
Dorchester Dri. se24.	19T 75	
Dorchester Gro. w4.	6P 58	
Dorchester St. n1.	20J 51	
Dordrecht Rd. w3.	6N 58	
Dore Av. e12.	32G 43	
Doreen Av. nw9.	5D 19	
Doria Rd. sw6.	10R 71	
Dorien Rd. sw20.	8Za 92	
Dorinda St. n7.	18G 36	
Doris Rd. e7.	29H 41	
Doris St. se11.	18P 62	
Dorking Rd. se8.	24Q 65	
Dorlcote Rd. sw18.	13U 72	
Dornberg Rd. se3.	29R 79	
Dorncliffe Rd. sw6.	10R 71	
Dornfell St. nw6.	10G 33	
Dornton Rd. sw12.	15W 84	
Dorothy Av. Wem.	2H 30	
Dorothy Rd. sw11.	13S 72	
Dorrington St. ec1.	18L 50	
Dors Clo. nw9.	5D 19	
Dorset Dri. Edg.	3Ac 13	
Dorset Pl. e15.	27G 40	
Dorset Pl. sw1.	16P 61	
Dorset Rd. e7.	30H 41	
Dorset Rd. n15.	20B 25	
Dorset Rd. sw8.	17Q 62	
Dorset Rd. sw19.	10Z 92	
Dorset Rd. w5.	1N 56	
Dorset Sq. nw1.	14K 49	
Dorset St. e1.	23M 52	
Dorset St. ec4.	18M 50	
Dorset St. n1.	20G 37	
Dorset St. w1.	14L 49	
Dorset Wk. sw8.	17Q 62	
Dorton Rd. Cro.	20Zh 91	
Dorton St. se15.	20Q 63	
Dorville Rd. se12.	28U 78	
Dorville Rd. w6.	7O 58	
Dothill Rd. se18.	34R 95	
Doughty Mews wc1.	17K 50	
Doughty St. wc1.	17K 50	
Douglas Av. Wem.	2G 30	
Douglas Pl. w2.	11M 48	
Douglas Rd. e16.	29L 55	
Douglas Rd. n1.	19H 37	
Douglas Rd. n22.	18Aa 16	
Douglas Rd. nw6.	10H 33	
Douglas Rd. Ilf.	36D 42	
Douglas Rd. Twi.	1aU 93	
Douglas St. se8.	25R 77	
Douglas St. sw1.	16P 61	
Douro Pl. w8.	11O 60	
Douro St. e3.	25J 53	
Dove Mews sw5.	12P 60	
Dove Row e2.	22J 52	
Dovecot Av. n22.	18A 24	
Dovedale Av. Har.	1B 18	
Dovedale Rd. se22.	22U 76	
Dover Rd. e12.	30E 41	
Dover Rd. se19.	20Y 86	
Dover St. w1.	15M 49	
Dovercourt Av. Cro.	18Zc 90	
Dovercourt Rd. se22.	20U 75	
Doverfield Rd. sw2.	17U 74	
Dover House Rd. sw15.	7T 70	
Doveridge Gdns. n13.	19Ac 16	
Dover Pk. Rd. sw15.	7U 70	
Doveton St. e1.	23K 52	
Dowanhill Rd. se6.	27W 89	
Dowgate Hill ec4.	20M 51	
Dowlas St. se5.	20Q 63	
Down Pl. w6.	7P 58	
Down St. se18.	34P 95	
Down St. w1.	15N 61	
Downage nw4.	8A 21	
Downes Ct. n21.	18Ae 16	
Downes Pl. se15.	22Q 64	
Downham Rd. w1.	20H 37	
Downhills Av. n15.	20A 85	
Downhills Pk. Rd. n15.	19A 25	
Downhurst Av. nw7.	5Ac 13	
Downing St. sw1.	16N 62	
Downs Rd. e5.	22F 38	
Downs Rd. Cro.	19Z 90	
Downsell Rd. e15.	27F 40	
Downsfield Rd. e17.	24C 27	
Downshall Av. Ilf.	35D 42	
Downshire Hill nw3.	13F 34	
Downside Cres. nw3.	14G 35	
Downs Pk. Rd. e8. 1-73 & 2-90. e5. 75, 92 & up.	21G 38	
Downsview Rd. se19.	19Z 90	
Downton Av. sw2.	17W 85	
Dowrey St. n1.	18H 36	
Dowsett Rd. n17.	21A 26	
Doyce St. se1.	19N 63	
Doyle Gdns. nw10.	7H 32	
Doyle Rd. se17.	14W 84	
D'Oyley St. sw1.	14O 61	
Doynton St. n19.	15E 35	
Draco St. se17.	19Q 63	
Dragon Rd. nw10.	5K 45	
Dragon Rd. se15.	20Q 63	
Drakefell Rd. se14. 1-87 & 2-134 se14. 89, 136 & up	23S 76	
Drakefield Rd. sw17.	14W 84	
Drant St. e1.	21L 51	
Draper St. se17.	19O 63	
Draper's Gdns. ec2.	20L 51	
Drapper's Rd. se16.	22O 64	
Draycott Rd. e11.	29C 29	
Draycott Av. sw3.	13O 60	
Draycott Av. Har.	1B 18	
Draycott Clo. Har.	1B 18	
Draycott Pl. sw3.	14P 61	
Draycott Ter. sw3.	14P 61	
Drayson Mews w8.	11N 60	
Drayton Av. w13.	1aM 94	
Drayton Gdns. n21	19Af 16	
Drayton Gdns. sw10.	12P 60	
Drayton Gdns. w13.	1aM 94	
Drayton Grn. w13.	1aM 94	
Drayton Pk. n5.	18G 36	
Drayton Rd. e11.	27D 28	
Drayton Rd. n17.	21A 25	
Drayton Rd. nw10.	6H 32	
Drayton Rd. w13.	1aL 94	
Drayton Rd. w13.	18Zf 91	
Drayton Bridge Rd. w7. 1-125 & 2-120 w13. Remainder.	1bM 94	
Drayton Grn. Rd. w13.	1aM 94	
Dreadnought St. se10.	28O 60	
Dresden Rd. n19.	16D 23	
Drew Rd. e16.	31N 67	
Drew St. e14.	26M 53	
Drewstead Rd. sw16.	16W 84	
Drewton St. e1.	23M 52	
Driffield Rd. e3.	24J 53	
Drive, The nw9.	6D 20	
Drive, The, e17.	26A 27	
Drive, The, e18.	29A 28	
Drive, The, n3.	11Ab 14	
Drive, The, n11.	16Ab 15	
Drive, The, nw11.	10C 21	
Drive, The, sw16.	17Zb 90	
Drive, The, sw20.	8Z 92	
Drive, The, w3.	5L 45	

Drive, The, w4.	6Q 58
Drive, The, Bar.	36H 43
Drive, The, Cro.	19Zb 90
Drive, The, Edg.	4Ac 13
Drive, The, Ilf.	32D 42
Drive, The, Mor.	12Zc 92
Drive, The, Wem.	5E 31
Drive St. sw8.	15R 73
Dromore Rd. sw15.	9U 71
Droop St. w10.	9K 47
Drovers Rd. Cro.	19Zg 91
Druce Rd. se21.	20U 75
Druid St. se1.	21O 63
Drummond Cres. nw1.	16K 50
Drummond Rd. e11.	30C 29
Drummond St. se16.	22O 64
Drummond Rd. Cro.	19Zf 91
Drummond St. nw1.	16K 49
Drury La. wc2.	17L 50
Drury Rd. Har.	1dC 12
Dryad St. sw15.	9S 71
Dryburgh Gdns. nw9.	4A 19
Dryburgh Rd. sw15.	8S 70
Dryden Av. w7.	1bL 94
Dryden Rd. sw19.	11Y 83
Dryden Rd. Har.	1bAa 12
Dryfield Clo. nw10.	5G 31
Dryfield Rd. Edg.	5Ac 13
Drylands Rd. n8.	17C 24
Drysdale Rd. se13.	26S 77
Drysdale St. n1.	20K 51
Ducal St. e2.	21K 51
Du Cane Rd. w12.	6M 46
Duchess Rd. w1.	15L 49
Duchy St. se1.	18N 62
Ducie St. sw4.	17T 74
Duckett Rd. n4.	18C 24
Duckett St. e1.	24L 52
Ducks Wk. Rich.	1T 49
Ducksfoot La. ec4.	20M 51
Duddon Hill La. nw10.	7F 32
Dudley Av. Har.	1A 18
Dudley Gdns. w13.	1aN 94
Dudley Gdns. Har.	1cD 12
Dudley Rd. e17.	25A 27
Dudley Rd. n2.	12Aa 14
Dudley Rd. nw6.	10J 47
Dudley Rd. sw19.	10Y 82
Dudley Rd. Har.	1dD 12
Dudley Rd. Ilf.	43F 43
Dudley Rd. Kew	3R 68
Dudley Rd. w2.	12L 48
Dudlington Rd. e5.	23E 38
Duff St. e14.	26M 53
Dufferin St. ec1.	19K 51
Duffield St. sw11.	13S 72
Dugdale St. se5.	18Q 62
Duke Rd. w4.	5P 57
Duke St. e1.	21L 51
Duke St. ec3.	21M 51
Duke St. sw1.	16N 61
Duke St. w1.	14M 49
Duke St. wc2.	17M 50
Duke St. Rich.	1T 68
Duke St. Hill se1.	20N 63
Dukes Av. n3.	11Aa 14
Duke's Av. n10.	15A 23
Duke's Av. w4.	5P 57
Duke's Av. Har.	1bA 12
Duke's La. w8.	11N 60
Duke's Mews w1.	14L 49
Dukes Rd. e6.	33J 43
Dukes Rd. w5.	3K 45
Dukes' Rd. wc1.	16K 50
Dukesthorpe Rd. se26.	23X 87
Dulas St. n4.	18D 24
Dulka Rd. sw11.	14U 73
Dulwich Com. se21.	20W 86
Dulwich Pk. Rd.se19.	20X 86
Dulwich Rd. se24.	18U 74
Dulwich Village se21.	20U 75
Dumbarton Rd. sw2.	17U 74
Dumont Rd. n16.	21E 37
Dunbar Av. sw16.	18Za 90
Dunbar Rd. e7.	29H 41
Dunbar Rd. n22.	18Aa 16
Dunbar St. se27.	19X 86
Dunboyne St. nw5.	14G 35
Duncan Gro.w3.	6L 45
Duncan Rd. e8.	22J 52
Duncan Rd. Rich.	2S 68
Duncan St. n1.	21M 51
Duncan St. e8.	22H 38
Duncan St. n1.	18J 50
Duncan Ter. n1.	18J 50
Duncannon St. wc2.	17M 50
Duncombe Hill se23.	24V 88
Duncombe Rd. n19.	16D 24
Dundalk Rd. se4.	24S 76
Dundas Rd. se15.	23S 76
Dundee Rd. e13.	29K 55
Dundonald Rd. nw10.	9J 47
Dundonald St. sw1.	16P 62
Dunedin Rd. e10.	26F 39
Dunedin Rd. Ilf.	34D 42
Dunfield Rd. se6.	26Y 88
Dunford Rd. n7.	18F 36
Dungarvan Av.sw15.	7S 70
Dunheved Rd. N.Cro.	18Zd 91
Dunheved Rd. S.Cro.	18Zd 91
Dunheved Rd.W.Cro.	18Zd 91
Dunholme Av. n9.	21Ad 17
Dunholme Rd. n9.	21Ad 17
Dunk St. e1.	22L 52
Dunkold Rd. se25.	19Zb 90
Dunkeld St. e14.	27M 54
Dunkirk St. se27.	19X 86
Dunlace Rd. e5.	23F 38
Dunloe Av. n15.	20A 25
Dunloe St. e2.	21J 51
Dunlop Pl. se16.	21O 64
Dunmore Rd. nw6.	9H 33
Dunmore Rd. sw20.	8Za 92
Dunmow Rd. e15.	27G 40
Dunn St. e8.	21G 37
Dunollie Rd. nw5.	10G 35
Dunoon Rd. se23.	23V 87
Dunraven Rd. w12.	7M 46
Dunsany Rd. w14.	9O 59
Dunsmure Rd. n16.	20D 25
Dunstable Rd. Rich.	2T 68
Dunstan Rd. nw11.	10D 21
Dunstan's Gro. se22.	22U 76
Dunstan's Rd. se22.	22U 76
Dunster Dri. nw9.	5D 19
Dunster Gdns. nw6.	10H 33
Dunston Rd. e8.	21J 51
Dunston St. e8.	21J 51
Dunton Rd. e10.	26D 27
Dunton Rd. se1.	21P 63
Duntshill Rd. sw18.	11V 83
Dupont Rd. sw20.	9Za 92
Dupont St. e14.	24L 53
Dupont St. e14.	24M 53
Duppas Rd. Cro.	18Zf 91
Duppas Hill La. Cro.	18Zg 91
Duppas Hill Rd. Cro.	18Zg 91
Duppas Hill Ter. Cro.	18Zf 91
Dupree Rd. se7.	29P 67
Durand Gdns. sw9.	17R 74
Durand Way nw10.	4H 31
Durant St. e2.	22K 52
Durban Rd. e15.	28K 54
Durban Rd. n17.	21Ab 17
Durban Rd. se27.	19X 86
Durban Rd. Ilf.	35D 42
Dure Pl. e1.	21L 52
Durham Gdns, Ilf.	31D 29
Durham Gro. e9.	23G 38
Durham Hill se12.	28X 89
Durham Rd. e12.	31G 41
Durham Rd. e16.	28L 54
Durham Rd. n2.	14A 23
Durham Rd. n7.	18E 36
Durham Rd. n15.	20A 25
Durham Rd.se18.	34Q 95
Durham Rd. sw20.	8Z 92
Durham Rd. w5.	1O 56
Durham Row e1.	24L 52
Durham St. se11.	17P 62
Durham Ter. w2.	11L 48
Durham Villas w8.	11N 59
Durley Rd. n16.	20D 25
Durlston Rd. e5.	22E 38
Durnford Rd. se10.	26Q 66
Durnford St. n15.	21C 25
Durning Rd. se19.	20Y 86
Durnsford Av. sw19.	10W 82
Durnsford Rd. n11.	16Aa 15
Durnsford Rd. sw19.	11W 82
Durrell Rd. sw6.	10R 71
Durrington Rd. e5.	24F 39
Durrington Pk. Av. sw19.	8Z 92
Durrington Pk. Rd. sw19.	8Z 92
Durward St. e1.	22L 52
Dutch Yd. sw18.	11T 71
Dutton St. se10.	26R 77
Duval St. e1.	21L 51
Dye House La. e3.	25J 53
Dyer's Bldgs. ec1.	18L 50
Dyer's Hall Rd. e11.	27E 40
Dyer's La. sw15.	8S 70
Dymock St. sw6.	11S 72
Dyne Rd. nw6.	10H 33
Dynevor Rd. n16.	21F 37
Dynevor Rd. Rich.	2T 68
Dynham Rd. nw6.	11H 33
Dyott St. wc1.	16L 50
Dysart St. ec2.	20L 51
Dyson Rd. e11.	28C 28
Dyson Rd. e15.	28H 41
Dysons Rd. n18.	22Ab 17
Eade Rd. n4.	19C 25
Eagle Av. n15.	21B 25
Eagle Hill se19.	19Z 90
Eagle La. e11.	29B 28
Eagle Rd. Wem.	2G 30
Eagle St. wc1.	17L 50
Eagle Wharf Rd. n1.	19J 51
Eagling Rd. e3.	26K 53
Ealdham Sq. se9.	30T 79
Ealing Common w5.	2M 44
Ealing Grn. w5.	1M 44
Ealing Rd. Bre.	2P 56
Ealing Rd. Wem.	2G 30
Ealing Pk. Gdns. w5.	1O 56
Eamont St. nw8.	13J 48

Eardley Cres. sw5. 11P 59
Eardley Rd. sw16. 16Y 84
Earl Cotts. se1. 21P 63
Earl Rd. se1. 21P 63
Earl Rd. sw14. 4S 69
Earl St. e15. 27H 40
Earl St. ec2. 20L 51
Earl St. nw8. 13L 48
Earl St. se18. 34P 95
Earl St. wc2. 16M 50
Earldom Rd. sw15. 8S 71
Earlham Gro. e7. 28G 40
Earlham Gro. n22. 18Aa 16
Earlham Rd. n22. 18Ab 16
Earls Cres. Har. 1bA 12
Earl's Ct. Gdns. sw5. 11P 60
Earl's Ct. Rd.
  w8. 1-109 & 2-138.
  sw5. 111, 140 & up. 11O 59
Earl's Ct. Sq. sw5. 11P 60
Earlsfield Rd. sw18. 11V 82
Earlsmead Rd. n15. 21B 25
Earlsmead Rd. nw10. 8J 46
Earlsthorpe Rd se26. 23Y 87
Earlstoke St. ec1. 19K 50
Earlswood Av. Cro. 18Zc 90
Earlswood St. se10. 28Q 66
Earsby St. w14. 10O 59
East Av. e12. 32H 43
East Av. e17. 26B 27
East Av. Cro. 17Zg 91
East Bank n16. 20D 25
East Gdns. sw17. 13Y 83
East Hill sw18. 11T 72
East Hill Wem. 3D 19
East La. se16. 21O 64
East La. Wem. 1E 30
East Pl. se27. 19X 86
East Rd. e15. 29J 54
East Rd. n1. 20K 51
East Rd. sw19. 12Y 83
East Rd. Edg. 5Ab 13
East Row w10. 10K 47
E. Smithfield e1. 21M 52
East St. e1. 21L 51
East St. ec2. 20L 51
East St. n1. 17H 36
East St. se7. 31O 67
East St. se17. 19P 63
East St. se27. 19X 86
East St. Bar. 34H 43
East Wk. Barn. 15Af 15
East Way sw20. 9Zc 92
Eastway e9. 25G 39
E. Acton La. w3. 6M 46
E. Arbour St. e1. 23L 52
Eastbourne Av. n9. 23Ad 17
Eastbourne Av. w3. 5M 45
Eastbourne Gdns. sw14.4S 69
Eastbourne Mews w2. 12L 48
Eastbourne Rd. e15. 28J 54
Eastbourne Rd. n15. 20C 25
Eastbourne Rd.sw17.14Y 84
Eastbourne Rd. w4. 5P 57
Eastbourne Rd. Bre. 1P 56
Eastbourne Ter. w2. 12L 48
Eastbrook Rd. se3. 30R 79
Eastbury Av. Bar. 35J 43
Eastbury Gro. w4. 6P 58
Eastbury St. Bar. 36J 43
Eastcastle St. w1. 16L 49
E. Chapel St. w1. 15N 61
Eastcheap ec3. 20M 51
Eastcombe Av. se7. 29Q 67
Eastcote St. sw9. 17S 74
Eastdene se15. 21Q 63

Eastdown Pk. se13. 27T 78
E.Dulwich Gro. se22. 20U 75
E. Dulwich Rd. se22. 21T 75
East End Rd. n2 & n3.
                    11Aa 14
Eastern Av. e11 & Ilf. 30C 29
Eastern Rd. e13. 30J 55
Eastern Rd. e17. 27C 28
Eastern Rd. n2. 14A 23
Eastern Rd. n22. 17Aa 16
Eastern Rd. se4. 25T .77
Easternville Gdns. Ilf.
                    34C 42
E. Ferry Rd. e14. 26O 65
Eastfield Rd. e17. 26B 27
Eastfield Rd. n8. 17A 24
Eastfield St. e14. 24L 53
Eastfields Rd. w3. 5L 45
E. Ham & Barking By-Pass
  e6. 31L 55
E. Harding St. ec4. 18L 50
E. Heath Rd. nw3. 12E 34
Eastholm nw11. 12B 22
E. India Dock Rd. e14.
                    25M 53
E. India Dock Wall Rd.
  e14. 27M 54
Eastlake Rd. se5. 19S 75
Eastleigh Clo. nw10. 6E 32
Eastman St. e1. 22L 52
Eastmearn Rd. se27. 19W 86
E. Mount St. e1. 22L 52
Eastney St. se10. 27Q 66
Easton St. wc1. 18K 50
E. Sheen Av. sw14. 5T 69
Eastside Rd. nw11. 10B 21
E. Surrey Gro. se15. 21Q 63
Eastview Av. sw18. 35R 95
Eastville Av. nw11. 10C 21
Eastward St. e3. 25L 53
Eastwood Rd. e16. 29N 67
Eastwood Rd. e18. 29A 29
Eastwood Rd. n10. 14A 23
Eastwood Rd. Ilf. 36D 42
Eastwood St. sw16. 15Y 84
Eatington Rd. e10. 27C 28
Eaton Av. n12. 12Ab 14
Eaton Gate sw1. 14O 61
Eaton Gro. n19. 16E 36
Eaton Mews N. sw1. 14O 61
Eaton Mews S. sw1. 14O 61
Eaton Pl. e9. 23H 38
Eaton Pl. n18. 21Ac 17
Eaton Pl. sw1. 14O 61
Eaton Rise w5. 1L 44
Eaton Rd. nw4. 9B 21
Eaton Rd. sw9. 18T 74
Eaton Row sw1. 15O 61
Eaton Sq. sw1. 14O 61
Eaton St. se1. 18N 62
Eaton Ter. sw1. 14O 61
Eaton Pk. Rd. n13. 18Ad 16
Eatonville Rd. sw17.14W 84
Ebbsfleet Rd. nw2. 9F 33
Ebenezer Rd. nw2. 11E 33
Ebenezer Row se11. 18P 62
Ebenezer St. n1. 19K 51
Eben St. sw18. 11T 72
Ebor St. e1. 21K 51
Ebrington Rd. Har. 1C 18
Ebson St. sw18. 15R 73
Ebsworth St. se23. 23V 87
Ebury Bridge sw1. 15P 61
Ebury Mews sw1. 15O 61
Ebury Sq. sw1. 15P 61
Ebury St. n19. 16E 35

Ebury St. sw1. 14P 61
Ebury Bridge Rd. sw1.
                    15P 61
Eccles Rd. sw11. 13T 73
Ecclesbourne Gdns. n13.
                    18Ac 16
Ecclesbourne Rd. n1. 19H 37
Ecclesbourne Rd. Cro.
                    19Zc 90
Eccleston Bridge sw1.15O 61
Eccleston Pl. sw1. 15O 61
Ecclestone Pl. Wem. 3F 30
Eccleston Rd. w13. 1bM 94
Eccleston Sq. sw1. 15P 61
Eccleston St. sw1. 15O 61
Eckington Rd. n15. 20C 25
Eckstein Rd. sw11. 13T 72
Eclipse Rd. e13. 29L 55
Edale Rd. se16. 23P 64
Edbrooke Rd. w9. 11K 47
Ediscombe Rd. sw6. 10R 71
Eddystone Rd. se4. 24U 77
Eden Clo. Wem. 2H 30
Eden Gro. n7. 18G 36
Eden Rd. e17. 26B 27
Eden Rd. se27. 19Y 85
Eden Rd. Cro. 19Zg 91
Eden St. nw1. 15K 49
Edenbridge Rd. e9. 23H 38
Edencourt Rd. sw16. 15Y 84
Edenham St. w10. 10K 47
Edenhurst Av. sw6. 10S 71
Edensor Rd. w4. 6Q 57
Edenvale St. sw6. 11S 72
Ederline Av. sw16. 17Zb 90
Edgar Rd. e3. 26K 53
Edgarley Ter. sw6. 9R 71
Edge Hill se18. 33Q 95
Edge Hill sw19. 8Z 92
Edgecombe Rd. se5. 20S 75
Edgefield Av. Bar. 36H 43
Edge Hill Av. n3. 11A 21
Edge Hill Rd. w13. 1L 44
Edgel St. sw18. 11T 72
Edgeley Rd. sw4. 16S 73
Edgeworth Av. nw4. 7B 20
Edgeworth Cres. nw4. 7B 20
Edgeworth Rd. se9. 30T 79
Edgware Rd.
  w2. 1-451 & 2-510. 13L 48
  nw2 & nw9. Part. 6B 20
Edgware Way Edg. 3Ad 13
Edgwarebury Gdns. Edg.
                    4Ac 13
Edgwarebury La. Edg.
                    3Af 13
Edinburgh Rd. e3. 24L 53
Edinburgh Rd. e13. 30J 55
Edinburgh Rd. e17. 25B 27
Edinburgh Rd. n18. 22Ac 17
Edinborough Rd. w7.1bN 94
Edison Rd. n8. 17C 24
Edith Grove sw10. 12Q 60
Edith Rd. e6. 31H 41
Edith Rd. e15. 27G 40
Edith Rd. n11. 17Ab 16
Edith Rd. n17. 22B 26
Edith Rd. se15. 23S 76
Edith Rd. se25. 20Zc 90
Edith Rd. sw19. 11Y 83
Edith Rd. w14. 9P 59
Edith Row sw6. 11R 72
Edith St. e2. 21J 52
Edith Ter. sw10. 12Q 60
Edith Villas w14. 10P 59

Edithna St. sw9.	17S 74	
Edmond Pl. ec1.	19L 51	
Edmund Rd. Mit.	13Zb 92	
Edmund St. se5.	20Q 63	
Edna Rd. sw20.	8Za 92	
Edna St. sw11.	13R 72	
Edney St. se26.	22X 87	
Edric Rd. se14.	23Q 64	
Edridge Rd. Cro.	19Zf 91	
Edrington Rd. se19.	21Z 90	
Edward Pl. se8.	25Q 65	
Edward Rd. e17.	23B 26	
Edward Rd. se20.	23Z 90	
Edward Rd. Cro.	20Zd 91	
Edward Rd. Har.	1cA 12	
Edward St. e1.	23K 52	
Edward St. e16.	29L 54	
Edward St. n1.	19J 51	
Edward St. nw1.	15K 49	
Edward St. se8. 1-95 & 2-86. se14. 88, 97 & up.	25Q 65	
Edward St. sw1.	16P 61	
Edwardes Sq w8.	10O 59	
Edward's La. n16.	20E 37	
Edward's Rd. e3.	24K 53	
Edward's Rd. s3.	17J 50	
Edwin Rd. Edg.	5Ab 13	
Edwin Rd. Twi.	1cV 93	
Edwin St. e16.	29L 54	
Edwina Gdns. Ilf.	31C 29	
Edwin's Row se15.	22Q 64	
Eele St. se8.	22L 52	
Effie Rd. sw6.	11Q 59	
Effingham Rd. n8.	18B 24	
Effingham Rd. se12.	28U 78	
Effingham Rd. Cro.	17Ze 91	
Effingham St. sw1.	15P 61	
Effort St. sw17.	13Y 83	
Effra Par. sw2.	18U 74	
Effra Rd. sw11.	17U 74	
Effra Rd. sw19.	11Y 82	
Egan St. se8.	22P 64	
Egbert Pl. nw1.	14H 35	
Egbert St. nw1.	14H 35	
Egerton Cres. sw3.	13O 60	
Egerton Gdns. nw4.	8B 20	
Egerton Gdns. nw10.	8H 33	
Egerton Gdns. sw3.	13O 60	
Egerton Gdns. sw13.	1aL 94	
Egerton Gdns. Ilf.	36F 42	
Egerton Rd. n16.	21C 25	
Egerton Rd. se10.	26R 77	
Egerton Rd. se25.	20Zb 90	
Egerton Rd. Twi.	1cU 93	
Egerton Rd. Wem.	3H 30	
Egerton Ter. sw3.	13O 60	
Egham Rd. e13.	30L 55	
Eglantine Rd. sw18.	11U 72	
Egleton Rd. e3.	26K 53	
Eglinton Hill se18.	33Q 95	
Eglinton Rd. se18.	33Q 95	
Egliston Rd. sw15.	8S 70	
Egmont St. se14.	23R 76	
Egremont Rd. se27.	18X 85	
Eider St. se17.	19P 63	
Eighth Av. e12.	32F 43	
Eileen Rd. se25.	20Zc 90	
Elaine Gro. nw5.	14F 35	
Elam St. se5.	19S 74	
Eland Rd. sw11.	14S 73	
Eland Rd. Cro.	18Zf 91	
Elbe St. sw6.	12R 72	
Elborough Rd. se25.	21Zc 90	
Elborough St. sw18.	10V 82	
Elcho St. sw11.	13Q 60	
Elcom St. w10.	10K 47	
Elcot Av. se15.	22Q 64	
Elder Av. n8.	17B 24	
Elder Rd. se27.	19Y 86	
Elder St. e1.	21L 51	
Elderberry Rd. w5.	2N 56	
Elderfield Rd. e5.	23F 38	
Elderton Rd. se26.	24X 88	
Eldon Av. Cro.	23Zf 91	
Eldon Pk. se25.	22Zb 90	
Eldon Rd. e16.	29M 54	
Eldon Rd. e17.	25B 27	
Eldon Rd. n9.	23Ae 17	
Eldon Rd. n22.	19Aa 16	
Eldon Rd. nw3.	13F 34	
Eldon Rd. w8.	11O 60	
Eldon St. ec2.	20L 51	
Eldred Rd. Bar.	35J 43	
Eldrick Rd. Edg.	5Ab 13	
Eldrick Wk. Edg.	5Ab 13	
Eldridge Rd. se16.	21O 64	
Eleanor Gro. sw13.	6S 70	
Eleanor Rd. e8.	22H 38	
Eleanor Rd. e15.	28H 40	
Eleanor Rd. n11.	17Ab 16	
Eleanor Rd. se18.	33P 95	
Eleanor St. e8.	25K 53	
Electric Av. sw9.	18T 74	
Elephant La. se16.	23N 64	
Elephant Rd. se17.	19O 63	
Eleray Rd. Ted.	1bY 93	
Elers Rd. w13.	1N 56	
Elfin Gro. Ted.	1bY 93	
Elfin Rd. se5.	19Q 63	
Elfindale Rd. se24.	19U 75	
Elfort Rd. n5.	18F 36	
Elfrida Cres. se6.	25X 88	
Elgar St. se16.	24O 65	
Elgin Av. w9.	11K 47	
Elgin Av. Har.	1aAa 12	
Elgin Cres. w11.	10M 47	
Elgin Mews w11.	10L 47	
Elgin Rd. n22.	16Aa 15	
Elgin Rd. Cro.	21Ze 91	
Elgin Rd. Ilf.	35E 42	
Elgin Ter. w9.	11J 48	
Eli St. w14.	10P 59	
Elim St. se1.	20O 63	
Eliot Bank se23.	22W 87	
Eliot Hill se13.	27S 78	
Eliot Pk. se13.	27S 78	
Eliot Pl. se3.	27S 78	
Eliot Vale se3.	27S 78	
Elizabeth Cotts. Kew	8R 68	
Elizabeth Mews nw3.	14G 35	
Elizabeth Pl. sw15.	10T 71	
Elizabeth Rd. e6.	31J 55	
Elizabeth Rd. n15.	21B 25	
Elizabeth St. sw1.	14O 61	
Ella Rd. n8.	17C 24	
Ellaline Rd. w6.	9Q 59	
Elland Rd. se15.	23T 76	
Ellen St. e1.	22M 52	
Ellenborough Rd. n19.	17E 36	
Ellenborough Rd. n22.	19Aa 16	
Ellerby St. sw6.	9R 71	
Ellerdale Rd. nw3.	12F 34	
Ellerdale St. se13.	26T 77	
Ellerdine Rd. Twi.	1dT 93	
Ellerman Av. se14.	25M 53	
Ellerslie Rd. w12.	8M 46	
Ellerslie Sq. sw4.	16T 74	
Ellerthorp St. e14.	26M 53	
Ellerton Rd. sw13.	7R 70	
Ellerton Rd. sw18.	12V 83	
Ellery St. se15.	22S 76	
Ellesborough Rd. n22.	17Aa 15	
Ellesmere Av. Edg.	5Ad 13	
Ellesmere Gdns. Ilf.	32C 42	
Ellesmere Rd. e3.	24J 53	
Ellesmere Rd. e16.	29N 67	
Ellesmere Rd. nw10.	7F 32	
Ellesmere Rd. w4.	5P 57	
Ellesmere St. e14.	26L 53	
Ellingort Rd. e8.	22H 38	
Ellingham Rd. e15.	27F 40	
Ellingham Rd. w12.	7N 58	
Ellington Rd. n10.	15B 23	
Ellington St. n7.	18G 36	
Elliot Rd. nw4.	8C 20	
Elliot Rd. Cro.	18Zc 90	
Elliott Rd. sw9.	18R 74	
Elliott Rd. w4.	6O 57	
Elliott's Row se11.	19O 62	
Ellis St. sw1.	14O 61	
Elliscombe Rd. se7.	30Q 67	
Ellison Rd. sw13.	6R 70	
Ellison Rd. sw16.	16Z 95	
Ellora Rd. sw16.	16Y 85	
Elm Av. w5.	2N 56	
Elm Bank Gdns. sw13.	6S 70	
Elm Clo. e11.	30C 29	
Elm Clo. sw20.	8Zb 92	
Elm Cres. w5.	2N 56	
Elm Gdns. n2.	12A 22	
Elm Gdns. w6.	9O 59	
Elm Gro. n8.	17C 24	
Elm Gro. nw2.	9F 33	
Elm Gro. se15.	21S 75	
Elm Gro. sw19.	9Z 90	
Elm Gro. w6.	9O 59	
Elm La. se6.	25W 88	
Elm Pk. sw2.	17U 74	
Elm Pl. sw7.	13P 60	
Elm Rd. e7.	29H 40	
Elm Rd. e11.	27E 40	
Elm Rd. e17.	27C 29	
Elm Rd. nw1.	16H 35	
Elm Rd. sw14.	4S 69	
Elm Rd. Cro.	10Zf 00	
Elm Rd. Wem.	2F 30	
Elm Row e1.	23M 52	
Elm Row nw3.	12E 34	
Elm St. wc1.	18K 50	
Elm Ter. nw11.	11E 33	
Elm Wlk. sw20.	8Zb 92	
Elm Way nw10.	6F 32	
Elmar Rd. n15.	20B 25	
Elmbank Way w7.	1cK 93	
Elmbourne Rd. sw17.	14X 84	
Elmcourt Rd. se27.	18W 85	
Elmcroft Av. e11.	30B 29	
Elmcroft Av. nw11.	10C 21	
Elmcroft Cres. nw11.	10C 21	
Elmcroft St. e5.	23F 38	
Elmdale Rd. n13.	18Ac 16	
Elmdale St. w6.	8P 59	
Elmdene Rd. se18.	33Q 95	
Elmer Gdns. Edg.	4Ab 13	
Elmer Rd. se6.	26V 88	
Elmers Rd. Cro.	21Zd 91	
Elmers End Rd. se20. 1-81 & 2-82 Cro. Remainder	22Za 90	
Elmfield Av. n8.	17B 24	
Elmfield Av. Ted.	1bX 93	
Elmfield Rd. e17.	23C 26	
Elmfield Rd. n2.	13A 22	

Elmfield Rd. sw17.	14W 84	
Elmgate Gdns. Edg.	5Ac 13	
Elmgrove Cres. Har.	1aB 12	
Elm Grove. sw13	7R 70	
Elm Grove Rd. w5.	2N 56	
Elm Grove Rd. Cro.	22Ze 91	
Elmgrove Rd. Har.	1bB 12	
Elmgrove Gdns. Har.	1aB 12	
Elmhall Gdns. E11.	30C 29	
Elmhurst Av. N2.	13A 22	
Elmhurst Rd. E7.	30H 41	
Elmhurst Rd. N17.	21Aa 17	
Elmhurst St. sw4.	16S 73	
Elmington Rd. SE5.	20R 75	
Elmira St. SE13.	26T 77	
Elmley St. SE18.	34P 95	
Elmore Rd. E11.	27F 40	
Elmore St. N1.	20H 37	
Elm Pk. Av. N15.	21C 26	
Elm Pk. Gdns. sw10.	12P 60	
Elm Pk. Rd. E10.	24D 27	
Elm Pk. Rd. N3.	10Ab 14	
Elm Pk. Rd. N21	19Ae 16	
Elm Pk. Rd. SE25.	21Zc 90	
Elm Pk. Rd. sw3.	12P 60	
Elms Av. N10.	15A 23	
Elms Av. NW4.	9B 21	
Elms Close NW4.	9B 21	
Elms Rd. SE21	20U 75	
Elms Rd. sw4.	15T 73	
Elmscott Rd. Bro.	28Y 89	
Elmsdale Rd. E17.	25B 27	
Elmshaw Rd. sw15	7T 70	
Elmside Rd. Wem.	3E 31	
Elmsleigh Av. Har.	1A 18	
Elmsleigh Rd. sw18.	12T 72	
Elmsleigh Rd. Twi.	1cV 93	
Elms Pk. Gdns. NW4.	9B 21	
Elmstead Av. Wem.	3D 18	
Elmstead Rd. Ilf.	35E 42	
Elmstone Rd. sw6.	10R 71	
Elm Tree Rd. NW8.	12K 48	
Elmtree Rd. Twi.	1cX 93	
Elmwood Av. N13.	17Ac 16	
Elmwood Av. Har.	1aB 12	
Elmwood Cres. NW9.	5A 19	
Elmwood Gdns. w7.	1cL 94	
Elmwood Rd. SE24.	19U 75	
Elmwood Rd. w4.	4P 57	
Elmwood Rd. Cro.	18Zd 91	
Elmworth Grove SE21.	19W 86	
Elnathan Mews w9.	11K 48	
Elphick St. E16	29M 54	
Elphinstone Rd. E17	25A 27	
Elphinstone St. N.5	19F 37	
Elric St. w6.	9P 59	
Elrington Rd. E8.	22G 38	
Elsa St. E14	24L 53	
Elsdale St. E9.	23H 38	
Elsden Rd. N17.	21Aa 17	
Elsenham Rd. E12.	32G 43	
Elsenham St. sw18.	10V 82	
Elsham Rd. E11.	28F 40	
Elsham Rd. w14.	9N 59	
Elsie Rd. SE22.	21T 75	
Elsiedene Rd. N21	20Af 16	
Elsiemaud Rd. SE4	25U 77	
Elsinore Rd. SE23	24W 88	
Elsley Rd. sw11.	14S 73	
Elspeth Rd. sw11	14T 73	
Elspeth Rd. Wem.	2F 30	
Elsted St. SE17	20P 63	
Elstree Gdns. N9.	22Ae 17	
Elstree Gdns. Ilf.	34G 43	
Elswick Rd. SE13.	26S 77	
Elswick St. sw6.	12R 72	
Elsworthy Rd. NW3	13H 34	
Elsworthy Ter. NW3.	13H 34	
Elsynge Rd. sw11.	12T 72	
Eltham Grn. SE9.	30U 79	
Eltham Hill SE9.	31U 79	
Eltham Rd.		
SE12. 1-101 & 2-116		
SE9. Remainder	29U 78	
Eltham St. SE17.	20P 63	
Eltham Grn. Rd. SE9.	30T 79	
Eltham Palace Rd. SE9.		
	30U 79	
Elthiron Rd. sw6.	11R 71	
Elthorne Av. w7.	1bN 94	
Elthorne Rd. N19.	16E 36	
Elthorne Rd. NW9.	5C 19	
Elthorne Way NW9.	5C 19	
Elthorne Pk. Rd. w7.	1bN 94	
Elthruda Rd. SE13.	27U 78	
Eltisley Rd. Ilf.	33F 43	
Elton Av. Wem.	1F 30	
Elton Pl. N16.	20G 37	
Elton St. N16	20G 37	
Eltringham St. sw18.	12T 72	
Elvaston Pl. sw7	12O 60	
Elvendon Rd. N13.	17Ab 16	
Elverson Rd. SE8.	26S 77	
Elverton St. sw1	16O 61	
Elvino Rd. SE26.	23Y 87	
Elwell Rd. sw4.	16R 74	
Elwin St. E2.	21K 52	
Elwood St. N5.	19F 37	
Ely Cotts. sw8.	17Q 62	
Ely Pl. EC1.	18L 50	
Ely Rd. E10	27C 28	
Ely Rd. Cro.	19Zc 90	
Ely Ter. E1.	23L 52	
Elyne Rd. N4.	18C 24	
Elystan Pl. sw3.	13P 60	
Elystan St. sw3.	13P 60	
Emanuel Av. w3.	5L 45	
Emba St. SE16	22O 64	
Embankment sw15	9S 71	
Embankment Gdns. sw3.		
	14Q 61	
Embankment, The, Twi.		
	1bV 93	
Embden St. sw6.	11R 72	
Embleton Rd. SE13.	26T 77	
Emerald St. wc1.	17L 50	
Emerson Rd. Ilf.	33D 42	
Emerson St. SE1.	19N 63	
Emery Hill St. sw1.	16O 61	
Emily Pl. N7.	18F 36	
Emily Rd. SE1.	21P 63	
Emily St. E16.	28M 54	
Emlyn Rd. w12.	6N 58	
Emma Rd. E13.	28K 54	
Emma St. E2.	22J 52	
Emma St. E16.	31N 67	
Emmanuel Rd. sw12.	15V 84	
Emmett St. E14.	25M 53	
Emmott St. E1.	24L 53	
Emperor's Gate sw7.	12O 60	
Empire Rd. Wem.	1H 30	
Empire Way Wem.	3F 31	
Empress Av. E12.	31E 41	
Empress Av. Ilf.	32E 42	
Empress St. SE17.	19Q 63	
Empson St. E3.	26L 53	
Emsworth St. sw2.	17W 85	
Emu Rd. sw8.	15S 73	
Ena Rd. sw16.	16Zb 90	
Enbrook St. w10.	10K 47	
Endell St. wc2.	17M 50	
Enderley Rd. Har.	1cAa 12	
Endersleigh Gdns. NW4.	7B 20	
Endive Pl. E14.	24M 53	
Endive St. E14.	24L 53	
Endlesham Rd. sw12.	14U 73	
Endsleigh Gdns. NW1.		
	16K 50	
Endsleigh Gdns. Ilf.	32E 42	
Endsleigh Rd. w13.	1aM 94	
Endsleigh St. wc1.	16K 50	
Endwell Rd. SE4.	24S 77	
Endymion Rd. N4.	18D 24	
Endymion Rd. sw2.	17U 74	
Enfield Rd. N1.	21H 37	
Enfield Rd. N8.	17B 24	
Enfield Rd. w3.	4N 57	
Enfield Rd. Bre.	1P 56	
Engadine St. sw18.	10V 82	
Engate St. SE13.	26T 77	
Engineer Rd. SE18.	33Q 95	
England's La. NW3.	14G 35	
Englefield Rd. N1.	20H 37	
Engleheart Rd. SE6.	26V 88	
Englewood Rd. sw12.	15U 73	
Enid St. SE16.	21O 63	
Enkel St. N7.	17F 36	
Enmore Av. SE25.	21Zc 90	
Enmore Gdns. sw14.	5T 69	
Enmore Rd. SE25.	21Zc 90	
Enmore Rd. sw15.	8T 70	
Ennerdale Av. Har.	1A 18	
Ennerdale Dri. NW9.	6B 20	
Ennerdale Rd. Kew.	3R 68	
Ennersdale Rd. SE13.	27U 78	
Ennis Rd. N4.	18D 24	
Ennis Rd. SE18.	34Q 95	
Ennismore Av. w4.	6O 58	
Ennismore Gdns. sw7.	13O 60	
Ennismore Gdns. Mews		
sw7.	13O 60	
Entick St. E2.	23K 52	
Epirus Rd. sw6.	10Q 59	
Epple Rd. sw6.	10R 71	
Epsom Rd. E10.	27C 28	
Epsom Rd. Cro.	17Zg 91	
Epworth St. EC1.	18L 50	
Erasmus St. sw1.	16P 62	
Eresby Rd. NW6.	11H 33	
Ergonwald St. w12.	6L 46	
Eric Rd. E7.	29F 40	
Eric Rd. NW10.	6G 32	
Eric St. E3.	24K 53	
Eridge Rd. w4.	5O 57	
Eridge Rd. Cro.	18Zc 90	
Erindale SE18.	35Q 95	
Erlanger Rd. SE14.	23R 76	
Erlesmere Gdns. w13.	1aN 94	
Ermine Rd. SE13.	26T 77	
Ernald Av. E6.	31J 43	
Erncroft Way Twi.	1bU 93	
Ernest Gdns. w4.	4Q 57	
Ernest Rd. E16.	28L 54	
Ernest St. E1.	24L 52	
Ernest St. E27.	19X 85	
Ernle Rd. sw20.	8Z 92	
Erpingham Rd. sw15.	8S 70	
Erridge Rd. sw19.	10Za 92	
Errington Rd. w9.	10K 47	
Errol St. EC1.	19L 51	
Erskine Hill NW11.	11B 22	
Erskine Rd. E17.	25B 27	
Erskine Rd. NW3.	14H 35	
Esher Rd. Ilf.	35F 42	
Esher St. sw1.	16O 62	
Esk Rd. E13.	29L 55	

INDEX TO STREETS

157

Eskdale Dri. NW9. 5B 19
Esmeralda Rd. SE1. 22P 64
Esmond Rd. NW6. 10H 33
Esmond Rd. W4. 5O 57
Esmond St. SW15. 9T 71
Esparto St. SW18. 11U 72
Essenden Gdns. N3. 11A 22
Essendine Rd. W9. 11K 48
Essex Gro. E17. 24B 27
Essex Gro. SE19. 20Y 86
Essex Pk. N3. 11Ab 14
Essex Pl. W4. 5O 57
Essex Rd. E10. 24C 27
Essex Rd. E12. 32G 43
Essex Rd. E17. 24C 28
Essex Rd. E18. 30A 29
Essex Rd. N1. 19H 37
Essex Rd. NW10. 6G 32
Essex Rd. W3. 4M 45
Essex Rd. Bar. 35H 43
Essex St. E2. 23K 52
Essex St. E7. 29G 41
Essex St. E8. 22H 38
Essex St. N1. 21J 51
Essex St. WC2. 18M 50
Essex Villas W8. 11N 59
Essex Pk. Mews W3. 6N 58
Essian St. E1. 24L 52
Estcourt Rd. SE25. 22Zd 91
Estcourt Rd. SW6. 10Q 59
Este Rd. SW11. 13S 72
Estelle Rd. NW3. 14F 35
Esther Rd. E11. 28D 28
Estreham Rd. SW16. 16Y 84
Eswyn Rd. SW17. 18X 84
Etchingham Rd. E15. 27F 40
Etchingham Pk. Rd. N3.
    12Ab 14
Ethel Rd. E16. 30M 55
Ethelbert Gdns. Ilf. 33C 42
Ethelbert Rd. SW20. 9Z 92
Ethelbert St. SW12. 15V 84
Ethelburga St. SW11. 13R 72
Ethelden Rd. W12. 8N 58
Etheldene Av. N10. 16B 23
Ethelm St. SE1. 18N 62
Ethelred St. SE11. 18P 62
Etherdon St. SE17. 20P 63
Etherley Rd. N15. 19B 25
Etherow St. SE22. 21U 75
Etherstone Grn. SW16. 17X 85
Etherstone Rd. SW16. 18X 85
Ethnard Rd. SE15. 22Q 64
Etloe Rd. E10. 25E 39
Eton Av. NW3. 13H 34
Eton Av. Wem. 1F 30
Eton Gro. NW9. 4A 19
Eton Gro. SE13. 28T 78
Eton Pl. NW3. 13H 34
Eton Rd. NW3. 14H 35
Eton Rd. SE18. 33P 95
Eton Rd. Ilf. 34G 43
Eton St. NW1. 14H 35
Eton St. SE18. 34P 95
Eton St. Rich. 2T 68
Eton Villas NW3. 14G 35
Eton College Rd. NW3. 14H 35
Etropol Rd. E5. 24T 30
Etruria St. SW8. 16R 73
Etta St. SE8. 24Q 65
Ettrick St. E14. 27M 54
Eugenia Rd. SE16. 23P 64
Eustace Rd. SW6. 11Q 59
Euston Bldgs. NW1. 16K 49
Euston Gro. NW1. 16K 49
Euston Rd. NW1. 15K 49

Euston Rd. Cro. 17Ze 91
Euston Sq. NW1. 16K 49
Euston St. NW1. 16K 49
Evandale Rd. SW9. 18R 74
Evangelist Rd. NW5. 15F 35
Evanston Gdns. Ilf. 31C 29
Eve Rd. E11. 28F 40
Eve Rd. E15. 28J 54
Eve Rd. N15. 21A 25
Evelina Rd. SE15. 22S 76
Evelina Rd. SE20. 23Z 90
Evelyn Av. NW9. 5A 19
Evelyn Gdns. SW7. 12P 60
Evelyn Gdns. Rich. 2S 68
Evelyn Gro. W5. 3N 56
Evelyn Rd. E16. 29N 67
Evelyn Rd. E17. 27B 28
Evelyn Rd. SW19. 11Y 83
Evelyn Rd. W4. 5O 57
Evelyn Rd. Rich. 2S 68
Evelyn St. N1. 20J 51
Evelyn St. SE8. 24P 64
Everard St. E1. 22M 52
Everdon Rd. SW13. 7Q 58
Everett Rd. NW10. 5J 45
Everett St. SW8. 16Q 62
Everilda St. N1. 18J 50
Evering Rd.
    N16. 1-183 & 2-158.
    E5. 160, 185 & up. 21F 37
Everington St. W6. 9Q 59
Everleigh St. N4. 18D 24
Eversfield Rd. Kew. 3R 68
Eversholt St. NW1. 16J 49
Evershot Rd. N4. 17D 24
Eversleigh Rd. E6. 31J 55
Eversleigh Rd. SW11. 14S 73
Eversley Av. Wem. 4D 19
Eversley Rd. SE7. 29Q 67
Eversley Rd. SE19. 19Z 90
Everthorpe Rd. SE15. 21P 76
Everton Bldgs. NW1. 15K 49
Everton Rd. Cro. 21Ze 91
Everington Rd. N10. 14Aa 15
Eversfield Gdns. NW7. 6Ab 13
Eversleigh Rd. N3. 11Ab 14
Evesham Av. E17. 26A 27
Evesham Rd. E15. 28H 40
Evesham Rd. N11. 16Ac 15
Evesham St. W11. 9M 47
Ewald Rd. SW6. 10S 71
Ewart Gro. N22. 18Aa 16
Ewart Rd. SE23. 23V 87
Ewell Pl. SE5. 20Q 63
Ewelme Rd. SE23. 23V 87
Ewer St. SE1. 19N 63
Ewhurst Rd. SE4. 25U 77
Ewing St. E3. 24K 53
Exbury Rd. SE6. 25W 88
Exchange St. EC1. 19K 51
Exeter Gdns. Ilf. 32D 42
Exeter Rd. E16. 29L 54
Exeter Rd. E17. 25B 27
Exeter Rd. N9. 23Ad 17
Exeter Rd. N14. 15Ae 15
Exeter Rd. NW2. 9G 33
Exeter Rd. Cro. 20Zd 91
Exeter St. NW8. 13K 48
Exeter St. WC2. 17M 50
Exhibition Rd. SW7. 13O 60
Exmoor St. W10. 9L 47
Exmouth Pl. E8. 22H 38
Exmouth Rd. E17. 25B 27
Exmouth St. E1. 23L 52
Exmouth St. NW1. 16K 49
Exmouth St. EC1. 18K 50

Exning Rd. E16. 28L 54
Exon St. SE17. 20P 63
Exton St. SE1. 18N 62
Eyhurst Clo. NW2. 8D 20
Eynella Rd. SE22. 21V 86
Eynham Rd. W12. 8L 46
Eynsford Rd. Ilf. 35E 42
Eyot Gdns. W6. 7P 58
Eyre St. Hill EC1. 18K 50
Eythorne Rd. SW9. 18R 74
Ezra St. N2. 21K 52

Faber Gdns. NW4. 7B 20
Fabian Rd. SW6. 10Q 59
Factory La. N17. 21A 26
Factory Rd. E16. 31N 67
Factory Sq. SW16. 16Z 90
Fair St. E1. 23L 52
Fair St. SE1. 21N 63
Fairbank St. N1. 20J 51
Fairbourne Rd. N15. 20A 25
Fairbridge Rd. N19. 16E 36
Fairbrook Rd. N13. 18Ac 16
Faircross Av. Bar. 34H 43
Fairfax Pl. NW6. 12H 34
Fairfax Rd. N8. 18B 24
Fairfax Rd. NW6. 12H 34
Fairfax Rd. W4. 6O 58
Fairfield Av. NW4. 8C 20
Fairfield Av. Edg. 4Ab 13
Fairfield Cres. Edg. 4Ab 13
Fairfield Dri. Wem. 1J 44
Fairfield Gdns. N8. 17B 24
Fairfield Path Cro. 20Zf 91
Fairfield Rd. E3. 25J 53
Fairfield Rd. E17. 24A 27
Fairfield Rd. N8. 17C 24
Fairfield Rd. N18. 22Ac 17
Fairfield Rd. SE7. 31O 67
Fairfield Rd. Cro. 20Zf 91
Fairfield Rd. Ilf. 33G 43
Fairfield St. SW18. 11T 72
Fairfields Clo. NW9. 5B 19
Fairfields Cres. NW9. 5B 19
Fairfoot Rd. E3. 25K 53
Fairford Gro. SE11. 18P 62
Fairgreen Rd. Cro. 18Zc 90
Fairhazel Gdns. NW6. 12G 34
Fairholm Gdns. N3. 10A 21
Fairholme Rd. W14. 10P 59
Fairholme Rd. Cro. 18Zd 91
Fairholme Rd. Har. 1bB 12
Fairholme Rd. Ilf. 32D 42
Fairholt Rd. N16. 20D 25
Fairland Rd. E15. 28H 40
Fairlands Av. Cro. 17Zc 90
Fairlawn Av. N2. 14A 23
Fairlawn Av. W4. 5O 57
Fairlawn Gro. W4. 5O 57
Fairlawn Pk. SE26. 24Y 88
Fairlawn Rd. SW19. 10Z 92
Fairlie Gdns. SE23. 23R 87
Fairlight Av. NW10. 6J 46
Fairlight Rd. SW17. 12X 83
Fairlop Rd. E11. 27D 28
Fairmead Gdns. Ilf. 31C 29
Fairmead Rd. N10. 17F 36
Fairmead Rd. Cro. 18Ze 91
Fairmile Av. SW16. 16Y 84
Fairmount Rd. SW2. 17U 74
Fairthorn Rd. SE7. 29P 67
Fairview Pl. SW2. 17V 85
Fair View Rd. N15. 21C 26

Fairview Rd. sw16.	17Za 90
Fairview Rd. Wem.	2G 30
Fairview Way Edg.	4Ad 13
Fairway sw20.	8Za 92
Fairway Av. nw9.	4A 19
Fairway Clo. nw11.	12C 22
Fairway Gdns. Ilf.	34G 43
Fairway, The, w3.	6L 46
Fairway, The, Edg.	5Ae 13
Fairway, The, Wem.	1D 18
Fairweather Rd. n16.	22C 26
Fairwyn Rd. se26.	24X 87
Faith St. e1.	23L 52
Falcon Ct. se1.	19N 63
Falcon Gro. sw11.	13S 72
Falcon Rd. sw11.	13S 72
Falcon Sq. ec1.	19L 51
Falcon St. e13.	29K 54
Falcon St. ec1.	19L 51
Falcon Ter. sw11.	13S 72
Falkirk St. n1.	21J 51
Falkland Av. n3.	11Ab 14
Falkland Av. n11.	15Ad 15
Falkland Pl. nw5.	15G 35
Falkland Rd. n8.	18B 24
Falkland Rd. nw5.	15G 35
Falkland Pk. Av. se25.	20Zb 90
Fallodon Way nw11.	11A 22
Fallow Ct. Av. n12.	12Ab 14
Fallsbrook Rd. sw16.	15Y 84
Falmer Rd. e17.	26A 27
Falmer Rd. n15.	20B 25
Falmouth Gdns. Ilf.	31B 29
Falmouth Rd. se1.	19O 63
Falmouth St. e15.	27G 40
Fambridge Rd. se25.	25Y 88
Fane Pl. w14.	10P 50
Fane St. w14.	10P 59
Fann St. ec1.	19L 51
Fanny Rd. sw13.	7P 58
Fanshaw St. n1.	20K 51
Fanshawe Av. Bar.	34H 43
Fanthorpe St. sw15.	8S 71
Faraday Rd. e15.	28H 40
Faraday Rd. sw19.	11Y 82
Faraday Rd. w3.	5M 45
Faraday Rd. w10.	10L 47
Faraday St. se17.	20P 63
Farewell Pl. Mit.	12Za 92
Farjeon Rd. se3.	31R 79
Farleigh Rd. n16.	21F 37
Farley Rd. se6.	26V 88
Farley Rd. se25.	21Zc 90
Farlow Rd. sw15.	9S 71
Farlton Rd. sw18.	11V 83
Farm Av. nw2.	10E 33
Farm Av. sw16.	17X 85
Farm La. sw6.	11Q 59
Farm Rd. n21.	19Ae 16
Farm Rd. Edg.	4Ac 13
Farm St. w1.	15M 49
Farm Wk. nw11.	11B 21
Farmcote Rd. se12.	29W 89
Farmdale Rd. se10.	29P 66
Farmer Rd. e10.	26D 27
Farmer St. w8.	11M 47
Farmer's Rd. se5.	19Q 62
Farmilo Rd. e17.	25D 27
Farmstead Rd. se6.	25Y 88
Farmstead Rd. Har.	1cAa 12
Farnaby Rd. se9.	30T 79
Farnan Av. e17.	26A 27
Farnan Rd. sw16.	17Y 85
Farnborough Av. e17.	24A 27
Farncombe St. se16.	22O 64
Farnfield St. e14.	26M 53
Farnham Pl. se1.	19N 63
Farnham Rd. Ilf.	36D 42
Farningham Rd. n17.	22Ab 17
Farnley Rd. se25.	20Zc 90
Faroe Rd. w14.	9O 59
Farquhar Rd. se19.	21Y 86
Farquhar Rd. sw19.	10W 82
Farquharson Rd. Cro.	19Ze 91
Farrance St. e14.	25M 53
Farrant Av. n22.	18Aa 16
Farrant St. w10.	10K 47
Farrar St. sw9.	18R 74
Farrer Rd. n8.	16B 24
Farrer Rd. Har.	2B 18
Farringdon Av. ec4.	18L 50
Farringdon Rd. ec1.	18K 50
Farringdon St. ec4.	18L 50
Farringford Rd. e15.	28H 40
Fashion St. e1.	21L 51
Fassett Rd. e8.	22G 38
Fassett Sq. e8.	22G 38
Fauconberg Rd. w4.	4Q 57
Faulkner St. se14.	23R 76
Faunce St. se17.	18P 62
Faustin Pl. se16.	24N 65
Pavart Rd. sw6.	11R 71
Faversham Rd. se6.	25V 88
Favonia St. e3.	26K 53
Fawcett Rd. se16.	23P 64
Fawcett Rd. Cro.	18Zf 91
Fawcett St. sw10.	12Q 60
Fawe St. e14.	26L 53
Fawe Pk. Rd. sw15.	10T 71
Fawley Rd. n17.	22B 26
Fawley Rd. nw6.	11G 34
Fawn Rd. e13.	30J 55
Fawnbrake Av. se24.	19T 74
Fawood Av. nw10.	5H 31
Faygate Rd. sw2.	17W 85
Fayland Av. sw16.	15Y 84
Fearnley Rd. se5.	20S 75
Fearon St. se10.	29P 66
Featherstone Bldgs. wc1.	17L 50
Featherstone St. ec1.	20K 51
Felbridge Av. Har.	1aAa 12
Felbrigge Rd. Ilf.	36E 42
Felday Rd. se13.	26U 77
Felden St. sw6.	10R 71
Felgate Mews w6.	8P 58
Felix Av. n8.	17C 24
Felix Rd. w13.	1aM 94
Felix St. e2.	22J 52
Felix St. se1.	17O 62
Felixstowe Rd. n9.	22Ac 17
Felixstowe Rd. n17.	21A 25
Felixstowe Rd. nw10.	8J 46
Fell Rd. Cro.	19Zf 91
Fell St. ec2.	19L 51
Fellbrigg Rd. se22.	21U 75
Fellbrigg St. e1.	22K 52
Fellows Rd. nw3.	13H 34
Fellows St. e2.	21J 51
Felsberg Rd. sw2.	17U 74
Felsham Rd. sw15.	9S 71
Felmingham Rd. se20.	22Zb 90
Felstead Rd. e11.	29D 29
Felstead Rd. e16.	31M 55
Felstead St. e9.	25H 39
Felton St. n1.	20J 51
Fen St. e16.	28M 54
Fenchurch Av. ec3.	20M 51
Fenchurch St. ec3.	20M 51
Fendall St. se1.	21O 63
Fenelon Rd. w14.	10P 59
Fenham Rd. se15.	22R 76
Fenn St. e9.	23G 38
Fenn St. n9.	22Ad 17
Fennell St. se18.	33Q 95
Fenner Rd. se16.	22O 64
Fenning St. se1.	20N 63
Fenstanton Rd. n12.	13Ac 14
Fentiman Rd. sw8.	17Q 62
Fenton Rd. n17.	19Ab 16
Fenton St. e1.	22M 52
Fenton's Av. e13.	29K 55
Fenwick Gro. se15.	21T 76
Fenwick Pl. sw9.	16S 74
Fenwick Rd. se15.	21T 76
Fenwick St. se18.	33Q 95
Ferdinand Clo. nw1.	15H 35
Ferdinand Pl. nw1.	15G 35
Ferdinand St. nw1.	15H 35
Fergus Rd. n5.	19G 37
Ferme Pk. Rd.	
n4. 1-53 & 2-66.	
n8. 55, 68 & up.	17C 24
Fermor Rd. se23.	24W 88
Fermoy Rd. w9.	10K 47
Fern St. e3.	25L 53
Fernbrook Rd. se13.	27U 78
Ferncliff Rd. e8.	22G 38
Ferncroft Av. n12.	14Ac 15
Ferncroft Av. nw3.	11F 34
Ferndale Av. e17.	27B 28
Ferndale Rd. e7.	30H 41
Ferndale Rd. e11.	28E 40
Ferndale Rd. n15.	21C 25
Ferndale Rd. se25.	22Zc 90
Ferndale Rd.	
sw4. 1-169 & 2-172.	
sw9. 171, 174 & up.	16T 74
Ferndale Ter. Har.	1bA 12
Ferndene Rd. se5.	19T 75
Ferney Rd. Bar.	15Af 13
Fernhall Dri. Ilf.	31C 29
Fernham Rd. Cro.	19Zb 90
Fernhead Rd. w9.	10J 47
Fernholme Rd. se15.	23T 76
Fernhurst Gdns. Edg.	3Ac 13
Fernhurst Rd. sw6.	10R 71
Fernhurst Rd. Cro.	22Ze 91
Fernlea Rd. sw12.	15V 84
Fernleigh Rd. n21.	18Ae 16
Ferns Rd. e15.	28H 40
Fernshaw Rd. sw10.	12Q 60
Fernside Av. Edg.	6Ad 13
Fernside Rd. sw12.	14V 84
Fernthorpe Rd. sw16.	15Y 84
Ferntower Rd. n5.	20G 37
Fernwood Av. sw16.	16X 85
Fernwood Cres. n20.	14Ad 15
Ferrers Rd. sw16.	16Y 85
Ferrier St. sw18.	11T 72
Ferring Clo. Har.	1dD 12
Ferris Rd. se22.	21T 76
Ferron Rd. e5.	22F 38
Ferry La. n17.	22A 26
Ferry La. Bre.	2Q 56
Ferry La. Kew.	3Q 56
Ferry Rd. sw13.	7Q 58
Ferry Rd. Ted.	1bX 93
Ferry Rd. Twi.	1aV 93
Ferry St. e14.	26P 65
Festing Rd. sw15.	9S 71
Fetter La. ec4.	18L 50
Ffinch St. se8.	25Q 65

Field Ct. wc1. 18L 50
Field La. Ted. 1bY 93
Field Pl. ec1. 18J 50
Field Rd. e7. 29F 40
Field Rd. n15. 20A 25
Field Rd. w6. 9P 59
Field St. wc1. 17J 50
Fieldgate St. e1. 22L 52
Fieldhouse Rd. sw12. 16V 84
Fielding Rd. w4. 5O 57
Fielding Rd. w14. 9O 59
Fieldside Rd. New Bec.
              27Y 89
Fieldview sw18. 12V 83
Field Way nw10. 5H 31
Fieldway Cres. n5. 18G 36
Fife Rd. e16. 29L 54
Fife Rd. n22. 19Aa 16
Fife Rd. sw14. 4T 69
Fifth Av. e12. 32F 43
Fifth Av. w10. 9K 47
Fifth Cross Rd. Twi. 1dW 93
Filey Av. n16. 21E 38
Fillebrook Rd. e11. 28D 28
Filmer Rd. sw6. 10R 71
Finborough Rd. sw10.
              11P 60
Finch Clo. nw10. 5G 31
Finch La. ec3. 20M 51
Finch St. e1. 21L 52
Finchley Av. n3. 10A 21
Finchley La. nw4. 9A 21
Finchley Pk. n12. 12Ad 14
Finchley Pl. nw8. 12J 48
Finchley Rd.
   nw8. 1-97 & 2-82.
   nw3. 84-378 & 99-617.
   nw2. 380-450 & 619-707.
   nw11, 452, 709 & up.
              11E 33
Finchley Rd. se17. 19Q 62
Finchley Way n3. 11Ab 14
Finck St. se1. 17O 62
Finden Rd. e7. 30G 41
Findhorn St. e14. 27M 54
Findon Rd. n9. 22Ae 17
Findon Rd. w12. 7N 58
Fingal St. se10. 28P 66
Finland Rd. se4. 24S 76
Finlay St. sw6. 9R 71
Finnis St. e2. 22K 52
Finsbury Av. ec2. 20L 51
Finsbury Circus ec2. 20L 51
Finsbury Mkt. ec2. 20L 51
Finsbury Pavement ec2.
              20L 51
Finsbury Rd. n22. 17Aa 16
Finsbury Sq. ec2. 20L 51
Finsbury St. ec2. 20L 51
Finsbury Pk. Av. n4. 19D 25
Finsbury Pk. Rd. n4. 19E 37
Finsen Rd. se5. 19S 75
Finstock Rd. w10. 9L 47
Fir St. se26. 22X 87
Firbank Rd. se15. 22S 76
Fircroft Rd. sw17. 13W 84
Firhill Rd. se6. 25X 88
Firs Av. n10. 15A 23
Firs La. n13 & n21. 19Ad 16
Firsby Rd. n16. 21D 26
Firscroft n13. 19Ad 16
Firs Pk. Av. n21. 20Ae 17
First Av. e12. 32G 43
First Av. e13. 29K 55
First Av. e17. 26B 27

First Av. n18. 23Ac 17
First Av. nw4. 9A 21
First Av. sw14. 6S 69
First Av. w3. 6M 46
First Av. w10. 10K 47
First St. sw3. 13O 60
First Way sw20. 8Za 92
First Cross Rd. Twi. 1cV 93
Firth Gdns. sw6. 9R 71
Fish St. Hill ec3. 20M 51
Fisher Rd. Har. 1bAa 12
Fisher St. e16. 29L 54
Fisher St. wc1. 17L 50
Fisher's La. w4. 5O 57
Fishmonger's Hall St. ec4.
              20M 51
Fishponds Rd. sw17. 13X 83
Fitzalan Rd. n3. 10A 21
Fitzalan St. se11. 18O 62
Fitzgeorge Av. w14. 9P 59
Fitzgerald Av. sw14. 6S 70
Fitzgerald Rd. e11. 29C 28
Fitzgerald Rd. sw14. 5S 69
Fitzhardinge St. w1. 14L 49
Fitzjames Av. w14. 10P 59
Fitz James Av. Cro. 21Zf 91
Fitzjohn's Av. nw3. 12F 34
Fitz Neal St. w12. 6L 46
Fitzroy Pk. n6. 14D 23
Fitzroy Pl. nw1. 15K 49
Fitzroy Rd. nw1. 14H 35
Fitzroy Sq. w1. 15K 49
Fitzroy St. w1. 16L 49
Fitzwarren Gdns. n19. 16D 23
Fitzwilliam Av. Rich. 2R 68
Fitzwilliam Rd. sw4. 15S 73
Fladbury Rd. n15. 20C 25
Fladgate Rd. e11. 28C 28
Flambard Rd. Har. 1aC 12
Flamborough St. e14. 23M 52
Flamstead Av. Wem. 1G 31
Flamstead Rd. se7. 31Q 67
Flanchford Rd. w12. 6O 58
Flanders Rd. w4. 6O 58
Flask St. e1. 21M 52
Flask Wk. nw3. 12F 34
Flavell Rd. sw18. 12T 72
Flaxman Rd. se5. 19S 75
Flaxman Ter. wc1. 16K 50
Flaxton Rd. se18. 35R 95
Fleeming Rd. e17. 25A 27
Fleet La. ec4. 18L 50
Fleet Rd. nw3. 14F 35
Fleet St. ec4. 18M 50
Fleetwood Rd. nw10. 7F 32
Fleetwood St. n16. 21E 37
Fleming Rd. se17. 19Q 62
Flemming St. n1. 21J 51
Flempton Rd. e10. 24D 27
Fletcher La. se1. 19N 63
Fletcher Rd. w4. 5N 57
Fletching Rd. e5. 23F 38
Fletton Rd. n11. 17Ab 16
Fleur de Lis St. e1. 21L 51
Flexmere Rd. n17. 20Aa 17
Flint St. se17. 20P 63
Flinton St. se17. 20P 63
Flitcroft St. wc2. 16M 50
Flockton St. se16. 21N 64
Flodden Rd. se5. 19R 75
Flood Wlk. sw3. 13P 60
Flora Gdns. w6. 7O 58
Floral St. wc2. 17M 50
Florence Gro. se14. 25R 77
Florence Rd. e6. 30J 55
Florence Rd. e11. 27E 40

Florence Rd. e13. 29K 54
Florence Rd. n4. 18D 24
Florence Rd. n18. 23Ac 17
Florence Rd. se14. 25R 77
Florence Rd. sw19. 11Y 82
Florence Rd. w4. 5N 57
Florence Rd. w5. 2M 44
Florence St. e16. 28K 54
Florence St. n1. 19H 37
Florence St. nw4. 8A 21
Florence Ter. se14. 25R 77
Floreston St. e1. 23L 52
Florian Rd. sw15. 10T 71
Florida Rd. Cro. 18Za 90
Florida St. e2. 22K 52
Florington Rd. n2. 14A 23
Floss St. sw15. 8S 70
Flower & Dean St. e1. 21L 51
Floyd Rd. se7. 30P 67
Foley Pl. sw8. 15S 73
Foley St. w1. 15L 49
Foliot St. w12. 6L 46
Folkestone Rd. e15. 28J 54
Folkestone Rd. e17. 26B 27
Folkestone Rd. n18. 22Ac 17
Folkington Corner n12.
              10Ac 14
Follett St. e14. 26M 53
Fontaine Rd. sw16. 17Z 90
Fontarabia Rd. sw11. 14T 73
Fontenoy Rd. sw12. 15W 84
Fonthill Rd. n4. 18E 36
Football La. Har. 1bD 12
Forburg Rd. n16. 22D 26
Ford Clo. Har. 1cC 12
Ford Rd. e3. 24J 53
Ford Sq. e1. 22L 52
Ford St. e3. 24J 53
Ford St. e16. 28M 54
Fordel Rd. se6. 27V 89
Fordham St. e1. 22L 52
Fordhook Av. w5. 3M 44
Fordingley Rd. w9. 10K 47
Fordington Rd. n6. 14B 23
Fordmill Rd. se6. 25W 88
Fords Gro. n21. 19Ae 16
Ford's Pk. Rd. e16. 29L 54
Fordwych Rd. nw2. 10F 33
Fordyce Rd. se13. 26U 78
Fore St. ec2. 20L 51
Fore St.
   n18. 1-269 & 2-276.
   n9. 271, 278 & up. 21Ab 17
Fore St. Av. ec2. 20L 51
Foreign St. se5. 19S 75
Forest Clo. e11. 29C 28
Forest Dale n14. 16Ad 15
Forest Dri. e12. 31F 41
Forest Dri. e. e11. 27D 28
Forest Dri. W. e11. 27D 28
Forest Gdns. n17. 21Aa 17
Forest Gate nw9. 6B 20
Forest Glade e11. 28C 28
Forest La,
   e15. 1-91.
   e7. 92 & up. 28G 40
Forest Rise e17. 27B 28
Forest Rd. e7. 29F 41
Forest Rd. e8. 21H 37
Forest Rd. e11. 27D 28
Forest Rd. e17. 23B 26
Forest Rd. n9. 23Ae 17
Forest Rd. Kew. 3Q 57
Forest St. e7. 29G 41
Forester Rd. se15. 22T 76
Forester St. e3. 24K 53

Foresters Dri. E17.   27B 28
Forest Hill Rd.
   SE22. 2-128 & 3-41
   SE23. 130 & up   22U 76
Forest View Av. E10. 27C 28
Forest View Rd. E12. 31F 41
Forfar Rd. N22.   19Aa 16
Forfar Rd. SW11.   14R 73
Formby Av. Har.   1A 18
Formosa St. W9.   12K 48
Forres Gdns. NW11. 11C 21
Forrest Gdus. SW16. 17Zb 90
Forest Clo. NW8.   12J 48
Forset St. W1.   13L 48
Forster Rd. E17.   24C 27
Forster Rd. N17.   21A 25
Forster Rd. Cro.   19Zd 91
Forston St. N1.   19J 51
Forsyte Cres. SE19. 20Za 90
Fort Rd. SE1.   21P 64
Fort St. E1.   21L 51
Fort St. E16.   30N 07
Forterie Gdns. Ilf. 36F 42
Fortescue Av. E8   22H 38
Fortescue Rd. SW19. 12Z 92
Fortescue Rd. Edg.   5Ab 13
Fortess Gro. NW5   15F 35
Fortess Rd. NW5.   15F 35
Forthbridge Rd. SW11.14T 73
Fortis Grn. Av. N2. 14A 23
Fortis Grn. Rd.
   N2. 1-75 & 2-64.
   N10. Part.   14A 23
Fortismere Av. N10. 15A 23
Fortnam Rd. N19   17E 36
Fortune St. EC1.   19K 51
Fortune Gate Rd. NW10.
               6H 32
Fortune Grn. Rd. NW6.
               11F 33
Forty Av. Wem.   3E 30
Forty Clo. Wem.   3E 30
Forty La. Wem.   4E 31
Forty Acre La. E16.   29L 54
Foscote Rd. NW4.   8C 20
Foskett Rd. SW6.   10S 71
Foss Av. Cro.   17Zh 91
Foss Rd. SW17.   12X 83
Fosdene Rd. SE7.   30Q 67
Fosse Way W13   1aK 94
Fossil Rd. SE13.   25T 77
Foster La. EC2.   19L 51
Foster Rd. E13.   29K 54
Foster Rd. W3.   6M 46
Foster Rd. W4.   5P 57
Foster St. E1.   22L 52
Foster St. NW4.   9B 21
Foubert's Pl. W1.   15M 49
Foulden Rd. N16.   21F 37
Foulis Ter. SW7.   12P 60
Foulser Rd. SW17.   14X 84
Foulsham Rd. Cro. 19Zb 90
Fount St. SW8.   16Q 62
Fountain Rd. SE19. 21X 86
Fountain Rd. SW17. 12X 83
Fountayne Rd. N15. 22B 26
Fountayne Rd. N16. 21E 38
Fournier St. E1.   21L 51
Fourth Av. E12.   32F 43
Fourth Av. W10.   10K 47
Fourth Cross Rd. Twi. 1dW93
Fowell St. W11.   9M 47
Fowler Rd. E7.   29F 40
Fowler Rd. N1.   19H 37
Fowler St. SE5.   20S 75
Fowler's Wk. W5.   2K 44

Fownes St. SW11.   13S 72
Fox Hill SE19.   20Z 90
Fox La. N13.   17Ae 16
Fox St. E2.   22K 52
Fox St. E16.   28L 54
Fox & Knot St. EC1. 18L 50
Foxberry Rd. SE4.   24T 77
Foxbourne Rd. SW17.14W 84
Foxglove St. W12.   6M 46
Foxham Rd. N19.   16F 35
Foxhill Gdns. SE19.   21Z 90
Foxley Rd. SW9.   18Q 62
Foxley Rd. Cro.   18Zb 90
Foxmole Rd. SE9.   31U 79
Foxmore St. SW11.   13R 73
Fox's La. E9.   23G 38
Foxwell St. SE4.   24S 76
Foyle Rd. N17.   22Aa 17
Foyle Rd. SE3.   28Q 66
Framfield Rd. N5.   19F 36
Framfield Rd. W7.   1bL 94
Frampton St. NW8. 13K 48
Frampton Pk. Rd. E9. 23H 38
Francemary Rd. SE4. 25U 77
Frances St. SE18.   32P 95
Franche Court Rd. SW17.
               12W 83
Francis Av. Har.   1aB 12
Francis Av. Ilf.   34E 42
Francis Gro. SW19. 10Y 82
Francis Rd. E10.   26E 39
Francis Rd. Cro.   18Zd 91
Francis Rd. Har.   1aB 12
Francis Rd. Wem.   1J 44
Francis St. E2.   21J 51
Francis St. E15.   28G 40
Francis St. N1.   18J 50
Francis St. SW1.   16O 61
Francis St. W2.   12L 48
Francis St. W6.   9P 59
Francis St. WC1.   16L 49
Francis Ter. N19.   16E 35
Franciscan Rd. SW17. 14X 84
Francklin Gdns. Edg. 4Ae 13
Franklin Rd. SE20.   23Z 90
Franconia Rd. SW4. 16U 73
Frank St. E13.   29L 55
Frank St. SE11.   17P 62
Frankfurt Rd. SE24. 19T 75
Frankham St. SE8.   25R 77
Franklin St. N15.   20C 25
Franklin St. E3.   26K 53
Franklin St. NW5.   15G 35
Franklin's Row SW3. 14P 61
Franklyn Rd. NW10. 6G 32
Frankton Rd. SE15. 21R 76
Franlau Cres. N13.   20Ac 16
Fransfield Gro. SE26. 22X 87
Frant Rd. Cro.   18Zc 90
Fraser Rd. E17.   26C 27
Fraser Rd. N9.   22Ad 17
Fraser Rd. Wem.   1H 30
Fraser St. W4.   6P 57
Frazier St. SE1.   18N 62
Frean St. SE16.   21O 64
Freda St. SE16.   21O 64
Frederick Cres. SW9. 18R 74
Frederick Pl. E3.   24K 53
Frederick Pl. E8.   21H 37
Frederick Rd. E16. 29M 55
Frederick Pl. SE18.   33Q 95
Frederick Rd. SE17. 19Q 62
Frederick St. E15.   27H 40
Frederick St. E17.   24C 27
Frederick St. N7.   17H 36

Frederick St. NW8.   13J 48
Frederick St. SW1.   16P 61
Frederick St. WC1.   17K 50
Frederick's Pl. E12. 12Ad 14
Freedom St. SW11.   14S 73
Free Grove Rd. N7. 17G 36
Freeland Rd. W5.   3M 44
Freeland St. SW11.   13R 72
Freeling St. N1.   17H 36
Freemasons Rd. E16. 29L 55
Freemasons Rd. Cro. 20Ze 91
Freke Rd. SW11.   14S 73
Fremantle St. SE17. 20P 63
Fremont St. E9.   23H 38
Frendsbury Rd. SE4. 23T 76
Frensham St. SE15.   22Q 64
Frere St. SW11.   13R 72
Freshford St. SW18. 12W 83
Freshwater Rd. SW17. 14Y 84
Frewin Rd. SW18.   12V 83
Friar St. EC4.   19M 51
Friar St. SE1.   19N 62
Friars Av. N20.   14Ad 15
Friars La. Rich.   1T 68
Friar's Rd. E6.   31J 55
Friars Way W3.   5M 45
Friars Pl. La. W3.   5M 45
Friars Stile Rd. Rich. 2U 94
Friary Rd. N12.   13Ac 14
Friary Rd. SE15.   22Q 64
Friary Rd. W3.   5L 45
Friary Way N12.   13Ac 14
Friday St. EC4.   19M 51
Friend St. EC1.   18K 50
Friendly St. SE8.   25R 77
Friends Rd. Cro.   19Zf 91
Friern Pk. N12.   13Ac 14
Friern Rd. SE22   21V 86
Friern Barnet La.
   N11.1-71 & 2-80.
   N20. 73, 136 & up. 13Ad 14
Friern Barnet Rd. N11.
               14Ac 15
Friern Watch Av. N12.
               12Ad 14
Frimley Gdns. Mit. 13Zb 92
Frimley Rd. Ilf.   35F 42
Frimley St. E1.   23K 52
Frinton Rd. E6.   31K 55
Frinton Rd. N15.   21C 25
Frinton Rd. SW17.   14Y 84
Friston St. SW6.   11S 72
Frith Rd. E11.   27F 40
Frith Rd. Cro.   19Zf 91
Frith St. W1.   16M 50
Frithville Gdns. W12. 8N 58
Frobisher Rd. N8.   18B 24
Frobisher St. SE10.   28Q 66
Frogley Rd. SE22.   21T 75
Frogmore SW18.   11T 71
Frognal NW3.   12F 34
Frognal Av. Har.   1bB 12
Frognal Gdns. NW3. 12F 34
Frognal La. NW3.   12F 34
Frognal Rise NW3.   12F 34
Frognal Way NW3.   12F 34
Froissart Rd. SE9.   31U 79
Frome Rd. N22.   19A 24
Frome St. N1.   19J 51
Froude St. SW8.   15S 73
Fry Rd. E6.   31H 41
Fryatt Rd. N17.   20Aa 17
Fryent Gro. NW9.   6C 20
Fryston Av. Cro.   21Zf 91
Fulbourne Rd. E17.   27A 28
Fulbourne St. E1.   22L 52

Fulbrook Rd. N19. 16F 35
Fulford St. SE16. 22A 64
Fulham Pl. W2. 13L 48
Fulham Rd.
 SW3. 1-267 & 2-132
 SW10. 134-366 & 273-459
 SW6. 392, 461 & up 10R 71
Fulham High St. SW6. 10S 71
Fulham Palace Rd.
 W6. 1-211 & 2-250
 SW6. 225, 286 & up 9P 59
Fulham Pk. Gdns. SW6.
 10R 71
Fulham Pk. Rd. SW6. 10R 71
Fuller St. E2. 21K 52
Fuller St. NW4. 8A 21
Fullerton Rd. SW18. 11T 72
Fullerton Rd. Cro. 20Zd 91
Fulready Rd. E10. 27C 28
Fulton St. E16. 28M 54
Fulwell Rd. Twi. 1dX 93
Fulwood Av. Wem. 3J 44
Fulwood Pl. WC1. 18L 50
Furber St. W6. 7O 58
Furley Rd. SE15. 22R 76
Furlong Rd. N7. 18G 36
Furmage St. SW18. 11U 72
Furneaux Av. SE27. 18Y 85
Furness Rd. NW10. 7J 46
Furness Rd. W6. 11R 72
Furnival St. EC4. 18L 50
Fursby Av. N3. 11Ac 14
Further Grn. Rd. SE6. 28V 89
Furze Rd. Cro. 19Zb 90
Furze St. E3. 25L 53
Furze St. W4. 6P 58
Furzedown Dri. SW17. 15Y 84
Furzedown Rd. SW17 15X 84
Furzefield Rd. SE3. 29Q 67
Fuse St. SE2. 36P 95
Fyfield Rd. E17. 27A 28
Fyfield Rd. SW9. 18S 74

Gabriel St. SE23 23V 87
Gaddesden Av. Wem. 3G 31
Gage St. WC1. 17L 50
Gainford St. N1. 18H 36
Gainsborough Av. E12.33G 43
Gainsborough Gdns. NW3.
 13F 34
Gainsborough Gdns. NW11.
 10C 21
Gainsborough Gdns. Edg.
 3Aa 13
Gainsborough Rd. E3.24K 53
Gainsborough Rd. E11.
 28D 28
Gainsborough Rd. E15.
 28K 54
Gainsborough Rd. N12.
 12Ac 14
Gainsborough Rd. W4. 6O 58
Gainsborough Rd. Kew.
 3R 68
Gainsford Rd. E17 25B 27
Gainsford St. SE1. 21N 63
Gairloch Rd. SE5. 20S 75
Gaisford St. NW5. 16G 35
Galatea Rd. SE15. 22S 76
Galbraith St. E14. 26O 65
Gale St. E3. 25L 53
Galena Rd. W6. 8O 58
Gale's Gdns E2. 22K 52
Galesbury Rd. SW18. 12U 72
Gallants Pk.Rd.Barn.14Ae 15

Gallery Rd. SE21. 20V 86
Galley Wall Rd. SE16.22P 64
Gallia Rd. N5. 19G 37
Galliard Rd. N9. 22Ae 17
Gallosson Rd. SE18. 35P 95
Galloway Rd. W12. 7M 46
Galpin's Rd. Cro. 16Zc 90
Galt St. E14. 24M 53
Galton St. W10 9K 47
Galveston Rd. SW15. 10T 71
Galway St. EC1. 19K 51
Gambetta St. SW8. 15S 73
Gambia St. SE1. 19N 63
Gambole Rd. SW17. 13X 83
Gamlen Rd. SW15. 9S 71
Gamuel Rd. E17. 25C 27
Gange St. SE5. 19Q 63
Ganton St. W1. 15M 49
Gantshill Cross Ilf. 33C 42
Gap Rd. SW19. 10X 82
Gard St. EC1. 19K 51
Garden La. SW2. 17V 85
Garden Rd. NW8. 12J 48
Garden Rd. SE15. 22T 76
Garden Rd. SE20. 23Za 90
Garden Rd. Rich. 3S 69
Garden Row SE1. 18O 62
Garden Row SE13 26S 77
Garden Row SW9. 17S 74
Garden St. E1. 23L 52
Garden St. SW1. 16P 61
Garden Way NW10. 5G 31
Gardener's Rd. E3. 24J 52
Gardens, The SE22. 21T 76
Gardiner Av. NW2. 8F 32
Gardner Rd. E13. 29L 55
Gardnor Rd. NW3. 12F 34
Gareth Gro. E12. 29X 89
Garfield Rd. E13. 28L 54
Garfield Rd. N11. 15Ac 15
Garfield Rd. SW11. 14S 73
Garfield Rd. SW19. 12Y 83
Garfield Rd. Twi. 1bV 93
Garford St. E14. 25M 53
Garibaldi St. SE15. 35P 95
Garland Rd. SE18. 34R 95
Garlies Rd. SE23. 24X 88
Garlick Hill EC4. 19M 51
Garlinge Rd. NW2. 10G 33
Garnault Pl. EC1. 18K 50
Garner St. E2. 22J 52
Garnet Rd. NW10. 6G 32
Garnet Rd. Cro. 19Zb 90
Garnett Rd. NW3. 14G 35
Garnham St. N16. 21E 37
Garnies St. SE15. 21Q 63
Garrard's Rd. SW16. 16X 84
Garratt Lane
 SW18. 1-643 & 2-480
 SW17. 482, 645 & up 11U 72
Garratt Rd. Edg. 4Ab 13
Garrett St. EC1. 19K 51
Garrick Av. NW11. 10C 21
Garrick Rd. NW9. 7C 20
Garrick St. WC2. 17M 50
Garsdale Rd. SE15. 22R 76
Garth Rd. NW11. 10E 33
Garth Way N12 13Ab 14
Garthorne Rd. SE23. 23V 87
Gartmoor Gdns. SW19.10V 82
Gartmore Rd. Ilf. 36E 42
Garton St. SW18. 11U 72
Garvan Rd. W6. 9Q 59
Garvary Rd. E16. 29M 55
Garway Rd. W2. 11M 48

Gascoigne Pl. E2. 21K 51
Gascoigne Rd. Bar. 34J 43
Gascony Av. NW6. 11H 33
Gascoyne Rd. E9. 24H 38
Gaselee E14. 27N 66
Gaskarth Rd. SW12. 15U 73
Gaskarth Rd. Edg. 5Aa 13
Gaskell Rd. N6. 14C 23
Gaskell St. SW4. 16R 74
Gassiot Rd. SW17. 14X 84
Gastein Rd. W6. 9P 59
Gataker St. SE16. 22O 64
Gatcombe Rd. N19. 16F 36
Gate St. WC2. 17L 50
Gateforth St. NW8. 13K 48
Gate House St. SW1. 16O 62
Gateley Rd. SW9. 17S 74
Gateside Rd. SW17. 13W 83
Gatestone Rd. SE19. 20Z 90
Gatliff Rd. SW1. 15P 61
Gatling Rd. SE2. 36Q 95
Gatton Rd. SW17. 13X 83
Gatwick Rd. SW18. 10V 82
Gauden Rd. SW4. 16S 73
Gaverick St. E14. 25O 65
Gavin St. SE18. 35P 95
Gawber St. E2. 23K 52
Gawthorne St. E3. 25J 53
Gay St. SW15. 9S 71
Gayfere St. SW1. 16O 62
Gayford Rd. W12. 7N 58
Gayhurst Rd. E8. 22H 38
Gaynesford Rd. SE23.23W 87
Gaysham Rd. Ilf. 33C 42
Gayton Cre. NW3. 13F 34
Gayton Rd. NW3. 12F 34
Gayton Rd. Har. 1bC 12
Gayville Rd. SW11. 14U 73
Gaywood Rd. E17. 25A 27
Gaywood St. SE1. 19O 62
Gaza st. SE17. 18P 62
Geary Rd. NW10. 7F 32
Gedeney Rd. N17 20Aa 16
Gedling St. SE1. 21O 63
Gee St. EC1. 19K 51
Gee St. NW1. 16J 49
Geere Rd. E15. 28J 54
Geldart Rd. SE15. 22R 76
Geldeston Rd. E5. 22E 38
Gellatly Rd. SE14. 23S 76
Gem St. E16. 30N 67
General Gordon Pl. SE3.
 30R 79
General Gordon Pl. SE18.
 33P 95
Genesta Rd. SE18. 33Q 95
Geneva Rd. SW9. 18T 74
Geneva Rd. Cro. 19Zc 90
Geneva Ter. SW9. 18T 74
Genista Rd. N18. 22Ac 17
Genoa Av. SW15. 8T 70
Genoa Rd. SE20. 22Za 90
Geoffrey Gdns. E6. 31K 55
Geoffrey Rd. SE4. 24S 77
George La. E11. 30C 29
George La. E18. 29A 29
George La. SE13. 26U 77
George Rd. Bre. 2P 56
George Row SE16. 21N 64
George Sq. N1. 20K 51
George St. E16. 28M 54
George St. SW18. 32P 95
George St. NW1. 16K 49
George St. W1. 14L 49
George St. W1. 15M 49
George St. W7. 1bM 94

George St. Bar.	34H	43
George St. Cro.	19Zf	91
George St. Rich.	1T	68
George's Rd. N7.	17G	36
Georgette Pl. SE10.	27R	78
Georgia Rd. Cro.	18Za	90
Georgian Court Wem.	4G	31
Georgiana St. NW1.	16H	35
Gerald Rd. E11.	29C	29
Gerald Rd. E16.	28K	54
Gerald Rd. SW1.	14O	61
Geraldine Rd. SW18.	12U	72
Geraldine Rd. Kew.	3P	57
Geraldine St. SE11.	18O	62
Gerard Rd. SW13.	6R	70
Gerard Rd. Har.	1aC	12
Gernon Rd. E3.	24J	53
Gerrard St. N1.	19J	51
Gerrard St. W1.	16M	50
Gerridge St. SE1.	18O	62
Gertrude St. SW10.	12Q	60
Gervase' Rd. Edg.	5Aa	13
Gervase St. SE15.	22Q	64
Ghent St. SE6.	25W	88
Gibbins Rd. E15.	27H	40
Gibbon Rd. SE15.	23S	76
Gibbon Rd. W3.	6M	45
Gibbon Wk. SW15.	7T	70
Gibbons Rd. NW10.	6G	31
Gibbs Av. SE19.	20Y	86
Gibbs Clo. SE19.	20Y	86
Gibbs Sq. SE19.	19Y	86
Gibraltar Wk. E2.	21K	52
Gibson Gdns. N16.	21E	37
Gibson Sq. N1.	18H	36
Gibson St. SE10.	27P	66
Gibson's Hill SE19.	18Z	90
Gideon Rd. SW11.	14S	73
Giesbach Rd. N19.	16E	35
Giffard Rd. N18.	21Ab	17
Giffin St. SE8.	25Q	65
Gifford Rd. N1.	17H	36
Gifford St. N1.	21J	51
Gift La. E15.	28J	54
Gilbert Gro. Edg.	5Aa	13
Gilbert Rd. SE11.	18P	62
Gilbert Rd. SW19.	12Z	92
Gilbert St. E15.	28F	40
Gilbert St. W1.	15M	49
Gilbert St. WC1.	17L	50
Gilbert Ter. SE16.	24O	65
Gilbey Rd. SW17.	13X	83
Gilda Cres. N16.	22E	38
Gildersome St. SE18.	33Q	95
Gilkes Cres. SE21	20U	75
Gill St. E14.	25M	53
Gillespie Rd. N5.	18F	36
Gillett Av. E6.	31J	55
Gillett Rd. Cro.	19Zc	90
Gillett St. N16.	21G	37
Gillian St. SE13	25T	77
Gillies St. NW5.	15G	35
Gillingham Rd. NW2.	10E	33
Gillingham Row WC2.	17M	50
Gillingham St. SW1.	15O	61
Gillman St. E2.	22J	52
Gillray sq. SW10	12Q	60
Gilmore Rd. SE13.	27T	78
Gilpin Av. SW14.	5T	69
Gilpin Cres. N18.	21Ac	17
Gilpin Gro. N18	21Ac	17
Gilpin Rd. E5.	24F	39
Gilsland Rd. Cro.	19Zc	90
Gilstead Rd. SW6.	11R	72
Gilston Rd. SW10.	12P	60
Giltspur St. EC1.	19L	51
Gipsy Hill SE19.	20Y	86
Gipsy La. SW15.	7S	70
Gipsy Rd. SE27.	19X	86
Giraud St. E14.	26M	53
Girdlers Rd. W14.	9O	59
Girdlestone Rd. N19.	16E	35
Girdwood Rd. SW18.	9V	82
Gironde Rd. SW6.	10Q	59
Girton Av. NW9.	4A	19
Girton Av. Wem.	1F	30
Girton Rd. SE26.	23Y	87
Gisburn Rd. N8.	18B	24
Gladding Rd. E12.	31F	41
Glade, The, Cro.	23Zc	91
Gladeside Cro.	23Zd	91
Gladesmore Rd. N15.	21C	25
Gladiator St. SE23.	24V	88
Glading Ter. N16.	21F	37
Gladsmuir Rd. N19.	16D	23
Gladstone Av. E12.	32H	43
Gladstone Av. N22.	18A	24
Gladstone Rd. E15.	28H	40
Gladstone Rd. SW19.	10Z	92
Gladstone Rd. W4.	5O	57
Gladstone Rd. Cro.	20Zd	91
Gladstone St. E11.	27F	40
Gladstone St. N19.	17E	36
Gladstone St. SE1.	18O	62
Gladstone Ter. sw8.	15R	73
Gladstone Pk. Gdns. NW2.	8E	32
Gladwell Rd. N8.	17C	24
Gladwyn Rd. sw15	9S	71
Gladys Rd. E10	25E	39
Gladys Rd. NW6.	11G	34
Glamis Rd. E1.	23M	52
Glamorgan St. SW1.	15P	61
Glaserton Rd. N16.	21D	25
Glasford St. SW17.	14Y	84
Glasgow Rd. E13.	29J	55
Glasgow Rd. N18.	22Ac	17
Glasgow Ter. SW1.	15P	61
Glaskin Mews. E5.	22G	38
Glaskin Rd. E9.	23H	38
Glaskin St. E9.	23H	38
Glass St. E2.	22K	52
Glasshill St. SE1.	19N	63
Glasshouse Fields E1.	23M	52
Glasshouse St. E1.	21M	52
Glasshouse St. W1.	16M	49
Glasshouse Wk. SE11.	17P	62
Glasslyn Rd. N8.	16B	24
Glastonbury St. NW6.	10G	33
Glaucus St. E3.	26L	53
Glazbury Rd. W14.	9P	59
Glebe Av. Har.	2A	18
Glebe Av. Mit.	13Za	92
Glebe Cres. NW4.	9A	21
Glebe Cres. Har.	2A	18
Glebe Pl. sw3.	13Q	60
Glebe Rd. E3.	26K	53
Glebe Rd. N8.	17B	24
Glebe Rd. SW13.	7R	70
Glebe Side Twi.	1bU	93
Glebe St. W4.	5P	57
Glebe St. SE16.	22O	64
Glebe, The, SE3.	28S	78
Glebelands Av. E18.	29A	29
Glebelands Av. Ilf.	35D	42
Gledhow Gdns. sw5.	12P	60
Gledstanes Rd. w14.	10P	59
Glen Gdns. Cro.	18Zf	91
Glen Rd. E13.,	30L	55
Glen Rd. E17.	25B	27
Glen St. NW1.	15K	49
Glen, The, Cro.	23Zf	91
Glen, The, Wem.	2F	30
Glenalmond Rd. Har.	2A	18
Glenarm Rd. E5.	23F	38
Glenavon Rd. E15.	28H	40
Glenbow Rd. Brom.	27Y	89
Glenbrook Rd. NW6.	11G	33
Glenburnie Rd. SW17.	13W	83
Glencairn Dri. w5.	1K	44
Glencairn Rd. sw16.	16Z	90
Glencoe Av. Ilf.	35D	42
Glencoe St. E14	27L	54
Glendale Av. N22	18Ab	16
Glendale Av. Edg.	3Ad	13
Glendall St. sw9.	17S	74
Glendarvon St. sw15.	9S	71
Glendish Rd. N17.	22Aa	17
Glendore Gdns. NW7.	6Ad	13
Glendower Pl. sw7.	12O	60
Glendower Rd. sw14.	5S	69
Glendown Rd. SE2.	36Q	95
Glendun Rd. w3.	6M	45
Gleneagle Rd. sw16.	16Y	84
Gleneldon Rd. sw16.	16X	85
Glenelg Rd. sw2.	16T	74
Glenfarg Rd. SE6.	27V	89
Glenfield Rd. sw12.	16V	84
Glenfield Rd. w13.	1aN	94
Glenfield Ter. w13.	1aN	94
Glenforth St. SE10.	28P	66
Glengall Causeway E14.	25O	65
Glengall Rd. E14.	25O	65
Glengall Rd. NW6.	10H	33
Glengall Rd. SE15.	21Q	63
Glengall Ter. SE15.	21Q	63
Glengarnock Av. E14.	27P	66
Glengarry Rd. SE22.	20T	75
Glenholm St. SE1.	19N	63
Glenhurst Av. NW5.	15F	35
Glenhurst Rd. Bre.	1P	56
Glenilla Rd. NW3.	13G	34
Glenister Rd. SE10.	28P	66
Glenloch Rd. NW3.	13G	34
Glenluce Rd. SE3.	29Q	66
Glenmore Rd. NW3.	13G	34
Glennie Rd. SE27.	18X	85
Glenny Rd. Bar.	34H	43
Glenparke Rd. E7.	30G	41
Glenrosa St. sw6.	12R	72
Glenroy St. w12.	8L	46
Glensdale Rd. SE4.	25T	77
Glenside Rd. SE18.	35P	95
Glentham Rd. sw13.	7P	58
Glenthorne Av. Cro.	22Ze	91
Glenthorne Rd. E17.	24B	27
Glenthorne Rd. N11.	14Ac	15
Glenthorne Rd. w6.	8O	58
Glenton Rd. SE13.	27T	78
Glentworth St. NW1.	14K	49
Glenview Rd. SE13.	27U	78
Glenville Gro. SE8.	25R	77
Glenwood Av. NW9.	6D	20
Glenwood Gro. NW9.	5D	19
Glenwood Rd. N15.	19B	25
Glenwood Rd. SE6.	25V	88
Glenwood Rd. Edg.	6Ae	13
Glenwood Way Cro.	23Zd	91
Gliddon Rd. w14.	9P	59
Globe Cre. E15.	28G	40
Globe La. SE18.	33O	95
Globe Rd. E13. E1.1-123 & 2-154 E2. 125, 156 & up	23K	52
Globe Rd. E15.	28G	40
Globe St. E1.	22N	64
Globe St. SE1.	19O	63

Gloucester Cres.nw1. 15H 35
Gloucester Gdns. nw11.
　　　　　　　10C 21
Gloucester Gdns Ilf. 32D 42
Gloucester Gate ᴀw1. 15J 49
Gloucester Gro. Edg. 5Aa 13
Gloucester Mews w2. 12L 48
Gloucester Pl. sᴇ10. 26R 78
Gloucester Pl w1. 14L 49
Gloucester Pl.Mews w1.14L 49
Gloucester Rd. ᴇ10. 25D 27
Gloucester Rd. ᴇ11. 30C 29
Gloucester Rd. ᴇ12. 32F 42
Gloucester Rd. ɴ4. 19E 37
Gloucester Rd. ɴ15. 20A 25
Gloucester Rd. ɴ17. 17E 36
Gloucester Rd. nw1. 14H 35
Gloucester Rd.sᴇ15. 20Q 63
Gloucester Rd. sw7. 12O 60
Gloucester Rd. w3. 5N 57
Gloucester Rd. w5. 1N 56
Gloucester Rd. Cro. 20Ze 91
Gloucester Rd. Kew. 3Q 57
Gloucester Rd. Ted. 1cY 93
Gloucester Sq. w2. 13M 48
Gloucester St. sw1. 15P 61
Gloucester Ter. w2. 12L 48
Gloucester Wlk. w8. 11N 59
Gloucester Way ᴇc1. 18K 50
Glover St. ᴇc2. 20K 51
Glycena Rd. sw11. 14S 73
Glyn Rd. ᴇ5. 23F 38
Glyn St. sᴇ11. 17P 62
Glynde St.sᴇ4. 25U 77
Glyndon Rd. sᴇ18. 34P 95
Glynfield Rd. nw10. 6H 32
Goat St. sᴇ1. 21N 63
Goda St. sᴇ11. 18P 62
Godalming Av. Cro. 16Zg 91
Godbold Rd. ᴇ15. 28K 54
Godfrey Av. Twi. 1cU 93
Godfrey Hill sᴇ18. 32P 95
Godfrey Rd. sᴇ18. 32P 95
Godfrey St. ᴇ15 27J 54
Godfrey St. sw3. 13P 60
Goding St.sᴇ11. 17P 62
Godley Rd. sw18 12V 83
Godliman St. ᴇc4. 19M 51
Godman Rd. sᴇ15. 22S 76
Godolphin Rd. w12. 8N 58
Godson Rd. Cro. 17Zf 91
Godson St. ɴ1. 18J 50
Godstone Rd. Twi. 1aU 93
Godwin Rd. ᴇ7. 30F 41
Golborne Gdns. w10. 10K 47
Golborne Rd. w10. 10K 47
Gold Hill nw7.
　　　　　　　6Ac 13
Gold St. ᴇ1. 23L 52
Goldbeaters Gro. nw7. 6Ac 13
Golden La. ᴇc1. 19K 51
Golden Manor w7. 1cM 94
Golden Sq. w1. 16M 49
Golders Clo. Edg. 5Ac 13
Golders Gdns. nw11. 10C 21
Golders Hill nw11. 11D 22
Golders Grn. Cre. nw11.
　　　　　　　11D 21
Golders Grn. Rd. nw11.10C21
Golders Manor Dri. nw11.
　　　　　　　9C 21
Golders Rise nw4. 9B 21
Goldhawk Rd.
　w12. 1-309 & 2-308.
　w6. 310, 311 & up. 7O 58
Goldhurst Ter. nw6. 12H 34

Goldie St. sᴇ5. 21Q 63
Goldington Cres.nw1. 16J 50
Goldington St. nw1. 16J 50
Goldney Rd. w9. 11K 47
Goldsboro' Rd. sw8. 16R 74
Goldsmith Av. nw9. 6B 20
Goldsmith Av. w3. 5M 45
Goldsmith La. nw9. 4A 19
Goldsmith Rd. ᴇ10. 26E 39
Goldsmith Rd. ᴇ12. 31G 43
Goldsmith Rd. ᴇ17. 24A 26
Goldsmith Rd. ɴ11. 14Ac 15
Goldsmith Rd. sᴇ15. 21R 76
Goldsmith Rd. w3. 5M 45
Goldsmith St. wc2. 17L 50
Goldsmith's Row ᴇ2. 22J 52
Goldsmith's Sq. ᴇ2. 22J 52
Goldwell Rd. Cro. 17Zb 90
Golf Rd. w5. 3L 44
Golf Rd. Ilf. 34F 42
Gomer Gdns. Ted. 1bY 93
Gomer Pl. Ted. 1bY 93
Gomer Rd. Ted. 1bY 93
Gomer Ter. ᴇ5. 23E 38
Gomm Rd. sᴇ16. 23O 64
Gomshall Av. Cro. 16Zg 91
Gondar Gdns. nw6. 10F 33
Gonsalva Rd. sw8. 15R 73
Gonville Rd. Cro. 17Zc 90
Gonville St. sw.6 10S 71
Goodall Rd. ᴇ11. 27F 40
Goodge St. ᴇc1. 18K 50
Goodenough Rd. sw19.10Z 92
Goodge St. w1. 16L 49
Goodhall St. nw10. 6J 46
Goodliff St. ᴇ14 26M 53
Goodinge Rd. n7. 17G 36
Goodman Rd. ᴇ10. 27D 28
Goodman's Yd. ᴇ1. 21M 51
Goodmayes Av. Ilf. 36D 42
Goodmayes La. Ilf. 36F 42
Goodmayes Rd. Ilf. 36E 42
Goodrich Rd.sᴇ22. 21U 76
Goodson Rd. nw10. 6H 32
Goodson Rd. sw6. 10Q 59
Goods Way nw1. 16J 50
Goodwin Rd. w12. 7N 58
Goodwin Rd. Cro. 18Zh 91
Goodwin St. ɴ4. 18E 36
Goodwood Rd.sᴇ14. 24R 77
Goodwyn Av. nw7. 6Ac 13
Goodwyns Vale n10. 15Aa 15
Goodyers Gdns. nw4. 9B 21
Goose Grn. sᴇ22. 21T 75
Gooseacre La. Har. 2B 18
Gopsall St. ɴ1. 20J 51
Gordon Av. sw14. 5S 69
Gordon Av. Twi. 1aT 93
Gordon Gro. sᴇ5. 18S 74
Gordon Pl. w8. 11N 60
Gordon Pl. wc1. 16K 50
Gordon Rd. ᴇ11. 29C 28
Gordon Rd. ᴇ12. 33F 42
Gordon Rd. ᴇ15. 27F 40
Gordon Rd. ᴇ17. 25C 27
Gordon Rd. ɴ3. 10Ab 14
Gordon Rd. ɴ8. 17B 24
Gordon Rd. ɴ9. 23Ae 17
Gordon Rd. ɴ11. 16Ab 15
Gordon Rd. ɴ16. 21F 37
Gordon Rd. sᴇ15. 22S 76
Gordon Rd. w4. 4P 57
Gordon Rd.
　w5. 1-95 & 2-84.
　w13. 86, 97 & up. 1M 24
Gordon Rd. Bar. 35J 43

Gordon Rd. Har. 1bA 12
Gordon Rd. Ilf. 34F 42
Gordon Rd. Kew. 3S 68
Gordon Sq. wc1. 16K 50
Gordon St. ᴇ13. '29K 54
Gordon St. ɴ1. 19J 51
Gordon St. wc1. 16K 50
Gordonbrock St. sᴇ4. 25U 77
Gordondale Rd. sw19 11W 82
Gordon House Rd. nw5.
　　　　　　　15F 35
Gore Rd. ᴇ9. 23J 52
Gore Rd. sw20. 8Za 92
Gore St. sw7. 12O 60
Goresbrook Rd. Bar. 37J 43
Goring Rd. n11. 16Ab 16
Goring St. ᴇ8. 22J 52
Gorleston Rd. n15. 20B 25
Gorleston St. w14. 10O 59
Gorse Rise sw17. 14Y 84
Gorst Rd. nw10. 5K 45
Gorst Rd. sw11. 13U 72
Gorsuch St. ᴇ2. 21J 51
Gosberton Rd. sw12. 14V 84
Goschen St. sᴇ5. 19Q 63
Gosedge Cres. Cro. 18Zg 91
Gosfield St. w1. 15L 49
Gosling Way sw9. 18R 74
Gospatrick Rd. n17 19Aa 16
Gospel Oak Gro. nw9. 14G 35
Gosport Rd. ᴇ17. 25B 27
Gossage Rd. sᴇ18. 34Q 95
Gosset St. ᴇ2. 21K 51
Gosterwood St. sᴇ8. 24Q 65
Goswell Rd. ᴇc1 19K 51
Goswell Ter. ᴇc1. 19K 50
Gotha St. ᴇ2. 23J 52
Gothic Rd. Twi. 1cW 93
Goudhurst Rd. Brom. 28Y 89
Gough Gro. ᴇ14. 25M 53
Gough Rd. ᴇ15. 28F 40
Gough Sq. ᴇc4. 18M 50
Gough St. sᴇ18. 33P 95
Gough St. wc1. 18K 50
Gould Rd. Twi. 1cV 93
Goulden St. sw11. 13R 72
Goulston St. ᴇ1. 21L 51
Goulton Rd. ᴇ5. 22F 38
Gourlay St. n15. 20C 25
Gowan Av. sw6. 9R 71
Gowan Rd. nw10. 8G 32
Gower Mews wc1. 16L 50
Gower Pl. wc1. 16K 49
Gower Rd. ᴇ7. 29H 41
Gower St. wc1. 16K 49
Gower's Wlk. ᴇ1. 21M 52
Gowlett Rd. sᴇ15. 21T 76
Gowrie Rd. sw11. 14S 73
Grace Rd. ᴇ15. 27H 40
Grace Rd. Cro. 19Zd 91
Grace St. ᴇ3. 26K 53
Grace St. ᴇ3. 18H 36
Gracechurch St. ᴇc3. 20M 51
Gracedale Rd. sw16. 15Y 84
Gracefield Gdns. sw16 17X 85
Grace's Alley ᴇ1. 22M 52
Grace's Mews sᴇ5. 20R 75
Grace's Rd. sᴇ5. 20R 75
Graemsdyke Av. sw14. 4S 69
Grafferton Rd. Cro. 19Zg 91
Grafton Cre. nw1. 15G 35
Grafton Pl. nw1. 16K 50
Grafton Rd. n7. 17F 36
Grafton Rd. nw5. 15G 35
Grafton Rd. w3. 5M 45
Grafton Rd. Cro. 18Ze 91

Grafton Rd. Har. 1cB 12
Grafton Sq. sw4. 15S 73
Grafton St. e1. 23K 52
Grafton St. w1. 15M 49
Grafton St.
wc1. 1-31&2-46
w1. 33, 48 & up 16K 49
Grafton Ter. nw5. 14G 35
Graham Av. w13. 1aN 94
Graham Rd. e8. 22G 38
Graham Rd. e13. 29K 54
Graham Rd. n15. 19A 25
Graham Rd. nw4. 8C 20
Graham Rd. sw19. 10Z 92
Graham Rd. w4. 5N 57
Graham Rd. Har. 1cA 12
Graham St. n1. 19J 51
Graham St. sw1. 14P 61
Grainger Rd. n22. 19Aa 16
Grainger St. se15. 22Q 64
Grampian Gdns. nw2 10D 21
Granard Rd. sw12. 13U 73
Granby St. e2. 21K 52
Granby Ter. nw1. 15J 49
Grand Av. ec3. 20M 51
Grand Av. n10. 15B 23
Grand Av. Wem. 3F 31
Grand Dri. sw20. 8Za 92
Grandison Rd. sw11. 14T 73
Grand Depo Rd. se18. 33Q 95
Grand Junc. Rd. w2. 13M 48
Granfield St. sw11. 13R 72
Grange Av. n12. 12Ac 14
Grange Av. se25. 20Za 90
Grange Clo. Edg. 5Ac 13
Grange Court w2. 17M 50
Grange Gdns. se25. 20Za 90
Grange Hill se25. 20Za 90
Grange Hill Edg. 5Ac 13
Grange Pk. w5. 2M 44
Grange Rd. e10. 26E 39
Grange Rd. e13. 29K 54
Grange Rd. e17. 24C 27
Grange Rd. n1. 19G 37
Grange Rd. n6. 14C 23
Grange Rd. n17. 22Ab 17
Grange Rd. nw1. 15H 35
Grange Rd. nw10. 8G 32
Grange Rd. se1. 21O 63
Grange Rd.
se25. 49-343.
se19. 345-361.
Cro. Remainder. 20Zb 90
Grange Rd. sw4. 15S 73
Grange Rd. sw13. 7R 70
Grange Rd. w4. 4P 57
Grange Rd. w5. 2M 44
Grange Rd. Edg. 6Ab 13
Grange Rd. Har. 1aB 12
Grange Rd. Har. 1cD 12
Grange Rd. Ilf. 33F 43
Grange St. n1. 20J 51
Grange The, se1. 21O 63
Grange The, sw19. 9Y 82
Grange The, Wem. 3H 31
Grange Wlk. se1. 21O 63
Grange Yd. se1. 21O 63
Grangecliffe Gdns. se25.
20Za 90
Grangecourt Rd. n16. 20D 25
Grangemill Rd. se6. 25W 88
Grangemill Way se6. 25W 88
Grange Pk. Rd. e10. 26E 39
Grange Pk. Rd. Cro. 19Zb 90
Grangeway nw6. 10H 33
Granleigh Rd. e11. 28E 40

Gransden Av. e8. 22H 38
Grant Rd. sw11. 12S 72
Grant Rd. Cro. 21Ze 93
Grant Rd. Har. 1bA 12
Grant St. e13. 29K 54
Grant St. n1. 18J 50
Grantbridge St. n1. 19J 51
Grantham Rd. e12. 33F 42
Grantham Rd. sw9. 17S 74
Grantham Rd. w4. 6Q 57
Granton Rd. Ilf. 36E 42
Grantully Rd. w9. 11K 48
Granville Av. n9. 23Ad 17
Granville Gdns. w5. 3M 44
Granville Pk. se13. 27S 78
Granville Pl. w1. 14M 49
Granville Rd. e16. 29L 54
Granville Rd. e17. 26C 27
Granville Rd. e18. 30A 29
Granville Rd. n4. 18C 24
Granville Rd. N12 12Ab 14
Granville Rd. n22. 19Aa 16
Granville Rd. nw2. 10D 21
Granville Rd. nw6. 11J 47
Granville Rd. se13. 26S 78
Granville Rd. sw18. 10U 71
Granville Rd. Ilf. 33E 42
Granville Sq. wc1. 18K 50
Granville St. e11. 27F 40
Grape St. wc2. 17L 50
Grasdene Rd. se18 36R 95
Grasmere Av. sw19 11Zb 92
Grasmere Av. w3. 5M 45
Grasmere Av. Har. 1C 18
Grasmere Gdns. Har.
1aAa 12
Grasmere Rd. e13. 29J 54
Grasmere Rd. n10. 15Aa 15
Grasmere Rd. n17. 21Ab 17
Grasmere Rd. se25 22Zc 90
Grasmere Rd. sw16.
17Y 85
Gratton Rd. w14. 9O 59
Gratton Ter. nw2. 9E 33
Gravel Hill n3. 10Aa. 14
Gravel La. e1. 21M 51
Gravel La. se1. 19N 63
Gravel Rd. Twi. 1cV 93
Gravelly Ride sw19. 6X 81
Graveney Rd. sw17. 13X 83
Gravesend Rd. w12. 7M 46
Gray St. e1. 22L 52
Gray St. e16. 31N 67
Gray St. se1. 18N 62
Graydon St. se18. 33Q 95
Graylands Rd. se15. 20Q 63
Grayling Rd. n16. 20E 37
Grayshott Rd. sw11. 14S 73
Gray's Inn wc1. 18L 50
Gray's Inn Rd. wc1. 17K 50
Gray's Inn Sq. wc1. 18L 50
Grazebrook Rd. n16. 20E 37
Gt. Arthur St. ec1. 19L 51
Gt. Bushey Dri. n20. 12Ae 14
Gt. Cambridge Rd. n17.
19A 25
Gt. Cambridge St. e2. 21J 52
Gt. Castle St. w1. 15L 49
Gt. Central St. nw1. 14L 49
Gt. Chapel St. w1. 16L 49
Gt. Chertsey Rd. w4. 5R 69
Gt. Church La. w6. 9P 59
Gt. College St. nw1. 16H 35
Gt. College St. sw1. 16O 62
Gt. Cumberland Pl. w1.
14L 49

Gt. Dover St. se1. 20O 6
Gt. Earl St. wc2. 17M 50
Gt. Eastern Rd. e15. 27H 40
Gt. Eastern St. ec2. 20K 51
Greatfields Rd. Bar. 35J 43
Gt. George St. sw1. 16N 62
Gt. James St. wc1. 17L 50
Gt. Marlborough St. w1.
15M 49
Gt. Maze Pond se1. 20N 63
Gt. New St. ec4. 18L 50
Gt. Newport St. wc2. 16M 50
Gt. North Rd. n2.. 14B 23
Gt. North Way nw4. 9A 21
Greatorex St. e1. 21L 52
Gt. Ormond St. wc1. 17L 50
Gt. Percy St. wc1. 18K 50
Gt. Peter St. sw1. 16O 62
Gt. Portland St. w1. 15L 49
Gt. Pulteny St. w1. 16M 49
Gt. Queen St. wc2. 17L 50
Gt. Russell St. wc1. 16L 50
Gt. St. Andrew St. wc2.
17M 50
Gt. St. Helen's ec3. 20M 51
Gt. Scotland Yd. sw1. 17N 62
Gt. Smith St. sw1. 16O 62
Gt. Stanhope St. w1. 14N 61
Gt. Suffolk St. se1. 19N 63
Gt. Sutton St. ec1. 19K 51
Gt. Swan Alley ec2. 20L 51
Gt. Tichfield St. w1. 15L 49
Gt. Tower St. ec3. 20M 51
Gt. Trinity La. ec4. 19M 51
Gt. Turnstile wc1. 17L 50
Gt. West Rd. Bre. 1P 56
Great Western Rd.
w9. 1-37 & 2-56.
w11. 60 & up. 10L 47
Gt. Winchester St. ec2.
20L 51
Gt. Windmill St. w1. 16M 49
Grecian Cres. se19. 18Y 85
Greek St. w1. 16M 50
Green Av. nw7. 6Ad 13
Green Av. w13. 1aO 94
Green Bank e1. 22N 64
Green Bank se1. 20N 63
Green Clo. nw9. 5B 19
Green Clo. nw11. 12C 22
Green End n21. 19Ae 16
Green La. n2. 12A 22
Green Lanes.
n16. 1-203 & 2-162.
n4. 182-430 & 205-531.
n8. 533-677 & 572-654.
n13. 1-615 & 2-64.
n21. 606-948 & 617-949.
18Ac 16
Green La. nw4. 9B 21
Green La. se19. 18Z 90
Green La. se20. 23Z 90
Green La. se22 & se5. 20T 75
Green La. sw19. 11W 82
Green La. w7. 1cN 94
Green La. Edg 3Ad 13
Green La. Ilf. 34E 42
Green Moor n21. 19Af 16
Green Rd. n20. 12Ad 14
Green St. e2. 23K 52
Green St.
e7. 1-283 & 2-304.
e13. 285, 306 & up. 30G 41
Green St. w1. 14M 49
Green St. w2. 13L 48
Green St. wc2. 16M 50

Green Ter. EC1. 18K 50
Green The E11. 29C 29
Green The E15. 28H 40
Green The N14. 22Ad 17
Green The N14. 17Ad 16
Green The N15. 21B 25
Green The SW20. 9Zb 92
Green The W3. 6L 46
Green The Twi. 1cV 93
Green Wk. SE1. 20O 63
Green Way SE9. 31U 79
Greenaway Gdns. NW3. 12F 34
Greenberry St. NW8. 13J 48
Greencoat Pl. SW1. 16O 61
Greencourt Av. Cro. 22Ze 91
Greencourt Av. Edg. 4Aa 13
Greencourt Gdns. Cro. 22Ze 91
Greencroft Gdns. NW6.
12H 34
Green Dragon La. Bre. 2P 56
Green Dragon Yd. E1. 21L 52
Green End Rd. W4. 6N 57
Greenfell St. SE10. 28O 66
Greenfield Gdns. NW2. 10E 33
Greenfield Rd. N15. 21B 25
Greenfield St. E1. 22L 52
Greenfield St. SE8. 24P 65
Greenford Av. W7. 1cK 93
Greengate St. E13. 29K 55
Greenhalgh Wk. NW11.
12B 22
Greenham Rd. N10. 15Aa 15
Greenheys Dri. E18. 29A 28
Greenhill Wem. 4D 19
Greenhill Cres. Har. 1bB 12
Greenhill Gro. E12. 31G 43
Greenhill Pk. NW10. 6H 32
Greenhill Rd. NW10. 6H 32
Greenhill Rd. Har. 1bB 12
Greenhill St. SE18. 32P 95
Green Hundred Rd. SE15.
22Q 64
Greenhurst Rd. SE27. 18Y 85
Greenland St. NW1. 15H 35
Green La. Gdns. Cro. 19Za 90
Greenlaw Pl. SE18. 32P 95
Greenlaw St. SE18. 32P 95
Greenleaf Rd. E6. 30J 55
Greenleaf Rd. E17. 25A 27
Green Man La. W13 1aM 94
Greenman St. N1. 19H 37
Greenpond Rd. E17. 24A 27
Green's End SE18. 33P 95
Greenside Rich. 1T 68
Greenside Rd. W12. 7N 58
Greenside Rd. Cro. 18Zd 91
Greenstead Gdns. SW15. 7T 70
Greenway N14. 17Ae 16
Greenway N20. 11Ae 14
Greenway SW20. 8Zb 92
Greenway Har. 1bAa 12
Greenway Har. 2B 18
Greenway Av. E17. 27B 28
Greenway Gdns. NW9. 5Aa 13
Greenway The NW9. 5Aa 13
Greenwell St. W1. 15K 49
Greenwich Rd. SE10. 26R 77
Greenwich Foot Tunnel
SE10. 26Q 65
Greenwood Clo. SW20. 9Zb 92
Greenwood Gdns. N13
19Ad 16
Greenwood Pl. NW5. 15F 35
Greenwood Rd. E8. 22G 38
Greenwood Rd. E13. 29J 54
Greenwood Rd. Cro. 18Zd 91

Greet Rd. Bre. 2P 56
Grena Rd. Rich. 3T 68
Grenaby Av. Cro. 19Zd 91
Grenaby Rd. Cro. 19Zd 91
Grenada Rd. SE7. 30R 79
Grenade St. E14. 25M 53
Grendon Gdns. Wem. 4E 31
Grenfell Gdns. Har. 2C 18
Grenfell Rd. W11. 9M 47
Grenoble Gdns. N13. 18Ab 16
Grenville Pl. SW7. 12O 60
Grenville Rd. N19. 17D 24
Grenville St. E16. 28M 54
Grenville St. WC1. 17K 50
Gresham Av. N20. 14Ad 15
Gresham Gdns. NW11. 10D 21
Gresham Rd. NW10. 6G 31
Gresham Rd. SW9. 18S 74
Gresham St. EC2. 19L 51
Gresley Rd. N19. 16D 23
Gresse St. W1. 16L 49
Gressenhall Rd. SW18. 10U 71
Greswell St. SW6. 9R 71
Greta Rd. Har. 1cA 12
Greville Pl. NW6. 11J 48
Greville Rd. E17. 27B 28
Greville Rd. NW6. 11J 48
Greville St. EC1. 18L 50
Grey Clo. NW11. 12C 22
Greycoat Pl. SW1. 16O 61
Greycoat St. SW1. 16O 61
Greycot Rd. Bec. 25Y 88
Grey Eagle St. E1. 21L 51
Greyhound Hill NW4. 8A 20
Greyhound La. SW16. 16Y 85
Geryhound Rd. N17. 21A 25
Greyhound Rd. NW10. 8J 46
Greyhound Rd.
W6. 1-183 & 2-136.
W14. 187 & up. 9Q 59
Greystone Gdns. Har. 1C 18
Greystone Gdns. Har. 1C 18
Greystone Gdns. Har. 1C 18
Greyswood St. SW16. 15Y 84
Grierson Rd. SE23. 23U 76
Griffin Rd. SE18. 34Q 95
Griffin St. SE1. 18N 62
Griffin Manor Way SE18.
35P 95
Griffith Rd. SW19. 11Z 92
Grigg's Pl. SE1. 20O 63
Griggs Rd. E10. 27C 28
Grimaldi St. N1. 17J 50
Grimsby St. E2. 21K 52
Grimston Rd. SW6. 10S 71
Grimwade Av. Cro. 21Zf 91
Grimwade Cres. SE15. 22S 76
Grimwood Rd. Twi. 1bU 93
Grindal St. SE1. 18N 62
Grinling Pl. SE8. 25Q 65
Grinstead Rd. SE8. 24P 65
Grittleton Av. NW10. 4G 31
Grittleton Rd. W9. 11K 47
Groombridge Rd. E9. 23H 38
Grosmont Rd. SE18. 36Q 95
Grosvenor Av. SW14. 5S 69
Grosvenor Cres. NW9. 4B 19
Grosvenor Cres. SW1. 14N 61
Grosvenor Cres. Mews SW1.
14N 61
Grosvenor Gdns. E6. 31K 55
Grosvenor Gdns. N10. 16A 23
Grosvenor Gdns. NW2. 9G 33
Grosvenor Gdns. NW11.
10B 21
Grosvenor Gdns. SW1. 15O 61
Grosvenor Gdns. SW14. 6S 69

Grosvenor Hill SW19. 9Y 82
Grosvenor Mews W1. 15M 49
Grosvenor Pk. SE5. 19Q 63
Grosvenor Pl. SW1. 15N 61
Grosvenor Rise E. E17.
26B 27
Grosvenor Rd. E6. 31J 55
Grosvenor Rd. E7. 30H 41
Grosvenor Rd. E10. 27D 28
Grosvenor Rd. N3. 11Ab 14
Grosvenor Rd. N5. 19G 37
Grosvenor Rd. N9. 22Ae 17
Grosvenor Rd. N10. 15Aa 15
Grosvenor Rd. SW1. 15P 61
Grosvenor Rd. W4. 4P 57
Grosvenor Rd. W7. 1bM 94
Grosvenor Rd. Bre. 2Q 56
Grosvenor Rd. Ilf. 34E 42
Grosvenor Rd. Rich. 2T 68
Grosvenor Rd. Twi. 1bV 93
Grosvenor Sq. W1. 14M 49
Grosvenor St. E1. 23L 52
Grosvenor St. SE5. 19Q 63
Grosvenor St. W1. 15M 49
Grosvenor Ter. SE5. 19Q 63
Grosvenor Pk. Rd. E17.

Groton Rd. SW18. 11W 83
Grotto Rd. Twi. 1bW 93
Grove Av. N3. 11Ab 14
Grove Av. N10. 16A 23
Grove Av. W7. 1bL 94
Grove Av. Twi. 1bV 93
Grove Cotts. SW3. 13P 60
Grove Ct. SE18. 33O 95
Grove Cres. E18. 29A 28
Grove Cres. NW9. 5A 19
Grove End E18. 28A 28
Grove Gdns. NW4. 7B 20
Grove Gdns. Twi. 1bX 93
Grove Hill E18. 28A 28
Grove Hill Har. 1bD 12
Grove La. N16. 21D 25
Grove La. SE5. 20R 75
Grove Mews W6. 8O 58
Grove Pk. E11. 29C 29
Grove Pk. NW9. 5A 19
Grove Pk. SE5. 20S 75
Grove Pass. E2. 22J 52
Grove Pl. W3. 5N 57
Grove Pl. W5. 2M 44
Grove Rd. E3. 24J 52
Grove Rd. E11. 28D 28
Grove Rd. E17. 26C 27
Grove Rd. E18. 28A 28
Grove Rd. N7. 17E 36
Grove Rd. N11. 15Ac 15
Grove Rd. N12. 13Ac 14
Grove Rd. N15. 20B 25
Grove Rd. NW2. 8G 32
Grove Rd. SW9. 17R 74
Grove Rd. SW12. 15V 84
Grove Rd. SW13. 6R 70
Grove Rd. SW19. 12Z 92
Grove Rd. W3. 5N 57
Grove Rd. W5. 2M 44
Grove Rd. Bre. 1P 56
Grove Rd. Cro. 17Zc 90
Grove Rd. Edg. 4Ac 13
Grove Rd. Twi. 1cW 93
Grove St. E1. 22M 52
Grove St. SE8. 24P 65
Grove Ter. NW5. 15F 35
Grove Ter. W14. 10P 59
Grove Ter. Twi. 1bX 93

Grove, The, E15.	28G 40	Gunterstone Rd. w14.	10P 59	Half Acre, Bre.	1Q 56
Grove, The, N3.	11Ab 14	Gunthorpe St. E1.	21L 51	Halfacre Rd. w7.	1cM 94
Grove, The, N4.	17D 24	Gunton Rd. E5.	22E 38	Half Moon Cres. N1.	18J 50
Grove, The, N6.	14D 23	Gunton Rd. sw17.	14Y 84	Half Moon La. se24.	19U 75
Grove, The, N8.	16B 24	Gurdon Rd. se7.	29Q 67	Half Moon Pass. E1.	21M 51
Grove, The, N13.	18Ac 16	Gurley St. E3.	26K 53	Half Moon St. w1.	15N 61
Grove, The, nw3.	12E 34	Gurney Cres. Cro.	17Ze 91	Halford Rd. E10.	27C 28
Grove, The, nw9.	5B 19	Gurney Dri. N2.	12B 22	Halford Rd. sw6.	11Q 59
Grove, The, nw11.	10C 21	Gurney Rd. E15.	28G 40	Halford Rd. Rich.	2T 68
Grove, The, se10.	27R 78	Gurney St. se17.	19O 63	Haliday Wlk. N1.	20G 37
Grove, The, sw10.	12P 60	Gutter La. EC2.	19L 51	Halidon St. E9.	23G 38
Grove, The, sw18.	12U 72	Guy St. se1.	20N 63	Halifax St. se26.	22X 87
Grove, The, w5.	2M 44	Guyscliff Rd. se13.	26U 77	Haling Pk. Rd. Cro.	18Zh 91
Grove, The, w6.	8O 58	Gwalior Rd. sw15.	9S 71	Halkin St. sw1.	14N 61
Grove, The, Edg.	4Ad 13	Gwendolen Av. sw15.	8T 71	Halkin St. W. sw1.	14O 61
Grove, The, Twi.	1bX 93	Gwendoline Av. E13.	30J 55	Hall Pl. w2.	12L 48
Grove, The, Wem.	4F 31	Gwendwr Rd. w14.	10P 59	Hall Rd. E6.	32J 43
Grove Vale se22.	21T 75	Gwydor Rd. Cro.	23Zb 90	Hall Rd. E11.	30C 29
Grove Villas E14.	26M 53	Gwynne Av. Cro.	23Zd 91	Hall Rd. E15.	27F 40
Grove Cres. Rd. E15.	27H 40	Gwynne Rd. sw11.	12R 72	Hall Rd. nw8.	12K 48
Grovedale Rd. N19.	16E 36	Gye St. se11.	17P 62	Hall Rd. se15.	23T 76
Grove End Rd. nw8.	12K 48	Gyllyngdune Gdns. Ilf.		Hall Rd. Twi.	1dT 93
Grove Green Rd. E11.	27D 28		36E 42	Hall St. E3.	25L 53
Grove Green Rd. E11.	27F 40			Hall St. EC1.	19K 51
Grove Hall Pk. E3.	26J 53	Haarlem Rd. w14.	9O 59	Hall St. N12.	12Ac 14
Grove Hill Rd. se5.	20S 75	Haberdasher St. N1.	20K 51	Hallam St. w1.	15L 49
Grovehill Rd. Har.	1bC 12	Hack Rd. E16.	29M 54	Halley Rd.	
Grove House Rd. n8.	17B 24	Hack St. E14.	26L 53	E7. 1-207 & 2-188	
Groveland Av. sw16.	17Z 90	Hackford Rd. sw9.	17R 74	E12. 190, 209 & up	30H 41
Grovelands Rd. n13.	18Ad 16	Hackney Gro. E8.	22H 38	Halley St. E14.	24L 53
Grovelands Rd. n15.	22C 26	Hackney Rd. E2.	21K 51	Hall Farm Dri. Twi.	1dU 93
Grove Pk. Gdns. w4.	4Q 57	Haddington Rd. se16.	27X 89	Halliburton Rd. Twi.	1aT 93
Grove Pk. Rd. n15.	21B 25	Haddo St. se10.	26Q 65	Halliford St. N1.	20H 37
Grove Pk. Rd. w4.	4Q 57	Haddonhall St. se1.	20O 63	Halliwell Rd. sw2.	17U 74
Grove Pk. Ter. w4.	4Q 57	Hadland St. se16.	23O 64	Halliwick Rd. n10.	14Aa 15
Grummant Rd. se15.	21R 75	Hadleigh Rd. n9.	22Af 17	Hallsville Rd. E16.	28M 54
Grundy St. E14.	26M 53	Hadleigh St. E1.	23K 52	Hallswelle Rd. nw11.	10B 21
Gruneisen Rd. n3.	11Ab 14	Hadley Gdns. w4.	5P 57	Halpin Pl. se17.	20P 63
Gubyon Av. se24.	19U 74	Hadley Rd. w13.	1N 56	Halsbury Rd. n18.	20Ab 17
Guerin St. E3.	25K 53	Hadley Rd. nw1.	15G 35	Halsbury Rd. w12.	7M 46
Guernsey Gro. se24.	19V 86	Hadlow Pl. se19.	21Z 90	Halse St. N7.	17G 36
Guernsey Rd. E11.	27E 40	Hadrian St. se10.	28P 66	Halsemere Av. sw18.	11W 83
Guernsey Rd. Ilf.	33G 43	Hadyn Pk. Rd. w12.	7N 58	Halsey St. sw3.	13O 61
Guest St. EC1.	19K 51	Hafer Rd. sw11.	13T 72	Halsmere Rd. se5.	19R 75
Guild Rd. se7.	31Q 67	Hafton Rd. se6.	28W 89	Halstead Gdns. n21.	20Ae 17
Guildersfield Rd. sw16.		Haggard Rd. Twi.	1aU 93	Halstead Rd. n21.	20Ae 17
	16Z 90	Haggerston Rd. E8.	21H 37	Halstead St. sw9.	17R 74
Guildford Pl. sw14.	5S 69	Hague St. E2.	22K 52	Halstow Rd. nw10.	9K 47
Guildford Rd. E14.	26L 53	Ha-Ha Rd. se18.	32Q 95	Halstow Rd. se10.	29Q 66
Guildford Rd. se10.	26R 77	Haig Rd. E13.	30K 55	Halton Rd. N1.	19H 37
Guildford Rd. sw8.	17R 74	Hailsham Ave. sw2.	17W 85	Hambalt Rd. sw4.	15U 73
Guildford Rd. Ilf.	35E 42	Hailsham Cres. Bar.	36G 43	Hamble St. sw6.	11S 72
Guildford St. se1.	19N 63	Haimo Rd. se9.	31U 79	Hambledon Rd. sw18.	10V 82
Guildford Way Cro.	17Zg 91	Hainault Rd. E10.	27D 28	Hambro' Rd. sw16.	16Y 84
Guildhouse St. sw1.	15P 61	Hainault St. Ilf.	34E 42	Hambrook Rd. se25.	22Zb 90
Guilford St. wc1.	17K 50	Haines St. sw8.	16Q 61	Hamfrith Rd. E15.	28G 40
Guilsborough Rd. nw10.		Hainthorpe Rd. se27.	18X 85	Hamilton Clo. nw8.	12K 48
	6H 32	Halcomb St. N1.	20J 51	Hamilton Cre. n13.	18Ac 16
Guion Rd. sw6.	10R 71	Haldane Rd. E6.	31K 55	Hamilton Gdns. nw8.	12J 48
Gumleigh Rd. w5.	1O 56	Haldane Rd. sw6.	10Q 59	Hamilton Gro. se27.	19X 86
Gun St. E1	21L 51	Haldon Rd. sw18.	10U 71	Hamilton Pl. w1.	15N 61
Gundulf St. se11.	18P 62	Hale Clo. nw7.	6Ac 13	Hamilton Rd. E3.	24K 52
Gunmaker's La. E3.	24J 53	Hale Dri. nw7.	5Ac 13	Hamilton Rd. E15.	28K 54
Gunners Rd. sw18.	12W 83	Hale Gdns. n17.	22A 26	Hamilton Rd. E17.	24A 27
Gunnersbury Av.		Hale Gdns. w3.	3M 45	Hamilton Rd. n2.	12A 22
w5. 1-119 & 2-114.		Hale La. nw7.	4Ac 13	Hamilton Rd. n5.	19F 37
w4. Part.		Hale Rd. n17.	22A 26	Hamilton Rd. nw10.	7F 32
w3. 127-137 & 144-248.		Hale St. E14.	26M 53	Hamilton Rd. nw11.	9C 21
	3M 44	Hale St. N1.	19J 51	Hamilton Rd. se27.	18U 74
Gunnersbury Cres. w3.	3N 57	Hale, The, n17.	22A 26	Hamilton Rd. se27.	20X 86
Gunnersbury Dri. w5.	3N 56	Hale End Rd. E17	22A 26	Hamilton Rd. sw19.	11Z 92
Gunnersbury Gdns w3.	3N 57	Halefield Rd. n17	22Aa 17	Hamilton Rd. w4.	6N 57
Gunnersbury La. w3.	3N 57	Halegrove Gdns. nw7.		Hamilton Rd. w5.	2M 44
Gunning St. se18.	35P 95		6Ac 13	Hamilton Rd. Bre.	1P 56
Gunter Gro. sw10	12Q 60	Hales St. se8.	25R 77	Hamilton Rd. Cro.	19Zb 90
Gunter Gro. Edg.	5Ab 13	Halesworth Rd. se13.	26S 77	Hamilton Rd. Har.	1bB 12

Hamilton Rd. Ilf. 33F 43
Hamilton Rd. Twi. 1cV 93
Hamilton St. nw1. 15H 35
Hamilton St. se8. 25Q 65
Hamilton Ter. nw8. 12J 48
Hamilton Way n3. 11Ab 14
Hamlet Gdns. w6. 7O 58
Hamlet Rd. se19. 21Z 90
Hammersmith Bridge
    w6. 7P 58
Hammersmith Rd.
    w14. 1-155 & 2-122
    w6. 124, 157 & up 9P 59
Hammersmith Bridge Rd.
    w6. 8P 58
Hammond St. nw5. 16G 35
Ham Pk. Rd.
    e15. 1-111 & 2-66.
    e7. 68, 113 & up. 28H 40
Hampden La. n17. 21Aa 17
Hampden Rd. n8. 18B 24
Hampden Rd. n10. 15Ab 15
Hampden Rd. n17. 22Aa 17
Hampden Rd. n19. 16E 36
Hampden Rd. Har. 1cAa 12
Hampden St. nw1. 16J 50
Hampden St. w2. 11L 48
Hampden Way n14. 15Ae 15
Hampshire Pl. s11. 17P 62
Hampshire St. nw5. 16G 36
Hampshire Hog La.
    w6. 7P 58
Hampstead Gdns. nw11.
    11C 21
Hampstead Grn. nw3. 13F 34
Hampstead La. n6. 13D 22
Hampstead Rd. nw1. 16J 49
Hampstead Sq. nw3. 12F 34
Hampstead Way nw11.
    11C 22
Hampstead High St. nw3.
    12F 34
Hampstead Hill Gdns. nw3.
    13F 34
Hampton Rd. e7. 30G 41
Hampton Rd. e11. 27E 40
Hampton Rd. w2. 11K 47
Hampton Rd. Cro. 19Zd 91
Hampton Rd. Ilf. 34F 43
Hampton Rd. Ted 1dV 93
Hampton Rd. Twi. 1dW 93
Hampton Sq. sw14. 5S 69
Hampton St. se17. 19P 63
Hamsell St. ec1. 19L 51
Hanbury Rd. n8. 18B 24
Hanbury Rd. n17 22A 26
Hanbury Rd. sw11. 14S 73
Hanbury Rd. w3. 4N 57
Hanbury St. e1. 22L 51
Hancock Rd. e3. 26K 53
Hancock Rd. se19. 19Z 90
Hand Court wc1. 17L 50
Handcroft Rd. Cro. 18Ze 91
Handel St. sw18. 11T 72
Handel St. wc1. 17K 50
Handel Way Edg. 4Ab 13
Handen Rd. se12. 28U 78
Handforth Rd. sw9. 18Q 62
Handley Rd. e9. 23H 38
Handley St. sw11. 13R 72
Handsworth Rd.n15. 20A 25
Hanger La. w5. 3K 44
Hanger Vale La. w5. 3L 44
Hankey Pl. se1. 20O 63
Hankins La. Edg. 6Ae 13
Hanley Rd. n4. 17D 24

Hanlon St. se8. 24P 65
Hannell Rd. sw6. 9Q 59
Hannen Rd. se27. 19X 85
Hannibal Rd. e1. 23L 52
Hanover Cotts. w6. 9P 59
Hanover Gdns. se11. 18Q 62
Hanover Gate nw8. 13K 48
Hanover Pk. se15. 22R 76
Hanover Rd. n15. 21B 26
Hanover Rd. nw10. 8H 33
Hanover Sq. w1. 15M 49
Hanover St. n1. 19J 51
Hanover St. nw5. 14G 35
Hanover St. se15. 21R 75
Hanover St. w1. 15M 49
Hanover Ter. nw1. 13K 49
Hanover Ter. w11. 10M 47
Hans Cre. sw1. 14O 61
Hans Pl. sw1. 14O 61
Hans Rd. sw3. 13O 60
Hansard Mews w14. 9N 59
Hansler Rd. se22. 21T 75
Hanson St. w1. 15L 49
Hanway Pl. w1. 16L 50
Hanway St. w1. 16L 50
Harad's Pl. e1. 22M 52
Harben Rd. nw8. 16S 73
Harberson Rd. e15. 28J 54
Harberson Rd. sw12. 15V 84
Harberton Rd. n19. 16D 23
Harbinger Rd. e14. 26P 65
Harbledown Rd.sw6.10R 71
Harbord St. sw6. 9R 71
HarboroughRd.sw16.17X 85
Harbour Rd. se5. 19S 75
Harbut Rd. sw11. 12T 72
Harcombe Rd. n16. 20F 37
Harcourt Av. e12. 32G 43
Harcourt Rd. e15. 28J 54
Harcourt Rd. n22. 16Aa 15
Harcourt Rd. se4. 24T 77
Harcourt Rd. Cro. 17Zd 91
Harcourt St. w1. 13L 48
Harcourt Ter. sw10. 12P 60
Hard St. se17. 19P 63
Hardcastle St. se15. 22R 76
Harden St. se18. 31P 67
Harden's Manor Way,sw7.
    31O 67
Harder's Rd. se15. 22R 76
Harders Rd. Mews se15.
    22R 76
Hardess St. se24. 19S 75
Hardinge Rd. n18. 20Ab 17
Hardinge Rd. nw10. 8J 46
Hardinge St. e1. 23M 52
Hardinge St. n1. 18H 36
Hardings La. se20. 23Z 90
Hardington St. nw8. 13L 48
Hardman Rd. se7. 29P 67
Hardwick Rd. w4. 5O 57
Hardwick St. ec1. 18K 50
Hardwicke Rd. n13 17Ab 16
Hardwicke St. Bar. 34J 43
Hardwidge St. se1. 20N 63
Hardy Rd. se3. 28Q 66
Hardy Rd. sw19. 11Z 92
Hare St. e1. 23 L 52
Hare St. e2. 21K 52
Hare St. se18. 33O 95
Hare Wlk. n1. 21J 51
Haredale Rd. se24. 19T 75
Harefield Mews se4. 24S 77
Harefield Rd. n8. 16B 24
Harefield Rd. n15 20C 25
Harefield Rd. se4. 24S 77

Harewood Av. nw1. 13K 48
Harewood Pl. nw1. 13L 48
Harewood Pl. w1. 15M 49
Harford St. e1. 24L 53
Harford Wlk. n2. 13B 22
Hargrave Rd. n19. 16E 35
Hargrave Pk. n19. 15E 35
Hargwyne St. sw9. 17S 74
Haringey Gro. n8. 18B 24
Haringey Pk. n8. 17C 24
Haringey Rd. n8. 17B 24
Harland Av. Cro. 21Zf 91
Harland Rd. se12. 29V 89
Harlech Rd. n14. 17Ad 16
Harlescott Rd. se15.
    23T 76
Harlesden Gdns. nw10 7H 32
Harlesden Rd. nw10. 7H 32
Harleton St. sw11. 13R 72
Harley Cre. Har. 1cA 12
Harley Gdns. sw10 12P 60
Harley Rd. nw3. 13H 34
Harley Rd. nw10. 6J 46
Harley Rd. Har. 1cA 12
Harley St. e3. 25K 53
Harley St. w1. 15L 49
Harleyford Mews se11.
    18Q 62
Harleyford Rd. se11.
    17P 62
Harleyford St. se11. 18Q 62
Harling St. se5. 20Q 63
Harman Dri. nw2. 10F 33
Harman St. n1. 21J 51
Harmood St. nw1. 15H 35
Harmsworth St.se17.18P 62
Harold Rd. e11 28E 40
Harold Rd. e13. 30J 55
Harold Rd. n8. 17B 24
Harold Rd. n15. 21B 26
Harold Rd. nw10. 5J 45
Harold Rd. se19. 20Z 90
Harold St. e2. 23J 52
Haroldstone Rd. e17. 24B 27
Harp La. ec3. 20M 51
Harpenden Rd. e12. 30E 41
Harpenden Rd.se27. 18W 85
Harper Rd. se1. 19O 63
Harpour Rd. Bar. 34H 43
Harpur St. wc1. 17L 50
Harraden Rd. se3. 30R 79
Harrap St. e14. 27M 54
Harriet St. sw1. 14O 61
Harriet Wk. sw1. 14O 61
Harringay Gdns. n15. 19B 25
Harringay Rd. n15. 19B 25
Harrington Gdns. sw7.
    12P 60
Harrington Hill e5. 23D 26
Harrington Rd. e11. 28D 28
Harrington Rd. n9. 22Ad 17
Harrington Rd. se18. 31O 67
Harrington Rd.se25.
    22Zc 90
Harrington Rd. sw7. 12O 60
Harrington Sq. nw1. 16J 49
Harrington St. nw1. 15J 49
Harris St. e17. 25D 27
Harris St. se5. 20Q 63
Harrison St. wc1. 17K 50
Harrison's Rise Cro. 18Zf 91
Harrow Alley e1. 21L 51
Harrow Dri. n9. 21Ae 17
Harrow Grn. e11. 28F 40
Harrow La. e14. 26M 53
Harrow Pk. Har. 1bD 12

Harrow Rd. E6. 31J 43
Harrow Rd. E11. 28F 40
Harrow Rd.
  w2. 1-281 & 2-322.
  w9. 283-419 & 324-570.
  w10. 421-625 & 572-742
  NW10. 639, 744 & up.
         8K 46
Harrow Rd. Bar. 35J 43
Harrow Rd. Ilf. 34G 43
Harrow Rd. Wem. 1F 30
Harrow St. NW1. 13L 48
Harrow View Har. 1cAa 12
Harroway Rd. SW11. 12S 72
Harrowby St. w1. 13L 48
Harrowdene Rd. Wem.
         2E 30
Harrowes Meade Edg.
         4Ad 13
Harrowgate Rd. E9. 24H 38
Harrowview Rd. w5. 1K 44
Hart Gro. w5. 3M 45
Hart St. EC2. 19L 51
Hart St. EC3. 20M 51
Hart St. wc1. 17L 50
Hart St. Bar. 34J 43
Hartfield Cres. SW19. 10Z 92
Hartfield Gro. SE20. 22Za 90
Hartfield Rd. SW19. 10Z 92
Hartfield Ter. E3. 25J 53
Hartford Av. Har. 1aA 12
Hartham Rd. N7. 17G 36
Hartham Rd. N17. 21Aa 17
Hartington Rd. E16. 29M 55
Hartington Rd. E17. 24C 27
Hartington Rd. N17. 21Aa 17
Hartington Rd. sw8. 16R 74
Hartington Rd. w4. 4Q 57
Hartington Rd. w13. 1aM 94
Hartington Rd. Twi. 1aU 93
Hartismere Rd. sw6. 10Q 59
Hartland Clo. Edg. 4Ae 13
Hartland Gdns. Edg. 4Ae 13
Hartland Gro. NW1. 15H 35
Hartland Rd. E15. 28H 40
Hartland Rd. N11. 14Ac 15
Hartland Rd. NW1. 15H 35
Hartland Rd. NW6. 10J 47
Hartley Av. E6. 31J 43
Hartley Rd. E11. 28D 28
Hartley Rd. Cro. 19Zd 91
Hartley St. E2. 23K 52
Hartnoll St. N7. 18G 36
Harton Rd. N9. 23Ad 17
Harton St. SE8. 25R 77
Hartopp Av. sw6. 10Q 59
Harts La. SE14. 24R 76
Harts La. Bar. 33H 43
Hartswood Rd. w12. 6N 58
Hartville Rd. SE18. 35P 95
Harvard Hill w4. 4P 57
Harvard La. w4. 4P 57
Harvard Rd. SE13. 26U 78
Harvard Rd. w4. 4P 57
Harvey Rd. E11. 28D 28
Harvey Rd. N8. 17B 24
Harvey Rd. SE5. 20R 75
Harvey Rd. Ilf. 33G 43
Harvist Rd. N7. 18F 36
Harvist Rd. NW6. 9J 47
Harwell Pass. N2. 14A 23
Harwood Rd. sw6. 11Q 60
Harwood Ter. sw6. 11R 72
Haselrigge Rd. sw4. 16T 74
Haseltine Rd. SE26. 24X 88
Hasker St. sw3. 13O 60

Haslam Pl. SE15. 21R 75
Haslemere Av. NW4. 9C 21
Haslemere Av.
  w13. 1-69 & 2-84.
  w7. 71, 86 & up. 1aO 94
Haslemere Av. Barn. 14Ae 15
Haslemere Av. Mit. 12Za 92
Haslemere Gdns. N3. 10A 21
Haslemere Gdns. Ilf. 36E 42
Haslemere Rd. N8. 17C 24
Haslemere Rd. Cro. 18Zc 90
Hassard St. E2. 21K 51
Hassendean Rd. SE3. 29Q 67
Hassett Rd. E9. 24G 38
Hassop Rd. NW2. 9F 33
Hasted Rd. SE7. 31P 67
Hastings Rd. E15. 28J 54
Hastings Rd. N11. 16Ac 15
Hastings Rd. w13. 1M 44
Hastings Rd. Cro. 20Ze 91
Hastings St. wc1. 17K 50
Hatch Rd. sw16. 16Za 90
Hatcham Rd. SE15. 23Q 64
Hatcham Pk. Rd. SE14.
         23R 76
Hatchard Rd. N19. 17E 36
Hatchcroft NW4. 8A 20
Hatfield Rd. E15. 28G 40
Hatfield Rd. w4. 5N 57
Hatfield Rd. w13. 1aM 94
Hatfield St. EC1. 19K 51
Hatfield St. SE1. 18N 62
Hatfield St. w6. 9P 59
Hathaway Rd. Cro. 18Ze 91
Hatherley Gdns. E6. 31K 55
Hatherley Gdns. N8. 17C 24
Hatherley Gro. w2. 11L 48
Hatherley Rd. E17. 25B 27
Hatherley Rd. Kew. 3R 68
Hatherley St. sw1. 16O 61
Hatherway Gdns. w13.
         1aL 94
Hathway St. SE15. 23S 76
Hatley Clo. N11. 14Ac 15
Hatley Rd. N4. 18E 36
Hatton Gdn. EC1. 18L 50
Hatton Rd. Cro. 18Ze 91
Hatton St. NW8. 13K 48
Hatton Wall EC1. 18L 50
Hauberk Rd. sw11. 13T 72
Havana Rd. sw19. 11W 82
Havannah St. E14. 25O 65
Havant Rd. E17. 27A 28
Havelock Pl. Har. 1bC 12
Havelock Rd. E9. 23H 38
Havelock Rd. N17. 22A 26
Havelock Rd. sw19. 11Y 83
Havelock Rd. w14. 9O 59
Havelock Rd. Cro. 21Ze 91
Havelock Rd. Har. 1bA 12
Havelock St. N1. 17H 36
Havelock St. SE23. 23W 87
Havelock Ter. sw8. 15R 73
Haven Grn. w5. 2L 44
Haven La. w5. 2L 44
Haverfield Gro. Kew 3Q 57
Haverford Way Edg. 3Aa 13
Haverhill Rd. sw12. 15V 84
Havering St. E1. 23M 52
Haverlock St. Ilf. 33E 42
Haverstock Hill NW3. 14G 35
Haverstock Pl. NW1. 15H 35
Haverstock Rd. NW5. 14G 35
Haverstock St. N1. 19J 51
Havil St. SE5. 20R 75
Hawarden Gro. SE24. 19V 86

Hawarden Rd. E17. 24B 26
Hawbridge Rd. E11. 27D 28
Hawes Rd. N18. 22Ab 17
Hawgood St. E3. 25L 53
Hawke Rd. SE19. 20Y 86
Hawker St. SE15. 21R 75
Hawkesbury Rd. sw15.
         7T 70
Hawkesfield Rd. SE23.
         24W 88
Hawkins Cres. Har. 1cC 12
Hawkins St. E1. 23L 52
Hawkshead Rd. NW10.
         6H 32
Hawkslade Rd. SE15. 23U 76
Hawksley Rd. N16. 20E 37
Hawksmoor St. w6. 9Q 59
Hawkstone Rd. SE16. 23P 64
Hawley Cres. NW1. 15H 35
Hawley Rd. NW1. 15H 35
Hawley St. NW1. 15H 35
Hawstead Rd. SE6. 26U 77
Hawthorn Av. Cro. 18Za 90
Hawthorn Av. Mit. 12Za 92
Hawthorn Gdns. w5. 2O 56
Hawthorn Gro. SE20. 22Z 90
Hawthorn Rd. E17. 25A 27
Hawthorn Rd. N8. 17A 24
Hawthorn Rd. N18. 21Ab 17
Hawthorn Rd. NW10. 7G 32
Hawthorne Av. N13. 17Ac 16
Hawthorne Rd. Har. 1aC 12
Hawthorne Rd. N1. 20G 37
Hawthorne Way N19.
         21Ad 17
Hay Hill w1. 15M 49
Hay La. NW9. 5B 19
Hay St. E2. 22J 52
Haycroft Gdns. NW10. 7H 32
Haycroft Rd. sw2. 17U 74
Hay Currie St. E14. 26L 53
Hayday Rd. E16. 29L 54
Haydock Rd. SE16. 23P 64
Haydon Sq. E1. 21M 51
Haydon St. E1. 21M 51
Haydon's Rd. sw19. 11Y 83
Haydons Pk. Rd. sw19.
         11Y 82
Hayes Cres. NW11. 10B 21
Hayes Pl. NW1. 13L 48
Hayland Clo. NW9. 5B 19
Hayles St. SE11. 18O 62
Hayling Rd. N16. 21G 37
Haymarket sw1. 16M 50
Haymerle Rd. SE15. 21Q 64
Hayne St. EC1. 19L 51
Haynes La. SE19. 20Z 90
Haynt Wk. sw20. 9Za 92
Hays La. SE1. 20N 63
Hay's Mews w1. 15M 49
Haysleigh Gdns. Cro. 22Za 90
Hayter Rd. sw2. 17T 74
Hayward's Pl. EC1. 18K 50
Haywards Rd. N20. 12Ae 14
Hazel Gdns. Edg. 4Ad 13
Hazel Gro. Wem. 2H 30
Hazel Rd. NW10. 8K 46
Hazelbourne Rd. sw12.
         15U 73
Hazelbury Grn. N9. 21Ad 17
Hazelbury Rd. N9. 21Ac 17
Hazelbury Rd. sw6. 11R 72
Hazeldean Rd. NW10. 6H 31
Hazeldon Rd. SE4. 24U 77
Hazelhurst Rd. sw17. 12X 83
Hazellville Rd. N19. 16D 24

Hazelmere Rd. nw6.	11J	47
Hazelmere Av. Mor.	11Zb	92
Hazelwood Cres. n13.	18Ad	16
Hazelwood Rd. e17.	24B	27
Hazewood La. n13.	18Ad	16
Hazledene Rd. w4.	4P	57
Hazledean Rd. Cro.	20Zf	91
Hazlemere Rd. n21.	19Ae	16
Hazlewell Rd. sw15.	8T	70
Hazlewood Cres. w10.	10K	47
Hazlitt Rd. w14.	9O	59
Headcorn Rd. n17.	21Ab	17
Headcorn Rd. Bro.	28Y	89
Headcorn Rd. Cro.	17Zc	92
Heading St. nw4.	8A	20
Headington Rd. sw18.		
	12W	83
Headley Av. Cro.	17Zg	91
Headley Dri. Ilf.	33C	42
Headley St. se15.	22S	76
Headstone Dri. Har.	1cA	12
Headstone Gdns. Har.	1cA	12
Headstone Rd. Har.	1cB	12
Headworth Rd. sw17.	11W	83
Healey St. nw1.	15G	35
Hearn St. e16.	28M	54
Hearn St. ec2.	20L	51
Hearne Rd. w4.	3P	57
Hearnville Rd. sw12.	14V	84
Heath Brow nw3.	12E	34
Heath Clo. nw11.	11D	22
Heath Croft nw11.	12D	22
Heath Dri. nw3.	11F	34
Heath Dri. sw20.	8Zb	92
Heath Gdns. Twi.	1bV	93
Heath Gro. se20.	23Z	90
Heath La. se3.	27S	78
Heath Rd. sw8.	15S	73
Heath Rd. Cro.	19Zb	90
Heath Rd. Har.	1dC	12
Heath Rd. Twi.	1cV	93
Heath St. e1.	23L	52
Heath St. nw3.	12E	34
Heath St. Bar.	34J	43
Heatham Pk. Twi.	1cV	93
Heathcote Rd. Twi.	1aU	93
Heathcote St. wc1.	17K	50
Heathcroft w5.	3K	44
Heathdene Rd. sw16.	17Z	90
Heather Gdns. nw11.	9C	21
Heather Rd. nw2.	7E	32
Heather Wk. Edg.	4Ac	13
Heatherley St. e5.	21F	38
Heatherpark Dri. Wem.		
	3H	31
Heathfield N. Twi.	1cU	93
Heathfield S. Twi.	1cU	93
Heathfield Av. sw18.	12U	72
Heathfield Gdns. nw11.		
	9C	21
Heathfield Gdns. w4.	5P	57
Heathfield Pk. nw2.	8G	33
Heathfield Rd. sw18.	12U	72
Heathfield Rd. w3.	4N	57
Heathfield Rd. Cro.	19Zg	91
Heathfield Ter. se18.	35Q	95
Heathfield Ter. w4.	5P	57
Heathgate nw11.	11C	22
Heath Hurst Rd. nw3.		
	13F	34
Heathland Rd. n16.	20D	25
Heathstan Rd. w12.	7M	46
Heathview Gdns. sw15.	8V	81
Heathview Rd. Cro.	18Zb	90
Heathville Rd. n19.	17D	24
Heathwall St. sw11.	14S	73
Heathwood Gdns. se7.	31P	67
Heaton Pl. e15.	27G	40
Heaton Rd. se15.	22S	76
Heaver Rd. sw11.	13S	72
Heavitree Rd. se18.	34Q	95
Hebdon Rd. sw17.	13X	83
Heber Rd. nw2.	9F	33
Heber Rd. se22.	21U	75
Hebron Rd. w6.	8O	58
Heckfield Pl. sw6.	10Q	59
Heckford St. e1.	23M	52
Hector St. se18.	35P	95
Heddon St. w1.	15M	49
Hedge La. n13.	18Ad	16
Hedgers Gro. e9.	24G	39
Hedgley St. se12.	28U	78
Heigham Rd. e6.	31H	41
Heiron St. se17.	19Q	63
Helder Gro. se12.	28V	89
Helen St. se18.	33P	95
Helena Rd. e13.	29K	54
Helena Rd. e17.	25C	27
Helena Rd. nw10.	8F	32
Helena Rd. w5.	2K	44
Helenslea Av. nw11.	11D	21
Helix Gdns. sw2.	17U	74
Helix Rd. sw2.	17U	74
Hellings St. e1.	22N	64
Helmet Row ec1.	19K	51
Helmsley St. e8.	22H	38
Helvetia St. se6.	24W	88
Hemans St. sw8.	16Q	62
Hemberton Rd. sw9.	17S	74
Heming Rd. Edg.	4Ab	13
Hemingford Rd. n1.	18H	36
Hemington Av. n11.	14Ac	15
Hemlock Rd. w12.	7M	46
Hemming St. e1.	22K	52
Hemp Row se17.	20P	63
Hempstead Rd. e17.	27A	28
Hemstal Rd. nw6.	11H	34
Hemsworth St. e16.	11L	54
Hemsworth St. n1.	20J	51
Henchman St. w12.	7L	46
Hendale Av. nw4.	8A	20
Henderson Rd. e7.	30G	41
Henderson Rd. n9.	22Ae	17
Henderson Rd. sw18.	13U	72
Henderson Rd. Cro.	19Zc	90
Hendham Rd. sw17.	13W	83
Hendon Av. n3.	10Aa	14
Hendon La. n3.	10Aa	14
Hendon Rd. n9.	22Ae	17
Hendon Way.		
nw2. 17-223 & 38-176.		
nw4. 200-236 & 307-371.		
	9C	21
Hendon Pk. Row nw11.		
	10C	21
Hendrick Av. sw12.	14U	73
Heneage La. ec3.	21M	51
Heneage St. e1.	21L	52
Henfield Rd. sw19.	10Za	92
Hengrave Rd. se23.	23V	87
Henley Rd. n18.	20Ad	17
Henley Rd. nw10.	8H	33
Henley Rd. Ilf.	34G	43
Henley St. sw11.	14R	73
Henniker Gdns. e6.	31K	55
Henniker Rd. e15.	27G	40
Henning St. sw11.	13R	72
Henningham Rd. n17.		
	20Aa	17
Henrietta Rd. n15.	20C	25
Henrietta St. e2.	21J	52
Henrietta St. w1.	15L	49
Henrietta St. wc2.	17M	50
Henry Rd. n4.	19D	25
Henry Rd. n15.	20C	25
Henry St. e14.	25L	53
Henry St. nw8.	13J	48
Henry St. se1.	20N	63
Henry St. se11.	17P	62
Henry St. se18.	32P	95
Henry St. wc1.	17K	50
Henryson Rd. se4.	25U	77
Henshall St. n1.	20G	37
Henshaw St. se17.	20O	63
Henslowe se22.	21U	76
Henson Av. nw2.	8F	32
Henstridge Pl. nw8.	13J	48
Henty Wlk. sw15.	7T	70
Henwick Rd. se9	31T	79
Henwood Rd. se16.	23O	64
Hepscott Rd. e9.	25H	39
Hepworth Rd. sw16.	16Z	90
Herbert Cres. sw1.	14O	61
Herbert Gdns. nw10.	8J	46
Herbert Rd. e12.	31G	43
Herbert Rd. e17.	25C	27
Herbert Rd. n9.	22Ad	17
Herbert Rd. n11.	17Ab	16
Herbert Rd. n15.	21B	26
Herbert Rd. nw9.	7C	20
Herbert Rd. se18.	33R	95
Herbert Rd. sw9.	17S	74
Herbert Rd. sw15.	10T	71
Herbert Rd. sw19.	10Z	92
Herbert Rd. Ilf.	35E	42
Herbert St. e13.	29K	55
Herbert St. n1.	20J	51
Herbert St. nw5.	14G	35
Herbrand St. wc1.	17K	50
Hercules Pl. n7.	17F	36
Hercules Rd. n.7.	17F	36
Hercules Rd. se1.	18O	62
Hereford Av. Bar.	14Ae	15
Hereford Gdns. Ilf.	32D	42
Hereford Pl. se14.	24Q	65
Hereford Rd. e11.	30C	29
Hereford Rd. w2.	11L	48
Hereford Rd. w3.	4M	45
Hereford Rd. w5.	1O	56
Hereford Sq. sw7.	12P	60
Hereford St. e2.	22K	52
Hereward Gdns. n13.	18Ac	16
Hereward Rd. sw17.	13X	83
Herga Rd. Har.	1bA	12
Heriot Pl. nw5.	14F	35
Heriot Rd. nw4.	9B	21
Hermes St. n1.	18J	50
Hermiston Av. n8.	17B	24
Hermit Rd. e16.	28K	54
Hermit St. ec1.	18K	50
Hermitage Clo. e18.	29B	28
Hermitage La. nw11.	11E	33
Hermitage La. sw16.	17Z	90
Hermitage La. Cro.	22Zd	91
Hermitage Rd. n4 & n15.		
	19C	25
Hermitage Rd. se19.	19Y	86
Hermitage St. w2.	12L	48
Hermitage, The, Rich.	2T	68
Hermitage Wlk. e18.	29B	28
Hermitage Wall e1.	22N	64
Herndon Rd. sw18.	11T	72
Herne Hill se24.	19U	75
Herne Pl. se24.	18U	74
Herne Hill Rd. se24	19T	75
Heron Rd. nw10.	6G	32
Heron Rd. se24.	19T	75
Heron Rd. Twi.	1aT	93

Herondale Av. sw18. 13V 83
Herongate Rd. e12. 30E 41
Herrick Rd. n5. 19E 37
Herrick St. sw1. 16P 62
Herries St. w10. 10J 47
Herring St. se5. 2CQ 63
Herschell Rd. se23. 23V 87
Hersee Pl. e2. 23K 52
Hertford Av. sw14. 5T 69
Hertford Rd. e6. 33H 43
Hertford Rd. n1. 21H 37
Hertford Rd. n2. 13A 22
Hertford St. e8. 21H 37
Hertford Rd. n9. 22Ad 17
Hertford Rd. Ilf. 35C 42
Hertford St. w1. 15N 61
Hertslet Rd. n7. 17F 36
Hervey Clo. n3. 11Aa 14
Hervey Pk. Rd. e17. 24B 27
Hervey Rd. se3. 29R 79
Hesketh Pl. w11. 9M 47
Hesketh Rd. e7. 29F 40
Heslop Rd. sw12. 14V 84
Hesper Mews sw5. 11P 60
Hesperus Cre. e14. 26P 65
Hessel Rd. w13. 1aN 94
Hessel St. e1. 22M 52
Hester Rd. sw11. 13Q 60
Hestercombe Av. sw6. 10R 71
Heston St. se8. 25R 77
Hetherington Rd. sw4. 16T 74
Hethpool St. w2. 12L 48
Hetley Rd. w12. 8N 58
Hetton St. w6. 8O 58
Heversham Rd. se18. 35P 95
Hewett St. ec2. 20K 51
Hewer St. w10. 9L 47
Hewish Rd. n18. 20Ac 17
Hewitt Av. n22. 18A 24
Hewitt Rd. n8. 18B 24
Hewlett Rd. e3. 24J 53
Hewling St. n16. 20F 37
Hewson St. se17. 19P 63
Hexham Rd. se27. 19W 86
Heybourn Rd. n17. 22Ab 17
Heybridge Av. sw16. 17Y 85
Heyford Av. sw8. 17Q 62
Heygate St. se17. 19P 63
Heysham Rd. n15. 20C 25
Heythorp St. sw18. 10V 82
Heyworth Rd. e5. 22F 38
Heyworth Rd. e15. 28G 40
Hibbert Rd. e17. 25D 27
Hibbert Rd. Har. 1bAa 12
Hibbert St. sw11. 12S 72
Hichisson Rd. se15. 23T 76
Hickey's Gro. Rich. 3T 68
Hickling Rd. Ilf. 33G 43
Hickling St. se16. 22O 64
Hicks St. se8. 24P 64
Hide Pl. sw1. 16P 61
Hide Rd. Har. 1cB 12
Hides St. n7. 18G 36
High Holborn wc1. 17L 50
High La. w7. 1cL 94
High Path sw19. 11Z 92
High Rd. E. Finch. n2. 13A 22
High Rd. Harlesden nw10.
7G 32
High Rd. Ilf. 33F 42
High Rd. Leyton
e15. 1-215 & 2-164
e10. 166, 217 & up 26E 39
High Rd. Leytonstone
e15. 122-166 & 233-243
e11. 168, 245 & up 28F 40

High Rd. New Southgate
n11. 15Ac 15
High Rd. Finchley
n2 & n12. 12Ac 14
High Rd. Tottenham
n15. 1-363 & 2-344.
n17. 346, 365 & up. 21C 25
High Rd. Wem. 2G 30
High Rd. Whetsone n12.
12Ad 14
High Rd. Willesden nw10.
7G 32
High Rd. Wood Green
n22. 18A 24
High St. Acton w3. 4N 57
High St. Barnes sw13. 6R 70
High St. Battersea sw11.
13R 72
High St. Bre. 1Q 56
High St. Cro. 19Zf 91
High St. Ealing w5. 2M 44
High St. Edg. 3Ac 13
High St. Harlesden nw10.
6J 46
High St. Har. 1bE 12
High St. Highgate n6. 15D 23
High St. Hornsey n8. 17B 24
High St. Lewisham se13.
26U 77
High St. Merton sw19. 11Z 92
High St. Mortlakesw14. 5S 69
High St. North
e6. 1-239 & 2-226
e12. 228, 241 & up 31G 41
High St. Finchley n12.
12Ac 14
High St. Norwood se25.
21Zb 90
High St. Penge se20. 22Z 90
High St. Plaistow e13. 29J 55
High St. St. John's Wood
nw8. 13J 48
High St. Sth. e6. 32J 43
High St. Southgate n14.
16Ae 15
High St. Stepney e1. 24L 52
High St. Stoke Newington
n16. 21F 37
High St Stratford e15. 26J 53
High St. Teddington 1bY 93
High St. Thornton Heath
Cro. 19Zb 92
High St. Walthamstow
e17. 24B 27
High St. Wanstead e11.
29C 28
High St. Wea. 1bAa 12
High St. Wem. 3F 30
High St. Wim. sw19. 9Y 82
High St. Woolwich se18.
32O 95
Higham St. e17. 24A 27
Higham Rd. n17. 20A 25
Higham Hill Rd. e17. 24A 27
Highbarrow Rd. Cro. 21Ze 91
Highbridge Rd. e6. 33J 43
Highbury Av. Cro. 18Za 90
Highbury Cre. 18G 36
Highbury Fields n5. 18G 36
Highbury Gdns. Ilf. 35E 42
Highbury Grange n5. 19F 37
Highbury Gro. n5. 19G 37
Highbury Hill n5. 18F 36
Highbury Pk. n5. 19F 37
Highbury Pl. n5. 19G 36
Highbury Quad. n5. 19F 37

Highbury Rd. sw19. 9Y 82
Highbury Ter. n5. 19G 36
Highbury New Pk. n5. 19G 37
Highbury Station Rd. n1.
18G 36
Highclere St. se26. 24X 87
Highcliffe Gdns. Ilf. 31C 29
Highcombe se7. 30Q 67
Highcroft nw9. 6B 20
Highcroft Av. Wem. 3H 31
Highcroft Gdns. nw11. 10C 21
Highcroft Rd. n19. 17D 24
High Cross Rd. n17. 21A 26
Highdown Rd. sw15. 7U 70
Highfield Av. nw9. 5B 19
Highfield Av. nw11. 9C 21
Highfield Av. Wem. 3E 30
Highfield Clo. nw9. 5B 19
Highfield Gdns. nw11. 10C 21
Highfield Hill se19. 20Z 90
Highfield Rd. n21. 19Ae 16
Highfield Rd. nw11. 10C 21
Highfield Rd. w3. 4L 45
Highgate Av. n6. 15C 23
Highgate Hill
n19. 1-99 & 2-90
n6. 92-130 15D 23
Highgate Rd. nw5. 15F 35
Highland Av. w7. 1cL 94
Highland Croft Bec. 26Y 88
Highland Rd. se19. 20Y 86
Highland St. e14. 26L 54
Highlands Av. w3. 4M 45
Highlands Gdns. Ilf. 32D 42
Highlands The. Edg. 4Aa 13
Highlever Rd. w10. 9L 47
Highmead Cres. Wem. 3G 30
High Meadow Cres. nw9.
5B 19
Highmore Rd. se3. 28Q 66
High Pk. Rd. Kew. 3R 69
Highstone Av. e11. 29C 28
Highview Av. Edg. 5Ad 13
High View Clo. se25. 21Za 90
High View Gdns. n3. 10A 21
High View Gdns. Edg. 5Ad 13
High View Rd. e18. 28A 28
High View Rd. se19. 20Z 90
High View Rd. w13. 1aL 94
Highway The. e1. 22M 52
Highweek Rd. n15. 21B 25
Highwood Av. n12. 12Ad 14
Highwood Gro. nw7. 6Ac 13
Highwood Rd. n19. 17F 36
Highworth Rd. n11. 16Ab 15
Highworth St. nw1. 18L 48
Hilary Rd. w12. 6M 46
Hilcot St. e8. 21H 37
Hilda Rd. e6. 31H 41
Hilda Rd. e16. 28L 54
Hilda Rd. sw9. 18R 74
Hilditch St. e14. 26M 54
Hildreth St. sw12. 14V 84
Hildyard Rd. sw6. 11Q 59
Hiley Rd. nw10. 8J 46
Hilgrove I nw6. 12H 34
Hill Clo. nw2. 8E 32
Hill Clo. nw11. 11C 22
Hill Cre. n20. 12Ae 14
Hill Cre. Har. 1aB 12
Hill Dri. nw9. 5D 19
Hill Dri. sw16. 17Zb 90
Hill Rise nw11. 12B 22
Hill Rd. n10. 14Aa 15
Hill Rd. nw8. 12J 48
Hill Rd. Har. 1aB 12

Hill Rd. Har. 1aE 12
Hill Side nw10. 5H 31
Hill Side sw19. 9Y 82
Hill St. E16. 29M 55
Hill St. se15. 21Q 64
Hill St. w1. 15N 61
Hill St. Rich. 1T 68
Hill Top N. w5. 3K 44
Hill Top S. w5. 3K 44
Hill Way nw9. 6D 20
Hillbrook Rd. sw17. 14X 84
Hillbury Av. Har. 1B 18
Hillbury Rd. sw17. 15W 84
Hillcote Av. sw16. 17Z 90
Hillcourt Av. n12. 12Ac 14
Hillcourt Rd. se22. 22U 76
Hillcrest Av. nw11. 10B 21
Hillcrest Av. Edg. 4Ad 13
Hillcrest Gdns. n3. 10A 21
Hill Crest Gdns. nw2. 7E 32
Hillcrest Rd. E17. 27A 28
Hillcrest Rd. E18. 29A 28
Hillcrest Rd. se26. 21Y 87
Hillcrest Rd. w3. 4N 57
Hillcrest Rd. w5. 2K 44
Hillcrest Rd. Bro. 29Y 89
Hillcroft Cres. w5. 2L 44
Hillcroft Cres. Wem. 3F 30
Hillcross Av. Mor. 9Zc 92
Hilldowne Rd. sw16. 17Z 90
Hilldrop Cres. n7. 16G 36
Hilldrop Rd. n7. 16G 36
Hillersdon Av. sw13. 7R 70
Hillery Rd. se17. 20P 63
Hill Farm Rd. w10. 9L 47
Hillfield Av. n8. 17B 24
Hillfield Av. nw9. 6B 20
Hillfield Av. Wem. 2G 30
Hillfield Clo. Har. 1dA 12
Hillfield Pk. n10. 15A 23
Hillfield Pk. n21. 18Ae 16
Hillfield Rd. nw6. 10F 33
Hill House Rd. sw16.
17Y 85
Hilliard's Court E1. 22N 64
Hillier Rd. sw11. 14U 73
Hillingdon St. se17. 19Q 63
Hillington Gdns. Ilf. 31A 29
Hillman St. E8. 22G 38
Hillmarton Rd. n7. 17G 36
Hillmore Gro. se26. 24Y 87
Hill Pl. St. E14. 25L 53
Hills Pl. w1. 15M 49
Hillsboro' Rd. se22. 20U 75
Hillside nw9. 5B 19
Hillside Av. n11. 14Ac 15
Hillside Av. Wem. 3F 30
Hillside Clo. sw20. 9Zb 92
Hillside Dri. Edg. 3Ac 13
Hillside Gdns. n6. 15C 23
Hillside Gdns. Edg. 3Ad 13
Hillside Gro. n14. 16Af 15
Hillside Rd. n15. 21C 25
Hillside Rd. sw2. 17W 85
Hillside Rd. sw2. 18V 85
Hillside Rd. w5. 2L 44
Hillside Rd. Cro. 18Zg 91
Hillside Way n9. 21Ad 17
Hillsleigh Rd. w8. 10N 59
Hillstowe St. E5. 23E 38
Hilltop nw11. 12A 22
Hilltop Rd. nw6. 11G 34
Hillview Av. Har. 2B 18
Hill View Cres. Ilf. 32C 42
Hill View Gdns. nw4. 9A 21
Hill View Gdns. nw9. 6B 19

Hill View Rd. Twi. 1bU 93
Hillway n6. 15E 35
Hilly Fields. Cres. se4. 25T 77
Hilmer St. w14 10P 59
Hilsea St. E5. 23F 38
Hilside Way n9. 21Ad 17
Hilton Av. n12. 13Ac 14
Hilton Rd. n7. 17F 36
Hilton St. E1. 23M 52
Himley Rd. sw17. 13Y 83
Hinchliffe St. sw1. 17O 62
Hinckley Rd. se15. 21T 76
Hind Gro. E14. 25M 53
Hinde St. w1. 14L 49
Hindes Rd. Har. 1cB 12
Hindle St. E8. 21F 37
Hindman's Rd. se22. 21U 76
Hindrey Pl. E5. 22G 38
Hindsley's Pl. se23. 23W 87
Hinstock Rd. se18. 34R 95
Hinton Rd. n18. 20Ac 17
Hinton Rd. se24. 19S 75
Hitcham Rd. E17. 24D 27
Hitherfield Rd. sw16.
17W 85
Hither Grn. La. se13.
27U 78
Hoadley Rd. sw16. 16W 84
Hobart Pl. sw1. 15O 61
Hobbes Wlk. sw15. 7U 70
Hobbs' Pl. n1. 20J 51
Hobday St. E14. 26L 53
Hobury St. sw10. 12Q 60
Hocker St. E2. 21K 51
Hockley Av. E6. 31J 43
Hockley St. E9. 23G 38
Hocroft Av. nw2. 10E 33
Hocroft Av. nw2. 10F 33
Hodford Rd. nw11. 11D 21
Hodson St. se17. 19P 63
Hoe St. E17. 25B 27
Hofland Rd. w14. 9O 59
Hogarth Av. w4. 6P 58
Hogarth Hill nw11. 11B 21
Hogarth La. w4. 6P 57
Hogarth Pl. w4. 6P 57
Hogarth Rd. sw5. 11P 60
Hogarth Rd. Edg. 4Aa 13
Holbeach Rd. se6. 25V 88
Holbeck Row se15. 22R 76
Holbein Pl. sw1. 14P 61
Holberton Gdns. nw10.
8J 46
Holborn EC1. 18L 50
Holborn Circus EC1. 18L 50
Holborn Rd. E13. 30L 55
Holborn Viaduct EC1. 18L 50
Holbrook Rd. E15. 28J 54
Holcombe Rd. n17. 21A 26
Holcombe Rd. Ilf. 33D 42
Holcombe St. w6. 8P 58
Holcombs St. se1. 20N 63
Holcroft Rd. E9. 23H 38
Holden Av. n12. 12Ac 14
Holden Av. nw9. 5D 19
Holden Rd. E3. 26K 53
Holden Rd. n12. 11Ac 14
Holden St. sw11. 14S 73
Holdenby Rd. se4. 24U 77
Holdenhurst Av. n12.
12Ab 14
Holdernesse Rd. sw17.
14W 84
Holders Hill Av. nw4. 9A 21
Holder's Hill Dri. nw4.
9A 21

Holdgate St. se7. 30O 67
Holford Pl. wc1. 18K 50
Holford Rd. nw3. 12E 34
Holford Sq. wc1. 18J 50
Holford St. E1. 23K 52
Holford St. wc1. 18J 50
Holgate Av. sw11. 12S 72
Holland Gro. sw9. 18Q 62
Holland La. w14. 10O 59
Holland Pk. w11. 10N 59
Holland Rd. E6. 32J 43
Holland Rd. n8. 17B 24
Holland Rd. n19. 17D 24
Holland Rd. nw10. 7J 46
Holland Rd. se25. 22Zc 90
Holland Rd. sw9. 18S 74
Holland Rd. w14. 9N 59
Holland Rd. Wem. 2G 30
Holland St. se1. 17R 74
Holland St. w8. 11N 59
Holland Ter. w3. 4N 57
Holland Wk. w8. 10N 59
Holland Pk. Av. w11. 9N 59
Holland Pk. Av. Ilf. 35C 42
Holland Pk. Gdns. w14.
9N 59
Holland Pk. Mews w11.
10N 59
Holland Pk. Rd. w14. 10O 59
Holland Villas Rd. w14.
9N 59
Hollen St. w1. 16L 49
Holles St. w1. 15L 49
Hollickwood Av. n12.
14Ab 15
Hollies Rd. w5. 1O 56
Hollingbourne Gdns. w13.
1aL 94
Hollingbourne Rd. se24.
19U 75
Hollingsworth St. n7.
18G 36
Hollington St. se5. 19Q 63
Holloway Pass. E1. 22L 52
Holloway Rd. E11. 28F 40
Holloway Rd.
n7. 2-596 & 13-479.
n19. 481, 598 & up. 16E 36
Holloway St. E1. 22L 52
Holly Hill nw3. 12F 34
Holly La. nw10. 6G 32
Holly Pk. n3. 11A 21
Holly Pk. n4. 17D 24
Holly Pl. nw3. 12F 34
Holly Rd. E11. 28D 28
Holly Rd. w4. 5O 57
Holly Rd. Twi. 1bV 93
Holly St. E8. 21H 37
Holly Ter. n20. 12Ae 14
Holly Wk. nw3. 12F 34
Hollybush Gdns. E2. 22K 52
Hollybush St. E13. 30K 55
Hollycroft Av. nw3. 11E 34
Hollycroft Av. Wem. 3E 30
Hollydale Rd. se15. 22R 76
Hollyfield Av. n11. 14Ac 15
Holly Lodge Gdns. n6.
14D 23
Holly Pk. Gdns. n3. 11A 21
Holly Pk. Rd. n11. 14Ac 15
Holly Pk. Rd. w7. 1bM 94
Hollywood Rd. sw10. 12P 60
Holman Rd. sw11. 12S 72
Holmbrook Dri. nw4. 9B 21
Holmbrook St. E9. 23G 38
Holmbury View E5. 22D 26

Holmbush Rd. sw15. 9U 71
Holmby St. se17. 20Q 63
Holmcote Gdns. n5. 19G 37
Holmdale Gdns. nw4. 9B 21
Holmdale Rd. n15. 21C 25
Holmdale Rd. nw6. 11G 33
Holmdene Av. se24. 19U 75
Holme Rd. e6. 32J 43
Holme Lacey Rd. se12.
28V 89
Holmes Av. e17. 25A 27
Holmes Rd. nw5. 15G 35
Holmes Rd. Twi. 1bW 93
Holmesdale Av. sw14. 4S 69
Holmesdale Rd. n6. 15C 23
Holmesdale Rd. n11. 15Ac 15
Holmesdale Rd. se25.
20Zc 90
Holmesdale Rd. Kew. 3R 68
Holmesley Rd. se23. 24U 76
Holmewood Gdns. sw2.
17V 85
Holmewood Rd. sw2. 17V 85
Holmfield Av. nw4. 9B 21
Holmleigh Rd. n16. 21D 25
Holms St. e2. 21J 52
Holmshaw Rd. se26. 24X 88
Holmside Rd. sw12. 14U 73
Holmstall Av. nw9. 5A 13
Holmwood Gdns. n3.
11Aa 14
Holmwood Gro. nw7. 6Ac 13
Holmwood Rd. se25.20Zb 90
Holmwood Rd. Ilf. 35E 42
Holmwood Rd. Mit. 12Zb 92
Holness Rd. e15. 28H 40
Holroyd Rd. sw15. 8T 70
Holt Rd. Wem. 1E 30
Holtham Rd. nw8. 12H 34
Holyoak Rd. se11. 18O 62
Holyoake Wk. w5. 1K 44
Holyport Rd. sw6. 9Q 59
Holyrood Gdns. nw9. 4A 13
Holywell La. ec2. 20K 51
Holywell Row ec2. 20K 51
Home Rd. sw11. 13R 72
Homecroft Rd. n22. 19Aa 16
Homecroft Rd. se26. 23Y 87
Homefield Clo. nw10. 5G 31
Homefield Gdns. Mit.
12Za 92
Homefield Rd. sw19. 9Y 82
Homefield Rd. w4. 6P 58
Homefield Rd. Edg. 5Ab 13
Homefield St. n1. 20J 51
Homeleigh Rd. se15. 23T 76
Home Pk. Rd. sw19. 10X 82
Homer Rd. e9. 24G 39
Homer Rd. Cro. 23Zd 91
Homer Row w1. 13L 48
Homer St. se1. 18O 62
Homer St. w1. 13L 48
Homerton Gro. e9. 23G 38
Homerton Rd. e9. 24G 39
Homerton Row e9. 23G 38
Homerton Ter. e9. 23G 38
Homerton High St. e9.
23G 38
Homestall Rd. se22. 22T 76
Homestead Pk. nw2. 7E 32
Homestead Rd. sw6. 10Q 59
Homeway, The, w7. 1cL 94
Homfray St. e9. 25G 39
Honduras St. ec1. 19K 51
Honeybourne Rd. nw6.
11G 34

Honeybrook Rd. sw12.
15V 84
Honeywell Rd. sw11. 13U 72
Honeywood Rd. nw10. 7J 46
Honiton Rd. nw6. 10J 47
Honiton St. se15. 22R 76
Honley Rd. se6. 26V 88
Honor Oak Pk. se23. 23U 76
Honor Oak Rise se23. 23U 76
Honor Oak Rd. se23. 22V 87
Hood Av. sw14. 4T 69
Hood St. se8. 24P 65
Hook Wk. Edg. 5Ab 13
Hookers Av. e17. 24A 26
Hook's Rd. se15. 22R 76
Hoop La. nw11. 11C 21
Hooper Rd. e16. 29M 55
Hooper St. e1. 21M 52
Hoopwick St. se8. 24P 05
Hope Rd. w13. 1aM 94
Hope St. e1. 21L 52
Hope St. n7. 18G 36
Hope St. sw11. 12S 72
Hopedale Rd. se7. 29Q 67
Hopefield Av. nw6. 10J 47
Hopgood St. w12. 8N 59
Hopkins St. w1. 16M 49
Hopper's Rd.
n13. 1-5 & 2-54.
n21. 7, 56 & up. 18Ad 16
Hopton Rd. sw16. 16Y 85
Hopton St. se1. 19N 63
Horace Rd. e7. 29F 41
Horace St. sw8. 17Q 62
Horatio St. e2. 21J 52
Horbury Cres. w11. 10M 47
Horbury Mews w11. 10M 47
Horder Rd. sw6. 10R 71
Hormead Rd. w9. 10K 47
Horn La. se10. 29P 66
Horn La. w3. 4M 45
Horn Pk. La. se12. 29U 79
Hornby Rd. se15. 20Q 63
Horncastle Rd. se12. 29V 89
Horney La. se1. 21O 63
Hornfair Rd. se7. 30Q 67
Horniman Dri. se23. 22V 87
Horns Rd. Ilf. 34C 42
Hornsey La. n6. 16D 23
Hornsey Rise n19. 17D 24
Hornsey St. n7. 18G 36
Hornsey Rd.
n7. 1-281 & 2-352.
n19. 283, 354 & up.18F 36
Hornsey La.Gdns.n6. 16D 23
Hornsey Pk. Rd. n8. 18A 24
Hornsey Rise Gdns. n19.
17D 24
Hornshay St. se15. 23Q 64
Hornton St. w8. 11N 59
Horsecroft Rd. Edg. 6Ab 13
Horsefield Gdns. se9. 31U 79
Horsefeld Rd. se9. 31U 79
Horseferry Rd. e14. 24M 53
Horseferry Rd. se10. 26Q 65
Horseferry Rd. sw1. 16O 62
Horse Guards Av. sw1.
17N 62
Horsell Rd. n5. 18G 36
Horsford Rd. sw2. 17T 74
Horselydown La. se1.21N 63
Horsley St. se17. 19Q 63
Horsham Av. n12. 14Ac 15
Horsman St. se5. 19Q 63
Horsmonden Rd. se4.24U 77
Hortensia Rd. sw10. 12Q 60

Horton Rd. e8. 22G 3�|
Horton St. se13. 26S 7⁌
Hosack Rd. sw17. 14W 84
Hosier La. ec1. 19L 50
Hosier St. se8. 25R 7⁊
Hoskins St. se10. 27Q 66
Hotham Rd. sw15. 8S 70
Hotham Rd. sw19. 12Z 92
Hotham St. e15. 27J 54
Hothfield Pl. se16. 23O 64
Hotspur St. se11. 18P 62
Houblon Rd. Rich. 2T 68
Houghton Pl. nw1. 16J 49
Houghton Rd. n15. 21B 25
Houghton St. wc2. 17M 50
Houlder Cres. Cro. 18Zh 91
Houndsditch e1. 20L 51
Houndsfield Rd. n9. 22Ae 17
Houston Rd. se23. 24W 88
Hove Av. e17. 25C 27
Hove St. se15. 22R 76
Hoveden Rd. nw2. 9F 33
Howard Clo. w3. 4L 45
Howard Rd. e11. 28E 40
Howard Rd. e17. 26A 27
Howard Rd. n15. 21C 25
Howard Rd. n16. 20F 37
Howard Rd. nw2. 9F 33
Howard Rd. se20. 23Z 90
Howard Rd. se25. 21Zc 90
Howard Rd. Bar. 34J 43
Howard Rd. Ilf. 33F 43
Howard St. sw8. 16R 73
Howard St. wc2. 18M 50
Howard Wk. n2. 12B 22
Howard's La. sw15. 8T 70
Howards Rd. e13. 29K 54
Howberry Rd. Cro. 19Za 90
Howbury Rd. se15. 23S 76
Howden Rd. se25. 21Za 90
Howden St. se15. 21S 76
Howe St. se10. 27Q 66
Howgate Rd. sw14. 5S 69
Howick Pl. sw1. 16O 61
Howie St. sw11. 13Q 60
Howitt Rd. nw3. 13G⁍34
Howland St. w1. 16L 49
Howletts Rd. se24. 19U 75
Howley Pl. se1. 18N 62
Howley Pl. w2. 12L 48
Howley Rd. Cro. 18Zf 91
Hows St. e2. 21J 51
Howsman Rd. sw13. 7Q 58
Howson Rd. se4. 24T 77
Hoxton Sq. n1. 20K 51
Hoxton St. n1. 20K 51
Hoy St. e16. 28M 54
Hoylake Rd. w3. 6L 46
Hoyland Rd. se15. 22Q 64
Hoyle Rd. sw17. 13Y 83
Hubbard Rd. se27. 19X 86
Hubbard St. e15. 28J 54
Hubert Gro. sw9. 17S 74
Hubert Rd. e6. 31K 55
Hubert Rd. sw19. 12Z 92
Huddart St. e3. 25L 53
Huddlestone Rd. e7. 29F 40
Huddlestone Rd. n7. 16F 35
Huddlestone Rd. nw2.8G 32
Hudson Rd. e16. 29L 54
Hudson Rd. se18. 34Q 95
Hudson's Pl. sw1. 15O 61
Huggin La. ec2. 19L 51
Huggin La. ec4. 19M 51
Hugh St. sw1. 15P 61
Hughan Rd. e15. 27G 40

Hughenden Av. Har. 1B 18
Hughenden Rd. w6. 7P 58
Hughes Fields SE8. 25Q 65
Hugo Rd. N19. 16F 35
Hugon Rd. sw6. 11S 72
Huguenot Pl. sw18. 12T 72
Huguenot Rd. SE15. 22S 76
Hull St. EC1. 19K 51
Hulse Av. Bar. 35H 43
Humber Rd. SE3. 28Q 66
Humber Rd. NW2. 8E 32
Humberstone Rd. E13. 30K 55
Humbolt Rd. w6. 9Q 59
Hume Rd. w11. 9N 59
Humes Av. w7. 1bN 94
Humphrey St. SE1. 21P 63
Hungerford Rd. N7. 17G 36
Hungerford St. E1. 22M 52
Hunsden Rd. SE14. 23Q 64
Hunslett St. E2. 23K 52
Hunt St. SE11. 17P 62
Hunt St. w4. 6P 57
Hunt St. w11. 9M 47
Hunter Rd. sw20. 8Z 92
Hunter Rd. Ilf. 33G 43
Hunter St. wc1. 17K 50
Hunters Gro. Har. 1A 18
Huntingdon Rd. N2. 13A 22
Huntingdon St. E16. 28M 54
Huntingdon St. N1. 17H 36
Huntingfield Rd. sw15. 7T 70
Huntley Rd. SE25. 20Zb 90
Huntley St. wc1. 16L 49
Hunton Ct. E1. 21L 52
Hunton St. E1. 22L 52
Hunts Mews E1. 21M 52
Huntsmoor Rd. sw18. 12T 72
Huntspill St. sw17. 12X 83
Hunts Slip Rd. se21. 20W 86
Huntsworth Mews NW1. 14K 49
Huntsworth Ter. NW8. 13K 48
Hurlbutt Pl. SE17. 19P 63
Hurley Rd. SE11. 18P 62
Hurlingham Gdns. sw6. 10S 71
Hurlingham Rd. sw6. 10S 71
Hurlock St. N5. 19F 37
Huron Rd. sw17. 14W 84
Hurst Clo. NW11. 11C 22
Hurst Rd. E17. 26A 27
Hurst Rd. N21. 18Ae 16
Hurst Rd. Cro. 19Zg 91
Hurst St. SE24. 18U 74
Hurstbourne Gdns. Bar. 35H 43
Hurstbourne Rd. SE23. 24W 88
Hurstdene Gdns. N15. 21C 25
Hurstway St. w11. 9M 47
Hurstwood Av. E18. 30B 29
Hurstwood Rd. NW11. 10B 21
Hutchings St. E14. 25O 65
Hutchison St. E1. 21L 51
Hutton Gro. N12. 12Ac 14
Hutton Rd. SE11. 17P 62
Huxbear St. SE4. 25U 77
Huxley Gdns. NW10. 3J 44
Huxley Pl. N13. 19Ad 16
Huxley Rd. E10. 26E 40
Huxley Rd. N18. 20Ad 17
Huxley St. w10. 9K 47
Hyacinth Rd. sw15. 7V 81

Hyde Cres. NW9. 6B 20
Hyde La. sw11. 13R 72
Hyde Way N9. 21Ad 17
Hyde Pk. Av. N21. 20Ae 16
Hyde Pk. Corner sw1. 14N 61
Hyde Pk. Gdns. SE1. 20Ae 16
Hyde Pk. Gdns. w2. 13M 48
Hyde Pk. Gate w7. 12N 60
Hyde Pk. Pl. w2. 13M 48
Hyde Pk. Sq. w2. 13M 48
Hyde Pk. St. w2. 13M 48
Hyde Pk. Ter. w2. 13M 48
Hyde Rd. N1. 20J 51
Hyde St. SE8. 25Q 65
Hyde The NW9. 5Aa 13
Hyde Vale SE10. 27R 78
Hyde's Pl. E. N1. 19H 37
Hyde's Pl. W. N1. 19H 37
Hydethorpe Av. N9. 21Ad 17
Hydethorpe Rd. sw12. 15V 84
Hylton St. SE18. 36P 95
Hyndman St. SE15. 22Q 64
Hyson Rd. SE16. 22P 64
Hythe Rd. NW10. 7K 46
Hythe Rd. SE25. 19Za 90

Iceland Rd. E3. 25J 53
Ickburgh Rd. E5. 22E 38
Ickworth Pk. Rd. E17. 24B 27
Ida Rd. N15. 20B 25
Ida St. E14. 26M 53
Idenden Cotts. SE10. 28P 66
Idlecombe Rd. sw17. 14Y 84
Idmiston Rd. E15. 28G 40
Idmiston Rd. se27. 19W 86
Idol La. EC3. 20M 51
Idonia St. SE8. 25Q 65
Ifley Rd. w6. 8O 58
Ifield Rd. sw10. 11Q 60
Ilbert St. w10. 9K 47
Ilchester Pl. w14. 10O 59
Ildersley Gro. SE21. 20W 86
Ilderton Rd. SE16. 23Q 64
Ilex Rd. NW10. 6G 32
Ilford La. Ilf. 33F 42
Ilfracombe Rd. SE12 28X 89
Iliffe St. SE17. 19P 63
Ilkley Rd. E16. 30L 55
Ilmington Rd. Har. 2C 18
Ilminster Gdns. sw11. 13T 72
Ilton Rd. E17. 25C 27
Ilva Pl. E8. 21H 37
Imperial Rd. N22. 17Aa 16
Imperial Rd. sw6. 11R 72
Imperial St. E3. 26K 53
Imperial Way Har. 2B 18.
Imperial Institute Rd. sw7. 12O 60
Inchmery Rd. SE6. 26W 88
Inderwick Rd. N8. 17B 24
India St. EC3. 21M 51
Indus Rd. SE7. 30R 79
Ingal Rd. E13. 29L 54
Ingate Pl. sw8. 15R 73
Ingatestone Rd. E12. 30E 41
Ingelow Rd. sw8. 15S 73
Ingersoll Rd. w12. 8N 58
Ingestre Pl. w1. 16M 49
Ingestre Rd. E7. 29F 41
Ingestre Rd. NW5. 15F 35
Ingham Rd. NW6. 11F 33
Inglebert St. EC1. 18J 50
Ingleborough St. sw9. 18R 74
Ingleby Rd. N7. 17E 36
Ingleby Rd. Ilf. 33E 42

Ingledew Rd. SE18. 35P 95
Inglehurst Gdns. Ilf. 32C 42
Inglemere Rd. SE23. 23X 87
Ingleside Gro. SE3. 28Q 66
Inglethorpe St. sw6. 9R 71
Ingleton Rd. N18. 22Ab 17
Ingleton St. sw9. 18R 74
Ingle Way N12. 13Ab 14
Inglewood Rd. NW6. 11G 34
Inglis Rd. w5. 3M 44
Inglis Rd. Cro. 21Ze 91
Inglis St. SE5. 19R 75
Ingoldisthorpe Gro. SE15. 21Q 63
Ingram Av. NW3. 12D 22
Ingram Rd. N2. 14B 23
Ingram Rd. Cro. 19Z 90
Ingrave St. sw11. 12S 72
Ingress St. w4. 6P 58
Inkerman Rd. NW5. 15G 35
Inkerman Ter. w8. 11O 59
Inman Rd. NW10. 6H 32
Inman Rd. sw18. 12V 83
Inner Circle NW1. 14K 49
Inner Temple EC4. 18M 50
Inner Pk. Rd. sw19. 9W 82
Innis Pl. SE17. 20P 63
Inniskilling Rd. E13. 30K 55
Instow Pl. N7. 18F 36
Inver Rd. E5. 23E 38
Inverine Rd. SE7. 30Q 67
Inverness Gdns. w8. 11N 60
Inverness Pl. w2. 11M 48
Inverness Rd. N18. 22Ac 17
Inverness St. NW1. 15H 35
Inverness Ter. w2. 12M 48
Inverton Rd. SE15. 23T 76
Invicta Rd. E16. 29M 54
Invicta Rd. SE3. 29Q 67
Inville Rd. SE17. 20P 63
Inworth St. sw11. 13R 72
Ion Rd. Cro. 19Za 90
Ion Sq. E2. 22J 52
Ipplepen Rd. N15. 21B 25
Ipswich Rd. E8. 22J 52
Irene Rd. sw6. 11R 71
Ireton St. E3. 25K 53
Irongate Wharf Rd. w2. 13L 48
Iron Mill Pl. sw18. 11U 72
Iron Mill Rd. sw18. 11U 72
Ironmonger La. EC2. 19M 51
Ironmonger Row EC1. 19K 51
Ironmonger St. EC1. 19K 51
Irvine Av. Har. 1aA 12
Irving Gro. sw9. 17S 74
Irwin Gdns. NW10. 8H 32
Irwin St. SE18. 35R 95
Isabel St. sw9. 17R 74
Isabella Rd. E9. 23G 38
Isabella St. SE1. 18N 62
Isis Rd. sw18. 12W 83
Isla St. SE18. 34Q 95
Island Row E14. 24M 53
Isledon Rd. N7. 18F 36
Islington Green N1. 18J 50
Islington High St. N1. 18J 50
Islip St. NW5. 16G 35
Ismailia Rd. E7. 29H 41
Ismailia Rd. sw6. 11S 72
Italian Wlk. SE11. 17P 62
Ivanhoe Dri. Har. 1aAa 12
Ivanhoe Rd. SE5. 20S 75
Iveagh Av. NW10. 3J 45
Iveagh Clo. NW10. 3J 45

Iveley Rd. sw4.	15S 73	
Iverna Court w8.	11O 60	
Iverna Gdns. w8.	11O 60	
Iverson Rd. nw6.	11G 33	
Ives St. sw3.	13O 60	
Ivimey St. e2.	22K 52	
Ivor Pl. nw1.	14K 49	
Ivor St. nw1.	15H 35	
Ivorydown se12.	29X 89	
Ivy Cres. w4.	4O 57	
Ivy Gdns. n8.	17C 24	
Ivy La. ec4.	19M 51	
Ivy La. n1.	20J 51	
Ivy Rd. e16.	29M 54	
Ivy Rd. e17.	26C 27	
Ivy Rd. n14.	16Af 15	
Ivy Rd. nw2	8F 32	
Ivy Rd. se4.	24T 77	
Ivy St. n1.	20J 51	
Ivy Ter. e5.	22D 26	
Ivydale Rd. se15.	23S 76	
Ivyday Gro. sw16	17X 85	
Ivydene Rd. e8.	22H 38	
Ivymount Rd. se27.	18X 85	
Ixworth Pl. sw3.	13P 60	
Jackson Rd. n7.	18F 36	
Jackson Rd. Bar.	35J 43	
Jackson St. se18.	33Q 95	
Jackson's La. n6.	1C 23	
Jacob St. se1.	21N 64	
Jacobin St. e2.	22J 52	
Jaffray Pl. se27.	19X 85	
Jamaica Rd. se16.	21O 64	
Jamaica Rd. Cro.	18Zd 91	
Jamaica St. e1.	23L 52	
James Av. nw2.	8F 33	
James Gdns. n22.	19Ab 16	
James La.		
e10. 1-122		
e11. 27-55.	27D 28	
James Pl. e1.	23M 52	
James' Pl. n17.	21Aa 17	
James St. e2.	23K 52	
James St. e13.	29L 55	
James St. n7.	18G 36	
James St. nw1.	15H 35	
James St. w1.	14L 49	
James St. w2.	12L 48	
James St. w3.	6P 58	
James St. wc2.	17M 50	
James St. Bar.	34H 43	
Jameson St. w8.	11M 47	
Jane St. e1.	22M 52	
Janet St. e14.	25O 65	
Janeway St. se16.	22O 64	
Janson Rd. e15.	28G 40	
Janson's Rd. n15.	21A 25	
Japan Cres. n4.	17D 24	
Jardin St. se5.	20Q 63	
Jarvis Rd. se22.	21T 75	
Jasmine Gro. se20.	22Za 90	
Jasper Rd. se19.	21Y 86	
Jay Mews nw7.	12N 60	
Jebb St. e3.	25J 53	
Jedburgh Rd. e13	30K 55	
Jedburgh St. sw11.	14T 73	
Jeddo Rd. w12.	6N 58	
Jefferson St. e3.	26K 53	
Jeffreys Rd. sw4.	16R 74	
Jeffreys St. nw1.	15H 35	
Jeken Rd. se9.	30T 79	
Jelf Rd. sw2.	18T 74	
Jellicoe Rd. n17.	20Aa 17	
Jenkins Rd. e13.	30L 55	
Jenner Rd. n16.	21E 38	
Jennet Rd. Cro.	17Zf 91	
Jennings Rd. se22.	21U 75	
Jephson Rd. e7.	30H 41	
Jephson St. se5.	20R 75	
Jeptha Rd. sw18.	1U 71	
Jerdan Pl. sw6.	11Q 59	
Jeremiah St. e14.	26M 53	
Jermyn St. sw1.	16M 49	
Jerningham Rd. se4.	24S 76	
Jerome St. e1.	21L 51	
Jerrard St. se13.	26S 77	
Jersey Rd. e11.	27E 40	
Jersey Rd. e16.	29M 55	
Jersey Rd. w7.	1aN 94	
Jersey Rd. Ilf.	33G 43	
Jersey St. e2.	22K 52	
Jervis Rd. sw6.	10Q 59	
Jesmond Av. Wem.	3G 31	
Jesmond Rd. Cro.	21Zd 91	
Jessamine Rd. w7.	1bM 94	
Jesse Rd. e10.	26E 39	
Jessica Rd. sw18.	12U 72	
Jessop Rd. se24.	19T 74	
Jewell Rd. e17.	25A 27	
Jewel St. e1.	23L 52	
Jewin Cres. ec1.	19L 51	
Jewin St. ec1.	19L 51	
Jewry St. ec3.	21M 51	
Jews' Row sw18.	11T 72	
Jews' Wlk. se26.	22X 87	
Jeymer Av. nw2.	8G 32	
Jeypore Rd. sw18.	12U 72	
Joan St. se1.	18N 62	
Jocelyn Rd. Rich.	2S 68	
Jocelyn St. se15.	21R 75	
Jockey's Fields wc1.	17L 50	
Jodrell Rd. e3.	25H 39	
Johanna St. se1.	18N 62	
John St. e15.	28J 54	
John St. ec3.	21M 51	
John St. se25.	21Zb 90	
John St. w1.	15M 49	
John St. wc1.	17L 50	
John St. wc2.	17M 50	
John Campbell Rd. n16.	21G 37	
John Carpenter St. ec4.	18M 50	
John Penn St. se13.	26R 77	
John Ruskin St. se5.	19Q 63	
John's Av. nw4.	8A 21	
John's Hill e1.	22M 52	
John's Mews wc1.	17L 50	
John's Pl. e1.	22L 52	
Johnson Rd. Cro.	19Zd 91	
Johnson St. e1.	22M 52	
Johnson St. e14.	26P 65	
Johnson St. nw1.	16J 49	
Johnson St. sw1.	16O 62	
Johnson's Pl. sw1.	15P 61	
Joiner St. se1.	20N 63	
Jonathan St. se11.	17P 62	
Jordan Rd. Wem.	1H 30	
Joseph St. e3.	25L 53	
Josephine Av. sw2.	17U 74	
Joshua St. e14.	26L 53	
Joubert St. sw11.	14S 73	
Jubilee Pl. sw3.	13P 60	
Jubilee St. e1.	23L 52	
Judd St. wc1.	17K 50	
Jude St. e16.	28M 54	
Judkin St. e14.	26O 65	
Juer St. sw11.	13Q 60	
Julia St. nw5.	14F 35	
Julian Av. w3.	4M 45	
Julien Rd. w5.	1O 56	
Junction App. se13.	26S 77	
Junction Rd. e10.	26E 39	
Junction Rd. e13.	30J 55	
Junction Rd. e15.	28G 40	
Junction Rd. n9.	22Ae 17	
Junction Rd. n17.	22A 26	
Junction Rd. n19.	16F 35	
Junction Rd. se8.	24P 65	
Junction Rd. w3.	4O 57	
Junction Rd. w5.	1O 56	
Junction Rd. Cro.	19Zh 91	
Junction St. e16.	28L 54	
Juniper St. e1.	23M 52	
Jupp Rd. e15.	27H 40	
Jupp's Rd. e3.	24K 53	
Jutland Rd. se6.	26V 88	
Juxon St. se11.	17O 62	
Kambala Rd. sw11.	13S 72	
Kangley Bridge Rd. se26.	24Y 88	
Kashgar Rd. se18.	36P 98	
Kashmir Rd. se7.	31R 79	
Kassala Rd. sw11.	14R 73	
Kate St. sw12.	14V 84	
Katherine Gdns. se9.	31T 79	
Katherine Rd.		
e6. 1-239 & 2-224.		
e7. 226, 241 & up.	30G 41	
Katherine Rd. Twi.	1bV 93	
Katherine St. Cro.	19Zf 91	
Kathleen Av. w3.	5K 45	
Kathleen Av. Wem.	2H 30	
Kathleen Rd. sw11.	13S 73	
Kay Rd. sw9.	17S 74	
Kay St. e2.	22J 52	
Kay St. e15.	27H 40	
Kean St. wc2.	17M 50	
Keats Gro. nw3.	13F 34	
Keble St. sw17.	12X 83	
Keedonwood Rd. Brom.	27Y 89	
Keeley Rd. Cro.	19Zf 91	
Keeley St. wc2.	17M 50	
Keeling Rd. se9.	30U 79	
Keemor St. se18.	33Q 95	
Keens Rd. Cro.	19Zg 91	
Keen's Yd. n5.	19G 37	
Keeton's Rd. se16.	22O 64	
Keildon Rd. sw11.	13T 72	
Keith Gro. w12.	7N 58	
Kelceda Clo. nw2.	8D 20	
Kelday Rd. e9.	25H 39	
Kelfield Gdns. w10.	9L 47	
Kell St. se1.	19O 63	
Kelland Rd. e13.	29K 55	
Kellerton Rd. se13.	27U 78	
Kellett Rd. sw2.	18T 74	
Kellino St. sw17.	13X 83	
Kelly Rd. e16.	29L 54	
Kelly St. nw1.	15G 35	
Kelmore Gro. se22.	21T 76	
Kelmscott Rd. sw11.	18U 72	
Kelross Rd. n5.	19F 37	
Kelso Pl. w8.	11O 60	
Kelson St. nw6.	10G 33	
Kelvedon Rd. sw6.	10R 71	
Kelvin Av. n13.	18Ab 16	
Kelvin Gro. se26.	22X 87	
Kelvin Rd. n5.	19F 37	
Kelvington Rd. se15.	23U 76	
Kemble Rd. n17.	21Aa 17	
Kemble Rd. se23.	23W 87	
Kemble Rd. Cro.	18Zf 91	

Kemble St. wc2. 17M 50
Kemerton Rd. se5. 19S 75
Kemerton Rd. Cro. 21Zd 91
Kemeys St. e9. 24G 39
Kempe Rd. nw6. 9J 47
Kempshott Rd. sw16. 16Z 90
Kemplay Rd. nw3. 13F 34
Kempsford Gdns. sw5. 11P 60
Kempsford Rd. se11. 18P 62
Kempshead Rd. se5. 21Q 63
Kempslade St. se8. 24P 65
Kempson Rd. sw6. 11R 72
Kempt St. se18. 33Q 95
Kempton Rd. e6. 32J 43
Kempton St. e16. 31N 67
Kemsing Rd. se10. 29Q 66
Kenbury St. se5. 19R 75
Kenchester St. sw8. 17Q 62
Kendal Av. n18. 20Ac 17
Kendal Av. w3. 4L 45
Kendal Av. Bar. 35J 43
Kendal Gdns. n18. 20Ac 17
Kendal Rd. nw10. 7F 32
Kendall Mews w1. 14L 49
Kender St. se14. 23R 76
Kendoa St. sw4. 16T 74
Kendrey Gdns. Twi. 1cU 93
Kenilford Rd. sw12. 15V 84
Kenilworth Av. e17. 26A 27
Kenilworth Av. sw19. 10X 82
Kenilworth Gdns. Ilf. 36E 42
Kenilworth Rd. e3. 24J 52
Kenilworth Rd. nw6. 10H 33
Kenilworth Rd. se20. 23Za 90
Kenilworth Rd. w9. ?M 44
Kenilworth St. w11. 9M 47
Kenley Gro. Cro. 18Zc 92
Kenley Rd. sw19. 10Za 92
Kenley Rd. Bre. 2P 56
Kenley Rd. Twi. 1aU 93
Kenley St. w11. 9M 47
Kenlor Rd. sw17. 12Y 83
Kenmare Gdns. n13. 19Ac 16
Kenmare Rd. Cro. 17Zd 91
Kenmere Gdns. Wem. 3H 31
Kenmont Gdns. nw10. 7J 46
Kenmore Av. Har. 1aA 12
Kenmore Gdns. Edg. 4Aa 13
Kenmore Rd. Har. 2A 18
Kenmure Rd. e8. 22G 38
Kennard Rd. e15. 27H 40
Kennard Rd. n11. 14Ac 15
Kennedy Rd. Bar. 35J 43
Kenneth Av. Ilf. 33F 43
Kenneth Cres. nw2. 8F 32
Kenneth Rd. w14. 10Q 59
Kennet Rd. w9. 10K 47
Kenning St. se16. 23N 64
Kenninghall Rd. e5. 22F 38
Kenninghall Rd. n18. 23Ac 17
Kennington Gro. se11. 17P 62
Kennington La. se11. 17P 62
Kennington Oval se11. 18Q 62
Kennington Rd.
se1. 1-69 & 2-64.
se11. 66, 71 & up. 18O 62
Kennington Pk. Gdns se11. 18Q 62
Kennington Pk. Pl. se11. 18P 62

Kennington Pk. Rd. se11. 18Q 62
Kensal Rd. w10. 9K 47
Kensington Av. e12. 32H 43
Kensington Av. Cro. 18Za 90
Kensington Ct. w8. 11N 60
Kensington Cres. w14. 10O 59
Kensington Gdns. Ilf. 32E 42
Kensington Gate w8. 12O 60
Kensington Gore sw7. 12N 60
Kensington Pl. sw1. 16O 62
Kensington Pl. w8. 11N 59
Kensington Rd. w8. 12N 60
Kensington Sq. w8. 11N 60
Kensington Ct. Pl. w8. 11O 60
Kensington Gdns. Sq. w2. 11M 48
Kensington High St. w8. 11N 60
Kensington Pal. Gdns. w8. 11N 60
Kensington Pk. Gdns. w11. 10M 47
Kensington Pk. Mews w11. 10M 47
Kensington Pk. Rd. w11. 10M 47
Kent Av. w13. 1aK 94
Kent Gdns w13. 1aK 94
Kent Rd. n15. 20B 25
Kent Rd. n21. 20Ae 17
Kent Rd. w4. 5O 57
Kent Rd. Kew 3Q 57
Kent St. e2. 21J 51
Kent St. e13. 30K 55
Kent Ter. nw1 13K 48
Kent House La. se26. 24Y 88
Kent House Rd. se26. 24Y 87
Kentmere Rd. se18. 35P 95
Kentish Town Rd.
nw1. 1-187 & 2-156.
nw5. 158, 189 & up. 15G 35
Kenton Av. Har. 1bC 12
Kenton Gdns. Har. 1B 18
Kenton La. nw9. 4B 19
Kenton La. Har. 1A 18
Kenton Rd. e9. 23H 38
Kenton Rd. Har. 1B 18
Kenton Rd. Har, 1bC 12
Kenton St. wc1. 17K 50
Kenton Pk. Av. Har. 2B 18
Kenton Pk. Clo. Har. 1B 18
Kenton Pk. Cres. 2A 18
Kenton Pk. Rd. Har. 1B 18
Kent View Gdns. Ilf. 35E 42
Kentwode Grn. sw13. 7Q 58
Kenver Av. n12. 13Ab 14
Kenward Rd. se9. 30U 79
Kenway Rd. sw5. 11O 60
Kenwood Rd. n6. 14C 23
Kenwood Rd. n9. 22Ae 17
Kenwyn Dri. nw2. 6E 32
Kenwyn Rd. sw4. 16T 74
Kenwyn Rd. sw20. 8Za 92
Kenya Rd. se7. 30R 79
Kenyon St. sw6. 9R 71
Keogh Rd. e15. 28G 40
Kepler Rd. sw4. 17T 74
Keppel Rd. e6. 32H 43

Keppel St. se1. 19N 62
Keppell St. wc1. 16L 50
Kerbela St. e2. 21K 52
Kerbey Rd. e14. 26M 53
Kerfield Cres. se5. 20R 75
Kerfield Pl. se5. 20R 75
Kerrison Pl. w5. 2M 44
Kerrison Rd. sw11. 13S 72
Kerrison Rd. w5. 2N 56
Kerry Rd. se14. 24Q 65
Kerry St. e16. 29M 54
Kersfield Rd. sw15. 9U 71
Kersley Mews sw11. 13R 72
Kersley Rd. n16. 21E 37
Kersley St. sw11. 13R 72
Keslake Rd. nw6. 9J 47
Keston Rd. n15. 20B 25
Keston Rd. se15. 21T 76
Keston Rd. Cro. 17Zd 91
Kestrel Av. se24. 19T 75
Keswick Gdns. Wem. 2F 30
Keswick Rd. sw11. 9U 71
Keswick Rd. sw19. 10Za 92
Kettlebaston Rd. e10. 24D 27
Kevelioc Rd. n17. 20Aa 16
Kew Bridge Kew. 3P 56
Kew Green Kew. 3Q 56
Kew Rd. Kew. 2S 68
Kew Bridge Rd. Kew. 3P 56
Kew Foot Rd. Rich. 2S 68
Kew Gdns. Rd. Kew. 3Q 56
Key St. e1. 23L 52
Keyes Rd. nw2. 9F 33
Keyse Rd. se1. 21O 63
Keymer Rd. sw2. 17W 85
Keynsham Gdns. se9. 31U 79
Keynsham Rd. se9. 31U 79
Keystone Cres. n1. 17J 50
Keyworth St. se1. 19O 63
Kezia St. se8. 24P 64
Killue ? Rd. cw17. 13X 83
Khartoum Rd. ?. 20K 55
Khartoum Rd. sw17. 12A 00
Khartoum Rd. Ilf. 33G 43
Khyber Rd. sw11. 13S 72
Kibworth St. sw8. 17Q 62
Kidbrooke Gdns. se3. 29S 78
Kidbrooke Gro. se3. 29R 79
Kidbrooke La. se3. 29S 79
Kidbrooke La. se9. 31T 79
Kidbrooke Way se3. 30S 79
Kidbrooke Pk. Rd. se3. 29R 79
Kidd St. se18. 31P 67
Kidderminster Rd. Cro. 19Ze 91
Kidderpore Av. nw3. 11F 34
Kidderpore Gdns nw3. 11F 34
Kilburn La.
w10. 1-271 & 2-300.
w9. 273, 302 & up. 9J 47
Kilburn Priory nw6. 11H 34
Kilburn Sq. nw6. 11H 33
Kilburn Vale nw6. 11H 34
Kilburn High Rd. nw6. 11H 33
Kilburn Pk. Rd. nw6. 11K 47
Kildare Gdns. w2. 11L 48
Kildare Ter. w2. 11L 48
Kildoran Rd. sw2. 16T 74
Kildowan Rd. Ilf. 36E 42
Kilgour Rd. se23. 24U 76
Kilkie St. sw6. 12S 72
Killarney Rd. sw18. 12U 72

Killearn Rd. se6. 27W 87
Killieser Av. sw2. 16W 85
Killowen Rd. e9. 23H 38
Killyon Rd. sw8. 16S 73
Kilmaine Rd. sw6. 10Q 59
Kilmarsh Rd. w6. 8O 58
Kilmartin Av. sw16. 17Zb 90
Kilmartin Rd. Ilf. 37E 42
Kilmington Rd. sw13. 7Q 58
Kilmorey Gdns. Twi. 1aT 93
Kilmorey Rd. Twi. 1aT 93
Kilmorie Rd. se23. 24W 88
Kilravock St. w10. 9K 47
Kilton St. sw11. 14R 73
Kimbell Gdns. sw6. 9R 71
Kimber Rd. sw18. 11V 82
Kimberley Av. e6. 31J 55
Kimberley Av. se15. 22S 76
Kimberley Av. Ilf. 35D 42
Kimberley Gdns. n4. 19C 25
Kimberley Rd. e11. 27E 40
Kimberley Rd. e16. 28K 54
Kimberley Rd. n17. 22A 26
Kimberley Rd. n18. 22Ab 17
Kimberley Rd. nw6. 10H 33
Kimberley Rd. sw9. 17S 74
Kimberley Rd. Cro. 18Zd 91
Kimpton Rd. se5. 20R 75
Kinburn St. se16. 23N 64
Kincaid Rd. se15. 22R 76
Kinder St. e1. 22M 52
Kinfauns Rd. sw2. 18W 85
Kinfauns Rd. Ilf. 37E 42
King Sq. ec1. 19K 51
King St. e1. 21M 51
King St. e10. 26D 27
King St. e13. 29L 54
King St. e14. 25M 53
King St. ec1. 18L 50
King St. ec2. 19M 51
King St. n2. 13A 22
King St. nw1. 16J 49
King St. sw1. 16N 61
King St. sw3. 13P 60
King St. w3. 4M 45
King St. w6. 7P 58
King St. w8. 11N 60
King St. wc2. 17M 50
King St. Rich. 1T 68
King St. Twi. 1bV 93
King Alfred Av. se6. 25X 88
King Arthur St. se15. 22R 76
King Charles St. sw1. 16N 62
King David La. e1. 23M 52
Kingdon Rd. nw6. 11G 34
King Edward Rd. e10. 26D 28
King Edward Rd. e17. 24A 27
King Edward St. e1. 22L 52
King Edward St. ec1. 19L 51
King Edward St. n1. 18J 50
King Edward Wk. se1. 18O 62
King Edward's Gdns. w3. 3N 57
King Edward's Gro. Twi. 1aY 93
King Edward's Rd.e9. 23H 38
King Edward's Rd. n9. 22Af 17
King Edward's Rd. Bar. 34J 43

Kingfield Rd. w5. 2K 44
Kingfield St. e14. 27P 66
King George St. se10. 26R 78
King George's Av. e16. 30M 55
King Henry St. n16. 20G 37
King Henry's Rd. nw3. 13H 34
King Henry's Wlk. n1. 20G 37
Kinghorn St. ec1. 19L 51
King James's Stairs e1. 23N 64
King James St. se1. 19O 63
King John St. e1. 23L 52
Kinglake St. se17. 20P 63
Kingley St. w1. 16M 49
King William St. ec4. 20M 51
King William St. se10. 26Q 66
Kings Av. n10. 15A 23
Kings Av. n21. 19Ae 16
King's Av. sw4. 1-145 & 2-108
sw12. 114, 147 & up 16V 84
King's Av. w5. 2L 44
King's Clo. nw4. 9B 21
King's Court se1. 19N 63
Kings Cross n1. 17J 50
Kings Dri. Edg. 3Ad 13
King's Dri. Wem. 4E 31
King's Gdns. Ilf. 34D 42
King's Highway se18. 35Q 95
King's Mews wc1. 17L 50
King's Pl. nw1. 16J 49
King's Pl. se1. 19O 63
King's Pl. w1. 14L 49
King's Rd. e6. 30J 55
King's Rd. e11. 28D 28
King's Rd. n4. 19E 37
King's Rd. n17. 21Aa 17
Kings Rd. n18. 22Ac 17
Kings Rd. n22. 18Aa 16
King's Rd. nw1. 16H 35
Kings Rd. nw10. 8H 32
King's Rd. se15. 22R 76
Kings Rd. se25. 21Zb 90
King's Rd.
sw3. 1-363 & 392
sw10. 365-539 & 394-552
sw6. 541, 554 & up 12Q 60
King's Rd. sw14. 5S 69
King's Rd. sw19. 10Y 82
Kings Rd. Bar. 34H 43
King's Rd. Ted. 1dX 93
King's Rd. Twi. 1aU 93
Kings St. n17. 21Aa 17
Kings Way Cro. 17Zg 91
King's Way Har. 1bA 12
King's Way Wem. 2F 30
King's Bench Wk. ec4. 18M 50
King's Bench St. se1. 19N 63
Kingsbridge Av. w3. 3N 56
Kingsbridge Rd. w10. 9L 47
Kingsbury La. nw9. 5E 31
Kingsbury Rd. n1. 21G 37
Kingsbury Rd. nw9. 4B 19
Kingscliffe Gdns. sw19. 10V 82
King's College Rd. nw3. 13H 34
Kingscote Rd. w4. 5O 57
Kingscote Rd. Cro. 22Ze 91
Kingscourt Rd. sw16. 16X 85
Kingscroft Rd. nw2. 10G 33

King's Cross Rd. wc1. 17K 50
Kingsdale Rd. se18. 35R 95
Kingsdale Rd. se20. 23Z 90
Kingsdown Av. w3. 6M 46
Kingsdown Av. w13. 1N 56
Kingsdown Rd. e11. 28F 40
Kingsdown Rd. n19. 17E 36
Kings Farm Av. Rich. 3S 68
Kingsfield Av. Har. 1dB 12
Kingsfield Rd. Har. 1cD 12
Kingsford St. nw5. 14G 35
Kingsgate Av. n3. 11A 22
Kingsgate Pl. nw6. 11H 33
Kingsgate Rd. nw6. 11H 33
Kingsground se9. 31U 79
Kingshill Av. Har. 1A 18
Kingshill Dri. Har. 1aAa 12
Kingsholm Gdns. se9. 31T 79
Kingshurst Rd. se12. 29V 89
Kingsland Grn. n16. 21G 37
Kingsland Rd.
e2. 1-283 & 2-240
e8. 242, 285 & up. 21J 51
Kingsland Rd. e13. 30K 55
Kingsland High St. e8. 21G 37
Kingsley Av. w13. 1aL 94
Kingsley Rd. e7. 29H 41
Kingsley Rd. n13. 18Ac 16
Kingsley Rd. nw6. 10H 33
Kingsley Rd. sw19. 11X 83
Kingsley Rd. Cro. 17Ze 91
Kingsley St. sw11. 14S 73
Kingsley Way nw11. 12B 22
Kingslyn Cres. sw19. 20Za 90
Kingsman St. se18. 32P 95
Kingsmead Av. nw9. 5C 19
Kingsmead Av. n9. 22Ae 17
Kingsmead Rd. sw2. 18W 85
Kingsmere Pk. nw9. 4D 19
Kingsmere Rd. sw19. 9W 82
Kingsmill Ter. nw8. 13J 48
Kings Ride Gate Rich. 3T 69
Kingsthorpe Rd. nw10. 5G 31
Kingsthorpe Rd. se26. 23X 87
Kingston By-Pass sw20. 6X 80
Kingston Hill Kin. 4Y 80
Kingston La. Twi. 1bY 93
Kingston Rd. n9. 22Ae 17
Kingston Rd. e11. 27F 40
Kingston Rd. sw20. 8Za 92
Kingston Rd. Ilf. 34F 43
Kingston Rd. Twi. 1aY 93
Kingston St. se17. 20P 63
Kingston Vale sw20. 5X 80
Kingstown St. nw1. 14H 35
Kingsway sw14. 4S 69
Kingsway wc2. 17L 50
Kingsway Cres. Har. 1dB 12
Kingswood Av. nw6. 10J 47
Kingswood Av. Cro. 18Zc 90
Kingswood Pl. se13. 28T 78
Kingswood Rd. se19. 20X 86
Kingswood Rd. se20 22Z 90
Kingswood Rd. sw2. 16U 74
Kingswood Rd. sw6. 9R 71
Kingswood Rd. sw19. 10Z 92
Kingswood Rd. w4. 4O 57
Kingswood Rd. Ilf. 36D 42
Kinloch Dri. nw9. 6C 19
Kinlock St. n7. 18F 36
Kinloss Gdns. n3. 10A 21
Kinnaird Av. w4. 4Q 57

Kinnear Rd. w12. 6N 58
Kinnerton St. sw1. 14N 61
Kinnoul Rd. w6. 9Q 59
Kinsale Rd. se15. 22T 76
Kintore St. se1. 21O 63
Kinveachy Gdns. se7. 31P 67
Kinver Rd. N. se26. 23X 87
Kinver Rd. S. se26. 23X 87
Kipling St. se1. 20N 63
Kirby Gro. se1. 20N 63
Kirby St. ec1. 18L 50
Kirchen Rd. w13. 1aM 94
Kirk La. se18. 34Q 95
Kirkby St. sw2. 16V 85
Kirkdale se26. 22X 87
Kirkdale Rd. e11. 28D 28
Kirkham St. se18. 35Q 95
Kirklees Rd. Cro. 17Zc 90
Kirkley Rd. sw19. 11Z 92
Kirk's Pl. e14. 24L 53
Kirkside Rd. se3. 29Q 66
Kirkstall Av. n15. 20B 25
Kirkstall Gdns. sw2. 16V 85
Kirkstall Rd. sw2. 16V 85
Kirkwall Pl. e2. 23K 52
Kirkwood Rd. se15. 22S 76
Kirtley Rd. se26. 24X 88
Kirtling St. sw8. 15Q 61
Kirton Rd. e13. 30J 55
Kitchener Rd. e7. 30H 41
Kitchener Rd. n2. 13A 22
Kitchener Rd. Cro. 19Zb 90
Kitson Rd. se5. 19Q 63
Kitto Rd. se14. 23S 76
Kiver Rd. n19. 17E 36
Klea Av. sw4. 15U 73
Knapmill Rd. se6. 05W 80
Knapmill Way se6. 25W 88
Knapp Rd. e3. 25L 53
Knaresborough Pl. sw5.
 11O 60
Knatchbull Rd. nw10. 5H 31
Knatchbull Rd. se5. 18R 74
Knebworth Rd. n16. 20F 37
Kneller Gdns. Twi. 1dT 93
Kneller Rd. se4. 24T 77
Kneller Rd. Twi. 1dU 93
Knightland Rd. e5. 22E 38
Knighton Pk. Rd. se26.
 23Y 87
Knighton Rd. e7. 29F 41
Knightrider St. ec4. 19M 51
Knights Av. w5. 2N 56
Knight's Hill se27. 18Y 85
Knights La. n9. 22Ad 17
Knight's Rd. e16. 29N 67
Knightsbridge
 sw1. 1-161 & 2-124
 sw7. 163 & up 14N 61
Knightsbridge Grn. 13N 61
Knight's Hill Sq. se27.
 18X 85
Knivett Rd. sw6. 11Q 59
Knockholt Rd. se9. 81U 79
Knoll Rd. sw18. 11U 72
Knollys Rd. sw16. 18X 85
Knott St. e1. 24L 52
Knott St. se8. 25Q 65
Knottisford St. e2. 23K 52
Knott's Grn. Rd. e10. 26C 27
Knowle Rd. sw9. 18S 74
Knowle Rd. Twi. 1cV 93
Knowles Hill Cres. se13.
 27U 78
Knowsley Rd. sw11. 13S 73

Knox Rd. e7. 29H 40
Knox Rd. sw11. 12S 72
Knox St. w1. 14L 49
Knoyle St. se14. 24Q 64
Knutsford St. sw8. 16R 73
Kohat St. sw19. 11Y 83
Kossuth St. se10. 28P 66
Kylemore Rd. nw6. 11G 33
Kymberley Rd. Har. 1bC 12
Kynaston Av. Cro. 19Zc 90
Kynaston Cres. Cro. 19Zc 90
Kynaston Rd. n16. 21E 38
Kynaston Bro. 29Y 89
Kynaston Rd. Cro. 19Zc 90
Kyrle Rd. sw11. 14U 73
Kyverdale Rd. n16. 21D 26

Laburnham Gdns. n21.
 19Ae 16
Laburnham Gro. n21. 19Ae 16
Laburnham Rd. n17. 20Ab 17
Laburnum Av. n9. 21Ad 17
Laburnum Rd. sw19. 12Z 92
Laburnum St. e2. 21J 51
Lacey St. e3. 25J 53
Lackington St. ec2. 20L 51
Lacland Pl. sw10. 12Q 60
Lacon Rd. se22. 21T 75
Lacy Rd. sw15. 9S 71
Ladas Rd. se27. 19Y 86
Ladbroke Cre. w11. 10L 47
Ladbroke Gdns. w11. 10M 47
Ladbroke Gro.
 w11. 1-137 & 2-108
 w10. 110, 139 & up 9K 47
Ladbroke Rd. w11. 10M 47
Ladbroke Sq. w11. 10M 47
Ladbroke Ter. w11. 10M 47
 10M 47
Ladbrook Rd. se25. 20Zb 90
Ladycroft Rd. se13. 25S 77
Lady Margaret Rd.
 nw5. 1-83 & 2-70.
 n19. 72, 87 & up 16F 35
Ladysmith Av. e6. 31J 55
Ladysmith Av. Ilf. 35D 42
Ladysmith Rd. e16. 28K 54
Ladysmith Rd. n17. 21A 26
Ladysmith Rd. n18. 22Ac 17
Ladysmith Rd. Har. 1bAa 12
Lady Somerset Rd. nw5.
 15F 35
Ladywell Pk. se13. 26U 77
Ladywell Rd. se13. 25T 77
Lafone St. se1. 21N 63
Lahore Rd. Cro. 20Zd 91
Lainson St. sw18. 10V 82
Laitwood Rd. sw12. 15V 84
Lake Rd. sw19. 10Y 82
Lake St. e1. 23M 52
Lake View Edg. 3Ac 13
Lakedale Rd. se18. 35Q 95
Lakefield Rd. n22. 19A 25
Lakefield Gdns. Cro. 18Zc 90
Lakehall Rd. Cro. 18Zc 90
Lake House Rd. e11. 29E 40
Lakeside Av. Ilf. 31B 29
Lakeside Rd. n13. 18Ad 16
Laleham Av. Edg. 5Ae 13
Laleham Rd. se6. 26V 88
Lalor St. sw6. 9R 71
Lamb La. e8. 22H 38
Lamb La. se10. 26Q 65
Lamb St. e1. 21L 51

Lamb Wlk. se1. 20O 63
Lamberhurst Rd. se27.
 18Y 85
Lambert Av. sw14. 3S 69
Lambert Rd. e16. 29M 55
Lambert Rd. n12. 13Ac 14
Lambert Rd. sw2. 17U 74
Lambert St. n1. 18H 36
Lambeth Bridge. sw1. 17O 62
Lambeth Hill ec4. 19M 51
Lambeth Rd. se1. 17O 62
Lambeth Rd. Cro. 18Ze 91
Lambeth Sq. se1. 18N 62
Lambeth St. e1. 21M 52
Lambeth Wlk. se11. 17O 62
Lambeth High St. se11.
 17O 62
Lambeth Palace Rd. se1.
 17O 62
Lamble St. nw5. 14F 35
Lambolle Pl. nw3. 13G 34
Lambolle Rd. nw3. 13G 34
Lambourn Rd. sw4. 15S 73
Lambourne Rd. Bar. 35H 43
Lambourne Rd. Ilf. 35E 42
Lambrooke Ter. sw6. 9R 71
Lambs Ct. wc1. 17L 50
Lamb's Passage ec1. 20L 51
Lamb's Conduit St. wc1.
 17L 50
Lambton Rd. n19. 17D 24
Lambton Rd. sw20. 8Z 92
Lamerock Rd. se12. 28X 89
Lamerton St. se8. 25Q 65
Lammas Rd. e9. 24H 38
Lammas Pk. Gdns. w5. 1N 56
Lammas Pk. Rd. w5. 1N 56
Lammermoor Rd. sw12.
 15V 84
Lamont Rd. sw10. 12Q 60
Lampeter St. n1. 20H 37
Lampmead Rd. se12. 28T 78
Lamprell St. e3. 25H 53
Lanark Pl. w9. 12K 48
Lanark Villas w9. 12K 48
Lanbury Rd. se15. 23T 76
Lancaster Av. e18. 30B 29
Lancaster Av. se27. 19W 86
Lancaster Av. sw19. 9X 82
Lancaster Av. Bar. 35H 43
Lancaster Dri. nw3. 13G 34
Lancaster Gdns. w13. 1aN 94
Lancaster Gate w2. 12M 48
Lancaster Gate Ter. w2.
 12M 48
Lancaster Gro. nw3. 13G 34
Lancaster Mews w2. 12M 48
Lancaster Mews w11. 10L 47
Lancaster Pl. wc2. 17M 50
Lancaster Rd. e7. 29H 41
Lancaster Rd. e11. 28E 40
Lancaster Rd. e17. 24A 26
Lancaster Rd. r4. 18D 24
Lancaster Rd. n11. 17Ab 16
Lancaster Rd. n18. 21Ac 17
Lancaster Rd. nw10. 7F 32
Lancaster Rd. se25. 21Zb 90
Lancaster Rd. sw19. 9Y 82
Lancaster Rd. w5. 2M 44
Lancaster Rd. w11. 10L 47
Lancaster St. se1. 19N 62
Lancaster St. w2. 12M 48
Lancaster Wlk. w2. 12M 48
Lance Rd. Har. 1dC 12
Lance St. e14. 25M 53
Lancefield St. w10. 10J 47

Lancell St. N16. 21E 37
Lancelot Av. Wem. 2F 30
Lancelot Cre. Wem. 2F 30
Lancelot Rd. sw7. 13N 60
Lancelot Rd. Wem. 2F 30
Lanchester Rd. N6. 14B 23
Lancing Gro. N9. 21Ae 17
Lancing Rd. Cro. 17Zd 91
Lancing Rd. Ilf. 34D 42
Lancing St. NW1. 16K 50
Landcroft Rd. SE22. 21U 75
Landells Rd. SE22 21U 75
Landfield St. E5. 21F 38
Landford Rd. sw15. 8S 70
Landgrove Rd. sw19. 10X 82
Landor Rd. sw9. 17S 74
Landor Rd. w12. 7N 58
Landridge Rd. sw6. 10R 71
Landrock Rd. N8. 17C 24
Landseer Av. E12. 33G 43
Landseer Clo. Edg. 4Aa 13
Landseer Rd. E3. 25K 53
Landseer Rd. N19. 17E 36
Landseer St. sw11. 14R 73
Lane Close NW2. 8E 32
Lane, The, NW8. 12J 48
Lanercost Rd. sw2. 18W 85
Lanfranc St. SE1. 18O 62
Langbourne Av. N6. 15E 35
Langdale Rd. SE10 26R 77
Langdale Rd. Cro. 18Zb 90
Langdale St. E1. 22M 52
Langdon Cres. E6. 33J 43
Langdon Dri. NW9. 5D 19
Langdon Rd. E6 33J 43
Langdon Rd. N19. 15E 35
Langdon Pk. Rd. N6. 15D 23
Langford Pl. NW8. 12J 48
Langford Rd. sw6. 11R 72
Langham Gdns. Edg. 5Ab 13
Langham Gdns. Wem. 1E 30
Langham Pl. w1. 15L 49
Langham Rd. N15. 19A 25
Langham Rd. sw20 8Z 92
Langham Rd. Edg. 5Ab 13
Langham Rd. Twi. 1aY 93
Langham St. w1. 15L 49
Langhedge La. N18. 21Ac 17
Langland Gdns. NW3. 12F 34
Langler Rd. NW10. 9J 47
Langley Dri. E11. 30D 29
Langley La. sw8. 17Q 62
Langley Pk. NW7. 6Ac 13
Langley Rd. sw19. 10Za 92
Langley St. wc2. 17M 50
Langmead St. SE27. 19X 85
Langroyd Rd. sw17. 14W 84
Langside Av. sw15. 7T 70
Langside Cre. N14. 16Ad 15
Langstone St. E14. 25L 53
Langthorne St. E15. 27H 40
Langthorne St. sw6. 9Q 59
Langton Av. N20. 13Af 14
Langton Rd. NW2. 8G 33
Langton Rd. SE23. 22V 87
Langton Rd. sw9. 18R 74
Langton St. sw10. 12Q 60
Lanhill Rd. w9. 11K 47
Lanier Rd. SE13. 27U 78
Lankaster Gdns. N2. 13Aa 14
Lanrick Rd. E14. 27L 54
Lansdown Pl. SE19. 20Z 90
Lansdown Rd. E7. 30H 41
Lansdowne Cres. w11. 10M 47
Lansdowne Gdns. sw8.
17R 74

Lansdowne Gro. NW10. 6F 32
Lansdowne Hill SE27. 18X 85
Lansdowne Mews w11.
10N 59
Lansdowne Pl. SE1. 20O 63
Lansdowne Pl. SE10. 27R 78
Lansdowne Pl. wc1. 17K 50
Lansdowne Rise w11. 10M 47
Lansdowne Rd. E8. 22H 38
Lansdowne Rd. E11. 28E 40
Lansdowne Rd. E16. 29M 54
Lansdowne Rd. E17. 25C 27
Lansdowne Rd. E18. 29A 29
Lansdowne Rd. N3. 11Ab 14
Lansdowne Rd. N10. 16A 23
Lansdowne Rd. N17. 21Aa 17
Lansdowne Rd. SE7. 30Q 67
Lansdowne Rd. sw8. 17R 74
Lansdowne Rd. sw20. 8Z 92
Lansdowne Rd. w11. 10M 47
Lansdowne Rd. Cro. 19Ze 91
Lansdowne Rd. Har. 1bC 12
Lansdowne Rd. Ilf. 35D 42
Lansfield Av. N18. 22Ac 17
Lanvanor Rd. SE15. 22S 76
Lapstone Gdns. Har. 1C 18
Larch Rd. NW2. 9F 33
Larch Rd. sw12. 15W 84
Larches Av. sw14. 5S 69
Larches The, N13. 19Ad 16
Larcom St. SE17. 19P 63
Larden Rd. w3. 6N 58
Lark Row E2. 23J 52
Larkbere Rd. se26. 24X 88
Larkfield Av. Har. 1A 18
Larkfield Rd. Rich. 2S 68
Larkhall La. sw4. 16R 74
Larkhall Rise sw4. 16S 73
Larkway Clo. NW9. 6B 19
Larnaca St. SE1. 21O 63
Larnach Rd. w6. 9Q 59
Larpent Av. sw15. 8T 70
Lascelles Av. Har. 1cC 12
Lascelles Rd. E11. 27E 40
Lascelles St. NW1. 13K 48
Lascotts Rd. N22. 18Ab 16
Lassell St. SE10. 27P 66
Latchmere Gro. sw11. 13S 72
Latchmere Rd. sw11. 13S 72
Latchmere St. sw11. 13R 72
Lateward Rd. Bre. 1Q 56
Latham Rd. Twi. 1bU 93
Latham St. E14. 25M 53
Latham Rd. E6. 32H 43
Latimer Av. E6. 32J 43
Latimer Rd. E7. 30F 41
Latimer Rd. sw19. 11Y 83
Latimer Rd.
w11. 1-123 & 2-120
w10. 122, 125 & up 9M 47
Latimer Rd. Twi. 1bX 93
Latimer St. E1. 23L 52
Latona Rd. SE15. 21Q 64
Latymer Rd. N9. 21Ae 17
Latymer Way N9. 20Ad 17
Laud St. SE11. 17P 62
Laud St. Cro. 19Zf 91
Lauderdale Rd. w9. 11K 48
Laughton Rd. N22. 18A 24
Launcelot St. SE1. 18N 62
Launceston Gdns. Wem.
1H 30
Launceston Pl. w8. 12O 60
Launceston Rd. Wem. 1H 30

Launch St. E14. 26O 65
Laundry Rd. w6. 9Q 59
Laundry Yd. sw1. 16O 62
Laura Pl. E5. 23F 38
Laura Rd. E10. 25E 39
Lauradale Rd. N2. 14A 23
Laurel Av. Twi. 1bV 93
Laurel Clo. Edg. 5Ad 13
Laurel Gdns. w7. 1cM 94
Laurel Gro. SE20. 22Z 90
Laurel Gro. SE26. 23Y 87
Laurel Rd. sw13. 7R 70
Laurel Rd. Ted. 1dY 93
Laurel St. E8. 21G 37
Laurel Ter. N17. 22Ab 17
Laurel Way N20. 11Ad 14
Laurence Pountney La.
EC4. 20M 51
Laurie Gro. SE14. 24R 77
Laurier Rd. Cro. 21Zd 91
Lauriston Rd. E9. 23H 38
Lauriston Rd. sw19. 8Y 82
Lausanne Rd. N8. 18B 24
Lausanne Rd. SE15. 23R 76
Lavell St. N16. 20F 37
Lavender Av. NW9. 5D 19
Lavender Av. Mit. 13Za 92
Lavender Gdns. sw11. 14T 73
Lavender Gro. E8. 21H 38
Lavender Hill sw11. 14S 73
Lavender Rd. sw11. 12S 72
Lavender Rd. Cro. 17Zd 91
Lavender Sweep sw11.
13T 72
Lavender Ter. sw11. 13S 72
Lavender Wlk. sw11. 14T 73
Lavengro Rd. SE27. 19W 86
Lavenham Rd. sw18. 10V 82
Lavers Rd. N16. 21E 37
Lavina Gro. N1. 17J 50
Lavington Rd. w13. 1aM 94
Lavington Rd. Cro. 17Zf 91
Lavington St. SE1. 19N 63
Law St. SE1. 20O 63
Lawes St. E3. 25L 53
Lawford Rd. NW5. 16G 35
Lawford Rd. w4. 5Q 57
Lawless St. E14. 28M 54
Lawley St. E5. 23F 38
Lawn Av. sw14. 5T 69
Lawn Cres. Kew. 3R 68
Lawn Gdns. w7. 1cM 94
Lawn La. sw8. 17Q 62
Lawn Rd. NW3. 14G 35
Lawn Ter. SE3. 28S 78
Lawn, The, w12. 8N 59
Lawrence Av. E2. 32F 42
Lawrence Av. N13. 19Ac 16
Lawrence Av. NW7. 6Ad 13
Lawrence Ct. NW7. 6Ac 13
Lawrence Cres. NW9. 4Aa 13
Lawrence La. EC2. 19M 51
Lawrence Rd. E3. 25K 53
Lawrence Rd. E6. 31J 55
Lawrence Rd. E13. 30J 55
Lawrence Rd. N15. 20B 25
Lawrence Rd. N16. 21E 37
Lawrence Rd. N18. 22Ac 17
Lawrence Rd. SE25. 21Zc 90
Lawrence Rd. w5. 1O 56
Lawrence St. E16. 28L 54
Lawrence St. sw3. 13Q 60
Lawrie Pk. Av. SE26.
22Y 87
Lawrie Pk. Cres. SE26.
22Y 87

Lawrie Pk. Gdns. se26.
    22Y 87
Lawrie Pk. Rd. se26. 22Y 87
Lawson St. se1. 20O 63
Lawton Rd. e3. 24K 53
Lawton Rd. e10. 26D 27
Layard Rd. se16. 22O 64
Layard Rd. Cro. 19Za 90
Laycock St. n1. 18H 36
Layer Gdns. w3. 3M 45
Laystall St. ec1. 18K 50
Layton Cres. Cro. 18Zg 91
Layton Rd. Bre. 1P 56
Layton's Bldgs. se1. 19N 63
Lea Bridge e5. 23E 38
Leabourne Rd. n16. 21C 26
Lea Bridge Gdns. e10.
    24D 27
Leabon St. e15. 28J 54
Lea Bridge Rd.
  e5. 1-47 & 2-150.
  e10. 49-713 & 152-738.
  e17. 715, 740 & up.
    23E 38
Leacroft Av. sw12. 14V 84
Lead St. e14. 26P 65
Leadale Rd.
  n16. 1-81 & 2-46.
  n15. 60, 93 & up. 22C 26
Leadenhall St. ec3. 20M 51
Leafield Rd. sw20. 10Za 92
Leage St. ec1. 19K 51
Leagrave St. e5. 23E 38
Lea Hall Rd. e10. 25D 27
Leahurst Rd. se13. 27U 78
Leake St. se1. 17N 62
Lealand Rd. n15. 21C 25
Leamington Av. n17. 27C 27
Leamington Av. Mor. 9Zb 91
Leamington Gdns. Ilf. 36E 42
Leamington Pk. w3. 5L 45
Leamington Rd. Villas w11.
    10L 47
Leamore St. w6. 8O 58
Leamouth Rd. e14. 27M 54
Leander Rd. sw2. 17U 74
Leander Rd. Cro. 17Zc 90
Leaside Av. n10. 14A 23
Leaside Rd. e5. 23E 38
Leasowes Rd. e10. 25D 27
Leather La. ec1. 18L 50
Leatherdale St. e1. 23K 52
Leather Market se1. 20O 63
Leathermarket St. se1.
    20N 63
Leathwaite Rd. sw11. 14T 73
Leathwell Rd. se8. 26S 77
Lebanon Gdns. sw18. 10U 71
Lebanon Pk. Twi. 1aV 93
Lebanon Rd. sw18. 10U 71
Lebanon Rd. Cro. 20Ze 91
Lebanon St. se17. 20P 63
Lechmere Rd. nw2. 8G 32
Leckford Rd. sw18. 12V 83
Leconfield Pass. sw13. 6S 70
Leconfield Rd. n5. 20F 37
Ledbury Rd. w11. 10L 47
Ledbury Rd. Cro. 19Zg 91
Ledbury St. se15. 22Q 64
Ledder Av. e12. 33G 43
Lee Green se3. 28T 78
Lee Park se3. 28T 78
Lee Rd. se3. 28T 78
Lee Rd. Wem. 1H 30
Lee St. e14. 25L 53

Lee St. n11. 15Ac 15
Lee Ter. se3. 27T 78
Lee St. se18. 34Q 95
Lee Church St. se13. 28T 78
Lee Conservancy Rd. e9.
    25G 39
Lee High Rd.
  se13. 1-231 & 2-332.
  se12. 233, 334 & up.
    27T 78
Leeds Rd. Ilf. 35E 42
Leeds St. n18. 22Ac 17
Leeke St. wc1. 17K 50
Leeland Rd. w13. 1aM 94
Lee's Pl. w1. 14M 49
Leeside Cres. nw11. 10C 21
Lefevre Rd. e3. 25J 53
Leffern Rd. w12. 7N 58
Lefroy Rd. w12. 6N 58
Legard Rd. n5. 19F 37
Legatt Rd. se9. 30U 79
Leggatt Gro. n12. 12Ac 14
Leggatt Rd. e15. 27J 54
Leghorn Rd. nw10. 7J 46
Leghorn Rd. se18. 35Q 95
Leicester Gdns. Ilf. 35D 42
Leicester Pl. wc2. 16M 50
Leicester Rd. e11. 30C 29
Leicester Rd. n2. 13A 23
Leicester Rd. nw10. 5G 31
Leicester Rd. Cro. 20Ze 91
Leicester Sq. wc2. 16M 50
Leicester St. e14. 27M 54
Leicester St. wc2. 16M 50
Leigh Av. Ilf. 31B 29
Leigh Gdns. nw10. 8J 47
Leigh Rd. e6. 32H 43
Leigh Rd. e10. 27D 28
Leigh Rd. n5. 19F 37
Leigh St. wc1. 17K 50
Leigh Hunt St. se1. 19N 62
Leigham Av. sw16. 17W 85
Leigham Vale
  sw16. 1-69.
  sw2. 70 & up. 18W 85
Leigham Ct. Rd. sw16.
    17W 85
Leighton Av. e12. 33G 43
Leighton Clo. Edg. 4Aa 13
Leighton Cres. nw5. 16G 35
Leighton Gdns. nw10. 8J 46
Leighton Gro. nw5. 16G 35
Leighton Rd. nw5. 16G 35
Leighton Rd. w13. 1aN 94
Leighton Rd. Har. 1cAa 12
Leighton Rd. E. Cro.
    18Ze 91
Leinster Av. sw14. 4S 69
Leinster Gdns. w2. 12M 48
Leinster Pl. w2. 12M 48
Leinster Rd. n10. 15B 23
Leinster Rd. nw6. 11J 47
Leinster Sq. w2. 11M 48
Leinster St. w2. 12L 48
Leinster Ter. w2. 12M 48
Leith Rd. n22. 19Aa 16
Leithcote Gdns. sw16.
    17X 85
Leitrim Gro. sw11. 14R 73
Leman St. e1. 21M 52
Leman Pass. e1. 21M 52
Lemna Rd. e11. 28D 28
Lemuel St. sw18. 11U 72
Lena Gdns. w6. 8O 59
Lenham St. se12. 28T 78
Lenham Rd. se25. 20Za 90

Lennard Pl. nw8. 13J 48
Lennard Rd. se20. 23Z 90
Lennard Rd. Cro. 19Ze 91
Lennox Av. e17. 25C 27
Lennox Gdns. nw10. 7F 32
Lennox Gdns. sw1. 13O 61
Lennox Gdns. Ilf. 32D 42
Lennox Rd. e17. 25C 27
Lennox Rd. n4. 18E 36
Lennox Gdns. Mews sw1.
    13O 60
Lens Rd. e7. 30H 41
Lenthall Rd. e8. 21H 37
Lenthorp Rd. se10. 28P 66
Lentmead Rd. se12. 28X 89
Lenton St. se18. 34P 95
Leo St. se15. 22Q 64
Leonard Rd. e7. 29F 40
Leonard Rd. n9. 21Ad 17
Leonard St. e16. 31N 67
Leonard St. ec2. 20K 51
Leopold Av. sw19. 10Y 82
Leopold Rd. e17. 25C 27
Leopold Rd. n2. 13A 22
Leopold Rd. n18. 23Ac 17
Leopold Rd. nw10. 6H 32
Leopold Rd. sw19. 10X 82
Leopold Rd. w5. 3M 44
Leopold St. e3. 25L 53
Leopold St. se11. 17P 62
Lepine Cotts. se27. 19X 86
Leppoc Rd. sw4. 16U 73
Leroy St. se1. 20O 63
Lesbia Rd. e5. 23G 38
Lescombe Clo. se23. 24X 88
Lescombe Rd. se23. 24X 88
Leslie Gro. Cro. 20Ze 91
Leslie Rd. e11. 27F 40
Leslie Rd. e16. 29M 55
Leslie Rd. n2. 13A 22
Leslie Rd. sf.1. 23L 52
Leslie Pk. Rd. Cro. 20Ze 91
Lesly St. n7. 17G 04
Lessada St. e3. 24J 52
Lessar Av. sw4. 15U 73
Lessing St. se23. 24V 87
Lessingham Av. sw17.
    14X 84
Lester Av. e15. 28K 54
Leswin Rd. n16. 21E 37
Letchford Gdns. nw10. 7J 44
Letchworth St. sw17. 13X 84
Lethben Gro. n3. 10B 21
Lethbridge Rd. se13. 26S 77
Lett Rd. e15. 27H 40
Letterstone Rd. sw6. 10Q 59
Lettice St. sw6. 10R 71
Lettsom St. se5. 20S 75
Leucha Rd. e17. 24C 27
Leven Rd. e14. 27L 54
Levendale Rd. se23. 24W 88
Lever St. ec1. 19K 51
Leverett St. sw3. 13O 60
Leverson St. sw16. 15Y 84
Leverton Pl. nw5. 15G 35
Leverton St. nw5. 15G 35
Levett Gdns. Ilf. 35F 43
Levett Rd. Bar. 35H 43
Lewes Rd. n12. 13Ac 15
Leweston Pl. n16. 21D 25
Lewgars Av. nw9. 5C 19
Lewin Rd. sw14. 5S 69
Lewin Rd. se16. 16Y 84
Lewis Cres. nw10. 5G 31
Lewis Gdns. n2. 13Aa 14
Lewis Gro. se13. 26T 78

Lewis Rd. SE5.   19S 75
Lewis Rd. Mit.   12Za 92
Lewis St. NW1.   15H 35
Lewisham Hill SE13.   26S 78
Lewisham Pk. SE13.   26U 77
Lewisham Rd. NW5.   15F 35
Lewisham Rd. SE13.   26S 77
Lewisham St. SW1.   16N 62
Lewisham High Rd.
  SE14. 1-169 & 2-158A.
  SE4. 160, 171 & up.
                        24R 77
Lewisham High St. SE13.
                        26U 77
Lexden Rd. W3.   4M 45
Lexham Gdns. W8.   11O 60
Lexham Mews W8.   11O 60
Lexington St. W1.   16M 49
Ley St. Ilf.   33E 42
Leyborne Av. W13.   1N 56
Leyborne Pk. Kew.   3Q 57
Leybourne Rd. E11.   28D 28
Leybourne Rd. NW1.   15H 35
Leyburn Rd. N18.   22Ab 17
Leyden St. E1.   21L 51
Leyes Rd. E16.   30M 55
Leyland Rd. SE12.   28U 78
Leyland Rd. SE14.   23Q 64
Leys The NW11.   12A 22
Leysfield Rd. W12.   7N 58
Leyspring Rd. E11.   28D 28
Leythe Rd. W3.   5N 57
Leyton Grn. E10.   26C 27
Leyton Rd. E15.   27G 40
Leyton Rd. SW19.   12Z 92
Leyton Sq. SE15.   21Q 64
Leyton Green Rd. E10.
                        26C 27
Leyton Pk. Rd. E10.   27E 40
Leytonstone Rd. E15.   28G 40
Liardet St. SE14.   24Q 65
Liberia Rd. N5.   19G 37
Liberty St. SW9.   17R 74
Libra Rd. E3.   25J 53
Libra Rd. E13.   29J 54
Library St. SE1.   18O 62
Lichfield Gdns. Rich.   2T 68
Lichfield Gro. N3.   11Aa 14
Lichfield Rd. E3.   24K 53
Lichfield Rd. E6.   31K 55
Lichfield Rd. NW2.   9F 33
Lichfield Rd. Kew.   3R 68
Liddell Gdns. NW10.   8J 47
Liddington Rd. E15.   28J 54
Liddon Rd. E13.   29K 55
Lidfield Rd. N16.   20F 37
Lidgate Rd. SE15.   21Q 63
Lidgold St. E1.   21L 52
Lidiard Rd. SW18.   12W 83
Lidlington Pl. NW1.   16J 49
Lidyard Rd. N19.   16D 23
Liffler Rd. SE18.   35P 95
Lifford St. SW15.   9T 71
Lightcliffe Rd. N13.   18Ad 16
Lightfoot Rd. N8.   17B 24
Lilac Gdns. W5.   2O 56
Lilac St. W12.   7M 46
Lilburne Gdns. SE9.   31U 79
Lilburne Rd. SE9.   31U 79
Lilford Rd. SE5.   18S 74
Lilian St. N16.   20E 37
Lillian Av. W3.   3N 57
Lillian Rd. SW13.   7P 58
Lillie Rd. SW6.   9Q 59
Lillie Wk. W6.   10Q 59
Lillieshall Rd. SW4.   15S 73

Lillington St. SW1.   16P 61
Lily Gdns. Wem.   1J 44
Lily Rd. E17.   26C 27
Lilyville Rd. SW6.   10R 71
Limburn Rd. SW11.   13T 72
Lime Gro. N20.   10Af 14
Lime Gro. W12.   8N 58
Lime St. E17.   24B 27
Lime St. EC3.   20M 51
Lime Wlk. W5.   2N 56
Limehouse Causeway E14.
                        25M 53
Limerston St. SW10.   12Q 60
Limes Av. N12.   12Ad 14
Limes Av. N7.   6Ac 13
Limes Av. NW1.   10C 21
Limes Av. SW13.   6R 70
Limes Av. Cro.   17Zf 91
Limes Gro. SE13.   26T 78
Limes Rd. Cro.   19Zd 91
Limesdale Gdns. NW9.   5Aa 13
Limesford Rd. SE15.   23T 76
Limes Av., The, N11.   15Ac 15
Limetree Av. SE20.   22Z 90
Limpsfield Av. Cro.   17Zc 90
Linacre Rd. NW2.   8G 32
Linchmere Rd. SE12.   28V 89
Lincoln Av. N14.   16Ad 15
Lincoln Gdns. Ilf.   32D 42
Lincoln Mews NW6.   10H 33
Lincoln Rd. E7.   31H 41
Lincoln Rd. E13.   29L 55
Lincoln Rd. N2.   13A 23
Lincoln Rd. SE25.   22Zb 90
Lincoln Rd. Wem.   2G 30
Lincoln St. E3.   25K 53
Lincoln St. E11.   27E 40
Lincoln St. SW3.   13P 60
Lincoln's Inn WC2.   18L 50
Lincoln's Inn Fields WC2.
                        17L 50
Lincombe Rd. SE12.   28X 89
Lind St. SE8.   25S 77
Linda St. SW11.   12S 72
Lindal Rd. SE4.   24U 77
Lindale St. E14.   26M 53
Linden Av. NW10.   9J 47
Linden Av. Cro.   18Zb 90
Linden Av. Wem.   3F 30
Linden Gdns. W2.   11M 48
Linden Gdns. W4.   5P 57
Linden Gro. SE15.   22T 76
Linden Gro. SE26.   23Z 90
Linden Gro. Twi.   1cX 93
Linden Lea N2.   12B 22
Linden Rd. E17.   25B 27
Linden Rd. N10.   15B 23
Linden Rd. N15.   19B 25
Lindfield Gdns. NW3.   12F 34
Lindfield Rd. W5.   1K 44
Lindfield Rd. Cro.   21Zd 91
Lindley Rd. E10.   26E 39
Lindley St. E1.   23L 52
Lindo St. SE15.   23S 76
Lindore Rd. SW11.   13T 72
Lindrop St. SW6.   12R 72
Lindsell Rd. Bar.   34J 43
Lindsell St. SE10.   26R 77
Lindsey St. EC1.   19L 51
Linford Rd. E17.   27A 28
Linford St. SW8.   15R 73
Ling Rd. E16.   29L 54
Lingards Rd. SE13.   27T 78
Lingen St. E3.   26K 53
Lingfield Gdns. N9.   23Af 17
Lingfield Rd. SW19.   9Y 82

Lingham St. SW9.   17S 74
Lingwell Rd. SW17.   13W 83
Lingwood Rd. E5.   22D 26
Linhope St. NW1.   14L 49
Link St. E9.   23G 38
Link, The, W3.   4L 45
Links Av. Mor.   10Zb 92
Links Dri. N20.   11Ae 14
Links Rd. NW2.   6E 32
Links Rd. SW17.   14Y 84
Links Rd. W3.   3L 45
Links, The, E17.   24B 27
Linkside N12.   11Ac 14
Linkway SW20.   8Zb 92
Linley Rd. N17.   20Aa 17
Linnell Clo. NW11.   11C 22
Linnell Dri. NW11.   11C 22
Linnell Rd. SE5.   20R 75
Linom Rd. SW4.   16T 74
Linscott Rd. E5.   23F 38
Linsey St. SE16.   21O 64
Linstead St. NW6.   11G 33
Lintaine Gro. W14.   10Q 59
Linthorpe Rd. N16.   21D 26
Linton Cres. N18.   21Ac 17
Linton Gro. SE27.   19Y 86
Linton Rd. Bar.   34H 43
Linton St. N1.   19J 51
Linver Rd. SW6.   10R 71
Linzee Rd. N8.   17B 24
Lion Rd. N9.   22Ad 17
Lion Rd. Cro.   19Zc 90
Lion Rd. Twi.   1bV 93
Lion St. SE17.   19O 63
Lionel Gdns. SE9.   31U 79
Lionel Mews W10.   9L 47
Lionel Rd. SE9.   31U 79
Lionel Rd. Bre.   3P 56
Lionel Rd. Kew.   2O 56
Liongate Gdns. Rich.   2S 68
Liphook Cre. SE23.   22R 87
Lisbon St. E1.   22L 52
Lisburne Rd. NW3.   14F 35
Lisford St. SE15.   21R 75
Lisgar Ter. W14.   10O 59
Liskeard Gdns. SE3.   29S 78
Lisle St. WC2.   16M 50
Lismore Circ. NW5.   14F 35
Lismore Rd. N15.   20A 25
Lismore Rd. NW5.   14F 35
Lissenden Gdns. NW5.   15F 35
Lisson Gro. NW1.   13K 48
Lisson St. NW1.   13L 48
Lister Gdns. N18.   19Ac 16
Lister Mews N7.   17F 36
Liston Rd. N17.   21Aa 17
Liston Rd. SW4.   15S 73
Listowel St. SW9.   18R 74
Listria Pk. N16.   21E 37
Litchfield Av. E15.   28H 40
Litchfield Gdns. NW10.
                        7G 32
Litchfield St. WC2.   16M 50
Litchfield Way NW11.   12B 22
Lithgow St. SW11.   12S 72
Lithos Rd. NW3.   12G 34
Litlington St. SE16.   22O 64
Little Britain EC1.   19L 51
Little Heath SE7.   32Q 95
Little Hill E5.   22D 26
Little St. EC1.   19K 50
Little Albany St. NW1.
                        15K 49
Little Bentinck St. W1.
                        15L 49
Little Bury St. N9.   20Ae 17

Little Cadogan Pl. sw1. 14O 61	Livingstone Rd. sw11. 12S 72	London Fields e8. 22H 38
Little Camden St. nw1. 16J 49	Livingstone Rd. Cro. 19Za 90	London Fields W. Side e8. 22H 38
Little Chester St. sw1.15O 61	Lizard St. ec1. 19K 51	London La. e8. 22H 38
Little Church St. nw8.13L 48	Lizban St. se3. 29R 79	London Rd. e5. 22F 38
Little College St. ec4.19M 51	Llanelly Rd. nw2. 11E 33	London Rd. e13. 29J 54
LittleCollege St. sw1. 17O 62	Llanover Rd. se18. 33R 95	London Rd. se1. 19O 62
Little Cross St. n1. 19H 37	Llanover St. Wem. 2E 30	London Rd. se23 22W 87
Little Dean St. w1. 16M 49	Llanvanor Rd. nw11. 11E 33	London Rd.
Little Ealing La. w5. 1O 56	Llewellyn St. se16. 21O 64	sw16. 1102-1544
Little Earl St. wc2. 16M 50	Lloyd Av. sw16. 17Za 90	& 1109-1599
Little Ebury St. sw1.14P 61	Lloyd Rd. e6. 32J 43	Cro. Remainder 17Za 90
Little Edward St. nw1. 15J 49	Lloyd Rd. e17. 24B 26	London Rd. Bar. 33J 43
Littlefield Rd. Edg. 5Ab 13	Lloyd Sq. wc1. 18K 50	London Rd. Har. 1cD 12
Little Fitzroy St. w1.15K 49	Lloyd St. wc1. 18K 50	London Rd. Mit. 13Zb 92
Little George St. sw1.16N 62	Lloyd Baker St. wc1. 18K 50	London Rd. Mor. 10Zc 92
Little Goodge St. w1. 16L 49	Lloyd's Av. ec3. 21M 51	London Rd. Twi. 1bU 93
Little Howland St. w1. 15L 49	Lloyd's Pl. sw3. 13O 60	London Rd. Wem. 2G 30
Little Ilf. La. e12. 32F 43	Lloyd's Row ec1. 18K 50	London St. e2. 22K 52
Little Marlborough St. w1. 15M 49	Lloyd's Wlk. Cro. 21Zg 91	London St. e14. 24M 53
Littlemore Rd. Ilf. 35F 42	Loampit Hill se13. 25S 77	London St. ec3. 20M 51
Little New St. ec4. 18L 50	Loampit Vale se13. 26S 77	London St. n1. 17J 50
Little Newport St. wc2. 16M 50	Loanda St. e8. 21H 37	London St. se10. 26Q 65
Little North St. nw8. 13K 48	Lochaber Rd. se13. 28T 78	London St. w2. 12L 48
Little Orford St. sw3. 13P 60	Lochaline St. w6. 8P 59	London Wall ec2. 20L 51
Little Portland St. w1. 15L 49	Lochinvar St. sw12. 15V 84	Long Acre wc2. 17M 50
Little Pulteney St. w1. 16M 49	Lochnagar St. e14. 26L 54	Long Dri. w3. 6L 46
Little Queen's Rd. Ted. 1cY 93	Lock Sq. se17. 19P 63	Long La. ec1. 19L 51
Little Randolph St. nw1. 16H 35	Locket Rd. Har. 1bAa 12	Long La.
Little Russell St. wc1. 16L 50	Lockhart St. e3. 25L 53	n3. 1-221 & 2-280.
Little St. Andrew St. wc2. 17M 50	Lockhurst St. e5. 23F 38	n2. 223, 282 & up. 12A 22
Little St. James's sw1. 15N 61	Lockington Rd. sw8. 15R 73	Long La. se1. 20N 63
Little Smith St. sw1. 16O 62	Lockner Rd. n1. 21H 37	Long La. Cro. 22Zd 91
Little Somerset St. e1.21M 51	Locksley St. e14. 25L 53	Long Rd. sw4. 15T 73
Little Stanhope St. w1. 15N 61	Lockwood Rd. se16. 22O 64	Long St. e2. 21K 51
Little Surrey St. se1. 18N 62	Lockwood Rd. Ilf. 34E 42	Long Yd. wc1. 17K 50
Little Titchfield St. w1. 15K 49	Lockyer St. se1. 20N 63	Longbeach Rd. sw11. 14S 73
Littleton Cres. Har. 1bE 12	Locton St. e3. 25J 53	Longbridge Rd. Bar. 34H 43
Littleton Rd. Har. 1aE 12	Loddiges Rd. e9. 23H 38	Longbridge Rd. Ilf. 36F 43
Little Trinity La. ec4. 19M 51	Loder St. se15. 22P 64	Longdown Rd. se6. 25X 88
Littleton St. sw18. 12W 83	Lodge Av. sw14 5S 69	Longfellow Rd. e3. 24K 53
Little Turner St. e1. 22M 52	Lodge Av. Bar. 36J 43	Longfellow Rd. e17. 25C 27
Little William St. se11. 18Q 62	Lodge Av. Cro. 17Zf 91	Longfield Av. e17. 24D 27
Little Winchester St. ec2. 20L 51	Lodge Av. Har. 2B 18	Longfield Av. w5. 1M 44
Littlewood Rd. se13. 27U 78	Lodge Clo. n18. 20Ac 16	Longfield Rd. w5. 1L 44
Livermere Rd. e8. 21H 37	Lodge Dri. n13. 18Ac 16	Longfield St. sw18. 10V 82
Liverpool Gro. se17. 19P 63	Lodge La. n12. 12Ac 14	Longfield Wk. w5. 1L 44
Liverpool Rd. e10. 27C 28	Lodge Pl. nw8. 13K 48	Longford St. nw1. 15K 49
Liverpool Rd. e16. 28L 54	Lodge Rd. nw4. 9A 21	Longhedge St. sw11. 14R 73
Liverpool Rd.	Lodge Rd. nw8. 13K 48	Longhill Rd. se6. 27W 89
n1. 1-393 & 2-296	Lodge Rd. Cro. 18Zd 91	Longhurst Rd. se13. 27U 78
n7. 298, 395 & up 18G 36	Lodge Rd. Ted. 1cY 93	Longlands Dri. n20. 12Ad 14
Liverpool Rd. w5. 2N 56	Lodore Gdns. nw9. 6B 20	Longley Av. Wem. 3H 30
Liverpool Rd. Cro. 19Zb 90	Lodore St. e14. 26M 53	Longley Rd. sw17. 13Y 83
Liverpool St. ec2. 20L 51	Loftie St. se16. 22N 64	Longley Rd. Cro. 18Ze 91
Liverpool St. n1. 18J 50	Lofting Rd. n1. 18H 36	Longley Rd. Har. 1cB 12
Liverpool St. wc1. 18K 50	Loftus Rd. w12. 8M 46	Longley St. se1. 21P 64
Livingstone Rd. e15. 27J 54	Logan Pl. w8. 11O 59	Longmead Rd. sw17. 13X 83
Livingstone Rd. e17. 26C 27	Logan Rd. n9. 23Ad 17	Longmoore St. sw1. 15P 61
Livingstone Rd. n13.17Ab 16	Lolesworth St. e1. 21L 51	Longnor Rd. e1. 24K 52
	Lollard St. se11. 18O 62	Longridge Rd. sw5. 11P 59
	Loman St. se1. 19N 63	Longstaff Cres. sw18. 11U 71
	Lombard Av. Ilf. 35E 42	Longstaff Rd. sw18. 11U 71
	Lombard St. ec4. 18M 50	Longstone Av. nw10. 7H 32
	Lombard Rd. se7. 29P 67	Longstone Rd. sw17. 15Y 84
	Lombard Rd. sw11. 12R 72	Longton Av. se26. 21X 87
	Lombard Rd. sw19. 11Za 92	Longton Gro. se26. 22X 87
	Lombard St. e1. 21L 52	Longville Rd. se11. 18O 62
	Lombard St. ec3. 20M 51	Longwood Dri. sw15. 7U 70
	Lomond Clo. Wem. 3H 30	Loning The nw9. 6A 20
	Lomond Gro. se5. 19Q 63	Lonsdale Av. e6. 31K 55
	Longcroft Rd. se5. 20Q 63	Lonsdale Av. Wem. 3G 30
	Londesborough Rd. n16. 20F 37	Lonsdale Cres. Ilf. 33C 42
	London Bridge ec4. 20N 63	Lonsdale Gdns. Cro. 17Zb 90
		Lonsdale Rd. e11. 29D 28
		Lonsdale Rd. nw6. 10J 47

Lonsdale Rd. se25. 22Zb 90
Lonsdale Rd. sw13. 6R 70
Lonsdale Rd. w4. 6O 58
Lonsdale Rd. w11. 10M 47
Lonsdale Sq. n1. 18H 36
Lopen Rd. n18. 20Ac 17
Loraine Pl. n7. 17F 36
Loraine Rd. n7. 17F 36
Loraine Rd. w4. 4Q 57
Lord North St. sw1. 17O 62
Lordship Gro. n16. 20E 37
Lordship La.
n17. 1-421 & 2-470.
n22. 423-741 & 478-748.
18Aa 16
Lordship La. se22. 21T 75
Lordship Pl. sw3. 13Q 6(
Lordship Pk. n16. 20E 37
Lordship Rd. n16. 20D 2?
Lordship Ter. n16. 20E 37
Lordsmead Rd. n17.
21Aa 17
Lorenco Rd. n17. 21Ab 17
Lorenzo St. wc1. 17J 5(
Loretto Gdns. Har. 2A 18
Loring Rd. n20. 13Ae 14
Loris Rd. w6. 8O 5?
Lorn Rd. sw9. 17R 7(
Lorne Av. Cro. 23Zd 9?
Lorne Clo. nw8. 13K 48
Lorne Gdns. w11. 9N 5?
Lorne Gdns. Cro. 23Zd 9?
Lorne Rd. e7. 30F 4?
Lorne Rd. e17. 25C 27
Lorne Rd. n4. 18D 2?
Lorne Rd. Har. 1bAa 1?
Lorrimore Rd. se17. 19Q 6?
Lorrimore Sq. se17. 19Q 6?
Lothair Rd. w5. 1N 5(
Lothair Rd. N. n4. 19C 2?
Lothair Rd. S. n4. 18C 24
Lothbury ec2. 20M 5?
Lothian Rd. sw9. 18R 74
Lothrop St. w10. 9K 47
Lots Rd. sw10. 12R 7?
Loubet St. sw17. 14Y 84
Loudoun Rd. nw8. 12H 34
Loudoun Rd. Mews nw8.
12H 34
Loughborough Pk. sw9.
18T 74
Loughborough Rd. sw9.
18S 74
Loughborough St. se11.
18P 62
Louisa St. e1. 23L 5?
Louise Rd. e15. 28G 4(
Louisville Rd. sw17. 14W 84
Louvaine Rd. sw11. 12T 72
Louvaine St. e1. 24L 53
Lovatt Clo. nw2. 7E 32
Love La. e1. 23M 52
Love La. e5. 22F 38
Love La. ec2. 19L 51
Love La. ec3. 20M 51
Love La. n17. 21Ab 17
Love La. se25. 22Zb 90
Love La. sw9. 17S 74
Love La. Mit. 13Zb 9?
Love Wk. se5. 19S 75
Loveday Rd. w13. 1aM 94
Lovegrove St. se1. 22Q 64
Lovelace Rd. se21. 19W 86
Lovelinch St. se15. 23Q 64
Loveridge Rd. nw6. 10G 33
Lovers Wk. n3. 11Ab 14

Lovers' Wk. w1. 14N 61
Lowden Rd. n9. 22Ae 17
Lowden Rd. se24. 19T 75
Lowder St. e1. 22N 64
Lowell St. e14. 24M 53
Lower Gro. sw18. 11U 72
Lower Mall w6. 8P 58
Lower Marsh se1. 18N 62
Lower Parkfields sw15. 8T 70
Lower Rd. e13. 29K 54
Lower Rd.
se16. 1-245 & 2-196.
se8. 198, 247 & up. 23O 64
Lower Rd. Har. 1cD 12
Lower Ter. nw3. 12F 34
Lower Adam St. wc2.
17M 50
Lower Addiscombe Rd. Cro.
20Ze 91
Lower Belgrave St. sw1.
15O 61
Lower Boston Rd. w7.
1cN 94
Lower Charles St. ec1.
18K 50
Lower Church St. Cro.
18Zf 91
Lower Clapton Rd. e5.
22F 33
Lower Common S. sw15.
8S 70
Lower Coombe St. Cro.
19Zg 91
Lower Downs Rd. sw20.
9Z 92
Lower Drummond St. nw1.
16K 50
Lower Grosvenor Pl. sw1.
15O 61
Lr. Harden St. se18. 31P 6?
Lr. James St. w1. 16M 49
Lr. John St. w1. 16M 49
Lower King St. nw1. 16J 49
Lr. Mortlake Rd. Rich. 2S 68
Lr. Pk. Rd. n11. 16Ac 15
Lr. Richmond Rd.
sw14. 1-173 & 2-58.
sw15. & Rich. remainder.
3S 69
Lr. Robert St. wc2. 17M 50
Lr. Seymour St. w1. 14L 49
Lr. Sloane St. sw1. 14P 61
Lr. Thames St. ec3. 20M 51
Lowfield Rd. nw6. 11G 33
Lowfield Rd. w3. 4L 45
Lowhall La. e17. 24C 27
Lowick Rd. Har. 1cA 12
Lowlands Rd. Har. 1cC 12
Lowman Rd. n7. 18F 36
Lowndes Pl. sw1. 14O 61
Lowndes Sq. sw1. 14N 61
Lowndes St. sw1. 14O 61
Lowood St. e1. 22M 52
Lowth Rd. se5. 19R 75
Lowther Hill se23. 24V 88
Lowther Rd. e17. 24A 27
Lowther Rd. n7. 18G 36
Lowther Rd. sw13. 6R 70
Loxford Av. e6. 31J 55
Loxford La. Ilf. 34G 43
Loxford Rd. Bar. 34H 43
Loxley Rd. sw18. 12V 83
Loxton Rd. se23. 23W 87
Loxwood Rd. n15. 20A 25
Luard St. n1. 17H 36
Lubbock St. se14. 23R 76

Lubeck St. sw11. 13S 72
Lucan Pl. sw3. 13P 60
Lucas Av. e13. 30J 55
Lucas Rd. e15. 27J 54
Lucas Rd. se17. 18Q 62
Lucas Rd. se20. 23Z 90
Lucas St. e1. 23M 52
Lucas St. se8. 25R 77
Lucerne Rd. n5. 19F 37
Lucerne Rd. Cro. 19Zc 90
Lucey Rd. se16. 21O 64
Lucian Rd. sw19. 11W 82
Lucien Rd. sw17. 14X 84
Lucknow St. se18. 35R 95
Lucy Cres. w3. 5K 45
Ludgate Circus ec4. 18M 50
Ludgate Hill ec4. 19M 50
Ludlow Rd. w5. 1K 44
Ludlow St. ec1. 19K 51
Ludlow Way n2. 12A 22
Ludwick Rd. se14. 24Q 65
Lugard Rd. se15. 22R 76
Luke St. ec2. 20K 51
Lullington Garth n12.
11Ac 14
Lullington Rd. se20. 21Z 90
Lulot St. n19. 15E 35
Lulworth Av. Har. 1C 18
Lulworth Rd. se15. 22S 76
Lumley St. w1. 14M 49
Luna Rd. Cro. 19Zb 90
Luna St. sw10. 12Q 60
Lundy St. w6. 9P 59
Lunham Rd. se19. 20Y 86
Lupton St. nw5. 16F 35
Lupus St. sw1. 15P 61
Lurgan Av. w6. 9Q 59
Lurgan St. w6. 9P 59
Lurline Gdns. sw11. 14R 73
Luscombe St. sw8. 17Q 62
Lushington Rd. nw10. 7J 14
Luther Rd. Ted. 1bY 93
Lutheran Pl. sw2. 17V 85
Luton Pl. se10. 27R 78
Luton Rd. e13. 29L 54
Luton Rd. e17. 24A 27
Luton St. nw8. 13K 48
Luttrel Av. sw15. 8T 70
Lutwyche Rd. se6. 24W 88
Luxemburg Gdns. w6. 9O 59
Luxford St. se16. 23P 64
Luxor St. se5. 19S 75
Lyal Mews sw1. 14O 61
Lyal Rd. e3. 24J 53
Lyal St. sw1. 14O 61
Lydden Gro. sw18. 11V 83
Lydden Rd. sw18. 11V 83
Lydeard Rd. e6. 32H 43
Lydford Av. n15. 20B 25
Lydford Rd. nw2. 9G 33
Lydford Rd. w9. 10K 47
Lyden Rd. sw4. 15S 73
Lydhurst Av. sw2. 17W 85
Lydia St. e1. 23L 52
Lyford Rd. sw18. 13V 83
Lyford St. se18. 31P 67
Lyham Rd. sw2. 16T 74
Lyme Gro. e9. 23H 38
Lyme St. nw1. 16H 35
Lyminge Gdns. sw18. 13V 83
Lymington Av. n22. 18A 24
Lymington Rd. nw6. 11G 34
Lynbridge Gdns. n13.
19Ac 16
Lyncroft Gdns. nw6. 11F 34

Lyncroft Gdns. w13. 1N 56
Lyndale nw2. 10F 33
Lyndale Av. nw2. 10E 33
Lyndhurst Av. n12. 14Ac 15
Lyndhurst Av. nw7. 6Ab 13
Lyndhurst Clo. nw10. 6E 31
Lyndhurst Dri. e10. 27D 28
Lyndhurst Gdns. nw3. 13G 34
Lyndhurst Gdns. Bar. 35G 43
Lyndhurst Gdns. Ilf. 35C 42
Lyndhurst Gro. se15. 20S 75
Lyndhurst Rd. n18. 22Ac 17
Lyndhurst Rd. n22. 18Ab 16
Lyndhurst Rd. nw3. 13G 34
Lyndhurst Rd. se15. 21R 75
Lyndhurst Rd. Cro. 18Z 90
Lyndhurst Sq. se15. 21R 75
Lyndhurst St. nw10. 6E 31
Lynedoch St. n1. 21J 51
Lynette Av. sw4. 15U 73
Lynford Gdns. Edg. 4Ad 13
Lynford Gdns. Ilf. 36E 42
Lynmouth Gdns.Wem.1H 30
Lynmouth Rd. e17. 24C 27
Lynmouth Rd. n2. 14A 23
Lynmouth Rd. n16. 21D 25
Lynmouth Rd. Wem. 1H 30
Lynn Rd. sw12. 15U 73
Lynn Rd. Ilf. 34D 42
Lynsted Gdns. se9. 31T 79
Lynton Av. nw9. 7B 20
Lynton Av. w13. 1aL 94
Lynton Cres. Ilf. 33C 42
Lynton Gdns. n9. 21Ae 17
Lynton Gdns. n11. 16Ab 15
Lynton Mead n20. 11Ad 14
Lynton Rd. e11. 27F 40
Lynton Rd. n8. 17B 24
Lynton Rd. nw6. 10J 47
Lynton Rd. se1. 21F 60
Lynton Rd. w3. 4M 45
Lynton Rd. Cro. 17Zd 91
Lynwood Gdns. Cro. 177g 91
Lynwood Rd. sw17. 14X 84
Lynwood Rd. w5. 2K 44
Lyon Rd. Har. 1bC 12
Lyon St. n1. 17H 36
Lyon Pk. Av. Wem. 2G 30
Lyon's Pl. nw8. 12K 48
Lyric Rd. sw13. 6R 70
Lysander Gro. n19. 16D 23
Lysia St. sw6. 9Q 59
Lysias Rd. sw12. 14U 73
Lysons Wk. sw15. 7T 70
Lytcott Gro. se22. 20U 75
Lyte St. e2. 23J 52
Lytham Gro. w5. 3J 44
Lytham St. se17. 19P 63
Lyttleton Rd. e10. 26F 39
Lyttleton Rd. n2. 12B 22
Lytton Av. n13. 18Ae 16
Lytton Gro. sw15. 9U 71
Lytton Rd. e11. 28D 28
Lyveden Rd. se3. 29R 79
Lyveden Rd. sw17. 13Y 83

Maberley Rd. se19. 21Za 90
Maberley Rd. Cro. 23Zb 90
Mabledon Pl. wc1. 16K 50
Mablethorpe Rd. sw6. 9Q 59
Mabley St. e9. 24G 39
Mabyn Rd. se18. 35P 95
Macaulay Rd. e6. 31J 52
Macaulay Rd. sw4. 15S 73
McCall Cres. se7. 31Q 67

Macclesfield Rd. se25.
    22Zc 90
Macclesfield St. ec1. 19K 51
Macclesfield St. w1. 16M 50
McCullum Rd. e3. 24J 53
McDermott Rd. se15. 21S 76
Macdonald Rd. e7. 29F 40
Macdonald Rd. n11. 14Ac 15
McDowall Rd. se5. 19R 75
Macduff Rd. sw11. 14R 73
Mace St. e2. 23J 52
Macfarlane Rd.w12. 8N 59
Machell Rd. se15. 23S 76
Mackay Rd. sw4. 15S 73
McKay Rd. sw19. 8Z 92
Mackenzie Rd. Cro. 23Za 90
McKerrell Rd. se15. 22R 76
Mackeson Rd. nw3. 14F 35
Mackie Rd. sw2. 18V 85
Macklin St. wc2. 17L 50
Macks Rd. se16. 22O 64
Maclaren St. e5. 24F 39
Maclean Rd. se23. 24U 76
Maclise Rd. w14. 9O 59
MacLeod St. se17. 19P 63
McNiel Rd. se5. 20S 75
Macoma Rd. se18. 34Q 95
Macoma Ter. se18. 34Q 95
Macready Pl. n7. 17F 36
Macroom Rd. w9. 10K 47
Macquarie Way e14. 26P 65
Maddams St. e3. 26L 53
Maddin Rd. se26. 24Y 88
Maddox St. w1. 15M 49
Madeira Av. e11. 27E 40
Madeira Rd. n13. 19Ad 16
Madeira Rd. sw16. 17Y 85
Madeley Rd. w5. 2L 44
Madeline Rd. se20. 21Z 90
Madras Pl. n7. 18G 36
Madras Rd. Ilf. 35H 40
Madrid Pl. sw8. 17Q 62
Madrid Rd. sw13. 7Q 58
Madron St. se17. 20P 63
Mafeking Av. e6. 31J 55
Mafeking Av. Bre. 2P 56
Mafeking Av. Ilf. 35D 42
Mafeking Rd. e16. 28K 54
Mafeking Rd. n17. 22A 26
Magdala Rd. n19. 15E 35
Magdalen Rd. sw18. 12V 83
Magdalen St. se1. 20N 63
Magee St. se11. 18Q 62
Magnolia Rd. w4. 4Q 57
Maguire St. se1. 21N 63
Maida Hill W. w2. 12L 48
Maida Vale w9. 12K 48
Maiden La. ec4. 19M 51
Maiden La. wc2. 17M 50
Maiden Rd. e15. 28H 40
Maidenhead Ct. ec1. 19L 51
Maidenstone Hill se10.
    26R 77
Maidman St. e3. 24K 53
Maid of Honour Row. Rich.
    1T 68
Maidstone Rd. n11. 16Ab 15
Maidstone St. e2. 22J 52
Maidstone Ter. n11. 16Ac 15
Maismore St. se15. 21Q 64
Maitland Rd. e15. 28H 40
Maitland Rd. se20. 23Z 90
Maitland Pk. Rd. nw3.
    14G 35
Maitland Pk. Villas nw3.
    14G 35

Maiwand Rd. e5. 24F 39
Maize Row e14. 25M 53
Majendie Rd. se18. 34Q 95
Major Rd. e15. 27G 40
Major Rd. se16. 22O 64
Makepeace Av. n6. 15E 35
Makins St. sw3. 13P 60
Malabar St. e14. 25O 65
Malay St. e1. 22N 64
Malbrook Rd. sw15. 8T 70
Malcolm Rd. se20. 22Z 90
Malcolm Rd. se25. 21Zd 91
Malcolm Rd. sw19. 9Y 82
Malcombe Cres. nw4. 7B 20
Malden Av. se25. 22Zb 90
Malden Cres. nw1. 15H 35
Malden Pl. nw5. 14G 35
Malden Rd. n9. 21Ad 17
Malden Rd. nw5. 14G 35
Malden Rd. w3. 5M 45
Malet St. wc1. 16L 50
Maley Av. se27. 19W 85
Malford Gro. e18. 29B 28
Malfort Rd. se5. 20S 75
Malham Rd. se23. 23V 87
Mall Rd. w6. 8P 58
Mall, The, n14. 17Ad 16
Mall, The, sw1. 16N 61
Mall, The, w5. 2M 44
Mall, The, w8. 11M 48
Mallard St. e9. 25G 39
Mallet Rd. se13. 27U 78
Mallinson Rd. sw11. 13T 72
Mallord St. sw3. 13P 60
Mallow St. ec1. 20K 51
Malmesbury Rd. e3. 25K 53
Malmesbury Rd. e16. 28L 54
Malmsey Pl. se11. 17P 62
Malpas Rd. se4. 24S 77
Malt St. se1. 21Q 64
Malta Rd. e10. 25D 27
Malta St. ec1. 19K 50
Maltby St. se1. 21O 63
Malton St. se18. 35Q 95
Malva Rd. sw18. 11U 72
Malvern Dri. Ilf. 36F 43
Malvern Gdns. nw2. 10D 21
Malvern Rd. e6. 31J 55
Malvern Rd. e8. 21H 38
Malvern Rd. e11. 28E 40
Malvern Rd. n8. 18A 24
Malvern Rd. n17. 21A 26
Malvern Rd. nw6. 10J 47
Malvern Rd. Cro. 18Zc 90
Malvern Ter. n1. 18H 36
Malvern Ter. n9. 21Ae 17
Malvern Ter. nw6. 10J 47
Malwood Rd. sw12. 15U 73
Malyons Rd. se13. 25U 77
Malyons Ter. se13. 25U 77
Manaton Rd. se15. 22S 76
Manbey Gro. e15. 28G 40
Manbey Rd. e15. 28G 40
Manbey St. e15. 28H 40
Manbey Pk. Rd. e15. 28G 40
Manby Rd. e15. 27F 40
Manchester Gro. e14. 26P 65
Manchester Rd. e14. 26O 66
Manchester Rd. n15. 20C 25
Manchester Rd. w10. 9M 47
Manchester Rd. Cro. 19Zb 90
Manchester Sq. w1. 14L 49
Manchester St. w1. 14L 49
Manchester St. we1. 17K 50
Manchuria Rd. sw11. 14U 73
Manciple St. se1. 20O 63

Mandalay Rd. sw4. 15U 73
Mandeville Av. n14. 16Ad 15
Mandeville Pl. w1. 14L 49
Mandeville St. e5. 24F 38
Mandrake Rd. sw17. 13W 83
Mandrell Rd. sw2. 16U 74
Manette St. w1. 16M 50
Manfred Rd. sw15. 10T 71
Manilla St. e14. 25N 65
Manisty St. e14. 26M 54
Manley St. nw1. 14H 35
Mann St. se17. 20P 63
Manners St. se1. 17N 62
Manning Gdns. Har. 2C 18
Mannock Rd. n22. 19A 25
Manns Rd. Edg. 4Ac 13
Manor Cotts. n2. 12Aa 14
Manor Dri. n14. 15Af 15
Manor Dri. n20 14Ad 15
Manor Dri. nw7. 6Ac 13
Manor Dri. Wem. 3F 30
Manor Fields sw15. 8U 71
Manor Gdns. n7. 17E 36
Manor Gdns. sw3. 13P 60
Manor Gdns. sw20. 10Za 92
Manor Gdns. w3. 3O 57
Manor Gdns. Rich. 3S 68
Manor Gro. se15. 23Q 64
Manor Gro. Rich. 3S 68
Manor House nw1. 9H 33
Manor La.
  se13. 1-59 & 2-86
  se12. 65-257 & 88-178
                      28U 78
Manor Mount se23. 23W 87
Manor Pk. se13. 27T 78
Manor Pk. Rich. 3S 68
Manor Pl. e8. 22G 38
Manor Pl. se17. 19P 63
Manor Pl. w2. 12L 48
Manor Rd. e10. 25D 27
Manor Rd.
  e15. 1-347 & 2-118
  e16. 401-463   28K 54
Manor Rd. n16. 20E 37
Manor Rd. n17. 22a 17
Manor Rd. n22. 17Ab 16
Manor Rd. se4. 25S 77
Manor Rd. se25. 21Zb 90
Manor Rd. sw20. 10Za 92
Manor Rd. w13. 1aM 94
Manor Rd. Bar. 36H 43
Manor Rd. Har. 1aB 12
Manor Rd. Rich. 3T 68
Manor Rd. Twi. 1bX 93
Manor St. sw3. 13P 60
Manor St. sw4. 16S 73
Manor Way se3. 28T 78
Manor Way nw9. 6A 20
Manor Way Cro. 20Zh 91
Manor Ct. Rd. w7. 1cM 94
Manor Farm Rd. Wem. 2H 30
Manor House Gdns. se13.
                      28U 78
Manor La. Ter. se13. 27T 78
Manor Pk. Cres. Edg. 4Ac 13
Manor Pk. Gdns. Edg. 4Ac 13
Manor Pk. Rd. e12. 31G 41
Manor Pk. Rd. n2. 12A 22
Manor Pk. Rd. nw10. 6H 32
Manresa Rd. sw3. 13P 60
Manse Rd. n16. 21F 37
Mansel Rd. sw19. 9Y 82
Mansell Rd. w3. 5N 57
Mansell St. e1. 21M 51
Mansfield Av. n15. 20B 25

Mansfield Rd. e11. 30C 29
Mansfield Rd. e17. 25B 27
Mansfield Rd. nw3. 14F 35
Mansfield Rd. Ilf. 33E 42
Mansfield St. e2. 21J 51
Mansfield St. w1. 15L 49
Mansford St. e2. 22J 52
Mansion St. se5. 19Q 63
Manson Pl. sw7. 12O 60
Manstone Rd. nw2. 10F 33
Mantell St. n1. 18J 50
Manthorp Rd. se18. 34S 95
Mantilla Rd. sw17. 14X 84
Mantle Rd. se4. 24S 77
Manton Rd. se2. 36P 95
Manton Rd. w7. 1bN 94
Mantua St. sw11. 13P 59
Manus Way n20. 12Ae 14
Manville Rd. sw17. 14W 84
Manwood Rd. se4. 25U 77
Mape St. e2. 22K 52
Mapesbury Rd. nw2. 9G 33
Maple Gdns. Edg. 6Ab 13
Maple Gro. w5. 2N 56
Maple Rd. e11. 28C 28
Maple Rd. se20. 22Za 90
Maple St. w1. 15L 49
Mapledale Av. Cro. 21Zf 91
Mapledene Rd. e8. 21H 37
Maplestead Rd. sw2. 17V 85
Maplethorpe Rd. Cro.
                      18Zb 90
Mapleton Rd. sw18. 11U 71
Maplin Rd. e16. 29M 55
Maplin St. e3. 24K 53
Marban Pl. w9. 10J 47
Marban Rd. w9. 10J 47
Marble Arch w1. 14M 49
Marble Hill Clo. Twi. 1aU 93
Marble Hill Gdns. Twi.
                      1aU 93
Marcellus Rd. n7. 17E 36
March Rd. Twi. 1bU 93
March St. e14. 26M 53
Marchant St. se14. 24Q 64
Marchmont St. wc1. 17K 50
March's Pl. sw15. 8S 70
Marchmont Rd. Rich. 2T 68
Marchwood Cres. w5. 1L 44
Marcia Rd. se1. 21P 63
Marcilly Rd. sw18. 12T 72
Marco Rd. w6. 8O 58
Marcus St. e15. 28J 54
Marcus St. sw18. 11U 72
Mardale Dri. nw9. 6B 19
Mardale St. w12. 8N 58
Mardell Rd. Cro. 23Zc 90
Marden Cres. Cro. 17Zd 91
Marden Rd. se16. 22O 64
Marden Rd. Cro. 17Zd 91
Marder Rd. w13. 1aN 94
Mare St. e8. 22J 52
Maresfield Gdns. nw3. 12G 34
Margaret St. e9. 23H 38
Margaret St. n16. 21E 37
Margaret St. w1. 15L 49
Margaretta Ter. sw3. 13P 60
Margaretting Rd. e12. 30E 41
Margate Rd. sw2. 16T 74
Margery St. wc1. 18K 50
Margery Pk. Rd. e7. 29H 40
Margravine Gdns. w6. 9P 59
Margravine Rd. w6. 9P 59
Marham Gdns. sw18. 13V 83
Maria St. e2. 21J 51
Maria St. e14. 25O 65

Maria Ter. e1. 23L 52
Marian Sq. e2. 22J 52
Marian St. e9. 23G 38
Marian Way nw10. 6H 32
Marigold St. se16. 22O 64
Marine St. se16. 21O 64
Marinefield Rd. sw6. 11R 72
Mariner St. e1. 22M 52
Marischal Rd. se13. 27T 78
Maritime St. e3. 25L 53
Marius Rd. sw17. 14W 84
Marjorie Gro. sw11. 14T 73
Mark La. ec3. 20M 51
Mark Rd. n22. 19Aa 16
Mark St. e15. 28H 40
Mark St. ec2. 20K 51
Market Hill se18. 33O 95
Market Mews w1. 15N 61
Market Pl. n2. 13A 22
Market Pl. w1. 15L 49
Market Pl. w3. 4N 57
Market Pl. Bre. 1Q 56
Market Rd. n7. 17G 36
Market Rd. Rich. 3S 69
Market St. e1. 24L 52
Market St. e6. 33J 43
Market St. ec2. 20L 51
Market St. n7. 17H 36
Market St. se18. 33P 95
Market St. sw1. 16M 49
Market St. w2. 13L 48
Markfield Rd. n15. 22B 26
Markham Sq. sw3. 13P 60
Markham St. sw3. 13P 60
Markhouse Av. e17. 24C 27
Markhouse Rd. e17. 24C 27
Markmanner Rd. e17. 24C 27
Marksbury Av. Kew 3S 69
Marl St. sw18. 11T 72
Marlborough Av. n14. 16Ad 15
Marlborough Av. Edg. 5Ad 13
Marlborough Cres. w4. 5O 57
Marlborough Gdns. n20.
                      14Ad 15
Marlborough Gate w2. 12N 61
Marlborough Hill nw8. 12J 48
Marlborough Hill Har. 1cB 12
Marlborough La. se7. 30R 79
Marlborough Pl. nw8. 12J 48
Marlborough Rd. e7. 30H 41
Marlborough Rd. e8. 22H 38
Marlborough Rd. e15. 28F 40
Marlborough Rd. e18. 29A 29
Marlborough Rd. n9. 21Ae 17
Marlborough Rd. n19. 16E 36
Marlborough Rd. n22.
                      17Ab 16
Marlborough Rd. se13.
                      27T 78
Marlborough Rd. sw19.
                      10W 82
Marlboro' Rd. sw19. 13Y 83
Marlborough Rd. w4. 4P 57
Marlborough Rd. w5. 2N 56
Marlborough Rd. Har. 1bA 12
Marlborough Rd. Rich. 2U 68
Marlborough Rd. sw3. 13P 60
Marler Rd. se23. 24W 88
Marloes Rd. w8. 11O 60
Marlow Cres. Twi. 1bU 93
Marlow Rd. e9. 23G 38
Marlow Rd. se20. 22Zb 90
Marlowe Rd. e17. 27B 28
Marlton St. se10. 28P 66
Marmadon Rd. se18. 35P 95
Marmion Rd. sw11. 14T 73

Marmont Rd. SE15. 22R 76
Marmora Rd.SE22. 22U 76
Marne Av. N11. 15A 15
Marne St. w10. 9J 47
Marner St. E3. 26K 53
Marney Rd. sw11. 14T 73
Marnock Rd. SE4. 24U 77
Maroon St. E14. 24L 53
Marquess Gro. N1. 20G 37
Marquess Rd. N1. 19H 37
Marquis Clo. Wem. 3H 31
Marquis Rd. N4. 18D 24
Marquis Rd. N22. 18Ab 16
Marquis Rd. NW1. 16G 36
Marriott Rd. N4. 17D 24
Marriot Rd. N10. 14Aa 15
Marryat St. w6. 8P 58
Marryatt Rd. sw19. 9X 82
Marsala Rd. SE13. 26T 77
Marsden Rd. N9. 22Ad 17
Marsden Rd. SE15. 21T 75
Marsden St. NW5. 14G 35
Marsh Hill E9. 24G 39
Marsh La. E10. 25E 39
Marsh La. NW7. 6Ad 13
Marshall Gdns.SE1. 18O 62
Marshall Pl.SE16. 21O 63
Marshall Rd. N17. 20Aa 17
Marshall St. w1. 16M 49
Marshalsea Rd.SE1. 19N 63
Marsham St. sw1. 16O 62
Marsh Farm Rd. Twi. 1cV 93
Marshfield St. E14. 26O 65
Marshgate La. E15. 26J 53
Marsland Rd. SE17. 19P 63
Marston Rd. Twi. 1aY 93
Martaban Rd. N16. 21E 37
Martell Rd. SE21. 19X 86
Martha St. E1. 23M 52
Martin Cres. Cro. 17Ze 91
Martin Gro. Mor. 10Zb 92
Martin La. EC4. 20M 51
Martin St. E15. 27H 40
Martin St. w10. 9M 47
Martin Way sw20. 267-313 & 274-324 9Za 92
Martindale Rd. E16. 29M 54
Martindale Rd. sw12. 15V 84
Martindale Rd. sw14. 4T 69
Martineau Rd. N5. 18F 36
Martlett Ct. wc2. 17M 50
Martley Dri. Ilf. 33C 42
Marton Rd. N16. 20E 37
Martyr's Pa. SE18. 32P 95
Marville Rd. sw6. 10Q 59
Marvin St. E8. 22G 38
Mary Pl. w11. 9M 47
Mary St. E16. 28L 54
Mary St. N1. 19J 51
Mary Ter. NW1. 15J 49
Mary Ann St. E1. 22M 52
Maryann's Bldgs.SE8. 25Q 65
Maryland Pk. E15. 28G 40
Maryland Rd. E15. 27G 40
Maryland Rd. N22. 18Ab 16
Maryland Rd. Cro. 18Za 90
Maryland Sq. E15. 28G 40
Maryland St. E15. 27G 40
Marylands Rd. w9. 11K 48
Marylebone La. w1. 15L 49
Marylebone Rd. NW1. 13L 48
Marylebone St. w1. 14L 49

Marylebone High St. w1. 14L 49
Maryon Gro. SE7. 31P 67
Maryon Rd. SE7. 31P 67
Maryon Rd. SE7. 31P 67
Maryon Rd. SE18. 32P 95
Mary's Ter. Twi. 1bV 93
Masbro' Rd.w14. 9O 59
Mascalls Rd. SE7. 30Q 67
Mascotte Rd. sw15. 9S 71
Mashie Rd. w3. 6L 46
Maskell Rd. sw17. 11X 83
Mason St. SE17. 20P 63
Masons Av. Cro. 19Zf 91
Masons Av. Har. 1bA 12
Mason's Grn. La. w3. 3K 45
Massie Rd. E8. 22G 38
Massinger St.SE17. 20P 63
Mast House Ter. E14. 25P 65
Masterman Rd. E6. 31K 55
Matcham Rd. E11. 28F 40
Matheson Rd. w14. 10P 59
Matilda St. E2. 22J 52
Matilda St. N1. 18H 36
Matlock Rd. E10. 27C 28
Matlock St. E14. 24L 53
Matlock St. SE16. 22O 64
Matthew Parker St.sw1. 16O 62
Matthews St. sw11. 18S 73
Matthews Pk. Rd.E15.28H 40
Matthias Rd. N16. 20G 37
Mattison Rd. N4. 18C 24
Mattock La. w5. 1-36 & 82-87 & w13. 37-81. 1M 44
Maud Rd. E10. 27F 40
Maud Rd. E13. 29J 54
Maud St. E16. 28L 54
Maude Rd. SE5. 20R 75
Maude Ter. E17. 24B 27
Mauleverer Rd. sw2. 16T 74
Maunder Rd. w7. 1bN 94
Maurice Av. N22. 19A 25
Maurice Wlk. NW11. 12D 22
Mauritius Rd. SE10. 28P 66
Maury Rd. N16. 22E 38
Mauve St. E14. 26L 53
Maverton Rd. E3. 25J 53
Mawbey Rd. SE1. 21P 63
Mawbey St. sw8. 17Q 62
Mawson Clo. sw20. 9Za 92
Mawson La. w4. 6P 58
Maxey Rd. SE18. 34P 95
Maxilla Gdns. w10. 9L 47
Maxted Pk. Har. 1bC 12
Maxted Rd. SE15. 21S 75
Maxwell Rd. sw6. 11Q 60
Maxwelton Av. NW7. 6Ac 13
May Gdns. Wem. 1J 44
May Rd. E10. 25E 39
May Rd. E13. 29J 55
May Rd. Twi. 1cV 93
May St. w14. 10P 59
Mayall Rd. SE24. 18T 74
Maybank Av. E18. 30A 29
Maybank Rd. E18. 29A 29
Maybury Gdns. NW10. 8G 32
Maybury Rd. E13. 30L 55
Maybury St. sw17. 13Y 83
Maycross Av. Mor. 10Zb 92
Mayday Rd. Cro. 18Zd 91
Maydwell St.SE17. 19Q 63
Mayerne Rd. SE9. 31U 79

Mayes Rd. N22. 18A 24
Mayesbrook Rd. Bar. 36J 43
Mayesbrook Rd. Ilf. 36F 42
Mayfair Av. Ilf. 32E 42
Mayfair Gdns.N17. 20Ab 16
Mayfield Av. N12. 12Ad 14
Mayfield Av. N14. 16Ae 15
Mayfield Av. w4. 6O 58
Mayfield Av. w13. 1aN 94
Mayfield Av. Har. 1aB 12
Mayfield Cres. Cro. 17Zc 90
Mayfield Gdns. NW4. 9C 21
Mayfield Gdns. w7. 1cL 94
Mayfield Rd. E8. 21H 37
Mayfield Rd. E13. 28L 54
Mayfield Rd. N8. 18C 24
Mayfield Rd. w3. 4M 45
Mayfield Rd. sw19. 10Z 92
Mayfield Rd. Cro. 17Zc 90
Mayfields Wem. 3D 19
Mayfields Clo. Wem. 3D 19
Mayflower Rd. sw9. 17S 74
Mayflower St. SE16. 23N 64
Mayford Rd. sw12. 14R 84
Mayford Rd. sw12. 14V 84
Maygood St. N1. 18J 50
Maygrove Rd. NW6. 10G 33
Moyhill Rd. SE7. 29O 67
Mayland St. E1. 23L 52
Maynard Rd. E17. 26B 28
Maynard Rd. SE16. 23O 64
Mayo Rd. NW10. 6G 32
Mayo Rd. Cro. 19Zc 90
Mayola Rd. E5. 23F 38
Mayow Rd. SE23. 1-69 & 2-24 SE26. 24a, 71& up 23X 87
May's Bldgs. wc2. 17M 50
Mays Rd. Twi. 1dX 93
Maysoule Rd. sw11. 12T 79
Mayton St. N7. 17F 00
Mayville Rd. E11. 28E 40
Mayville Rd. Ilf. 33G 43
Mayville St. N16. 20G 37
Maze Hill SE10. 1-25 & 2-10 SE3. Remainder 27Q 66
Maze Pond SE1. 20N 63
Maze Rd. Kew 3Q 57
Maze Row E14. 24M 53
Mazenod Av. NW6. 11H 34
Mead Pl. E9. 23G 38
Mead Pl. Cro. 18Ze 91
Mead Plat w10. 5G 31
Mead Row SE1. 18O 62
Mead Way Har. 2C 18
Meadow Clo. sw20. 8Zb 92
Meadow Gdns. Edg. 5Ac 13
Meadow Garth NW10. 5G 31
Meadow Pl. sw8. 17Q 62
Meadow Rd. sw8. 17Q 62
Meadow Rd. sw19. 12Z 92
Meadow Rd. Bar. 36H 43
Meadow Row SE1. 19O 63
Meadow Side SE9. 30T 79
Meadow St. Cro. 19Zf 91
Meadow Way NW9. 6B 19
Meadow Way Wem. 2F 30
Meadow Bank Rd. NW9. 5C 19
Meadowcourt Rd. SE3.28T 78
Meadowcroft Rd. N13. 18Ad 16
Meadow Way The, Har. 1bAa 12

Meads La. Ilf. 35D 42
Meads Rd. N22. 19A 24
Meads Rd. Edg. 3Ab 13
Meads The NW7. 6Ac 13
Meadvale Rd. w5. 1K 44
Meadvale Rd. Cro. 21Zd 91
Meadway N9. 20Af 17
Meadway N14. 17Ae 16
Meadway NW7. 6Ae 13
Meadway NW11. 11C 22
Meadway sw20. 8Zb 92
Meadway Ilf. 35F 43
Meadway Twi. 1dV 93
Meadway Clo. NW11. 12C 22
Meadway Gate NW11. 11C 22
Meanley Rd. E12. 31G 43
Meard's St.w1. 16M 49
Meath Gdns. E2. 23K 52
Meath Rd. E15. 28J 54
Meath Rd. Ilf. 34F 42
Meath St. sw11. 15R 73
Mecklenburgh Sq. wc1. 17K 50
Medburn St. NW1. 16J 50
Medcroft Gdns. sw14. 4T 69
Medfield St. sw15. 7U 70
Medhurst Rd. E3. 24J 53
Median Rd. E5. 23F 38
Medina Rd. N7. 18E 36
Medland St. E14. 24M 53
Medlar St. se5. 19R 75
Medley Rd. NW6. 11G 33
Medora Rd. sw2. 17U 74
Medusa Rd. se6. 26U 77
Medway Rd. E3. 24J 53
Medway St. sw1. 16O 62
Medwin St. sw4. 17T 74
Meek St. sw10. 12Q 60
Meeson Rd. E15. 28H 40
Meeson St. E5. 24F 39
Meetinghouse Alley E1. 22N 64
Meeting House La. se15. 22R 76
Mehetabel Rd. E9. 23G 38
Melbourne Av. N13. 18Ab 16
Melbourne Av. w13. 1aM 94
Melbourne Gro. se22. 20T 75
Melbourne Pl. wc2. 17M 50
Melbourne Rd. E6. 32J 43
Melbourne Rd. E10. 26D 27
Melbourne Rd. E17. 24B 27
Melbourne Rd. sw19. 11Z 92
Melbourne Rd. Ilf. 33D 42
Melbourne Sq. sw9. 18R 74
Melbury Ct. w8. 10O 59
Melbury Rd. w14. 10O 59
Melcombe Pl. NW1. 14L 49
Melcombe St. NW1. 14L 49
Meldrum Rd. Ilf. 37E 42
Melford Av. Bar. 35G 43
Melford Rd. E11. 28E 40
Melford Rd. E13. 29K 54
Melford Rd. E17. 24B 27
Melford Rd. se22. 22V 87
Melford Rd. Ilf. 35E 42
Melfort Av. Cro. 18Zb 90
Melfort Rd. Cro. 18Zb 90
Melgund Rd. N5. 18G 36
Melina Pl. NW8. 12K 48
Melina Rd. w12. 7N 58
Melior St. se1. 20N 63
Melling St. se18. 35Q 95
Mellington St. E5. 21F 38
Mellish St. E14. 25O 65
Mellison Rd. sw17. 13Y 83

Mellitus St. w12. 6L 46
Melody Rd. sw18. 12T 72
Melon Rd. se15. 21R 76
Melrose Av. N22 19Aa 16
Melrose Av. NW2. 8F 32
Melrose Av. sw16. 17Zb 90
Melrose Av. sw19. 10W 82
Melrose Gdns. NW9. 4A 13
Melrose Gdns. w6. 8O 59
Melrose Rd. sw13. 6R 70
Melrose Rd. sw18. 10U 71
Melrose Rd. sw19. 10Za 92
Melrose Rd. w3. 4O 57
Melrose Ter. w6. 8O 59
Melton Rd. N15. 21B 25
Melton St. NW1. 16K 49
Melton St. w6. 9P 59
Melville Av. Cro. 21Zh 91
Melville Rd. E17. 25A 27
Melville Rd. NW10. 5H 31
Melville Rd. sw13. 7R 70
Melvin Rd. se20. 22Za 90
Memorial Av. E15. 28K 54
Mendip Rd. sw11. 12S 72
Mendora Rd. sw6. 10Q 59
Menelik Rd. NW2. 10F 33
Menotti St. E2. 22K 52
Mentmore Clo. Har. 1C 18
Mentmore Ter. E8. 22H 38
Mentone Av. N5. 19F 37
Meon Rd. w3. 5N 57
Mepham St. se1. 18N 62
Mercer St. E1. 23M 52
Mercer St. wc2. 17M 50
Merceron St. E1. 22L 52
Mercers Rd. N19. 16F 36
Merchant St. E3. 25K 53
Merchiston Rd. se6. 27V 89
Mercia Gro. se13. 27T 78
Mercy Ter. se4. 26T 77
Merebank La. Cro. 17Zg 91
Meredith Av. NW2. 8F 33
Meredith St. E13. 29K 55
Meredith St. Ec1. 18K 50
Meredyth Rd. sw13. 7R 70
Mereway Rd. Twi. 1cV 93
Merfield Rd. se9. 30T 79
Meridian Rd. se7. 31R 79
Merivale Rd. sw15. 9S 71
Merivale Rd. Har. 1cC 12
Merlin Cres. Edg. 3Ab 13
Merlin Rd. E12. 31E 41
Mermaid Ct. se1. 20N 63
Merrick Sq. se1. 19O 63
Merriman St. se3. 30R 79
Merrington Rd. sw6. 11Q 59
Merritt Rd. se4. 24U 77
Merrivale Av. Ilf. 31B 29
Merrow St. se17. 19P 63
Mersey Av. E17. 25A 27
Mersey St. w10. 9M 47
Mersham Dri. NW9. 4B 19
Mersham Rd. Cro. 19Zb 90
Merthyr Ter. sw13. 8Q 58
Merton Av. w4. 6O 58
Merton La. N6. 14E 35
Merton Pl. se18. 26R 77
Merton Rise NW3. 13H 34
Merton Rd. E17. 26C 27
Merton Rd. se25. 21Zc 90
Merton Rd. sw18. 10U 71
Merton Rd. sw19. 11Z 92
Merton Rd. w8. 11O 60
Merton Rd. Bar. 36H 43
Merton Rd. Ilf. 36D 42
Merton Rd. Har. 1cD 12

Merton HallGdns.sw19.9Z 92
Merton Hall Rd. sw19. 9Z 92
Merttins Rd. se15. 23T 76
Mervan Rd. sw2. 18T 74
Mervyn Rd. w13. 1aN 94
Messaline Av. w3. 5M 45
Messent Rd. se9. 30U 79
Messina Av. NW6. 11H 33
Meteor St. sw11. 14T 73
Methley St. se11. 18P 62
Methuen Pk. N10. 15A 23
Methuen Rd. Edg. 4Ab 13
Methwold Rd. w10. 9L 47
Mexfield Rd. sw15. 10T 71
Meymott St. se1. 18N 62
Meynell Cres. E9. 23H 38
Meynell Gdns. E9. 23H 38
Meynell Rd. E9. 24H 38
Meyrick Rd. NW10. 7G 32
Meyrick Rd. sw11. 12S 72
Miall Rd. se26. 24X 88
Michael Rd. se25. 20Zb 90
Micheldever Rd. se12.28U 78
Michelham Gdns. Twi. 1bW 93
Michigan Av. E12. 32F 43
Micklethwaite Rd. sw6. 11Q 59
Middle La. N8. 17B 24
Middle La. Ted. 1bY 93
Middle Rd. E13. 29K 54
Middle Rd. Har. 1cD 12
Middle Row w10. 9K 47
Middle St. E8. 21F 37
Middle St. Ec1. 19L 51
Middle St. se15. 21R 75
Middle St. sw7. 13O 60
Middle St. Cro. 19Zf 91
Middleham Gdns. N18. 22Ab 17
Middleham Rd. N18. 22Ab 17
Middle New St. Ec4. 18L 50
Middle Pk. Av. se9. 30U 79
Middlesex St. E1. 21L 51
Middlesex St. N7. 17E 36
Middlesex Wharf E5. 23E 38
Middle Temple La. Ec4. 18M 50
Middleton Gdns. Ilf. 33C 42
Middleton Rd. E8. 21H 37
Middleton Rd. N7. 17G 36
Middleton Rd. NW11. 11C 22
Middleton Rd. sw18. 27T 78
Middleton St. E2. 22K 52
Middleway NW11. 12B 22
Middle Way, The, Har. 1bAa 12
Midholm NW11. 12B 22
Midholm Wem. 4D 19
Midhope St. wc1. 17K 50
Midhurst Av. N2. 14A 23
Midhurst Av. Cro. 18Zd 91
Midhurst Rd. w13. 1aN 94
Midland Rd. E10. 26D 28
Midland Rd. NW1. 16J 50
Midland Ter. NW10. 6K 46
Midland Brent Ter. NW2. 9D 21
Midmoor Rd. sw12. 16V 84
Midmoor Rd. sw20. 9Z 91
Milborne Gro. sw10. 12P 60
Milborough Cres. se12. 28V 89
Milcote St. se1. 18O 62
Mildenhall Rd. E5. 23F 38
Mildmay Av. N1. 20G 37

Street	Ref	Page
Mildmay Gro. N1.	20G	37
Mildmay Pk. N1.	20G	37
Mildmay Rd. N1.	20G	37
Mildmay St. N1.	20G	37
Mile End Rd.		
E1. 1-357 & 2-510.		
E3. 359, 510A & up.		
	23L	52
Miles La. EC4.	20M	51
Miles La. Mit.	12Zb	92
Miles Pl. NW8.	13K	48
Miles St. SE10.	28Q	66
Miles St. SW8.	17Q	62
Miles St. W6.	7P	58
Miles Way N20.	14Ae	15
Milestone Rd. SE19.	21Z	90
Milfoil St. W12.	7M	46
Milford Gdns. Edg.	4Ab	13
Milford La. WC2.	18M	50
Milford Rd. W13.	1aM	94
Milford St. SW8.	15S	73
Milk St. EC2.	19M	51
Milk Yd. E1.	23N	64
Milkwood Rd. SE24.	18U	74
Mill La. NW6.	10G	33
Mill La. NW7.	6Ad	13
Mill La. Cro.	17Zt	91
Mill Ridge Edg.	3Ac	13
Mill Rd. E16.	30N	67
Mill Rd. SE13.	26T	77
Mill Rd. sw19.	12Z	92
Mill Rd. Ilf.	33F	42
Mill Row N1.	20J	51
Mill St. SE1.	21N	63
Mill St. w1.	15M	49
Millais Gdns. Edg.	4Aa	13
Millais Rd. E11.	27F	40
Millais St. SE5.	19Q	63
Millard Rd. N16.	21G	37
Millbank SW1.	17O	62
Millbrook Rd. N9.	23Ac	17
Millbrook Rd. SW9.	18S	74
Milledge St. SE16.	22P	64
Miller Rd. SE19.	12Y	83
Miller Rd. Cro.	17Ze	91
Miller St. NW1.	15J	49
Miller's Av. E8.	21F	37
Miller's Ter. E8.	21F	37
Millfield Av. N6.	14E	35
Millfield Rd. N18.	20Ac	17
Millfield Rd. Edg.	5Aa	13
Millfields Rd. E5.	23F	38
Millgrove St. sw11.	14R	73
Mill Hill Gro. w3.	4N	57
Mill Hill Pl. w1.	15L	49
Mill Hill Rd. sw13.	7S	70
Mill Hill Rd. w3.	4N	57
Millicent Rd. E10.	25D	27
Milling Gro. Edg.	6Ab	13
Millman St. wc1.	17K	50
Mills Gro. E14.	26L	53
Millstream Rd. SE1.	21O	63
Millwood St. w10.	9L	47
Milman Rd. NW6.	9J	47
Milman's St. sw10.	12Q	60
Milne Gdns. SE9.	31U	79
Milner Dri. Twi.	1dU	93
Milner Rd. E15.	28K	54
Milner Rd. sw19.	11Z	92
Milner Rd. Cro.	19Zb	90
Milner Sq. N1.	18H	36
Milner St. sw3.	13O	60
Milnthorpe Rd. w4.	5P	57
Milo Rd. SE22.	21U	75
Milson Rd. w14.	9O	59
Milstead St. sw2.	16U	74
Milton Av. E6.	31H	41
Milton Av. N6.	16D	23
Milton Av. NW9.	5A	19
Milton Av. NW10.	5H	31
Milton Av. Cro.	20Ze	91
Milton Cres. Ilf.	34D	42
Milton Gro. N11.	16Ac	15
Milton Gro. N19.	16E	36
Milton Pk. N6.	16C	23
Milton Pl. E14.	26L	53
Milton Pl. NW1.	14K	49
Milton Rd. E13.	29J	54
Milton Rd. E17.	25B	27
Milton Rd. N6.	16D	23
Milton Rd. N15.	19A	25
Milton Rd. N16.	20F	37
Milton Rd. N18.	21Ab	17
Milton Rd. NW9.	7C	20
Milton Rd. SE24.	18U	74
Milton Rd. sw14.	5S	69
Milton Rd. sw19.	11Y	83
Milton Rd. w3.	5M	45
Milton Rd. w7.	1bM	94
Milton Rd. Cro.	20Ze	91
Milton Rd. Har.	1bA	12
Milton St. E13.	29J	54
Milton St. EC2.	19L	51
Milton St. sw8.	16R	73
Milton Ct. Rd. SE14.	24Q	65
Milverton Gdns. Ilf.	36E	42
Milverton Rd. NW6.	9H	33
Milward St. SE11.	18P	62
Milward St. E1.	22L	52
Milward St. SE8.	33Q	95
Mimosa St. sw6.	10R	71
Mina Rd. SE17.	20P	63
Mina Rd. sw19.	11Z	92
Minard Rd. SE13.	27V	89
Minchenden Cres. N14.		
	16Ad	15
Minden Rd. SE20.	22Z	90
Minehead Rd. sw16.	17Y	85
Mineral St. SE18.	35P	95
Minerva Rd. NW10.	5K	45
Minerva St. E2.	22J	52
Minet Av. NW10.	6J	46
Minet Gro. NW10.	6J	46
Minford Gdns. w14.	9N	59
Miniver St. SE1.	19N	62
Minnow St. SE17.	20P	63
Minories E1.	21M	51
Minson Rd. E9.	23H	38
Minster Rd. N15.	20C	25
Minster Rd. NW2.	10G	33
Mint St. SE1.	19N	63
Mint Wk. Cro.	19Zf	91
Mintern St. N1.	20J	51
Minto St. SE1.	20O	63
Mirabel Rd. sw6.	10Q	59
Miranda Rd. N19.	16D	23
Miriam Rd. SE18.	35P	95
Mission Gro. E17.	25B	27
Mission Pl. SE16.	22O	64
Misteurs Bldgs. SE16.	23N	64
Mitcham La. sw16.	15Y	84
Mitcham Rd. sw17.	13Y	83
Mitcham Rd. Cro.	17Zd	91
Mitcham Rd. Ilf.	36D	42
Mitcham St. NW1.	13L	48
Mitchell Rd. N13.	19Ac	16
Mitchell St. EC1.	19K	51
Mitchell Way NW10.	5G	31
Mitchley Rd. N17.	21A	26
Mitford Rd. N19.	17E	36
Mitre Ct. EC4.	18M	50
Mitre St. EC3.	21M	51
Mitre St. SE1.	18N	62
Moat Dri. Har.	1cA	12
Moat Pl. sw9.	17S	74
Modbury St. NW5.	14G	35
Modder Pl. sw15.	9S	71
Model Bldgs. wc1.	18K	50
Model Cotts. sw14.	5S	69
Moffat Rd. N13.	17Ab	16
Moffat Rd. sw17.	13X	83
Moffatt Rd. Cro.	19Za	90
Mogden La. Twi.	1cT	93
Moity Rd. E14.	25O	65
Molesford Rd. sw6.	11R	71
Molesworth St. SE13.	26T	77
Mollison Way Edg.	3Aa	13
Molyneux St. w1.	13L	48
Mona Rd. SE15.	23R	76
Mona St. E16.	28L	54
Monck St. sw1.	16O	62
Moncrieff St. SE15.	22S	76
Monega Rd.		
E7. 1-203 & 2-204.		
E12. 205, 206 & up.		
	30H	41
Moness St. E14.	27M	54
Moneyer St. N1.	20K	51
Monier Rd. E3.	25H	39
Monk St. SE18.	33P	95
Monkleigh Rd. Mor.	9Zb	92
Monks Dri. w3.	3L	45
Monks Pk. Wem.	4G	31
Monkton St. SE11.	18O	62
Monkville Av. NW11.	10B	21
Monkwell St. EC2.	19L	51
Monmouth Av. E18.	30B	29
Monmouth Rd. N9.	22Ae	17
Monmouth Rd. w2.	11M	48
Monnery Rd. N19.	16E	35
Monnow Rd. SE1.	21P	64
Monsell Rd. N4.	18R	36
Monsey St. E1.	14L	50
Monson Rd. NW10.	7J	46
Monson Rd. SE14.	23R	76
Montacute Rd. SE6.	24V	88
Montagu Cres. N18.	22Ac	17
Montagu Gdns. N18.		
	22Ac	17
Montagu Pl. w1.	14L	49
Montagu Rd. N9 & N18.		
	23Ac	17
Montagu Rd. NW4.	7C	20
Montagu Sq. w1.	14L	49
Montagu St. w1.	14L	49
Montagu St. w6.	9P	59
Montague Av. SE4.	25T	77
Montague Av. w7.	1bN	94
Montague Clo. SE1.	20N	63
Montague Gdns. w3.	3M	45
Montague Pl. E14.	26M	53
Montague Pl. wc1.	16L	50
Montague Rd. E8.	22G	38
Montague Rd. E11.	28E	40
Montague Rd. N8.	17B	24
Montague Rd. N15.	21B	26
Montague Rd. sw19.	11Z	92
Montague Rd. w7.	1bN	94
Montague Rd. w13.	1L	44
Montague Rd. Cro.	18Ze	91
Montague St. wc1.	17L	50
Montana Rd. sw17.	14X	84
Montana Rd. sw20.	8Z	92
Montcalm Rd. SE7.	31Q	67
Montclare St. E2.	21K	51
Monteagle Av. Bar.	34H	43
Monteagle St. E1.	24L	53

Montefiore St. sw8. 15S 73
Monteith Rd. E3. 24J 53
Montem Rd. se23. 24V 88
Montem St. N4. 17D 24
Montenotte Rd. N8. 16C 23
Montesquieu st. E16. 28L 54
Montford Pl. se11. 18P 62
Montgomery Rd. w4. 5O 57
Montgomery Rd. Edg.
   3Ab 13
Montgomery St. w6. 9P 59
Montholme Rd. sw11. 14U 73
Montolieu Gdns. sw15. 8T 70
Montpelier Av. w5. 1L 44
Montpelier Gdns. E6. 31K 55
Montpelier Pl. sw7. 13O 60
Montpelier Rise nw11.
   10C 21
Montpelier Rd. N2. 12Aa 14
Montpelier Rd. N19. 17E 36
Montpelier Rd. nw5. 16F 35
Montpelier Rd. se15. 22R 76
Montpelier Rd. w5. 1L 44
Montpelier Rd. w6. 8P 59
Montpelier Rd. Twi. 1aU 93
Montpelier Row se3. 28S 78
Montpelier Row sw7. 13O 60
Montpelier Sq. sw7. 13O 60
Montpelier St. se17. 19Q 63
Montpelier St. sw7. 13O 60
Montrave Rd. se20. 23Z 90
Montreal Pl. wc2. 17M 50
Montreal Rd. Ilf. 34D 42
Montrell Rd. sw2. 16V 85
Montrose Av. nw6. . 10J 47
Montrose Av. Edg. 6Aa 13
Montrose Cres. N12. 12Ab 14
Montrose Cres. Wem. 2G 30
Montrose Pl. sw1. 14O 61
Montrose Rd. Har. 1bAa 12
Montserrat Rd. sw15. 9T 71
Monument St. ec3. 20M 51
Monza St. E1. 23N 64
Moodkee St. se16. 23O 64
Moody St. E1. 23K 52
Mooltan St. w14. 10Q 59
Moon St. N1. 18H 36
Moor La. ec2. 20L 51
Moor St. w1. 13L 48
Moor St. w1. 16M 50
Moorcroft Rd. sw16. 16W 85
Moordown se18. 33R 95
Moore St. sw3. 14O 61
Moore Pk. Rd. sw6. 11Q 60
Moorfield Av. w5. 2K 44
Moorfields ec2. 20L 51
Moorgate ec2. 20L 51
Moor Mead Rd. Twi. 1aU 93
Moorside Rd. se12. 28X 89
Mora Rd. nw2. 8F 33
Mora St. ec1. 19K 51
Morant St. E14. 25M 53
Morat St. sw9. 17R 74
Moravian St. E2. 23K 52
Moray Mews n7. 18E 36
Moray Rd. n4. 18E 36
Mordaunt Rd. nw10. 5H 31
Mordaunt St. sw9. 17S 74
Morden Gdns. Mit. 12Zb 92
Morden Gro. se13. 26S 77
Morden Hill se13. 26S 77
Morden La. se10. 26R 77
Morden Rd. se3. 29S 78
Morden Rd. sw19. 11Z 92
Morden Rd. Mor. 12Zb 92
Morden St. se13. 26R 77

Morden Hall Rd. Mor.
   11Zb 92
Morden Wharf Rd. se10.
   28O 66
Mordon Rd. Ilf. 36D 42
Morecambe St. se17. 19P 63
Moreland Rd. Har. 2B 18
Moreland St. ec1. 19K 51
Moreland St. n4. 18E 36
Morella Rd. sw12. 18U 73
Moremead Rd. se6. 25X 88
Morena St. se6. 26V 88
Moresby Rd. e5. 22D 26
Moreton Pl. sw1. 16P 61
Moreton Rd. n15. 20C 25
Moreton Rd. Cro. 19Zg 91
Moreton St. sw1. 16P 61
Moreton Ter. sw1. 16P 61
Morgan Av. E17. 27B 28
Morgan Rd. n7. 18G 36
Morgan St. E3. 24K 53
Morgan St. E16. 28L 54
Morgan's La. se1. 20N 63
Morgan's Wk. sw11. 13Q 60
Morie St. sw18. 11T 72
Morieux Rd. E10. 25D 27
Moring Rd. sw17. 14X 84
Morland Av. Cro. 20Ze 91
Morland Clo. nw11. 12D 22
Morland Rd. E17. 24C 26
Morland Rd. Cro. 20Ze 91
Morland Rd. Ilf. 33E 42
Morley Av. n18. 22Ac 17
Morley Av. n22. 18Aa 16
Morley Cres. Har 1A 18
Morley Rd. E10. 27E 40
Morley Rd. E15. 28J 54
Morley Rd. se7. 29P 67
Morley Rd. se13. 26T 78
Morley Rd. Bar. 34J 43
Morley St. se1. 18O 62
Morna Rd. se5. 19R 75
Morning La. E9. 23G 38
Mornington Av. w14. 10P 59
Mornington Av. Ilf. 33D 42
Mornington Cres. nw1. 15J 49
Mornington Pl. nw1. 15J 49
Mornington Rd. E3. 25K 53
Mornington Rd. E11. 28E 40
Mornington Rd. E11. 29C 29
Mornington Rd. nw1. 15J 49
Mornington Rd. se8. 25R 77
Mornington Rd. nw1. 15J 49
Morocco St. se1. 20O 63
Morpeth Rd. E9. 23J 52
Morpeth St. E2. 23K 52
Morpeth Ter. sw1. 15O 61
Morras Gdns. Ilf. 36F 42
Morris Av. E12. 32G 43
Morris Rd. E14. 26L 53
Morris Rd. E15. 28F 40
Morris St. E1 22M 52
Morris St. se18. 31P 67
Morrish Rd. sw2. 17V 85
Morrison Av. n15. 20A 25
Morrison St. sw11. 14S 73
Morshead Rd. w9. 11K 48
Mortham St. E15. 27J 54
Mortimer Cres. nw6. 11J 48
Mortimer Mkt. wc1. 16K 49
Mortimer Pl. nw6. 11J 48
Mortimer Rd. n1. 20H 37
Mortimer Rd. nw10. 8J 47
Mortimer Rd. w13. 1L 44
Mortimer St. w1. 15L 49
Mortlake Rd. E16. 30M 55

Mortlake Rd. Ilf. 34G 43
Mortlake Rd. Kew. 3Q 57
Mortlock Gdns. se15. 22R 76
Morton Cres. n14. 16Ad 15
Morton Pl. se1. 18O 62
Morton Rd. E15. 28H 40
Morton Rd. n1. 19H 37
Morton Way n14. 16Ad 15
Morval Rd. sw2. 18U 74
Morven Rd. sw17. 13W 83
Morville Rd. E8. 25J 53
Morville St. E3. 25J 53
Morwell St. wc1. 16L 50
Moscow Rd. w2. 11M 48
Mosedale St. se5. 20R 75
Moselle Av. n22. 18Aa 16
Moselle St. n17. 21Ab 17
Moss St. E2. 23K 52
Mossbury Rd. sw11. 13S 72
Mossford St. E3. 24K 53
Moss Hall Cres. n12. 12Ab 14
Moss Hall Gro. n12. 12Ac 14
Mossington Rd. se16. 22P 64
Mosslea Rd. se20. 23Z 90
Mossop St. sw3. 13O 60
Mossville Gdns. Mor. 10Zb 92
Mostyn Av. Wem. 3F 30
Mostyn Gdns. nw10. 9J 47
Mostyn Gro. E3. 25J 53
Mostyn Rd. sw9. 18R 74
Mostyn Rd. sw19. 10Za 92
Mostyn Rd. Edg. 6Ab 13
Motcomb St. sw1. 14O 61
Motley St. ec2. 20K 51
Motley St. sw8. 15R 73
Moundfield Rd. n16. 22C 26
Mount Av. w5. 1L 44
Mount Dri. Wem. 5D 19
Mount Gro. Edg. 5Ad 13
Mount Pleasant se18. 33P 95
Mount Pleasant wc1. 18K 49
Mount Pleasant Wem. 2H 30
Mount Rd. nw2. 8E 32
Mount Rd. nw4. 7C 20
Mount Rd. nw19. 11W 82
Mount Rd. Mit. 12Za 92
Mount Row w1. 15M 49
Mount St. E1. 22L 52
Mount St. E2. 21K 51
Mount St. se7. 31P 67
Mount St. w1. 14M 49
Mount, The, nw3. 12F 34
Mount, The, se26. 22X 87
Mount, The, Wem. 4D 19
Mount Vernon nw3. 12F 34
Mount Villas se27. 18X 85
Mount Adon Pk. se22. 21V 87
Mount Ash Rd. se26 22X 87
Mountbell Rd. Har. 1aAa 12
Mountearl Rd. sw16. 17W 85
Mount Ephraim La. sw16.
   16W 85
Mount Ephraim Rd. sw16.
   16W 85
Mountfield Rd. n3. 11A 21
Mountfield Rd. w5. 2L 44
Mountford Cres. n1. 18H 36
Mountford Rd. E8. 21G 38
Mount Gro. Rd. E11. 27D 28
Mountgrove Rd. n5. 19E 37
Mount Nod Rd. sw16.
   17W 85
Mount Nod Sq. se13. 26S 77
Mount Pk. Av. Har. 1cE 12
Mount Pk. Cres. w5. 2L 44

Mount Pk. Rd. w5.	2L 44	
Mount Pk. Rd. Har.	1cE 12	
Mount Pleasant Hill E5.	23E 38	
Mount Pleasant Lane E5.	22E 38	
Mount Pleasant Rd. N4.	18E 24	
Mount Pleasant Rd. N17.	20A 25	
Mount Pleasant Rd. Nw10.	8H 33	
Mount Pleasant Rd. SE13.	26U 77	
Mount Pleasant Rd. w5.	1K 44	
Mount Pleasant Villas N4.	17C 24	
Mount Pond Rd. SE3.	28S 78	
Mt. Stewart Av. Har.	2C 18	
Mount View Rd. N4.	17C 24	
Mt. View Rd. Nw9.	5B 19	
Movers La. Bar.	35J 43	
Mowbray Rd. Nw6.	10G 33	
Mowbray Rd. SE19.	21Z 90	
Mowbray Rd. Edg.	4Ad 13	
Mowlem St. E2.	22J 52	
Mowll St. Sw9.	18R 74	
Moye St. E2.	22J 52	
Moyers Rd. E10.	27D 28	
Moylan Rd. w6.	9Q 59	
Moyser Rd. Sw16.	15Y 84	
Mozart St. w10.	10K 47	
Muirdown Av. Sw14.	5T 69	
Muirfield w3.	6L 46	
Muirkirk Rd. SE6.	27W 89	
Mulberry Ct. E1.	22L 52	
Mulberry Wlk. Sw10.	13P 60	
Mulgrave Rd. Nw10.	7H 32	
Mulgrave Rd. SE18.	10Q 59	
Mulgrave Rd. w5.	2K 44	
Mulgrave Rd. Cro.	19Zf 91	
Mulkern Rd. N19.	16D 24	
Mullins Path Sw14.	5S 69	
Multon Rd. Sw18.	12V 83	
Muncaster Rd. Sw11.	14T 73	
Mund St. w14.	10P 59	
Mundania Rd. SE22.	22U 76	
Mundella Rd. Sw8.	16R 73	
Munden St. w14.	9O 59	
Mundford Rd. E5.	23E 38	
Munro Mews w10.	10L 47	
Munster Gdns. N13.	19Ac 16	
Munster Rd. Sw6.	10R 71	
Munster Rd. Twi.	1aY 93	
Munster Sq. Nw1.	15K 49	
Munton Rd. SE17.	19O 63	
Murchison Rd. E10.	26E 39	
Murchison Rd. w10.	9K 47	
Muriel St. N1.	18J 50	
Murillo Rd. SE13.	27T 78	
Murphy St. SE1.	18O 62	
Murray Mews Nw1.	16H 36	
Murray Rd. Sw19.	8Y 82	
Murray Rd. w5.	1O 56	
Murray St. N1.	20J 51	
Murray St. Nw1.	16H 35	
Murton St. EC1.	19K 51	
Musard Rd. w6.	9Q 59	
Muschamp Rd. SE15.	21S 75	
Muscovy St. EC3.	21M 51	
Museum St. wc1.	17H 50	
Musgrave Cres. Sw6.	11R 72	
Musgrove Rd. SE14.	24R 76	
Musjid Rd. Sw11.	13S 72	
Muston Rd. E5.	22E 38	
Muswell Av. N10.	15A 23	
Muswell Hill N10.	15A 23	
Muswell Rd. N10.	15A 23	
Muswell Hill Pl. N10.	15A 23	
Muswell Hill Rd.		
N6. 1&2-40.		
N10. 3, 42 & up.	15C 23	
Mutrix Rd. Nw6.	11H 34	
Myatt Rd. Sw9.	18R 74	
Mycenae Rd. SE3.	29Q 66	
Myddleton Pk. N20.	13Ad 14	
Myddleton Rd. N8.	17A 24	
Myddleton Rd. N22	17Ab 16	
Myddleton Sq. EC1.	18J 50	
Myddleton St. EC1.	18K 50	
Mylne St. EC1.	18J 50	
Myra St. E15.	28J 54	
Myra St. SE2.	36P 95	
Myrdle St. E1.	22L 52	
Myron Pl. SE13.	27T 78	
Myrtle Gdns. w7.	1cM 94	
Myrtle Gro. SE26.	23Y 87	
Myrtle Rd. E17.	24C 27	
Myrtle Rd. w3.	5M 45	
Myrtle Rd. Ilf.	33E 42	
Myrtle St. N1.	20J 51	
Myrtle St. SE8.	33P 95	
Myrtledene Rd. SE2.	36P 95	
Mysore Rd. Sw11.	14T 73	
Myton Rd. SE21.	19X 86	
Nadine St. SE7.	30Q 67	
Nailour St. N7.	17H 36	
Nairn St. E14.	27L 54	
Nairne Gro. SE24.	20T 75	
Namton Dri. Cro.	17Zb 90	
Nankin St. E14.	25M 53	
Nansen Rd. E15.	27J 54	
Nansen Rd. Sw11.	14S 73	
Nant Rd. Nw11.	10D 33	
Napier Av. Sw6.	10S 71	
Napier Rd. E6.	32J 43	
Napier Rd. E11.	28F 40	
Napier Rd. E15.	28J 54	
Napier Rd. N15.	21A 25	
Napier Rd. Nw10.	8J 46	
Napier Rd. w14.	10O 59	
Napier Rd. Wem.	2G 30	
Napier St. N1.	19J 51	
Napier St. SE8.	25Q 65	
Napier Ter. N1.	18H 36	
Napoleon Rd. Twi.	1aU 93	
Narbonne Av. Sw4.	15U 73	
Narborough St. Sw6.	11S 72	
Narcissus Rd. Nw6.	11G 33	
Narford Rd. E5.	22E 38	
Narrow St. E14.	24M 53	
Nascot St. w12.	8L 46	
Naseby Rd. SE19.	20Y 86	
Nash Rd. SE4.	24T 76	
Nasmyth St. w6.	8O 58	
Nassau Rd. Sw13.	6R 70	
Nassau St. w1.	15L 49	
Nassington Rd. Nw3.	14F 35	
Natal Rd. N11.	17Ab 16	
Natal Rd. Sw16.	16Y 84	
Natal Rd. Cro.	19Zb 90	
Natal Rd. Ilf.	33G 43	
Naval Row E14.	27M 54	
Navarino Gro. E8.	22G 38	
Navarino Rd. E8.	22G 38	
Navarre Rd. E6.	32J 43	
Navarre St. E2.	21K 51	
Navy St. Sw4.	16S 73	
Naylor Rd. N20.	12Ae 14	
Naylor Rd. SE15.	22Q 64	
Neal Clo. N2.	12A 22	
Neal St. wc2.	17M 50	
Nealden St. Sw9.	17S 74	
Neasden La. Nw10.	6F 32	
Neate St. SE5.	20Q 63	
Neath Pl. E1.	22L 52	
Nebraska St. SE1.	19N 63	
Neckinger, SE1.	21O 63	
Neckinger St. SE1.	21O 63	
Needham Ter. Nw2.	9E 33	
Neeld Cres. Nw4.	8B 20	
Neeld Cres. Wem.	3G 31	
Nelgarde Rd. SE6.	25V 88	
Nella Rd. w6.	9Q 59	
Nelldale Rd. SE16.	22P 64	
Nelson Pl. N1.	19J 51	
Nelson Rd. E11.	29B 29	
Nelson Rd. N8.	17C 24	
Nelson Rd. N9.	22Ad 17	
Nelson Rd. N15.	21B 25	
Nelson Rd. Sw19.	11Z 92	
Nelson Rd. Har.	1cD 12	
Nelson Sq. SE1.	19N 62	
Nelson St. E1.	22L 52	
Nelson St. E2.	22J 52	
Nelson St. E6.	32J 43	
Nelson St. E16.	28M 54	
Nelson St. Nw1.	15J 49	
Nelson St. SE10.	26Q 78	
Nelson St. SE18.	33O 95	
Nelson St. Bar.	34H 43	
Nelson Ter. N1.	19J 51	
Nelson Gro. Rd. Sw19.	11Z 92	
Nelson's Row Sw4.	16T 73	
Nemoure Rd. w3.	4M 45	
Nepaul Rd. Sw11.	13S 72	
Nepean St. Sw15.	7U 70	
Neptune St. E1.	22M 52	
Neptune St. SE16.	23O 64	
Nisbet Rd. SE9	31T 79	
Neston Rd. SE10.	23N 64	
Nether St.		
N12. 1-175 & 2-124.		
N3. 126-284 & 177-407.	11Aa 14	
Netheravon Rd. w4.	6P 58	
Netheravon Rd. w7.	1bM 94	
Netherbury Rd. w5.	1O 56	
Netherby Rd. SE23.	22V 87	
Nethercourt Av. N3.	11Ac 14	
Netherfield Gdns. Bar.	35H 43	
Netherfield Rd. N12.	12Ac 14	
Netherfield Rd. Sw17.	14W 84	
Netherford Rd. Sw4.	15S 73	
Netherhall Gdns. Nw3.	12G 34	
Netherton Gro. Sw10.	12Q 60	
Netherton Rd. N15.	20C 25	
Netherton Rd. Twi.	1aT 93	
Netherwood Rd. w14.	9O 59	
Netherwood St. Nw6.	10G 33	
Netley Rd. E17.	25B 27	
Netley Rd. Bre.	2P 56	
Netley Rd. Ilf.	35C 42	
Netley St. Nw1.	15K 49	
Netley St. w9.	11K 48	
Nettleden Av. Wem.	3G 31	
Nettleden Cres. Wem.	3G 31	
Nettleton Rd. SE14.	24R 76	
Neuchatel Rd. SE6.	24W 88	
Nevada St. SE10.	27O 66	
Nevern Pl. Sw5.	11P 59	
Nevern Rd. Sw5.	11P 59	

Nevern Sq. sw5.	11P 59	
Nevill Rd. N16.	21F 37	
Neville Dri. Nw11.	12C 22	
Neville Rd. E7.	29H 41	
Neville Rd. Nw6.	10J 47	
Neville Rd. w5.	1K 44	
Neville Rd. Cro.	20Zd 91	
Neville St. SE11.	17P 62	
Neville St. sw7.	12P 60	
Neville Ter. sw7.	12P 60	
Nevis Rd. sw17.	14W 84	
New End Nw3.	12F 34	
New Pl. SE16.	22O 64	
New Rd. E1.	22L 52	
New Rd. E16.	27L 54	
New Rd N8.	17B 24	
New Rd. N9.	22Ad 17	
New Rd. N17.	21Aa 16	
New Rd. N22.	19Aa 16	
New Rd. SE18.	33P 95	
New Rd. Bre.	2P 56	
New Rd. Ilf.	35E 42	
New Sq. wc2.	18L 50	
New St. E15.	27H 40	
New St. EC2.	21L 51	
New St. SE17.	18P 62	
New St. sw1.	16O 61	
New St. Sq.EC4.	18L 50	
Newark Cres. Nw10.	5J 45	
Newark St. E1.	22L 52	
New Barn St. E13.	29L 55	
Newbold St. E1.	23L 52	
Newbold Rd. SE15.	22R 76	
New Bond St. w1.	15M 49	
New Brent St. Nw4.	9B 21	
New Bridge St. EC4.	18M 50	
New Broad St. EC2.	20L 51	
Newburgh Rd. w3.	4M 45	
New Burlington St. w1.	15M 49	
Newburn St. SE11.	17P 62	
Newbury Rd. Ilf.	35C 42	
Newbury St. EC1.	19L 51	
Newby Pl. E14.	26M 53	
Newby St. sw8.	15S 73	
New Castle Pl. E1.	21L 51	
New Castle St. E1.	21L 51	
Newcastle St. SE10	27P 66	
New Cavendish St.w1.	15L 49	
New Charles St. EC1.	19K 51	
New Church Rd. SE5.	20Q 63	
New City Rd. E13.	30K 55	
Newcombe Pk. Nw7.	6Ac 13	
Newcombe St. w8.	11M 47	
Newcomen Rd. E11.	28F 40	
Newcomen Rd. sw11.	12S 72	
Newcomen St. SE1.	20N 63	
New Compton St. wc2.	16M 50	
Newcourt St. Nw8.	13J 48	
New Cross Rd. SE14.	24R 76	
New End Sq. Nw3.	12F 34	
Newgate St. EC1.	19L 51	
New Goulston St. E1.	21L 51	
New Gravel La. E1.	23M 52	
Newhall St. N1.	19H 37	
Newham's Row E1.	20O 63	
Newhaven Gdns. SE9.	31T 79	
Newhaven Rd. SE25.	20Zc 90	
Newick Rd. E5.	22F 38	
Newington Butts.		
SE11. 1-24 & up.		
SE1. 2-22.	19O 63	
Newington Causeway SE1.		
	19O 63	
Newington Cres. SE17.19P 62		

Newington Green.		
N1. 1-14.		
N16. 15 & up.	20G 37	
Newington Green Rd. N1.		
	20G 37	
New Inn Yd. EC2.	21K 51	
New James St.SE15.	22S 76	
New Kent Rd. SE1.	19O 63	
New King St. SE8.	25Q 65	
New King's Rd. sw6.	10R 71	
Newland Gdns. w13.	1aN 94	
Newland Rd. N8.	17A 24	
Newlands Pk. SE26.	23V 87	
Newlands Rd sw16.	17Za 90	
Newling St. E2.	21K 51	
New London St. EC3.	20M 51	
Newlyn Rd. N17.	21Aa 17	
Newman Rd. E13.	29K 55	
Newman St. w1.	16L 49	
Newnham Rd. N22.	18Aa 16	
Newnham St. E1.	21M 51	
Newnham Ter. SE1.	18O 62	
New North Rd. N1.	20J 51	
New North St. wc1.	17L 50	
New Oak Rd. N2.	12A 22	
New Oxford St. wc1.	17L 50	
New Palace Yd. sw1.	17N 62	
New Pk. Rd. sw2.	16V 85	
Newport Rd. E10.	27E 40	
Newport Rd. sw13.	7R 70	
Newport St. SE11.	17O 62	
New Providence St. E15.		
	27G 40	
Newquay Rd. SE6.	26W 88	
New Quebec St. w1.	14L 49	
New River Cres.N13.19Ac 16		
Newry Rd. Twi.	1aT 93	
Newsam Rd. N15.	20B 25	
New Scotland Yd. sw1.		
	17N 62	
Newstead Rd. SE12.	28V 89	
Newton Av. N10.	15Aa 15	
Newton Av. w3.	5N 57	
Newton Gro. w4.	6O 57	
Newton Rd. E15.	27G 40	
Newton Rd. N15.	21B 26	
Newton Rd. Nw2.	8E 32	
Newton Rd. sw19.	9Z 92	
Newton Rd. w2.	11L 48	
Newton Rd. Har.	1bAa 12	
Newton Rd. Wem.	3H 30	
Newton St. E16.	28M 54	
Newton St. N1.	20J 51	
Newton St. wc2.	17L 50	
Newtown Way N18.	19Ac 16	
Newtown St. sw11.	15R 73	
New Trinity Rd. N2.	13A 22	
New Tyssen St. E2.	21K 52	
New Union St. EC2.	20L 51	
New Wanstead E11.	29C 28	
New Way Rd. Nw9.	6B 20	
New Wharf Rd. N1.	17J 50	
Niagara Av. w5.	1O 56	
Nibthwaite Rd. Har.	1bB 12	
Nicholas Gdns. w5.	1N 56	
Nicholas La. EC4.	20M 51	
Nicholas St. E1.	23K 52	
Nicholas St. N1.	20J 51	
Nicholay Rd. N19.	16D 24	
Nicholl Sq. EC1.	19L 51	
Nicholl St. E2.	22J 52	
Nichols Sq. E2.	21J 51	
Nicholson Rd. E17.	24B 27	
Nicholson Rd. Cro.	21Ze 91	
Nicholson St. SE1.	18N 62	
Nicoll Pl. Nw4.	8C 20	

Nicoll Rd. Nw10.	6H 32	
Nicosia Rd. sw18.	13V 83	
Niederwald Rd. SE26.24X 87		
Nigel Rd. E7.	31G 41	
Nigel Rd. SE15.	22S 76	
Nigeria Rd. SE7.	30R 79	
Nightingale Gro. SE13. 27U 78		
Nightingale La. E1.	21M 52	
Nightingale La. E11.	29C 29	
Nightingale La. N8.	17B 24	
Nightingale La. SE10.	27R 78	
Nightingale La.		
sw4. 1-25		
sw12. 2, 27 & up	14U 73	
Nightingale La. Rich.	2U 68	
Nightingale Pl. SE18	33Q 95	
Nightingale Rd. E5.	22F 38	
Nightingale Rd. N22.17Aa 16		
Nightingale Rd. Nw10.	7J 46	
Nightingale Rd. w7.	1bM 94	
Nightingale Sq. sw12.	14V 84	
Nightingale Vale SE18. 33Q 95		
Nightingale Wk.sw12.15U 73		
Nile Rd. E13.	30K 55	
Nile St. N1.	20K 51	
Nile St. SE18.	33O 95	
Nile Ter. SE15.	21P 63	
Nimrod Rd. sw16.	15Y 84	
Nine Elms La. sw8.	16Q 61	
Nisbet St. E9.	24G 38	
Nithdale Rd. SE18.	33R 95	
Niton Rd. Rich.	3S 69	
Niton St. sw6.	9Q 59	
Noble St. EC2.	19L 51	
Noel Rd. w3.	4L 45	
Noel St. N1.	19J 51	
Noel St. SE1.	20O 63	
Noel St. w1.	16M 49	
Noel Pk. Rd. N22.	18A 24	
Nolton Pl. Edg.	3Aa 13	
Norah St. E2.	22K 52	
Norbroke St. w12.	6M 46	
Norbury Av. Cro.	17Za 90	
Norbury Clo. SE19.	18Z 90	
Norbury Cres. sw16.	17Za 90	
Norbury Hill SE19.	18Z 90	
Norbury Rd. Cro.	19Zb 90	
Norbury Ct. Rd. sw16.		
	17Za 90	
Norbury Croft Rd. SE19.		
	18Z 90	
Norcombe Gdns. Har.	1B 18	
Norcott Rd. N16.	22E 38	
Norcutt Rd. Twi.	1cV 93	
Norfolk Av. N13.	19Ab 16	
Norfolk Av. N15.	21C 25	
Norfolk Cres. w2.	13L 48	
Norfolk Rd. E6.	32J 43	
Norfolk Rd. E8.	21G 38	
Norfolk Rd. N1.	20H 37	
Norfolk Rd. Nw8.	13J 48	
Norfolk Rd. Nw10.	6H 32	
Norfolk Rd. sw19.	13Y 83	
Norfolk Rd. Bar.	35H 43	
Norfolk Rd. Cro.	19Zb 90	
Norfolk Rd. Ilf.	35D 42	
Norfolk Row SE11.	17O 62	
Norfolk Sq. w2.	13L 48	
Norfolk St. E1.	23K 52	
Norfolk St. E7.	29G 41	
Norfolk St. N1.	19H 37	
Norfolk St. SE1.	18N 62	
Norfolk St. w1.	14M 49	
Norfolk St. wc2.	18M 50	
Norfolk House Rd. sw16.		
	16W 85	

Norgrove St. sw12. 14V 84
Norhyrst Av. se25. 21Zb 90
Norland Gdns. w11. 9N 59
Norland Rd. w11. 9N 59
Norland Sq. w11. 10N 59
Norlington Rd.
 e11. 1-55 & 2-28.
 e10. 30, 57 & up. 27D 28
Norman Av. n22. 19Aa 16
Norman Av. Twi. 1aU 95
Norman Rd. e3. 24J 53
Norman Rd. e11. 27E 40
Norman Rd. n15. 21B 26
Norman Rd. se10. 26Q 65
Norman Rd. sw19. 12Z 92
Norman Rd. Cro. 18Zc 90
Norman Rd. Ilf. 33G 43
Norman St. e1. 19K 51
Norman Way n14. 17Ad 16
Norman Way w3. 4L 45
Normanby Rd. nw10. 7F 32
Normand Rd. w14. 10P 59
Normandy Rd. sw9. 18R 74
Normandy St. e16. 29M 55
Normanhurst Rd. sw2.
 17W 85
Norman's Bldgs. ec1. 19K 51
Normansmead nw10. 5G 31
Normanton Av. sw19. 10W 82
Normanton Rd. Cro. 20Zh 91
Normanton St. se23.
 23W 87
Norrice Lea n2. 13B 22
Norris Rd. e3. 26K 53
Norris St. e1. 20J 51
Norris St. sw1. 16M 50
Norroy Rd. sw15. 9T 71
North Av. n18. 22Ac 17
North Av. w10. 1aL 94
North Av. Kew. 0P 68
North Bank nw8. 13K 48
North Clo. sw20. 9Zb 92
North Cres. n3. 10A 21
North Dri. sw16. 15X 84
North End. Cro. 19Ze 91
North Gdns. sw19. 12Z 92
North Gate nw8. 13J 49
North Gro. n6. 14D 23
North Gro. n15. 20B 25
North Hill n6. 14C 23
North La. Ted. 1bY 93
North Pass. sw18. 11T 71
North Pl. e1. 22L 52
North Pl. Ted. 1aY 93
North Quay e1. 22M 52
North Rd. e17. 27B 28
North Rd. n6. 15D 23
North Rd. n7. 17G 36
North Rd. n9. 22Ae 17
North Rd. sw4. 16T 74
North Rd. sw19. 12Y 83
North Rd. w5. 1O 56
North Rd. Bre. 2P 56
North Rd. Edg. 4Ab 13
North Rd. Ilf. 35E 42
North Rd. Rich. 3S 68
North Row w1. 14M 49
North Side sw18. 12T 72
North Sq. nw11. 11B 22
North St. e8. 22J 52
North St. e13. 29J 55
North St. nw4. 9B 21
North St. se1. 18O 62
North St. se7. 30O 67
North St. sw4. 15S 73
North St. sw10. 11Q 60

North St. Bar. 33H 43
North Ter. sw3. 13O 60
North View w5. 1K 44
North Villas nw1. 16G 36
North Wk. w2. 12M 48
North Way nw6. 4A 19
North Way sw20. 9Zb 92
North Wood nw3. 13D 22
North Access Rd. e17 24C 26
North Acton Rd. nw10. 5J 45
Northall St. sw9. 17R 74
Northam St. se13. 26S 77
Northampton Pk. n1. 20G 37
Northampton Pl. se17.
 20P 63
Northampton Rd. ec1.
 18K 50
Northampton Rd. Cro.
 21Ze 91
Northampton Sq. ec1. 19K 50
Northampton St. e1. 22L 52
Northampton St. ec1. 18K 50
Northampton St. n1. 19H 37
North Audley St. w1. 14M 49
North Birbeck Rd. e11.
 27F 40
Northborough Rd. sw16.
 16Za 90
Northbrook Rd. n22. 17Ab 16
Northbrook Rd. se13. 27U 78
Northbrook Rd. Cro. 19Zc 90
Northbrook Rd. Ilf. 33E 42
Northburgh St. ec1. 19K 51
North Circular Rd.
 nw10. 2-98
 nw2. 431-705 & 560-912
 5G 31
 nw11. 1-31 & 2-74
 n3. n12. n13. Remainder
 10A 21
North Common Rd. w5.
 2M 44
Northcote Av. w5. 2M 44
Northcote Av. Twi. 1bT 93
Northcote Rd. e17. 24B 27
Northcote Rd. nw10. 6H 32
Northcote Rd. sw11. 13T 72
Northcote Rd. Twi. 1aT 93
Northcott Av. n22. 17Aa 16
Northcroft Rd. w13. 1aN 94
North Cross Rd. se22.
 21T 75
Northdene Gdns. n15. 21C 25
Northdown St. n1. 17J 50
N. Earnhay Wk. Mor. 9Zb 92
North East Pass. e1. 22M 52
North End Rd.
 nw11. 1-145 & 2-90.
 nw3. Part. 11D 22
North End Rd.
 w14. 1-311 & 2-234
 sw6. 238, 313 & up 10P 59
Northern Av. n9. 21Ad 17
Northern Rd. e13. 30J 55
Northey St. e14. 24M 53
Northfield Av.
 w13. 1-249 & 2-242.
 w5. 244, 251 & up. 1aN 94
Northfield Rd. e6. 32H 43
Northfield Rd. n16. 21D 25
Northfield Rd. w13. 1aN 94
Northfields Rd. w3. 4L 45
North Hill Av. n6. 14C 23
Northington St. wc1. 17L 50

N. Kent Gro. se18. 32P 95
Northlands St. se5. 19S 75
Northolme Edg. 5Ad 13
Northolme Gdns. Edg.
 4Ab 13
Northolme Rd. n5. 19F 37
Northolt Rd. Har. 1dE 12
Northover se12. 28X 89
North Pole Rd. w10. 8L 46
Northport St. n1. 20J 51
Northstead Rd. sw2. 18W 85
Northumberland Alley ec3.
 21M 51
Northumberland Av. e12.
 30E 41
Northumberland Av. wc2.
 17N 62
Northumberland Gdns. n9.
 21Ad 17
Northumberland Gro. n17.
 22Ab 17
Northumberland Pk. n17.
 21Ab 17
Northumberland Pl. w2.
 11L 47
Northumberland Rd. e17.
 25D 27
Northumberland St. e14.
 25M 53
NorthumberlandSt.w1.14L 49
Northumberland St. wc2.
 17N 62
N. View Cres. nw10. 6F 32
Northview Dri. Ilf. 31A 29
North View Rd. n8. 16A 24
Northway nw11. 12B 22
Northway Rd. se5. 19S 75
Northway Rd. Cro. 21Zd 91
North Wharf Rd. w2. 12L 48
Northwick Av. Har. 1aC 12
Northwick Circle Har. 1B 18
Northwick Ter. nw8. 12K 48
Northwick Ter. Mews. nw8.
 12K 48
Northwick Wk. Har. 1bC 12
Northwick Pk. Rd. Har.
 1bB 12
Northwold Rd.
 n16. 1-67 & 2-34
 e5. 36, 69 & up 21E 37
Northwood Rd. n6. 15C 23
Northwood Rd. se23 24W 88
Northwood Rd. Cro. 19Za 90
North Woolwich Rd. e16.
 29N 66
Norton Folgate e1. 21L 51
Norton Gdns. sw16 16Za 90
Norton Rd. e10. 25D 27
Norton Rd. Wem. 2G 30
Norton St. e2. 23J 52
Norval Rd. Har. 1aD 12
Norway St. se10. 26Q 65
Norwich Rd. e7. 29G 40
Norwich Rd. e8. 22J 52
Norwich Rd. Cro. 19Zb 90
Norwich St. ec4. 18L 50
Norwich Wk. Edg. 5Ab 13
Norwood Av. Wem. 3H 30
Norwood Rd.
 se24. 1-339 & 4-150
 se27. 152, 341 & up 18W 85
Norwood High St. se27.
 19X 86
Notley St. se5. 20Q 63
Nottingham Av. e16. 30L 55
Nottingham Pl. e1. 22L 52

Nottingham Pl. w1. 14L 49
Nottingham Rd. E10. 27C 28
Nottingham Rd. sw17. 13V 83
Nottingham Rd. Cro. 19Zg 91
Nottingham St. w1. 14L 49
Notting Hill Gate w11.
    11M 47
Nova Rd. Cro. 18Ze 91
Novello St. sw6. 11R 71
Nowell Rd. sw13. 7Q 58
Noyna Rd. sw17. 14W 84
Nuding Rd. se13. 25S 77
Nugent Rd. N19. 17D 24
Nugent Rd. se25. 20Zb 90
Nugent Ter. nw8. 12J 48
Nunhead Cres. se15. 22T 76
Nunhead Grn. se15. 22S 76
Nunhead Gro. se15. 22S 76
Nunhead La. se15. 22T 76
Nursery Av. Cro. 23Zf 91
Nursery Clo. Cro. 23Zf 91
Nursery La. E7. 29G 41
Nursery Rd. N2. 12Aa 14
Nursery Rd. N14. 16Af 15
Nursery Rd. sw9. 17T 74
Nursery Rd. sw19. 11Za 92
Nursery Rd. Cro. 19Zc 90
Nursery Row se17. 19P 63
Nursery St. N17. 21Aa 17
Nursery St. sw8. 15S 73
Nutbourne St. w10. 9J 47
Nutbrook St. se15. 21S 76
Nutfield Gdns. Ilf. 36E 42
Nutfield Rd. E15. 27F 40
Nutfield Rd. se22. 21T 75
Nutfield Rd. nw2. 7E 32
Nutfield Rd. Cro. 18Zb 90
Nutford Pl. w1. 13L 48
Nuthurst Av. sw2. 17W 85
Nutley Ter. nw3. 12G 34
Nutmel Av. sw14. 5T 69
Nutt St. se15. 21Q 63
Nuttall St. N1. 21J 51
Nutwell St. sw17. 13Y 83
Nyanza St. se18. 35R 95
Nye St. E14. 26M 53
Nylands Av. Kew. 3R 69
Nynehead St. se14. 24Q 65
Nyon Gro. se6. 24W 88

Oak Av. N8. 17B 24
Oak Av. N10. 15Ab 15
Oak Av. N17. 20Ab 17
Oak Cres. E16. 28L 54
Oak Gdns. Edg. 5Aa 13
Oak Gro. nw2. 9F 33
Oak Gro. se20. 22Za 90
Oak La. E14. 24M 53
Oak La. N2. 13Aa 14
Oak La. N11. 17Ab 16
Oak La. Twi. 1aV 93
Oak La. Twi. 1cT 93
Oak Rd. E16. 28L 54
Oak Rd. nw10. 6G 32
Oak St. se18. 31P 67
Oak St. w5. 2M 44
Oak Village nw5. 14F 35
Oak Way sw20. 8Zb 92
Oakbank Gro. se24. 19T 75
Oakbury Rd. sw6. 11S 72
Oakcroft Rd. se13. 27S 78
Oakdale N14. 15Ae 15
Oakdale Av. E18. 30A 29
Oakdale Av. Har. 2B 18
Oakdale Rd. E7. 30H 41
Oakdale Rd. E11. 27E 40

Oakdale Rd. N4. 20C 25
Oakdale Rd. sw16. 17Y 85
Oakden St. se11. 18O 62
Oakdene Pk. N3. 11Ab 14
Oakeshott Av. N6. 15E 35
Oakfield Av. Har. 1A 18
Oakfield Cres. nw5. 14G 35
Oakfield Rd. E5. 22F 38
Oakfield Rd. E6. 31J 55
Oakfield Rd. E17. 24A 27
Oakfield Rd. N3. 12Aa 14
Oak Field Rd. N4. 18C 24
Oakfield Rd. N4. 20C 25
Oakfield Rd. N14. 17Ad 16
Oakfield Rd. se20. 22Z 90
Oakfield Rd. sw19. 9W 82
Oakfield Rd. Cro. 19Ze 91
Oakfield St. sw10. 12Q 60
Oakfields Rd. nw11. 10B 21
Oakfields Rd. Ilf. 34F 42
Oakford Rd. nw5. 15F 35
Oak Grove Rd. se20. 22Za 90
Oak Hall Rd. E11. 30C 29
Oakhill Av. nw3. 11F 34
Oak Hill Pk. nw3. 12F 34
Oakhill Rd. sw15. 10T 71
Oakhill Rd. sw16. 17Za 90
Oak Hill Way nw3. 12F 34
Oakhurst Gro. se22. 21T 76
Oakhurst Rd. E7. 29G 41
Oakington Av. Wem. 3E 30
Oakington Manor Dri.
    Wem. 3F 31
Oakington Rd. w9. 11K 48
Oakington Way N8. 17C 24
Oaklands N21. 18Ae 16
Oaklands Av. Cro. 17Zb 90
Oaklands Gro. w12. 7M 46
Oaklands Rd. nw2. 9F 33
Oaklands Rd. sw14. 5S 69
Oaklands Rd. w7. 1bN 94
Oaklands Pk. Av. Ilf. 34E 42
Oakleigh Av. N20. 13Ae 14
Oakleigh Av. Edg. 4Aa 13
Oakleigh Ct. nw6. 5Aa 13
Oakleigh Cres. N20. 14Ad 15
Oakleigh Gdns. N8. 17B 24
Oakleigh Gdns. N20. 13Ae 14
Oakleigh Gdns. Edg. 3Ac 13
Oakleigh Pk. N. N20. 13Ae 14
Oakleigh Pk. S. N20. 13Af 14
Oakleigh Rd. N. N20. 13A 14
Oakleigh Rd. S. N11. 15Ad 15
Oakley Av. w5. 3M 45
Oakley Av. Bar. 36H 43
Oakley Cres. EC1. 19J 51
Oakley Gdns. sw3. 13Q 60
Oakley Pl. se1. 21P 63
Oakley Rd. N1. 20H 37
Oakley Rd. se25. 22Zc 90
Oakley Rd. sw19. 9V 82
Oakley Rd. Har. 1cB 12
Oakley Sq. nw1. 16J 49
Oakley St. se1. 18O 62
Oakley St. sw3. 13P 60
Oakmead Gdns. Edg. 5Ad 13
Oakmead Rd. sw12. 14V 84
Oakmere Rd. se2. 36Q 95
Oakridge Rd. Brom. 27Y 89
Oaks Av. se27. 20Y 86
Oaks La. Ilf. 35C 42
Oaks Rd. Cro. 22Zg 91
Oaksford Av. se26. 22X 87
Oakthorpe Rd. N13. 18Ac 16
Oaktree Av. N13. 19Ad 16
Oak Tree Dell nw9. 5B 19

Oaktree Dri. N20. 12Ae 14
Oak Tree Rd. nw8. 13K 48
Oakwood Av. Mit. 12Za 92
Oakwood Ct. w14. 10O 59
Oakwood Dri. Edg. 5Ac 13
Oakwood Gdns. Ilf. 36E 42
Oakwood Rd. nw11. 11B 22
Oakwood Rd. Cro. 18Zd 91
Oakworth Rd. w10. 9L 47
Oareboro' Rd. se8. 24Q 65
Oat La. EC2. 19L 51
Oatland Rise E17. 24A 27
Oban Rd. E13. 30K 55
Oban Rd. se25. 20Zb 90
Oban St. E14. 27L 54
Oberstein Rd. sw11. 12T 72
Observatory Gdns. w8.
    11N 59
Observatory Rd. sw14. 4T 69
Occupation Rd. w5. 2O 56
Ocean St. E1. 24L 52
Ockendon Rd. N1. 20H 37
Ockley Rd. sw16. 16X 85
Ockley Rd. Cro. 17Zd 91
Octavia St. sw11. 13R 72
Octavius St. se8. 25Q 65
Odell St. se5. 21P 63
Odessa Rd. E7. 28F 40
Odessa Rd. nw10. 7J 46
Odessa St. se16. 24O 65
Odger St. sw11. 14S 73
Offerton Rd. sw4. 16S 73
Offham Slope N12. 11Ac 14
Offley Rd. sw9. 18Q 62
Offord Rd. N1. 18H 36
Offord St. N1. 18H 36
Ogilby St. se18. 32P 95
Oglander Rd. se15. 21T 75
Ogle St. w1. 15L 49
Ohio Rd. E13. 28L 54
Oil Mill La. w6. 7P 58
Okeburn Rd. sw17. 14Y 84
Okehampton Rd. nw10. 9J 47
Olaf St. w11. 9M 47
Old Bailey EC4. 19M 50
Old Change se4. 19M 51
Old Jewry EC2. 20L 51
Old Rd. se13. 28T 78
Old Sq. wc2. 18L 50
Old St. E13. 30J 55
Old St. EC1. 19K 51
Old Town sw4. 15S 73
Old Town Cro. 18Zf 91
Oldberry Rd. nw7. 6Ab 13
Old Bethnal Green Rd. E2.
    22K 52
Old Bond St. w1. 15M 49
Oldborough Rd. Wem. 1E 30
Old Broad St. EC2. 20L 51
Old Bromley Rd. Bec. 27Y 89
Old Brompton Rd. sw5.
    & sw7. 11P 60
Old Burlington St. w1.
    15M 49
Oldbury Pl. w1. 14L 49
Old Castle St. E1. 21L 51
Old Cavendish St. w1. 15L 49
Old Church La. nw9. 5E 31
Old Church Rd. E1. 23L 52
Old Church St. sw3. 13P 60
Old Compton St. w1. 16M 50
Old Court Pl. w8. 11N 60
Old Deer Pk. Gdns. Rich.
    2S 68
Old Devonshire Rd. sw12.
    15V 84

Old Dover Rd. se3. 29R 79
Oldfield Gro. se16. 23P 64
Oldfield Rd. n16. 20F 37
Oldfield Rd. nw10. 6G 33
Oldfield Rd. sw19. 9Y 82
Oldfield Rd. w12. 6N 58
Old Ford Rd.
  e2. 1-211 & 2-232.
  e3. 213, 234 & up. 23J 52
Old Gloucester St. wc1.
             17L 50
Old Gravel La. e1. 22N 64
Oldham's Ter. w3. 4N 57
Oldhill Pl. e5. 21D 26
Oldhill St. n16. 21D 26
Old James St. se15. 22S 76
Old Kent Rd.
  se1. 1-587 & 2-588.
  se15. 589, 590 & up.
             20O 63
Old Manor La. se16. 23P 64
Old Mill Rd. se18. 35Q 95
Old Montague St. e1. 21L 52
Old Nichol St. e2. 21K 51
Old Oak La. nw10. 6K 46
Old Oak Rd. w3. 6M 46
Old Oak Common La. w3.
            6K 46
Old Palace La. Rich. 1T 68
Old Palace Rd. Cro. 18Zf 91
Old Palace Yd. sw1. 17O 62
Old Palace Yd. Rich. 1T 68
Old Paradise St. se11. 17O 62
Old Pk. Av. sw12. 14U 73
Old Pk. Rd. n13. 18Ad 16
Old Pye St. sw1. 16O 62
Old Quebec St. w1. 14M 49
Old Rd. sw1. 16N 62
Oldridge Rd. sw12. 11V 97
Old S. Lambeth Rd. sw8.
            17Q 62
Oldstead Rd. se6. 27X 89
Old Swan La. ec4. 20M 51
Old Woolwich Rd. se10.
            27Q 66
Oley Pl. e1. 23L 52
Olga St. e3. 24J 53
Olinda Rd. n16. 21C 25
Oliphant St. w10. 9J 47
Olive Rd. e13. 30K 55
Olive Rd. nw2. 8F 32
Olive Rd. sw19. 12Z 92
Olive Rd. w5. 2O 56
Oliver Av. se25. 21Zb 90
Oliver Gro. se25. 21Zb 90
Oliver Rd. e10. 26E 39
Oliver Rd. e17. 27B 28
Oliver St. se18. 34P 95
Olivette St. sw15. 9S 71
Ollerton Rd. n11. 16Ac 15
Olmar St. se1. 21Q 64
Olney St. se17. 19P 63
Olven Rd. se18. 34R 95
Oman Av. nw2. 8F 32
Ommaney Rd. se14. 24R 76
Ondine Rd. se15. 21T 75
Ongar Rd. sw6. 11Q 59
Onra Rd. e17. 25D 27
Onslow Av. Rich. 2T 68
Onslow Cres. sw7. 13O 60
Onslow Gdns. e18. 30A 29
Onslow Gdns. n10. 15B 23
Onslow Gdns. sw7. 12P 60
Onslow Pl. sw7. 13P 60
Onslow Rd. Cro. 17Ze 91

Onslow Sq. sw7. 13P 60
Onslow St. ec1. 18L 50
Ontario St. se1. 19O 63
Opal St. se11. 18P 62
Openview sw18. 12V 83
Ophir Ter. se15. 21R 75
Oppidans Rd. nw3. 14H 35
Orange Pl. se16. 23O 64
Orange St. e2. 21K 52
Orange St. wc2. 16M 50
Orange Hill Rd. Edg. 5Ab 13
Orb St. se17. 20P 63
Orbain Rd. sw6. 10Q 59
Orchard Av. n3. 11A 21
Orchard Clo. sw20. 8Zb 92
Orchard Clo .Wem. 2H 30
Orchard Cres. Edg. 5Ac 13
Orchard Dri. Edg. 3Ac 13
Orchard Gate Wem. 1G 30
Orchard Gro. Edg. 4Ab 13
Orchard Hill se13. 26S 77
Orchard Pl. e14. 28M 54
Orchard Pl. n17. 21Aa 17
Orchard Rise Rich. 4T 69
Orchard Rd. n6. 15C 23
Orchard Rd. Bre. 1P 56
Orchard Rd. Rich. 3S 68
Orchard Rd. Twi. 1aT 93
Orchard Rd. e17. 24B 27
Orchard St. sw1. 16O 62
Orchard St. w1. 14M 49
Orchard, The. nw11. 11B 21
Orchard, The. w4. 5O 57
Orchardson St. nw8. 13K 48
Orchid St. w12. 7M 46
Orcus St. nw8. 13K 48
Orde Hall St. wc1. 17L 50
Ordell Rd. e3. 25J 53
Ordnance Hill nw8. 13J 48
Ordnance Rd. e16. 09M 54
Ordnance Rd. se10. 27O 66
Ordnance Rd. se18. 33R 95
Oregon Av. e12. 32F 43
Orford Gdns. Twi. 1bW 93
Orford Rd. n17. 26B 27
Orford Rd. e18. 29A 29
Orford St. sw3. 13P 60
Oriel Pl. nw3. 12F 34
Oriel Rd. e9. 24G 38
Orient St. se11. 18O 62
Oriental Rd. e16. 31N 67
Oriental St. e14. 25M 53
Orissa Rd. se18. 35P 95
Orkney St. sw11. 14R 73
Orlando Rd. sw4. 15S 73
Orleans Rd. n19. 10D 24
Orleans Rd. se19. 20Z 90
Orleans Rd. Twi. 1aU 93
Orleston Rd. n7. 18G 36
Orlop St. se10. 27Q 66
Ormanton Rd. se26. 22X 87
Orme Sq. w2. 11M 48
Ormeley Rd. sw12. 15V 84
Ormiston Rd. se10. 29Q 66
Ormiston Rd. w12. 7M 46
Ormond Clo. wc1. 17L 50
Ormond Gate sw3. 14P 61
Ormond Rd. n19. 17D 24
Ormond Rd. Rich. 1T 68
Ormonde Rd. sw14. 4S 69
Ormonde Ter. nw8. 14J 49
Ormsby St. e2. 21J 51
Ormside St. se15. 22Q 64
Ornan Rd. nw3. 13G 34
Orpheus St. se5. 19R 75

Orpingley Rd. n7. 17E 36
Orpington Gdns. n18.
           20Ad 17
Orpington Rd. n21. 19Ae 16
Orsett St. se11. 17P 62
Orsett Ter. w2. 12L 48
Orton St. e1. 22N 64
Orville Rd. sw11. 13R 72
Orwell Rd. e13. 30J 55
Osbaldeston Rd. n16. 21E 38
Osberton Rd. se12. 29U 78
Osborn Pl. e1. 21L 52
Osborn St. e1. 21L 52
Osborn Ter. se12. 28T 78
Osborne Gro. n4. 18D 24
Osborne Rd. e7. 29G 41
Osborne Rd. e9. 25G 39
Osborne Rd. e10. 26E 39
Osborne Rd. n4. 18D 24
Osborne Rd. n13. 18Ad 16
Osborne Rd. nw2. 8G 32
Osborne Rd. w3. 4N 57
Osborne Rd. Cro. 19Za 90
Osborne St. se17. 20P 63
Oscar St. se8. 25R 77
Oseney Cres. nw5. 16G 35
Osidge La. Barn. 16Ae 15
Osman Rd. n9. 22Ad 17
Osman Rd. n15. 20C 25
Osman Rd. w6. 8O 59
Osnaburgh St. nw1. 15K 49
Osprey St. se16. 23O 64
Ospringe Rd. nw5. 16F 35
Ossian Rd. n4. 17D 24
Ossington St. w2. 11M 48
Ossleton Way nw11. 12B 22
Ossory Rd. se1. 21Q 64
Ossulston St. nw1. 16J 50
Ostade Rd. sw2. 17V 85
Osterley Gdns. Cro. 19Za 90
Osterley Pk. se16. 20F 37
Osterley Pk. View Rd. w7.
           1bN 94
Oswald St. e5. 24F 38
Oswin St. se11. 19O 62
Oswyth Rd. se5. 20R 75
Otford Cres. se4. 24U 77
Otis St. e3. 26K 53
Otley App. Ilf. 33C 42
Otley Dri. Ilf. 33C 42
Otley Rd. e16. 30M 55
Otley Ter. e5. 23E 38
Ottaway St. e5. 22F 38
Otterburn St. sw17. 14Y 84
Otterden St. se6. 25X 88
Otto St. se17. 18Q 62
Oulton Cres. Bar. 36G 43
Oulton Rd. n15. 20B 25
Oulton St. sw11. 14R 73
Ouseley Rd. sw12. 14V 84
Outer Circle nw1. 14K 49
Outgate Rd. nw10. 6G 32
Outram Rd. e6. 31J 55
Outram Rd. n22. 16Aa 15
Outram Rd. Cro. 21Ze 91
Outram St. n1. 17H 36
Outram St. e13. 29L 55
Oval Pl. sw8. 17Q 62
Oval Rd. nw1. 15H 35
Oval Rd. Cro. 20Ze 91
Oval, The. e2. 22J 52
Overbrae Bec. 25Y 88
Overbury Rd. n15. 20C 25
Overbury St. e5. 24F 38
Overcliff Rd. se13. 25S 77
Overdale Rd. w5. 1O 56

Overdown Rd. se6.	25X 88	
Overhill Rd. se22.	21V 87	
Overstone Rd. w6.	8O 58	
Overton Dri. e11.	29D 29	
Overton Rd. e10.	24D 27	
Overton Rd. sw9.	18S 74	
Overtons Yd. Cro.	19Zf 91	
Ovington Gdns. sw3.	13O 60	
Ovington Sq. sw3.	13O 60	
Ovington St. sw3.	13O 60	
Owen Rd. n13.	19Ac 16	
Owen St. ec1.	18J 50	
Owen's Row ec1.	18J 50	
Oxberry Av. sw6.	9R 71	
Oxendon St. sw1.	16M 50	
Oxenford St. se15.	21T 75	
Oxford Av. sw20.	9Za 92	
Oxford Circus w1.	15L 49	
Oxford Gdns. n21.	20Af 16	
Oxford Gdns. w4.	4P 57	
Oxford Gdns. w10.	9L 47	
Oxford Rd. e15.	27H 40	
Oxford Rd. n1.	20H 37	
Oxford Rd. n4.	18D 24	
Oxford Rd. n9.	22Ae 17	
Oxford Rd. nw6.	11J 48	
Oxford Rd. se19.	20Y 92	
Oxford Rd. sw15.	9T 71	
Oxford Rd. w4.	4P 57	
Oxford Rd. w5.	2M 44	
Oxford Rd. Har.	1bA 12	
Oxford Rd. Har.	1cB 12	
Oxford Rd. Ilf.	34G 43	
Oxford Rd. Twi.	1cX 93	
Oxford Sq. w2.	13M 48	
Oxford St. e1.	22L 52	
Oxford St. w1.	14M 49	
Oxford Ter. w2.	13L 48	
Oxgate Gdns. nw2.	8E 32	
Oxgate La. nw2.	8D 20	
Oxley St. se1.	21O 64	
Oxonian St. se22.	21T 75	
Pacific Rd. e16.	29M 54	
Packington Rd. w3.	4O 57	
Packington St. n1.	19J 51	
Paddenswick Rd. w6.	7O 58	
Paddington Grn. w2.	12L 48	
Paddington St. n4.	18E 36	
Paddington St. w1.	14L 49	
Paddock Rd. nw2.	7E 32	
Paddocks, The, Wem.	4D 19	
Padua Rd. se20.	22Za 90	
Page Cres. Cro.	18Zg 91	
Page St. sw1.	16O 62	
Page Grn. Rd. n15.	21B 26	
Page Gro. Ter. n15.	21B 25	
Pagehurst Rd. Cro.	22Zd 91	
Page's Hill n10.	15A 23	
Page's La. n10.	15A 23	
Page's Wlk. se1.	20O 63	
Paget Rd. n16.	20D 25	
Paget Rd. se18.	33R 95	
Paget Rd. Ilf.	33G 43	
Paget St. ec1.	18K 50	
Pagnell St. se14.	24R 77	
Pagoda Av. Rich.	2S 68	
Paignton Rd. n15.	20C 25	
Paisley Rd. n22.	19Aa 16	
Pakeman St. n7.	17F 36	
Pakenham St. wc1.	18K 50	
Palace Av. w8.	11N 60	
Palace Court w2.	11M 48	
Palace Ct. Har.	2C 18	
Palace Gate w8.	12N 60	
Palace Rd. e9.	23H 38	

Palace Rd. n8.	17B 24	
Palace Rd. n11.	17Ab 16	
Palace Rd. se19.	21Z 90	
Palace Rd. sw2.	17V 85	
Palace Sq. se19.	21Z 90	
Palace St. sw1.	15O 61	
Palace Ct. Gdns. n10.	15A 23	
Palace Gdns. Mews w8.		
	11M 48	
Palace Gdns. Ter. w8.	11N 60	
Palace Gates Rd. n22.		
	17Aa 15	
Palamos Rd. e10.	25D 27	
Palatine Rd. n16.	21F 37	
Palermo Rd. nw10.	7J 46	
Palestine Gro. Mit.	12Za 92	
Palewell Pk. sw14.	5T 69	
Palewell Common Rd. sw14.		
	5T 69	
Palfrey Pl. sw8.	17Q 62	
Palgrave Rd. w12.	6O 58	
Palissy St. e2.	21K 51	
Palliser Rd. w14.	9P 59	
Pall Mall sw1.	16N 61	
Pall Mall E. sw1.	16M 50	
Palm St. e3.	24K 52	
Palmer Pl. n7.	18G 36	
Palmer Rd. e13.	30L 55	
Palmer St. e1.	21L 51	
Palmer St. se1.	18N 62	
Palmer St. sw1.	16O 61	
Palmer's Rd. e2.	24K 52	
Palmers Rd. n11.	15Ac 15	
Palmers Rd. sw14.	4S 69	
Palmers Rd. sw16.	17Za 90	
Palmerston Cres. n13.		
	18Ac 16	
Palmerston Cres. se18.		
	34Q 95	
Palmerston Gro. sw19.	11Z 92	
Palmerston Rd. e7.	30G 41	
Palmerston Rd. e17.	25B 27	
Palmerston Rd. n22.	17Ab 16	
Palmerston Rd. nw6.	10H 33	
Palmerston Rd. sw14.	4T 69	
Palmerston Rd. sw18.	11U 71	
Palmerston Rd. sw19.	10Z 92	
Palmerston Rd. w3.	4N 57	
Palmerston Rd. Har.	1bA 12	
Palmerston Rd. Twi.	1cU 93	
Pamber St. w10.	9L 47	
Pancras La. ec4.	19M 51	
Pancras Rd. nw1.	16J 50	
Pancras St. wc1.	16L 49	
Pandora Rd. nw6.	11G 33	
Pangbourne Av. w10.	9L 47	
Panmure Rd. se26.	22X 87	
Pansy Gdns. w12.	7M 46	
Panton St. sw1.	16M 50	
Paper St. ec1.	19L 51	
Paradise Rd. n5.	19F 37	
Paradise Rd. sw4.	16R 74	
Paradise Rd. Rich.	2T 68	
Paradise Row w6.	7O 58	
Paradise St. ec2.	20K 51	
Paradise St. se16.	22O 64	
Paradise St. w1.	14L 49	
Paradise Wk. sw3.	14Q 61	
Paragon Pl. se3.	28S 78	
Paragon Rd. e9.	23G 38	
Paragon Row se17.	19P 63	
Paragon, The, se3.	29S 78	
Parbury Rd. se23.	24U 76	
Parchmore Rd. Cro.	19Zb 90	
Pardon St. ec1.	19K 51	
Pardoner St. se1.	20O 63	

Parfett St. e1.	22L 52	
Parfitt Rd. se16.	22P 64	
Parfrey St. w6.	9P 59	
Parham Dri. Ilf.	33C 42	
Parian St. e14.	27M 54	
Paris Gdn. se1.	18N 62	
Paris St. se1.	17O 62	
Paris Ter. e14.	25M 53	
Parish La. se20.	23Z 90	
Parish St. se1.	20N 63	
Park Av. e6.	33J 43	
Park Av. e15.	28H 40	
Park Av. n3.	12Aa 14	
Park Av. n13.	18Ad 16	
Park Av. n18.	22Ac 17	
Park Av. n22.	17Aa 16	
Park Av. nw2.	8F 32	
Park Av. nw11.	11D 22	
Park Av. sw14.	5T 69	
Park Av. w5.	3J 44	
Park Av. Bar.	34H 43	
Park Av. Ilf.	33E 42	
Park Av. N. n8.	16B 24	
Park Av. S. n8.	16B 24	
Park Chase Wem.	3F 30	
Park Clo. nw2.	8E 32	
Park Clo. nw10.	3J 44	
Park Cres. n3.	12Ab 14	
Park Cres. w1.	15K 49	
Park Dri nw11.	11D 22	
Park Dri. sw14.	5T 69	
Park Dri. w3.	3O 57	
Park Gdns. nw9.	4A 19	
Park Gro. e15.	29J 54	
Park Gro. sw11.	14R 73	
Park Gro. Edg.	3Ac 13	
Park Hill sw4.	16T 74	
Park Hill w5.	2L 44	
Park Hill Rich.	2U 68	
Park La. n9.	21Ad 17	
Park La. n16.	20F 37	
Park La. n17.	21Aa 17	
Park La. se7.	31R 79	
Park La. se18.	32Q 95	
Park La. w1.	14M 49	
Park La. Cro.	19Zf 91	
Park La. Rich.	1S 68	
Park La. Ted.	1cY 93	
Park La. Wem.	2F 30	
Park Mews nw6.	11J 47	
Park Parade nw10.	7J 46	
Park Pl. se10.	27Q 66	
Park Pl. sw1.	15N 61	
Park Pl. sw4.	16T 73	
Park Pl. w3.	3O 57	
Park Pl. w5.	2M 44	
Park Pl. Wem.	3F 30	
Park Rd. e3.	24L 53	
Park Rd. e6.	30J 55	
Park Rd. e10.	26E 39	
Park Rd. e12.	30E 41	
Park Rd. e15.	29J 54	
Park Rd. e17.	25B 27	
Park Rd. n2.	13A 22	
Park Rd. n8.	16B 23	
Park Rd. n11.	17Ab 16	
Park Rd. n14.	17Af 16	
Park Rd. n15.	19B 25	
Park Rd. n18.	21Ac 17	
Park Rd.		
nw1. 1-77 & 2-98		
nw8. 100, 105 & up	13K 48	
Park Rd. nw4.	8C 20	
Park Rd. nw9.	5C 19	
Park Rd. nw10.	6H 32	
Park Rd. nw10.	6J 46	

Park Rd. se14. 24R 77
Park Rd. se18. 34P 95
Park Rd. se21. 19W 86
Park Rd. se23. 23W 87
Park Rd. se25. 20Zb 90
Park Rd. sw11. 13Q 60
Park Rd. sw19. 10Y 82
Park Rd. sw19. 13Y 83
Park Rd. w4. 5Q 57
Park Rd. w7. 1bM 94
Park Rd. Ilf. 34F 42
Park Rd. Rich. 2T 68
Park Rd. Ted. 1bY 93
Park Rd. Wem. 2G 30
Park Rd. E. w3. 4N 57
Park Rd. N. w3. 4N 57
Park Row se10. 27Q 66
Park Sq. nw1. 15K 49
Park Sq. W. nw1. 15K 49
Park St. e2. 23K 52
Park St. e14. 25M 53
Park St. n1. 18H 36
Park St. n16. 20E 37
Park St. nw1. 15J 49
Park St. se1. 19N 63
Park St. se10. 27Q 66
Park St. se13. 26U 77
Park St. w1. 14M 49
Park St. w10. 8L 47
Park St. Cro. 19Zf 91
Park St. Ted. 1cY 93
Park, The, n6. 15C 23
Park, The, nw11. 12D 22
Park, The, w5. 2N 56
Park View n21. 17Af 16
Park View w3. 5L 45
Park View Wem. 4F 31
Park Wk. n6. 15C 23
Park Wk. sw10. 12Q 60
Park Way sw10. 17AP 19
Park Way n20. 14Ad 15
Park Way nw11. 10B 21
Park Way sw20. 8Zb 92
Park Way Edg. 5Aa 13
Park Av. Rd. n17. 22Aa 17
Parkcroft Rd. se12. 28V 89
Parkdale Rd. se18. 35Q 95
Parke Rd. sw13. 7R 70
Parker Rd. Cro. 19Zg 91
Parker St. e16. 31N 67
Parker St. wc2. 17L 50
Parker's Row se1. 21O 64
Parkfield Av. Har. 1dAa 12
Parkfield Cres. Har. 1dAa 12
Parkfield Rd. nw10. 8G 32
Parkfield Rd. Har. 1dE 12
Parkfield St. n1. 18J 50
Parkfields sw15. 8T 70
Parkfields Av. nw9. 6D 19
Park Gate Gdns. sw14. 5S 69
Park Gro. Rd. e11. 28E 40
Park Hall Rd. n2. 14A 23
Parkham St. sw11. 13T 72
Park Hill Rise Cro. 20Zf 91
Parkhill Rd. nw3. 14G 35
Park Hill Rd. Cro. 20Zf 91
Parkholm Rd. e8. 21H 38
Parkhouse St. se5. 20Q 63
Parkhurst Av. e12. 33F 42
Parkhurst Rd. n7. 17F 36
Parkhurst Rd. n11. 15Ac 15
Parkhurst Rd. n17. 21A 26
Parkhurst Rd. n22. 18Ab 16
Parklands Rd. sw16. 15Y 84
Parklands Dri. n3. 10A 21
Parkleigh Rd. sw19. 11Za 92

Parkmead sw15. 7U 70
Park Pl. Pass. sw7. 13N 61
Park Pl. Villas w2. 12L 48
Parkridings n8. 18A 27
Park Rise Rd. se23. 24V 88
Park Royal Rd. nw10. 5K 45
Parkshot Rich. 2S 68
Parkside n2. 8F 32
Parkside n3. 12Ab 14
Parkside nw2. 8F 32
Parkside Av. sw19. 8X 82
Parkside Dri. Edg. 4Ad 13
Parkside Gdns. sw19. 8X 82
Parkside Gdns. Barn. 14Af 15
Parkside St. sw11. 14R 73
Parkside Way Har. 1dA 12
Parkstead Rd. sw15. 7T 70
Parkstone Av. n18. 21Ab 17
Parkstone Rd. e17. 27A 28
Parkstone Rd. se15. 22S 76
Parkthorne Rd. sw12. 16V 84
Parkview Cres. n11. 15Ad 15
Park View Gdns. nw4. 9B 21
Park View Rd. n3. 12Aa 14
Park View Rd. n17. 22A 26
Park View Rd. nw10. 7F 32
Park View Rd. w5. 2L 44
Parkview Rd. Cro. 21Ze 91
Park Village E. nw1. 15J 49
Park Village W. nw1. 15J 49
Parkville Rd. sw6. 10Q 59
Parkway Ilf. 36F 42
Parliament Hill nw3. 14F 35
Parliament Sq. sw1. 17N 62
Parliament St. sw1. 17N 62
Parma Cres. sw11. 13T 72
Parmiter St. e2. 23J 52
Parnell Rd. e3. 25J 53
Parnham St. e14. 24M 53
Parolles Rd. n19. 16D 23
Parr Rd. e6. 31J 55
Parr St. n1. 20J 51
Parr Rd. se25. 20Zb 90
Parsifal Rd. nw6. 11F 34
Parson St. nw4. 9A 21
Parsonage St. e14. 27P 66
Parsons Cres. Edg. 4Ae 13
Parson's Grn. sw6. 10R 71
Parson's Hill se18. 32P 95
Parson's Mead Cro. 18Ze 91
Parson's Grn.La.sw6. 10R 71
Parthenia Rd. sw6. 11R 71
Parton St. wc1. 17L 50
Parvin St. sw8. 16R 73
Pascal St. sw8. 16Q 62
Pascoe Rd. se13. 27U 78
Pasley Rd. se17. 19P 63
Pasquir Rd. e17. 24A 27
Passmore Gdns. n11. 16Ab 15
Passmore St. sw1. 14P 61
Pasteur Gdns. n18. 19Ac 16
Pasteur St. e1. 22L 52
Pastor St. se11. 19O 63
Pasture Rd. se6. 28W 89
Pasture Rd. Har. 1aE 12
Pater St. w8. 11O 59
Paternoster Row ec4. 19M 51
Paternoster Sq. ec4. 19L 51
Pathfield Rd. sw16. 16Y 85
Patience Rd. sw11. 13S 72
Patmore St. sw8. 15R 73
Patmos Rd. sw9. 18R 74
Paton St. ec1. 19K 51
Patrick Rd. e13. 30K 55

Patriot Sq. e2. 23J 52
Patshull Pl. nw5. 16G 35
Patshull Rd. nw5. 16G 35
Patten Alley Rich. 2T 68
Patten Rd. sw18. 13V 83
Pattenden Rd. se6. 25W 88
Patterson Rd. se19. 21Z 90
Pattison Rd. nw2. 11E 34
Pattison Rd. se18. 34P 95
Pattison St. e1. 23L 52
Paul St. e15. 27H 40
Paul St. ec2. 20K 51
Paulet Rd. se5. 19R 74
Paulin St. se1. 21O 63
Paul's Alley ec1. 19L 51
Paul's Pass se1. 19O 63
Paultons Sq. sw3. 13Q 60
Paultons St. sw3. 13Q 60
Pauntley St. n19. 16D 23
Pavement, The, sw4. 15T 73
Pavilion Rd. sw1. 14O 61
Pawleyne Rd. se20. 23Z 90
Pawsons Rd. Cro. 19Zd 91
Paxford Rd. Har. 1aD 12
Paxford Rd. Wem. 1E 30
Paxton Pl. se27. 20X 86
Paxton Rd. n17. 21Ab 17
Paxton Rd. w4. 6P 57
Payne Rd. e3. 26J 53
Payne St. n1. 18J 50
Payne St. se8. 25Q 65
Paynesfield Av. sw14. 5S 69
Peabody Av. sw1. 15P 61
Peabody Sq. se1. 18N 62
Peabody Trust Cotts. n17.
20Aa 17
Peach St. w10. 9K 47
Peacock St. se17. 19P 63
Peak, The, se26. 23X 87
Peak Hill se26. 23X 87
Peak Hill Av. se26. 23X 87
Peak Hill Gdns. se26. 23X 87
Peaketon Av. Ilf. 31B 29
Peall Rd. Cro. 17Zd 91
Pear Clo. nw9. 5B 19
Pearcefield Av. se23. 23W 87
Pearcroft Rd. e11. 27E 40
Peardon St. sw8. 15S 73
Pearfield Rd. se23. 24W 87
Pearl Rd. e17. 25A 27
Pearl St. e1. 22N 64
Pearman Pl. se1. 18O 62
Pearscroft Rd. sw6. 11R 72
Pearson Rd. e2. 21J 51
Pearson St. se10. 26Q 65
Pearson St. sw11. 13S 72
Pear Tree St. ec1. 19K 51
Pear Tree St. se1. 18N 62
Pebworth Rd. Har. 1aE 12
Peckford Pl. sw9. 18S 74
Peckham Gro. se15. 20Q 63
Peckham Rd.
se5. 1-93 & 2-84.
se15. 86, 95 & up. 20R 75
Peckham Rye
se15. 1-259 & 2-132.
se22. 134 & up. 22T 76
Peckham High St. se15.
21R 76
Peckham Pk. Rd. se15.
22Q 64
Peckwater St. nw5. 16G 35
Pedley St. e1. 21K 52
Pedro St. e5. 24F 38
Pedworth Rd. se16. 23P 64
Peek Cres. sw19. 9X 82

Peel Gro. E2. 23J 52
Peel Rd. NW6. 10J 47
Peel Rd. Har. 1bA 12
Peel Rd. Wem. 1E 30
Peel St. w8 11N 59
Peerless St. EC1. 20K 51
Pegwell St. NW1. 13L 48
Pegwell St. SE18. 35R 95
Pekin St. E14. 25M 53
Peldon Av. Rich. 3T 68
Pelham Av. Bar. 35J 43
Pelham Cres. sw7. 13P 60
Pelham Pl. sw7. 13O 60
Pelham Rd. E18. 29A 29
Pelham Rd. N15. 21B 25
Pelham Rd. N22. 18A 24
Pelham Rd. sw19. 10Z 92
Pelham Rd. Cro. 23Za 90
Pelham Rd. Ilf. 35E 42
Pelham St. E1. 22L 52
Pelham St. sw7. 13O 60
Pell St. E1. 22M 52
Pellant Rd. sw6. 10Q 59
Pellatt Gro. N22. 18Aa 16
Pellatt Rd. SE22. 21U 75
Pellerin Rd. N16. 21G 37
Pelling St. E14. 25M 53
Pellipar Rd. SE18. 32P 95
Pelly Rd. E13. 29J 55
Pelton Rd. SE10. 27P 66
Pembar Av. E17. 24A 27
Pember Rd. NW10. 9K 47
Pemberton Gdns. N19. 16E 35
Pemberton Rd. N4. 18C 24
Pemberton Ter. N19. 16E 35
Pembridge Cres. w11. 11M 47
Pembridge Gdns. w2. 11M 47
Pembridge Pl. w2. 11M 47
Pembridge Rd. w11. 11M 47
Pembridge Sq. w2. 11M 47
Pembridge Villas w11.
11M 47
Pembroke Av. Har. 1aA 12
Pembroke Gdns. w8. 10O 59
Pembroke Mews N. sw1.
14N 61
Pembroke Pl. w8. 11O 59
Pembroke Pl. Edg. 4Ab 13
Pembroke Rd. E17. 26B 27
Pembroke Rd. N8. 17A 24
Pembroke Rd. N10. 15Aa 15
Pembroke Rd. N15. 21B 25
Pembroke Rd. SE25. 20Zc 90
Pembroke Rd. w8. 10O 59
Pembroke Rd. Ilf. 36D 42
Pembroke Rd. Wem. 2E 30
Pembroke Sq. w8. 11O 59
Pembroke St. N1. 17H 36
Pembroke Villas w8. 11O 59
Pembroke Villas Rich. 1T 68
Pembury Gro. E5. 22G 38
Pembury Rd. E5. 22G 38
Pembury Rd. N17. 21Aa 17
Pembury Rd. SE25. 21Zc 90
Pemdevon Rd. Cro. 18Zd 91
Pemell's Pl. SE15. 22R 76
Penally Pl. N1. 20K 51
Penang St. E1. 22N 64
Penarth St. SE15. 23Q 64
Penberth Rd. SE6. 26V 89
Penda Rd. E5. 24F 39
Pendarves Rd. sw20. 8Z 92
Pendennis Rd. N15. 20A 25
Pendennis Rd. sw16. 17X 85
Pender St. SE8. 25Q 65
Penderry Rise SE6. 27V 89

Pendle Rd. sw16. 15Y 84
Pendlestone Rd. E17. 26C 27
Pendragon Rd. SE12. 28X 89
Pendrell Rd. SE4. 24S 76
Pendrell St. SE18. 35Q 95
Penerley Rd. SE6. 26V 88
Penfold Pl. NW1. 13L 48
Penfold St.
NW. 1-11 & 2-28.
NW8. 13, 30 & up. 13K 48
Penford Gds. SE9. 31T 79
Penford St. SE5. 18R 74
Penge La. SE20. 23Z 90
Penge Rd. E13. 30J 55
Penge Rd.
SE25. 1-81 & 2-70.
SE20. 72, 83 & up. 21Zb 90
Penistone Rd. sw16. 16Z 90
Penn Clo. Har. 1B 18
Penn Rd. N7. 17F 36
Penn St. N1. 20J 51
Pennack Rd. SE15. 21Q 63
Pennant Mews w8. 11O 60
Pennard Rd. w12. 8N 59
Pennethorne Rd. SE15.
22R 76
Pennine Dri. NW2. 9E 33
Pennington St. E1. 22M 52
Pennyfields E14. 25M 53
Penpoll Rd. E8. 22G 38
Penrhyn Cres. sw14. 5T 69
Penrith Rd. N15. 20B 25
Penrith Rd. Cro. 19Za 90
Penrith St. sw16. 15Y 84
Penrose Gro. SE17. 19P 63
Penrose St. SE17. 19P 63
Penry Rd. SE1. 21P 64
Penryn St. NW1. 16J 49
Pensbury St. sw8. 16R 73
Pensford Av. Kew 3R 69
Penshurst Gdns. Edg. 4Ac 13
Penshurst Rd. E9. 23H 38
Penshurst Rd. Cro. 18Zc 90
Pentland St. sw18. 11U 72
Pentlow St. sw15. 8S 71
Pentney Rd. sw12. 15V 84
Penton Gro. N1. 18J 50
Penton Pl. SE17. 19P 63
Penton Rise wc1. 18J 50
Penton St. N1. 18J 50
Pentonville Rd. N1. 17J 50
Pentridge St. SE15. 21R 75
Pentyre Av. N18. 20Ac 17
Penwith Rd. sw18. 11W 82
Penwortham Rd. sw16.
15Y 84
Penylan Pl. Edg. 4Ab 13
Penywern Rd. sw5. 11P 60
Penzance Pl. w11. 10M 47
Pepler Rd. SE15. 21P 63
Peploe Rd. NW6. 9J 47
Pepper St. SE1. 19N 63
Pepys Rd. SE14. 23R 76
Pepys Rd. sw20. 8Z 92
Pepys St. EC3. 21M 51
Perceval Av. NW3. 13G 34
Perch St. E8. 21F 37
Percival Rd. sw14. 4T 69
Percival St. EC1. 19K 50
Percy Circus wc1. 18K 50
Percy Rd. E9. 23H 38
Percy Rd. E11. 28D 28
Percy Rd. E16. 28L 54
Percy Rd. N12. 12Ac 14
Percy Rd. N21. 20Ae 16
Percy Rd. NW6. 11J 47

Percy Rd. SE20. 23Za 90
Percy Rd. SE25. 21Zc 90
Percy Rd. w12. 7N 58
Percy Rd. Ilf. 36D 42
Percy St. E11. 27E 40
Percy St. w1. 16L 49
Percy Ter. E9. 25G 39
Percy Villas w8. 11N 59
Pereira St. E1. 22K 52
Perham Rd. w14. 10P 59
Perimeade Rd. Wem. 1J 44
Periton Rd. SE9. 30T 79
Perivale La. Wem. 2J 44
Perkin's Rents sw1. 16O 62
Perran Rd. sw2. 18W 85
Perrers Rd. w6. 8O 58
Perring St. E3. 25L 53
Perrins Ct. NW3. 12F 34
Perrin's La. NW3. 12F 34
Perrin's Wk. NW3. 12F 34
Perry Gdns. N9. 20Ad 17
Perry Hill SE6. 24X 88
Perry Rise SE23. 24X 88
Perry Vale SE23. 23W 87
Perrymans Farm Rd. Ilf.
34C 42
Perrymead St. sw6. 11R 72
Perryn Rd. w3. 5M 45
Perth Av. NW9. 6C 19
Perth Rd. E10. 24D 27
Perth Rd. E13. 29K 55
Perth Rd. N4. 18D 24
Perth Rd. N22. 19Aa 16
Perth Rd. Bar. 35J 43
Perth Rd. Ilf. 33C 42
Perth St. E1. 23L 52
Perth Ter. Ilf. 34D 42
Peter Av. NW10. 8H 32
Peter St. E2. 21K 51
Peter St. E3. 26K 53
Peter St. E16. 28L 54
Peter St. w1. 16M 49
Peterborough Rd. E10.
27C 28
Peterborough Rd. sw6.
11S 71
Peterborough Rd. Har. 1bD 12
Peterborough Villas sw6.
11R 72
Petergate sw11. 12T 72
Peter's La. EC1. 19L 50
Petersfield Clo. N18. 19Ac 16
Petersfield Rd. w3. 5N 57
Petersham Mews sw7.12O 60
Petherton Rd. N5. 20C 37
Petley Rd. w6. 9Q 59
Peto Pl. NW1. 15K 49
Peto St. E16. 28M 54
Pett St. SE18. 31P 67
Petty France sw1. 16O 61
Petworth Rd. N12. 13Ac 15
Petworth St. sw11. 13R 72
Petyward sw3. 13P 60
Pevensey Rd. E7. 29F 40
Pevensey Rd. N11. 16Ac 15
Pevensey Rd. sw17. 12X 83
Peveril St. sw11. 13R 72
Peyton Pl. SE10. 26R 77
Phelp St. SE17. 20Q 63
Phene St. sw3. 13Q 60
Philbeach Gdns. sw5. 10P 59
Philip La. EC2. 19L 51
Philip La. N15. 20B 25
Philip Rd. SE15. 22S 76
Philip St. E1. 22M 52

Philip St. E13.	29L 54	Pitt St. SE15.	21R 75
Philip Ter. W2.	11L 48	Pitt St. W1.	16L 49
Philippa Gdns. SE9.	30U 79	Pitt St. W8.	11N 60
Phillimore Gdns. NW10.		Pitt's Head Mews W1.	
	8H 32		15N 61
Phillimore Gdns. W8.	11N 59	Pixley St. E14.	25L 53
Phillimore Wk. W8.	11N 59	Plaistow Gro. E15.	28J 54
Phillip St. N1.	20J 51	Plaistow Rd. E15.	28J 54
Philpot La. EC3.	20M 51	Plaistow Pk. Rd. E13.	29J 55
Philpot St. E1.	22L 52	Planet St. E1.	22M 52
Phipp St. EC2.	20K 51	Plashet Gro. E6.	31H 41
Phipps Bridge Rd. Mit.		Plashet La. E6.	31J 55
	12Za 92	Plashet Rd. E13.	29H 41
Phoebe St. E14.	25M 53	Plassy Rd. SE6.	26V 88
Phœbeth Rd. SE4.	25U 77	Plato Rd. SW2.	17T 74
Phœnix Pl. WC1.	18K 50	Platt St. NW1.	16J 50
Phœnix Rd. SE20.	23Z 90	Platt, The, SW15.	9S 71
Phœnix St. N1.	16J 50	Platt's La. NW3.	11E 34
Phœnix Yd. W1.	15L 49	Playfair St. W6.	8P 59
Phyllis Av. Mor.	8Zc 92	Playfield Cres. SE22.	20U 75
Piccadilly W1.	15N 61	Playfield Rd. Edg.	5Aa 13
Piccadilly Circus W1.	16M 49	Playford Rd. N4.	18E 36
Pickard St. EC1.	19K 51	Play Green Way SE6.	25X 88
Pickering St. N1.	19H 37	Playhouse Yd. EC4.	19M 50
Pickets St. SW12.	14V 84	Pleasance Rd. SW15.	7T 70
Pickle Herring St. SE1.		Pleasance, The, SW15.	7T 70
	21N 63	Pleasant Pl. N1.	19H 37
Pickwick Rd. SE21.	20U 75	Pleasant Pl. SW4.	16T 73
Pickwick St. SE1.	19N 63	Pleasant Way NW1.	1J 44
Picton Pl. W1.	14L 49	Plevna Cres. N15.	21C 26
Picton St. SE5.	20R 75	Plevna Rd. N15.	20C 26
Piedmont Rd. SE18.	35Q 95	Plevna St. E14.	26O 65
Pier St. E14.	27P 66	Pleydell Av. E19.	21Z 90
Piercefield St. NW5.	14G 35	Pleydell Av. W6.	6O 58
Piermont Rd. SE22.	22U 76	Plimsoll Rd. N4.	19E 36
Pierrepoint Rd. W3.	4M 45	Plimsoll St. E14.	26M 53
Pigott St. E14.	25M 53	Plough Alley E1.	22N 64
Pilgrim Hill SE27.	19X 86	Plough Ct. EC4.	18L 50
Pilgrim St. W4.	19M 50	Plough La. E9.	23G 38
Pilgrimage St. SE1.	19O 63	Plough La. SE22.	21U 75
Pilgrim's La. NW3.	13F 34	Plough La. SW17.	
Pilgrim's Way, Cro.	21Zb 91	& SW19.	11X 82
Pilkington Rd. SE15.	22S 76	Plough Rd. SE16.	24P 65
Pimlico Rd. SW1.	14P 61	Plough Rd. SW11.	12S 72
Pimlico Wk. N1.	20J 51	Plough St. E1.	21L 52
Pinchin St. E1.	22M 52	Plough Ter. SW11.	12T 72
Pincott Rd. SW19.	11Z 92	Plover St. E9.	25G 39
Pindar St. EC2.	20L 51	Plum Garth, Bre.	2O 56
Pindock Mews W9.	11K 48	Plum La. SE18.	33R 95
Pine Gro. N4.	17E 36	Plumber's Row E1.	22L 52
Pine Gro. N20.	11Af 14	Plumbridge St. SE10.	26R 77
Pine Coombe, Cro.	23Zg 91	Plumstead Rd. SE18.	33P 95
Pine Rd. NW2.	9F 33	Plum Tree Ct. EC4.	18L 50
Pine St. EC1.	18K 50	Plumstead Common Rd.	
Pinfold Rd. SW16.	16X 85	SE18.	33Q 95
Pink's Row EC1.	19K 51	Plumstead High St. SE18.	
Pinnell Rd. SE9.	31T 79		35P 95
Pinner Rd. Har.	1dB 12	Plymouth Rd. E16.	29L 54
Pinner View Har.	1dA 12	Plympton Av. NW6.	10H 33
Pinner Pk. Av. Har.	1dAa 12	Plympton Rd. NW6.	10H 33
Pinner Pk. Gns. Har.	1cAa 12	Plympton St. NW8.	13K 48
Piquet Rd. SE20.	22Za 90	Pocock St. SE1.	19N 63
Pirbright Rd. SW18.	10V 82	Podmore Rd. SW18.	12T 72
Pitcairn St. SW8.	15S 73	Poet's Rd. N5.	20G 37
Pitchford St. E15.	27H 40	Point Hill SE10.	26R 78
Pitfield St. N1.	20K 51	Point Pleasant SW18.	10T 71
Pitfield Way NW10.	5G 31	Poland St. W1.	16M 49
Pitfold Rd. SE6.	29V 89	Pole St. E1.	23L 52
Pitlake Bridge, Cro.	18Ze 91	Pollard Rd. NW9.	7C 20
Pitman St. SE5.	19O 63	Pollard Row E2.	22K 52
Pitsea Pl. E1.	23M 52	Pollard St. E2.	22K 52
Pitshanger La. W5.	1K 44	Pollards Cres. SW16.	16Zb 90
Pitshanger Rd. W13.	1aK 94	Pollards Hill, E. SW16.	
Pitt Cres. SW19.	11X 82		17Zb 90
Pitt Rd. Cro.	19Zc 90	Pollards Hill, N. SW16.	
Pitt St. E16.	28L 54		17Zb 90
Pollards Hill, S. SW16.			
	17Zb 90		
Pollards Hill, W. SW16.			
	17Zb 90		
Pollards Rd. N20.	13Ad 14		
Pollards Wood Rd. Cro.			
	16Zb 90		
Pollen St. W1.	15M 49		
Pollock Rd. SE17.	19O 63		
Polstead Rd. SE6.	25V 88		
Polthorne St. SE18.	34P 95		
Polworth Rd. SW16.	17Y 85		
Polytechnic St. SE18.	33P 95		
Pomeroy St. SE14.	23R 76		
Pomfret Rd. SE5.	18S 74		
Pond Cotts. SE21.	20W 86		
Pond Pl. SW3.	13P 60		
Pond Rd. E15.	28J 54		
Pond Rd. SE3.	28S 78		
Pond Sq. N6.	15D 23		
Pond St. NW3.	13F 34		
Pont St. Mews SW1.	13O 61		
Pont St. SW1.	14O 61		
Ponler St. E1.	22M 52		
Ponsard Rd. NW10.	8J 46		
Ponsonby Pl. SW1.	16P 62		
Ponsonby Rd. SW15.	7V 81		
Ponsonby Ter. SW1.	16P 62		
Pont St. SW1.	14O 61		
Ponton Rd. SW8.	16Q 62		
Ponton St. SW8.	16Q 62		
Poole Rd. E9.	23H 38		
Poole St. N1.	20J 51		
Pooles Pk. N4.	18E 36		
Poolsford Rd. NW9.	6A 20		
Pope St. SE1.	21O 63		
Popes Av. Twi.	1cV 93		
Popes Gro. Twi.	1aW 93		
Pope's La. W5.	2O 56		
Pope's Rd. SW9.	18S 74		
Popham Rd. N1.	19H 37		
Popham St. N1.	19H 37		
Poplar Gro. W6.	8N 59		
Poplar Pl. W2.	11M 48		
Poplar Rd. SW19.	10Za 92		
Poplar Wk. SE24.	19T 75		
Poplar Wk. Cro.	19Ze 91		
Poplar High St. E14.	26M 53		
Poplar Wk. Rd. SE24.	19T 75		
Poplar's Av. NW2.	8G 32		
Poplars Rd. E17.	26C 27		
Poppleton Rd. E11.	28C 28		
Porchester Gdns. W2.	11M 48		
Porchester Pl. W2.	13L 48		
Porchester Rd. W2.	11L 48		
Porchester Sq. W2.	11L 48		
Porchester St. W2.	13L 48		
Porchester Ter. W2.	12L 48		
Porden Rd. SW2.	17T 74		
Porlock Av. Har.	1dD 12		
Porlock Rd. N9.	21Af 17		
Porlock St. W10.	9K 47		
Porson St. SE13.	26S 77		
Porten Rd. W14.	9O 59		
Porteus Rd. W2.	12L 48		
Porthcawe Rd. SE26.	24X 88		
Portinscale Rd. SW15.	10U 71		
Portland Av. N16.	21D 25		
Portland Gdns. N4.	19C 25		
Portland Pl. W1.	15L 49		
Portland Pl.N. SW8.	17R 74		
Portland Pl. S. SW8.	17R 74		
Portland Rd. E16.	29M 54		
Portland Rd. N4.	19D 25		
Portland Rd. N15.	21B 25		
Portland Rd. W11.	10M 47		

Portland Rd. Cro. 21Zb 90
Portland Rd. Mit. 13Za 92
Portland St. E1. 24M 52
Portland St. SE17. 20P 63
Portland Ter. NW8. 13J 48
Portland Ter. Rich. 1T 68
Portman Av. sw14. 5S 69
Portman Bldgs. NW1. 13K 48
Portman Dri. Ilf. 31A 29
Portman Gdns. NW9. 5A 13
Portman Mans. w1. 14L 49
Portman Mews N. w1. 14L 49
Portman Mews S. w1. 14M 49
Portman Pl. E2. 23K 52
Portman Sq. w1. 14L 49
Portman St. w1. 14M 49
Portnall Rd. w9. 10J 47
Portobello Rd.
 w11. 1-275 & 2-262
 w10. 264, 277 & up 10L 47
Portpool La. EC1. 18L 50
Portree St. E14. 27M 54
Portsdown Av. NW11. 10C 21
Portsdown Mews NW6. 11J 48
Portsdown Pl.NW6. 11J 48
Portsdown Rd. w9. 11J 48
Portsea Pl. w2. 13M 48
Portslade Rd. sw8. 15R 73
Portsmouth St. wc2. 17M 50
Portugal St. wc2. 17M 50
Portway E15. 28H 40
Potier St. SE1. 20O 63
Pott St. E2. 22K 52
Potter's Fields SE1. 21N 63
Pottery La. w11. 10M 47
Pottery Rd. Bre. 2P 56
Pottery St. SE16. 22N 64
Poulett Gdns. Twi. 1bV 93
Poulett Rd. E6. 32J 43
Poultry EC2. 20M 51
Pound La. NW10. 7G 32
Pound Pk. Rd. SE7. 31P 67
Pountney Rd. sw11. 14S 73
Pourland Wk. Edg. 5Ac 13
Powell Rd. E5. 22F 38
Powell Rd. w4. 6P 57
Powell St. EC1. 19K 51
Powell's Wk. w4. 6Q 58
Power Rd. w4. 3O 57
Power St. sw8. 15R 73
Power's Pl. SE14. 23R 76
Powerscroft Rd. E5. 23F 38
Powis Gdns. NW11. 10C 21
Powis Gdns. w11. 10L 47
Powis La. N13. 17Ac 16
Powis Mews w11. 10L 47
Powis Rd. wc1. 17L 50
Powis Rd. E3. 26K 53
Powis Sq. w11. 10L 47
Powis St. SE18. 33P 95
Powis Ter. w11. 10L 47
Powlett Pl. NW1. 15H 35
Pownall Rd. E8. 21J 52
Pownall Rd. sw6. 10Q 59
Poynders Rd. sw4. 15U 73
Poynings Rd. N19. 16E 35
Poynings Way N12. 11Ac 14
Poynton Rd. N17. 22Aa 17
Poyntz Rd. sw11. 14S 73
Poyser St. E2. 22J 52
Praed St. w2. 13L 48
Pragell St. E13. 30K 55
Prague St. sw2. 17U 74
Prah Rd. N4. 18E 36
Prairie St. sw8. 15S 73
Pratt St. NW1. 15J 49

Pratt St. SE11. 17O 62
Prebend Gdns.
 w4. 1-37 & 2-40
 w6. 39, 42 & up 6O 58
Prebend St. N1. 19J 51
Prentis Rd. sw16. 16X 84
Presburg St. E5. 23F 38
Prescelly Pl. Edg. 3Aa 13
Prescot St. E1. 21M 52
Prescott Pl. sw4. 16S 73
President St. EC1. 19K 51
Pressland St. w10. 10K 47
Prestage St. E14. 27M 54
Prestbury Rd. E7. 30H 41
Prested Rd. sw11. 13T 72
Preston Clo. Twi. 1cW 93
Preston Dri. E11. 30C 29
Preston Gdns. NW10. 6G 32
Preston Gdns. Ilf. 32C 42
Preston Pl. Rich. 2T 68
Preston Rd. E11. 28C 28
Preston Rd. E15. 27J 54
Preston Rd. sw19. 18Y 85
Preston St. E2. 23K 52
Preston's Rd. E14. 26M 54
Prestwood Av. Har. 1aB 12
Prestwood Clo. Har. 1A 18
Pretoria Av. E17. 24B 27
Pretoria Rd. E11. 27D 28
Pretoria Rd. E16. 28K 54
Pretoria Rd. N17 & N18.
 21Ab 17
Pretoria Rd. sw16. 15Y 84
Pretoria Rd. Ilf. 33G 43
Price's St. SE1. 19N 62
Prideaux Pl. wc1. 18K 50
Prideaux Rd. sw9. 17S 74
Pridham Rd. E. Cro. 19Zc 90
Pridham Rd. W. Cro. 19Zc 90
Priestfield Rd. SE23. 24X 88
Priestley St. sw4. 23G 38
Priest's Bridge sw14 & 15.
 6S 70
Prima Rd. sw9. 18Q 62
Primrose Ct. E18. 30A 29
Primrose Rd. E10. 26E 39
Primrose Rd. E18. 30A 29
Primrose Way Wem. 1J 44
Primrose St. EC2. 20L 51
Primrose Hill Rd. NW3.
 14H 35
Primula St. w12. 7M 46
Prince Rd. SE25. 20Zc 90
Prince St. SE8. 25Q 65
Prince Arthur Rd. NW3.
 12F 34
Prince Consort Rd. sw7.
 12O 60
Prince Edward Rd. E9.25G 39
Prince George Rd.N16.21F 37
Prince George's Av. sw20.
 8Za 92
Prince George's Rd. sw19.
 13Z 92
Prince John Rd. sE9. 31U 79
Princelet St. E1. 21L 52
Prince of Wales Cres. NW1.
 15G 35
Prince of Wales Dri. sw11.
 14R 73
Prince of Wales Rd. E16.
 30M 55
Prince of Wales Rd. NW4.
 8A 20
Prince of Wales Rd. NW5.
 15G 35

Prince of Wales Ter. w4.
 6P 57
Prince of Wales Ter. w8.
 11N 60
Prince Regent's Lane
 E13. 1-279 & 2-250.
 E16.258,323 & up. 30K 55
Prince's Av. N3. 11Aa 14
Prince's Av. N10. 15A 23
Prince's Av. N13. 18Ac 16
Prince's Av. N22 16Aa 15
Prince's Av. NW9. 3B 19
Prince's Av. w3. 3O 57
Prince's Clo. Edg. 4Ac 13
Prince's Court E2. 21K 51
Princes Ct. Wem. 2F 30
Prince's Dri. Har. 1bA 12
Princes Gdns. sw7. 13O 60
Princes Gdns. w3. 4L 45
Princes Gdns. w5. 1K 44
Princes Gate sw7. 13N 60
Princes Mews w2. 13O 60
Princes Pl. w11. 9N 59
Princes Pl. w13. 1M 44
Princes Rd. SE11. 17P 62
Princes Rd. SE13. 26S 78
Princes Rd. SE18. 33Q 95
Princes Rd. SE20. 23Z 90
Prince's Rd. sw14. 5S 69
Princes Rd. sw19. 9V 82
Princes Rd. sw19. 10Y 82
Princes Rd. w1. 10M 47
Princes Rd. Kew 3Q 56
Prince's Rd. Rich. 2T 68
Princes Rd. Twi. 1dX 93
Princes Row sw1. 15O 61
Princes Sq. E1. 22M 52
Prince's Sq. w2. 11M 48
Princes St. EC2. 20M 51
Princes St. N17. 21Ab 17
Princes St. sw1. 16N 62
Princes St. w1. 15L 49
Princes St. w1. 15M 49
Prince's Way Cro. 17Zh 91
Princes Pk. Av. NW11.10B 21
Princess Pl. SE1. 19O 63
Princess Rd. N4. 19E 37
Princess Rd. NW1. 14H 35
Princess Rd. NW6. 11J 47
Princess Rd. Cro. 19Zd 91
Princess St. NW8. 13K 48
Princess May Rd. N16.21F 37
Princethorpe Rd. SE26.
 23X 87
Princeton St. wc1. 17L 50
Priolo Rd. SE7. 30Q 67
Prior St. SE10. 26R 77
Prioress St. SE1. 20O 63
Priors Croft E17. 24A 27
Priory Av. E17. 25B 27
Priory Av. N8. 16B 24
Priory Ct. sw8. 16R 74
Priory Gdns. N6. 15C 23
Priory Gdns sw13. 6S 70
Priory Gro. sw8. 16R 74
Priory Gro. sw10. 12P 60
Priory La. SE3. 28T 78
Priory La. sw15. 6U 70
Priory Pl. NW1. 15H 35
Priory Rd. E6. 31J 55
Priory Rd. N8. 16B 24
Priory Rd. N15. 20C 25
Priory Rd. NW6. 11H 34
Priory Rd. sw19. 12Z 92
Priory Rd. w4. 5O 57

Priory Rd. Bar. 34H 43
Priory Rd. Cro. 17Zd 91
Priory Rd. Kew. 3Q 57
Priory St. E3. 26K 53
Priory Ter. NW6. 11H 34
Priory Pk.Rd. NW6. 10H 33
Priscilla Rd. E3. 26K 53
Pritchard's Rd. E2. 22J 52
Priter Rd. SE16. 22O 64
Probert Rd. sw2. 18T 74
Probyn Rd. sw2. 18W 85
Progress Way Cro. 17Ze 91
Promenade w4. 6R 70
Promenade App. Rd. w4. 6Q 57
Prospect Hill E17. 26B 27
Prospect Pl. N1. 18H 36
Prospect Pl. N2. 13A 22
Prospect Pl. N17 21Aa 17
Prospect Pl. SE14. 23R 76
Prospect Rd. E17. 25C 27
Prospect Rd. NW2. 11E 33
Prospect Rd.SE26. 22X 87
Prospect St. SE16. 22O 64
Prospect Ter. wc1. 17K 50
Prospect Vale SE18. 31P 67
Prospero Rd. N19. 16D 23
Prothero Gdns. NW4. 8B 20
Protheroe Rd. sw6. 10Q 59
Prout Gro. NW10. 6F 32
Prout Rd. E5. 22E 38
Provence St. N1. 19J 51
Providence Pl. NW6. 11G 34
Providence Pl. w1. 14M 49
Providence Pl. w12. 9N 59
Providence St. E1. 22M 52
Provost Rd. NW3. 14H 35
Provost St. N1. 20J 51
Pudsom St. F1 22N 64
Pudding La. EC3. 20M 51
Pudding Mill La. E15. 26J 53
Pulborough Rd. sw18. 10V 82
Pulford St. sw1. 16P 61
Pulross Rd. sw9. 17S 74
Pulteney Rd. E18. 29A 29
Pulteney St. N1. 18J 50
Pulteney Ter. N1. 18H 36
Pulton Pl. sw6. 11Q 59
Puma Ct. E1. 21L 51
Pump Pail Cro. 19Zf 91
Pumping Station Rd. w4. 6Q 58
Punderson's Gdns. E2. 22K 52
Purbeck Dri. NW2. 9D 21
Purbrook St. SE1. 21O 63
Purcell Cre. sw6. 9Q 59
Purcell St. N1. 20J 51
Purcells Av. Edg. 4Ac 13
Purchese St. NW1. 16J 50
Purdy St. E3. 26K 53
Purley Av. NW2. 10E 33
Purley Rd. N9. 20Ad 17
Purley Way Cro. 17Zg 91
Purnell Pl. SE16. 23N 64
Purneys Rd. SE9. 30T 79
Purrett Rd. SE18. 36Q 95
Purser's Cross Rd. sw6. 10R 71
Purves Rd. NW10. 8J 44
Putney Bridge sw6. 9S 71
Putney Heath sw15. 7 U 70
Putney Hill sw15. 9U 71
Putney BridgeApp.sw6.9S 71
Putney Bridge Rd.
  sw18. 1-73 & 2-114
  sw15. 75, 116 & up 10T 71

Putney Heath La. sw15. 9U 71
Putney High St. sw15. 9T 71
Putney Pk. Av. sw15. 7T 70
Putney Pk. La. sw15. 7T 70
Pyecombe Corner N12. 11Ad 14
Pymmes Gdns. N. N9. 21Ad 17
Pymmes Gdns. S. N9. 21Ad 17
Pymmes Rd. N13. 17Ab 16
Pymmes Grn. Rd. N11. 15Ad 15
Pyrland Rd. N5. 20G 37
Pyrland Rd. Rich. 3U 68
Pyrmont Gro. SE27. 18X 85
Pyrmont Rd. w4. 3P 57
Pyrmont Rd. Ilf. 34E 42
Pytchley Rd. SE5. 20S 75
Quadrant Gro. NW5. 14G 35
Quadrant Rd. N1. 19H 37
Quadrant Rd. Cro. 18Zc 90
Quadrant Rd. Rich. 2T 68
Quadrant St. E16. 27L 54
Quadrant, The, sw19. 9Z 92
Quadrant, The, Rich. 2T 68
Quainton St. NW10. 5E 31
Quaker St. E1. 21L 51
Quantock Gdns. NW2. 9D 33
Quarrendon St. sw6. 11R 71
Quarry Rd. sw18. 12U 72
Quebec Rd. Ilf. 34D 42
Queen Sq. wc1. 17L 50
Queen St. E1. 22L 52
Queen St. F.15. 27G 40
Queen St. EC4. 19M 51
Queen St. NW1. 16J 49
Queen St. w1. 15N 61
Queen St. WC. n18
Queen St. Cro. 19Zf 91
Queen St. Pl. EC4. 19M 51
Queen Adelaide Rd. SE20. 23Z 90
Queen Anne Rd. E9. 23H 38
Queen Anne St. w1. 15L 49
Queen Anne's Gdns. w4. 6O 58
Queen Anne's Gdns. w5. 2N 56
Queen Anne's Gate sw1. 16N 61
Queen Anne's Gro. N9. 20Af 17
Queen Anne's Gro. w4. 6O 57
Queen Anne's Gro. w5. 2N 56
Queen Elizabeth Dri. N14. 17Ae 16
Queen Elizabeth Rd. E17. 24A 27
Queen Elizabeth St. SE1. 21N 63
Queen Elizabeth's Wk. N16. 20E 37
Queenhithe EC4. 19M 51
Queen Margaret's Gro. N1. 20G 37
Queens Av. N3. 12Ab 14
Queen's Av. N10. 15A 23
Queens Av. N20. 13Ae 14
Queen's Av. N21. 19Ae 16
Queen's Circus sw11. 15R 73
Queen's Clo. Edg. 4Ac 13
Queen's Ct. SE1. 19N 63

Queen's Ct. Wem. 2E 30
Queen's Cres. NW5. 14G 35
Queen's Dri. w5. 3L 44
Queen's Gdns. NW4. 9B 21
Queen's Gdns. w2. 12M 48
Queen's Gdns. w5. 1K 44
Queen's Gate sw7. 12O 60
Queen's Pl. N1. 19H 37
Queen's Pl. sw8. 15S 73
Queen's Pl. w11. 9N 59
Queen's Ride sw13. 7S 70
Queen's Rd. E8. 21H 38
Queen's Rd. E11. 27D 28
Queen's Rd. E13. 29J 55
Queen's Rd. E17. 25C 27
Queens Rd. N2. 12Aa 14
Queen's Rd. N4. 19E 37
Queens Rd. N9. 22Ad 17
Queens Rd. N11. 17Ab 16
Queen's Rd. NW4. 8B 21
Queen's Rd. NW8. 13J 48
Queen's Rd.
  SE15. 1-289 & 2-222.
  SE14. 291, 224 & up.
22R 76
Queen's Rd. SE19. 19Y 85
Queens Rd. SE25. 21Zb 90
Queen's Rd. sw8. 15S 73
Queens Rd. sw14. 5S 69
Queens Rd. sw19. 10Y 82
Queen's Rd. w2. 11M 48
Queens Rd. w5. 2L 44
Queens Rd. Bar. 34H 43
Queen's Rd. Cro. 18Zd 91
Queens Rd. Ilf. 34E 42
Queen's Rd. Mit. 12Za 92
Queen's Rd. Mor. 11Zb 92
Queen's Rd. Ted. 1cY 93
Queen's Rd. Twi. 1bV 93
Queens Row SE17. 19Q 63
Queen's St. N18. 21Ab 17
Queen's Wk. NW8. n18
Queen's Wk. sw1. 15N 61
Queen's Wk. w5. 1K 44
Queen's Wk. Har. 1cA 12
Queensberry Mews sw7. 12O 60
Queensberry Pl. sw7. 12O 60
Queensborough Ter. w2. 12M 48
Queensbury Rd. NW9. 5C 19
Queensbury Rd. Wem. 3J 44
Queensbury St. N1. 19H 37
Queen's Club Gdns. w14. 10Q 59
Queenscroft Rd. SE9. 31U 79
Queensdale Rd. w11. 9N 59
Queensdown Rd. E5. 22F 38
Queensferry Rd. E16. 29M 54
Queen's Gate Gdns. sw7. 12O 60
Queen's Gate Mews sw7. 12O 60
Queen's Gate Pl. sw7. 12O 60
Queen's Gate Pl. Mews sw7. 12O 60
Queen's Gate Ter. sw7. 12O 60
Queen's Head St. N1. 19J 51
Queensland Av. N18. 20Ab 16
Queensland Av. sw19. 11Z 92
Queensland Rd. N7. 18F 36
Queensmere Rd sw19. 8W 82
Queensmill Rd sw6. 9Q 59
Queen's Ter. Mews sw7. 12O 60

Queensthorpe Gdns. N3.
    11A 22
Queensthorpe Rd. SE26.
    23X 87
Queensville Rd. SW12. 16V 84
Queensway, Cro. 17Zh 91
Queer.swell Av. N20. 14Ad 15
Qu.eenswood Av. Cro.
    18Zc 90
Queens Wood Rd. N6. 15C 23
Queenswood Rd. SE23.
    24X 87
Queen Victoria St. EC4.
    19M 51
Quemerford Rd. N7. 17F 36
Quentin Rd. SE13. 28T 78
Quernmore Rd. N4. 18C 24
Querrin St. SW6. 12S 72
Quex Rd. NW6. 11H 34
Quick Rd. W4. 6P 57
Quickett St. E3. 25K 53
Quicks Rd. SW19. 11Z 92
Quill La. SW15. 9S 71
Quilp St. SE1. 19N 63
Quintin Av. SW20. 9Za 92
Quilter St. E2. 21K 52
Quinton St. SW18. 12W 83
Quixley St. E14. 27M 54
Quorn Rd. SE5. 20T 75

Raasay St. SW10. 12Q 60
Rabbits Rd. E12. 32F 43
Raby St. E14. 24M 53
Rackham St. W10. 9L 47
Racton Rd. SW6. 10Q 59
Radbourne Av. W5. 1O 56
Radbourne Rd. SW12. 16V 84
Radcliffe Av. NW10. 7J 46
Radcliffe Rd. N21. 19Ae 16
Radcliffe Rd. Cro. 21Zf 91
Radcliffe Rd. Har. 1aAa 12
Raddington Rd. W10. 10L 47
Radford Rd. SE13. 27U 78
Radipole Rd. SW6. 10R 71
Radley Av. Ilf. 36F 43
Radley Rd. N17. 21Aa 17
Radlix Rd. E10. 25D 27
Radnor Av. Har. 1cB 12
Radnor Gdns. Twi. 1bV 93
Radnor Pl. W2. 13L 48
Radnor Rd. NW6. 10H 33
Radnor Rd. Har. 1cB 12
Radnor Rd. Twi. 1bW 93
Radnor St. E13. 29J 55
Radnor St. EC1. 19K 51
Radnor St. SE15. 21Q 64
Radnor St. SW3. 13P 60
Radnor Ter. SW8. 17Q 62
Radnor Ter. W14. 10O 59
Radstock Av. Har. 1aA 12
Radstock St. SW11. 13Q 60
Raeburn Av. Edg. 3Aa 13
Raeburn Clo. NW11. 12C 22
Raeburn St. SW2. 17T 74
Raft Rd. SW18. 11T 71
Raglan Rd. E17. 27B 28
Raglan Rd. SE18. 33P 95
Raglan St. NW5. 15G 35
Raglan St. SE23. 23W 87
Rahere St. EC1. 19K 51
Railey Mews NW5. 15F 35
Railton Rd. SE24. 18T 74
Railway App. Twi. 1bV 93
Railway App. SE1. 20N 63
Railway Av. SE16. 23N 64
Railway Cotts. Wem. 2G 30

Railway Gro. SE14. 24R 77
Railway Pl. E2. 23K 52
Railway Pl. EC3. 21M 51
Railway Rd. Twi. 1cX 93
Railway Side SW13. 6S 70
Railway St. N1. 17J 50
Railway St. SW13. 6S 70
Railway Ter. SE13. 26U 77
Railway Yd. SE16. 24P 65
Rainbow St. SE5. 20Q 63
Raine St. E1. 22N 64
Rainham Rd. NW10. 9K 47
Rainton Rd. SE7. 29P 67
Rainville Rd. W6. 8Q 59
Raith Av. N14. 16Ad 15
Raleana Rd. E14. 27N 66
Raleigh Clo. NW4. 8B 21
Raleigh Dri. N20. 14Ad 15
Raleigh Rd. N8. 18B 24
Raleigh Rd. SE20. 23Z 90
Raleigh Rd. Rich. 3S 68
Raleigh St. N1. 19J 51
Raleigh Way N14. 17Ae 16
Ralph St. N7. 18F 36
Ralph St. SE1. 19O 63
Ram Sq. SW18. 11T 72
Ramillies Pl. W1. 15M 49
Ramillies Rd. W4. 5O 57
Ramillies St. W1. 15M 49
Rampayne St. SW1. 16P 61
Ramsay Rd. E7. 28F 40
Ramsay Rd. W3. 5N 57
Ramsdale Rd. SW17. 14Y 84
Ramsden Rd. N11. 14Ac 15
Ramsden Rd. SW12. 14U 73
Ramsey Rd. NW9. 7C 20
Ramsey St. Cro. 17Zd 91
Ramsey St. E2. 22K 52
Ramsgate St. E8. 21G 37
Rancliffe Gdns. SE9. 31T 79
Rancliffe Rd. E6. 31K 55
Randall Av. NW2. 6E 32
Randall Pl. SE10. 26Q 65
Randall Rd. SE11. 17P 62
Randall St. E16. 27L 54
Randall St. SW11. 13R 72
Randell's Rd. N1. 17H 36
Randlesdown Rd. SE6.
    25X 88
Randolph Cres. W9. 12K 48
Randolph Gdns. NW6.
    11J 48
Randolph Mews W9. 12K 48
Randolph Rd. E16. 30M 55
Randolph Rd. E17. 26B 27
Randolph Rd. W9. 12K 48
Randolph St. NW1. 16H 35
Ranelagh Av. N22. 17Aa 16
Ranelagh Av. SW6. 10S 71
Ranelagh Av. SW13. 7R 70
Ranelagh Bridge W2. 12L 48
Ranelagh Clo. Edg. 4Ad 13
Ranelagh Dri. Edg. 3Ad 13
Ranelagh Dri. Twi. 1aT 93
Ranelagh Gdns. SW6. 10S 71
Ranelagh Gdns. SW13. 7R 70
Ranelagh Gdns. Ilf. 32D 42
Ranelagh Gro. SW1. 10S 71
Ranelagh Gro. SW1. 14P 61
Ranelagh Rd. E6. 32J 43
Ranelagh Rd. E11. 28F 40
Ranelagh Rd. E15. 28J 54
Ranelagh Rd. N15. 21A 25
Ranelagh Rd. NW10. 6J 46
Ranelagh Rd. SW1. 16P 61
Ranelagh Rd. W2. 11L 48

Ranelagh Rd. W5. 2N 56
Ranelagh Rd. Wem. 2G 30
Ranger Rd. SE19. 21Y 86
Rangefield Rd. Brom. 27Y 89
Rangemoor Rd. N15. 21B 26
Ranger Rd. SE19. 21Y 90
Rannoch Rd. W6. 8Q 59
Rannock Av. NW9. 6C 19
Ransom Rd. SE7. 30P 67
Ranulf Rd. NW2. 10F 33
Ranwell St. E3. 24J 53
Ranworth Rd. N9. 23Ad 17
Raphael St. SW7. 13N 60
Rashleigh St. SW8. 15S 73
Rasper Rd. N20. 13Ad 14
Rastell Av. SW2. 16W 84
Ratcliff Rd. E7. 30G 41
Ratcliff St. E1. 22M 52
Ratcliffe Cross St. E1. 23M 52
Rathbone Pl. W1. 16L 49
Rathbone St. E16. 28L 54
Rathbone St. W1. 16L 49
Rathcoole Av. N8. 18B 24
Rathcoole Gdns. N8. 18B 24
Rathfern Rd. SE6. 25W 88
Rathgar Av. W13. 1N 56
Rathmore Rd. SE7. 30P 67
Rattray Rd. SW2. 18T 74
Raul Rd. SE15. 22R 76
Raveley St. NW5. 16F 35
Raven Row E1. 22L 52
Ravenet St. SW11. 15R 73
Ravenfield Rd. SW17. 14X 84
Ravenhill Rd. E13. 30J 55
Ravenna Rd. SW15. 9T 71
Ravensbourne Gdns. W13.
    1aL 94
Ravensbourne Pk. SE6.
    25V 88
Ravensbourne Pk. Cres. SE6.
    25V 88
Ravensbourne Rd. SE6.
    24V 88
Ravensbourne Rd. Twi.
    1aU 93
Ravensbury Gro. Mit.
    12Zb 92
Ravensbury Path Mit.
    12Zb 92
Ravensbury Rd. SW18.
    11W 82
Ravenscourt Av. W6. 7O 58
Ravenscourt Gdns. W6. 7O 58
Ravenscourt Pk. W6. 7O 58
Ravenscourt Rd. Kew. 4O 57
Ravenscourt Sq. W6. 7O 58
Ravenscraig Rd. N11.
    16Ad 15
Ravenscroft Av. NW11.
    10C 21
Ravenscroft Rd. E16. 29L 54
Ravenscroft Rd. SE20.
    23Za 90
Ravenscroft St. E2. 21J 51
Ravensdale Av. N12. 12Ac 14
Ravensdale Rd. N16. 21C 25
Ravensdon St. SE11. 18P 62
Ravenshaw St. NW6. 10G 33
Ravenshurst Av. NW4. 8A 21
Ravenslea Rd. SW12. 14V 84
Ravenstone Rd. E15. 28G 40
Ravenstone Rd. N8. 18A 24
Ravenstone Rd. NW9. 7C 20
Ravenstone St. SW12. 14V 84
Ravenswood Rd. E17.
    26B 27

Ravenswood Rd. sw12. 15V 84
Ravenswood Rd. Cro. 18Zf 91
Ravensworth Rd. nw10. 8J 46
Raverley St. e3. 26K 53
Ravey St. ec2. 20K 51
Ravine Gro. se18. 35Q 95
Rawlings St. sw3. 13O 60
Rawson St. sw11. 14R 73
Rawstone Pl. ec1. 18K 50
Rawstorne St. ec1. 18K 50
Ray St. ec1. 18K 50
Raydon St. n19. 15E 35
Rayleigh Rd. sw19. 10Z 92
Rayleigh Rd. w14. 9O 59
Raymead Av. Cro. 18Zc 90
Raymede St. w10. 9K 47
Raymond Av. e18. 28A 28
Raymond Av. w13. 1aO 94
Raymond Bldgs. wc1. 18L 50
Raymond Rd. e13. 30J 55
Raymond Rd. sw19. 9Y 82
Raymond Rd. Ilf. 34D 42
Raymond St. e1. 22N 64
Raymouth Rd. se16. 22P 64
Rayner St. e9. 23H 38
Rayner's Rd. sw15. 9T 71
Raynham Av. n18. 22Ab 17
Raynham Rd. n18. 22Ac 17
Raynham Rd. w6. 8O 58
Raynham Ter. n18. 22Ac 17
Rays Av. n18. 23Ac 17
Rays Rd. n18. 23Ac 17
Raywood St. sw8. 15R 73
Reading La. e8. 22H 38
Reaston St. se14. 23R 76
Reckitt Rd. w4. 6P 57
Record St. se15. 22Q 64
Recovery St. sw17. 13Y 83
Recreation St. se26. 23X 87
Rectory Cres. e11. 30C 29
Rectory Gdns. n8. 17B 24
Rectory Gdns. Edg. 4Ac 13
Rectory Gro. se18. 32P 95
Rectory Gro. sw4. 15S 73
Rectory La. sw17. 14Y 84
Rectory Pl. se18. 32P 95
Rectory Rd. e12. 32G 43
Rectory Rd. e17. 26B 27
Rectory Rd. n8. 17B 24
Rectory Rd. n16. 21E 37
Rectory Rd. sw6. 10R 71
Rectory Rd. sw13. 7R 70
Rectory Rd. w3. 4M 45
Rectory Sq. e1. 23L 52
Reculver Rd. se16. 23P 64
Redan St. w14. 9O 59
Redan Ter. se5. 19S 75
Redberry Gro. se26. 23X 87
Red Bridge La. e11. 30C 29
Redbridge La. Ilf. 31C 42
Redbourne Av. n3. 11Aa 14
Redburn St. sw3. 13P 61
Redcar St. se5. 19Q 63
Redcliffe Gdns. sw10. 11P 60
Redcliffe Gdns. Ilf. 32D 42
Redcliffe Mews sw10. 11P 60
Redcliffe Rd. sw10. 12P 60
Redcliffe Sq. sw10. 11P 60
Redcliffe St. sw10. 11P 60
Redcly ffe Rd. e6. 30J 55
Redcross St. ec1. 19L 51
Redcross St. se1. 19N 63

Reddins Rd. se15. 21Q 64
Redesdale St. sw3. 13P 60
Redfern Rd. nw10. 6H 32
Redfield La. sw5. 11O 60
Redford Av. Cro. 17Zc 90
Redgrave Rd. sw15. 9S 71
Redhill Dri. nw9. 5Aa 13
Redhill St. nw1. 15J 49
Redington Gdns. nw3. 12F 34
Redington Rd. nw3. 11E 34
Red Lion Ct. ec4. 18M 50
Red Lion Hill n2. 13A 22
Red Lion La. se18. 33R 95
Red Lion Mkt. ec1. 19L 51
Red Lion Pass. wc1. 17L 50
Red Lion Pl. wc1. 17L 50
Red Lion Row se17. 19Q 63
Red Lion Sq. wc1. 17L 50
Red Lion St. e1. 22N 64
Red Lion St. se18. 33P 95
Red Lion St. wc1. 17L 50
Red Lion St. Rich. 1T 68
Redman's Rd. e1. 23L 52
Redmead La. e1. 22N 64
Redmore Rd. w6. 8O 58
Rednall Ter. w6. 9P 59
Red Post Hill.
  se21. 1-5 & 2-12.
  se24. 7, 14 & up. 19T 75
Redriff La. se16. 24N 65
Redriff Rd. se16. 23O 64
Redriffe Rd. e13. 28J 54
Redston Rd. n8. 16B 24
Redvers Rd. n22. 18Aa 16
Redvers St. n1. 21J 51
Redwald Rd. e5. 24F 38
Redway Dri. Twi. 1dU 93
Reece Mews sw7. 12O 60
Reed Ct. se16. 23P 64
Reedham St. se15. 21S 76
Reedholm Villas n16.
  20F 37
Reed's Pl. nw1. 15H 35
Reedworth St. se11. 18P 62
Reeves Av. nw9. 5C 19
Reeves Mews w1. 14M 49
Reeve's Pl. n1. 20J 51
Reeve's Rd. e3. 26K 53
Reform Pl. sw19. 11Z 92
Reform Rd. sw11. 14R 73
Reform Row n17. 21A 26
Regal Way Har. 2B 18
Regency Pl. sw1. 16O 62
Regency St. sw1. 16O 62
Regent Clo. Har. 2C 18
Regent Rd. se24. 18U 74
Regent Sq. wc1. 17K 50
Regent St. n1. 19K 51
Regent St. nw10. 9K 47
Regent St. se10. 26R 77
Regent St.
  sw1. 1-37 & 2-36.
  w1. 39, 44 & up. 15M 49
Regent St. w4. 3P 57
Regent Dock Rd. e14.
  25N 65
Regent's Row e8. 21J 52
Regent's Pk. Rd. n3. 10A 21
Regent's Pk. Rd. nw1.
  14H 35
Regina Rd. n4. 18D 24
Regina Rd. w13. 1aN 94
Regina Ter. w13. 1aM 94
Reginald Rd. e7. 29H 40
Reginald Rd. se8. 25R 77

Reginald Sq. se8. 25R 77
Reidhaven Rd. se18. 35P 95
Reigate Rd. se12. 28X 89
Reigate Rd. Ilf. 36E 42
Reigate Way Cro. 16Zg 91
Reighton Rd. e5. 22E 38
Relf Rd. se15. 21S 76
Rembrandt Rd. se13. 27T 78
Remington St. n1. 19J 51
Remus Rd. e3. 25H 39
Renbold Pl. se10. 26R 77
Reno St. e14. 24L 53
Rendel Rd. e16. 29M 54
Rendle St. w10. 9L 47
Rendlesham Rd e5. 22F 38
Renforth St. se16. 23O 64
Renfrew Rd. se11. 18P 62
Renmuir St. sw17. 14Y 84
Rennell St. se13. 26T 77
Renness Rd. e17. 24A 27
Rensburg Rd. e17. 24C 26
Renshaw St. sw8. 15S 73
Renters Av. nw4. 9C 21
Rephidim St. se1. 20O 63
Replingham Rd. sw18. 10V 82
Reporton Rd. sw6. 10R 71
Repository Rd. se18. 32P 95
Repton St. e14. 24L 53
Reservoir Rd. se4. 24S 76
Retcar St. n19. 15E 35
Retford St. n1. 20J 51
Retreat Pl. e9. 23G 38
Retreat The, se3. 26U 78
Retreat The, se15. 23R 76
Retreat The, Cro. 19Zb 90
Revelon Rd. se4. 24T 76
Revelstoke Rd. sw18. 10W 82
Reverdy Rd. se1. 21P 64
Revesby St. se17. 19P 63
Review Rd. nw2. 7E 32
Reydon Av e11. 30C 29
Reynardson Rd n17.
  20Ab 16
Reynolds Av. e12. 33G 43
Reynolds Clo. nw11. 12D 22
Reynolds Dri. Edg. 4Aa 13
Reynolds' Rd. e15. 28H 40
Reynold's Rd. se15. 23T 76
Reynold's Rd. w4. 5N 57
Rheidol Ter. n1. 19J 51
Rhodes Av. n22. 15Aa 15
Rhodes St. n7. 17G 36
Rhodesia Rd. e11. 27E 40
Rhodesia Rd. sw9. 17S 74
Rhodeswell Rd. e14. 24L 53
Rhyl St. nw5. 14G 35
Rhyme Rd. se13. 26T 77
Rhys Av. n11. 17Ab 16
Ribblesdale Rd. n8. 18B 24
Ribblesdale Rd. sw16. 15Y 84
Ribstone St. e9. 23G 38
Ricardo St. e14. 26M 53
Richard St. e1. 22M 52
Richard St. e16. 29L 54
Richard St. n1. 18J 50
Richard's Pl. e17. 25B 27
Richard's Pl. sw3. 13O 60
Richardson Rd. e15. 28J 45
Richardson St. se1. 20N 63
Richborne Ter. sw8. 17Q 62
Richborough Rd. nw2. 9F 33
Richford Rd. e15. 28J 54
Richford St. w6. 8N 58
Richmond Av. nw10. 8G 32
Richmond Av. sw20. 9Za 92
Richmond Cres. n1. 18H 36

Richmond Gdns. nw4. 8B 20
Richmond Gdns. w12. 9N 59
Richmond Pl. se18. 34P 95
Richmond Pl. sw8. 16R 73
Richmond Rd. e7. 30G 41
Richmond Rd. e8. 21H 37
Richmond Rd. e11. 27E 40
Richmond Rd. e11. 29E 40
Richmond Rd. e17. 25C 27
Richmond Rd. n1. 18H 36
Richmond Rd. n11. 17Ab 16
Richmond Rd. n15. 20C 25
Richmond Rd. sw5. 11P 60
Richmond Rd. sw20. 8Za 92
Richmond Rd. w2. 11L 47
Richmond Rd. w5. 2N 56
Richmond Rd.
  w12. 1-15 & 2-52.
  w14. 23, 52a & up. 9N 59
Richmond Rd. Cro. 18Zb 90
Richmond Rd. Edg. 4Aa 13
Richmond Rd. Ilf. 34E 42
Richmond Rd. Twi. 1aV 93
Richmond St. e13. 29J 55
Richmond St. n1. 17H 36
Richmond St. se11. 18O 62
Richmond Ter. sw1. 17N 62
Richmond Pk. Rd. sw14.
  5T 69
Rickett St. sw6. 11P 59
Riddell St. se5. 21R 75
Ride, The, Bre. 1P 56
Rideout St. se18. 32P 95
Ridgdale St. e3. 26J 53
Ridge Av. n21. 20Af 16
Ridge Clo. nw9. 6B 19
Ridge Hill nw11. 10D 21
Ridge Rd. n8. 18C 24
Ridge Rd. n21. 20Ae 17
Ridge St. se16. 22P 64
Ridgemount Av. Cro.
  23Ze 91
Ridgeview Rd. n20. 12Ad 14
Ridgeway n3. 11Ab 14
Ridgeway n14. 17Ae 16
Ridgeway sw20. 8Z 92
Ridgeway, The, n11. 14Ae 15
Ridgeway, The, nw9. 6B 20
Ridgeway, The, nw11. 10D 21
Ridgeway, The, w3. 3N 57
Ridgeway, The, Cro. 17Zf 91
Ridgeway, The, Har. 1C 18
Ridgmount Gdns. wc1.
  16L 49
Ridgmount Gdns. Edg.
  5Ad 13
Ridgmount Rd. sw18.
  11U 72
Ridgmount St. wc1. 16L 50
Ridgway sw19. 9Y 82
Ridgway Gdns. sw19. 8Z 92
Ridgway Pl. sw19. 9Y 82
Ridgway Pl. S. sw19. 9Y 82
Ridgway Rd. sw9. 18S 74
Riding, The, nw11. 10D 21
Riding, The, w5. 3K 44
Riding House St. w1. 15L 49
Ridings Rd. Kin. 5Y 80
Ridings, The, w5. 3L 44
Ridley Av. w13. 1aO 94
Ridley Rd. e7. 30F 41
Ridley Rd. e8. 21G 37
Ridley Rd. nw10. 7J 46
Ridley Rd. sw19. 11Z 92
Ridsdale Rd. se20. 22Z 90
Riffel Rd. nw2. 8G 32

Rifle St. e14. 26L 53
Rigault Rd. sw6. 10R 71
Rigden St. e14. 26M 53
Rigeley Rd. nw10. 7J 46
Riggindale Rd. sw16. 16X 84
Rignold Rd. se5. 20S 75
Riles Rd. e13. 29J 54
Riley Rd. se1. 21O 63
Riley St. sw10. 12Q 60
Ring, The, w2. 13M 48
Ringcroft St. n7. 18G 36
Ringford Rd. sw18. 10U 71
Ringmer Av. sw6. 10R 71
Ringmore Rise se23. 22R 87
Ringslade Rd. n22. 18Aa 16
Ringstead Rd. se6. 26V 88
Ringwood Av. n2. 14A 23
Ringwood Av. Cro. 17Zd 91
Ringwood Rd. e17. 25C 27
Ringwood Way n21. 19Ae 16
Ripley Gdns. sw14. 5S 69
Ripley Rd. e16. 30M 55
Ripley Rd. Ilf. 35E 42
Ripley St. se1. 19O 63
Ripon Gdns. Ilf. 31D 29
Ripon Gdns. Ilf. 31D 42
Ripon Rd. n9. 22Af 17
Ripon Rd. n15. 20A 25
Ripon Rd. se18. 33Q 95
Ripple Rd. Bar. 34J 43
Ripplevale Gro. n1. 18H 36
Rippolson Rd. se18. 36Q 95
Rippoth Rd. e3. 25H 39
Risborough St. se1. 19N 63
Risdon St. se16. 23O 64
Rise, The, e11. 29C 28
Rise, The, n13. 18Ac 16
Rise, The, nw10. 6E 31
Rise, The, Edg. 4Ac 13
Riseholme St. e9. 24G 39
Riseldine Rd. se23. 24U 76
Risinghill St. n1. 18J 50
Risingholme Rd. Har.
  1bAa 12
Risings, The, e17. 27B 28
Risley Av. n17. 19Aa 16
Rita Av. Ilf. 31B 29
Rita Rd. sw8. 17Q 62
Ritchie Rd. Cro. 22Zd 91
Ritchies Rd. n15. 19B 25
Ritchings Av. e17. 24B 27
Ritherdon Rd. sw17. 14W 84
Ritson Rd. e8. 21G 38
Ritter St. se18. 33Q 95
River Av. n13. 19Ad 16
River St. ec1. 18K 50
River St. n1. 19H 37
River St. sw15. 9S 71
River Ter. w6. 8P 58
River Way sw10. 28O 66
Rivercourt Rd. w6. 7P 58
Riverdale Rd. se18. 35Q 95
Riverhall St. sw8. 16Q 62
River Pk. n22. 18Aa 16
Riversdale Rd. n5. 19E 37
Riverside se7. 30O 67
Riverside Twi. 1aV 93
Riverside Gdns. w6. 8P 58
Riverside Rd. sw17. 11X 83
River View Gdns. sw13.
  8P 58
River View Gdns. Twi.
  1bW 93
River View Gro. w4. 4Q 57

River View Pk. se6. 25W 88
River View Rd. w4. 4Q 57
Riverway n13. 18Ac 16
Rivet St. se1. 21P 64
Rivett St. e16. 29M 54
Rivington Av. Ilf. 31A 29
Rivington St. ec2. 20K 51
Rivulet Rd. n17. 19Ab 16
Rixsen Rd. e12. 32G 43
Roach Rd. e3. 25H 39
Road's Pl. n19. 17E 36
Roan St. se10. 26Q 65
Robert St. e2. 22K 52
Robert St. e14. 25M 53
Robert St. n1. 19J 51
Robert St. nw1. 15K 49
Robert St. se18. 34P 95
Robert St. wc1. 17L 50
Robert St. wc2. 17M 50
Robertson Rd. e15. 27J 54
Robertson St. sw8. 15S 73
Robeson St. e3. 25L 53
Robin Gro. n6. 14E 35
Robin Gro. Bre. 1Q 56
Robinhood La. e14. 27M 54
Robin Hood La. sw20. 5X 80
Robin Hood Rd. sw19. 6X 81
Robinson Rd. e2. 23J 52
Robinson Rd. sw17. 13Y 83
Robsart St. sw9. 18S 74
Robson Av. nw10. 7H 32
Robson Rd. se27. 19X 86
Roch Av. Edg. 3Aa 13
Rochdale Rd. e17. 25D 27
Roche Rd. sw16. 17Za 90
Rochelle St. e2. 21K 51
Rochester Av. e13. 30J 55
Rochester Gdns. Ilf. 32D 42
Rochester Mews nw1. 16H 35
Rochester Pl. nw1. 16H 35
Rochester Rd. nw1. 15H 35
Rochester Row sw1. 16O 61
Rochester Sq. nw1. 16H 35
Rochester St. sw1. 16O 61
Rochester Ter. nw1. 15H 35
Rochester Way.
  se3. 1-325 & 2-364.
  se9. 327-617 & 366-666.
  30S 79
Rochford St. nw5. 14G 35
Rochford Way Cro. 16Zd 91
Rock Av. sw6. 10Q 59
Rock Hill se26. 21X 86
Rock Rd. e5. 24F 39
Rock St. n4. 18E 36
Rockbourne Rd. se23.
  23W 87
Rockhall Rd. nw2. 9F 33
Rockingham St. se1. 19O 63
Rockland Rd. sw15. 9T 71
Rockley Rd. w14. 9N 59
Rockmead Rd. e9. 24H 38
Rockmount Rd. se18. 36Q 95
Rockmount Rd. se19. 20Z 90
Rocks La. sw13. 7R 70
Rockwells Pl. se22. 22U 76
Rocliffe St. n1. 19J 51
Rodborough Mews w9.
  10K 47
Rodborough Rd. nw11.
  11D 21
Roden St. n7. 17F 36
Roden St. Ilf. 33F 42
Rodenhurst Rd. sw4. 16U 73
Roderick Rd. nw3. 14F 35
Roding La. Ilf. 31B 29

Roding Rd. E5. 24F 38
Rodmarton Mews w1. 14L 49
Rodmell Slope N12. 11Ac 14
Rodmere St. SE10. 28P 66
Rodney Pl. SE17. 19O 63
Rodney Rd. E11. 29B 29
Rodney Rd. SE17. 19P 63
Rodney Rd. Mit. 13Za 92
Rodney St. N1. 18J 50
Rodney St. SE18. 33O 95
Rodway Rd. SW15. 7U 70
Rodwell Rd. SE22. 21U 77
Roe End NW9. 5A 19
Roe Green NW9. 5B 19
Roe La. NW9. 4A 19
Roedean Cres. SW15. 5U 69
Roehampton Clo. SW15.
       7T 70
Roehampton Gate SW15.
       5U 69
Roehampton La. SW15.
       7T 70
Roehampton St. SW1. 16P 62
Roehampton High St. SW15.
       7U 70
Roffey St. E14. 26O 65
Rogers Rd. SW17. 13X 83
Rojack Rd. SE23. 23V 87
Rokeby Rd. SE4. 24S 77
Rokeby Rd. Har. 1cA 12
Rokeby St. E15. 27J 54
Rokesly Av. N8. 17B 24
Roland Gdns. SW7. 12P 60
Roland Rd. E17. 27B 28
Rolfe Rd. SE7. 31P 67
Rollins St. SE15. 23Q 64
Rollo St. SW11. 14R 73
Rolls Rd. SE1. 21P 63
Rollscourt Av. SE24. 19T 75
Rolt St. SE8. 24O 65
Rolma Rd. E17. 01A 07
Roman Rd. E3. 24J 53
Roman Rd. E6. 31L 55
Roman Rd. N7. 17G 36
Roman Rd. N10. 15Ab 15
Roman Rd. SE19. 20Y 86
Roman Rd. W4. 6O 58
Roman Rd. Ilf. 33G 43
Roman Bath St. EC1. 19L 51
Romberg Rd. SW17. 14X 84
Romborough Way SE13.
       26U 77
Romer Pl. SE13. 26T 77
Romeyn Rd. SW16. 17X 85
Romford Rd.
  E15. 1-191 & 2-166A.
  E7. 168-544 & 193-607.
  E12. 546, 609 & up. 31F 42
Romford St. E1. 22L 52
Romford St. Bar. 34H 43
Romilly Rd. N4. 18E 36
Rommany Rd. SE27. 19X 86
Romney Clo. NW11. 12D 22
Romney Rd. SE10. 27Q 66
Romney St. SW1. 16O 62
Romola Rd. SE24. 18V 85
Rona Rd. NW3. 14F 35
Ronald Av. E15. 28K 54
Ronald St. E1. 23M 52
Ronalds Rd. N5. 18G 36
Rondu Rd. NW2. 9F 33
Ronver Rd. SE12. 28V 89
Rood La. EC3. 20M 51
Rook St. E14. 26M 53
Rookery Rd. SW4. 15T 73
Rookery Way NW9. 6B 20

Rookfield Av. N10. 16B 23
Rookfield Clo. N10. 16B 23
Rookstone Rd. SW17. 13Y 83
Rookwood Rd. N16. 21C 26
Ropemaker St. EC2. 20L 51
Ropemakers Fields E14.
       25M 53
Roper La. SE1. 21N 63
Ropery St. E3. 25L 53
Rope Yd. Rails SE18. 33O 95
Ropley St. E2. 21J 52
Ropner Pl. E14. 25M 53
Rosaline Rd. SW6. 10Q 59
Rosaville Rd. SW6. 10Q 59
Roscoe St. E16. 28M 54
Roscoe St. EC1. 19K 51
Rose Alley SE1. 19N 63
Rose Av. E18. 30A 29
Rose Gdns. W5. 2O 56
Rose Glen NW9. 5A 19
Rose La. E14. 24M 58
Rose & Crown La. W6. 9P 59
Rosebank Gro. E17. 25A 27
Rosebank Rd. E3. 24J 53
Rosebank Rd. E17. 26C 27
Rosebank Rd. W7. 1bN 94
Roseberry Gdns. N4. 19C 25
Roseberry Pl. E8. 21H 37
Roseberry Rd. N10. 16A 23
Roseberry Rd. SE16. 22P 64
Rosebery Av. E12. 32H 43
Rosebery Av. EC1. 18K 50
Rosebery Av. N10. 15Aa 15
Rosebery Av. N17. 22Aa 17
Rosebery Av. Cro. 19Za 90
Rosebery Gdns. N8. 17B 24
Rosebery Gdns. w13. 1aL 94
Rosebery Rd. N9. 22Ad 17
Rosebery Rd. SW2. 16U 74
Rosebury Rd. E9. 25H 39
Rosecourt Rd. Cro. 17Za 91
Rosecroft Av. NW3. 11E 34
Rosecroft Gdns. NW2. 7E 32
Rosedale Cotts. w7. 1bN 94
Rosedale Rd. E7. 30G 41
Rosedale Rd. Rich. 2S 68
Rosedene Av. SW16. 17X 85
Rosedene Av. Cro. 17Zd 91
Rosedew Rd. W6. 9Q 59
Roseford Gdns. w12. 9N 59
Roseford Ter. w12. 9N 59
Rose Hill Rd. SW18. 12U 72
Roseleigh Av. N5. 19F 37
Rosemary Av. N2. 12Aa 14
Rosemary Av. N9. 22Ae 17
Rosemary Dri. Ilf. 31C 29
Rosemary Rd. SE15. 21Q 63
Rosemary St. N1. 20H 37
Rosemead Av. Wem. 3F 30
Rosemont Av. N12. 12Ac 14
Rosemont Rd. NW3. 12G 34
Rosemont Rd. w3. 4M 45
Rosemont Rd. Rich. 2U 68
Rosemount Rd. w13. 1aL 94
Rosenau Cres. SW11. 13R 72
Rosenau Rd. SW11. 13R 72
Rosendale Rd.
  SE21. 1-245 & 2-248.
  SE24. 250, 279 & up.
       19V 86
Roseneath Av. N21. 19Ae 16
Roseneath Rd. SW11. 14U 73
Rosenthal Rd. SE6. 26V 88
Rosenthorpe Rd. SE15.
       23U 76

Roserton St. E14. 26O 65
Rosery, The, Cro. 23Zd 91
Rosetta St. SW8. 17Q 62
Rosevine Rd. SW20. 8Za 92
Roseway SE21. 20U 75
Rosewell Av. SW4. 17U 74
Rosher Rd. E15. 27H 40
Roskell Rd. SW15. 9S 71
Roslin Rd. w3. 4O 57
Roslin Way Bro. 29Y 89
Roslyn Av. SE5. 19S 75
Roslyn Clo. Mit. 12Za 92
Roslyn Rd. N15. 20B 25
Rosmead Rd. W11. 10M 47
Rosoman St. EC1. 18K 50
Ross Rd. E15. 27J 54
Ross Rd. SE25. 20Zb 90
Ross St. SW1. 15P 61
Rossall Cres. W5. 3J 44
Rossdale Dri. NW9. 5D 19
Rossdale Rd. SW15. 8S 71
Rossington St. E5. 22E 38
Rossiter Rd. SW12. 15V 84
Rosslyn Av. SW13. 6S 70
Rosslyn Cres. Har. 1bB 12
Rosslyn Cres. Wem. 2E 30
Rosslyn Cres. N. Har. 1bA 12
Rosslyn Cres. S. Har. 1bB 12
Rosslyn Hill NW3. 13F 34
Rosslyn Rd. E17. 27B 28
Rosslyn Rd. Bar. 34H 43
Rossmore Rd. NW1. 13K 48
Rostella Rd. SW17. 12X 83
Rostrevor Av. N15. 21C 25
Rostrevor Rd. SW6. 10R 71
Rostrevor Rd. SW19. 10Y 82
Rotary St. SE1. 19O 62
Rothbury Rd. E9. 25H 39
Rotherfield St. N1. 19H 37
Rotherhithe St. SE16. 23N 64
Rotherhithe New Rd. SE16.
       22P 64
Rotherhithe Old Rd. SE16.
       23O 64
Rothermere Rd. Cro. 17Zh 91
Rotherwick Hill w5. 3K 44
Rotherwick Rd. NW11.
       11D 22
Rotherwood Rd. SW15. 9S 71
Rothesay Av. SW14. 4S 69
Rothesay Av. SW20. 9Za 92
Rothesay Rd. SE25. 20Zc 90
Rothsay Rd. E7. 30H 41
Rothsay St. SE1. 20O 63
Rothschild Rd. w4. 4O 57
Rothschild St. SE27. 19X 86
Rothwell St. NW1. 14H 35
Rotten Row SW7. 13N 60
Rovel Rd. SE16. 21O 64
Round Hill SE26. 22W 87
Roundell St. SW8. 15S 73
Roundtable Rd. SE12.
       28X 89
Roundway, The, N17. 19Aa 16
Roundwood Rd. NW10. 6G 32
Rounton Rd. E3. 25K 53
Roupell Rd. SW2. 17V 85
Roupell St. SE1. 18N 62
Routh Rd. SW18. 13V 83
Rowallan Rd. SW6. 9Q 59
Rowan Rd. w6. 9O 59
Rowans, The, N13. 19Ad 16
Rowantree Clo. N21. 20Ae 17
Rowantree Rd. N21. 20Ae 17
Rowben Clo. N20. 12Ae 14
Rowcross St. SE1. 21P 63

Rowdon Av. nw10.	8H 32
Rowena Cres. sw11.	13S 72
Rowfant Rd. sw17.	14W 84
Rowhill Rd. e5.	22F 38
Rowland Av. Har.	1A 18
Rowland Gro. se26.	22X 87
Rowland Hill Av. n17.	
	20Ab 16
Rowlett St. e14.	26M 54
Rowley Clo. Wem.	3H 30
Rowley Rd. n15.	19B 25
Rowsell St. e3.	25L 53
Rowsley Av. nw4.	8A 21
Rowton Rd. se18.	34R 95
Roxborough Av. Har. 1cC 12	
Roxborough Pk. Har. 1cC 12	
Roxborough Rd. Har. 1cB 12	
Roxburgh Rd. se27.	18Y 85
Roxeth Hill, Har.	1cD 12
Roxley Rd. se13.	26U 77
Roxwell Rd. w12.	7N 58
Royal Av. sw3.	14P 61
Royal Circus se27.	18X 85
Royal Cres. w11.	9N 59
Royal Hill se10.	26R 77
Royal Mews sw1.	15O 61
Royal Parade se3.	28S 78
Royal Rd. e16.	30M 55
Royal Rd. se17.	18Q 62
Royal Rd. Twi.	1cX 93
Royal St. se1.	17O 62
Royal Ter. se17.	18Q 62
Royal Hospital Rd. sw3.	
	14P 61
Royal Mint St. e1.	21M 51
Royal Oak Rd. e8.	22G 38
Royal Oak Rd. se22.	22U 76
Royal Oak Wk. n1.	20K 51
Royal Victor Pl. e3.	24J 52
Roydene Rd. se18.	35Q 95
Roydon St. sw11.	15R 73
Royle Cres. w13.	1aK 94
Royston Rd. se20.	23Za 90
Royston Rd. Rich.	2T 68
Royston St. e2.	23K 52
Rozel Rd. sw4.	15S 73
Rubens St. se6.	25W 88
Ruby Rd. e17.	25A 27
Ruby St. se15.	22Q 64
Ruby Triangle se5.	20S 75
Ruckholt Rd. e10.	26F 39
Rucklidge Av. nw10.	7J 46
Rudall Cres. nw3.	13F 34
Ruddigore Rd. se14.	24Q 65
Rudford Rd. se16.	23P 64
Rudloe Rd. sw12.	15U 73
Rudolph Rd. e13.	29K 54
Rudolph Rd. nw6.	11J 48
Rudyard Gro. Edg.	5Ac 13
Rufford St. n1.	17H 36
Rugby Av. n9.	21Ae 17
Rugby Av. Wem.	1F 30
Rugby Rd. nw9.	4A 19
Rugby Rd. w4.	6N 57
Rugby Rd. Twi.	1cT 93
Rugby St. wc1.	17L 50
Rugg St. e14.	25M 53
Ruislip St. sw17.	13X 84
Rumsey Rd. sw9.	17S 74
Runcorn Pl. w11.	9M 47
Rundell Cres. nw4.	8B 20
Rundell Rd. w9.	11K 48
Runham St. se17.	20P 63
Runton St. n19.	16D 24
Rupack St. se16.	23N 64
Rupert Av. Wem.	2G 30

Rupert Rd. n19.	16E 36
Rupert Rd. nw6.	10J 47
Rupert Rd. w4.	6O 58
Rupert St. e1.	21M 52
Rupert St. w1.	16M 49
Rural Pl. se14.	23R 76
Rusham Rd. sw12.	14U 73
Rushcroft Rd. sw2.	18T 74
Rushey Green se6.	26V 88
Rushford Rd. se4.	25U 77
Rushgrove Av. nw9.	6B 20
Rush Hill Rd. sw11.	14S 73
Rushmore Cres. e5.	23F 38
Rushmore Rd. e5.	23F 38
Rusholme Rd. sw15.	9U 71
Rushout Av. Har.	1aC 12
Rushton St. n1.	20J 51
Rushworth St. se1.	19N 63
Ruskin Av. e12.	31G 43
Ruskin Av. Kew.	3Q 57
Ruskin Clo. nw11.	11C 22
Ruskin Rd. n17.	21Aa 17
Ruskin St. sw8.	15R 73
Ruskin Wk. se24.	19U 75
Rusland Rd. Har.	1bA 12
Rusper Rd. n22.	19A 25
Russel Clo. nw10.	5H 31
Russell Av. n22.	19A 24
Russell Gdns. nw11.	10C 21
Russell Gdns. w14.	9O 59
Russell Gro. nw7.	6Ad 13
Russell Gro. sw9.	18R 74
Russell La. n20.	14Ae 15
Russell Rd. e10.	26C 27
Russell Rd. e16.	29M 55
Russell Rd. e17.	25A 27
Russell Rd. n7.	18E 36
Russell Rd. n8.	16C 24
Russell Rd. n13.	17Ab 16
Russell Rd. n15.	20C 25
Russell Rd. n20.	13Ae 15
Russell Rd. nw9.	7C 20
Russell Rd. se15.	22S 76
Russell Rd. sw19.	10Z 92
Russell Rd. w14.	10O 59
Russell Rd. Cro.	20Zd 91
Russell Rd. Twi.	1bU 93
Russell Sq. wc1.	17L 50
Russell St. e1.	22L 52
Russell St. e13.	29J 55
Russell St. se26.	22X 87
Russell St. wc2.	17M 50
Russell's Footpath sw16.	
	17Y 85
Russia La. e2.	23J 52
Russia Row ec2.	19M 51
Rust Sq. se5.	19Q 63
Rusthall Av. w4.	5O 57
Ruston St. e3.	25J 53
Rutford Rd. sw16.	16Y 85
Ruth St. e15.	27G 40
Rutherford St. sw1.	16O 62
Rutherglen Rd. se2.	36Q 95
Ruthin Rd. se3.	29Q 66
Rutland Gdns. n4.	19C 25
Rutland Gdns. sw7.	13N 60
Rutland Gdns. Cro.	20Zg 91
Rutland Gate sw7.	13N 60
Rutland Pk. nw2.	8G 33
Rutland Pk. se6.	24W 88
Rutland Rd. e7.	31H 41
Rutland Rd. e9.	23J 52
Rutland Rd. e11.	30B 29
Rutland Rd. e17.	25C 27
Rutland Rd. se6.	25W 88

Rutland Rd. sw19.	13Z 92
Rutland Rd. w6.	8P 58
Rutland Rd. Har.	1cB 12
Rutland Rd. Ilf.	33F 42
Rutland Rd. Twi.	1dW 93
Rutland St. e1.	22L 52
Rutland St. nw1.	15J 49
Rutland St. sw7.	13O 60
Rutland St. sw8.	17Q 62
Rutt's Ter. se15.	23R 76
Ruvigny Gdns. sw15.	9S 71
Rydal Gdns. nw9.	6B 20
Rydal Rd. sw16.	16X 84
Ryde Vale Rd. sw12.	15W 84
Ryder St. sw1.	16N 61
Ryder's Ter. nw8.	12J 48
Rydon Cres. ec1.	18K 50
Rydon St. n1.	19J 51
Rye Dale se22.	22U 76
Rye La. se15.	21R 76
Rye Rd. se15.	23T 76
Ryecroft Rd. se13.	27U 78
Ryecroft Rd. sw16.	18Y 85
Ryecroft St. sw6.	11R 72
Rye Hill Pk. se15.	22T 76
Ryfold Rd. sw19.	10W 82
Rygate St. e1.	22N 64
Ryhope Rd. n11.	15Ad 15
Rylands Rd. nw5.	15G 35
Rylands Rd. nw5.	7E 32
Rylett Cres. w12.	6N 58
Rylett Rd. w12.	7N 58
Rylston Rd. sw6.	10Q 59
Rymer Rd. Cro.	20Zd 90
Rymer St. se24.	18U 75
Sabbarton St. e14.	25L 53
Sabine Rd. sw11.	14S 73
Sable St. n1.	19H 37
Sach Rd. e5.	22E 38
Sackville Gdns. Ilf.	32D 42
Sackville St. w1.	16M 49
Saddlescombe Way n12.	
	11Ac 14
Sadler St. ec1.	18K 50
Saffron St. ec1.	18L 50
Sage St. e1.	23M 52
Sail St. se11.	17O 62
Sainfoin Rd. sw17.	14W 84
Sainsbury Rd. se19.	20Y 86
St. Agnes Pl. se11.	18Q 62
St. Aidan's Rd. se22.	22U 76
St. Alban's Av. w4.	5O 57
St. Alban's Cres. n22.	
	18Aa 16
St. Albans Gdns. Twi.	
	1bX 93
St. Alban's Pl. n1.	18J 50
St. Alban's Rd. nw5.	15E 85
St. Alban's Rd. nw10.	6H 32
St. Alban's Rd. w8.	11O 60
St.'Alban's Rd. Ilf.	36E 42
St. Alban's St. se1.	18O 62
St. Alban's St. sw1.	16M 49
St. Alfege Rd. se7.	31Q 67
St. Alphonsus Rd. sw4.	
	16T 73
St. Andrew St. wc2.	16M 50
St. Andrew's Clo. nw2.	
	8E 32
St. Andrew's Hill ec4.	
	19M 51
St. Andrew's Pl. nw1.	
	15K 49
St. Andrew's Rd. e11.	
	28C 28

St. Andrew's Rd. E13.
                        30K 55
St. Andrew's Rd. E17. 24A 27
St. Andrew's Rd. N16.
                        20D 25
St. Andrew's Rd. NW10.
                        8G 32
St. Andrew's Rd. NW11.
                        10C 21
St. Andrew's Rd. W3. 6L 46
St. Andrew's Rd. W14. 9Q 59
St. Andrew's Rd. Ilf. 32D 42
St. Andrew's St. EC4. 18L 50
St. Anne St. E14.   25M 53
St. Anne's Ct. W1.   16M 49
St. Annes Gdns. W5.   3J 44
St. Anne's Rd. E11.   27E 40
St. Ann's Hill SW18. 11U 72
St. Ann's Rd. E3.   24L 53
St. Ann's Rd. N8.   17B 24
St. Ann's Rd. N9.   21Ae 17
St. Ann's Rd. N15.   20B 25
St. Ann's Rd. SW9.   18R 74
St. Ann's Rd. SW13.   6R 70
St. Ann's Rd. W11.   9M 47
St. Ann's Rd. Bar.   34J 43
St. Ann's Rd. Har.   1bC 12
St. Anns Rd. Wem.   2F 30
St. Ann's Rd. SW1.   16O 62
St. Ann's Ter. NW8.   13J 48
St. Ann's Villas W11. 9N 59
St. Ann's Pk. Rd. SW18.
                      12U 72
St. Antony's Rd. E7. 29H 41
St. Asaph Rd. SE4.   23S 76
St. Aubyn's Rd. SE19. 20Z 90
St. Augustine's Av. W5. 2J 44
St. Augustine's Av. Wem.
                       2E 30
St. Augustine's Rd. NW1.
                      16H 36
St. Austell Rd. SE13. 27S 78
St. Awdry's Rd. Bar. 34H 43
St. Barnabas St. SW1. 14P 61
St. Bernard's Rd. E6. 31J 55
St. Bride St. EC4.   18L 50
St. Chad's Pl. WC1.   17K 50
St. Charles Sq. W10.   9L 47
St. Clare St. E1.   21M 51
St. Clement St. N7.   18H 36
St. Cloud Rd. SE27.   19X 86
St. Christopher's Pl. W1.
                      15L 49
St. Cuthbert's Rd. NW2.
                      10G 33
St. Cyprian's St. SW17.
                      13X 83
St. David St. SE1.   19O 63
St. David's Pl. NW4.   8C 20
St. Denis Rd. SE27.   19X 86
St. Donatt's Rd. SE14.
                      24R 77
St. Dunstan's Av. W3. 5M 45
St. Dunstan's Gdns. W3.
                       5M 45
St. Dunstan's Hill EC3.
                      20M 51
St. Dunstan's Rd. E3. 24L 53
St. Dunstan's Rd. E7. 30G 41
St. Dunstan's Rd. W6. 9P 59
St. Dunstan's Rd. W7. 1cN 94
St. Edmund's Rd. N9.
                      22Ae 17
St. Edmunds Rd. Ilf. 32C 42
St. Edmund's Ter. NW8.
                      13J 49

St. Elmo Rd. W12.   7N 58
St. Erkenwald Rd. Bar.
                      34J 43
St. Ervan's Rd. W10. 10L 47
St. Faith's Rd. SE21. 18V 85
St. Fillans Rd. SE6. 27V 89
St. Gabriel St. SE11. 19O 63
St. Gabriel's Rd. NW2. 9G 33
St. George's Av. E7. 30H 41
St. George's Av. N7. 16F 36
St. George's Av. NW9. 5A 19
St. George's Av. W5.   1N 56
St. George's Circus SE1.
                      18O 62
St. George's Mkt. SE1. 19O 63
St. George's Rd. E7. 30H 41
St. George's Rd. E10. 27E 40
St. George's Rd. N9. 22Ad 17
St. George's Rd. N13.
                      18Ad 16
St. George's Rd. N15. 20B 25
St. George's Rd. NW1. 14H 35
St. George's Rd. NW11.
                      10C 21
St. George's Rd. SE1. 18O 62
St. George's Rd. SW1. 15P 61
St. George's Rd. SW19.
                      10Y 82
St. George's Rd. W4.   5N 57
St. George's Rd. W7. 1bM 94
St. George's Rd. Ilf. 32D 42
St. George's Rd. Rich. 3S 68
St. George's Rd. Twi. 1aT 93
St. George's Sq. E7. 30H 41
St. George's Sq. SW1. 16P 61
St. George's Ter. NW1.
                      14H 35
St. George's Way SE15.
                      20Q 63
St. Helen's Cres. SW16.
                      17Za 90
St. German's Pl. SE3. 20R 78
St. German's Rd. SE23.
                      24V 88
St. Giles Rd. SE5.   20R 75
St. Giles High St. WC2.
                      16L 50
St. Gothard's Rd. SE27.
                      19X 86
St. Helena Rd. SE16. 23P 64
St. Helena St. WC1.   18K 50
St. Helen's Gdns. W10. 9L 47
St. Helen's Pl. EC3. 20L 51
St. Helen's Rd. SW16.
                      17Za 90
St. Helens Rd. Ilf.   32C 42
St. Helier Av. Mor.   12Zc 92
St. Heliers Rd. E10. 26C 27
St. Hugh's Rd. SE20. 22Z 90
St. James Av. N20.   13Ad 14
St. James Av. W13.   1aM 94
St. James Rd. N9.   22Ad 17
St. James's SE14.   24R 77
St. James's Cres. SW9.
                      18S 74
St. James's Gdns. NW5.
                      14G 35
St. James's Gdns. Wem.
                       2H 30
St. James's La. N10. 15B 23
St. James's Gro. SW11.
                      14R 73
St. James's Mews NW8.
                      14J 49
St. James's Pk. Cro. 19Zd 91
St. James's Pl. SE18. 33Q 95

St. James's Pl. SW1. 15N 61
St. James's Pl. W11. 10M 47
St. James's Rd. E2.   23J 52
St. James's Rd. E15. 28G 40
St. James's Rd. N7.   18G 36
St. James's Rd. SW17. 13V 83
St. James's Rd.
   SE16. 1-167 & 2-144.
   SE1. 146, 169 & up. 22P 64
St. James's Rd. Cro 19Zd 91
St. James's Sq. SW1. 16N 61
St. James's Sq. W11.   9M 47
St. James's St. E17. 24C 27
St. James's St. EC1. 18K 50
St. James's St. N1.   19J 51
St. James's St. SW1. 15N 61
St. James's St. W6.   8P 58
St. James's Villas SE18.
                      34Q 95
St. James's Wk. EC1. 18K 50
St. John St. EC1.   18K 50
St. John's Av. N11.   14Ac 15
St. John's Av. NW10.   6H 32
St. John's Clo. Wem.   2F 30
St. John's Cres. SW9. 18S 74
St. John's Gdns. W11. 10M 47
St. Johns Gro. Cro.   18Zf 91
St. John's Gro. Rich. 2S 68
St. John's Hill SW11. 12T 72
St. John's La. EC1.   19L 50
St. John's Pk. N19.   16E 35
St. John's Pk. SE3.   29R 78
St. John's Rd. E6.   31J 43
St. John's Rd. E16.   29M 54
St. John's Rd. E17.   26A 27
St. John's Rd. N1.   20J 51
St. John's Rd. N9.   21Ae 17
St. John's Rd. N15.   20C 25
St. John's Rd. N19.   16D 24
St. John's Rd. NW11. 10C 21
St. John's Rd. SE20. 23Z 90
St. John's Rd. SE23. 24V 90
St. John's Rd. SW11. 13T 72
St. John's Rd. SW15.   9T 71
St. John's Rd. W13.   1aM 94
St. John's Rd. Bar.   35J 43
St. John's Rd. Cro.   18Zf 91
St. John's Rd. Har.   1bC 12
St. John's Rd. Ilf.   35D 42
St. John's Rd. Rich.   2S 68
St. John's Rd. Wem.   2F 30
St. John's Sq. EC1.   18K 50
St. John's Ter. E7.   30G 41
St. John's Ter. SE18. 34Q 95
St. John's Vale SE8. 25S 77
St. John's Villas N19. 16E 36
St. John's Church Rd. E9.
                      23G 38
St. John's Hill Gro. SW11.
                      12T 72
St. John's Pk. Rd. SE3.
                      29R 78
St. John's Wood Pk. NW8.
                      13H 34
St. John's Wood Rd. NW8.
                      13K 48
St. John's Wood Ter. NW8.
                      13J 48
St. Joseph's Rd. N8. 17B 24
St. Joseph's Rd. N9. 23Ae 17
St. Joseph's St. SW8. 15R 73
St. Jude St. N16.   21G 37
St. Jude's St. E2.   22J 52
St. Julian's Rd. NW6. 10H 33
St. Julian's Farm Rd. SE27.
                      18X 85

St. Katherine's Way E1. 21N 63
St. Kilda Rd. w13. 1aN 94
St. Kilda's Rd. N16. 20D 25
St. Kilda's Rd. Har. 1cB 12
St. Lawrence Rd. sw9. 18R 74
St. Lawrence Rd. w10. 10L 47
St. Lawrence St. E14. 27N 66
St. Leonard's Av. E14. 26M 53
St. Leonards Av. Har. 1B 18
St. Leonard's Gdns. Ilf. 34G 43
St. Leonards Rd. E14. 26L 53
St. Leonards Rd. NW10. 5K 45
Sr. Leonard's Rd. sw14. 4S 69
St. Leonard's Rd. w13. 1M 44
St. Leonards Rd. Cro. 18Zf 91
St. Leonard's Sq. NW5. 15G 35
St. Leonard's St. E3. 26K 53
St. Leonards Ter. sw3. 14P 61
St. Loo Av. sw3. 13Q 60
St. Louis Rd. sE27. 19X 86
St. Loy's Rd. N17. 21A 25
St. Luke's Mews w11. 10L 47
St. Luke's Rd. sw4. 16T 74
St. Luke's Rd. w11. 10L 47
St. Lukes Sq. E16. 28M 54
St. Malo Av. N9. 23Ad 17
St. Margaret's Av. N15. 19B 25
St. Margaret's Av. N20. 12Ae 14
St. Margaret's Ct. sE1. 19N 63
St. Margaret's Dri. Twi. 1aT 93
St. Margaret's Gro. sE18. 34Q 95
St. Margaret's Gro. Twi. 1aU 93
St. Margaret's Path sE18. 32O 95
St. Margaret's Rd. E12. 30E 41
St. Margaret's Rd. N15. 21A 25
St. Margaret's Rd. NW10. 8J 46
St. Margaret's Rd. sE4. 24T 77
St. Margaret's Rd. w7. 1cN 94
St. Margaret's Rd. Bar. 34J 43
St. Margaret's Rd. Cro. 23Zc 90
St. Margaret's Rd. Edg. 4Ac 13
St. Margaret's Rd. Twi. 1aT 93
St. Margaret's Ter. sE18. 34Q 95
St. Margaret's Ter. w3. 4N 57
St. Mark St. E1. 21M 52
St. Mark's Cres. NW1. 15H 35
St. Mark's Gro. sw10. 11Q 60

St. Mark's Rd. E8. 21G 37
St. Mark's Rd. sE13. 27T 78
St. Marks Rd. sE25. 21Zb 90
St. Mark's Rd. sw10. 11Q 60
St. Mark's Rd. w7. 1cN 94
St. Mark's Rd. w11. 1-53 & 2-22. w10. 24, 55 & up. 9L 47
St. Martin's Av. E6. 31J 55
St. Martin's Ct. wc2. 16M 50
St. Martin's La. wc2. 16M 50
St. Martins-le-Grand Ec1. 19L 51
St. Martin's Pl. wc2. 16M 50
St. Martin's Rd. N9. 22Ad 17
St. Martin's Rd. sw9. 17R 74
St. Martin's St. wc2. 16M 50
Saint Mary Axe Ec3. 20M 51
St. Mary St. E1. 22L 52
St. Mary St. sE18. 32P 95
St. Mary's Av. E11. 30D 29
St. Mary's Av. Ted. 1bY 93
St. Mary's Cres. Nw4. 8A 20
St. Mary's Gdns. sE11. 18O 62
St. Mary's Gro. sw15. 7S 70
St. Mary's Gro. w4. 4P 57
St. Mary's Gro. Rich. 3S 68
St. Mary's Rd. E10. 26E 40
St. Mary's Rd. E13. 29J 55
St. Mary's Rd. E17. 26B 27
St. Mary's Rd. N1. 19G 37
St. Mary's Rd. N8. 17B 24
St. Mary's Rd. N9. 23Ae 17
St. Mary's Rd. Nw10. 6H 32
St. Mary's Rd. Nw11. 10C 21
St. Mary's Rd. sE15. 23R 76
St. Mary's Rd. sE25. 20Zb 90
St. Mary's Rd. sw19. 10Y 82
St. Mary's Rd. w5. 1N 56
St. Mary's Rd. w11. 10L 47
St. Mary's Rd. Bar. 34J 43
St. Mary's Rd. Ilf. 34E 42
St. Mary's Sq. w2. 12L 48
St. Mary's Ter. w2. 12L 48
St. Mary Abbot's Pl. w8. 10O 59
St. Mary at Hill Ec3. 20M 51
St. Marychurch St. sE16. 23N 64
St. Matthews Rd. sw2. 17T 74
St. Matthew's Rd. w5. 2M 44
St. Maur Rd. sw6. 10R 71
St. Michael Ter. N22. 17Aa 15
St. Michaels Rd. N22. 18Ab 16
St. Michaels Rd. NW2. 8F 32
St. Michael's Rd. sw9. 17R 74
St. Mildred's Rd. sE12. 28V 89
St. Nicholas Rd. sE18. 36P 95
St. Nicholas Rd. sw17. 14W 84
St. Nicholas St. sE4. 25R 77
St. Norbert Rd. sE4. 23T 76
St. Olaf's Rd. sw6. 10Q 59
St. Olave's Rd. E6. 33J 43
St. Oswald's Pl. sE11. 17P 62
St. Oswald's Rd. Cro. 18Z 90
St. Oswulf St. sw1. 16P 62
St. Paul St. N1. 19J 51
St. Paul's Av. Nw2. 8G 32

St. Paul's Churchyd. Ec4. 19M 51
St. Paul's Cres. Nw1. 16H 36
St. Paul's Pl. N1. 20G 37
St. Paul's Rd. E3. 25L 53
St. Paul's Rd. N1. 19G 37
St. Paul's Rd. N11. 15Ac 15
St. Paul's Rd. N17. 22Aa 17
St. Paul's Rd. Nw1. 16H 35
St. Paul's Rd. sE17. 19P 62
St. Paul's Rd. Bar. 34J 43
St. Paul's Rd. Bre. 1Q 56
St. Paul's Rd. Cro. 19Zb 90
St. Paul's Rd. Rich. 2S 68
St. Peter St. E2. 22J 52
St. Peters Av. E17. 27B 28
St. Peter's Av. N18. 22Ac 17
St. Peter's Gro. w6. 7P 58
St. Peter's Pl. sw11. 12T 72
St. Peter's Rd. N7. 17F 36
St. Peter's Rd. E1. 23K 52
St. Peter's Rd. w6. 23Ae 17
St. Peter's Rd. w6. 7P 58
St. Peter's Rd. Cro. 19Zg 91
St. Peter's Rd. Twi. 1aT 93
St. Peter's Sq. E2. 22J 52
St. Peter's Sq. w6. 7P 58
St. Peter's St. N1. 19J 51
St. Peter's St. Cro. 19Zg 91
St. Peter's Villas w6. 7P 58
St. Peter's Way N1. 21H 37
St. Petersburgh Pl. w2. 11M 48
St. Philip Sq. sw8. 15R 73
St. Philip St. N1. 19J 51
St. Philip St. sw8. 15S 73
St. Philip's Rd. E8. 22H 38
St. Quintin Av. w10. 9L 47
St. Raphaels Way Nw10. 5G 31
St. Rule St. sw8. 15S 73
St. Saviour's Rd. sw2. 17U 74
St. Saviours Rd. Cro. 19Zd 91
St. Silas St. Nw5. 14G 35
St. Simon's Av. sw15. 8T 71
St. Stephen's Av. w12. 8N 58
St. Stephen's Av. w13. 1aL 94
St. Stephen's Rd. E3. 24J 53
St. Stephen's Rd. E6. 30H 41
St. Stephen's Rd. E17. 26C 27
St. Stephen's Rd. sE13. 26S 78
St. Stephen's Rd. w2. 11L 47
St. Stephens Rd. w13. 1L 44
St. Stephen's Sq. sE1. 20O 63
St. Stephen's Sq. w2. 11L 47
St. Stephen's Ter. sw8. 17R 74
St. Swithin's La. Ec4. 20M 51
St. Thomas' Gdns. Nw5. 14G 35
St. Thomas Rd. E16. 29M 54
St. Thomas Rd. Nw10. 6H 32
St. Thomas's Gdns. Ilf. 34G 43
St. Thomas's Pl. E9. 23H 38
St. Thomas's Rd. E3. 24L 53
St. Thomas's Rd. N4. 18E 36
St. Thomas's Rd. sw6. 10Q 59
St. Thomas's Sq. E9. 23H 38
St. Thomas's St. sE1. 20N 63
St. Vincent St. w1. 14L 49

t. Winifred's Rd. Twi. 1aY 98
Salamanca St. SE11. 17P 62
Salcombe Rd. E17. 25D 27
Salcot Rd. Cro. 16Zf 91
Salcott Rd. SW11. 13T 72
Sale St. E2. 22K 52
Sale St. W2. 13L 48
Salehurst Rd. SE4. 24U 77
Salem Pl. W6. 8O 58
Salem Pl. Cro. 18Zf 91
Salem Rd. W2. 11M 48
Salford Rd. SW2. 16V 84
Salisbury Av. N3. 10A 21
Salisbury Av. Bar. 35H 43
Salisbury Pl. W1. 14L 49
Salisbury Rd. E7. 29H 40
Salisbury Rd. E10 27E 40
Salisbury Rd. E12. 31G 41
Salisbury Rd. E17. 26C 28
Salisbury Rd. N4. 19B 25
Salisbury Rd. N9. 22Ad 17
Salisbury Rd. N19. 16E 36
Salisbury Rd. N22. 18Aa 16
Salisbury Rd. SE25. 21Zd 91
Salisbury Rd. SW19 9Z 92
Salisbury Rd. W13. 1aN 94
Salisbury Rd. Har. 1cB 12
Salisbury Rd. Ilf. 35E 42
Salisbury Rd. Rich. 2S 68
Salisbury Row SE17. 20P 63
Salisbury Sq. EC4. 18M 50
Salisbury St. E3. 24L 53
Salisbury St. N1. 20J 51
Salisbury St. NW8. 13K 48
Salisbury St. W3. 5N 57
Salmen Rd. E13. 28K 54
Salmon La. E14. 24M 53
Salmon St. NW9. 4D 19
Salmon St. NW10. 4D 19
Salmon's Rd. N9. 22Ae 17
Salop Rd. E17. 24C 26
Saltcoats Rd. W4. 6N 57
Salter St. E14. 25M 53
Salterford Rd. SW17. 14Y 84
Salter's Hill SE19. 19Y 86
Salters Rd. E17. 27B 28
Salterton Rd. N7. 17E 36
Saltoun Rd. SW2. 18T 74
Saltram Cres. W9. 10J 47
Saltwell St. E14. 25M 53
Salusbury Rd. NW6. 10H 33
Salvador SW17. 13Y 83
Salvin Rd. SW15. 9S 71
Salvin St. SW8. 16R 73
Salway Rd. E15. 27H 40
Samford St. NW8. 13K 48
Samos Rd. SE20. 22Za 90
Samson St. E13. 30J 55
Samuda St. E14. 26O 66
Samuel St. E14. 24L 53
Samuel St. SE18. 32P 95
Sancroft St. SE11. 17P 62
Sanctuary St. SE1. 19N 63
Sand St. SE18. 31P 67
Sandal Rd. N18. 22Ac 17
Sandal St. E15. 27J 54
Sandall Rd. NW5. 16G 35
Sandall Rd. W5. 2K 44
Sandbach Pl. SE18. 34P 95
Sandbourne Av. SW19. 11Za 92
Sandbourne Rd. SE4. 24S 77
Sandbrook Rd. N16. 20F 37
Sandcroft Rd. Har. 1aAa 12
Sandell St. SE1. 18N 62

Sander St. E1. 22M 52
Sanderstead Av. NW2. 10E 33
Sanderstead Rd. E10. 24D 27
Sandfield Gdns. Cro. 18Zb 90
Sandfield Rd. Cro. 19Zb 90
Sandford Av. N22. 19Aa 16
Sandford Row, SE17. 20P 63
Sandford St. E16. 29M 54
Sandford St. SW6. 12Q 60
Sandgate St. SE15. 22Q 64
Sandhurst Dri. Ilf. 36G 43
Sandhurst Rd. NW9. 3A 19
Sandhurst Rd. SE6. 27V 89
Sandilands Cro. 21Zf 91
Sandilands Rd. SW6. 11R 72
Sandison St. SE15. 21S 75
Sandland St. WC1. 17L 50
Sandmere Rd. SW4. 16T 74
Sandover Rd. SE5. 20Q 63
Sandown Pl. SW18. 11U 72
Sandown Rd. SE25. 22Zc 90
Sandpits Rd. Cro. 23Zg 91
Sandringham Av. SW20. 9Za 92
Sandringham Gdns. N8. 17C 24
Sandringham Gdns. N12. 13Ab 14
Sandringham Rd. E7. 30G 41
Sandringham Rd. E8. 21G 37
Sandringham Rd. E10. 27C 28
Sandringham Rd. N17. 19A 25
Sandringham Rd. NW2. 8G 32
Sandringham Rd. NW11. 10C 21
Sandringham Rd. Bar. 36H 43
Sandringham Rd. Bro. 29Y 89
Sandringham Rd. Cro. 19Zc 90
Sandrock Rd. SE13. 25S 77
Sands End La. SW6. 11R 72
Sandtoft Rd. SE7. 29Q 67
Sandwell Cres. NW6. 11G 34
Sandwich St. WC1. 17K 50
Sandy Rd. NW3. 11E 34
Sandycombe Rd. Kew. 3S 68
Sandycombe Rd. Twi. 1aU 93
Sandy Hill Av. SE18. 33Q 90
Sandy Hill Rd. SE18. 33P 95
Sandhill Rd. Ilf. 33F 43
Sandys Row E1. 22L 51
Sanford La. N16. 21E 37
Sanford St. SE14. 24Q 64
Sanford Ter. N16. 21E 37
Sangley Rd. SE6. 26V 88
Sangley Rd. SE25. 20Zb 90
Sangora Rd. SW11. 13T 72
Sans Wk. EC1. 18K 50
Sansom Rd. E11. 28E 40
Sansom St. SE5. 20R 75
Santley St. SW4. 17T 74
Santos Rd. SW18. 10T 71
Sarah St. E16. 28M 54
Saratoga Rd. E5. 23F 38
Sardinia St. WC2. 17L 50
Sard's Rents SE1. 21N 63
Sarre Rd. NW2. 10F 33
Sarsfeld Rd. SW12. 14V 84
Sarsfield Rd. Wem. 1J 44
Sartor Rd. SE15. 23T 76

Satchwell St. E2. 21K 52
Saul St. E1. 21L 52
Saunders Rd. SE18. 36Q 95
Saunders Rd. W11. 9N 59
Saunders St. SE11. 18O 62
Savage Gdns. EC3. 21M 51
Savernake Rd. NW3. 14F 35
Savile Row W1. 15M 49
Saville Pl. SE11. 18O 62
Saville Rd. E16. 31N 67
Saville Rd. W4. 5O 57
Saville Rd. Twi. 1bV 93
Savona Pl. SW8. 15Q 61
Savona St. SW8. 15Q 61
Savoy Clo. Edg. 4Ac 13
Savoy Hill WC2. 17M 50
Savoy St. WC2. 17M 50
Savoy Way WC2. 17M 50
Sawley Rd. W12. 7M 46
Sawyer St. SE1. 19N 63
Saxby St. SW2. 16U 74
Saxon Dri. W3. 4L 45
Saxon Rd. E3. 24J 53
Saxon Rd. N22. 19Aa 16
Saxon Rd. SE25. 19Zc 90
Saxon Rd. Ilf. 33G 43
Sayer St. SE17. 19O 63
Sayes St. SE8. 24P 65
Sayes Ct. Gdns. SE8. 25Q 65
Sayes Ct. St. SE8. 25Q 65
Scales Rd. N17. 21A 26
Scandrett St. E1. 22N 64
Scarborough Rd. E11. 27D 28
Scarborough Rd. N4. 18D 24
Scarborough St. E1. 21M 51
Scarbrook Rd. Cro. 19Zf 91
Scarle Rd. Wem. 2G 30
Scarsdale Rd. SE5. 20Q 63
Scarsdale Villas W8. 11O 60
Scarth Rd. SW13. 7S 70
Scawen Rd. SE8. 24P 64
Scawfell St. E2. 21J 52
Sceptre St. E1. 23K 52
Scholars Rd. SW12. 15V 84
Scholefield Rd. N19. 16D 36
Scholey St. SW11. 13R 72
School Alley, Twi. 1aV 93
School Rd. E12. 32F 43
School Rd. NW10. 5K 45
School Way N12. 13Ab 14
Schoolhouse La. E1. 23M 52
Schubert Rd. SW15. 10T 71
Scipio St. SE15. 21Q 63
Sclater St. E1. 21K 51
Scoresby St. SE1. 18N 62
Scotsdale Rd. SE12. 29U 79
Scotch Common W13. 1aK 94
Scotland Grn. N17. 21Aa 17
Scotswood St. EC1. 18K 50
Scott St. E1. 22K 52
Scott St. E16. 29M 54
Scott Ellis Gdns. NW8. 12K 48
Scott's Rd. E10. 26E 40
Scott's Rd. W12. 8N 58
Scovell Rd. SE1. 19O 63
Scrafton Rd. Ilf. 33F 42
Scrooby St. SE6. 26V 88
Scrubs La.
NW10. 1-123 & 2-148.
W10. 125, 150 & up. 7K 46
Scrutton St. EC2. 20K 51
Scudamore La. NW9. 5A 19
Scurr St. E14. 26M 53
Scutari Rd. SE22. 22U 76
Scylla Rd. SE15. 22S 76

Seabright St. E2. 22K 52
Seacoal La. EC4. 18M 50
Seafield Rd. N11. 16Ac 15
Seaford Rd. E17. 26B 27
Seaford Rd. N15. 20B 25
Seaford Rd. W13. 1aM 94
Seaford St. WC1. 17K 50
Seaforth Gdns. N21. 18Af 16
Seagrave Rd. SW6. 11Q 59
Seagry Rd. E11. 29C 29
Seaham St. SW8. 16Q 62
Seal St. E8. 21F 37
Seamore Pl. W1. 15N 61
Searle St. SW11. 13R 72
Searles St. SE1. 20O 63
Sears St. SE5. 19Q 63
Seaton Rd. Ilf. 35G 43
Seaton Rd. Wem. 2J 44
Seaton St. E13. 29L 55
Seaton St. NW1. 15K 49
Seaton St. SW10. 12Q 60
Sebastian St. EC1. 19K 51
Sebastopol Rd. N9. 22Ad 17
Sebbon St. N1. 19H 37
Sebert Rd. E7. 29G 41
Secker St. SE1. 18N 62
Second Av. E12. 32F 43
Second Av. E13. 29K 54
Second Av. E17. 26B 27
Second Av. N18. 23Ac 17
Second Av. NW4. 9A 21
Second Av. W14. 6S 69
Second Av. W3. 6N 58
Second Av. W10. 10K 47
Second Cross Rd. Twi. 1cV 93
Secretan Rd. SE5. 20Q 63
Sedan St. SE17. 20P 63
Sedgeford Rd. W12. 7M 46
Sedgemere Av. N2. 12A 22
Sedgeway SE6. 28W 89
Sedgmoor Pl. SE5. 20R 75
Sedgwick Rd. E10. 26E 39
Sedgwick St. E9. 23G 38
Sedleigh Rd. SW18. 10U 71
Sedlescombe Rd. SW6. 10Q 59
Sedley Pl. W1. 15M 49
Seely Rd. SW17. 14Y 84
Seething La. EC3. 21M 51
Sefton Av. NW7. 5Ac 13
Sefton Av. Har. 1cAa 12
Sefton Rd. Cro. 21Ze 91
Sefton St. SW15. 8S 70
Sekforde St. EC1. 18K 50
Selborne Av. E17. 25B 27
Selborne Gdns. NW4. 7A 20
Selborne Rd. E12. 33F 42
Selborne Rd. E17. 25B 27
Selborne Rd. N14. 17Ad 16
Selborne Rd. N22. 17Aa 16
Selborne Rd. SE5. 19R 75
Selborne Rd. Cro. 20Zf 91
Selborne Rd. Ilf. 33E 42
Selby Av. NW10. 6G 32
Selby Rd. E11. 28F 40
Selby Rd. E13. 30L 55
Selby Rd. N17. 20Ab 17
Selby Rd. SE20. 22Za 90
Selby Rd. W5. 1K 44
Selby St. E1. 22L 52
Selcroft Rd. SE10. 28P 66
Selden Rd. SE15. 23S 76
Selhurst Pl. Cro. 20Zd 91
Selhurst Rd. N9. 20Ad 17
Selhurst Rd. Cro. 20Zc 90
Selhurst New Rd. Cro.
                    20Zd 91

Selkirk Rd. SW17. 13X 83
Sellincourt Rd. SW17. 13Y 83
Sellons Av. NW10. 7H 32
Selman St. E9. 24G 39
Selsdon Rd. E11. 29D 28
Selsdon Rd. E13. 30J 55
Selsdon Rd. NW2. 7E 32
Selsdon Rd. SE27. 18X 85
Selsdon Rd. Cro. 19Zg 91
Selsey St. E14. 25L 53
Selvage La. Edg. 6Ad 13
Selwood Pl. SW7. 12P 60
Selwood Rd. Cro. 22Ze 91
Selworthy Rd. SE6. 24X 88
Selwyn Av. Ilf. 35C 42
Selwyn Av. Rich. 2S 68
Selwyn Rd. E3. 24J 53
Selwyn Rd. E13. 29J 55
Selwyn Rd. NW10. 6H 31
Semley Pl. SW1. 15P 61
Semley Rd. SW16. 17Za 90
Senate St. SE15. 23S 76
Seneca Rd. SW4. 17T 74
Seneca Rd. Cro. 19Zc 90
Senegal Rd. SE16. 23P 64
Senior St. W2. 11L 48
Senlac Rd. SE12. 29W 89
Senrab St. E1. 23L 52
Sergeants Inn EC4. 18M 50
Serle St. WC2. 18L 50
Serpentine Rd. W2. 13N 60
Seth St. SE16. 23N 64
Settle Rd. E13. 29J 54
Settles St. E1. 22L 52
Settrington Rd. SW6. 11S 72
Seven Dials WC2. 17M 50
Seven Kings Rd. Ilf. 36E 42
Seven Oaks Rd. SE4. 24U 77
Seven Sisters Rd.
    N7. 1-163 & 2-188A.
    N4. 165-331 & 190-486.
    N15. No. 333, Rem. in Tot.
                    18E 36
Seventh Av. E12. 32F 43
Severn Way NW10. 6F 32
Severne St. E1. 22M 52
Severus Rd. SW11. 13T 72
Seville St. SW1. 14N 61
Sevington Rd. NW4. 8C 20
Sevington St. W9. 11K 48
Seward St. EC1. 19K 51
Seward Rd. W7. 1aN 94
Sewardstone Rd. E2. 23J 52
Sewdley St. E5. 23F 38
Sewell St. E13. 29K 55
Seymour Av. N17. 22A 26
Seymour Gdns. Ilf. 32E 42
Seymour Gdns. Twi. 1aV 93
Seymour Mews W1. 14L 49
Seymour Pl. SW10. 12P 60
Seymour Pl. W1. 14L 49
Seymour Rd. E6. 31J 55
Seymour Rd. E10. 25D 27
Seymour Rd. N3. 12Ab 14
Seymour Rd. N8. 18B 24
Seymour Rd. N9. 23Ad 17
Seymour Rd. SW18. 10U 71
Seymour Rd. SW19. 9W 82
Seymour Rd. W4. 5O 57
Seymour St. NW1. 16J 49
Seymour St. SE8. 25R 77
Seymour St.
    W1. 1-59 & 2-68.
    W2. 63, 70 & up. 14M 49
Seymour Villas SE20. 22Za 90
Seyssell St. E14. 27P 66

Shaa Rd. W3. 5M 45
Shacklegate Rd. Twi. 1cX 93
Shacklewell La. E8. 21G 37
Shacklewell Row E8. 21F 37
Shacklewell St. E2. 21K 51
Shad Thames SE1. 21N 63
Shadwell Pl. E1. 22M 52
Shaftesbury Av. E13. 29J 55
Shaftesbury Av.
    W1. 1-113 & 2-136.
    WC2. 115, 138 & up.
                    16M 50
Shaftesbury Av. Har. 1dD 12
Shaftesbury Av. Har. 2B 18
Shaftesbury Av. E7. 30H 41
Shaftesbury Av. E10. 25E 39
Shaftesbury Av. E17. 26C 27
Shaftesbury Rd. N18.
                    21Ab 17
Shaftesbury Rd. N19. 17D 24
Shaftesbury Rd. W3. 4O 57
Shaftesbury Rd. W6. 7O 58
Shaftesbury Rd. W14. 10O 59
Shaftesbury Rd. Bar. 34J 43
Shaftesbury Rd. Rich.
                    2S 68
Shaftesbury Rd. E. W6.
                    7O 58
Shaftesbury St. N1. 20J 51
Shafton Rd. E9. 23H 38
Shakespeare Av. N11. 16Ac 15
Shakespeare Av. NW10. 5H 31
Shakespeare Cres. E12.
                    32H 43
Shakespeare Rd. E17.
                    24A 26
Shakespeare Rd. N16. 20F 37
Shakespeare Rd. SE24.
                    18U 74
Shakespeare Rd. W3. 5M 45
Shakespeare Rd. W7. 1bM 94
Shakespeare St. N18. 21Ab 17
Shalcomb St. SW10. 12Q 60
Shaldon Dri. Mor. 9Zc 92
Shalimar Gdns. W3. 4M 45
Shalimar Rd. W3. 4M 45
Shalstone Rd. SW14. 4S 69
Shamrock Rd. Cro. 17Zc 90
Shamrock St. SW4. 16S 73
Shamrock Way N14. 15Ae 15
Shand St. SE1. 20N 63
Shandon Rd. SW4. 15U 73
Shandy St. E1. 24L 52
Shanklin Rd. N8. 16C 24
Shanklin Rd. N15. 22B 26
Shap St. E2. 21J 51
Shard Rd. SE15. 22R 76
Shardcroft Av. SE24. 16U 74
Shardeloes Rd. SE14. 24S 77
Shard's Sq. SE15. 22Q 64
Sharon Rd. W4. 5P 57
Sharples Hall St. NW1.
                    14H 35
Sharratt St. SE15. 23Q 64
Sharsted St. SE17. 18P 62
Shaw Rd. SE12. 28X 89
Shawbrooke Rd. SE9. 30U 79
Shawbury Rd. SE22. 21T 75
Shawfield St. SW3. 13P 60
Sheaveshill Av. NW9. 6A 20
Sheba St. E1. 21L 51
Sheen Gro. N1. 18H 36
Sheen La. SW14. 5S 69
Sheen Pk. Rich. 2T 68
Sheen Rd. Rich. 2T 68
Sheen Way Cro. 17Zg 91

Sheen Common Dri. Rich. 3T 69
Sheendale Rd. Rich. 2S 68
Sheen Gate Gdns. sw14. 4T 69
Sheep La. E8. 22J 52
Sheepcote La. sw11. 14S 73
Sheepcote Rd. Har. 1bC 12
Sheffield Ter. w8. 11N 59
Shelbourne Rd. N17. 22Aa 17
Shelburne Rd. N7. 18F 36
Shelbury Rd. SE22. 22U 76
Sheldon Av. N6. 14C 23
Sheldon Rd. N18. 21Ac 17
Sheldon Rd. NW2. 9F 33
Sheldon St. w2. 12L 48
Sheldon St. Cro. 19Zf 91
Shelgate Rd. sw11. 13T 73
Shell Rd. SE13. 25T 77
Shelley Av. E12. 31H 41
Shelley Gdns. Wem. 1E 30
Shelley Rd. E10. 26D 27
Shelley Rd. NW10. 5H 31
Shelley Rd. Har. 1bA 12
Shellgrove Rd. N16. 21G 37
Shellwood Rd. sw11. 14S 73
Shelton Rd. sw19. 10Z 92
Shene St. EC1. 19K 51
Shenfield Pl. E3. 26K 53
Shenley Rd. SE5. 20R 75
Shenton St. SE15. 22Q 64
Shepherd Mkt. w1. 15N 61
Shepherd St. E1. 21L 51
Shepherd St. w1. 15N 61
Shepherdess Wk. N1. 19J 51
Shepherds Hill N6. 15C 23
Shepherd's La. E9. 23G 38
Shepherd's Wk. NW3. 13F 34
Shepherd's Bush Green w12. 9N 59
Shepherd's Bush Rd. w6. 9O 59
Sheppard St. E16. 28L 54
Shepperd St. E3. 26L 53
Shepperton Rd. N1. 19H 37
Sherard Rd. SE9. 31U 79
Sherborne Gdns. w13. 1aL 94
Sherborne St. N1. 20H 37
Sherborough Rd. N15. 21C 25
Sherbourne Gdns. NW9. 4A 19
Sherbrook Gdns. N21. 19Af 16
Sherbrooke Rd. sw6. 10Q 59
Shere Rd. SE8. 24Q 65
Sheridan Gdns. Har. 1C 18
Sheridan Rd. E7. 29F 40
Sheridan Rd. E12. 32G 43
Sheridan Rd. sw19. 10Za 92
Sheridan Rd. Rich. 1aW 93
Sheridan St. E1. 23M 52
Sheringham Av. E12. 32F 43
Sheringham Rd. N7. 18G 36
Sheringham Rd. SE20. 22Zb 90
Sheringham St. NW1. 13L 48
Sherington Rd. SE7. 29Q 67
Sherland Rd. Twi. 1bV 93
Sherman St. E3. 26K 53
Shernhall St. E17. 26B 28
Sherrard Rd.
  E7. 1-195 & 2-210.
  E12. 197, 212 & up. 30G 41
Sherrick Green Rd. NW10. 8F 32
Sherriff Rd. NW6. 11G 34

Sherringham Av. N17. 22Aa 17
Sherwin Rd. SE14. 23R 76
Sherwood Av. E18. 30B 29
Sherwood Gdns. Bar. 34H 43
Sherwood Rd. NW4. 9A 21
Sherwood Rd. Cro. 22Ze 91
Sherwood Rd. Har. 1dE 12
Sherwood St. N20. 13Ad 14
Sherwood St. w1. 16M 49
Shetland St. E2. 22K 52
Shields St. SE15. 21Q 63
Shillington St. sw11. 13S 72
Shillitoe Rd. N13. 19Ac 16
Shinfield St. w12. 8L 46
Ship Alley E1. 22M 52
Ship La. sw14. 5S 69
Ship La. w6. 8P 58
Ship St. E1. 22N 64
Ship St. E14. 27P 66
Ship St. E16. 28L 54
Ship St. SE8. 25R 77
Shipka Rd. sw12. 15V 84
Shipman Rd. E16. 30M 55
Shipman Rd. SE23. 23W 87
Shipton St. E2. 21J 52
Shipwright St. E16. 27L 54
Shirbutt St. E14. 26M 53
Shirehall Clo. NW4. 9B 21
Shirehall Gdns. NW4. 9C 21
Shirehall La. NW4. 9C 21
Shirehall Pk. NW4. 9C 21
Shirland Mews w9. 10K 47
Shirland Rd. w9. 11K 47
Shirley Av. Cro. 22Ze 91
Shirley Gdns. w7. 1bM 94
Shirley Gdns. Bar. 35G 43
Shirley Gro. sw11. 14S 73
Shirley Rd. E15. 28H 40
Shirley Rd. w4. 5N 57
Shirley Rd. Cro. 22Ze 91
Shirley St. E16. 28M 54
Shirley Church Rd. Cro. 23Zf 91
Shirley Hills Rd. Cro. 23Zg 91
Shirley Pk. Rd. Cro. 22Ze 91
Shirlock Rd. NW3. 14F 35
Shobden Rd. N17. 20Aa 17
Shoe La. EC4. 18L 50
Shoebury Rd. E6. 32H 43
Shooters Av. Har. 1A 18
Shooters Hill Rd.
  SE3. 1-227 & 2-166.
  SE18. 168, 229 & up. 27R 78
Shoot-up Hill NW2. 10G 33
Shore Pl. E9. 23H 38
Shore Rd. E9. 23H 38
Shoreditch High St. E1. 21K 51
Shoreham St. sw18. 11T 72
Shorncliffe Rd. SE1. 21P 63
Shorndean St. SE6. 26V 89
Shorrold's Rd. sw6. 10Q 59
Short Rd. E11. 28E 40
Short Rd. E17. 27B 28
Short Rd. w4. 6P 57
Short St. E11. 27F 40
Short St. EC2. 20L 51
Short St. N1. 20K 51
Short St. N18. 21Ab 17
Short St. SE1. 18N 62
Shorter St. E1. 22M 52
Shortlands Clo. N18. 20Ad 17
Shortlands Rd. E10. 26D 27

Shorts Croft NW9. 4A 19
Shorts Gdns. wc2. 17M 50
Shotley St. w6. 9P 59
Shottendane Rd. sw6. 10R 71
Shottlefield Av. sw14. 5S 69
Shoudham St. w1. 13L 48
Shoulder of Mutton Alley E14. 24M 53
Shrewsbury Av. sw14. 5T 69
Shrewsbury Av. Har. 2A 18
Shrewsbury Rd. E7. 31G 41
Shrewsbury Rd. N11. 16Ac 15
Shrewsbury Rd. NW10. 5H 31
Shrewsbury Rd. w2. 11L 47
Shroton St. NW1. 13L 48
Shrubberies,The,E18. 29A 29
Shrubbery Cres. sw16. 16X 85
Shrubbery Gdns. N21. 19Af 16
Shrubbery Rd. N9. 22Ad 17
Shrubbery Rd. SE13. 26S 77
Shrubland Rd. E8. 21H 38
Shrubland Rd. E10. 25C 27
Shrubland Rd. E17. 25C 27
Shuttleworth Rd. sw11. 13R 72
Sibella Rd. sw4. 16S 73
Sibley Gro. E12. 32H 43
Sidbury St. sw6. 9R 71
Sidcup Rd.
  SE12. 2-160.
  SE9. 501-873 & 540-898. 30U 79
Siddons La. NW7. 14K 49
Siddons Rd. N17. 22Aa 17
Siddons Rd. SE23. 24W 87
Siddons Rd. Cro. 18Zf 91
Side Rd. E17. 24B 27
Sidmouth Rd. E10. 26E 40
Sidmouth Rd. NW2. 8H 33
Sidmouth St. wc1. 17K 50
Sidney Av. N13. 18Ac 16
Sidney Rd. E7. 29F 41
Sidney Rd. E9. 24G 39
Sidney Rd. N22. 17Ab 16
Sidney Rd. SE25. 21Zc 90
Sidney Rd. sw9. 17S 74
Sidney Rd. Har. 1cA 12
Sidney Rd. Twi. 1aU 93
Sidney Sq. E1. 23L 52
Sidney St. E1. 23L 52
Sidney St. E2. 23J 52
Sidney St. E16. 29M 54
Sidney St. NW1. 16J 49
Sidworth St. E8. 22H 38
Siebert Rd. SE3. 29Q 67
Siemens Rd. SE18. 31O 67
Sigdon Rd. E8. 22G 38
Sigismund St. SE10. 28O 66
Sign Rd. Twi. 1aV 93
Silas St. E3. 24L 53
Silchester Mews w10. 9L 47
Silchester Rd. w10. 9M 47
Silchester St. w10. 9M 47
Silchester Ter. w10. 9M 47
Silcote Rd. SE5. 20Q 63
Silex St. SE1. 19N 63
Silk St. EC2. 19L 51
Silkfield Av. NW9. 6B 20
Silk Mills Path SE13. 26S 77
Silkstream Rd. Edg. 5Aa 13
Silsoe Rd. N22. 18A 24
Silver Cres. w4. 4O 57
Silver Pl. w1. 16M 49
Silver St. E1. 23L 52

Silver St. ec2. 19L 51
Silver St. n18. 20Ac 17
Silver St. wc1. 17L 50
Silver Wk. se16. 24N 65
Silverdale se26. 23X 87
Silverdale Rd. Cro. 18Zf 91
Silverleigh Rd. Cro. 17Zc 90
Silverlock St. se16. 23P 64
Silvermere Rd. se6. 25V 88
Silverthorne Rd. sw8.
14S 73
Silverton St. w6. 9Q 59
Silvertown Way e6. 28M 54
Silvester Rd. se22. 21U 75
Silvio St. w14. 10Q 59
Silwood St. se16. 23P 64
Simla St. se14. 24Q 65
Slaidburn St. sw10. 12Q 60
Slaithwaite Rd. se13. 26T 78
Simmons Way n20. 14Ae 15
Simonds Rd. e10. 25E 39
Simpson St. sw8. 16Q 62
Simpson St. sw11. 13S 72
Sinclair Gdns. w14. 9N 59
Sinclair Gro. nw11. 9C 21
Sinclair Rd. w14. 9O 59
Singapore Rd. w13. 1aM 94
Singer St. ec2. 20K 51
Single St. e3. 24K 53
Singleton Scarpe n12.
11Ac 14
Sirdar Rd. n22. 19A 25
Sirdar Rd. w11. 9M 47
Sisley Rd. Bar. 35J 43
Sispara Gdns. sw18. 10U 71
Sissinghurst Rd. Cro.
21Zd 91
Sisters Av. sw11. 14T 73
Sistova Rd. sw12. 15V 84
Siward Rd. n17. 20Aa 17
Siward Rd. sw17. 11W 83
Sixth Av. e12. 32F 43
Sixth Av. w10. 9K 47
Sixth Cross Rd. Twi. 1dW 93
Skardu Rd. nw2. 9F 33
Skeena Hill sw18. 9V 82
Skeffington Rd. e6. 32K 43
Skelbrook St. sw18. 11W 83
Skelgill Rd. sw15. 10T 71
Skelton Rd. e7. 29H 41
Skelton's La. e10. 26D 27
Skelwith Rd. w6. 8Q 59
Skidmore St. e1. 24L 52
Skiers St. e15. 27J 54
Skin Mkt. Pl. se1. 19M 51
Skinner St. ec1. 18K 50
Skipton St. se1. 19O 63
Slade, The, se18. 35Q 95
Sladedale Rd. se18. 35Q 95
Slaney Pl. n7. 18F 36
Sleaford St. sw8. 15Q 61
Slipper's Pl. se16. 22O 64
Sloane Av. sw3. 13P 60
Sloane Ct. E. sw3. 14P 61
Sloane Ct. W. sw3. 14P 61
Sloane Gdns. sw1. 14P 61
Sloane Sq. sw1. 14P 61
Sloane St. sw1. 14O 61
Sloane Ter. sw1. 14O 61
Slough La. nw9. 5C 19
Smalley Rd. sw16. 21E 37
Smallwood Rd. sw17. 12X 83
Smart St. e2. 23K 52
Smart's Pl. wc2. 17L 50
Smeaton Rd. sw18. 10V 82
Smedley St. sw8. 16R 74

Smeed Rd. e3. 25H 39
Smith Sq. sw1. 17O 62
Smith St. e1. 23L 52
Smith St. sw3. 13P 61
Smith Ter. sw3. 13P 61
Smithson Rd. n17. 20Aa 17
Smyrk's Rd. se17. 20P 63
Smyrna Rd. nw6. 11H 33
Snaresbrook Rd. e11. 28B 28
Snarsgate St. w10. 8L 47
Snead St. se14. 24R 77
Sneath Av. nw11. 10C 21
Snells Pk. n18. 21Ab 17
Sneyd Rd. nw2. 8F 33
Snow Hill ec1. 18L 50
Snowbury Rd. sw6. 11S 72
Snow's Fields se1. 20N 63
Soames St. se15. 21S 75
Soho Sq. w1. 16L 50
Soho St. w1. 16L 50
Solander St. e1. 22M 52
Solent Rd. nw6. 11G 33
Solna Rd. n21. 20Ae 17
Solomon's Pass. se15. 22T 76
Solon Rd. sw2. 17T 74
Solon New Rd. sw4. 16T 74
Solway Rd. n22. 19Aa 16
Solway Rd. se22. 21T 76
Somali Rd. nw2. 10F 33
Somerby Rd. Bar. 34H 43
Somerfield Rd. n4. 19E 37
Somerford Gro. n16. 21F 37
Somerford Gro. n17. 22Ab 17
Somerford St. e1. 22K 52
Somerleyton Rd. sw9. 18T 74
Somers Pl. sw2. 17U 74
Somers Pl. w2. 13L 48
Somers Rd. e17. 25B 27
Somers Rd. sw2 17U 74
Somerset Gdns. Twi. 1cX 93
Somerset Rd. e17. 25C 27
Somerset Rd. n17. 21A 26
Somerset Rd. n18. 21Ac 17
Somerset Rd. sw19. 9X 82
Somerset Rd. w4. 5N 57
Somerset Rd. w13. 1M 44
Somerset Rd. Bre. 1Q 56
Somerset Rd. Twi. 1cX 93
Somerset St. w1. 14M 49
Somerton Av. sw14. 4S 69
Somerton Rd. nw2. 9E 33
Somerton Rd. se15. 22T 76
Somerville Rd. se14. 23R 76
Sonderburg Rd. n7. 18E 36
Sondes St. se17. 20Q 63
Sonia Gdns. nw10. 7F 32
Sonning St. n7. 18G 36
Sophia Rd. e10. 26D 27
Sophia Rd. e16. 29L 55
Sophia St. e14. 26M 53
Sotheby Rd. n5. 19F 37
Sotheron Rd. sw6. 11Q 60
Soudan Rd. sw11. 14R 73
South Clo. n6. 15C 23
South Cres. n3. 10A 21
South Cres. se13. 26R 77
South Cres. wc1. 16L 50
South End Cro. 19Zg 91
South Gdns. sw19. 12Z 92
South Gro. e3. 24K 53
South Gro. e17. 24C 27
South Gro. n6. 15D 23
South Gro.n15. 20B 25
South Gro. se15. 21S 76
South Parade sw3. 13P 60
South Parade w4. 5O 57

South Park. sw6. 11S 72
South Pl. ec2. 20L 51
South Pl. se17. 18Q 62
South Rd. n9. 22Ae 17
South Rd. n11. 15Ac 15
South Rd. se23. 23W 87
South Rd. sw19. 12Y 83
South Rd. w5. 2O 56
South Rd. Edg. 4Aa 13
South Rd. Twi. 1dW 93
South Row se3. 28S 78
South Row w10. 9K 47
South Side sw19. 8Y 82
South Side w6. 6O 58
South Sq. nw11. 11C 22
South Sq. wc1. 18L 50
South St. e15. 28G 40
South St. ec2. 20L 51
South St. n1. 19H 37
South St. se10. 26R 77
South St. sw7. 13O 60
South St. sw10. 11Q 60
South St. w1. 14M 49
South Vale se19. 20Z 90
South Villas nw1. 16G 36
South Way sw20. 8Zc 92
S. Access Rd. e17. 24C 27
Southam St. w10. 10K 47
Southampton Bldgs. wc2.
18L 50
Southampton Rd. nw5.
14G 35
Southampton Row wc1.
17L 50
Southampton Sq. wc1.
15L 49
Southampton St. n1. 17J 50
Southampton St. w1. 15K 49
Southampton St. wc1. 17L 50
Southampton St. wc2.
17M 50
Southampton Way se5.
20Q 63
South Audley St. w1. 14M 49
South Birkbeck Rd. e11.
27F 40
South Bolton Gdns. sw5.
12P 60
Southborough Rd. e9.
23H 38
Southbourne Av. nw9.
5Aa 13
Southbourne Gdns. Ilf.
34G 43
Southbridge Rd. Cro.
19Zg 91
Southbrook Rd. se12. 28U 78
Southbrook Rd. se16.
16Za 90
Southbrook St. w12. 8N 58
South Bruton Mews w1.
15M 49
Southcombe St. w14. 9O 59
Southcote Rd. e17. 24B 27
Southcote Rd. n19. 16F 35
Southcote Rd. se25. 22Zc 90
Southcroft Rd.
sw17. 1-161 & 2-248.
sw16. 163, 250 & up.
14Y 84
South Croxted Rd. se21.
20X 75
Southdean Gdns. sw19.
10W 82
Southdown Rd. sw20. 9Za 92
Southdown Rd. w7. 1bO 94

S. Ealing Rd. w5. 1N 56
S. Eastern Av. N9. 21Ad 17
S. Eaton Pl. sw1. 14O 61
South End Green nw3.
　　　　　　　　　13F 34
Southend La. se6. 24T 88
Southend Rd. e6. 32H 43
Southend Rd. e18. 30A 29
South End Rd. nw3. 13F 34
Southern Av. se25. 21Zb 90
Southern Rd. e13. 30J 55
Southern Rd. n2. 14B 23
Southern St. n1. 17J 50
Southerton Rd. w6. 8O 58
Southesk Rd. e7. 30H 41
Southesk St. sw9. 17S 74
Southey Rd. n15. 20B 25
Southey Rd. sw19. 11Z 92
Southey St. se20. 23Z 90
Southfield Gdns. Twi. 1cX 93
Southfield Rd. w4. 5N 57
Southfields nw4. 8A 20
Southfields Rd. sw18. 10U 71
Southgate Gro. n1. 20H 37
Southgate Rd. n1. 20H 37
S. Hill Av. Har. 1bE 12
South Hill Pk. nw3. 13F 34
South Hill Pk. Gdns. nw3.
　　　　　　　　　13F 34
Southill St. e14. 26M 53
South Island Pl. sw9. 18Q 62
South Lambeth Rd. sw8.
　　　　　　　　　17Q 62
Southland Rd. se18. 36R 95
Southland Way Twi. 1dT 93
Southmead Rd. sw19. 9V 82
South Molton La. w1. 15M 49
South Molton Rd. e16.
　　　　　　　　　29L 55
South Molton St. w1. 15M 49
S. Norwood Hill Cro. 20Za 90
Southolm St. sw11. 15R 73
Southover n12. 11Ac 14
Southover Bro. 29Y 89
South Pk. Cres. se6. 28V 89
S. Pk. Cres. Ilf. 35F 42
S. Pk. Dri. Ilf. 35E 42
South Pk. Rd. sw19. 10Y 82
S. Pk. Rd. Ilf. 35F 42
S. Pk. Ter. Ilf. 35F 42
South Pk. Hill Rd. Cro.
　　　　　　　　　20Zg 91
Southport Rd. se18. 34P 95
Southsea Rd. Cro. 18Ze 91
Southvale Rd. se3. 28S 78
S. View Av. nw10. 6F 32
S. View Clo. nw10. 6F 32
Southview Cres. Ilf. 33C 42
Southview Dri. e18. 30A 29
South View Rd. n8. 17A 24
Southview Rd. se6. 27X 89
Southville sw8. 16R 74
Southwark Bridge ec4.
　　　　　　　　　19M 51
Southwark Gro. se1. 19N 63
Southwark St. se1. 19N 63
Southwark Bridge Rd. se1.
　　　　　　　　　19N 63
Southwark Pk. Rd. se16.
　　　　　　　　　22P 64
Southway n20. 11Ae 14
Southway nw11. 12B 22
Southwell Gdns. sw7. 12O 60
Southwell Gro. Rd. e11.
　　　　　　　　　28E 40
Southwell Rd. Cro. 17Zd 91

South West Rd. e11. 27D 28
S. Western Rd. Twi. 1aU 93
South Wharf Rd. w2. 13L 48
Southwick Cres. w2. 13M 48
Southwick Pl. w2. 13M 48
Southwick St. w2. 13L 48
Southwold Rd. e5. 22E 38
Southwood Av. n6. 15C 23
Southwood La. n6. 15D 23
Southwood Lawn Rd. n6.
　　　　　　　　　15C 23
Spa Clo. se25. 20Za 90
Spa Hill se19. 19Za 90
Spa Rd. se16. 21O 63
Spalding Rd. sw17. 15Y 84
Spanby Rd. e3. 25K 53
Spaniards Clo. nw11. 12D 22
Spaniards Rd. nw3. 12B 34
Spaniards, The, nw11. 12D 22
Spanish Pl. w1. 14L 49
Spanish Rd. sw18. 12T 72
Spark Bridge Rd. Har.
　　　　　　　　　1bA 12
Sparrick's Row se1. 20N 63
Sparsholt Rd. n19. 17D 24
Sparsholt Rd. Bar. 35J 43
Sparta St. se10. 26R 77
Spear Mews sw5. 11P 59
Spearman St. se18. 33Q 95
Speenham Rd. sw9. 18S 74
Speech St. se1. 19O 63
Speedwell St. se8. 25R 77
Speke Rd. sw11. 12S 72
Speke Rd. Cro. 19Za 90
Speldhurst Rd. e9. 23H 38
Speldhurst Rd. w4. 5N 57
Spelman St. e1. 22L 52
Spencer Av. n13. 18Ab 16
Spencer Clo. nw10. 3J 44
Spencer Dri. n2. 12C 22
Spencer Gdns. sw14. 4T 69
Spencer Hill sw19. 9Y 82
Spencer Pk. sw18. 12T 72
Spencer Rd. e6. 31J 55
Spencer Rd. n7. 18F 36
Spencer Rd. n8. 17B 24
Spencer Rd. n11. 15Ad 15
Spencer Rd. n17. 22Aa 17
Spencer Rd. nw5. 15F 35
Spencer Rd. sw15. 9T 71
Spencer Rd. sw18. 12T 72
Spencer Rd. sw20. 8Za 92
Spencer Rd. w3. 5M 45
Spencer Rd. w4. 5Q 57
Spencer Rd. Cro. 20Zg 91
Spencer Rd. Har. 1bAa 12
Spencer Rd. Ilf. 36D 42
Spencer Rd. Twi. 1cW 93
Spencer St. e1. 23M 52
Spencer St. ec1. 19K 50
Spencer St. n1. 19H 37
Spencer Hill Rd. sw19. 9Z 92
Spenlow St. e14. 25L 53
Spenser Rd. n16. 20F 37
Spenser Rd. se24. 18U 74
Spenser St. sw1. 16O 61
Speranza St. se18. 35Q 95
Sperling Rd. n17. 21A 25
Spey St. e14. 26L 53
Spezia Rd. nw10. 7J 46
Spicer St. sw11. 13R 72
Spigurnell Rd. n17. 20Aa 16
Spital Sq. e1. 21L 51
Spital St. e1. 21L 52
Splidts St. e1. 22M 52
Spondon Rd. n15. 22B 26

Sportsbank St. se6. 26V 88
Spotton's Gro. n17. 19Aa 16
Spratley's Row e14. 25N 65
Spray St. se18. 33P 95
Sprimount Pl. sw3. 13P 60
Spring Gdns. sw1. 16N 62
Spring Gro. w4. 3P 56
Spring Hill e5. 22D 26
Spring La. e5. 22D 26
Spring La. se25. 22Zd 91
Spring Pl. nw5. 15G 35
Spring St. e3. 25J 53
Spring St. n1. 19H 37
Spring St. se8. 25R 77
Spring St. w2. 12M 48
Springall St. se15. 22R 76
Springbank Rd. se13. 27U 78
Springbridge Rd. w5. 2M 44
Springcroft Av. n2. 14A 23
Springdale Rd. n16. 20F 37
Springfield e5. 22D 26
Springfield Av. n10. 16A 23
Springfield Av. sw20. 9Za 92
Springfield Dri. Ilf. 34C 42
Springfield Gdns. e5. 22D 26
Springfield Gdns. nw6.
　　　　　　　　　11J 48
Springfield Gdns. nw9. 6B 19
Springfield La. nw6. 11J 48
Springfield Mt. nw9. 6B 20
Springfield Pk. e5. 22D 26
Springfield Rd. e6. 32H 43
Springfield Rd. e17. 24C 27
Springfield Rd. n11. 15Ac 15
Springfield Rd. n15. 21B 26
Springfield Rd. nw8. 12H 34
Springfield Rd. se26. 22Y 87
Springfield Rd. sw19. 10Y 82
Springfield Rd. w7. 1bM 94
Springfield Rd. Cro. 19Za 90
Springfield Rd. Har. 1bB 12
Springfield Rd. Twi. 1bY 93
Springfield Pk. Cres. se6.
　　　　　　　　　25V 88
Spring Gdn. Pl. e1. 24L 52
Springrice Rd. se13. 27U 78
Spring Gro. Rd. Rich. 2T 68
Spring Pk. Av. Cro. 23Zf 91
Spring Pk. Rd. Cro. 23Zf 91
Spring Vale Av. Bre. 2P 56
Springwell Av. nw10. 7H 32
Springwell Clo. sw16. 17X 85
Springwell Rd. sw16. 17X 85
Sprowston Rd. e7. 29G 41
Spruce Hills Rd. e17. 26A 27
Sprules Rd. se4. 24S 77
Spur Rd. n15. 20B 25
Spurgeon St. se1. 20O 63
Spurling Rd. se22. 21T 75
Spurstowe Rd. e8. 22G 38
Spurstowe Ter. e8. 22G 38
Squarey St. sw17. 12X 83
Squires La. n3. 11Aa 14
Squire's Mt. nw3. 13E 34
Squirries St. e2. 22K 52
Stable Yard sw1. 16N 61
Stacey St. wc2. 16M 50
Stadium St. sw10. 12Q 60
Staff St. ec1. 20K 51
Staffa Rd. e10. 24D 27
Stafford Gdns. Cro. 17Zg 91
Stafford Mews nw6. 11J 47
Stafford Mews Rich. 2U 68
Stafford Pl. sw1. 15O 61
Stafford Rd. e3. 25J 53

Stafford Rd. E7. 31H 41
Stafford Rd. E17. 25C 27
Stafford Rd. NW6. 11J 47
Stafford Rd. Cro. 17Zg 91
Stafford St. SE15. 22R 76
Stafford St. W1. 15M 49
Stafford Ter. W8. 11N 59
Stag Clo. Edg. 5Aa 13
Stag La.
NW9. 139-359 & 192-364
4Aa 13
Stag La. SW15. 6X 81
Stag Ride SW19. 6X 81
Staines Rd. Ilf. 34G 43
Staines Rd. Twi. 1dV 93
Stainforth Rd. E17. 26B 27
Stainforth Rd. Ilf. 35D 42
Staining La. EC2. 19M 51
Stainsbury St. E2. 23K 52
Stainsby Rd. E14. 25M 53
Stainton Rd. SE6. 27V 89
Stalbridge St. NW1. 13L 48
Stalham St. SE16. 22O 64
Stamford Gro. E. N16.
21D 26
Stamford Gro. W. N16.
21D 26
Stamford Hill N16. 21D 25
Stamford Rd. E6. 31J 55
Stamford Rd. N1. 21H 51
Stamford Rd. N15. 21B 26
Stamford Rd. SW6. 11Q 60
Stamford St. SE1. 18N 62
Stamford Brook Av. W6.
7O 58
Stamford Brook Rd. W6.
6O 58
Stanbridge Rd. SW15. 8S 71
Stanbury Rd. SE15. 22R 76
Stancroft NW9. 6B 20
Standard Rd. NW10. 5K 45
Standard St. SE1. 20O 63
Standen Rd. SW18. 10V 82
Standish Rd. W6. 7P 58
Stanfield Rd. E3. 24J 53
Stanford Rd. N11. 14Ac 15
Stanford Rd. SW16. 17Za 90
Stanford Rd. W8. 11O 60
Stanford St. SW1. 16P 61
Stangate SE1. 17O 62
Stangate St. SE1. 17O 62
Stanger Rd. SE25. 21Zc 90
Stanhope Av. N3. 11A 21
Stanhope Av. Har. 1cAa 12
Stanhope Gdns. N4. 19C 25
Stanhope Gdns. N6. 15C 23
Stanhope Gdns. SW7. 12O 60
Stanhope Gdns. Ilf. 32D 42
Stanhope Gate W1. 14N 61
StanhopeMewsE.sw7. 12O 60
StanhopeMewsS.sw7. 12O 60
Stanhope Pl. W2. 13L 49
Stanhope Rd. E17. 26B 27
Stanhope Rd. N6. 16C 23
Stanhope Rd. N12. 12Ac 14
Stanhope Rd. Cro. 20Zf 91
Stanhope Rd. NW1. 15K 49
Stanhope St. SE8. 25R 77
Stanhope St. W2. 13L 48
Stanlake Rd. W12. 8N 58
Stanlake Villas W12. 8N 58
Stanley Av. Wem. 2H 30
Stanley Cres. W11. 10M 47
Stanley Gdns. NW2. 9G 33
Stanley Gdns. NW3. 13G 35

Stanley Gdns. W3. 6N 57
Stanley Gdns. W11. 10M 47
Stanley Gro. N17. 21Aa 17
Stanley Gro. Cro. 18Zd 91
Stanley Pl. SW1. 15P 61
Stanley Rd. E12. 31G 43
Stanley Rd. E10. 26C 27
Stanley Rd. E15. 27J 54
Stanley Rd. N1. 21G 37
Stanley Rd. N2. 13A 22
Stanley Rd. N9. 21Ae 17
Stanley Rd. N10. 15Ab 15
Stanley Rd. N11. 16Ac 15
Stanley Rd. N15. 19B 25
Stanley Rd. NW9. 7C 20
Stanley Rd. SW6. 11R 72
Stanley Rd. SW14. 4T 69
Stanley Rd. SW19. 10Y 82
Stanley Rd. W3. 4O 57
Stanley Rd. Cro. 18Zd 91
Stanley Rd. Har. 1dE 12
Stanley Rd. Ilf. 34E 42
Stanley Rd. Mor. 11Zb 92
Stanley Rd. Twi. 1cW 93
Stanley Rd. Wem. 3G 31
Stanley St. SE8. 25R 77
Stanley St. SW8. 14S 73
Stanley Ter. N19. 17E 36
Stanley Villas SW4. 17R 74
Stanley Gdns. Rd. Twi.
1cX 93
Stanley Pk. Rd. Wem. 3H 30
Stanmer St. SW11. 13R 72
Stanmore Gdns. Rich. 3S 68
Stanmore Rd. E11. 29D 28
Stanmore Rd. N15. 19B 25
Stanmore Rd. Rich. 2S 68
Stanmore St. N1. 17H 36
Stannard Rd. E8. 21G 38
Stannary St. SE11. 18P 62
Stansfield Rd. SW9. 17S 74
Stanstead Rd.
SE23. 1-819 & 2-302.
SE6. 304, 321 & up. 24V 87
Stanthorpe Rd. SW16.16X 85
Stanton Rd. SW13. 6R 70
Stanton Rd. SW20. 8Za 92
Stanton Rd. Cro. 19Ze 91
Stanton Sq. SE26. 24X 88
Stanton St. SE15. 21R 75
Stanway Gdns. W3. 3M 45
Stanway Gdns. Edg. 5Ac 13
Stanwick Rd. W14. 10P 59
Stanworth St. SE1. 21O 63
Stapenhill Rd. Har. 1aE 12
Staple Inn WC2. 18L 50
Staple Inn Bldgs. WC1.
18L 50
Staple St. SE1. 20O 63
Stapleford Rd. Wem. 2G 30
Staplehurst Rd. SE13.27U 78
Stapleton Rd. SW17. 14W 84
Stapleton Hall Rd. N4.
18D 24
Star La. E16. 29L 54
Star Rd. W14. 10P 59
Star St. E16. 28L 54
Star St. W2. 13L 48
Star Yard WC2. 18L 50
Star & Garter Hill Rich.
2U 68
Statham Gro. N16. 20F 37
Statham Gro. N18. 20Ac 17
Statham St. W2. 12L 48
Station App. Har. 1bC 12
Station App. Wem. 1G 30

Station Cres. N15. 21B 25
Station Cres. Wem. 1G 30
Station Gro. Wem. 2G 30
Station Path W12. 8N 58
Station Rd. E7. 29F 41
Station Rd. E10. 27F 40
Station Rd. E12. 31F 41
Station Rd. E15. 27H 40
Station Rd. E17. 24C 27
Station Rd. N3. 11Aa 14
Station Rd. N4. 18E 36
Station Rd. N11. 15Ac 15
Station Rd. N17. 22A 26
Station Rd. N18. 21Ac 17
Station Rd. N21. 19Ae 16
Station Rd. N22. 17Aa 16
Station Rd. NW2. 8G 33
Station Rd. NW4. 7C 20
Station Rd. NW7. 6Ac 13
Station Rd. NW10. 6J 46
Station Rd. NW10. 9J 47
Station Rd. SE3. 29Q 66
Station Rd. SE6. 25V 88
Station Rd. SE16. 21O 63
Station Rd. SE20. 23Y 92
Station Rd. SE22. 21T 75
Station Rd. SE25. 21Zb 90
Station Rd. SW13. 6R 70
Station Rd. SW19. 10Z 92
Station Rd. W5. 3L 44
Station Rd. W7. 1cM 94
Station Rd. W12. 7N 58
Station Rd. Cro. 19Ze 91
Station Rd. Edg. 4Ac 13
Station Rd. Har. 1bA 12
Station Rd. Ilf. 33E 42
Station Rd. Kew. 3R 68
Station Rd. Ted. 1bY 93
Station Rd. Twi. 1bV 93
Station St. E15. 27H 40
Station Ter. SE5. 19R 75
Station Yd. Twi. 1bV 93
Staunton St. SE8. 25Q 65
Staveley Gdns. W4. 5R 69
Staveley Rd. SE12. 22R 76
Staveley Rd. W4. 5Q 57
Staverton Rd. NW2. 8H 32
Stavordale Rd. N5. 18F 36
Stayner's Rd. E1. 23L 52
Steadman St. EC1. 19K 51
Stean St. E8. 21H 37
Stebbing St. W11. 9M 47
Stebondale St. E14. 26P 66
Steedman St. SE17. 19P 63
Steeds Rd. N10. 14Aa 15
Steele Rd. E11. 28F 40
Steele Rd. E15. 28J 54
Steele Rd. N17. 21A 25
Steele Rd. NW10. 5J 45
Steele Rd. W4. 5O 57
Steele's Rd. NW3. 14G 35
Steel's La. E1. 23M 52
Steep Hill SW16. 16X 85
Steeplestone Clo. N18.
19Ac 16
Steerforth St. SW18. 11W 83
Stella Rd. SW17. 14Y 84
Stembridge Rd. SE20.
22Za 90
Stephen St. W1. 16L 49
Stephendale Rd. SW6. 11S 72
Stephen's Rd. E15. 28J 54
Stephenson St. E16. 27L 54
Stephenson St. NW10. 6J 46
Stepney Causeway E1.
23M 52

Stepney Green E1.	23L 52
Stepney High St. E1.	24L 52
Sterndale Rd. w14.	9O 59
Sterne St. w12.	9N 59
Sternhall La. SE15.	22S 76
Sternhold Av. sw2.	16W 84
Sterry Rd. Bar.	36J 43
Sterry St. SE1.	20N 63
Stevenage Rd. E6.	32H 43
Stevenage Rd. sw6.	9R 71
Stevens Av. E9.	23G 38
Stevens St. SE1.	21O 63
Steventon Rd. w12.	7M 46
Steward St. E1.	21L 51
Steward Rd. E15.	27F 40
Stewart St. E14.	26O 66
Stewart's Clo. NW9.	5C 19
Stewart's Gro. sw3.	13P 60
Stewart's La. sw8.	15R 73
Stewarts Pl. sw2.	17U 74
Stewart's Rd. sw8.	15R 73
Stewartsby Clo. N18.	19Ac 16
Steyne Rd. w3.	4M 45
Steynings Way N12.	11Ac 14
Stibbington St. NW1.	16J 49
Stile Hall Gdns. w4.	3P 57
Stillingfleet Rd. sw13.	7Q 58
Stillington St. sw1.	16O 61
Stillness Rd. SE23.	24U 77
Stirling Rd. E13.	29J 55
Stirling Rd. E17.	24A 27
Stirling Rd. N17.	22Aa 17
Stirling Rd. N22.	18Aa 16
Stirling Rd. sw9.	17S 74
Stirling Rd. w3.	4O 57
Stirling Rd. Har.	1bA 12
Stock St. E13.	29K 54
Stockdale Rd. E8.	16R 73
Stockfield Rd. sw16.	17W 85
Stockholm Rd. SE16.	23Q 64
Stockmar Rd. E9.	23G 38
Stock Orchard Cres. N7.	17F 36
Stock Orchard St. N7.	17G 36
Stockton Rd. N17.	19Aa 16
Stockton Rd. N18.	22Ab 17
Stockwell Av. sw9.	17S 74
Stockwell Green sw9.	17S 74
Stockwell Rd. sw9.	17S 74
Stockwell St. SE10.	27Q 66
Stockwell Ter. sw9.	17R 74
Stockwell Pk. Cres. sw9.	17R 74
Stockwell Pk. Rd. sw9.	17R 74
Stockwell Pk. Wk. sw9.	18S 74
Stodart Rd. SE20.	22Za 90
Stokenchurch St. sw6.	11R 72
Stoke Newington Common N16.	21E 38
Stoke Newington Rd. N16.	21F 37
Stokesley St. w12.	7L 46
Stonard Rd. N13.	18Ad 16
Stondon Pk. SE23.	24U 76
Stone Bldgs. wc2.	18L 50
Stonebridge Pk. NW10.	5H 31
Stonebridge Rd. N15.	21B 25
Stonebridge Way NW10.	4G 31
Stonecroft Way Cro.	16Zd 91
Stonecutter St. EC4.	18L 50
Stonefield St. N1.	18H 36
Stonehall Av. Ilf.	31C 29
Stoneham Rd. E5.	22E 38
Stoneham Rd. N11.	16Ac 15
Stonehill Rd. sw14.	5T 69
Stonehill Rd. w4.	4P 57
Stoneleigh St. w11.	9M 47
Stoneleys Rd. N17.	21A 26
Stonell's Rd. sw11.	14U 73
Stones End St. SE1.	19O 63
Stoney La. E1.	21L 51
Stoney St. SE1.	19N 63
Stoneyfield Gdns. Edg.	5Ad 13
Stoneyfield La. Edg.	5Ad 13
Stonhouse St. sw4.	16S 73
Stonor Rd. w14.	10O 59
Stopford Rd. E13.	29J 55
Stopford Rd. SE17.	19P 63
Store St. E15.	27G 40
Store St. wc1.	16L 50
Storey Rd. E17.	25B 27
Storey Rd. N6.	14C 23
Stories Rd. SE5.	20S 75
Stork Rd. E7.	29H 40
Stork's Rd. SE16.	22O 64
Storksmead Rd. Edg.	6Ab 13
Stormont Rd. N6.	14D 23
Stormont Rd. sw11.	14S 73
Storrington Rd. Cro.	21Ze 91
Story St. N1.	17H 36
Stour Rd. E3.	25H 39
Stourcliffe St. w1.	14L 49
Stowage SE8.	25Q 65
Stowe Gdns. N9.	21Ae 17
Stowe Rd. w12.	8N 58
Stracey Rd. E7.	29F 41
Stracey Rd. NW10.	5H 31
Stradbroke Rd. N5.	19F 37
Stradella Rd. SE24.	19U 75
Strafford Rd. w3.	4N 57
Strafford Rd. Twi.	1aU 93
Strafford St. E14.	25N 65
Strahan Rd. E3.	24K 53
Straightsmouth SE10.	26Q 65
Strand wc2.	17M 50
Strand La. wc2.	17M 50
Strand on the Green w4.	3P 57
Stratfield Rd. E3.	26K 53
Stratford Gro. sw15.	9T 71
Stratford Pl. NW1.	16H 35
Stratford Pl. w1.	15M 49
Stratford Rd. E13.	29J 54
Stratford Rd. NW4.	9B 21
Stratford Rd. w8.	11O 59
Stratford Rd. Cro.	18Zb 90
Strathaven Rd. SE12.	30U 79
Strathblaine Rd. sw11.	13T 72
Strathearn Rd. sw19.	10X 82
Strathfield Gdns. Bar.	35H 43
Strathleven Rd. sw2.	17T 74
Strathmore Gdns. N3.	11Aa 14
Strathmore Gdns. Edg.	4Aa 13
Strathmore Rd. sw19.	11W 82
Strathmore Rd. Cro.	19Zd 91
Strathmore Rd. Twi.	1cX 93
Strathnairn St. SE1.	22P 64
Strathray Gdns. NW3.	13G 34
Strathville Rd. sw18.	11W 82
Strathyre Av. sw16.	17Zb 90
Stratton Dri. Bar.	35G 43
Stratton Rd. sw19.	10Za 92
Stratton St. w1.	15N 61
Strattondale St. E14.	26O 65
Strauss Rd. w3.	5N 57
Strawberry Vale N2.	13Aa 14
Strawberry Vale Twi.	1bW 93
Strawberry Hill Rd. Twi.	1aW 93
Streatfield Av. E6.	32J 43
Streatfield Rd. Har.	1A 18
Streatfield St. E14.	25L 53
Streatham Common sw16.	17Y 85
Streatham Common S. sw16.	17Y 85
Streatham Hill sw2.	17W 85
Streatham Pl. sw2.	16V 85
Streatham St. wc1.	17L 50
Streatham High Rd. sw16.	16Y 85
Streathbourne Rd. sw17.	14W 84
Streatley Pl. NW3.	12F 34
Streatley Rd. NW6.	10H 33
Strelley Way w3.	6M 45
Stretton Rd. Cro.	20Zd 91
Strickland St. SE8.	25R 77
Strode Rd. E7.	29F 41
Strode Rd. NW10.	7G 32
Strode Rd. sw6.	9Q 59
Strone Rd. E7. 1-209 & 2-216. E12. 211, 218 & up.	30H 41
Stronsa Rd. w12.	16N 58
Stroud Rd. Cro.	22Zd 91
Stroud Green Rd. N4.	18D 24
Strutton Ground sw1.	16O 61
Strype St. E1.	21L 51
Stuart Av. NW9.	7C 20
Stuart Av. w5.	3N 56
Stuart Cres. N22.	18Aa 16
Stuart Rd. SE15.	23T 76
Stuart Rd. sw19.	10W 82
Stuart Rd. w3.	4M 45
Stuart Rd. Bar.	36H 43
Stuart Rd. Cro.	19Zb 90
Stuart Rd. Har.	1bA 12
Stucley Pl. NW1.	15H 35
Studd St. N1.	18H 36
Studdridge St. sw6.	11R 71
Studholme St. SE15.	22R 76
Studland Rd. SE26.	23Y 87
Studland Rd. w7.	1cL 94
Studland St. w6.	8O 58
Studley Dri. Ilf.	31C 29
Studley Rd. E7.	30H 41
Studley Rd. sw4.	17R 74
Studley Grange Rd. w7.	1bN 94
Stukeley Rd. E7.	30H 41
Sturdy Rd. SE15.	22S 76
Sturge Av. E17.	26A 27
Sturge St. SE1.	19N 63
Sturgeon Rd. SE17.	19P 63
Sturgess Av. NW4.	8C 20
Sturry St. E14.	26M 53
Sturt St. N1.	19J 51
Stutfield St. E1.	22M 52
Styman St. N1.	20K 51
Sudbourne Rd. sw2.	17T 74
Sudbrooke Rd. sw12.	14U 73
Sudbury Av. Wem.	1E 30
Sudbury Cres. Bro.	29Y 89
Sudbury Hill Har.	1bE 1

Sudbury St. se1. 17O 62
Sudbury Ct. Dri. Har. 1aE 12
Sudbury Ct. Rd. Har. 1aE 12
Sudeley St. n1. 19J 51
Sudlow Rd. sw18. 11T 71
Sudrey St. se1. 19N 63
Suffield Rd. n15. 21B 25
Suffield Rd. se17. 19P 63
Suffield Rd. se20. 22Zb 90
Suffolk Gro. se16. 23P 64
Suffolk La. ec4. 20M 51
Suffolk Rd. e8. 22J 52
Suffolk Rd. e13. 29K 54
Suffolk Rd. n15. 20C 25
Suffolk Rd. nw10. 6H 32
Suffolk Rd. se25. 21Zb 90
Suffolk Rd. sw13. 7Q 58
Suffolk Rd. Bar. 35H 43
Suffolk Rd. Ilf. 35C 42
Suffolk St. e7. 29G 41
Suffolk St. sw1. 16M 50
Suffolk Pk. Rd. e17. 24B 27
Sugar House La. e15. 26J 54
Sugden Rd. sw11. 14S 73
Sulgrave Rd. w6. 8O 59
Sulina Rd. sw2. 16V 85
Sullivan Rd. sw6. 11S 71
Sultan Rd. e11. 29B 29
Sultan St. se5. 19Q 63
Sumatra Rd. nw6. 11G 33
Sumburgh Rd. sw12. 14U 73
Summer St. e3. 25J 53
Summer St. se8. 25R 77
Summerfield Av. nw6. 10J 47
Summerfield St. se12. 28V 89
Summerhill Rd. n15. 20B 25
Summerhouse Rd. n16.
 21E 37
Summerland Gdns. n10.
 15A 23
Summerlands Av. w3. 4M 45
Summerlee Av. n2. 14A 23
Summerley St. sw18. 11W 83
Summers La. n12. 13Ab 14
Summersby Rd. n6. 15C 23
Summerstown w17. 12X 83
Summit Av. nw9. 5B 19
Summit Clo. nw9. 6B 19
Summit Dri. Ilf. 31A 29
Summit Rd. e17. 26B 27
Summit Way n14. 15Ae 15
Sumner Pl. sw7. 12P 60
Sumner Rd. se15. 21Q 63
Sumner Rd. Cro. 18Ze 91
Sumner Rd. Har. 1dC 12
Sumner St. se1. 19N 63
Sumner Ter. sw7. 13P 60
Sun La. se3. 29R 79
Sun St. ec2. 20L 51
Sun St. Pass. ec2. 20L 51
Sunbeam Rd. nw10. 5K 45
Sunbury Av. nw7. 6Ac 13
Sunbury Av. sw14. 5T 69
Sunbury Gdns. nw7. 5Ac 13
Sunbury La. sw11. 13R 72
Sunbury St. se18. 32P 95
Sunderland Rd. se23. 23W 87
Sunderland Rd. w5. 1O 56
Sunderland Ter. w2. 11L 48
Sundew Av. w12. 7M 46
Sundial Av. se25. 21Zb 90
Sundorne Rd. se7. 30Q 67
Sundown Pl. Ilf. 33F 42
Sunfields Pl. se3. 29R 79
unleigh Rd. Wem. 2H 30
anning Rd. Cro. 21Zd 91

Sunningdale n14. 17Ac 16
Sunningdale Av. w3. 6M 46
Sunningdale Av. Bar. 34J 43
Sunningfields Rd. nw4.
 8A 20
Sunning Hill Rd. se13.
 26S 77
Sunny Bank se25. 21Zb 90
Sunny Cres. nw10. 4H 31
Sunny Gdns. nw4. 8A 20
Sunny Hill nw4. 8A 20
Sunny View nw9. 5B 19
Sunny Way n12. 13Ab 14
Sunnycourt Rd. se25.
 21Zb 90
Sunnydale Gdns. nw7.
 6Ac 13
Sunnydene St. se26. 24X 87
Sunnyhill Gdns. Edg. 5Ad 13
Sunnyhill Rd. sw16. 17X 85
Sunnymead Rd nw9 5C 19
Sunnymead Rd sw15. 7T 70
Sunnyside sw19. 9Y 82
Sunnyside Rd. e10. 25D 27
Sunnyside Rd. n9. 21Ad 17
Sunnyside Rd. n19. 16D 24
Sunnyside Rd. nw2. 11E 33
Sunnyside Rd. w5. 1N 56
Sunnyside Rd. Ilf. 34F 42
Sunnyside Rd. Twi. 1cX 93
Sunray Av. se24. 19T 75
Sunridge Rd. Cro. 21Ze 91
Sunset Gdns. se25. 20Za 90
Sunset Rd. se5. 19T 75
Sunwell St. se15. 22R 76
Surat St. e2. 23K 52
Surr St. n7 17G 36
Surrendale Pl. w9. 11K 48
Surrey Cres. w4. 3P 57
Surrey Gro. se17. 20P 63
Surrey La. sw11. 13R 72
Surrey La. S. sw11. 13R 72
Surrey Rd. se15. 23T 76
Surrey Rd. Bar. 35J 43
Surrey Row se1. 19N 62
Surrey Sq. se17. 20P 63
Surrey St. e13. 30K 55
Surrey St. wc2. 17M 50
Surrey St. se17. 19Zf 91
Surrey Ter. se17. 20P 63
Susannah St. e14. 26M 53
Sussex Gdns. w2. 12M 48
Sussex Gro. sw9. 18T 74
Sussex Pl. nw1. 14K 49
Sussex Pl. sw7. 12P 60
Sussex Pl. w2. 13M 48
Sussex Pl. w6. 8P 58
Sussex Rd. e6. 33J 43
Sussex Rd. n7. 17E 36
Sussex Rd. sw9. 18T 74
Sussex Rd. Cro. 19Zh 91
Sussex Rd. Har. 1dB 12
Sussex Sq. w2. 13M 48
Sussex St. e13. 30K 55
Sussex St. e14. 25M 53
Sussex St. sw1. 15P 61
Sutcliff Clo. nw11. 12B 22
Sutcliffe Rd. se18. 35Q 95
Sutherland Av. w9. 11K 48
Sutherland Av. w13. 1aL 94
Sutherland Gdns. sw14.
 6S 69
Sutherland Gro. sw18.
 10U 71
Sutherland Gro. Twi. 1cX 93
Sutherland Pl. w2. 11L 47

Sutherland Rd. e3. 25J 53
Sutherland Rd. e17. 24A 27
Sutherland Rd. n9. 22Ae 17
Sutherland Rd. n17. 22Aa 17
Sutherland Rd. w4. 6P 57
Sutherland Rd. w13. 1aL 94
Sutherland Rd. Cro. 18Zd 91
Sutherland Sq. se17. 19P 63
Sutherland St. sw1. 15P 61
Sutherland Ter. sw1. 15P 61
Sutherland Wk. se17. 19P 63
Sutlej Rd. se7. 30R 79
Sutterton St. n7. 17H 36
Sutton Ct. w4. 4Q 57
Sutton La. w4. 4P 57
Sutton Pl. e9. 23G 38
Sutton Rd. n10. 14Aa 15
Sutton Rd. n15. 20C 25
Sutton Rd. e13. 29L 54
Sutton Rd. Bar. 35J 43
Sutton St. e1. 17N 62
Sutton St. w1. 16L 50
Sutton St. E. e1. 23M 52
Sutton Way w10. 8K 46
Sutton Ct. Rd. e13. 30K 55
Sutton Ct. Rd. w4. 4Q 57
Swaby Rd. sw18. 12W 83
Swaffield Rd. sw18. 11U 72
Swain Rd. Cro. 19Zc 90
Swain's La. n6. 15E 35
Swainson Rd. w3. 6N 58
Swale St. e14. 25M 53
Swallands Rd. se6. 25X 88
Swallow St. w1. 16M 49
Swallowfield Rd. se7. 30Q 67
Swan La. ec4. 20M 51
Swan La. n20. 12Ad 14
Swan Mead se1. 20O 63
Swan Rd. se16. 23N 64
Swan St. e1. 21M 51
Swan St. se1. 19O 63
Swan Wk. sw3. 14Q 61
Swanage Rd. sw18. 12U 72
Swanscombe Rd. w4. 6P 58
Swanscombe St. e16. 28L 54
Swaton Rd. e3. 25K 53
Sweet Briar Gro. n9. 21Ad 17
Sweet Briar Wk. n18.
 21Ac 17
Swete St. e13. 29K 55
Swetenham Pl. se18. 34P 95
Swift St. sw6. 10R 71
Swinbrook Rd. w10. 10L 47
Swinburne Av. e12. 32G 43
Swinburne Rd. sw15. 7T 70
Swinderby Rd. Wem. 2G 30
Swindon St. w12. 8N 58
Swingate La. se18. 35R 95
Swinnerton St. e9. 24G 39
Swinton St. wc1. 17K 50
Sybourn St. e17. 25D 27
Sycamore Av. w5. 2O 56
Sycamore Way Cro. 17Zc 90
Sydenham Av. se26. 22Y 87
Sydenham Hill.
 se26. 1-61 & 2-48.
 se23. 50, 63 & up. 21X 86
Sydenham Pk. se26. 22X 87
Sydenham Rise se23. 22W 87
Sydenham Rd. se26. 23Y 87
Sydenham Rd. Cro. 19Ze 91
Sydenham Pk. Rd. se26.
 23X 87
Sydner Rd. n16. 21F 37
Sydney Gro. nw4. 8B 21
Sydney Pl. sw7. 13P 60

Sydney Rd. E11.	29F 41	
Sydney Rd. N8.	18A 24	
Sydney Rd. N10.	15Aa 15	
Sydney Rd. sw20.	9Za 92	
Sydney Rd. w13.	1aN 94	
Sydney Rd. Rich.	2T 68	
Sydney Rd. Ted.	1bY 93	
Sydney St. sw3.	13P 60	
Sylvan Av. N3.	11Aa 14	
Sylvan Av. N22.	18Ab 16	
Sylvan Av. NW7.	6Ac 13	
Sylvan Gro. se15.	22Q 64	
Sylvan Hill se19.	20Z 90	
Sylvan Rd. E7.	29G 41	
Sylvan Rd. E11.	29C 29	
Sylvan Rd. E17.	25B 27	
Sylvan Rd. se19.	21Za 90	
Sylvan Rd. Ilf.	34E 42	
Sylvester Rd. E8.	22G 38	
Sylvester Rd. E17.	25C 27	
Sylvester Rd. N2.	12Aa 14	
Sylvester Rd. Wem.	1F 30	
Sylvia Gdns. Wem.	4G 31	
Symons St. sw3.	14P 61	
Tabard St. se1.	20O 63	
Tabernacle St. ec2.	20K 51	
Tabley Rd. N7.	17F 36	
Tabor Gro. sw19.	9Z 92	
Tabor Rd. w6.	8O 58	
Tachbrook St. sw1.	16P 61	
Tadema Rd. sw10.	12Q 60	
Tadmor St. w12.	9N 59	
Tadworth Rd. NW2.	7E 32	
Tagg St. E2.	23J 52	
Tait Rd. Cro.	20Zd 91	
Tait St. E1.	22M 52	
Talavera Pl. E2.	22J 52	
Talbot Av. N2.	13A 22	
Talbot Cres. NW4.	7B 20	
Talbot Gdns. Ilf.	36E 42	
Talbot Gro. w10.	9M 47	
Talbot Rd. E6.	32J 43	
Talbot Rd. E7.	29F 41	
Talbot Rd. N6.	14C 23	
Talbot Rd. N15.	21B 25	
Talbot Rd. N22.	16Aa 15	
Talbot Rd. NW10.	6G 32	
Talbot Rd. se25.	20Zc 90	
Talbot Rd.		
w2. 1-97 & 2-102		
w11. 97A, 104 & up.	10L 47	
Talbot Rd. w13.	1aM 94	
Talbot Rd. Har.	1bAa 12	
Talbot Rd. Twi.	1cV 93	
Talbot Rd. Wem.	2G 30	
Talbot Sq. w2.	12M 48	
Talbot Yard se1.	20N 63	
Talfourd Pl. se15.	21R 75	
Talfourd Rd. se15.	21R 75	
Talgarth Rd. w14.	10P 59	
Tallis Gro. se7.	30Q 67	
Tallis St. ec4.	18M 50	
Talma Rd. sw2.	18T 74	
Talwin St. E3.	26K 53	
Tamar St. E15.	28J 54	
Tamar St. se7.	31P 67	
Tamarisk Sq. w12.	7M 46	
Tamworth Pl. Cro.	18Zf 91	
Tamworth Rd. Cro.	18Zf 91	
Tamworth St. sw6.	11Q 59	
Tancred Rd. N4.	19C 24	
Tanfield Av. NW2.	6F 32	
Tanfield Rd. Cro.	19Zg 91	
Tangier Rd. Rich.	3S 69	
Tankridge Rd. NW2.	8E 32	
Tanner St. se1.	20N 63	
Tanner St. Bar.	34H 43	
Tanner's Hill se8.	25R 77	
Tannsfeld Rd. se26.	23Y 87	
Tanswell St. se1.	18N 62	
Tantallon Rd. sw12.	14V 84	
Tanza Rd. NW3.	14F 35	
Tapley St. E14.	26M 53	
Taplow St. N1.	19J 51	
Tapp St. E1.	22K 52	
Tappesfield Rd. se15.	22S 76	
Tarbert Rd. se22.	20T 75	
Tariff Rd. N17.	22Ab 17	
Tarling St. E1.	23M 52	
Tarlton St. N1.	20J 51	
Tarn St. se1.	19O 63	
Tarver Rd. se17.	19P 63	
Tasman Rd. sw9.	17S 74	
Tasmania Av. N18.	19Ab 16	
Tasso Rd. w6.	9Q 59	
Tatam Rd. NW10.	5G 31	
Tate St. se11.	17P 62	
Tatnell Rd. se23.	24U 76	
Tatum St. se17.	20P 63	
Taunton Pl. NW1.	30K 49	
Taunton Rd. se12.	28U 78	
Tavistock Av. E17.	24A 27	
Tavistock Cres. w11.	10L 47	
Tavistock Gdns. Ilf.	35F 43	
Tavistock Gro. Cro.	19Ze 91	
Tavistock Pl. wc1.	17K 50	
Tavistock Rd. E7.	28F 40	
Tavistock Rd. E15.	28H 40	
Tavistock Rd. E18.	29B 29	
Tavistock Rd. N4.	20C 25	
Tavistock Rd. NW10.	6J 46	
Tavistock Rd. w11.	10L 47	
Tavistock Rd. Cro.	19Ze 91	
Tavistock Sq. wc1.	16K 50	
Tavistock St. wc2.	17M 50	
Tavistock Ter. N19.	17E 36	
Taviton St. wc1.	16K 50	
Tayben Rd. Twi.	1cU 93	
Taybridge Rd. sw11.	14S 73	
Taylor Av. Kew	4R 69	
Taylor St. se18.	33P 95	
Taylors La. NW10.	6G 32	
Taylor's La. se26.	22X 87	
Taymount Rise se23.	22W 87	
Teale St. E2.	22J 52	
Teddington Pk. Twi.	1bX 93	
Teddington Pk. Rd. Twi.		
	1bX 93	
Tedworth Sq. sw3.	14P 61	
Tee, The, w3.	6L 46	
Teesdale Rd. E11.	28C 28	
Teesdale St. E2.	22J 52	
Teignmouth Rd. NW2.	9G 33	
Telegraph Hill se14.	23S 76	
Telegraph St. ec2.	20L 51	
Telfer St. ec1.	19K 51	
Telferscot Rd. sw12.	16V 84	
Telford Av. sw2.	16V 85	
Telford Rd. N11.	16Ab 15	
Telford Rd. NW9.	7C 20	
Telford Rd. w10.	9L 47	
Tell Gro. se22.	21T 75	
Temeraire St. se16.	23N 64	
Temperley Rd. sw12.	14V 84	
Temperance St. E9.	23G 38	
Templar St. se5.	18R 74	
Templar's Av. NW11.	10C 21	
Templars Cres. N3.	11Aa 14	
Temple Av. ec4.	18M 50	
Temple Av. N20.	13Af 14	
Temple Gdns. NW11.	10C 21	
Temple Grove NW11.	11C 21	
Temple La. ec4.	18M 50	
Temple Pl. wc2.	18M 50	
Temple Rd. NW2.	8E 33	
Temple Rd. w4.	4O 57	
Temple Rd. w5.	1O 56	
Temple Rd. Cro.	19Zg 91	
Temple Rd. Kew	3S 68	
Temple Sheen sw14.	4T 69	
Temple St. E2.	22J 52	
Temple St. E8.	21H 37	
Temple St. E11.	28F 40	
Temple, The, ec4.	18M 50	
Templecourt Mews E9.		
	23H 38	
Temple Fortune Hill NW11.		
	11B 22	
Temple Fortune La. NW11.		
	11C 21	
Temple Mills La. E15.	26F 39	
Temple Mills Rd. E9.	26F 39	
Temple Sheen Rd. sw14.		
	4T 69	
Templeton Clo. se19.		
	20Za 90	
Templeton Pl. sw5.	11P 59	
Templeton Rd. N15.	20C 25	
Templewood Av. NW3.		
	12E 34	
Templewood Gdns. NW3.		
	12F 34	
Tenby Av. Har.	1aAa 12	
Tenby Rd. E17.	24B 26	
Tenby Rd. Edg.	3Aa 13	
Tench St. E1.	22N 64	
Tenda Rd. se1.	22P 64	
Tenham Av. sw2.	16W 84	
Tenison St. se1.	17N 62	
Tennison Rd. se25.	21Zc 90	
Tennyson Av. E11.	29D 29	
Tennyson Av. E12.	31H 41	
Tennyson Av. NW9.	5A 19	
Tennyson Av. Mor.	8Zc 92	
Tennyson Av. Twi.	1bV 93	
Tennyson Av. E15.	28H 40	
Tennyson Rd. E17.	25C 27	
Tennyson Rd. NW6.	10H 33	
Tennyson Rd. se20.	23Z 90	
Tennyson Rd. sw19.	11Y 83	
Tennyson Rd. w7.	1bM 94	
Tennyson St. sw8.	15S 73	
Tent St. E1.	22K 52	
Tenter St. E. E1.	21M 51	
Tenter St. N. E1.	21M 51	
Tenter St. S. E1.	21M 51	
Tenter St. W. E1.	21M 51	
Tenter St. ec2.	20L 51	
Tenterden Dri. NW4.	9A 21	
Tenterden Gro. NW4.	9A 21	
Tenterden Rd. N17.	21Ab 17	
Tenterden Rd. Cro.	21Zd 91	
Tenterden St. w1.	15M 49	
Terminus Pl. sw1.	15O 61	
Terrace Gdns. sw13.	6R 70	
Terrace Rd. E9.	23H 38	
Terrace Rd. E13.	29J 55	
Terrapin Rd. sw17.	15W 84	
Terrick Rd. N22.	17Aa 15	
Terront Rd. N15.	19B 25	
Testerton St. w11.	9M 47	
Tetcott Rd. sw10.	12Q 60	
Tetherdown N10.	15A 22	
Tetley St. E14.	26M 53	
Tevan Rd. Cro.	21Ze 91	
Teviot St. E14.	26L 53	

Tewkesbury Av. se23.	22R 87
Tewkesbury Gdns. nw9.	4A 19
Tewkesbury Rd. n15.	20C 25
Tewkesbury Ter. n11.	16Ab 15
Tewson Rd. se18.	35P 95
Teynton Ter. n17.	19Aa 16
Thackeray Av. n17.	22A 26
Thackeray Rd. e6.	31J 55
Thackeray Rd. sw8.	15S 73
Thackeray St. w8.	11N 60
Thames Bank sw14.	4R 69
Thames Pl. e14.	25M 53
Thames Rd. e16.	31N 67
Thames Rd. w4.	3P 57
Thames St. se10.	26Q 65
Thane Villas n7.	18E 36
Thanet Pl. Cro.	19Zg 91
Thanet St. wc1.	17K 50
Thavies Inn ec1.	18L 50
Thayer St. w1.	14L 49
Theatre St. sw11.	14S 73
Theberton St. n1.	18H 36
Theobald Rd. e17.	25D 27
Theobald Rd. Cro.	18Ze 91
Theobald St. se1.	20O 63
Theobalds Av. n12.	12Ad 14
Theobalds Rd. wc1.	17L 50
Theodore Rd. se13.	27U 78
Therapia La. Cro.	16Zd 91
Therapia Rd. se22.	22U 76
Theresa Mews w6.	7P 58
Thermopylæ Gate e14.	26P 65
Thessaly Rd. sw8.	15Q 61
Thessaly Sq. sw8.	16R 73
Theydon Rd. e3.	24J 53
Theydon Rd. e5.	23E 38
Theydon St. e17.	24D 27
Thicket Gro. se20.	21Z 90
Thicket Rd. se20.	21Z 90
Third Av. e12.	32F 43
Third Av. e13.	29K 55
Third Av. e17.	26B 27
Third Av. w3.	6N 58
Third Av. w10.	10J 47
Third Cross Rd. Twi.	1cV 93
Thirleby Pl. sw1.	16O 61
Thirleby Rd. sw1.	16O 61
Thirleby Rd. Edg.	5Aa 13
Thirlemere Rd. sw16.	16X 84
Thirlmere Av. Wem.	1J 44
Thirlmere Rd. n10.	15Aa 15
Thirsk Rd. sw11.	14S 73
Thirsk Rd. se25.	20Zb 90
Thirza St. e1.	23M 52
Thistle Gro. sw10.	12P 60
Thistlewaite Rd. e5.	23F 38
Thomas' La. se13.	25V 88
Thomas St. e14.	25L 53
Thomas St. se18.	33P 95
Thomas St. w1.	15M 49
Thomas Doyle St. se1.	19O 62
Thompson Av. Kew	3S 69
Thompson Rd. se22.	21U 75
Thomson Cres. Cro.	17Ze 91
Thomson Rd. Har.	1bA 12
Thorburn Sq. se1.	21P 64
Thornaby Gdns. n18.	22Ab 17
Thornbury Rd. sw2.	16U 74
Thornby Rd. e5.	23F 38
Thorncliffe Rd. sw2.	16U 74
Thorncombe Rd. se22.	20T 75
Thorncroft St. sw8.	16Q 62
Thorndean St. sw18.	11W 83
Thorndike St. sw1.	16P 61
Thorne Pass. sw18.	6S 70
Thorne Rd. sw8.	17R 74
Thorne St. sw13.	6S 70
Thornedene Av. Barn.	14Ae 15
Thorney Hedge Rd. w4.	4O 57
Thornfield Rd. w12.	8N 58
Thornford Rd. se13.	26U 78
Thorngate Rd. w9.	11K 48
Thorngrove Rd. e13.	30J 55
Thornham Gro. e15.	27G 40
Thornham St. se10.	26Q 65
Thornhaugh St. w1.	14L 49
Thornhill Av. se18.	35R 95
Thornhill Bridge Pl. n1.	17J 50
Thornhill Cres. n1.	17H 36
Thornhill Gdns. Bar.	35H 43
Thornhill Rd. e10.	26E 39
Thornhill Rd. n1.	18H 36
Thornhill Rd. Cro.	19Zd 91
Thornhill Sq. n1.	17H 36
Thornlaw Rd. se27.	18X 85
Thornloe Gdns. Cro.	18Zh 91
Thornsbeach Rd. se6.	26W 88
Thornsett Rd. se20.	22Zb 91
Thornsett Rd. sw18.	11V 83
Thornton Av. sw2.	16V 85
Thornton Av. w4.	6O 58
Thornton Av. Cro.	17Zd 91
Thornton Hill sw19.	9Z 92
Thornton Rd. e11.	27E 40
Thornton Rd. sw12.	16V 84
Thornton Rd. sw14.	5S 69
Thornton Rd. sw19.	9Y 82
Thornton Rd. Bro.	29Y 89
Thornton Rd. Cro.	17Zd 91
Thornton Rd. Ilf.	33F 43
Thornton St. e16.	29L 54
Thornton St. se16.	20P 63
Thornton St. sw9.	18S 74
Thornton Way nw11.	12J 23
Thorntree Rd. se7.	31Q 67
Thornville St. se8.	25R 77
Thornwood Rd. se13.	28U 78
Thorold Rd. n22.	17Ab 16
Thorold Rd. Ilf.	34E 42
Thorold St. e2.	21K 52
Thorparch Rd. sw8.	16R 74
Thorpe Mews w10.	10L 47
Thorpe Rd. e6.	32J 43
Thorpe Rd. e7.	29F 40
Thorpe Rd. n15.	21C 25
Thorpe Rd. Bar.	34H 43
Thorpebank Rd. w12.	7M 46
Thorpedale Rd. n4.	17D 24
Thorpewood Av. se26	22W 87
Thorverton Rd. nw2.	9E 33
Thrale Rd. sw16.	15Y 84
Thrale St. se1.	19N 63
Thrawl St. e1.	21L 51
Threadneedle St. ec2.	20M 51
Three Colt St. e14.	25M 53
Three Colts La. e2.	22K 52
Three Cranes La. ec4.	19M 51
Three Mill La. e3.	26K 53
Three Oak La. se1.	21N 63
Thresher Pl. w11.	9M 4?
Throgmorton Av. ec2.	20L 5?
Throgmorton Rd. e16.	30M 5?
Throgmorton Sq. ec2.	20M 5?
Thrush St. se17.	19P 6?
Thurland Rd. se16.	22O 6?
Thurlby Rd. se27.	18X 8?
Thurlby Rd. Wem.	2G 3?
Thurleigh Av. sw12.	14U 7?
Thurleigh Rd. sw12.	14U 7?
Thurlestone Av. n12.	14Ab 1?
Thurlestone Rd. se27.	18X 8?
Thurloe Pl. sw7.	13O 6?
Thurloe Sq. sw7.	13O 6?
Thurlow Gdns. Wem.	2F 3?
Thurlow Hill se21.	19W 8?
Thurlow Pk. Rd. se21.	19W 8?
Thurlow Pl. e2.	23K 5?
Thurlow Rd. nw3.	13F 3?
Thurlow Rd. w7.	1aN 9?
Thurlow St. se17.	20P 6?
Thurlow St. sw8.	16R 7?
Thurlstone Av. Ilf.	35F 4?
Thurso St. e14.	12X 8?
Thurston Rd. se13.	26S 7?
Thyra Gro. n12.	12Ab 1?
Tibbatt's Rd. e3.	26K 5?
Tibberton Sq. n1.	19H 3?
Tiber St. n1.	17J 5?
Ticehurst Rd. se6.	24W 8?
Tidal Basin Rd. e16.	28M 5?
Tidbury St. sw8.	15R 7?
Tidemore St. sw8.	15Q 6?
Tideswell Rd. sw15.	8T 7?
Tidey St. e3.	25L 5?
Tierney Rd. sw2.	16V 8?
Tile Yd. e14.	25M 5?
Tilehurst Gdns. Ilf.	34G 4?
Tilehurst Rd. sw18.	12V 8?
Tilekiln La. n6.	15D 2?
Tileyard Rd. n7.	17H 3?
Tilia Rd. e5.	22F 3?
Tilæ Rd. se18.	35Q 9?
Tillingbourne Gdns. n3.	11A 2?
Tillingham Way n12.	11Ad 1?
Tillman St. e1.	22M 5?
Tillotson Rd. n9.	21Ae 1?
Tillotson Rd. Ilf.	33D 4?
Tillotson St. e1.	23L 5?
Tilney Rd. e11.	30C 2?
Tilney St. w1.	14N 6?
Tilson Gdns. sw2.	16V 8?
Tilson Rd. n17.	22Aa 1?
Tilson Rd. se15.	21Q 6?
Tilton St. sw6.	10Q 5?
Timbercroft La. se18.	35R 9?
Timberwharf Rd. n16.	22C 2?
Tindal St. sw9.	18R 7?
Tinderbox Alley sw14.	5S 6?
Tintagel Cres. se22.	21T 7?
Tintern Av. nw9.	4A 1?
Tintern Rd. n22.	19Aa 1?
Tintern St. sw4.	17T 7?
Tinto Rd. e16.	29L 5?
Tinworth St. se11.	17P 6?
Tipthorpe Rd. sw11.	14S 7?
Tiptree St. wc2.	18M 5?
Tisdall Pl. se17.	20P 6?
Tissington St. se16.	23P 6?

Titchborne St. w2. 13L 48
Titchfield Rd. nw8. 14J 49
Titchfield Ter. nw8. 13J 49
Titchwell Rd. sw18. 12V 83
Tite St. sw3. 14P 61
Tiverton Rd. n15. 20C 25
Tiverton Rd. n18. 20Ac 17
Tiverton Rd. nw10. 9H 33
Tiverton Rd. Wem. 2J 44
Tiverton St. se1. 19O 63
Tivoli Rd. n8. 16B 24
Tivoli Rd. se27. 19Y 86
Tobago St. e14. 25N 65
Tokenhouse Yd. ec2. 20L 51
Tokyngton Av. Wem. 3G 31
Tollet St. e1. 23K 52
Tollington Pk. n4. 17E 36
Tollington Pl. n4. 17E 36
Tollington Rd. n7. 17F 36
Tolmer's Sq. nw1. 16K 49
Tolverne Rd. sw20. 8Za 92
Tomlin's Gro. e3. 25K 53
Tomlin's Ter. e14. 24L 53
Tompion St. ec1. 19K 50
Tonbridge Cres. Har. 2A 18
Tonbridge St. wc1. 17K 50
Tonsley Hill sw18. 11T 72
Tonsley Pl. sw18. 11T 72
Tonsley Rd. sw18. 11T 72
Tooke St. e14. 25O 65
Tooley St. se1. 20N 63
Toorack Rd. Har. 1cAa 12
Tooting Gro. sw17. 13Y 83
Tooting Bec Gdns. sw16.
16X 85
Tooting Bec Rd. sw17.
14X 84
Tooting High St. sw17.
13Y 83
Topaz St. se11. 18O 62
Topham Sq. n17. 19Aa 16
Topham St. ec1. 18K 50
Topley St. se9. 30T 79
Topsfield Rd. n8. 17B 24
Topsham Rd. sw17. 14X 84
Tor Gdns. w8. 11N 59
Torbay Rd. nw6. 10H 33
Torbay St. nw1. 15H 35
Tormount Rd. se18. 35Q 95
Toronto Av. e12. 32F 42
Toronto Rd. e11. 27F 40
Toronto Rd. Ilf. 34D 42
Torquay St. w2. 11L 48
Torr Rd. se20. 23Z 90
Torrens Rd. e15. 28G 40
Torrens Rd. sw2. 17T 74
Torrens Sq. e15. 28G 40
Torrens St. ec1. 18J 50
Torriano Av. nw5. 16G 35
Torriano Gdns. nw5. 16G 36
Torridge Rd. Cro. 18Zc 90
Torridon Rd.
se13. 1 & 3.
se6. 2, 5 & up. 27V 89
Torrington Av. n11. 16Ab 15
Torrington Av. n12. 13Ac 14
Torrington Gdns. Wem.
1H 30
Torrington Gro. n12. 13Ac 14
Torrington Pk. n12. 12Ac 14
Torrington Pl. wc1. 16K 50
Torrington Sq. wc1. 16L 50
Torrington Rd. Wem. 1H 30
Torver Rd. Har. 1bB 12
Torwood Rd. sw15. 7U 70
Tothill St. sw1. 16O 62

Totnes Rd. e16. 29L 55
Tottenham La. n8. 17B 24
Tottenham Rd. n1. 20G 37
Tottenham Rd. n13. 18Ab 16
Tottenham St. w1. 16L 49
Tottenham St. w10. 10K 47
Tottenham Ct. Rd. w1.
16L 49
Tottenham High Rd.
n15. 1-363 & 2-344.
n17. 346, 365 & up.
21Aa 17
Totterdown St. sw17. 13X 83
Totteridge La. n20. 10Ae 14
Totteridge Rd. sw11. 13S 72
Totton Rd. Cro. 18Zb 90
Totty St. e3. 24J 52
Toulmin St. se1. 19N 63
Toulon St. se5. 19Q 63
Tournay Rd. sw6. 10Q 59
Tower Bridge e1. 21N 63
Tower Hill ec3. 21M 51
Tower Rd. nw10. 7G 32
Tower Rd. Twi. 1aW 93
Tower St. e8. 22H 38
Tower St. wc2. 16M 50
Tower Bridge App. e1.
21M 51
Tower Bridge Rd. se1.
20O 63
Tower Gdns. Rd. n17.
19Aa 16
Tower Hamlets Rd. e7.
29G 40
Tower Hamlets Rd. e17.
25A 27
Town Rd. n9. 22Ad 17
Town Hall Av. w4. 5P 57
Town Hall Rd. sw11. 14S 73
Townholm Cres. w7. 1bN 94
Townley Rd. se22. 20U 75
Townley St. se17. 20P 63
Townmead Rd. sw6. 12S 72
Townsend Av. n14. 17Ac 16
Townsend La. nw9. 6C 19
Townsend Rd. n15. 21C 25
Townsend St. se17. 20P 63
Townshend Cotts. nw8.
13J 48
Townshend Rd. nw8. 13J 48
Townshend Rd. Rich. 2T 68
Townshend Ter. Rich. 2S 68
Towton Rd. se27. 19W 86
Toynbee Rd. sw19. 9Z 92
Tracey St. se11. 18P 62
Tracy Av. nw2. 8F 32
Tradescant Rd. sw8. 17Q 62
Trafalgar Av. se15. 21Q 63
Trafalgar Gro. se10. 27Q 66
Trafalgar Pl. n18. 22Ac 17
Trafalgar Rd. e8. 21H 37
Trafalgar Rd. se10. 27Q 66
Trafalgar Rd. sw19. 11Z 92
Trafalgar Rd. Twi. 1cW 93
Trafalgar Sq. e1. 24L 52
Trafalgar Sq.
sw1. No. 5.
wc2. Remainder. 16M 50
Trafalgar Sq. sw3. 13P 60
Trafalgar St. se17. 19P 63
Trafalgar St. Bar. 34H 43
Trafford Rd. Cro. 17Zc 90
Tramway Rd. n9. 23Af 17
Tranquil Vale se3. 28S 78
Tranmere Rd. sw18. 12W 83
Tranton Rd. se16. 22O 64

Travers Rd. n7. 18E 36
Treadgold St. w11. 9M 47
Treadway St. e2. 22J 52
Trebovir Rd. sw5. 11P 59
Treby St. e3. 24K 53
Tredegar Rd. e3. 25J 53
Tredegar Sq. e3. 24K 53
Trederwen Rd. e8. 22H 38
Tredown Rd. se26. 23Y 87
Tree Rd. e16. 30M 55
Treen Av. sw13. 6S 70
Trefoil Rd. sw18. 12U 72
Tregaron Av. n8. 17C 24
Tregarvon Rd. sw11. 14T 73
Tregenna St. sw2. 17U 77
Trego Rd. e9. 25H 39
Tregothnan Rd. sw9. 17S 74
Tregunter Rd. sw10. 12P 60
Trehern Rd. sw14. 5S 69
Treherne Rd. sw9. 18R 74
Trehurst St. e5. 24F 39
Trelawn Rd. e10. 27F 40
Trelawn Rd. sw2. 18T 74
Trelawney Rd. e9. 23G 38
Tremadoc Rd. sw4. 16T 74
Tremaine Rd. se20. 22Za 90
Tremlett Gro. n19. 16E 35
Trenance Gdns. Ilf. 36F 42
Trenholme Rd. se20. 22Z 90
Trenmar Gdns. nw10. 8J 46
Trent Av. w5. 1N 56
Trent Rd. sw2. 17U 74
Trentham St. sw18. 10V 82
Treport St. sw18. 11U 72
Tresco Gdns. Ilf. 36E 42
Tresco Rd. se15. 22T 76
Tresham Av. e9. 23G 38
Tresham Rd. Bar. 36H 43
Tressillian Cres. se4. 25S 77
Tressillian Rd. se4. 25T 77
Tretawn Gdns. nw7. 6Ad 13
Tretawn Pk. nw7. 6Ad 13
Trevanion Rd. w14. 10P 59
Treve Av. Har. 1cC 12
Trevelyan Av. e12. 32G 43
Trevelyan Cres. Har. 2C 18
Trevelyan Gdns. nw10.
8H 33
Trevelyan Rd. e15. 28F 40
Trevelyan Rd. sw17. 13Y 83
Treveris St. se1. 18N 62
Treverton St. w10. 9K 47
Treville St. sw15. 7U 70
Trevince Rd. sw20. 8Za 92
Trevithick St. se8. 25Q 65
Trevor Gdns. Edg. 5Aa 13
Trevor Pl. sw7. 13N 60
Trevor Rd. sw19. 9Z 92
Trevor Rd. Edg. 6Aa 13
Trevor Sq. sw3. 13P 60
Trevor Sq. sw7. 13O 60
Trevor St. w1. 16M 49
Trevor St. sw1. 16N 61
Trewint St. sw18. 11W 83
Trewsbury Rd. se26. 23Y 87
Triangle Rd. e8. 22H 38
Triangle, The, e8. 22H 38
Trident St. se16. 23O 64
Trig La. ec4. 19M 51
Trigon Gro. sw8. 17Q 62
Trigon Rd. sw8. 17Q 62
Trilby Rd. se23. 23W 87
Trim St. se14. 24Q 65
Trinder Rd. n19. 17D 24
Tring Av. w5. 3M 44
Tring Av. Wem. 3G 31

Trinidad St. E14.	25M 53
Trinity Av. N2.	13A 22
Trinity Gdns. sw9.	17T 74
Trinity Gro. SE10.	26R 77
Trinity Pl. EC3.	21M 51
Trinity Pl. N1.	20J 51
Trinity Rise sw2.	18V 85
Trinity Rd. N22.	17Aa 16
Trinity Rd.	
sw17. 1-259 & 2-236.	
sw18. 238, 261 & up.	
	12U 72
Trinity Rd. N2.	13A 22
Trinity Rd. sw19.	11Y 82
Trinity Rd. Rich.	3S 68
Trinity Sq. EC3.	21M 51
Trinity Sq. SE1.	19O 63
Trinity St. E11.	27F 40
Trinity St. E16.	28L 54
Trinity St. N1.	18J 50
Trinity St. SE1.	19O 63
Trinity St. SE18.	31O 67
Trio Pl. SE1.	19O 63
Tristram Rd. SE12.	28X 89
Tritton Rd. SE21.	19X 86
Trollope St. sw8.	15S 73
Troon St. E1.	24M 52
Trossachs Rd. SE22.	20T 75
Trothy Rd. SE1.	22P 64
Trott St. sw11.	13R 72
Trotyl Ter. SE2.	36P 95
Troughton Rd. SE7.	30P 67
Troutbeck Rd. SE14.	24R 76
Trouville Rd. sw4.	15U 73
Trowbridge Rd. E9.	25G 39
Troy Rd. SE19.	20Z 90
Troy St. SE18.	33P 95
Troy Town SE15.	21S 76
Trulock Rd. N17.	22Ab 17
Truman's Rd. N16.	21G 37
Trump St. EC2.	19M 51
Trumpington Rd. E7.	
	28F 40
Trundley's Rd. SE8.	23P 64
Trundley's Ter. SE8.	23P 64
Truro Rd. E17.	25B 27
Truro Rd. N22.	17Aa 16
Truro Rd. Ilf.	32D 42
Truro St. Nw5.	14G 35
Trussley Rd. w6.	8O 58
Tryon St. sw3.	13P 61
Tuam Rd. SE18.	34Q 95
Tubbs Rd. Nw10.	7J 46
Tucker St. E16.	27L 54
Tudor Clo. Nw9.	5D 19
Tudor Ct. E17.	24C 27
Tudor Ct. Wem.	4G 31
Tudor Gdns. Nw9.	5E 31
Tudor Gdns. sw13.	6S 70
Tudor Gdns. w3.	4L 45
Tudor Gro. E9.	23H 38
Tudor Rd. E6.	30J 55
Tudor Rd. E9.	23H 38
Tudor Rd. N9.	23Af 17
Tudor Rd. SE19.	21Z 90
Tudor Rd. SE25.	22Zc 90
Tudor Rd. Bar.	36J 43
Tudor Rd. Har.	1cAa 12
Tudor St. EC4.	18M 50
Tudor Way N14.	17Ae 16
Tudor Way w3.	3N 56
Tufnell Pk. Rd.	
N7. 1-217 & 2-210.	
N19. 212, 219 & up. 16F 35	
Tufton St. sw1.	16O 62
Tugela Rd. Cro.	19Zd 91

Tugela St. SE6.	25W 88
Tuilerie St. E2.	21J 52
Tulip Pl. SE8.	22O 64
Tulse Hill sw2.	18U 74
Tulsemere Rd. SE27.	19W 86
Tunis Rd. w12.	8M 46
Tunley Rd. Nw10.	6H 32
Tunley Rd. sw17.	14W 84
Tunmarsh La. E13.	30K 55
Tunnel App. E14.	24M 52
Tunnel App. E14.	27M 54
Tunnel Av. SE10.	28O 66
Tunnel Rd. SE16.	23N 64
Tunstall Rd. sw9.	17T 74
Tunstall Rd. Cro.	20Ze 91
Tupman Pl. SE1.	19N 63
Turin St. E2.	22K 52
Turk's Row sw3.	14P 61
Turle Rd. N4.	17E 36
Turner Clo. Nw11.	12C 22
Turner Dri. Nw11.	12C 22
Turner Pl. N1.	19J 51
Turner Rd. E17.	26B 28
Turner Sq. N1.	20J 51
Turner St. N1.	22L 52
Turner St. E1.	22L 52
Turner St. E16.	28M 54
Turner's Rd. E3.	24L 53
Turner's Wood Nw11.	12D 22
Turneville Rd. w14.	10P 59
Turney Rd. SE21.	19V 86
Turnham Rd. SE4.	24T 76
Turnham Grn. Ter. w4.	6O 58
Turnmill St. EC1.	18L 50
Turnpike La. N8.	18A 24
Turquand St. SE17.	19P 63
Turret Gro. sw4.	15S 73
Turtle Rd. sw17.	11W 83
Turton Rd. Wem.	2F 30
Tuscan Rd. SE18.	35Q 95
Tuscan St. E2.	23K 52
Tuskar St. SE10.	28Q 66
Tustin St. SE15.	22Q 64
Tweed St. sw8.	16Q 61
Tweedmouth Rd. E13.	29J 55
Twickenham Bridge Rich.	
	1T 68
Twickenham Rd. E11.	27E 40
Twickenham Rd. Rich.	1T 68
Twickenham Rd. Ted.	
	1bX 93
Twickenham Rd. Twi.	
	1bT 93
Twilley St. sw18.	11V 83
Twine Ct. E1.	23M 52
Twineham Green N12.	
	11Ad 14
Twining St. wc2.	17M 50
Twisden Rd. Nw5.	15F 35
Twybridge Way Nw10.	5H 31
Twyford Av. N2.	14A 23
Twyford Av. w3.	3M 45
Twyford Cres. w3.	3M 45
Twyford St. E16.	31N 67
Twyford St. N1.	17H 36
Twyford Abbey Rd. w5.	
	3J 44
Tyas Rd. E16.	28L 54
Tybenham Rd. sw19.	
	10Za 92
Tyburn La. Har.	1bC 12
Tye St. E14.	24L 53
Tyer's Gateway SE1.	20N 63
Tyers St. SE11.	17P 62
Tyers Ter. E11.	17P 62
Tylecroft Rd. sw16.	16Za 90
Tyler St. SE10.	28Q 66

Tylney Rd. E11.	30F 41
Tyndale Mews N1.	19H 37
Tyndale Pl. N1.	19H 37
Tyndale Ter. N1.	19H 37
Tyndall Rd. E10.	26E 40
Tyne Rd. Ilf.	34E 42
Tyneham Rd. sw11.	14S 73
Tynemouth Rd. N15.	21B 26
Tynemouth St. sw6.	12R 72
Tynte St. E9.	24G 39
Type St. E2.	23J 52
Tyrawley Rd. sw6.	11R 72
Tyrrel Rd. SE22.	21T 76
Tyrrell St. E2.	21K 52
Tyrwhitt Rd. SE4.	25S 77
Tysoe St. wc1.	18K 50
Tyson Rd. SE23.	23V 87
Tyssen Pass. E8.	21G 37
Tyssen Rd. N16.	21F 37
Tyssen St. E2.	21K 52
Tyssen St. E8.	21G 37
Tyssen St. N1.	20J 51
Tytherton Rd. N19.	16F 36
Uamvar St. E14.	26L 53
Udney Pk. Rd. Twi.	1bY 93
Uffington Rd. Nw10.	7H 32
Uffington Rd. SE27.	18X 85
Ufford St. SE1.	18N 62
Ufton Gro. N1.	20H 37
Ufton Rd. N1.	20H 37
Uganda St. sw17.	13X 83
Ullathorne Rd. sw16.	15X 84
Ulleswater Rd. N14.	17Ad 16
Ullin St. E14.	26L 53
Ullswater Rd. SE27.	18W 85
Ullswater Rd. sw13.	7Q 58
Ulric St. SE5.	19Q 63
Ulster Gdns. N13.	19Ac 16
Ulster Ter. Nw1.	15K 49
Ulundi Rd. SE3.	28Q 66
Ulva Rd. sw15.	9T 71
Ulverscroft Rd. SE22.	21U 75
Ulverston Rd. E17.	27A 28
Ulverstone Rd. SE27.	18W 85
Ulysses Rd. Nw6.	10F 33
Umberston St. E1.	22M 52
Umbria St. sw15.	7U 70
Umfreville Rd. N4.	18C 24
Uncerne Av. N14.	15Ad 15
Undercliff Rd. SE13.	25S 77
Underhill Rd. SE22.	22V 87
Undershaw Rd. SE12.	28X 89
Underwood St. E1.	22L 52
Underwood St. N1.	20K 51
Undine St. sw17.	13Y 83
Union Ct. w6.	8P 59
Union Gro. sw8.	16R 73
Union Mews N7.	18G 36
Union Rd. E11.	27F 40
Union Rd. E17.	24C 27
Union Rd. N7.	16F 35
Union Rd. N11.	16Ac 15
Union Rd. N16.	21F 37
Union Rd.	
sw4. 1-93 & 2-102.	
sw8. 95, 104 & up. 16S 74	
Union Rd. Cro.	19Zd 91
Union Rd. Wem.	2G 30
Union Row N18.	21Ab 17
Union Sq. N1.	19J 51
Union St. E2.	21K 51
Union St. E14.	26M 54
Union St. E15.	27J 54
Union St. EC4.	18L 51

Union St. N1. 19J 51
Union St. SE1. 19N 63
Union St. SE1. 33P 95
Union St. sw4. 16S 74
Union St. w1. 15L 49
Union St. Bar. 33H 43
Union Wharf SE10. 27P 66
Univerity Rd. sw19. 12Y 83
University St. wc1. 16K 49
Unwin Rd. SE15. 21Q 64
Upbrook Mews w2. 12M 48
Upcerne Rd. sw10. 12Q 60
Upcott St. SE15. 23Q 64
Upcroft Av. Edg. 5Ac 13
Upfield Cro. 22Zf 91
Uphall Av. Ilf. 33F 42
Uphall Rd. Ilf. 33F 42
Upham Pk. Rd. w4. 6O 58
Uphill Dri. NW7. 6Ac 13
Uphill Gro. NW7. 6Ad 13
Uphill Rd. NW7. 6Ad 13
Upland Rd. SE22. 21V 76
Upland Rd. Cro. 19Zh 91
Uplands Rd. N8. 18C 24
Uplands Rd. Barn. 15Ae 15
Upney La. Bar. 35G 43
Upr. Ground SE1. 18M 50
Upr. Gro. SE25. 20Zb 90
Upr. Mall w6. 7P 58
Upr. Marsh SE1. 17O 62
Upr. Rd. E13. 29K 54
Upper St. N1. 18J 50
Upper Ter. NW3. 12E 34
Upr. Addison Gdns. w14.
9N 59
Upr. Bedford Pl. wc1. 16K 50
Upr. Belgrave St. sw1.
15O 61
Upr. Berkeley St. w1. 14L 49
Upr. Beulah Hill SE19.
20Z 90
Upr. Brockley Rd. SE4.
24S 77
Upr. Brook Mews w2. 12M 48
Upr. Brook St. w1. 14M 49
Upr. Cavendish Av. N3.
11A 21
Upr. Cheyne Row sw3.
13Q 60
Upr. Clapton Rd. E5. 22E 38
Upr. Coombe St. Cro. 19Zg 91
Upr. Grosvenor St. w1.
14M 49
Upr. Grotto Rd. Twi. 1bW 93
Upr. Harley St. NW1. 15K 49
Upr. Hornsey Rise N19.
17D 24
Upr. James St. w1. 16M 49
Upr. John St. w1. 16M 49
Upr. Montagu St. w1. 14L 49
Upr. North St. E14. 25M 53
Upr. Pk. Dri. Ilf. 34C 42
Upr. Pk. Rd. N11. 16Ac 15
Upr. Pk. Rd. NW3. 14G 35
Upr. Phillimore Gdns. w8.
11N 59
Upr. Richmond Rd. sw14 &
sw15. 4S 69
Upr. Shirley Rd. Cro. 23Z 91
Upr. Thames St. EC4. 19M 51
Upr. Tollington Pk. N4.
18D 24
Upr. Tooting Pk. sw17.
14W 84
Upr. Tooting Rd. sw17.
14X 84

Upr. Tulse Hill sw2. 17V 85
Upr. Walthamstow Rd. E17.
27B 28
Upr. Wimpole St. w1. 15L 49
Upr. Woburn Pl. wc1.
16K 50
Upperton Rd. E13. 30K 55
Uppingham Av. Har. 1A 18
Upsdell Av. N13. 18Ab 16
Upstall St. SE5. 19R 74
Upton Av. E7. 29H 41
Upton Gdns. Har. 1B 18
Upton La. E7. 29G 41
Upton Rd. N18. 22Ac 17
Upton Rd. SE18. 34Q 95
Upton Rd. Cro. 19Za 90
Upton Pk. Rd. E7. 30H 41
Upway N12. 13Ab 14
Upwood Rd. SE12. 29U 78
Upwood Rd. sw16. 17Za 90
Ursula St. sw11. 13R 72
Urswick Rd. E9. 23G 38
Usher Rd. E3. 25J 53
Usk Rd. sw11. 12T 72
Usk St. E2. 23K 52
Usk St. E16. 28M 54
Uverdale Rd. sw10. 12Q 60
Uxbridge Rd.
w5. 1-113 & 2-58. 1M 44
w13. 60-162 & 115-217.
w7. 1-219 & 2-202.
w12. 1-289 & 2-492.
w3. 305-389 & 310-370.
Uxbridge St. SE1. 19O 63
Uxbridge St. w8. 11N 59

Vale Gro. N4. 19C 25
Vale Gro. w3. 5N 57
Vale Rd. E7. 29G 41
Vale Rd. N4. 19C 25
Vale Royal N7. 17H 36
Vale Ter. N4. 19C 25
Vale, The, N10. 15Aa 15
Vale, The, N14. 17Ae 16
Vale, The, NW2. 10E 33
Vale, The, NW11. 10D 21
Vale, The, sw3. 12P 60
Vale, The, w3. 16N 58
Vale, The, Cro. 23Zf 91
Valentine Pl. SE1. 18N 62
Valentine Rd. E9. 23H 38
Valentine Row SE1. 18N 62
Valentines Rd. Ilf. .33E 42
Valeswood Rd. Bro. 28Y 89
Valetta Gro. E13. 29J 54
Valetta Rd. w3. 6N 58
Valetta St. EC1. 19K 50
Valette St. E9. 23G 38
Vallance Rd.
E1. 1-121 & 2-168.
E2. 123, 170 & up. 22L 52
Vallance Rd. N22. 16Aa 15
Vallance St. E1. 22K 52
Vallentin Rd. E17. 27B 28
Valley Av. N12. 13Ac 14
Valley Dri. NW9. 4B 19
Valley Gdns. sw19. 12Z 92
Valley Gdns. Wem. 3G 30
Valley Rd. sw16. 17Y 85
Valley Wk. Cro. 22Ze 91

Valleyfields Rd. sw16.17Y 85
Valliere Rd. NW10. 7J 16
Vallis Way w13. 1aK 94
Valmar Rd. SE5. 19R 75
Valnay St. sw17. 13Y 83
Vambery Rd. SE18. 34Q 95
Vanbrugh Fields SE3. 28Q 66
Vanbrugh Hill.
SE3. 1-31 & 2-44.
SE10. 48, 53 & up. 28Q 66
Vanbrugh Pk. SE3. 28R 78
Vanbrugh Rd. w4. 5O 57
Vanbrugh Ter. SE3. 28R 78
Vanbrugh Pk. Rd. SE3.
28Q 66
Vanbrugh Pk. Rd. W. SE3.
28R 78
Vance St. SE14. 24R 77
Vancouver Rd. SE23. 24W 88
Vancouver Rd. Edg. 4Ab 13
Vanderbilt Rd. sw18. 11V 83
Vandon St. sw1. 16O 61
Vandy St. EC2. 20L 51
Van Dyke Cres. sE9. 31U 79
Vanguard St. SE8. 25R 77
Vansittart Rd. E7. 29F 40
Vansittart St. SE14. 24Q 65
Vanston Pl. sw6. 11Q 59
Vant Rd. sw17. 14Y 84
Varcoe Rd. SE16. 22Q 64
Varden St. E1. 22L 52
Vardens Rd. sw11. 12T 72
Varley Rd. E16. 30M 55
Varna Rd. sw6. 10Q 59
Vartry Rd. N15. 20C 25
Vassall Rd. sw9. 18R 74
Vauban St. SE16. 21O 63
Vaughan Av. NW4. 7B 20
Vaughan Av. w6. 6O 58
Vaughan Gdns. Ilf. 32D 42
Vaughan Rd. E15. 28H 40
Vaughan Rd. SE5. 19S 75
Vaughan Rd. Har. 1dC 12
Vauxhall Bridge sw1. 16P 62
Vauxhall Gro. sw8. 17Q 62
Vauxhall St. SE11. 17P 62
Vauxhall Wk. SE11. 17P 62
Vauxhall Bridge Rd. sw1.
16P 61
Veda Rd. SE3. 25T 77
Venables St. NW8. 13K 48
Venetia Rd. N4. 19C 25
Venetia Rd. w5. 1N 56
Venetian Rd. SE5. 19S 75
Venn St. sw4. 16S 73
Venner Rd. SE26. 23Y 87
Ventnor Dri. N20. 11Ad 14
Ventnor Gdns. Bar. 35G 43
Ventnor Rd. SE14. 23R 76
Venue St. E14. 26L 53
Vera Rd. sw6. 10R 71
Verbena Gdns. w6. 7P 58
Verdayne Av. Cro. 23Ze 91
Verdun Rd. sw13. 7Q 58
Verdun Rd. SE18. 36R 95
Vere St. w1. 15M 49
Vereker Rd. w14. 10P 59
Vermont Rd. SE19. 20Z 90
Vermont St. sw18. 11U 72
Verney Rd. SE16. 22P 64
Verney St. NW10. 5E 31
Vernham Rd. SE18. 34Q 95
Vernon Av. sw20. 8Za 92
Vernon Rise wc1. 17K 50
Vernon Rd. E3. 25J 53
Vernon Rd. E11. 28D 28

220   INDEX TO STREETS

Vernon Rd. E12. 32G 43
Vernon Rd. E15. 28H 40
Vernon Rd. E17. 25B 27
Vernon Rd. sw14. 5S 69
Vernon Rd. Ilf. 36E 42
Vernon Sq. wc1. 17K 50
Vernon St. w14. 10O 59
Verona Rd. E7. 29H 41
Verona St.sw11. 12S 72
Veronica Rd. sw17. 15W 84
Verran Rd. sw12. 14V 84
Versailles Rd. SE20. 21Z 90
Verulam Av. 17. 24C 27
Verulam St. EC1. 18L 50
Vesey St. E14. 26M 53
Vespan Rd. w12. 7N 58
Vesta Rd. SE4. 24S 76
Vestris Rd. SE23. 23W 87
Vestry Rd. E17. 26B 27
Vestry Rd. SE5. 20R 75
Vestry St. N1. 20K 51
Vevey St. SE6. 24W 88
Viaduct St. E2. 22K 52
Vian St. SE13. 26S 77
Vicarage Cres. sw11. 12R 72
Vicarage Gdns. w8. 11N 60
Vicarage Gate w8. 11N 60
Vicarage Gro. N17. 22Aa 17
Vicarage Gro. SE5. 20R 75
Vicarage La. E15. 28H 40
Vicarage La. Ilf. 34E 42
Vicarage Pk. SE18. 34Q 95
Vicarage Rd. E10. 26D 27
Vicarage Rd. E15. 28H 40
Vicarage Rd. N17. 22Aa 17
Vicarage Rd. Nw4. 7C 20
Vicarage Rd. Nw10. 6G 32
Vicarage Rd. SE18. 34P 95
Vicarage Rd. sw14. 5T 69
Vicarage Rd. Cro. 18Zf 91
Vicarage Rd. Ted. 1bX 93
Vicarage Rd. Twi. 1cV 93
Vicarage Way nw10. 6E 31
Vicars Hill SE13. 25T 77
Vicar's Rd. nw5. 14G 35
Vicar's Moor La. N21.
  19Af 16
Vicary St. sw2. 17U 74
Vicat St. sw10. 12Q 60
Viceroy Rd. sw8. 16R 74
Victor Rd. N7. 18E 36
Victor Rd. Nw10. 8J 46
Victor Rd. SE20. 23Z 90
Victor Rd. Har. 1dA 12
Victor Rd. Twi. 1cX 93
Victoria Av. E6. 31J 55
Victoria Av. N3. 11Aa 14
Victoria Av. Wem. 4G 31
Victoria Cres. N15. 20B 25
Victoria Cres. SE19. 20Y 86
Victoria Cres. sw19. 10Z 92
Victoria Dri. sw19. 9V 82
Victoria Gdns. w11. 10M 47
Victoria Gro. N16. 21F 37
Victoria Gro. w8. 12O 60
Victoria Gro. W. N16. 21F 37
Victoria Mews Nw6. 11H 33
Victoria Pl. N7. 18F 36
Victoria Pl. SE15. 22Q 64
Victoria Pl. SE19. 20Z 90
Victoria Pl. SE27. 19X 86
Victoria Pl. w2. 11L 47
Victoria Pl. Cro. 18Zg 91
Victoria Rise sw4. 15S 73
Victoria Rd. E11. 27F 40
Victoria Rd. E13. 29J 54

Victoria Rd. E17. 27A 28
Victoria Rd. E18. 30A 29
Victoria Rd. N4. 18D 24
Victoria Rd. N7. 18G 36
Victoria Rd. N9 & N18.
  21Ac 17
Victoria Rd. N15. 21B 26
Victoria Rd. N16. 21F 37
Victoria Rd. N22. 16Aa 15
Victoria Rd. NW1. 15H 35
Victoria Rd. NW4. 9B 21
Victoria Rd. NW6. 10J 47
Victoria Rd. NW10. 5K 45
Victoria Rd. SE7. 30Q 67
Victoria Rd. SE15. 21S 75
Victoria Rd. sw14. 5S 69
Victoria Rd. w5. 1L 44
Victoria Rd. w8. 12O 60
Victoria Rd. Bar. 33H 43
Victoria Rd. Kew. 3R 68
Victoria Rd. Ted. 1bY 93
Victoria Rd. Twi. 1aU 93
Victoria Sq. sw1. 15O 61
Victoria St. E15. 28H 40
Victoria St. sw1. 15O 61
Victoria St. w2. 12L 48
Victoria Ter. N4. 18D 24
Victoria Ter. Har. 1cD 12
Victoria Villas Nw6. 11H 33
Victoria Villas Rich. 3S 68
Victoria Dock Rd. E16.
  30M 54
Victoria Pk. Rd. E9. 24H 38
Victoria Pk. Sq. E2. 23K 52
Victory Rd. sw19. 11Z 92
View Clo. Har. 1cA 12
View Rd. N6. 14C 23
Viewfield Rd. sw18. 10U 71
Viewland Rd. SE18. 35Q 95
Vigo St. w1. 16M 49
Villa Rd. sw9. 18S 74
Villa St. SE17. 20P 63
Villacourt Rd. SE18. 36R 95
Village, The, SE7. 30Q 67
Village Way nw10. 5E 31
Village Way sw22. 20U 75
Villas Rd. SE18. 34P 95
Villiers Rd. nw2. 7G 32
Villiers St. wc2. 17M 50
Villiers Rd. Cro. 23Zb 90
Vince St. EC1. 20K 51
Vincent Gdns. Nw2. 7E 32
Vincent Rd. N15. 19B 25
Vincent Rd. N22. 18Aa 16
Vincent Rd. Cro. 20Ze 91
Vincent Rd. Wem. 3H 30
Vincent Sq. sw1. 16O 61
Vincent St. E16. 28L 54
Vincent St. sw1. 16O 62
Vincent Ter. N1. 19J 51
Vine Av. N3. 11Aa 14
Vine Ct. E1. 22L 52
Vine Gdns. Ilf. 34G 43
Vine La. SE1. 20N 63
Vine Rd. E15. 28H 40
Vine Rd. sw13. 6S 70
Vine St. EC3. 21M 51
Vine St. w1. 16M 49
Vineyard Pass. Rich. 2T 68
Vineyard Path sw14. 5S 69
Vineyard, The, Rich. 2T 68
Vineyard Hil Rd. sw19.
  10X 82
Vining St. sw9. 18T 74
Viola Sq. w12. 7M 46
Violet Gdns. Cro. 18Zh 91

Violet Hill nw8. 12J 48
Violet La. Cro. 18Zh 91
Violet Rd. E3. 26L 53
Violet Rd. E17. 25C 27
Violet Rd. E18. 30A 29
Virginia Rd. Cro. 18Za 90
Virginia St. E1. 22M 52
Virginia Rd. E2. 21K 51
Vista Dri. Ilf. 31B 29
Vista Way Har. 2C 18
Vittoria St. N1. 18J 50
Vivian Av. Nw4. 8B 20
Vivian Av. Wem. 4G 31
Vivian Gdns. Wem. 3F 31
Vivian Rd. E3. 24J 53
Vivian Rd. SE15. 22S 76
Vivian Way N2. 13B 22
Voltaire Rd. sw4. 16S 73
Voluntary Pl. E11. 29C 28
Vorley Rd. N19. 16E 35
Voss St. sw16. 17Z 90
Voss St. E2. 22K 52
Vowler St. SE17. 19P 63
Vulcan Rd. SE4. 24S 77
Vulcan St. E14. 25M 53
Vyner Rd. w3. 5M 45
Vyner St. E2. 22J 52

Wadding St. SE17. 19P 63
Waddington Rd. E15. 27G 40
Waddington St. E15. 27G 40
Waddon Clo. Cro. 18Zf 91
Waddon Rd. Cro. 18Zf 91
Waddon Ct. Rd. Cro. 17Zg 91
Waddon New Rd. Cro.
  18Zf 91
Wade Rd. E16. 30M 55
Wade St. E14. 26M 53
Wade's Gro. N21. 18Af 16
Wades La. Twi. 1bX 93
Wade's Pl. E14. 26M 53
Wadeson St. E2. 22J 52
Wadham Gdns. Nw3. 13H 34
Wadhurst Rd. sw8. 15R 73
Wadhurst Rd. w4. 5O 57
Wadley Rd. E11. 28D 28
Wadsworth Rd. Wem. 1J 44
Waggon La. N17. 21Ab 17
Waghorn Rd. E13. 30J 55
Waghorn St. SE15. 21S 76
Wagner St. SE15. 23Q 64
Waite Pl. SE17. 19O 63
Waite St. SE15. 21Q 63
Waite Davies Rd. SE12.
  28V 89
Wake St. SE11. 17O 62
Wakefield Gdns. Ilf. 31D 29
Wakefield Rd. N11. 17Ac 16
Wakefield Rd. N15. 21B 25
Wakefield Rd. Rich. 1T 68
Wakefield St. E6. 31J 55
Wakefield St. N18. 22Ac 17
Wakefield St. wc1. 17K 50
Wakeham St N1. 20G 37
Wakehurst Rd. sw11. 13T 72
Wakelin Rd. E15. 28J 54
Wakeling St. E14. 24M 52
Wakeman Rd. nw10. 9K 47
Wakemans Hill Av. nw9.
  5B 19
Wakering Rd. Bar. 34H 43
Wakley St. EC1. 19J 50
Walborough Rd. N22.
  17Aa 16
Walbrook EC4. 20M 51

Walburgh St. E1. 22M 52
Walcorde Av. SE17. 19P 63
Walcot Sq. SE11. 18O 62
Waldeck Gro. SE27. 18X 85
Waldeck Rd. N15. 19A 25
Waldeck Rd. w4. 3P 57
Waldeck Rd. w13. 1L 44
Waldegrave Gdns. Twi.
　　1bW 93
Waldegrave Pk. Twi. 1bX 93
Waldegrave Rd. N8. 18A 24
Waldegrave Rd. SE19. 21Z 90
Waldegrave Rd. w5. 3M 44
Waldegrave Rd. Twi. 1bX 93
Waldemar Av. sw6. 9R 71
Waldemar Av. w13. 1N 56
Waldemar Rd. sw19. 10X 82
Walden Av. N13. 19Ac 16
Walden St. E1. 22L 52
Waldenshaw Rd. SE23.
　　22W 87
Waldo Rd. NW10. 7J 46
Waldram Rd. SE23. 23W 87
Waldron Rd. sw18. 12W 83
Waldron Rd. Har. 1cD 12
Waldrons, The, Cro. 18Zg 91
Walerand Rd. SE13. 27S 78
Wales Farm Rd. w3. 5L 45
Waley St. E1. 24L 52
Walford Rd. N16. 21F 37
Walham Av. sw6. 10Q 59
Walham Gro. sw6. 11Q 59
Walker St. E14. 25L 53
Walks, The, N2. 13A 22
Wall St. N1. 20G 37
Wallace Pl. N1. 19G 37
Wallace Rd. E15. 28K 54
Wallace Rd. N1. 19G 37
Wallbutton Rd. SE4. 24S 76
Wall End Rd. E6. 32H 43
Waller Rd. SE14. 23R 76
Wallerton Gdns. sw14. 5T 69
Wallflower St. w12. 7M 46
Wallgrave Rd. sw5. 11O 60
Wallingford Av. w10. 9L 47
Wallington Rd. Ilf. 36D 42
Wallis Rd. E9. 25H 39
Wallwood Rd. E11. 27D 28
Wallwood St. E14. 25L 53
Walm La. NW2. 9O 33
Walmer Gdns. w13. 1aN 94
Walmer Rd. SE18. 34P 95
Walmer Rd.
　　w10. 1-143 & 2-132.
　　w11. 134, 145 & up. 9M 47
Walmer Ter. SE18. 34P 95
Walmington Fold N12.
　　11Ac 14
Walnut Tree Rd. SE10.
　　28Q 66
Walnut Tree Rd. Bre. 2P 56
Walnut Tree Wk. SE11.
　　18O 62
Walpole Av. Kew. 2R 68
Walpole Cres. Ted. 1cY 93
Walpole Gdns. w4. 4P 57
Walpole Gdns. Twi. 1cW 93
Wa.pole Pl. SE18. 33P 95
Walpole Rd. E6. 30H 41
Walpole Rd. E17. 24B 27
Walpole Rd. N17. 19A 25
Walpole Rd. SE14. 24R 77
Walpole Rd. sw19. 12Y 83
Walpole Rd. Cro. 19Ze 91
Walpole Rd. Ted. 1cY 93
Walpole Rd. Twi. 1cW 93

Walpole St. sw3. 14P 61
Walrond Av. Wem. 3G 30
Walsham Rd. SE14. 23S 76
Walsingham Rd. E5. 22F 38
Walter St. E1. 24L 52
Walter St. E2. 23K 52
Walter Wk. Edg. 5Ac 13
Walters Rd. SE25. 20Zc 90
Walterton Rd. w9. 10K 47
Waltham Av. NW9. 4B 19
Waltham Dri. NW9. 4Aa 13
Waltheof Av. N17. 20Aa 16
Waltheof Gdns. N17. 20Aa 16
Walton Clo. NW2. 8E 32
Walton Clo. Har. 1cA 12
Walton Dri. Har. 1cA 12
Walton Gdns. w3. 4L 45
Walton Rd. E12. 33F 42
Walton Rd. E13. 30J 55
Walton Rd. N15. 21B 26
Walton Rd. Har. 1cA 12
Walton St. sw3. 13O 60
Walton Way w3. 4L 45
Walworth Rd. SE17. 19P 63
Wandle Bank sw19. 12Z 92
Wandle Rd. sw17. 13W 83
Wandle Rd. sw19. 12Z 92
Wandle Rd. Cro. 19Zf 91
Wandle Rd. Mor. 12Zc 92
Wandon Rd. sw6. 11Q 60
Wandsworth Bridge sw18.
　　11S 72
Wandsworth Plain sw18.
　　11T 71
Wandsworth Rd. sw8. 15S 73
Wandsworth Bridge Rd.
　　sw6. 11R 72
Wandsworth Common, W.
　　Side, sw18. 12T 72
Wandsworth High St.
　　sw18. 11T 71
Wanless Rd. SE24. 19S 75
Wanlip Rd. E13. 30K 55
Wansbeck Rd. E9. 25H 39
Wansey St. SE17. 19P 63
Wanstead La. Ilf. 31C 29
Wanstead Rd. E12. 31F 41
Wanstead Pk. Av. E12.
　　31E 41
Wanstead Pk. Av. Ilf. 31C 29
Wantage Rd. SE12. 28U 78
Wapping Wall E1. 23N 64
Wapping Dock St. E1. 24L 52
Wapping High St. E1. 22N 64
Warbeck Rd. w12. 8N 58
Warberry Rd. N22. 17Aa 16
Warboys App. Kin. 4Y 80
Warboys Rd. Kin. 4Y 80
Warburton Rd. E8. 22H 38
Ward Rd. E15. 27H 40
Ward Rd. N19. 16F 35
Ward St. SE11. 17P 62
Warden Rd. NW5. 15G 35
Wardle St. E9. 23G 38
Wardley St. sw18. 11V 83
Wardo Av. sw6. 9R 71
Wardour St. w1. 16M 49
Wards Rd. E. Ilf. 35D 42
Wards Rd. W. Ilf. 34D 42
Ware St. N1. 21J 51
Warfield Rd. NW10. 9K 47
Wargrave Av. N15. 21C 25
Warham Rd. N4. 18B 24
Warham Rd. Cro. 18Zg 91
Warham Rd. Har. 1bAa 12
Warham St. SE5. 18O 62

Warkworth Rd. N17. 20Aa 17
Warley St. E2. 23K 52
Warlingham Rd. Cro.
　　18Zb 90
Warlock Rd. w9. 10K 47
Warlter's Mews N7. 17F 36
Warlter's Rd. N7. 17F 36
Warltersville Rd. N19.
　　17D 24
Warmington Rd. SE24.
　　19U 75
Warmington St. E13. 29K 54
Warminster Rd. SE25.
　　21Zb 90
Warminster Sq. SE25. 21Za 90
Warndon St. SE16. 23P 64
Warneford St. E9. 22H 38
Warner Pl. E2. 22J 52
Warner Rd. E17. 24B 27
Warner Rd. N8. 16B 24
Warner Rd. SE5. 19R 75
Warner St. Ec1. 18K 50
Warner St. N7. 18G 36
Warnham Rd. N12. 13Ac 14
Warple Rd. sw18. 11T 72
Warple Way sw18. 11T 72
Warple Way w3. 6N 57
Warren Av. sw14. 4S 69
Warren La. SE18. 33O 95
Warren Rd. E10. 27E 40
Warren Rd. E11. 30C 29
Warren Rd. NW2. 7E 32
Warren Rd. sw19. 13Y 83
Warren Rd. Cro. 20Ze 91
Warren Rd. Kin. 4Y 80
Warren Rd. Twi. 1dU 93
Warren St. w1. 15K 49
Warren, The, E12. 32F 43
Warrender Rd. N19. 16F 35
Warriner Gdns. sw11. 14R 73
Warrington Cres. w9. 12K 48
Warrington Rd. Cro. 18Zf 91
Warrington Rd. Har. 1bB 12
Warrior Rd. SE5. 19Q 63
Warsill St. sw11. 14R 73
Warton Rd. E15. 26H 40
Warwick Av.
　　w2. 1-5b & 2-16.
　　w9. 7, 18 & up. 12K 48
Warwick Av. Edg. 5Ad 13
Warwick Ct. wc1. 18L 50
Warwick Cres. w2. 12L 48
Warwick Dene w5. 2N 56
Warwick Gdns. N4. 19C 25
Warwick Gdns. sw14. 10O 59
Warwick Gdns. Ilf. 33E 42
Warwick La. Ec4. 19L 51
Warwick Pl. w9. 12L 48
Warwick Rd. E5. 22E 38
Warwick Rd. E11. 30C 29
Warwick Rd. E12. 31G 43
Warwick Rd. E15. 29H 40
Warwick Rd. N11. 16Ab 15
Warwick Rd. N18. 21Ac 17
Warwick Rd. SE20. 22Zb 90
Warwick Rd.
　　sw5. 1-133 & 2-76.
　　w14. 80, 135 & up. 10O 59
Warwick Rd. w5. 2N 56
Warwick Rd. Cro. 17Zb 90
Warwick Rd. Twi. 1cV 93
Warwick Row sw1. 15O 61
Warwick Sq. Ec4. 19M 51
Warwick Sq. sw1. 15P 61
Warwick Sq. SE8. 25Q 65
Warwick St. SE18. 32P 95

Warwick St. sw1. 15P 61
Warwick St. w1. 16M 49
Warwick Ter. se18. 34Q 95
Warwickshire Rd. n16.
    21F 37
Washington Av. e12. 32F 43
Washington Rd. e18. 28A 28
Washington Rd. sw13. 7Q 58
Washington St. e3. 26K 53
Wastdale Rd. se23. 23V 87
Watcombe Pl. se25. 22Zc 90
Watcombe Rd. se25. 22Zc 90
Water La. e15. 28G 40
Water La. ec3. 20M 51
Water La. ec4. 18M 50
Water La. sw2. 17U 74
Water La. Ilf. 35F 42
Water La. Rich. 1T 68
Water Side sw18. 11T 72
Water St. wc2. 18M 50
Waterbank Rd. se6. 26X 88
Waterdale Rd. se2. 36Q 95
Waterden Rd. e9. 25G 39
Waterfall Rd.
  n11. 1-127 & 2-46.
  n14. Remainder. 15Ac 15
Waterfall Rd. sw19. 12Y 83
Waterford Rd. sw6. 11Q 60
Watergate ec4. 18M 50
Watergate St. se8. 25Q 65
Waterloo Bridge wc2.
    17M 50
Waterloo Pl. sw1. 16N 50
Waterloo Pl. Kew. 3Q 56
Waterloo Rd. e2. 23J 52
Waterloo Rd. e6. 30H 41
Waterloo Rd. e10. 25D 27
Waterloo Rd. nw2. 7D 20
Waterloo Rd. se1. 18N 62
Waterloo Sq. se1. 19R 75
Waterloo St. e1. 21H 37
Waterloo St. e14. 24M 53
Waterloo St. ec1. 19K 51
Waterloo St. w6. 8P 58
Waterloo Ter. n1. 18H 36
Waterlow Rd. n19. 16D 23
Watermead Rd. se8. 26X 88
Water Tower Hill Cro.
    20Zg 91
Waterworks Rd. sw2. 17U 74
Waterworks Yd. Cro. 19Zf 91
Watery La. sw20. 10Za 92
Wateville Rd. n17. 20Aa 16
Watford Rd. e16. 29L 55
Watford Rd. Har. 1aC 12
Watford Villas sw11. 13R 72
Watford Way.
  nw4. 1-487 & 2-402.
  nw7. 450, 488 & up. 8B 20
Watling Av. Edg. 5Aa 13
Watling St. ec4. 19M 51
Watlington Gro. se26.
    24Y 87
Watney Pass. e1. 22M 52
Watney Rd. sw14. 4S 69
Watney St. e1. 22M 52
Watson Av. e6. 33H 43
Watson St. e13. 29J 55
Watson St. n16. 20F 37
Watson's Pl. n1. 21J 51
Watsons Rd. n22. 18Aa 16
Watson's St. se8. 25R 77
Wattisfield Rd. e5. 23E 38
Watts Gro. e3. 26L 53
Watts La. Twi. 1bX 93

Watts St. e1. 22N 64
Wavel Mews nw6. 11H 34
Wavendon Av. w4. 5P 57
Waveney Av. se15. 22T 76
Waverley Av. Wem. 3G 30
Waverley Gro. nw4. 9A 21
Waverley Pl. nw8. 12J 48
Waverley Rd. e17. 27A 28
Waverley Rd. n8. 17C 24
Waverley Rd. n17. 21A 26
Waverley Rd. se18. 34Q 95
Waverley Rd. se25. 22Zb 92
Waverley Rd. w2. 11L 47
Waverton St. w1. 15M 49
Wavertree Rd. e18. 29A 29
Wavertree Rd. sw2. 17W 85
Waxlow Rd. nw10. 5J 45
Waxwell Ter. se1. 17O 62
Wayford St. sw11. 13S 72
Wayland Av. e8. 22G 38
Wayland Rd. sw11. 12S 72
Waynflete St. sw18. 12W 83
Wayside nw11. 10D 21
Wayside sw14. 4T 69
Weald La. Har. 1cAa 12
Weardale Rd. se13. 27T 77
Wearside Rd. se13. 26T 77
Weaver St. e1. 21L 52
Webb St. e13. 29K 54
Webb St. se1. 20O 63
Webber Row se1. 18O 62
Webber St. se1. 18N 62
Webb's Rd. sw11. 13T 72
Webster Gdns. w5. 2M 44
Webster Rd. e11. 27F 40
Webster Rd. se16. 22O 64
Wedderburn Rd. nw3. 13G 34
Wedderburn Rd. Bar. 35J 43
Wedlake St. w10. 10K 47
Wedmore Gdns. n19. 16E 36
Wedmore St. n19. 16E 36
Weech St. nw6. 11F 33
Weedington Rd. nw5. 15G 35
Weigall Rd. se2. 29T 79
Weighouse St. w1. 15M 49
Weighton Rd. se20. 22Za 90
Weimar St. sw15. 9S 71
Weirdale Av. Barn. 14Ae 15
Weirhall Av. n18. 20Ab 17
Weirhall Gdns. n18. 20Ac 17
Weirhall Rd. n18. 20Ab 17
Weiss Rd. sw15. 9S 71
Welbeck Rd. e6. 31K 55
Welbeck St. w1. 15L 49
Welbeck Way w1. 15L 49
Welbourne Rd. n17. 21A 26
Welbury St. e8. 21H 37
Welby Mews w11. 10M 47
Welby St. se5. 19R 75
Welfare Rd. e15. 28H 40
Welford Ter. sw6. 9Q 59
Welham Rd.
  sw16. 1-129 & 2-34.
  sw17. 50, 143 & up.
    14Y 84
Well La. sw14. 4T 69
Well Pass. nw3. 13F 34
Well Rd. nw3. 12F 34
Well St. e1. 22M 52
Well St. e9. 23H 38
Well St. e15. 28G 40
Well St. ec1. 19L 51
Well Wk. nw3. 13F 34
Wellacre Rd. Har. 1B 18
Welland St. se10. 26Q 65
Wellclose Sq. e1. 22M 52

Welldon Cres. Har. 1cB 12
Weller St. se1. 19N 63
Wellesley Av. w6. 7O 58
Wellesley Cres. Twi. 1cW 93
Wellesley Gro. Cro. 19Ze 91
Wellesley Rd. e11. 28E 40
Wellesley Rd. e17. 25C 27
Wellesley Rd. n22. 18Aa 16
Wellesley Rd. nw5. 14G 35
Wellesley Rd. w4. 4P 57
Wellesley Rd. Cro. 19Ze 91
Wellesley Rd. Har. 1bB 12
Wellesley Rd. Ilf. 33E 42
Wellesley Rd. Twi. 1cW 93
Wellesley St. e1. 23L 52
Wellesley St. n1. 19K 51
Wellesley Ct. Ilf. Cro.
    19Zf 91
Wellfield Av. n10. 15A 23
Wellfield Rd. sw16. 17X 85
Wellgarth Rd. nw11. 12D 22
Wellington Av. n15. 22C 26
Wellington Gdns. Twi.
    1dX 93
Wellington Pl. nw8. 13J 48
Wellington Rd. e3. 25K 53
Wellington Rd. e6. 32J 43
Wellington Rd. e7. 29G 40
Wellington Rd. e10. 24D 27
Wellington Rd. e11. 29C 29
Wellington Rd. e17. 24B 27
Wellington Rd. n7. 17G 36
Wellington Rd. n9. 21Af 19
Wellington Rd. n9. 23Ad 17
Wellington Rd. n16. 21F 37
Wellington Rd. nw8. 13J 48
Wellington Rd. nw10. 9K 47
Wellington Rd. se15.
    23R 76
Wellington Rd. sw19.
    11W 82
Wellington Rd. w5. 1O 56
Wellington Rd. w6. 8P 58
Wellington Rd. Cro. 18Zd 91
Wellington Rd. Har. 1cA 12
Wellington Rd. Twi. 1dX 93
Wellington Row e2. 21K 52
Wellington Sq. sw3. 14P 61
Wellington St. e16. 27L 54
Wellington St. se8. 25Q 65
Wellington St. se18. 33P 95
Wellington St. wc2. 17M 50
Wellington Ter. Har. 1cD 12
Wellmeadow Rd. w7. 1aO 94
Wells Cres. se5. 20R 75
Wells Gdns. Ilf 31D 42
Wells Mews w1. 16L 49
Wells Pl. se5. 20R 75
Wells Pl. w5. 2M 44
Wells Rise nw8. 14J 49
Wells Rd. w12. 8N 58
Wells St. e14. 26M 54
Wells St. se5. 20Q 63
Wells St. w1. 16L 49
Wells Ter. n4. 18E 36
Wells Ter. se16. 23O 64
Wells House Rd. nw10.
    6K 46
Wells Pk. Rd. se26. 21X 87
Wellwood Rd. Ilf. 36D 42
Welsford St. se1. 21P 64
Welsh St. ec1. 20K 51
Welshpool St. e8. 22H 38
Weltje Rd. w6. 7P 58
Wembley Hill Rd. Wem.
    3F 30

Wembley Pk. Dri. Wem.
    3E 30
Wembley Way Wem. 4G 31
Wembury Rd. N6. 15D 23
Wemlock Rd. Edg. 5Ab 13
Wemyss Rd. SE3. 28S 78
Wendell Rd. W12. 6N 58
Wendon St. E3. 25J 53
Wendover Rd. SE9. 31T 79
Wendover Rd. NW10. 7J 46
Wendy Clo. Wem. 2H 30
Wenlock Rd. N1. 19J 51
Wenlock St. N1. 20J 51
Wennington Rd. E3. 24J 52
Wensley Rd. N18. 22Ab 17
Wentworth Av. N3. 11Ab 14
Wentworth Gdns. N13.
    19Ad 16
Wentworth Rd. E12. 31G 41
Wentworth Pk. N3. 11Ab 14
Wentworth Rd. NW11.
    10C 21
Wentworth Rd. Cro. 18Zd 91
Wentworth St. E1. 21L 51
Werley Av. SW6. 10Q 59
Wernbrook St. SE18. 34Q 95
Werndee Rd. SE25. 21Zc 90
Werrington St. NW1. 16J 49
Werter Rd. SW15. 9T 71
Wesley Av. NW10. 5J 45
Wesley Rd. E10. 26D 28
Wesley Rd. NW10. 5H 31
Wessex Av. SW19. 11Zb 92
Wessex Bldgs. N19. 16E 36
Wessex Gdns. NW11. 10D 21
Wessex Way NW11. 10D 21
West Av. E17. 26B 27
West Av. N3. 11Ab 14
West Av. NW4. 9B 21
West Av. Cro. 16Zg 91
West Av. Cro. 23J 40
West Bank N16. 20D 25
West Clo. Wem. 3D 18
West Ct. Wem. 1E 30
West Drive SW16. 15X 84
West Gdns. SW17. 13Y 83
West Hill N6. 14E 35
West Hill SE26. 22X 87
West Hill.
    SW18. 1-61 & 2-70.
    SW15. 63, 72 & up. 9U 71
West Hill Har. 1cD 12
West Hill Wem. 3D 18
West La. SE16. 22O 64
West Pl. SW15. 9T 71
West Rd. E15 29J 54
West Rd. N17. 22Ab 17
West Rd. SW4. 16T 74
West Rd. SW14. 4S 69
West Rd. W5. 2L 44
West Rd. Ted. 1aY 93
West Row W10. 9K 47
West Side SW18. 12U 72
W. Smithfield EC1. 19L 51
West Sq. SE11. 18O 62
West St. E1. 21L 51
West St. E11. 28E 40
West St. E15. 27G 40
West St. E17. 26C 27
West St. EC2. 20L 51
West St. N9. 21Ad 17
West St. E7. 31P 67
West St. W1. 16M 49
West St. WC2. 16M 50
West St. Cro. 19Zg 91
West St. Har. 1cD 12

West View NW4. 8B 21
West Wk. Barn. 15Af 15
West Way N3. 11Ab 14
West Way NW10. 6E 31
West Way SW20. 8Zb 92
West Way Edg. 4Ac 13
W. Arbour St. E1. 23L 52
W. Avenue Rd. E17. 26B 27
W. Barnes La. Mor. 8Zb 92
W. Beech Rd. N22. 18A 24
Westbere Rd. NW2. 10F 33
Westbourne Av. W3. 5M 45
Westbourne Cres. W2. 12M 48
Westbourne Gdns. W2.
    11L 48
Westbourne Gro.
    W2. 1-137 & 2-112.
    W11. 114, 139 & up.
    11M 47
Westbourne Rd. N7. 18G 36
Westbourne Rd. SE20.
    23Y 92
Westbourne Rd. SE23.
    23W 87
Westbourne Rd. SE26.
    23Y 87
Westbourne Rd. Cro.
    21Zd 91
Westbourne Sq. W2. 11L 48
Westbourne St. SW1. 14P 61
Westbourne St. W2. 12M 48
Westbourne Ter. W2. 12L 48
Westbourne Gro. Ter. W2.
    11L 48
Westbourne Pk. Cres. W2.
    11L 48
Westbourne Pk. Rd. W2.
    11L 48
Westbourne Pk. Villas W2.
    11L 48
Westbourne Ter. Rd. W2.
    12L 48
Westbrook Rd. SE3. 29S 79
Westbrook Rd. Cro. 19Za 90
Westbury Av. N22. 19A 25
Westbury Av. Wem. 2G 30
Westbury Gro. N12. 11Ac 14
Westbury Rd. E7. 30G 41
Westbury Rd. E17. 25B 27
Westbury Rd. N11. 17Ab 16
Westbury Rd. N12. 11Ac 14
Westbury Rd. NW10. 6G 32
Westbury Rd. SE20. 23Za 90
Westbury Rd. W2. 11L 48
Westbury Rd. W5. 2L 44
Westbury Rd. Bar. 34J 43
Westbury Rd. Cro. 19Zd 91
Westbury Rd. Ilf. 32E 42
Westbury Rd. Wem. 2G 30
Westbury St. SW8. 15S 73
West Chapel St. W1. 15N 61
Westcombe Av. Cro. 17Zd 91
Westcombe Hill.
    SE10. 1-21 & 2-62.
    SE3. 21A, 64 & up. 29Q 66
Westcombe Pk. Rd. SE3.
    28Q 66
Westcote Rd. SW16. 15Y 84
Westcott St. SE1. 20O 63
Westcroft Gdns. Mor. 9Zb 92
Westcroft Sq. W6. 7O 58
W. Cromwell Rd. SW5.
    11O 59
Westdale Rd. SE18. 33Q 95
Westdown Rd. E15. 26F 40
Westdown Rd. SE6. 25V 88

W. Eaton Pl. SW1. 14O 61
Westella Rd. NW10. 6H 32
West End Av. E10. 27C 28
West End La. NW6. 11G 34
Westerdale Rd. SE10. 29Q 66
Westerfield Rd. N15. 21B 25
Westerham Av. N9. 20Ad 17
Westerham Rd. E10. 26C 27
Westerly Cres. SE26. 24Y 88
Western Av. N9. 20Ad 17
Western Av. NW11. 9C 21
Western Av.
    W3. 1-297 & 2-156.
    W5. Remainder. 1J 44
Western Gdns. W5. 3M 45
Western La. SW12. 14U 73
Western Rd. E13. 30J 55
Western Rd. E17. 27C 28
Western Rd. N2. 14A 23
Western Rd. N22. 17A 24
Western Rd. SW9. 18S 74
Western Rd. W5. 2M 44
Western Rd. Mit. 12Za 92
Western St. E15. 27H 40
Western Ter. W11. 10M 47
Westernville Gdns. Ilf.
    34D 42
Westfield Gdns. Har. 2B 18
W. Ferry Rd. E14. 25O 65
Westfield Rd. N8. 17B 24
Westfield Rd. W13. 1aM 94
Westfield Rd. Cro. 18Zf 91
Westfield Rd. Edg. 6Ad 13
Westfield Rd. Har. 2B 18
Westfield St. SE18. 31P 67
Westfields Rd. W3. 4L 45
Westgate Rd. SE25. 22Zc 90
Westgate St. E8. 22H 38
Westgate Ter. SW10. 11P 60
West Green Rd. N15. 19B 25
Westhall Rd. SE5. 19Q 63
West Hall Rd. SW14. 4R 69
W. Halfn La. N19. 16H 40
W. Hampstead Mews NW6.
    11G 34
West Heath Av. NW11.
    11D 22
West Heath Clo. NW11. 11E 34
West Heath Dri. NW11.
    11D 22
West Heath Rd. NW3. 11E 34
West Hill Rd. SW18. 10U 71
West Hill Way N20. 11Ae 14
Westholm NW11. 11B 22
Westhorne Av. SE9. 30U 79
Westhorpe St. SW15. 8S 71
W. India Dock Rd. E14.
    25M 53
Westlake Rd. SE16. 23P 64
Westlands Ter. SW12. 15U 73
Westlea Rd. W7. 1bO 94
Westleigh Av. SW15. 8U 70
Westleigh Gdns. Edg. 4Aa 13
W. Lodge Av. W3. 3M 45
Westmacott St. SE5. 20Q 63
Westmead SW15. 7U 70
Westmere Dri. Edg. 5Ae 13
Westminster Av. Cro.
    18Za 90
Westminster Bridge SW1.
    17N 62
Westminster Bridge Rd.
    SE1. 18O 62
Westminster Dri. N13.
    17Ac 16
Westminster Rd. N9. 23Ae 17

Westminster Rd. w7. 1bN 94
Westminster Bridge Rd.
se1. 17N 62
Westmoreland Pl. n1.
20K 51
Westmoreland Pl. sw1.
15P 61
Westmoreland Rd. se17.
20Q 63
Westmoreland Rd. sw13.
7R 70
Westmoreland Rd. w2.
11L 47
Westmoreland St. sw1.
15P 61
Westmoreland St. w1.
15L 49
Westoe Rd. n9. 22Ad 17
Weston Clo. n18. 20Ad 17
Weston Dri. Har. 1aAa 12
Weston Pk. n8. 17C 24
Weston Pl. se1. 21N 63
Weston Rd. w4. 4O 57
Weston St. se1. 21N 63
Weston St. wc1. 17J 50
Westover Rd. sw18. 12U 72
Westow Hill se19. 20Y 86
Westow St. se19. 20Z 90
West Pk. Av. Kew. 3R 69
West Pk. Rd. Kew. 3R 69
Westport Rd. e13. 30L 55
Westrow Dri. Bar. 36G 43
Westrow Gdns. Ilf. 36E 42
W. Sheen Vale Rich. 2S 68
Westview Dri. Ilf. 31A 29
Westville Rd. w12. 7N 58
Westward Way Har. 2C 18
Westway.
w3. 1-297 & 2-156.
w5. 158, 299 & up. 7M 46
Westwell Rd. sw16. 16Y 85
Westwick Gdns. w14. 9N 59
Westwood Pk. se23. 22V 87
Westwood Rd. e16. 29N 67
Westwood Rd. se26. 22Y 87
Westwood Rd. sw13. 6S 70
Westwood Rd. Ilf. 36D 42
Wetherby Gdns. sw5. 12P 60
Wetherby Pl. sw7. 12P 60
Wetherby Rd. sw5. 11P 60
Wetherden St. e17. 25D 27
Wetherell Rd. e9. 24H 38
Wetherill Rd. n10. 15Aa 15
Wexford Rd. sw12. 13V 84
Weybourne St. sw18. 11W 83
Weybridge Rd. Cro. 18Zc 90
Weybridge St. sw11. 14R 73
Weyman Rd. se3. 30R 79
Weymouth Av. nw7. 6Ac 13
Weymouth Av. w5. 1O 56
Weymouth Mews w1. 15L 49
Weymouth St. w1. 15L 49
Weymouth Ter. e2. 21J 51
Whalebone La. e15. 28H 40
Wharf La. Twi. 1bV 93
Wharf Rd. e2. 22J 52
Wharf Rd. e14. 26P 66
Wharf Rd. e15. 27J 54
Wharf Rd. n1. 20J 51
Wharf Rd. nw1. 17J 50
Wharf Rd. w10. 9M 47
Wharf St. e16. 28L 54
Wharfdale Rd. n1. 17J 50
Wharfedale Gdns. Cro.
17Zb 90
Wharfedale St. sw10. 11P 60

Wharncliffe Gdns. nw8.
12K 48
Wharncliffe Gdns. se25.
20Za 90
Wharncliffe Rd. se25.
20Zb 90
Wharton St. wc1. 18K 50
Whateley Rd. se22. 21U 75
Whatley Av. sw20. 9Zb 92
Whatman Rd. se23. 23V 76
Wheathill Rd. se20. 22Zb 90
Wheatlands St. sw17.
14W 84
Wheatley Gdns. n9. 20Ad 17
Wheatsheaf La. sw8. 17Q 62
Wheatsheaf Ter. sw6. 10Q 59
Wheatstone Rd. w10. 10L 47
Wheler St. e1. 21L 51
Whellock Rd. w4. 6N 58
Whetstone Pk. wc2. 17L 50
Whewell Rd. n19. 17E 36
Whidbourne St. wc1. 17K 50
Whinyates Rd. se9. 31T 79
Whipps Cross e17. 27B 28
Whipps Cross Rd. e11.
28C 28
Whiskin St. ec1. 18K 50
Whistler Gdns. Edg. 3Aa 13
Whistler St. n5. 18F 36
Whiston St. e2. 22J 52
Whitbread Rd. se4. 24T 77
Whitburn Rd. se13. 26T 77
Whitby Av. nw10. 4J 45
Whitby Gdns. nw9. 4A 19
Whitby St. e1. 21K 51
Whitcher Pl. nw5. 16H 35
Whitcher St. se14. 24Q 64
Whitchurch La. Edg. 3Ab 13
Whitcomb St. wc2. 16M 50
White Rd. e15. 28H 40
White St. ec2. 20L 51
Whitechapel Rd. e1. 22L 52
Whitechapel High St. e1.
21L 51
White Conduit St. n1. 18J 50
Whitecross Pl. ec2. 20L 51
Whitecross St. ec1. 19L 51
Whitefriars Av. Har. 1cAa 12
Whitefriars Dri. Har 1cAa 12
Whitefriars St. ec4. 18M 50
Whitehall sw1. 17N 62
Whitehall Ct. sw1. 17N 62
Whitehall Gdns. sw1. 17N 62
Whitehall Gdns. w3. 3N 57
Whitehall Gdns. w4. 4P 57
Whitehall Pk. n19. 16D 23
Whitehall Pl. sw1. 17N 62
Whitehall Rd. w7. 1bN 94
Whitehall Rd. Cro. 17Zc 90
Whitehall Rd. Har. 1cC 12
Whitehall St. n17. 21Ab 17
Whitehall Pk. Rd. w4. 4P 57
White Hart La. n17 & n22.
18Aa 16
White Hart La. sw13. 6S 70
White Hart Rd. se18. 35P 95
White Hart St. se11. 18P 62
Whitehaven St. nw8. 13L 48
Whitehead St. e1. 23L 52
Whitehead's Gro. sw3.
13P 60
White Horse La. e1. 23L 52
Whitehorse La. se25. 20Zb 90
Whitehorse Rd. Cro. 19Zd 91
White Horse St. e1. 24L 52
White Horse St. w1. 15N 61

Whitehouse Way n14.
15Ad 15
Whiteley Rd. se19. 20Y 86
White Lion St. e1. 21L 51
White Lion St. n1. 18J 50
White Lion St. wc2. 16M 50
White Post La. e9. 25H 39
Whites Av. Ilf. 35C 42
White's Grounds se1.
20N 63
White's Row e1. 21L 51
White's Sq. sw4. 16T 74
Whitestile Rd. Bre. 1P 56
Whitethorn Gdns. Cro.
22Ze 91
Whitethorn St. e3. 25L 53
Whitfield Pl. w1. 16L 49
Whitfield Rd. e6. 30H 41
Whitfield St. ec2. 20K 51
Whitfield St. w1. 16L 49
Whitgift Av. Cro. 18Zh 91
Whitgift St. se11. 17O 62
Whitgift St. Cro. 19Zf 91
Whiting St. se1. 18N 62
Whitman Rd. e8. 24K 53
Whitmore Gdns. nw10. 8J 47
Whitmore Rd. n1. 20J 51
Whitmore Rd. Har. 1dC 12
Whitney Av. Ilf. 31B 29
Whitney Rd. e10. 26D 27
Whitstable St. se1. 21O 63
Whitta Rd. e12. 31F 41
Whittaker Rd. e6. 30H 41
Whittell Gdns. se26. 22X 87
Whittingstall Rd. sw6.
10R 71
Whittington Rd. n22.
17Ab 16
Whittington Rd. se15.
22R 76
Whittlesey St. se1. 18N 62
Whitton Av. Wem. 1G 30
Whitton Dene Twi. 1dT 93
Whitton Rd. Twi. 1bU 93
Whitwell Rd. e13. 29K 54
Whitworth Pl. se18. 33P 95
Whitworth St. se10. 28P 66
Whitworth Rd. se18. 33R 95
Whitworth Rd. se25.
20Zb 90
Whorlton Rd. se15. 22S 76
Whymark Av. n22. 18A 24
Whyteville Rd. e7. 30G 41
Wick La. e3. 25H 39
Wick Rd. e9. 24G 39
Wick Rd. e16. 28M 54
Wicker St. e1. 22M 52
Wickersley Rd. sw11. 14S 73
Wickford St. e1. 23K 52
Wickham Gdns. se4. 24T 77
Wickham La. se2. 36Q 95
Wickham Rd. se4. 24T 77
Wickham Rd. Cro. 23Zf 91
Wickham Rd. Har. 1cAa 12
Wickham St. se11. 17P 62
Wickliffe Av. n3. 10A 21
Wickliffe Gdns. Wem. 4D 19
Wicklow St. wc1. 17K 50
Wickwood St. se5. 19S 75
Widdenham Rd. n7. 17F 36
Widdin St. e15. 27H 40
Widecombe Way n2. 13B 22
Widegate St. e1. 21L 51
Widley Rd. w9. 11K 48
Wigan St. sw6. 11R 72
Wiggington Av. Wem. 4G 31

Wightman Rd.
n4. 1-131 & 2-138.
n8. 133, 140 & up.   18B 24
Wightman St. e16.   29M 55
Wigmore Pl. w1.   15L 49
Wigmore St. w1.   15L 49
Wigram Rd. e11.   3CC 29
Wigram Sq. e17.   27A 28
Wigston Rd. e13.   30K 55
Wilberforce Rd. nw9.   7C 20
Wilberforce Rd. n4.   19D 37
Wilberforce St. e16.   28M 54
Wilbury Way n18.   20Ac 17
Wilcox Rd. sw8.   17Q 62
Wilcox Rd. Twi.   1cX 93
Wild Ct. wc2.   17M 50
Wild Hatch nw11.   11C 22
Wild St. wc2.   17M 50
Wilderton Rd. n16.   21D 25
Wildfell Rd. se6.   26V 88
Wilditch St. sw11.   17O 62
Wild's Rents se1.   20O 63
Wildwood Gro. nw3.   12D 22
Wildwood Rd. nw11.   12C 22
Wilford Rd. Cro.   19Zd 91
Wilford St. se1.   2CO 63
Wilfred Gdns. w3.   5K 45
Wilfred St. sw1.   15O 61
Wilkes St. e1.   21L 51
Wilkin St. nw5.   15G 35
Wilkinson St. sw8.   17Q 62
Wilks Pl. n1.   20J 51
Willard St. sw8.   15S 73
Willcott Rd. w3.   4N 57
Will Crooks Gdns. se9.
                         30T 79
Willenhall Rd. se18.   33Q 95
Willes Rd. nw5.   15G 35
Willesden La.
nw6. 1-221 & 2-244.
nw2. 212, 223 & up.   9G 33
Willesden La. w3.   5L 45
Willett Rd. Cro.   17Zc 90
William Mews sw1.   14N 61
William Rd. sw19.   9Z 92
William St. e1.   22M 52
William St. e10.   26C 27
William St. e15.   27H 40
William St. n12.   12Ac 14
William St. n17.   21Ab 17
William St. nw1.   15K 49
William St. se18.   33P 95
William St. sw1.   14N 61
William St. w4.   6P 58
William St. Bar.   34H 43
William IV St. wc2.   17M 50
Wm. Morris Clo. e17.   25A 27
Williams Gro. n22.   18Aa 16
Williams La. sw14.   4S 69
Williams Rd. w13.   1aM 94
Williamson St. n7.   17F 36
Willifield Way nw11.
                         11B 21
Willingdon Rd. n22.   19A 25
Willingham Ter. nw5.
                         16G 35
Willington Rd. sw9.   17S 74
Willis Rd. e15.   28J 54
Willis Rd. Cro.   19Zd 91
Willis St. e14.   26M 53
Willoughby Gro. n17.
                         22Ab 17
Willoughby La. n17.   22Ab 17
Willoughby Rd. n8.   18A 24
Willoughby Rd. nw3.   13F 34
Willoughby Rd. w3.   6N 58

Willoughby Pk. Rd. n17.
                         22Ab 17
Willow Av. sw13.   6S 70
Willow Gro. e13.   29J 54
Willow Pl. sw1.   16O 61
Willow Rd. nw3.   13F 34
Willow Rd. w5.   2N 56
Willow St. e1.   23K 52
Willow St. ec2.   20K 51
Willow Vale w12.   7M 46
Willow Wk. e17.   25B 27
Willow Wk. n2.   13Aa 14
Willow Wk. n15.   19A 25
Willow Wk. nw5.   15F 35
Willow Wk. se1.   21O 63
Willow Wk. se6.   25V 88
Willow Wk. se26.   22X 87
Willow Wk. Ilf.   33E 42
Willow Way n3.   11Ab 14
Willow Bridge Rd. n1.
                         19H 37
Willowbrook Rd. se15.
                         21Q 63
Willowcourt Av. Har.   1B 18
Wilman Gro. e8.   22H 38
Wilmer Gdns. n1.   20J 51
Wilmer Way n14.   16Ac 16
Wilmington Av. w4.   5Q 57
Wilmington Gdns. Bar.
                         34H 43
Wilmington Sq. wc1.   18K 50
Wilmot Pl. nw1.   16H 35
Wilmot Rd. e10.   26E 39
Wilmot Rd. n15.   20A 25
Wilmot St. e2.   22K 52
Wilmount St. se18.   33P 95
Wilna Rd. sw18.   11V 83
Wilsham St. w11.   9M 17
Wilson Gro. se16.   22O 64
Wilson Rd. e6.   31K 55
Wilson Rd. se5.   20R 75
Wilson Rd. Har.   1aC 19
Wilson Rd. Ilf.   32D 42
Wilson St. e3.   25L 53
Wilson St. e13.   29J 54
Wilson St. e17.   26B 27
Wilson St. ec2.   20L 51
Wilson St. n21.   18Af 16
Wilson St. se14.   25R 77
Wilson St. wc1.   18K 50
Wilson St. wc2.   17M 50
Wilson's Rd. w6.   9P 59
Wilton Av. w4.   6P 58
Wilton Av. Rich.   3S 68
Wilton Cres. sw1.   14N 61
Wilton Cres. sw19.   10Z 92
Wilton Gro. sw19.   10Z 91
Wilton Mews sw1.   15O 61
Wilton Pl. sw1.   14N 61
Wilton Rd. e8.   22G 38
Wilton Rd. n10.   14Aa 15
Wilton Rd. sw1.   15O 61
Wilton Rd. sw19.   13Z 92
Wilton Rd. Ilf.   33F 43
Wilton Sq. n1.   20J 51
Wilton St. sw1.   15O 61
Wilton Cres. Mews sw1.
                         14N 61
Wiltshire Rd. Cro.   18Zd 90
Wiltshire Rd. sw9.   18S 74
Wiltshire Row n1.   20J 51
Wimbart Sq. sw2.   17V 85
Wimbledon Rd. sw17.
                         12X 83
Wimbledon Hill Rd. sw19.
                          9Y 82

Wimbledon Pk. Rd.
sw18. 1-257 & 2-248.
sw19. 250, 259 & up.
                          9W 82
Wimbledon Pk. Side sw19.
                          8W 82
Wimbolt St. e2.   22K 52
Wimborne Dri. nw9.   4A 19
Wimborne Gdns. w13.   1aL 94
Wimbourne Rd. n15.   20A 25
Wimbourne St. n1.   20J 51
Wimpole Mews w1.   15L 49
Wimpole St. w1.   15L 49
Wincanton Rd. sw18.   10U 71
Winchcomb Gdns. se9.
                         31T 79
Winchelsea Rd. e7.   29F 40
Winchelsea Rd. n17.   21A 25
Winchelsea Rd. nw10.   6H 31
Winchendon Rd. sw6.
                         10R 71
Winchendon Rd. Twi.   1cX 93
Winchester Av. nw6.   10H 33
Winchester Av. nw9.   3A 19
Winchester Mews nw3.
                         13H 34
Winchester Pl. n6.   15D 23
Winchester Rd. n6.   15D 23
Winchester Rd. n9.   21Ae 17
Winchester Rd. nw3.   13H 34
Winchester Rd. Ilf.   34R 42
Winchester Rd. Twi.   1aU 93
Winchester Sq. se1.   20N 63
Winchester St. e2.   22K 52
Winchester St. e16.   31N 67
Winchester St. n1.   17J 50
Winchester St. sw1.   15P 61
Winchester St. w3.   5N 57
Winchester Wk. se1.   20N 63
Winchfield Clo. Har.   1B 18
Winchfield Rd. se26.   24Y 88
Winchmore Hill Rd. n14
& n21.   17Ao 16
Wincott St. se11.   18F 62
Windermere Av. n3.   11A 22
Windermere Av. nw6.   10J 47
Windermere Av. sw19.
                         11Zb 92
Windermere Gdns. Ilf.
                         32C 42
Windermere Rd. n10.
                         15Aa 15
Windermere Rd. n19.   16E 35
Windermere Rd. w5.   1N 56
Windermere Rd. Cro.   21Ze 91
Winders Rd. sw11.   13R 72
Windmill Gro. Cro.   19Zd 91
Windmill Hill nw3.   12E 34
Windmill La. e15.   27G 40
Windmill La. se8.   24P 65
Windmill Pl. sw4.   15T 73
Windmill Rd. n18.   20Ac 17
Windmill Rd. sw4.   15U 73
Windmill Rd. sw18.   12U 72
Windmill Rd. w4.   6P 57
Windmill Rd. w5 & Bre.
                         1O 56
Windmill Rd. Cro.   19Zd 91
Windmill Row se11.   18P 62
Windmill St. se1.   18N 62
Windmill St. w1.   16L 49
Windover Av. nw9.   5A 19
Windsor Av. Edg.   4Ad 13
Windsor Gro. se27.   19X 86
Windsor Pl. n1.   21K 51
Windsor Rd. e7.   30G 41

Windsor Rd. E10. 26E 39
Windsor Rd. E11. 29E 41
Windsor Rd. N7. 17E 36
Windsor Rd. N13. 18Ad 16
Windsor Rd. N17. 22A 26
Windsor Rd. NW2. 8G 32
Windsor Rd. W5. 2M 44
Windsor Rd. Cro. 18Za 90
Windsor Rd. Har. 1cAa 12
Windsor Rd. Ilf. 34F 43
Windsor Rd. Kew. 3R 68
Windsor Rd. Twi. 1cX 93
Windsor St. N1. 19J 51
Windsor Ter. N1. 19K 51
Windsor Ter. NW3. 13F 34
Windsor Wk SE5. 20S 75
Windus Rd. N16. 21E 37
Wine Office Ct. EC4. 18M 50
Winforton St. SE10. 26R 77
Winfrith Rd. SW18. 11V 83
Wingate Rd. W6. 7O 58
Wingate Rd. Ilf. 33G 43
Wingfield Rd. E15. 28G 40
Wingfield Rd. E17. 26B 27
Wingfield St. SE15. 21S 76
Wingford Rd. SW2. 16U 74
Wingmore Rd. N17. 21Ab 17
Wingmore Rd. SE24. 19S 75
Wingrave Rd. W6. 8Q 59
Winifred Rd. SW19. 10Z 92
Winkfield Rd. E13. 29K 55
Winkfield Rd. N22. 18Aa 16
Winlaton Rd. SE6. 27Y 89
Winnington Rd. NW3. 13C 22
Winns Av. E17. 25A 27
Winns Ter. E17. 25A 27
Winscombe St. N19. 15E 35
Winscombe Way W5. 1K 44
Winsford Rd. SE6. 24X 88
Winsham Gro. SW11. 14U 73
Winslade Rd. SW2. 17T 74
Winslow Rd. W6. 8P 59
Winstanley Rd. SW11. 13S 72
Winstead St. SW11. 13R 72
Winston Rd. N16. 20F 37
Winstone Av. NW9. 6C 20
Winter Av. E6. 32J 43
Winterbourne Rd. SE6.
24R 88
Winterbourne Rd. Cro.
18Zb 90
Winterbrook Rd. SE24.
19U 75
Winterstoke Rd. SE6. 24V 88
Winterton St. E1. 22M 52
Winterwell St. SW2. 17T 74
Winthorpe Rd. SW15. 10T 71
Winthrop St. E1. 22L 52
Winton Av. N11. 16Ab 15
Winton Rd. E16. 30M 55
Winwood St. E1. 23L 52
Wisbech Rd. SE25. 20Zc 90
Wise Rd. E15. 27J 54
Wiseman Rd. E10. 25E 39
Wiseton Rd. SW17. 13V 83
Wisley Rd. SW11. 14U 73
Wisteria Rd. SE13. 27T 78
Witchampton St. N1. 20J 51
Witham Rd. SE20. 22Zb 90
Witham St. N1. 20J 51
Witherby Clo. Cro. 20Zg 91
Witherington Rd. N5. 18G 36
Witley Rd. N19. 16E 35
Wittersham Rd. Bro. 28Y 89
Wivenhoe Rd. SE15. 22S 76
Wiverton Rd. SE26. 23Y 87

Wix's La. SW4. 15T 73
Woburn Bldgs. WC1. 16K 50
Woburn Mews WC1. 16K 50
Woburn Pl. WC1. 17K 50
Woburn Rd. Cro. 19Ze 91
Woburn Sq. WC1. 16K 50
Wodeham St. E1. 22L 52
Wolcot St. NW1. 16J 50
Wolfe Cres. SE7. 31P 67
Wolferton Rd. E12. 32F 43
Wolfington Rd. SE27. 18X 85
Wolmer Clo. Edg. 4Ad 13
Wolmer Gdns. Edg. 4Ae 13
Wolseley Av. SW19. 10W 82
Wolseley Gdns. W4. 4P 57
Wolseley Rd. E7. 30H 41
Wolseley Rd. N8. 16C 24
Wolseley Rd. N22. 17Aa 16
Wolseley Rd. W4. 5O 57
Wolseley Rd. Har. 1bA 12
Wolseley St. SE1. 21N 64
Wolsey Av. E17. 25A 27
Wolsey Gro. Edg. 6Ab 13
Wolsey Rd. N1. 20G 37
Wolsey St. E1. 23L 52
Wolstonbury N12. 11Ac 14
Wolverley St. E2. 22K 52
Wolverton Gdns. W5. 3M 44
Wolverton Gdns. W6. 9O 59
Womersley Rd. N8. 17C 24
Wontner Rd. SW17. 14W 84
Wood Clo. NW9. 5C 19
Wood Clo. Har. 1cC 12
Wood La. N6. 15C 23
Wood La. NW9. 5D 19
Wood La. W12. 8M 47
Wood St. E2. 22K 52
Wood St. E16. 30M 55
Wood St. E17. 27B 28
Wood St. EC2. 19L 51
Wood St. SE11. 17P 62
Wood St. SE18. 32P 95
Wood St. SE27. 19X 86
Wood St. SW1. 16O 62
Wood St. W4. 6P 58
Wood Vale N10. 16B 23
Wood Vale SE23. 22V 87
Wood Wharf SE10. 26Q 65
Woodbank Rd. SE12. 28X 89
Woodbastwick Rd. SE26.
24Y 87
Woodberry Av. N21. 18Ae 16
Woodberry Av. Har. 1dA 12
Woodberry Cres. N10. 15A 23
Woodberry Down N4. 19D 25
Woodberry Gdns. N12.
12Ab 14
Woodberry Gro. N4. 19D 25
Woodberry Gro. N12.
12Ab 14
Woodberry Way N12.
12Ab 14
Woodbine Gro. E9. 23G 38
Woodbine Gro. SE20. 22Z 90
Woodbine Pl. E11. 29C 29
Woodborough Rd. SW15.
7T 70
Woodbourne Av. SW16.
16X 85
Woodbridge Rd. Bar. 36G 43
Woodbridge St. EC1. 18K 50
Woodbrook Rd. SE2. 36Q 95
Woodbury Clo. Cro. 21Zf 91
Woodbury Rd. E17. 26B 27
Woodbury St. SW17. 13Y 83
Woodchester St. W2. 11L 48

Woodchurch Rd. NW6.
11H 34
Woodcock Dell Har. 1C 18
Woodcock Hill Har. 1B 18
Woodcombe Cres. SE23.
23V 87
Woodcote Pl. SE27. 19Y 85
Woodcote Rd. E11. 29D 28
Woodcote Rd. Cro. 18Zc 90
Woodcroft N21. 18Ae 16
Woodcroft Av. NW7. 6Ab 13
Woodfall St. SW3. 14P 61
Woodfield Av. NW9. 6B 20
Woodfield Av. SW16. 16W 84
Woodfield Av. W5. 1K 44
Woodfield Av. Wem. 1E 30
Woodfield Cres. W5. 1K 44
Woodfield Cres. W9. 11K 47
Woodfield Dri. Barn. 14Af 15
Woodfield Gdns. W7. 1cK 94
Woodfield Pl. W9. 10K 47
Woodfield Rd. W5. 1K 44
Woodfield Rd. W9. 10L 47
Woodfield Way N11. 16Ab 15
Woodford Av. Ilf. 33C 42
Woodford Rd. E7. 29F 41
Woodford Rd. E11. 29C 28
Woodford Bridge Rd. Ilf.
31B 29
Woodford New Rd. E17.
28B 28
Woodgate St. SW8. 16Q 62
Woodgrange Av. N12.
13Ab 14
Woodgrange Av. W5. 3M 44
Woodgrange Av. Har. 1B 18
Woodgrange Rd. E7. 29G 41
Woodham Rd. SE6. 26X 88
Woodhayes Rd. SW19. 8Y 81
Woodhayes Rd. SW20. 8Z 92
Woodheyes Rd. NW10.
6G 31
Woodhouse Gro. E12. 31H 41
Woodhouse Rd. E11. 28F 40
Woodhouse Rd. N12. 13Ac 14
Woodhurst Rd. SE2. 36P 95
Woodhurst Rd. W3. 5M 45
Woodin St. E14. 26N 53
Woodland Gdns. N10. 15B 23
Woodland Gro. SE10. 28Q 66
Woodland Hill SE19. 20Y 86
Woodland Pl. SE10. 27Q 66
Woodland Rise N10. 15B 23
Woodland Rd. N11. 15Ac 15
Woodland Rd. N16. 20E 37
Woodland Rd. SE19. 20Y 86
Woodland Rd. Cro. 18Zc 90
Woodland St. E8. 21H 37
Woodland St. SE10. 27Q 66
Woodland Ter. SE7. 31P 67
Woodland Way N21. 18Ad 16
Woodland Way Mor. 10Zb 92
Woodlands NW4. 10B 21
Woodlands SW20. 8Zb 92
Woodlands Av. E11. 30E 41
Woodlands Av. N3. 12Ab 14
Woodlands Rd. E11. 28E 40
Woodlands Rd. E17. 27A 28
Woodlands Rd. N9. 23Ae 17
Woodlands Rd. SW13. 6S 70
Woodlands Rd. Har. 1bB 12
Woodlands Rd. Ilf. 34E 42
Woodlands St. SE13. 27V 89
Woodlands, The, N14. 15Ae 15
Woodlands Way SW15.
10T 71

Woodlands Pk. Rd. N15.
    19B 25
Woodlands Pk. Rd. SE10.
    28Q 66
Woodlawn Rd. SW6. 9Q 59
Woodlea Rd. N16. 20E 37
Woodleigh Av. N12. 14Ac 15
Woodmere Av. Cro. 23Zd 91
Woodmere Clo. Cro. 23Zd 91
Woodmere Gdns. Cro.
    23Ze 91
Woodnook Rd. SW16. 15Y 84
Woodpecker Rd. SE14.
    24Q 65
Woodquest Rd. SE24. 19U 75
Woodriffe Rd. E11. 27D 28
Woodrow SE18. 32P 95
Wood's Bldgs. E1. 22L 52
Wood's Mews W1. 14M 49
Wood's Pl. SE1. 20O 63
Woods Rd. SE15. 22R 76
Woodside NW11. 11B 22
Woodside SW19. 10Y 82
Woodside Av. N6. 14B 23
Woodside Av. N12. 12Ac 14
Woodside Av. SE25. 22Zd 91
Woodside Clo. Wem. 2H 30
Woodside End Wem. 2H 30
Woodside Gdns. N17. 21A 25
Woodside Green Cro. 22Zd 91
Woodside Gro. N12. 12Ad 14
Woodside La. N12. 12Ad 14
Woodside Pk. SE25. 22Zc 90
Woodside Pl. Wem 2H 30
Woodside Rd. E13. 30L 55
Woodside Rd. N22. 18Ab 16
Woodside Rd. SE25. 22Zd 91
Woodside Rd. Wem. 2H 30
Woodside Ct. Rd. Cro.
    21Ze 91
Woodside Grange Rd. N12.
    12Ad 14
Woodside Pk. Av. E17.
    27D 28
Woodside Pk. Rd. N12.
    12Ac 14
Woodsome Rd. NW5. 15E 35
Woodspring Rd. SW19.
    9W 82
Woodstock Av. NW11.
    10C 21
Woodstock Av. W13. 1aN 94
Woodstock Av. Twi. 1bT 93
Woodstock Gdns. Ilf. 36E 42
Woodstock Rd. E7. 30H 41
Woodstock Rd. E17. 27A 28
Woodstock Rd. N4. 18D 24
Woodstock Rd. NW11.
    10D 21
Woodstock Rd. W4. 6O 58
Woodstock Rd. W12. 9N 59
Woodstock Rd. Cro. 19Zf 91
Woodstock Rd. Wem. 3H 30
Woodstock St. E16. 28L 54
Woodstock St. W1. 15M 49
Woodstock Ter. E14. 26M 53
Woodthorpe Rd. SW15. 8T 70
Woodvale Av. SE25. 21Zb 90
Woodville Gdns. NW11. 9C 21
Woodville Gdns. W5. 2L 44
Woodville Gro. N15. 20B 25
Woodville Rd. E11. 28D 28
Woodville Rd. E17. 24B 27
Woodville Rd. E18. 30A 29
Woodville Rd. N16. 20G 37
Woodville Rd. N22. 18Ab 16

Woodville Rd. NW11. 10C 21
Woodville Rd. W5. 2L 44
Woodville Rd. Cro. 19Zb 90
Woodville Rd. Mor. 10Zb 92
Woodward Av. NW4. 7B 20
Woodwarde Rd. SE22.
    20U 75
Woodway Cres. Har. 1aB 12
Woodwell St. SW18. 12T 72
Woodyates St. SE6. 29V 89
Wool Rd. SW19. 8Z 92
Woolacombe Rd. SE3. 30S 79
Woolaston Rd. N4. 18C 24
Wooler St. SE17. 20P 63
Wolf St. SE1. 21O 63
Woollett St. E14. 26M 53
Woolmer Gdns. N18. 22A 17
Woolmer Rd. N18. 22Ac 17
Woolmore St. E14. 26M 54
Woolneigh St. SW6. 11S 72
Woolstone Rd. SE23. 24W 88
Woolwich Common SE18.
    32R 95
Woolwich Rd
  SE10 1-265 & 2-160.
  SE7. 162-754 & 267-833.
    29P 67
Wootton St. SE1. 18N 62
Worbeck Rd. SE20. 22Za 90
Worcester Av. N17. 22Ab 17
Worcester Gdns. Ilf. 32D 42
Worcester Rd. E12. 32F 42
Worcester Rd. SW19. 10Y 82
Worcester St. E1. 22N 64
Worcester St. SW1. 16P 61
Wordsworth Av. E12. 31H 41
Wordsworth Av. E18. 29A 28
Wordsworth Rd. N16. 20F 37
Wordsworth Rd. SE20.
    23Z 90
Wordsworth Rd. Har. 1bA 12
Wordsworth Wk. NW11.
    11B 21
Worfield St. SW11. 13R 72
Worland Rd. E15. 28H 40
World's End Pass. SW10.
    12Q 60
Worlidge St. W6. 8P 58
Worlingham Rd. SE22.
    21T 75
Wormholt Rd. W12. 7M 46
Wormwood St. EC2. 20L 51
Wornington Rd. W10. 10L 47
Woronzow Rd. NW8. 13J 48
Worple Av. SW20. 9Z 92
Worple Av. Twi. 1bT 93
Worple Rd. SW19. 9Y 82
Worple Rd. SW20. 8Za 92
Worple St. SW14. 5S 69
Worple Way Rich. 2T 68
Worple Way N. SW14. 5S 69
Worple Way S. SW14. 5S 69
Worship St. EC2. 20L 51
Worslade Rd. SW17. 12X 83
Worsley Rd. E11. 28F 40
Worsley Rd. NW3. 13F 34
Worsley Bridge Rd. SE26.
    25Y 88
Wortley Rd. E6. 31H 41
Wortly Rd. Cro. 17Zd 91
Wotton Rd. NW2. 8E 32
Wotton Rd. SE8. 24Q 65
Wouldham St. E16. 28M 54
Wragby Rd. E11. 28F 40
Wray Cres. N4. 17E 36
Wreckin Rd. SE18. 34R 95

Wren Av. NW2. 8F 33
Wren Rd. SE5. 20R 75
Wren St. WC1. 17K 50
Wrentham Av. NW10. 9J 47
Wrexham Rd. E3. 25J 53
Wricklemarsn Rd. SE3.
    30S 79
Wrigglesworth St. SE14.
    23Q 64
Wright's Bldgs. SE1. 20O 63
Wright's La. W8. 11O 60
Wright's Rd. E3. 24J 53
Wrights Rd. SE25. 20Zb 90
Wright's Wk. SW14. 5S 69
Wrotham Rd. NW1. 16H 35
Wrottesley Rd. NW10. 7J 46
Wrottesley Rd. SE18. 34Q 95
Wroughton Rd. SW11.
    14U 73
Wroughton Ter. NW4. 8A 20
Wroxham Gdns. N11.
    16Ab 15
Wroxton Rd. SE15. 22S 76
Wulfstan St. W12. 6L 46
Wyatt Pk. Rd. SW2. 17W 85
Wyatt Rd. E7. 29H 41
Wyatt Rd. N5. 19E 37
Wyatts La. E17. 27A 28
Wybert St. NW1. 15K 49
Wyborne Way NW10. 5H 31
Wyclif St. EC1. 18K 50
Wycliffe Rd. E15. 26G 39
Wycliffe Rd. SW11. 14S 73
Wycliffe Rd. SW19. 11Y 83
Wycombe Gdns. NW11.
    11D 21
Wycombe Rd. N17. 22Aa 17
Wydehurst Rd. Cro. 22Zd 91
Wye St. SW11. 12S 72
Wyfold Rd. SW6. 9R 71
Wyford Rd. Ilf. 34G 43
Wyke Dri. Edg. 8Aj 18
Wyke Rd. E3. 25H 39
Wyke Rd. SW20. 8Za 92
Wykeham Rd. NW4. 8B 20
Wykeham Rd. Har. 1aA 12
Wyld Way Wem. 4G 31
Wyldes Clo. NW11. 12D 22
Wyleu St. SE23. 24V 87
Wymering Rd. W9. 11K 48
Wymond St. SW15. 8S 71
Wynchgate N14. 17Ae 16
Wyndale Av. NW9. 4B 19
Wyndcliff Rd. SE7. 29Q 67
Wyndham Cres. N19. 16F 35
Wyndham Pl. W1. 14L 49
Wyndham Rd. E6. 31H 41
Wyndham Rd. SE5. 19Q 63
Wyndham Rd. W13. 1aN 94
Wyndham Rd. Rich. 3S 68
Wyndham St. W1. 14L 49
Wyneham Rd. SE24. 19U 75
Wynell Rd. SE23. 23X 87
Wynford Rd. N1. 18J 50
Wynne Rd. SW9. 18S 74
Wynne Ter. SW9. 18S 74
Wynnstay Gdns. W8. 11O 59
Wynter St. SW11. 12T 72
Wynton Pl. W3. 4L 45
Wynyatt St. EC1. 18K 50
Wythes Rd. E16. 31N 67
Wythfield Rd. SE7. 30Q 67
Wyvil Rd. SW8. 17Q 62
Wyvis St. E14. 26L 53

Yabsley St. E14. 27N 66

Yalding Rd. se16.	21O 64	
Yalford St. e1.	22L 52	
Yardley St. wc1.	18K 50	
Yateley St. se18.	31O 67	
Yattan St. e14.	26L 53	
Yeatman Rd. n6.	14C 23	
Yeldham Rd. w6.	9P 59	
Yelverton Rd. sw11.	12S 72	
Yeo St. e3.	26L 53	
Yeoman St. se8.	24P 64	
Yeoman's Row sw3.	13O 60	
Yeovil Pl. sw8.	16R 73	
Yeovil St. sw8.	16R 73	
Yerbury Rd. n19.	16E 36	
Yew Gro. nw2.	9F 33	
Yew Wk. Har.	1cD 12	
Yewtree Clo. n21.	18Ae 16	
Yew Tree Rd. w12.	7M 46	
Yewfield Rd. nw10.	6G 32	
Yolande Gdns se9.	31U 79	
Yonge Pk. n4.	18E 36	
York Av. se17.	19P 63	
York Av. sw14.	4T 69	
York Av. w7.	1bM 94	
York Bldgs. wc2.	17M 50	
York Gate nw1.	14K 49	
York Gro. se15.	23R 76	
York Hill se27.	18W 85	

York Pl. sw11.	12S 72	
York Pl. w6.	8P 58	
York Pl. wc2.	17M 50	
York Rise nw5.	15F 35	
York Rd. e7.	29H 40	
York Rd. e10.	26F 39	
York Rd. e14.	24M 53	
York Rd. e17.	24C 26	
York Rd. n1.	17H 36	
York Rd. n18.	z2Ab 17	
York Rd. n21.	20Af 17	
York Rd. nw9.	7C 20	
York Rd. se1.	17N 62	
York Rd. sw11. 1-367 & 2-260.	11T 72	
sw18. 262, 369 & up.		
York Rd. sw19.	11Y 83	
York Rd. w3.	5L 45	
York Rd. w5.	1O 56	
York Rd. Bre.	1P 56	
York Rd. Cro.	18Zd 91	
York Rd. Ilf.	33E 42	
York Rd. Twi.	1cX 93	
York Rd. By-Pass sw18.	11T 71	
York Row e2.	21J 51	
York Sq. e14.	24M 53	

York St. e16.	28M 54	
York St. w1.	14L 49	
York St. w1.	16M 49	
York St. wc2.	17M 50	
York St. Twi.	1bV 93	
York Ter. nw1.	14K 49	
York Ter. sw4.	16S 74	
York Way n20.	14Ad 15	
Yorkshire Gdns. n18.	22Ac 17	
Yorkton St. e2.	21J 52	
Young St. e16.	29M 55	
Young St. w8.	11N 60	
Youngs Rd Ilf.	34C 42	
Yoxley Dri. Ilf.	34C 42	
Yukon Rd. sw12.	15U 73	
Yuletide Rd.nw10.	6G 32	
Zampa Rd. se16.	23P 64	
Zennor Rd. sw12.	15V 84	
Zenoria St. se22.	21T 75	
Zermatt Rd. Cro.	19Zc 90	
Zetland St. e14.	26L 53	
Zion Pl. Cro.	19Zc 90	
Zion Rd. Cro.	19Zc 90	
Zoar St. se1.	19N 63	
Zoffany St. n19.	16E 36	